CHANGING PLACES

Changing Places

*History, Community, and Identity
in Northeastern Ontario*

KERRY ABEL

McGill-Queen's University Press
Montreal & Kingston · London · Ithaca

© McGill-Queen's University Press 2006
ISBN-13: 978-0-7735-3038-6   ISBN-10: 0-7735-3038-X (cloth)
ISBN-13: 978-0-7735-3071-3   ISBN-10: 0-7735-3071-1 (paper)

Legal deposit second quarter 2006
Bibliothèque nationale du Québec

Printed in Canada on acid-free paper that is 100% ancient forest free
(100% post-consumer recycled), processed chlorine free

This book has been published with the help of a grant from the
Canadian Federation for the Humanities and Social Sciences,
through the Aid to Scholarly Publications Programme, using funds
provided by the Social Sciences and Humanities Research Council of
Canada.

McGill-Queen's University Press acknowledges the support of the
Canada Council for the Arts for our publishing program. We also
acknowledge the financial support of the Government of Canada
through the Book Publishing Industry Development Program
(BPIDP) for our publishing activities.

Library and Archives Canada Cataloguing in Publication

Abel, Kerry M. (Kerry Margaret)
   Changing places : history, community, and identity in northeastern
Ontario / Kerry Abel.

Includes bibliographical references and index.
ISBN-13: 978-0-7735-3038-6   ISBN-10: 0-7735-3038-X (bnd)
ISBN-13: 978-0-7735-3071-3   ISBN-10: 0-7735-3071-1 (pbk)

1. Porcupine Region (Ont.) – History – 20th century.
2. Community – Ontario – Porcupine Region.   I. Title.

HN110.O5A24 2006   971.3'142   C2005–907363–2

Typeset in 10/12 Baskerville by True to Type

Contents

Illustrations and Maps

ILLUSTRATIONS

MAPS

Tables and Figures

Preface

The twentieth century, born in a celebration of the promise of humanity's progress to utopia, grew up amidst a ghastly display of inhumanity on a scale hitherto unimaginable. From the slaughter of a generation on the fields of Flanders, to mass murder coldly calculated and savagely personal, to the threat of global annihilation by nuclear weapons, our lives have been shaped by fear, conflict, and horror. It is scarcely surprising that scholars have focused on understanding the roots of disunity and the means by which power has been exercised both directly to impose will and indirectly to ensure the continuing complicity of those who carry out the orders or those who simply look away.

One important aspect of these conflicts has been the struggle over cultural identity. As old colonial systems and empires disintegrate, new global economies are connecting or reconnecting groups that have scarcely yet come to terms with their place in a postcolonial world. The once colonized are asserting ethnic identities and proclaim their re-emergence as "nations" – nations that are deemed to have existed before the imposition of imperial authority and now derive their claim to legitimacy from cultural rather than political or economic roots. Multi-ethnic states, allegedly the "unnatural" creation of colonial powers, dissolve into more "natural" divisions, defined as communities rooted deep in historical tradition, cultural tradition, and group self-interest – or at least according to the deeply felt beliefs of those participating in the process. Meanwhile, the former colonial powers are responding in the hope of maintaining their claim to legitimacy. Now the nation-state must be multicultural, open to diversity. Political and economic stability can be achieved only if cultural assimilation is abandoned. In order to do business, global economic leaders need to adapt new strategies. But for all the superficial openness to cultural diversity, the new imperialism is using very similar tools to those of the old. Economic and political systems continue to be linked to and reinforced by

cultural ideas. The new multicultural society is no longer defined in ethnic
or religious terms, but instead seen as a culture of consumerism that sub-
scribes to the philosophy of liberal capitalism, with its curious blend of
individual liberty and mass conformity. Although the world is still divided
into "us" and "other," the definitions of "us" have changed.

So while conflict was a hallmark of the twentieth century (and promises
to continue to shape the twenty-first), a sense of belonging to a group has
been equally important. We need to understand how consensus can be
built and how a sense of community is developed. How do people maintain or modify a sense of shared identity in the face of challenges and historical changes? As economic systems and technological discoveries
expand the territorial and intellectual range of our experience and contacts, how do we make sense of the new, the different, the potentially dangerous? Often, of course, we simply put up the defences and turn inward
– or lash outward – to prevent that change. But occasionally we look for
accommodation and accept something of the new, with consequences
that are sometimes hoped for and often unexpected. It is with these questions that this study is preoccupied: How do communities form? How do
people come to believe that they have something in common, and how is
this belief sustained over time? Why does a sense of community form in
some places and not in others?

In order to explore these questions, this book focuses on a region in
northeastern Ontario that forms a triangle bounded by the towns of
Timmins–South Porcupine, Iroquois Falls, and Matheson. Initially a cross-
road for several major Aboriginal cultural groups, the region was drawn
into an even broader international system in the seventeenth century as
English, French, and Iroquois entrepreneurs moved in on its fur
resources. In the early twentieth century it became the focal point for the
rapid development of three new economic activities: mining, pulp and
paper, and agriculture. The Aboriginal population and the well-established fur trade society were suddenly flooded by newcomers from a wide
variety of cultural backgrounds, including English- and French-speaking
Canadians, Italians, Finns, Ukrainians, Chinese, Poles, Russians, Croatians,
Slavs, Scots, Irish, and Cornish. They found themselves in towns created
almost overnight or on isolated homesteads hacked out of the bush. They
were subject to the vicissitudes of a resource-based economy and the promotional claims of an empire-building provincial government that bor-
dered on the criminally misleading. The process by which first the Aboriginal people and then the newcomers adapted to these conditions is, in
part, a process of community formation. Individuals coalesced into
groups, developing a sense of unique, shared identity, a sense of entitlement, and a belief in the legitimacy of what they had created. Who was
excluded is just as important as who was included.

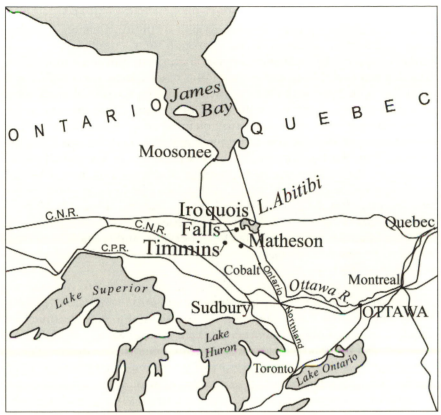

Map 1   The Place (by Thai-Nguyen Nyguyen)

   This book can be read in two ways. Readers interested in local history itself should find the stories they seek in chapters 1 to 12. Those interested in the ways in which these stories can be interpreted and analysed will find a discussion of the subject in the remainder of this preface and in the conclusion. If you don't like theory, you have been warned – skip ahead to chapter 1!

The obvious place to begin a community-formation study seems to be with the question, "What do we mean by 'community'?" The answer is neither obvious nor simple. Human beings are social animals. We cannot survive alone, either as individuals or as a species. But coming to terms with what it means to be part of a group is not as easily understood as the fact that we find ourselves in groups. Philosophers of all cultures and ages have struggled with the question; and the late-nineteenth-century concept of "social science" developed in no small measure around the attempts of

various philosophers to find new language and new methods to explore
the idea of group – whether it was a society, a culture, a nation, or fellow
participants in an economic system. Through the twentieth century, sociologists in particular tackled the idea of community, turning it into a football that was tossed back and forth among many hands, some skilled and
some less skilled, through changing weather (from the dismal mucky days
of war to the dry warmth of smug good times) and from one end of the
playing field to the other. Each pair of hands that touched the ball, of
course, had perceived it from a unique angle and hoped to put a magnificent spin on the toss that would shape the course of the game forever.
Ultimately, the ball became so badly worn that it no longer even looked
like a football, and a new generation of players declared it worthless for
further play. Defining "community" as an exercise in uncovering its
essence, or "real" form, is undoubtedly pointless. Nevertheless, something
called community seems to exist. The experience and symbolism of community continue to play a major role in the human experience. Thus, community deserves to be reconsidered.

   The debates about the nature of community in social science can be
read as part of a larger historical process of attempts to come to terms with
modernity, with its fascinating blend of post-Enlightenment rationalism
and faith in the promise of science and technology, its industrial capitalism, and its liberal individualism. In the nineteenth century, the idea of
community was first proposed as part of a critique of modernism. Then
the modernists themselves appropriated it as part of their justification for
the validity of the modernist world view. Today it is being used by a new
generation of fin-de-siècle critics of modernism, but in a very different way
from the nineteenth-century critique. It is worth tracing these changing
theories about community because all of them, in one way or another,
have shaped our basic assumptions about what it means to identify ourselves as part of a group.

   The German sociologist Ferdinand Tönnies (1855–1936), in an
attempt to characterize the changes brought to his country by industrialization, provided the vocabulary in his 1887 study, *Gemeinschaft und
Gesellschaft* (much to the confusion of generations of English-speaking
undergraduates).[1] For Tönnies, *Gesellschaft* was the social system of industrial capitalism, a large-scale social system rooted in science and scholarship and held together by law and contractual relations that sustained
business and international trade; it took its form in the modern state.
Gemeinschaft, in contrast, was the pre-industrial, small-scale social system of
the family, collective relations, folk culture, and religion, sustained by a
home-based economy and characterized by personal relationships. The
tendency of *Gesellschaft* was to individualism, exploitation, and alienation,
leaving the way open to struggle and conflict, whereas *Gemeinschaft* tended

to promote social unity, relative permanence, and peaceful relations. While Tönnies rejected the criticism that he was breaking the cardinal rule of the new social "science" by judging *Gemeinschaft* as a more desirable social system,[2] it is clear that he did indeed lament the passing of an old way of life. He certainly provided other critics of modernism with both concepts and vocabulary. To the conservative and romantic traditions of the nineteenth and twentieth centuries, community was a place of home and hearth, a world we had lost. The idea echoes strongly in contemporary popular and journalistic culture. Modern life leaves us alone, alienated, and adrift because modernity has torn up the roots of community.

Others of Tönnies's generation, who have come to be known as the Founding Fathers of Sociology, developed more general ideas about social groups. French scholar Émile Durkheim (1858–1917) devoted his life to challenging such English-speaking philosophers as Jeremy Bentham and John Stuart Mill, whose utilitarianism was rooted in *individual* action. Durkheim proposed instead that human behaviour was either derived from or shaped by its *social* context. Hence, the only worthwhile object of study was the community. Durkheim laid the basis in his work on this subject for what became the tradition of structuralism. Societies, he argued, were held together by systems and patterns of organization that could be identified and studied. Like Tönnies, he saw two fundamental patterns: the "mechanical solidarity" of "primitive" societies (in which individuals shared beliefs and work patterns, so societies held together) and the "organic solidarity" of urban-industrial society (in which individuals were much more diversified). Unlike Tönnies, however, Durkheim did not see industrial society as doomed to conflict and division; rather, individuals would eventually learn that the economy made them dependent on one another and on the state, and thus community would prevail.[3]

For Durkheim and many others, community was not a specific type of social organization; it was a general category to be analysed. University of Toronto political scientist R.M. MacIver (1882–1970) provided one of the clearest examples of this approach in his 1917 publication, *Community: A Sociological Study*. The purpose of the study, he wrote, was to look for the "fundamental laws of social development"; he found three in the structures that created community.[4] Better known is the work of German sociologist Max Weber (1864–1920). His more wide-ranging and subtle corpus of writing, by its nature, opened the door to decades of competing interpretations and critiques. Nonetheless, Weber's search for universal laws of human behaviour and his emphasis on collectives legitimized and encouraged the structuralist approach to community. The emerging discipline of anthropology also developed a taste for structuralism. Marcel Mauss (1872–1950), a student of Durkheim's, and then Claude Lévi-Strauss (b. 1908) looked at specific behaviours such as gift-giving, kinship

systems, and the exchange of women as means by which social networks
are established and reinforced, thereby ensuring social cohesion.5 Lévi-
Strauss used his studies of "primitive" and "advanced" societies to search
for common structures which he believed were shared by all humanity
because they were rooted in the operations of the human brain. The analysis of myth was one of his main interests because he believed that myth
represented relationships among human beings and between us and our
surroundings, and hence reflected the hidden code of universal structure.
Myth was a conscious manifestation of an unconscious meaning, just as
kinship systems reflect the internal logic of human society.

Karl Marx (1818–1883) and Friedrich Engels (1820–1895) gave structuralism a powerful variant. Primacy, for them, lay in the economic structures that shaped human relations, which in turn shaped the broad
processes of history itself. There have been endless debates over the extent
to which Marx believed that the economic system actually determined all
of human experience, but there is little debate that Marxism has been pro-
foundly influential in both the abstract world of the academic and the
practical world of modern politics. The ideas of class and class struggle
have been particularly important.

Responses to structuralism took several forms. One of the most influential came to be known as structural functionalism, perhaps best known
in the work of American sociologist Talcott Parsons (1902–1979).
Parsons accepted the idea that there were social systems or structures that
determined the nature of community. But he was also interested in how
people acted in relation to one another through work, through "obligations" imposed by authorities of various kinds, and through what he
called "the communicative complex," meaning messages and their means
of transmission.[6] Community was not just a group defined by territorial
limits or social systems but was also defined by relationships that shaped
its functioning.

The idea of relationships shaping community was taken even further by
the cultural ecologists. Somewhat confusingly, the term is used in both
sociology and anthropology but with different meanings. In sociology, it is
generally associated with the Chicago School (so named because of the
influential role of the sociology department at the university there). Using
a biological analogy, these scholars wrote of society as a web of individuals
living in mutual interdependence in the same way as biological organisms
do. Hence, both competition and cooperation characterize human relationships. The focus of the Chicago School was the city, and its practition-
ers pursued an almost ethnographic method of observing and analysing
specific groups (doctors, Jews, the homeless). Anthropologists studying
Aboriginal peoples of North America began to use the term "cultural
ecology" in a different sense. For those like American scholar Julian

Steward (1902–1972) at the University of Illinois, it meant the study of relationships between the physical environment and cultural arrangements. In both cases, however, societies were not just networks or systems; they were also relationships and interactions.

The idea of relationships was also adopted and adapted by various heirs to the Marxist tradition. One of the most influential was English historian E.P. Thompson (1924–1993) who, in *The Making of the English Working Class*,7 rejected the idea that class was a "thing" definable merely by its relationship to the system of production. Instead, Thompson proposed that "class is a social and cultural formation ... which cannot be defined abstractly, or in isolation, but only in terms of relationship with other classes ... [through] the medium of *time* – that is, action and reaction, change and conflict."8 English working people, he demonstrated, had a significant hand in their own "making" of a class identity.

Another branch of theory that contributed to the scientific effort to understand groups developed through a trajectory that was eventually dubbed semiotics (or the "sign and symbol" school). Its adherents proposed that communication was one of the systems that other structuralists had overlooked. Swiss linguist Ferdinand de Saussure (1857–1913) argued that language itself could be understood as a system. Language, he suggested, was composed of signs, which are arbitrary concepts that refer to ideas and images that exist "outside" language. It was he who coined the term "semiotics" (sometimes translated as "semiology") when expounding his "science of signs." Signs, he proposed, were used according to universal principles or laws that could be uncovered.9 The concept was expanded and explored by numerous disciples, including Roland Barthes (1915–1980), who proposed that a "sign" did not have to be just language but could be any social product: clothing fashions, stories, pictures.10 Anthropologist Clifford Geertz (b. 1926) used the principles of semiotics to argue that cultures could be interpreted in the same way as texts; at the heart of a culture, as at the heart of a text, was a coherent system of symbols that made the world both knowable and meaningful.11 Symbolic meaning had entered the lexicon as another aspect of the dynamics that held groups together.

For other twentieth-century scholars, the stress on relationships or systems of meaning was troubling because it seemed to leave insufficient room for the actions of individual human beings as social "agents." Structures and formal relationships were abstractions, the "hidden hand," suspiciously like older religious ideas about the will of God or predestination. Where did free will enter the picture? The search for agency took scholarship in several directions. One of these has come to be known as the school of social construction. Human beings create their own environments and circumstances by imaging meanings. Benedict Anderson (b.

1936) applied the concept to the phenomenon of nationalism in *Imagined Communities*.[12] Scholars of race and gender proposed that these categories, too, were socially constructed, usually to serve the purposes of those in power. Social psychology emerged as a subdiscipline amidst a debate over whether groups were anything more than a collection of individuals and to what extent individual minds were shaped by the collectivity to which they belonged.[13]

These main threads of twentieth-century theory (structuralism, symbolism, constructivism) were woven together most influentially in the work of French sociologist Pierre Bourdieu (1930–2002). He once called his ideas "constructivist structuralism," by which he meant he believed both that the social world included "objective structures," which exist independently of human consciousness and shape or limit our behaviour and thoughts, and that at the same time the social world is shaped by human agency. Human beings have ideas and relate to one another in ways that shape our experience of groups just as much as the structures or systems that provide the bones of the group. As "social agents," Bourdieu proposed, people "are not automata regulated like clocks, in accordance with laws which they do not understand." Rather, we "put into action" principles created through "habitus": ideas and behaviours "acquired through experience."[14] Bourdieu also believed that symbolism played a crucial role in the process. Thus, for Bourdieu, social groups are created and shaped by "agents" (human actors) who "construct" their societies through "practice" (repeated actions), using, in part, "symbolic representations."

If one looks carefully at the history of the idea of community (or indeed, of the social sciences more generally) as presented in the standard undergraduate textbooks, it becomes clear that the men – and indeed they are all male – who are selected as founding fathers and leading lights (in other words, the canon), for the period stretching from the late nineteenth century to the late twentieth century, represent variations on a theme. From Durkheim to Bourdieu, they have accepted the modernist idea of the importance of the individual and thus are trying (at least implicitly) to explain how group life/community is possible. They have rejected Tönnies's characterization of community as something lost to the industrial world. They admit the problems and tensions that arise in the new order, but they see in its very structures the hope for reconciliation of difference. Community becomes a community of shared interests in which human beings, as more or less free agents, recognize what they share and work together to build satisfying societies. In 1978 an American sociologist noted that although one of his predecessors had listed some ninety-four definitions of "community," one could still conclude that "the most common sociological definitions used today tend to focus on a community as an aggregate of people who share a common interest in a particular locality."[15] Community was no longer something that declined or disappeared in the process of modernization; rather, it changed as the economic system changed. Indeed, some took the idea even further: British cultural theorist Raymond Williams (1921–88) once played with the idea that modern life had actually generated a *greater* sense of community: "In many villages, community only became a reality when economic and political rights were fought for and partially gained, in the recognition of unions, in the extension of the franchise, and in the possibility of entry into new representative and democratic institutions. In many thousands of cases, there is more community in the modern village, as a result of this process of new legal and democratic rights, than at any point in the recorded or imagined past."[16] Modernity had appropriated the idea of community.

Meanwhile, through the 1960s and 1970s a rebellion was afoot, first in French intellectual circles and then spreading across the Atlantic to North America. The term "postmodernism" means different things to different people (perhaps entirely appropriately, given some of its main tenets), but generally it is used to refer to an attempt to "deconstruct" the modernism which our society takes too much for granted. The network of ideas, behaviours, economic systems, and political structures that constitute modernism is neither natural nor inevitable and indeed can be downright dangerous, argue the postmodernists. Jean-François Lyotard (1924–1998), in *La condition postmoderne*, proposed that we need to consider ideas such as progress, scientific rationalism, and even Marxism as "metanarratives" – big stories told in such a way as to validate them as the only reasonable ways of knowing.[17] Jacques Derrida (1930–2005) argued, in a wide range of publications, that any text contains hidden meanings built up through the hidden logic of signs and signifiers, and that the entire process can and should be "deconstructed" to reveal the concealed. He and other theorists then turned even more directly to language itself as the source of modernist ideas. Building on Ferdinand de Saussure's concept that language has both individual and social dimensions, proponents of what has come to be known as "the linguistic turn" have argued variously either that language limits our thinking or that it is everything, constituting our entire understanding of ourselves and our world. There is no "reality" that exists outside language. In Derrida's famous phrase, "There is nothing outside of the text."[18] As political scientist Walter Truett Anderson once put it, "Reality isn't what it used to be."[19]

The idea that language and discourse (social discussions structured by hidden rules) are central to knowledge led to a range of analytic works, including those of Michel Foucault (1926–1984), who studied ideas about prisons and mental illness, and gave us the phrase "discursive formation" to describe statements that are actually patterns of meaning that generate social roles, behaviours, and knowledge. The last, for Foucault, was an important form of power in society.[20] Judith Butler (b. 1956), an American philosopher, contributed to feminist theory with the idea that not only is language important in the construction of gender but the performance of speech is central to the process; in other words, making a statement is the performance of an action.[21] Postcolonial theory also found language and power theories useful. Edward Saïd (1935–2003) argued that imperialism became part of the Western experience through the novel and other literature and in the process came to be seen as "natural" and "legitimate" among Westerners, who accepted the idea that the colonized were inherently inferior "others."[22]

Other postmodernists chose the more explicit question of community as their focus. And here we return (in a sense) full circle to Tönnies and his use of "community" as an idea through which modernism might be critiqued. For the postmodernists, however, "community" has itself become a modernist concept, a "discursive formation" that is used to legitimize liberalism, power relations, or the economic system. In the words of feminist scholar Miranda Joseph, liberalism "imagines" that "the public is a sphere of abstract citizenship in which private interests ... are left behind in the construction of a larger political community." Thus, modernism proposes that the public sphere is a "site" of consensus and community.[23] But as feminists and victims of other forms of oppression have argued, this "consensus" is an illusion and the discourses that create the illusion are themselves the source of oppression. The community is not a "natural" or inevitable human experience; rather, it is a very specific manifestation of modernity – one that has created enormous pain for many.

Reactions to postmodern theory have been varied and vigorous. In some circles it has been swallowed whole and with enthusiasm. Others see it merely as "old wine in new bottles" or simply as empty bottles ("the emperor has no clothes" school). Many, especially among Canadian historians, simply choose to ignore it. But others have recognized in postmodern theory a fundamental challenge to the form, content, and practice of social science as a scholarly pursuit. If we can no longer accept without question such concepts as "nation" or the idea that there might be a single shared "reality," whither social science?

One of the most interesting responses to this problem has been the growing attention to the question of identity. For those who reject the extremes of postmodern theory but agree that we need to take into account ideas, imaginings, and symbolic thinking (and not just physical realities), one can still grapple with the dimensions and meaning of experience by examining the ways in which we do in fact seem to construct a sense of who we are. We create and repeat stories (narratives). We adopt symbols and metaphors that seem to provide meaning or emotional satisfaction. We participate in rituals and act out our ideas in other ways (performance), thereby creating or reinforcing both ideas and social networks. We create boundaries to distinguish ourselves from others. Our bodies and our physical surroundings are real, but how we see them and how we express our relationships with them can vary. We construct memories of our personal and collective pasts, perhaps to make our present meaningful, perhaps to legitimize our behaviour, perhaps as a credible explanation to obscure our terror of the unknown. And, obviously, a sense of collective identity and the "identity politics" it can generate are major forces in the contemporary world. Explaining these identities provides a justification for social science practice and avoids both the absurdities of extreme postmodernism and the increasing dissatisfaction with the implications of empiricism and essentialism.

Studies of identity are now found across the disciplines and in a variety of forms. Those inclined to believe that the individual should be the starting point have explored ways in which personality and psychology contribute to social formations. Those inclined to believe that language is the core of human experience have emphasized the ways in which shared discourses contribute to the development of collective identities. Those who want to put time into the equation have studied the role of memory in shaping identity; history becomes both a socially constructed "thing" and a central process in contemporary experience. Identity is not only understood in multiple ways; it is also understood as multifaceted and shifting in our own experience. We see ourselves in many ways: as individuals, in our varied relationships with others nearby (woman, wife, daughter, mother), in our place in an economic system (worker, consumer, entrepreneur, manager), in our place in a political system (citizen, social democrat, voter, Canadian). These multiple identities may conflict; there may be no logic in the ways we reconcile the differences in the several we maintain at one time. Nevertheless, identity is clearly important both to individuals and to societies and cultures.

This book is an examination of the process by which the people of Porcupine–Iroquois Falls developed changing ideas about "community" and how some came to define themselves as participants in a select group with a shared sense of identity, entitlement, and legitimacy. The focus of the book is the social process of community formation, but this process cannot be understood independently of the economic, political, historical, and environmental systems and structures in which people lead their lives. Community is not a "thing"; it is an ongoing historical process that incorporates imagined ideals, economic, political, and social structures inherited from other times and places, individual responses to the unanticipated or accidental, the unexpected consequences of human interaction, and relationships with the physical environment, both real and imagined. This study is an examination not just of historical "reality" but also of the ways in which people manipulated and constructed their realities to suit local needs and purposes. And while it examines a particular place, the story is not purely a local one, for events in Europe, Asia, and North America more broadly provided a constant influence. But the point is not to demonstrate the extent to which a local (micro) study can be extrapolated into general (macro) interpretations. Rather, my interest is in what a local study can tell us about the processes of human interaction – including both the local/unique and the wider context, interaction with the world.

A debate in the 1990s among academic historians in North America over the relative merits of social and "national" history, or of "little" stories and "big" ones, really served primarily to illustrate how historians have failed to find ways in which to incorporate into one effective interpretive device, the many levels upon which we all live. Usually we simply abandon the challenge by arguing that there is no one big story, just many little ones. So one might well ask, What is the purpose of yet another "small" study – and, indeed, one of an even more "limited identity," in Maurice Careless's famous phrase? Why look at a place that is completely unknown to many Canadians, a place with fewer residents than the city of Lethbridge, Alberta? The answer has three parts.

First, this subregion deserves to be better known, for its history has always been directly connected to events that made Canada what it is today. If you read a newspaper, wear gold jewellery, appreciate Canadian figure skating or hockey, have heard (or heard of) Shania Twain, live in a planned community, or have had occasion to bewail the policies of the Bank of Canada, your life has been affected by this region.[24] The city of Toronto can trace many of the roots of its dominance over the Canadian economy to this place, as can more individual entrepreneurial dynasties, such as those founded by Roy Thomson and by the Timmins brothers through their Hollinger investments. What kind of place could give rise to such a variety of stories? What kind of community sustained both the economic and the personal dimensions necessary for these outcomes? Clearly, Canadians ought to be better acquainted with this piece of our inheritance.

Second, the region provides a sort of laboratory in which the big, abstract questions can be asked on a smaller, more manageable scale: How can the idea of community be studied, and how do local identities emerge? I am not suggesting that Porcupine–Iroquois Falls is a microcosm of Canada or that patterns that develop locally can be extrapolated to the national stage. The local certainly does, at times, seem to share the characteristics of the national. But there are factors that make it unique – in the individual personalities, the circumstances of the local physical environment, and the chance events that happen only here and demand a local response. If history is, as Donald Creighton liked to say, the interplay of character and circumstance, local history shows us that those characters and circumstances can be derived locally, regionally, nationally, and internationally.

Third, the study of the history of Porcupine–Iroquois Falls is a worthy object simply in its own terms. "National" history, or "big" history, or even "total" history is not the only legitimate undertaking for our generation of historians. The local also is important, because our human experience happens as much at the local level as at the national or international (and perhaps more so).

The chapters are divided into three sections. In part 1, readers are introduced to the physical environment, the community that evolved out of the fur trade economy, and the story of the sudden changes (both planned and unplanned) that accompanied the northward push of Empire Ontario in the early twentieth century. Part 2 examines the key elements that contributed to the new society that displaced that of the fur trade – new economic forces, immigration, labour, political organization, and social structures. The third part examines the forces that tended to divide the residents in this new world, the forces that made it possible for them to come together, and ultimately the process by which they first imagined and then built a sense of community. The elements of this sense of community are described and analysed.

The book explores the ideas of community in the region as they evolved from the late eighteenth century to the early 1950s. This particular starting point was chosen because it was the earliest era for which sufficient sources (documentary and oral) could be obtained. The closing date was chosen because the mid-1950s represented both the beginning of a long decline in the gold-mining sector and the end of one community-building process, which was symbolized by the decision in 1954 that Timmins now required its first home for the elderly. After that time, a new stage in the evolution of community emerged, awaiting the examination of future historians.

This project began as a much narrower local history, but as it expanded, more and more people provided valuable assistance. The Social Sciences and Humanities Research Council of Canada and Carleton University provided important funding. Michael Devine of Toronto generously shared with me his personal historical collection and memories of Iroquois Falls. Robin Ormerod of the Timmins Museum and Nancy Renwick of the Iroquois Falls Pioneer Museum assisted above and beyond the call of duty (and the ladies at the Dev II provided the best lunches I have ever enjoyed on a research trip!). Judith Beattie of the Hudson's Bay Company Archives and the reading room staff at the Archives of Ontario kindly put up with my requests for obscure material and were unfailingly helpful in finding it. Kevin Stanton, then at the University of Colorado at Boulder, did some excellent research work for me

in the Western Federation of Miners archival collection, and Leena Sillanpää provided me with some important Finnish translations. Olaf Pollon of
Montreal, Nora Lake of Timmins, Phyllis Bray of Kingston, M.K. Abel of
Sudbury, and several people who prefer to remain anonymous shared
their experiences, knowledge, and opinions. Among my professional col-
leagues, I am grateful for inspiration, assistance, and encouragement from
Marilyn Barber, Gerald Friesen, Duncan McDowall, Charlene Porsild,
Deborah Gorham, Fred Goodwin, Jill St Germain ("Is it done yet?"), and
particularly Sandra Campbell (with her unfailing eye for wonderful obitu-
aries). Thanks also to Christine Earl of the Carleton University Geography
Department, to Thai-Nguyen Nguyen, who produced the maps, to Joan
McGilvray of McGill-Queen's, and particularly to Carlotta Lemieux, whose
eagle editorial eye has made this a much better book.

I lived at one of the mining "properties" just outside Timmins for two
years of my childhood. At the age of eleven, I thought "The Porcupine"
was the most magical place on earth, with its exotic smells of forest and
mine, the haunting remains of foundations that hinted at past dramas and
mysteries, and the fascinating array of schoolyard companions, with such
names as DiMarco, Sauvé, Heinonen, and Boychuk, who brought strange
and wonderful things to the lunchroom in their little metal boxes. Now it
is all a little less mysterious and a great deal less glamorous, but it still
retains its magic for me. I hope that readers will discover a little of this
magic in these pages – for, after all, there is more than a little sleight of
hand in both the process of community formation and the scholarly reconstruction of that process.

A NOTE ON SPELLING

Anishinabe, meaning "the people," has been rendered in many ways. The
spelling used here is purely an arbitrary choice, based on how it sounds to
my ear.

Mattagami is sometimes spelled Matagami but the officially recognized
spelling is used here because it was the most common variant in the historical record.

Ojibwa and *Ojibway* are currently competing for the "correct" spelling, but
I have chosen the former, since it was the most commonly used form in
northeastern Ontario during the period covered in this book.

Temiskaming The Ontario government insists on spelling this Timiskaming, but because it was spelled Temiskaming (in English) and Témiscamingue (in French), during most of the period covered in this book, the
older English spelling is used.

PART ONE

CHAPTER ONE

The Place

It has become almost commonplace to hear that history is about time and geography is about space. Yet none of us experiences time as disembodied from place, and indeed our understanding of time is often shaped by the space in which we experience it. No history can be fully appreciated if it is divorced from the place in which the story unfolds, and in the case of our story, the events that unfold are shaped as much by the place as by the people who lived in it. The particular combination of natural resources available here dictated the basic skeleton of the economy even as government policies and individual human choices modified how that economy shifted in shape over time. The climate and very bones of the land dictated how people could move about and live, either as submitting to these dictates or finding ways to overcome them. Even the visual appearance of the place had an impact on how people saw themselves and defined their relationship to others. Thus, in order to understand the community that evolved here, we need to begin by understanding the space in which it developed.

It is a bright warm day in early June 1906, and a little party of canoeists are busily packing and arranging supplies at their campground on the shore of Bay Lake.[1] Across the sparkling water they can just see the cluster of cabins and shacks that seem to have appeared from nowhere on the east shore of the lake where the newly laid railway tracks pass. There is the smell of freshly sawn lumber in the air, and the birds' songs are drowned by the rhythmic screams of saws ripping through logs at the two sawmills that are competing with one another to spew out yet more timbers. The canoeists sniff the unfamiliar smells anxiously; the white men claim to be building a new town, but so far the canoeists have seen only destruction as the tall pines come crashing down to clear a swath through traplines and campgrounds for the railway and to feed the voracious appetite of the saws. So they are glad to have accepted the commission that has brought them to within sight of this strange place now called Latchford. Last year, after repeated petitioning, the king had finally sent a party to discuss a treaty with the Anishinabe, but white men with their usual arrogance, had misjudged the length of time required to travel through the bush and had not managed to visit all the posts, as promised, before winter loomed; so the people had decided to wait no longer and had made their way to fall hunting grounds to lay in supplies. Now the treaty party was coming back, and the canoeists had agreed to take on the important task of conducting them safely up the Montreal River to the designated meeting place at Fort Matachewan. They are hoping that the treaty will protect their hunting grounds from the greed of the newcomers and create a partnership through which decisions about sharing the resources can be made to mutual advantage. So they are preparing for this historic trip while waiting for the treaty party to arrive on the train.

Finally everyone is gathered, and on June 15 the party, heavily loaded with bales and boxes, pushes off from Latchford and heads north. The day is hot, still, and sultry, and the deep waters of the Montreal River look black and glassy, reflecting the dense thickets of alders and other bushes crowding the shores. The shrubbery forms almost impenetrable walls along the river here, creating the illusion that the travellers are alone in an endless berth of greenery. Yet behind the bushes that line the shore are glimpses of a world beyond, where the great pine forests are giving way to the spindly spruce of the boreal zone. Here, giant red pines stand boldly against the creeping northlands, with their birch groves, thin tall black spruce, and poplars chatting in the slightest summer breeze.

As the party heads upriver, rolling hills signal the rise toward the height of land and the Arctic watershed. These are ancient hills of granite and gneiss, formed an almost inconceivable two billion years ago as massive volcanic eruptions convulsed the surface of the planet. Over the ages, they were enveloped by layers of sedimentary deposits worked by unknown oceans, and finally were scoured by glaciers that stripped away the sediment of millennia and laid bare once again the great igneous and metamorphic mounds that had for so long remained hidden. Gradually, the rocks were embraced by northern forests that provided home and shelter to an increasing diversity of wildlife. Moose, caribou, and bear settled here alongside hares, wolves, lynx, muskrat, beaver, skunks, raccoons, and chipmunks. Birds as varied as the great blue heron and black-capped chickadee found a niche, while grouse, jays, and ducks have settled too, and great flocks of geese migrate seasonally through the region. The acid soil is ideal for raspberries, and sandy pockets left by eons of ice and water are filled with blueberry bushes. Everywhere there is water – countless lakes and rivers teeming with pike, pickerel, and occasionally sturgeon. Marshlands abound, punctuated with patches of bulrushes and water lilies, home to frogs, dragonflies, and turtles, and with depths of thick, black, organic material that has rotted through the ages and settled to the bottom to create a rich nutrient base for the next generation.

The waters provide almost endless opportunities for the breeding of insects; mosquitoes and blackflies are everywhere. As the paddlers search for a first-night camping spot, they meet two canoes of prospectors heading downstream who claim it is impossible to travel any farther because the bugs are swarming guard over the secrets of the upriver country. That night the campers build a smoky smudge fire to keep the bugs at bay; the government men retreat beneath mosquito netting. For the next three days, the hot, sultry weather provides a perfect opportunity for the bugs to feast on the travellers. "Well," jokes one of the paddlers, "they can't get any worse. There would not be room for any more."

On the third day out of Latchford, the canoes slip almost noiselessly into Elk Lake, a long, narrow, water-filled valley between hills that rise steeply from the inky black water. The summer stillness is broken only by thunder rolling ominously in the distance. Little do any of the paddlers realize that very soon the lake will be echoing with the shouts and hammers of prospectors (and later by businessmen and women), building a base from which to explore for gold or make a fortune from those who find it. Fortunately, for now, the storm does not break and the paddlers make good time, drawing up to the shore at Fort Matachewan just as the sun is sinking behind the western hills.

Matachewan is a beautiful place. The rolling hills tumble straight into the river, which turns abruptly among them to find its way south. It has long been an important meeting place for the Anishinabe, so here the Hudson's Bay Company (HBC) erected a small post, consisting of a store, a warehouse, and a trader's house. The buildings sit on the slope of one of the hills, overlooking chattering little rapids and the fine country beyond. Above the post are two lakes nestled into the hills, with Anishinabe tents dotting the slopes around them. Below, the river broadens, and on a still day its waters are glassy but mysteriously dark, as if hiding a great secret deep below the surface mirror. Today, Matachewan is bustling with activity in anticipation of the treaty party's arrival. A volley of gunfire greets the canoes, and the excited shouts of children accompany Stephen Lafricain of the HBC as he makes his way down to greet the canoes as they pull ashore. The formalities may begin.

West of Matachewan (less than a hundred kilometres as the raven flies) is Mattagami Post, where the treaty party has arranged to meet other Anishinabe. The rocky bones of the land lie roughly north-south between the two posts, making an overland trip slow and exhausting – scrambling up and down the rocky outcrops from one creek or river valley to the next,

through thick bush or across spongy marshes. So travellers must take a
longer route that takes advantage of the waterways as much as possible. To
reach Mattagami, Anishinabe and their trade partners paddle their canoes
north from Matachewan, then portage across a series of well-developed
trails over the height of land into the Hudson Bay drainage basin. There,
they re-launch their canoes into what the newcomers call the Nighthawk
River, and continue north into Nighthawk Lake, formerly known as Piscoutagamy. Along the route the rolling hills begin to spread down into
flatter ground. Here, the soil changes to heavy clay, laid down by the
melting glaciers of the last ice age as the silt they had churned up slowly
settled to the bottom of the great glacial lake Barlow-Ojibway. The clay
deposits here can be surprisingly deep and provide a rock-hard surface for
easy travel on the portages when the weather has been dry. But after a rain-
storm the clay becomes an almost impassable gumbo that packs around
moccasined feet in great clods, drying to form concrete castings if not
scraped away in time. On the more level terrain, lake waters can spread
widely across the land, free of the long narrow gouges in the rocks that
restrict their movement elsewhere. Thus, Nighthawk Lake is a large but
relatively shallow body of water, dotted with islands that look like bristly
bootbrushes dropped at random from above. From here, travellers can
continue north to Frederick House Lake, then down the Frederick House
River to the Moose River, and thence all the way to James Bay.

But if we are heading for Mattagami Post, we must turn west at
Nighthawk Lake and take advantage of the portage route cut by the HBC
to provide access to the Mattagami River.[2] First, we go up a river that is
scarcely more than a creek flowing into the northwest bay of the big lake;
then overland to a little lake (later called Three Nations) for a short
paddle to the next portage, which leads to Porcupine River. More
upstream paddling brings us to Porcupine Lake, which is small enough
that the far shore is clearly visible but large enough that our shouts cannot
be heard across it. Its shoreline is flat and unremarkable, but the patches
of marsh that punctuate it have attracted moose, which browse lazily
among the rushes and lilies. From the south end of Porcupine Lake we
strike overland again, through the forest of spruce and fragrant balsam
that lies between Porcupine and what will soon be known as Pearl Lake.
The land here is less dramatic than that around Matachewan, perhaps
because the rocks rise and fall more gradually and provide none of the
sweeping vistas that so appeal to the romantic eye. Nevertheless, if you
know where to look, there is much to fascinate.

Just east of our route, hidden in secret places among the trees, lies a
series of little lakes known as "kettle lakes," which record a lengthy natural
history for those literate in the language of the land. Ten to twelve thousand years ago the glaciers had largely retreated through here, but the

process was not simply a smooth gradual melting, as many people imagine. Large chunks of ice tended to get trapped in the mountains of sand that were also getting dropped behind; thus insulated, these chunks remained as "icebergs" while the new land above them dried out and warmed. Over time, these chunks finally melted, leaving deep basins behind them, isolated from one another and from the rivers and streams that followed the depressions in the ancient, now-exposed granite. Gradually, these basins filled with water from springs, and beautiful little lakes were formed, their sandy banks dropping rapidly away into unseen depths as much as thirty metres below. With no real inlet and no outlet at all, the kettles were filled only by springs or by rainfall, leaving them vulnerable to the vagaries of the seasons. Wetland plants soon established themselves around the kettles, forming floating platforms that edged delicately and ever so gradually over the water. As thousands of years passed, some of the shallower kettles were completely covered by these spongy rafts of determined plants. In turn, the rafts supported ever-larger species of plants, from woody ground cover to bushes. Eventually some of the kettles were fully drained and were invaded by the surrounding forest. Others remain perfect jewels of deep, dark water nestled among the spruce and aspen. Sheltered from winds and untroubled by currents, their surfaces are mirrors reflecting the deep green of the forest. A hike of only a few kilometres through this magical landscape will reveal kettles in all stages of their history.

Directly along our current route, the land around us seems to be a great pine forest at one moment and subarctic taiga the next. We are in the transition zone between two major ecosystems. Groves of trembling aspen and birch litter the forest floor with their leaves and support a carpet of ferns, woody plants, fungi, and small berries. A short distance farther on, we are surrounded by an almost gothic cathedral of black spruce, with their long narrow trunks shooting straight up from the forest floor to a canopy of whispering green needles far above our heads. The ground here is carpeted with spreading mosses and lichens that look almost like a cultivated lawn, quite unlike the bushy thickets below the deciduous trees. Then we make another turn and we are atop a rocky outcrop, exposed to the full strength of the sun but looking down into a cool, shaded bog, where pitcher plants and Labrador tea abound. The hammering of a pileated woodpecker echoes through the trees, almost drowning out the snap of a branch that betrays the presence of a lynx.

Unknown to our travellers in 1906, the ground beneath our feet holds a tremendous secret. Zig-zagging through the ancient grainy rocks called gneisses are veins of sparkling white quartz. And scattered within these veins are tiny specks of gold, each in itself scarcely large enough to notice; but because the veins are so extensive, the flecks in their aggregate constitute a major treasure. There are other secrets in the rocks as well: sulphide deposits harbouring silver, copper, zinc, nickel, and perhaps even diamonds.

We cannot tarry long, for business awaits us at Mattagami Post. A few minutes' paddle across Pearl Lake takes us to a creek that brings us to yet another small lake (soon to be re-christened Gillies Lake). There is one final portage beyond Gillies Lake but it is across a mercifully flat plain, and the route is clearly marked by others who have gone before us on this important commercial route. Finally, across the flats, we arrive at the Mattagami River, one of the most important river systems that cuts through this land. As a major tributary of the Moose, you could paddle downstream from here directly to James Bay, through four hundred or more kilometres of boreal forest spilling out from the Canadian Shield onto the Hudson Bay Lowlands. That great sedimentary basin, washed and rolled by melting glaciers and ancient ocean shorelines, is dotted with millions of ponds and bogs that give way to muddy flatlands along the seacoast.

But we are not going to the seacoast. Instead, at the Mattagami River, we turn upstream and head directly for Mattagami Post. Along our route here, the clay soil is replaced by beautiful fine sand that once formed the shoreline of an ancient glacial lake. The sand is covered by a very thin and dark organic mat that holds it in place, except where spring rains have cut through it and created little gullies or sand cliffs cascading into the river. Stands of red and white pine, much like those supported farther south, are common here, as is the crooked jack pine. The river at first twists and turns as it meanders through the flat plains, but then the ground begins to rise, forcing the river to cascade down through boulders and through narrowings between rocky outcrops. Unlike the black waters of the Montreal River, these waters are clear and transparent; on a sunny day they reflect the glorious blue of the sky and sparkle in the breezes with a million dancing lights. About a day's paddle from our last overland portage, the river widens to form a long crooked lake nestled among the pine trees and sandy beaches, fed by dozens of streams flowing down from the height of land just beyond the lake. The lake is deep and well supplied with a variety of species of fish, some growing to tremendous size. The surrounding bush is well known for its rabbits, partridges, moose, and, at one time, caribou, so the area around Mattagami Lake has attracted a sizable portion of the region's Anishinabe. It has also become home to an important HBC trading post, strategically situated on a long sandy point jutting into the lake. By the 1880s, the HBC had built here a large and comfortable home for the chief trader, a row of smaller houses for the post "servants" (labourers), and the requisite storehouses and trading buildings. A few acres nearby had been cleared to grow potatoes and turnips, as well as hay for the four head of cattle kept here. While an experiment with oats had failed utterly and the barley crop could charitably be described as poor, the root vegetables did very well and the hay flourished. A little Anglican church and house for its missionary rounded out the site.[3]

This is the destination of our 1906 treaty party, but instead of the long roundabout traditional route that we have just taken through the Porcupine country, they have chosen a new option. The recently constructed Canadian Pacific Railway permits a more direct and comfortable route, striking northwest from Sudbury into the uplands, along the Spanish River, and then across the undulating hills to Chapleau, which has already become a bustling divisional point and the seat of the Anglican bishop of Moosonee. About midway between Sudbury and Chapleau is a little siding called Biscotasing, chosen by the HBC as its new jumping-off point to supply Mattagami Post in order to avoid the 400–kilometre trek from Moose Factory. So it is here that the treaty commissioners meet a different party of native guides on 4 July 1906. They unload their packs and packages from the train, repack everything into canoes, and head down a newly cleared series of fourteen portages on the three-day trip to Mattagami Lake.

The new route foreshadows major changes that are about to be visited on the land and its inhabitants. At Biscotasing, even the city-bred treaty men complain of the constant rumbling of trains that pass through, day and night. Meanwhile, the carousing of residents drunk on easily available whisky offends their Methodist sensitivities.[4] Along the route to Mattagami Post, they see evidence of the work of government survey parties; and they meet a provincial fire ranger who has been assigned to protect the valuable timber for the benefit of big logging companies, which are sending crews farther and farther into the bush in search of stands of pine like those they have already stripped from the Ottawa Valley to the east and the Muskoka region to the south. If the treaty party had followed the old fur trade route through the Porcupine country to the north, it would have met still more surveyors laying out townships in anticipation of agricultural development. Indeed, a handful of hopeful farmers have already visited the area and are eyeing the flood plain of the Mattagami River at the foot of the HBC portage as a likely spot. Moreover, some prospectors are not as easily deterred by the blackflies as the treaty party was on the Montreal River in June. Whispers of change are everywhere.

Even for those who knew it was coming, the abruptness of the change is cause for astonishment. Three years after the treaty, in the summer of 1908, the Canadian government sends another official expedition; it is to deal with the complaints at Lake Abitibi about the implementation of the 1905 treaty.[5] This time, the party travels in comfort on the newly constructed Temiskaming and Northern Ontario Railway (TNO) from North Bay to McDougall's Chutes, now officially called Matheson. There they meet their lead canoeist, Bazil McDougall, who complains that a townsite is being developed on his family's land in spite of guarantees he obtained from the surveyors. Everywhere there are people, cutting back the dense vegetation and dragging in wagonloads of provisions and building materials. Railway construction camps dot the bush well back from the tracks, where the sounds of English, French, Italian, and Ukrainian are replacing the Ojibwa, Cree, and Algonquin once heard here. The Black River, once the main canoe route to the Abitibi River from this region, has been taken over by motorized boats and even an optimistically named "steamer," which runs between the rapids on the Black and the falls on the Abitibi, carrying supplies and men to feed the voracious appetite of construction projects on both the TNO and the National Transcontinental Railway to the north. The Black River is not large, so the heavy traffic gives a real sense of congestion. It beats out the new rhythms of life coming to dominate the land.

The little flotilla of canoes makes its way through the river traffic and reaches the junction of the Black and Abitibi Rivers, the meeting place of two ancient and important transportation highways through the region. A few hours' paddle downstream from here would take them to the beautiful and historic Iroquois Falls, where the waters of the Abitibi River divide around an island and cascade in two great rushes down a series of rocky ledges on their way to the northern ocean. At the foot of the falls, the foaming waters dash against two small islands blocking their path, churning and retreating before finding their way again. Here, the shores of the river are well wooded with spruce, birch, and poplar. Above the falls, the river is often clogged with driftwood, evidence of the great spring floods that annually claw away at the riverbanks and redistribute the forest. But our canoeists have no time for sightseeing. There is business requiring attention elsewhere, and they turn up the Abitibi River towards its source.[6]

Here the river tumbles along through the boulders, necessitating several portages, where sandflies plague the trekkers. Then the terrain begins to roughen, and high bluffs line the route. Atop one bluff, a large rock (perhaps deposited by an ancient glacier) attracts the attention of the paddlers, who inform the government party that this is Old Woman's Rock (or Granny's Rock), named to honour an old blind Anishinabe woman who was pushed from it to her death in the waters below by her people's enemies, the Iroquois. The paddlers stop and reverently sprinkle tobacco on the waters to honour her spirit. A few hours later, the party reaches what they call Couchiching Falls, a picturesque series of falls and rapids that carry the waters of the Abitibi bubbling and chattering down a drop of about fourteen metres. Great flocks of gulls circle below the falls, diving for fish and occasionally stopping to paddle in the shoals or preen on the rocks as they have done for thousands of years.

Above the falls, though, things look very different. A large log building has been put up to accommodate the transcontinental railway construction crews, who are busily making timber for ties. A tramway has been laid to track around the falls. And the pungent smell of horse manure is everywhere as dozens of teams labour, even on this grey wet day, to haul their loads back and forth. So much brush is lying along the sides of the Abitibi River, left over from timber cutting, that our canoeists find it difficult to land and investigate the camp before they portage around the falls.

The canoeists make good time now, paddling up the Abitibi unimpeded by rapids. They reach the great inland sea that is Lake Abitibi in time for lunch. It is a beautiful day and the Lower Lake is perfectly calm, its mirrored surface reflecting the rich blue of the sky and the spiked green-black silhouettes of the many little islands that dot the lake. But on the shores of the lake, the calm has been broken by the buzz of human industry. On one bank, a large steamboat is under construction. Nearby, a sawmill is churning out boards – and dumping the refuse in the river so that its mouth is choked with debris – a metaphor for what is to come. For now, though, the Anishinabe are pleased to take advantage of the employment offered at the mill, and the lead paddler Bazil McDougall greets many old friends as the party passes by.

The paddlers head for the narrows that separate the lower and upper bodies of Lake Abitibi, then point their canoes eastward. The lake can be a real challenge to paddlers in delicate birchbark canoes, for it is large enough to generate heavy swells on windy or stormy days. Often, travellers must seek shelter and wait it out (fortunately, the lake is dotted with islands suitable for the purpose). Our party is lucky and makes a smooth crossing, passing the invisible boundary that now marks Quebec from Ontario. Despite its invisibility, the boundary is destined to have a tremendous impact on the lives of the Native people of the region, for it now marks the boundary between those with whom the Canadian government has established a treaty and those whom it has decided to exclude. A little more than two days' paddling from the confluence of the Black and Abitibi Rivers, the commissioners and their guides reach their destination at the HBC post of Fort Abitibi, now situated at the east end of the lake. Here they are greeted with the usual volleys of friendly gunfire and a feast. There have been trading posts at various places on this great lake since 1686. Here, in order to engage the trade of Native bands from several nations, the French competed against the English, the North West Company competed against the Hudson's Bay Company, and the Hudson's Bay Company competed against independent traders such as the Dokis family. Little do the 1908 inhabitants of the post know that within six years this long history will end and Fort Abitibi will disappear, defeated by the competition of the transcontinental railway. The new town of La Sarre will become the shipment point for furs and trade goods, while the growing settlement of farmer-colonizers along the rail route will eventually help to change the fur trade forever.

Our journey has taken us through a region of lakes, rocks, swamplands, and seemingly endless forests, which in the long days of summer seems welcoming to the Canadian visitors and is a land of plenty for those who know its secrets. But the winters here are long, hard, and very cold, forcing human adaptation to the extremes of a continental interior. This is the Subarctic, after all. January temperatures average between −30° and −20° (Celsius) while days of −40° are not uncommon. In the deep, still iciness of those midwinter days, smoke rises in columns straight into the heavens and the snow echoes hollowly beneath the foot, while the breath hangs visibly in the air, coating whiskers or fur-trimmed hoods with layers of white crystals. Some of the coldest temperatures in Ontario have been recorded in this region, including a low of −58.3° at Iroquois Falls in 1935. In some seasons, the snowfall can be exceptionally heavy, because parts of the area lie in a snowbelt that sweeps inland from the Great Lakes. Winds pick up moisture from Lake Huron (and occasionally Lake Superior) and drop it in deep blankets to the northeast. Because significant winter thaws are rare, the snow simply accumulates, sometimes to heights of several metres. Winter comes early and lingers late. The average frost-free season is officially eighty days within a hundred-day growing season – less than half of what it is in Toronto and three-quarters of what it is on the Canadian prairies. There is insufficient time for wheat, corn, and canola to ripen; only root vegetables and short-season varieties of other crops will grow successfully. And the frost-free period can be unpredictable. In 1918 there were only eleven days from the last "spring" frost to the first "fall" frost.[7]

The heavy winter snows are only part of the annual precipitation, which is considerable, with a yearly average of seventy-five to eighty-five centimetres; about half of it occurs during the growing season. Unfortunately for aspiring farmers, the heaviest rains tend to come at precisely the wrong time: in the fall when dry days are needed for ripening and harvesting. Spring rains are light and erratic. Furthermore, the heavy clay soil in the eastern part of the region does not drain easily, so the moisture collects in pockets. Peat bogs are scattered everywhere, fed and replenished by the drenching rain and melting snow. Elsewhere, the sandy pockets of land drain all too well, conspiring equally effectively to limit their fertility.

Fire is, next to climate and soil perhaps, the most fundamental force that has moulded this landscape throughout the millennia. Fire is necessary for the regeneration of such prevalent species as the black spruce and jack pine, because these trees store their seeds in their cones for the life of the tree, dropping them only at death; the heat of the fires opens the cones and the next generation is released. Other boreal forest species, such as the trembling aspen, seem to rise magically from the blackened charcoal on the forest floor, spreading a fine green mist punctuated by the vibrant pink of the fireweed flower. Scientists talk of natural "fire cycles" that seem to recur regularly to regenerate and remake the forest in a dramatic rush of fiery vortices. In some parts of the region, the fire cycle appears to be as much as a hundred and fifty years, meaning that the forests can be as old as a hundred and fifty or two hundred years.[8] The spindly trunks are a reflection of the poor soil and harsh climate, not the age of the trees.

It is a land where the basic elements of nature are constantly in view, from the ice-scoured ancient rocks to the fire-blackened patches where once stood a mysterious dark forest of black spruce and red berries. The harsh conditions do not provide a comfortable life for the animals and birds that inhabit the region, but there is a surprising richness and diversity nonetheless. Those who have merely driven along Highway 11 or taken the train through the area and complain of the tedious rolling panorama of "nothing but rocks and trees, then more rocks and trees" have really not been looking very closely. This was a land that sustained an Aboriginal population for thousands of years, shaping them and in turn being shaped by them. It was a land that seemed to promise endless opportunity for Canadians at the beginning of the twentieth century. And for the hopefuls who settled here, it was a landscape that they came to see as unique and their own, one that shaped them as much as they reshaped it. In the ebb and flow of human populations through the region lies a fascinating story of imposition and adaptation, conflict and community.

CHAPTER TWO

The First Communities

The region has always been a meeting place – a place for travellers, traders, adventurers, and families to come together and exchange goods, experiences, and ideas. For several thousand years, people have made their permanent homes here while others have come and gone as sojourners, weaving a complex pattern into the fabric of a life based on the resources of the land. Some inhabitants have made visible changes to the landscape while others faded in and out of the bush almost imperceptibly. In the same way, some are more visible to the historian than others. But something of the story of all can be reconstructed.

Ten thousand years ago, according to geological theory, northeastern Ontario was still covered by a great mass of ice known as the Laurentide Ice Sheet. It was the last remaining major extension of the polar glaciation of the Wisconsian Ice Age, and it was retreating as the climate warmed. By nine thousand years ago, a huge inland lake had formed along the southern edge of the melting ice sheet. Later named glacial lake Barlow-Ojibway, its bed would become the base for the Clay Belt of northern Ontario and Quebec. Two thousand years later, the ice sheet had retreated to patches in the Arctic, the glacial lakes had drained, and spruce and jack pine were beginning to establish themselves. Along with them came animal populations and the first people.

We know surprisingly little about the first human beings to inhabit the region. Archaeologists have dubbed them the Shield Archaic cultures. For four thousand years they lived across the rocky highlands in family bands, fishing, gathering plants, and hunting caribou and other large game. They made stone tools but also learned to work the copper found at the head of Lake Superior into points for their hunting spears. Trade networks were established to pass along the valuable copper. People may have kept dogs, and they probably cooked their food using the technique of heated stones dropped in their pots. But beyond these sketchy details we really know very little, and there is considerable debate among archaeologists about their history.[1]

Gradually, by about two thousand years ago, the people of the region began to adopt new technologies, undoubtedly because they invented better ways of managing, but also because they met other people and exchanged ideas. Archaeologists have called this era the Initial Woodland Period and sometimes refer to the people as being of the Laurel cultures. Stone tools were smaller and more finely worked; the bow and arrow was probably adopted, just as it was being adopted elsewhere across the continent. Pottery was imported from neighbours to the south, southwest, and southeast, and intermarriage with them brought the region knowledge of pottery skills and a range of styles. Other southern customs, such as the construction of burial mounds, apparently were not adopted. Copper continued to be used for tools and artwork, and silver from the Cobalt area was traded with southern neighbours. People continued to hunt large game, such as caribou and moose, but smaller animals, such as beaver and muskrat, were also economically important. Fishing and gathering remained mainstays of the diet. North of the height of land, resources were not as rich and travel southward was more difficult, which probably explains why there were fewer cultural changes evident there during this period.[2]

By about a thousand years ago, there had been sufficient cultural changes for archaeologists to apply a new name to the era (the Terminal Woodland) and to the culture (Algonkian). More clear-cut variations in language, tools, and artistic styles emerged. We really have no idea how the people themselves defined their community boundaries, but it seems that environmental realities helped to delineate certain cultural regions. Since people travelled primarily in the summer along river routes, the height of land that divides the Hudson Bay drainage system from the Great Lakes system made it difficult to travel from north to south. Within each watershed, the patterns of river formation meant that travel from east to west (or vice versa) also was awkward. It appears that people tended to focus most of their lives on subregions related to specific rivers or lakes; they probably related most strongly with their immediate neighbours in similar ecosystems. Thus, somewhat separate regional "communities" seem to have emerged in the areas north and south of the height of land. Anthropologists later named these groups Ojibwa (south of the height of land), Cree (north in the lowlands), and Algonquin (in the lands bordering the Ottawa River drainage system). Linguists hypothesize that these groups spoke increasingly diverse languages that originated in a single "parent" language spoken some 2,500 to 3,000 years ago.[3] As people expanded their territories and populations, linguistic changes accompanied the cultural.

Despite this internal regional diversity, people continued to trade and interact across significant distances. For much of the year they lived in small camps that were probably made up of two to four families, but in summer they congregated at favourite rivers or lakes to fish, gossip, exchange information, and enjoy themselves. Life could be dangerous and difficult, but women still found the time to develop exquisite artwork, such as porcupine quillwork on special-occasion clothing. Trading parties set off for distant points to exchange raw materials, tools, household goods, and information. Thus, no family group was completely isolated or disconnected from the wider world. Society was organized around family relationships, but individuals enjoyed considerable freedom to make decisions about where or how to hunt, where to settle, or how to conduct political and diplomatic affairs. A thousand years ago in northeastern Ontario there were many small autonomous communities, but each recognized a connection to a broader regional population of similar communities, and each was also connected to the outside world through trade, intermarriage, and travel.[4] It was a cosmopolitan society that was by no means isolated or inward-looking.

By the sixteenth century, the rumbling of distant changes had begun to echo through the region, adding yet more cultural, economic, and political variations to the mix. Long before anyone had actually seen a European, goods and possibly diseases that had originated across the Atlantic began to make their way along the established trade routes into northeastern Ontario. Stories must also have begun to filter into the region about newcomers and about the political alliances and warfare going on in the lower Ottawa and upper St Lawrence river valleys as the Algonquin and Iroquois jockeyed for control of the trade routes to the interior. In 1600 the French opened a trading post at Tadoussac on the north shore of the St Lawrence, and this initiated a major expansion of trade in which the Algonquin became major players through the interior all the way to James Bay. Then, after about 1615, a new access route was opened to the southwest, when the Nipissing and their partners in the Huron Confederacy began to take over the trade that the Algonquin had controlled. The Nipissing preferred a more westerly route through their own homelands, which drew people along the Mattagami and Abitibi rivers (as far as James Bay) into the trade network.

Meanwhile, the member nations of the Iroquois Confederacy were taking advantage of their strategically located lands to play the British and the French off against each other in the trade and politics of eastern North America. In the 1630s a series of devastating epidemics swept through the villages of the St Lawrence–Great Lakes lowlands, and the Iroquois seized the opportunity to harass and scatter the Huron and Nipissing who controlled access to the northern trade. By 1650–51 the Iroquois had largely succeeded. The once powerful Huron Confederacy had crumbled. Between 1654 and 1658 a brief peace permitted some trading to be resumed, but in 1658 the Iroquois renewed their attacks on the French and their trading partners, and this time succeeded in scattering the Montagnais people who lived along the Mistassini River and traded at Tadoussac. Many Montagnais fled north to James Bay, convinced that the Iroquois were following. As a Jesuit priest recorded in the summer of 1661, the Iroquois had attacked and completely routed one of the nations north of Tadoussac "so terrifying all the surrounding tribes that they have all dispersed in quest of other and more remote mountains, and of rocks more difficult of access, where their lives may be safe. The panic is said to have spread even to the Sea-coast."[5] Indeed, the Iroquois may have followed at least as far as Lake Nemiscau, which drains into James Bay through the Rupert River: a French expedition in 1671 reported the remains of an Iroquois fort at that place dating from about 1664 and positioned so as to command control of all access points on that key transportation route.[6]

Meanwhile, the Iroquois turned their attention to another important route into the north: the Ottawa River. A series of portages from its headwaters allowed access across the height of land to the Abitibi River and thence to James Bay. According to oral tradition, the Iroquois expanded their southern raids into the north along this route, initiating an era of tension and hostilities in the region that lasted well into the nineteenth century. One of the episodes (for which we have no confirmable date) took place at the site of the lovely waterfall on the upper Abitibi River. Versions of the event vary, but all tell of a successful ruse which the northern people used to defeat the Iroquois. A large Iroquois war party in canoes was spotted upriver, and they were either led or driven over the falls to their death.[7] The victory was commemorated in a new name for the site: Iroquois Falls.

While the Iroquois were pressing the various northern nations on all sides and the French were struggling to reopen their lucrative fur trade, the English were awakening to the commercial and territorial possibilities of what is now Northern Ontario. The French entrepreneurs Pierre-Ésprit Radisson and Médart Chouart des Groseilliers, unable to interest any French financial backers in opening trade north of Lake Superior, approached some London entrepreneurs who agreed to experiment with a sea voyage into James Bay in 1668. This voyage, of the *Nonsuch*, was fortuitously timed because the Iroquois had recently agreed to a truce, and the crew of the *Nonsuch* found the people gathered on the James Bay coast enthusiastic about having a new trade opportunity so close to home. In 1670 the Hudson's Bay Company was given its official royal charter, and Charles Fort was constructed at the mouth of what the English dubbed the Rupert River.

Now the French were roused to action. In 1671–72 an expedition led by a Jesuit father, Charles Albanel, travelled the route from Tadoussac to James Bay, ostensibly to carry the message of Christianity, but also to report on what was happening and to encourage the Native people to maintain their trading alliances with the French. In 1673, as the English were building a second post at the mouth of the Moose River on James Bay, the French decided to move into the territory by establishing trading posts at the headwaters of the rivers flowing into James Bay. After all, the richest fur country was here, in the interior, not in the swampy lowlands on the shores of the bay. One of the first of these posts was established on Nighthawk Lake in 1673; it was known initially as Fort Piscoutagamy and later as Fort St Germain.[8] Direct contact in the region bordering the height of land had been made between Europeans and Aboriginal peoples, ushering in a period of two hundred years in which a new community would gradually take shape.

This French trade was very small at first, but business families in Quebec and France soon worked to make it more organized and extensive, and to challenge the claims of the English through the Hudson's Bay Company to both the territory and the furs. In 1682, Charles Aubert de la Chesnaye formed the Compagnie du Nord to promote more systematic trade; the following year the Compagnie issued a licence to the Sieur d'Argenteuil for the construction of new posts in the Temiskaming and Abitibi regions.[9] In 1685 the king of France issued the Compagnie du Nord its own royal charter for the Hudson Bay trade, directly challenging the HBC.[10] Permission was then granted for two more posts on Lake Abitibi.[11]

Armed with the official state support, the Compagnie arranged for a military expedition. More than a hundred men under the command of Pierre, Chevalier de Troyes, assisted by the Jesuit father Antoine Silvy, paddled up the Ottawa and down the Abitibi to James Bay in 1686, seizing the HBC posts at Moose, Rupert, and Albany. De Troyes also oversaw the establishment of a new post on Lake Abitibi, on the east shore at the mouth of the Abitibi River. A second post was built some fifty kilometres away on the southwest shore of the lake where it narrows to join the lower lake.[12] The northern peoples were clearly pleased to have new trading opportunities closer to home; they would no longer have to go all the way to Tadoussac,[13] or face the Iroquois, who were renewing their raids along the Ottawa River in an attempt to regain control. For the next ten years the region was engulfed in conflict. The English recaptured their positions at Albany and Moose; the French took Fort Nelson. The Iroquois sent raiding parties up the Ottawa. Finally, in 1696, in the hope of cutting their losses and restoring a measure of peace, French officials ordered that all the interior posts be closed – the expectation being that Native middlemen would bring the furs from the northern interior down to Montreal. Four years later, the Compagnie du Nord's charter was revoked.

Much to their surprise, the French discovered that the Native middlemen now preferred to take their furs north to the HBC posts on Hudson Bay instead of coming to Montreal. To try to regain control, a French expedition attempted in 1709 to capture Fort Albany; its failure forced the French to turn again to the potential of the Abitibi-Temiskaming region. Several French traders headed into the area illegally between 1714 and 1718, and their success convinced the governor of New France, the Marquis de Vaudreuil, to reconsider the policy that had banned interior posts. In 1720 he ordered a small military expedition to Temiskaming to negotiate an alliance with the Aboriginal people of the district. Paul Guillet accompanied the party to supervise the construction of a licensed post not far from the mouth of the Montreal River on Lake Temiskaming. Guillet then constructed a second post on Lake Abitibi and travelled through the region from Lake Huron to Abitibi to introduce the French trade again. He was so successful that some Montreal traders complained that he was interfering with their profits. Clearly, northern trappers and middlemen preferred to deal with Guillet rather than risk the journey to Montreal. Although the Montreal lobby succeeded in having Guillet's licence revoked briefly, Vaudreuil reinstated it because he saw Guillet's operations as a strategic challenge to the English.[14] It seemed that the French had come back to stay. Indeed, the Hudson's Bay Company was so concerned that in 1730 it reopened its post at Moose Fort, proposing to offer better goods and better prices.

For almost thirty years the French and English competed for the business of the First Nations of the northern interior. Fur trade partnerships were cemented with political alliances and with marriages between the French and Aboriginal trading families. Small groups began to congregate seasonally around the posts, while others began to settle more permanently in the vicinity of the HBC posts on James Bay, where they could get regular employment, supplying the Englishmen with meat and fish. Relationships were not always peaceful, however. In 1754, the HBC traders at Henley House (200 kilometres up the Albany River from its mouth) were killed by a group of Cree men in a disagreement over the way the post was being managed. On the east side of the bay, conflict was almost perpetual between the Cree and Inuit over access to land and resources. And between 1744 and 1748 the French and English were at war in Europe, disrupting the availability of trade goods and thus interfering with the trade.

In spite of the problems, life for the people of the Mattagami and Abitibi area must have been exciting during that era. They found themselves at the intersection of the English and French trading zones, with a clear choice of partners. Their location gave them the upper hand in a complex relationship. Unfortunately, very little knowledge remains either orally or in the documentary record of events in the region in the mid-eighteenth century. The Abitibi post was not the largest of the French interior posts, but it was strategically located and a significant supplier to the important Temiskaming post. Officers in charge of the HBC post at Moose were anxious to learn more about the First Nations of the upper Abitibi and Mattagami in order to attract them to James Bay. But the canny Native traders along the lower reaches of the rivers guarded that knowledge closely so as to maintain their position of strength as middlemen.

If the patterns of participation in the trade here were similar to those in areas for which more information has survived, we can speculate that the trade brought changes to people's lives in some cases but reinforced older traditions in others. Not everyone would have chosen to join the trade, and most of those who did simply added it to their annual round of activities. Such trade goods as metal pots and knives were valued, but guns were notoriously unreliable and ammunition was awkward to carry on regular travels. Women likely welcomed the availability of cloth and beads that could be used to create the artwork with which they decorated clothing and household articles; they may even have enjoyed increased leisure time to produce more elaborate decorative arts now that they could obtain ready-made utensils such as pots. As happened elsewhere once the fur trade economy had been introduced, there appears to have been an increase in artistic and decorative production, incorporating new materials and techniques with older ones. During this era too, new marriage opportunities were presented through both fur trade alliances and personal encounters as people travelled more widely to and from the posts. So along with the tension and hostilities of fur trade competition, new opportunities were available.

The fur traders also brought new patterns of domestic life to the little posts and outposts which they established through the region, although life was very different at the French and English posts. The Hudson's Bay Company, anxious to avoid unnecessary expenses and potential disciplinary problems, decided in these early years to require its employees to live celibate lives, eschewing personal relationships with Aboriginal women; HBC officials also seem to have been concerned that Native women might be acting as spies for the French. The French traders out of Quebec saw the matter of intermarriage very differently. The fur trade offered not only a chance to get rich and live an adventurous life but also an opportunity for freedom and personal indulgence. Even more importantly, the French traders soon realized that their Native contacts expected kinship alliances as part of a trade relationship, and marriage *à la façon du pays* became an important part of their system in this part of the country as much as elsewhere. However, these relationships could be problematic. In 1714 the HBC claimed that the French traders had undercut their own business "through jealousy" created out of these marriages.[15]

Although during this period the HBC officially forbade relationships between its men and Native women, there are hints in the records that the rules were made to be broken. When de Troyes captured Moose Fort in 1686, he claimed to have found two Native women in the men's rooms, and in 1735 a young Native girl died in a fire there.[16] Certainly, the men hungered for female companionship. In the spring of 1735 the Moose Fort bricklayer James Norton conducted a sort of "work to rule" campaign to protest the disciplinary regime at the post; in a confrontation with his superior, he "swore that he would lay with all the Women that came if he could spare so much provisions to give them."[17] Undoubtedly, many more relationships between HBC men and Native women were established than company officials would admit.

Nevertheless, during the first half of the eighteenth century, most of the fur trade posts could scarcely be considered new communities; they were too small and temporary to lay the foundations for any sort of lasting social patterns. Only Moose Fort had any sense of permanency about it. There the men lived in a strictly regulated society which historian Jennifer Brown once called "military monasticism."[18] A hierarchy much like a military chain of command was used to maintain control; every man had his place, in both the work and the society, and discipline could be harsh. Attendance at prayers was required, and men needed permission to leave the post. In spite of the regulations, there were problems as the men rebelled or as occasional violence erupted. When William Bevan corrected sailor John Smith for his "mutinous manner" one day in 1732, Smith "run Directly & took up a Hatchet" to threaten the officer and deny Bevan's right to order him about.[19] Bricklayer James Norton, when asked by Bevan to perform some tasks other than bricklaying, "Cursed me & called me all the Ill names that could be thought of ... And turned up his Shirt tail & clap't his hand on his backside & bid me kiss that."[20] The men realized that they had options; at least one disgruntled employee threatened to "go to the french"[21] if he did not get his way with the senior officer.

In the world beyond the posts the fur trade slipped easily, in some ways, into the existing community structure of the region, since people had long been travellers and traders, accustomed to meeting new neighbours and negotiating political, economic, and personal relationships with them. English, Scottish, and French Canadian fur traders were, in one sense, just new groups of contacts. In other ways, however, the fur trade did introduce some new elements into community life. Settlements were established that would eventually lay the groundwork for new patterns of social relations; opportunities for economic diversification opened up, and conflicts with roots in faraway lands were introduced. Overall, though, it seemed as if the changes might be accommodated and unwanted disruptions minimized.

By the late 1750s, a major change began to destabilize this new society. England and France were again at war, and this time they were fighting significant battles in North America. French businessmen began to withdraw from the northern trade in 1758, finding it difficult to obtain and transport the necessary merchandise; apparently, between 1760 and 1763 there was little trade of any description. And, of course, New France then fell to the British. Initially, the HBC seems to have believed that its monopoly trading rights would now be recognized throughout the lands draining into Hudson Bay, but a number of Anglo-American and Scottish entrepreneurs decided otherwise. By 1764, individual traders based in Montreal had begun to fan out through the region, reoccupying trading territories that the French had abandoned, and interfering successfully in the flow of furs to Moose Fort. The Abitibi trade was one of the prizes. Possibly as early as 1764, William Grant, supplied by Richard Dobie of Montreal, began operations at Abitibi;[22] certainly, in 1768 the HBC officer at Moose Fort was complaining of the success of this new post.[23]

At length, the HBC decided it could no longer afford to sit in its bayside posts and wait for the Aboriginal traders to come. In 1774 John Thomas was sent up the Moose River to investigate the situation in the Abitibi country as part of a series of forays from Hudson Bay posts, and within two years the company had begun to construct inland posts at strategic locations. In 1782 Philip Turnor and George Donald were commissioned to survey the route from Moose Fort up the Abitibi River, and two years later Turnor and Germain Maugenest were sent to establish the first HBC post on Lake Abitibi. However, the area's Native people persuaded them to locate farther west at the junction of the Abitibi and Pusquachagama (or Piscoutagamy) rivers. In 1785 Turnor moved the post to a more convenient location on the nearby lake, which he named Frederick in honour of King George III's second son; the post was christened Frederick House. It was used as a base to challenge Montreal traders working out of Abitibi and "Langue de Terre" on the Montreal River. Frederick House certainly succeeded in annoying the Canadian traders, but as a commercial venture it was on shaky ground, since the HBC still had much to learn about inland trade techniques. The governing council in London complained of the "great Expence without any real profit,"[24] and Turnor was sent to explore a route to Lake Temiskaming to try to encourage Native traders from that region as well as from Abitibi to come to Frederick House with their furs.

In 1790 Richard Dobie of Montreal sold his Abitibi-Temiskaming trading interests to Grant, Campion, and Company, who decided to mount a determined commercial campaign against the HBC at Frederick House. In 1792 they built a post on Devil's Island, directly across from the HBC, and its newly appointed manager, Isaac Constant, set to work with vigorous

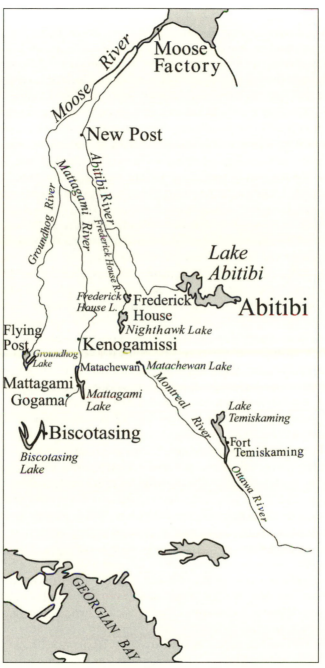

Map 2   Fur trade posts and routes (by Thai-Nguyen Nyguyen)

enthusiasm.[25] Trade at the HBC post trickled away, and in the spring of 1794 the London Council wrote to John Thomas at Moose Fort, "We clearly see that Frederick House is of very little consequence, relinquish it therefore as soon as possible & settle a good House at Abbitibbi."[26] The HBC men at Moose disagreed with the plan, believing that Frederick House was too important to close, so they kept it open for strategic reasons. Possibly to placate the London Council, Thomas did agree to send a trading party to Lake Abitibi under Robert Folster to establish a second post not far from the site of the post that Turnor and Maugenest had operated in 1784. But within weeks, a party of Canadian traders had arrived at Abitibi and begun construction of a new post of their own "nearly alongside" the HBC buildings.[27]

As part of the intensifying competition, smaller outposts began to proliferate throughout the region. That same year (1794), the HBC sent John Mannall to Lake Kenogamissi, where he built a post near the source of the Mattagami River, about sixty-five kilometres southwest of Frederick House. Three months later, Donald McKay established its competition still farther inland on Mattagami Lake. Meanwhile, the powerful new North West Company (NWC), formed through a series of amalgamations of Montreal trading houses, bought Grant, Campion, and Company's posts in the Abitibi-Temiskaming region. The presence of the NWC intensified the action. The NWC built two new posts on Lake Abitibi and in 1796 experimented with bringing the first large canoes up as far as the Abitibi posts, in an attempt to meet the competition presented by the HBC, which was able to import a larger range of trade goods through its seaport at Moose Fort. In 1798 the NWC sent an expedition of Iroquois traders from the Montreal area to Moose Fort with the aim of opening NWC trade right on the doorstep of the HBC's district headquarters.[28] Although the HBC confiscated these interlopers' trade goods on the grounds that the HBC had a legal monopoly on trade there, the audacity of the move forced the HBC to admit that negotiations might be in order, and in 1799 an abortive attempt was made to divide the region's trade between the two companies.

Expansion and tension continued. The NWC built posts at Flying Post on Groundhog Lake (1800), near Moose Fort on James Bay (1800), on Charlton Island in James Bay (1803), at Lake Nemiscau (1804), and at a half-dozen outpost locations along James Bay and up the rivers. The HBC responded with new posts at Fort George (1803) and Kenogamissi (1807), and reorganized the administration of the region, which became part of the HBC's Southern Department, governed through Lachine (1810). Finally, both companies admitted that there were too many posts in the Abitibi region, and the NWC agreed to close its Devil's Island post if the HBC closed its Abitibi House. The deal gave the HBC control at Frederick House Lake and the NWC control at one end of Lake Abitibi; each party agreed not to interfere with the other at Kenogamissi and Flying Post.[29]

The arrangement did not satisfy some Native traders. Sometime during the winter of 1812–13, a group of Abitibi people attacked the HBC post at Frederick House, killing the manager Alexander Belly, the labourers Hugh Slater and Robert Sabiston, and an elderly Native man and his wife who were living at the post. An important HBC trading partner named Teckanartiqua, his wife, and their baby were also killed, apparently in an ambush as they approached the post. Another man and three children were later reported missing and presumed dead in the massacre, but their bodies were never found. The post's stores were ransacked and vandalized.[30] The perpetrators had sent a very clear message to the HBC. Since the area's Native traders refused to return to trade at the post, it was temporarily closed. It reopened in 1817 as an outpost of Kenogamissi, but after a fire in 1820, Frederick House was closed permanently.

Meanwhile, the HBC attempted to make up for the loss by opening a post in 1814 upriver from Kenogamissi on Mattagami Lake. The following year, unknown arsonists looted and destroyed it. Angus Cameron, the rival NWC trader at the lake, noted with smug delight in his journal on 18 May 1815: "I had the satisfaction of seeing the English Decamp this morning without a single skin of any kind excepting their own Hunt. I cannot help feeling some exultation at their entire want of success ... A number of circumstances conspired against them, [including] their extreme want of provisions, their own Indians having Deserted to this post & raised the most unfavourable reports against them."[31] The HBC made a half-hearted attempt to reopen the post but finally admitted defeat in 1817.

The HBC encountered disaster elsewhere as well. In 1816 four of its employees in the Kenogamissi area were killed in various accidents, and in 1820 two of its New Brunswick House staff were murdered. An epidemic on Kenogamissi Lake in 1817–18 killed a number of Native people; the following year others were "tormented with a dreadful disorder" that had arrived through Fort Temiskaming and killed a number of prominent hunters.[32] The NWC was forced to close its post at Kenogamissi in consequence. Fur returns were dropping off everywhere, and it was not simply because the Native trappers were too sick or fed up to trade. There was growing evidence that the beaver population of the region was in serious decline.

With the proliferation of personnel and posts between 1760 and 1821, the fur trade economy had an increasing impact on the social landscape. While many Native families continued to live their lives in their seasonal bush camps, a growing number decided to settle down near the larger posts to take advantage of the opportunities for providing the Europeans with food and clothing. Eventually they became known as the "Home Guard." Another social circle was emerging within the posts as more traders married local women and raised their children in the routines of post life; these children often grew up to be traders themselves (or wives of traders), establishing extended networks of relatives throughout the region. And, of course, the single men who staffed the posts and outposts formed their own society to make the hard work and long winters tolerable.

Intermarriage in the new social landscape took place at all levels. At one end is the story of the Cameron family. Aeneas Cameron (c.1757–1822) arrived in Montreal in the late 1780s and was hired by a Nor'Wester, Richard Dobie, to go to Fort Abitibi; by 1798 Cameron was a full-fledged partner in the company. He encouraged his nephew Angus Cameron (c.1785–1876) to join the fur trade, and Angus was sent to the NWC post at Mattagami in 1801. He served in that region for the next eighteen years. Angus also rose to the ranks of partnership in the NWC, and after the 1821 merger with the HBC he became a chief trader. Angus married a Native woman sometime during his service in the region. They had at least three children – Sophia, Elizabeth, and Alexander – who moved to Scotland in the early 1840s to join their father's relatives. Sophia apparently never married, living at home with her father and his second (Scottish) wife. She and her brother Alexander died of tuberculosis within two years of one another. Elizabeth married a local clergyman, James Grant.[33]

In a very different social role were the Beads and Lawson families. Both were founded by HBC labourers based initially at Moose Fort. In 1793 John Lawson was a member of the party sent by the HBC to re-establish a presence on Lake Abitibi; both he and Beads undoubtedly had many opportunities to travel through the region. Somewhere along the line, they established partnerships with Native women. Beads's sons, John and Charles (born c. 1787), both elected to join the HBC as labourers and, like their father, were based for a time at Moose. It was probably there that (in 1805) Charles Beads married Eleanor Lawson *à la façon du pays*. Charles and Eleanor worked as a team, Eleanor assisting at the fall fishery and making clothing as they were posted successively to Frederick House, Moose, Kenogamissi, and Abitibi. "The only blemish to his Character as a Servant," wrote his supervisor Richard Good at Kenogamissi, "is inebriation." His brother John was more independent-minded and a thorn in the side of his supervisors. Good reported that John had "conducted himself much to the discredit of himself & the service, by his constant visiting our Opponents [the NWC] without leave, and neither reproofs or blows availing any thing with him."[34]

Charles and Eleanor had five children: Charlotte (born 1817), Margaret, Henry (born 1823), Charles (born 1827), and William (born 1829). Margaret died as a child in 1822. Charles junior followed his father into HBC employ but died at the age of seventeen following a painful illness that was probably tuberculosis.[35] The lives of the others are not

known. Undoubtedly they became a part of the growing population iden-
tified sometimes as "Native" and at other times as "Métis." Not all of these
children melted into the region's Aboriginal population, however.
Through their work with the HBC, they followed life patterns more like the
European HBC servants. Thomas Moore, born circa 1820 at Moose Factory
to an HBC factor, worked in the area for forty years before retiring to
Mowat's Landing. One of his sons (Joseph) also worked for the HBC, at
Moose Factory and Abitibi, before taking up residence near Timmins at
Wawaitin Falls. Another son moved east into northern Quebec, and a third
went west to Manitoba.[36] In one way or another, family networks were
extended across the North as the century wore on.

Life at the posts revolved around the changing seasonal requirements of
the trade. As soon as weather permitted in the spring, the men were sent
out to cut firewood or to dig patches of ground in preparation for planting the potatoes and oats which the companies optimistically hoped would
supplement their provisions. In most years, the crops were not put in until
early July. Summers were dedicated to tending the crops, collecting yet
more firewood, and making repairs to the post buildings. At some of the
HBC posts, only a small complement of men were kept over the summer;
the rest were sent north to Moose Factory, where supplies were more plentiful and the men could be put to work on the many chores necessitated
by this larger establishment. In the fall they returned to the inland posts as
activity quickened in anticipation of the winter trading visits of the area's
Native trade partners. Crops were harvested and men set off to the goose
hunt or fall fishery to put in supplies for the long winter. After the snow
had fallen, some of the men continued to hunt or set rabbit snares, though
more often the posts relied on Native hunters to bring in supplies of
meat.[37]

The arrival of trading parties was, of course, the highlight of the work
life at each post and was no small part of its social life too. With the intense
competition between the Hudson's Bay Company and the Nor'Westers,
EuroCanadian traders worked hard to cultivate Native trade partners, and
the Native traders worked hard to play the competitors off against one
another. Native traders demanded gifts of brandy and tobacco as a symbol
of goodwill, and the EuroCanadians learned to comply – otherwise there
would be no trade. The HBC designated influential Native men as trading
"captains," men such as Muntango, who was welcomed to Moose in 1733
with a reputation for being "a Great man with the French." Governor
Joseph Adams instructed his officers "to take abundance of notice of & use
him kindly." One of them "had a Capt[ns] Coat made for him & laced it as
handsom as could be & gave it him, on w[ch] he Promised Great things."[38]
Trading parties might call in at any time of the year, but they came in
largest numbers in spring and fall (in the years before 1821). At Frederick

House in 1804–5, for example, the HBC took in most of its furs in September–October and April. A trading party typically consisted of two or three families, though sometimes only the men came with the furs, leaving their families camped out of sight of the post. Mostly they brought furs, but occasionally they brought welcome fresh meat.[39] There was invariably some haggling over the price of both the furs and the trade goods. The HBC devised a scheme of valuing furs and other products relative to the value of one large prime beaver pelt, which was called one "Made Beaver." So, for example, when Shappokeeshichwescum brought a canoe to Frederick House in the summer of 1789, the HBC paid him fifteen Made Beaver for it.[40] A decade later at that post, a mid-size black bear skin was valued at two Made Beaver, a prime grey fox at three Made Beaver, a large muskrat at one-sixth of a Made Beaver, and castoreum (a substance secreted by beavers and used in such things as perfume manufacturing) at three pounds per Made Beaver.[41] Imported trade goods were priced using the same system. So, at Frederick House in 1799–1800, a steel trap cost three Made Beaver, a four-foot gun cost twelve Made Beaver, an ice chisel cost half a Made Beaver, and a gallon of brandy could be had for four Made Beaver. The most popular goods in the region were clearly the tools of the trade: guns and ammunition, steel traps, fishing twine, and ice chisels. But a few luxuries were also in demand, including shirts, blankets, and, above all, brandy.

The trading itself was adapted to the ceremonies that the Aboriginal population considered appropriate for such occasions. Trading parties were greeted with a ritual volley of gunshots, followed by diplomatic exchanges of speeches and gifts; and after the business had been conducted, there might be smoking, drinking, and feasting – though in some years during the intensely competitive period, a trading party might prefer a surreptitious entry and exit to avoid tipping its hand to the rival company. Some people might agree to take on a little goose hunting or fishing to supply the post. This, too, was time for discussions about marriages and family alliances, or to pass on news that bound the people of the region together in shared knowledge.

Company employees did not simply sit at their posts awaiting the arrival of these trading parties. Long supply lines from James Bay (for the HBC) and Montreal (for the NWC) meant that many men spent weeks at a time on transport brigade duties. Long winters meant enormous demands on local wood supplies for heating fuel, and as time went by, men had to travel farther from the posts to obtain the necessary supplies. Meanwhile, other men spent considerable time hunting geese or fishing to feed the post. The life of the fur trade labourer was certainly hard and often dangerous. In the HBC's Kenogamissi District, no fewer than four died in the line of duty in the winter of 1816–17. James Gaddy and Robert Gill died of starvation while travelling north to Moose Factory; provisions intended to last for two weeks had apparently run out, and the two men had failed to procure more food. Robert Linna fell through the ice while en route from Mattagami to Kenogamissi Post and succumbed a few days later. George Geddy died at Frederick House Lake, apparently of severe frostbite.[42] Some of these deaths might have been the result of bad management, as Nor'Wester Angus Cameron at Mattagami believed. The "Hudsons Bay Company's Barbarity to their people is inexpressible & deserves the most serious consideration of those who have it in their power to punish such an atrocity," he wrote in February 1817. "Among eleven men exclusive of women & children they had not provisions sufficient for two of them for the Winter."[43] Hard physical labour also meant that injury was an ever-present possibility, and even apparently minor incidents could prove serious, as in the case of John Clouston at Frederick House in 1799. A log fell from the woodpile where he was working, breaking his leg, and for a time it appeared that he would die, "as no Assistance [could] be got from any Surgeon" and winter was too close at hand to send him to Moose Factory for help. Fortunately, although Clouston suffered a long convalescence, he did ultimately recover.[44]

The hard life did have its compensations, however. For a boy from a struggling Orkney family, the pay was good, and with few opportunities to spend his earnings, he could save significant sums before returning home. In the mid-eighteenth century, a labourer earned £10 to £14 a year at major HBC posts; basic room and board was provided free.[45] A century later, wages continued to be good. Historian Philip Goldring calculated that a Scottish crofter would have to take on a part-time fishing job as well as his farm in order to make as much as an HBC labourer made in a year.[46] From time to time, the company offered bonuses for extra work or hardship, as an incentive to get men to work at the less comfortable inland posts; and it offered "bounties" on furs produced (a measure introduced in the region in 1779).[47] The HBC also attempted to maintain a variety of provisions from home at the posts, including "Cheshire & gloucester cheese" at Kenogamissi in 1794–95 and sugar at Frederick House in 1793–94. Possibly only the man in charge was entitled to the expensive tea, chocolate, and coffee listed in the Frederick House accounts, but every man received a weekly allowance of brandy on Saturdays.[48] Major holidays, such as Christmas and New Year's Day, were celebrated with special meals, music, and dancing, while others, including St Andrew's Day and St George's Day, provided an excuse for special activities, like the target-shooting competition at Frederick House in the late 1780s.[49] The freedom, camaraderie, adventure, and opportunity for personal advancement clearly compensated for the hardships and occasional tragedies. It was a pattern that would be repeated in the twentieth-century resource-extraction economy.

Although the competition between the HBC and Canadian traders during the period 1760–1821 presented excellent opportunities for Native trappers, it also brought a significant social disruptor: alcohol. As early as 1769, alcohol had become a problem at Moose. The HBC's London Council ordered the Moose Council to stop providing it in trade for provisions and otherwise "to let them have as little Brandy or Spiritous Liquors as possible."[50] But as Canadian traders also began importing alcohol, the HBC men concluded that they would lose all hope of trade if they did not offer it as well. Canadian rum and British brandy were used as a gift (like tobacco) to encourage Native traders to choose one side over the other, or were provided as an "extra" during the trading to ensure that the traders went away happy. Unfortunately, women as well as men eventually began to drink excessively, and reports that visitors were "drunk and troublesome" began to punctuate the post journals. The consequences ranged from minor mishaps (a smashed table at Frederick House in 1791) to the troubling (all but three men too drunk to hunt for their families at Kenogamissi in 1814) to the tragic (a drowning at Abitibi in 1797 when a father was too drunk to manage his canoe, though his wife and child were saved).[51]

By the early years of the nineteenth century, the unique circumstances of the fur trade economy were producing a new community in the region that incorporated features of the older Aboriginal society with the ideas and needs of the newcomers. The first bond was one of kinship. As historian Jennifer Brown noted, by then "a considerable mixed-blood population in areas bordering on the southern and western fringes of the Cree territories near Hudson Bay" had developed,[52] and although there were clear differences in social patterns between the HBC and NWC, family networks had emerged across the region that reflected both social and economic participation in a common way of life. The second bond was one of shared distance. Traders were physically removed and probably intellectually distanced from colonial centres of administrative, political, and economic power. Senior officers might have only an annual correspondence; the average labourer had even less contact. British law had little influence here. Rather, authority was personal and limited, requiring compromise and appeal to a shared sense of purpose. In part by historical accident and in part by necessity, it was an authority more akin to Aboriginal traditions in the region. The third bond was one of shared experience. The dangers and hardships of a life that depended so much on the vagaries of country-food resources, combined with the conflicts engendered by corporate competition, alcohol, and Native politics, gave men and women a set of life experiences unique to the time and place. These were experiences that set not only those of European ancestry apart from their heritage but also changed the lives of the Native and mixed-blood members of the new community.

Of course, this emerging community was not a phenomenon unique to this region. The expanding fur trade was creating variations on it across the continent. The fierce competition between the HBC and NWC was a major factor in this expansion, as the corporations leapfrogged one another westward and northward in search of ever more sources of fur. In the end, the costs of this competition mounted to the point of unacceptability, and in 1821 the two companies negotiated a truce, in which they agreed to merge under the name of the Hudson's Bay Company and to reorganize the trade on a more economic (and profitable) basis.

In the Abitibi-Temiskaming region, as elsewhere, the merger meant the closing of the many small outposts and the elimination of duplicate posts at key locations. Many labourers, canoesmen, and others were laid off. Some may have remained in the area; others moved away in search of new opportunities. A smaller, leaner HBC now operated posts at Lake Abitibi, "Matawagamingue" on the Mattagami River (using the old NWC post buildings there), and at Flying Post on the Groundhog River. The Mattagami post, under Angus Cameron, was made the headquarters of what became a thriving Kenogamissi District, which ranged east to the Temiskaming and Abitibi people's hunting grounds, north to the Moose Factory District, west to the New Brunswick House District (on the Kenogami River), and south to Sault Ste Marie. A small farm helped to supply potatoes and other vegetables to the staff.[53] At Abitibi, Alexander Christie oversaw an establishment that included cattle as well as a vegetable garden. It served people from downstream along the Abitibi River and other smaller rivers that drain into the lake. Occasionally, visitors came from as far north as Hannah Bay (at the southern end of James Bay).[54] The post at Abitibi was established as headquarters for the Abitibi River District (which included Fort Abitibi, Fort Temiskaming, and Grand Lac).

If the two companies had hoped that their merger would eliminate competition, they soon discovered they had miscalculated. Almost immediately, "free traders" began to move into the margins of the region to siphon off the furs. For Mattagami Post, competition came first from the south, where new traders established themselves from 1824 on the north shore of Lake Huron and in 1825 at Whitefish Lake, an important gathering place just inland from the north end of Georgian Bay. Native people from the Mattagami District found it convenient to visit these traders. An additional draw was the presence of British officials at nearby Drummond Island. Here, the British had established a centre for the administration of Indian affairs, and each year they presented gifts to the Aboriginal population who lived in the still-uneasy border region between the United States and British North America, in an attempt to secure and maintain the Aboriginal alliance that had been so important during the War of 1812. The annual ceremony surrounding this gift-giving had become an important social and political event for the region's First Nations. In 1827 the HBC decided to build a post at Whitefish Lake to take advantage of the annual gatherings in the region and, it hoped, to cut off the supply of furs to the new competition.

Another competitive push came from the southeast, affecting both the Abitibi and Mattagami posts. In 1825 Clark Ross travelled up the Ottawa River from the Lake of Two Mountains near Montreal to open trade on the Montreal River, halfway between Temiskaming and Mattagami.[55] The following year a group of Iroquois traders from Montreal came right to Abitibi to challenge the HBC. Although these competitors were never well-organized or consistent visitors, they did prove to be a continual annoyance to the HBC and a useful tool for First Nations traders, who could (and did) use their presence to manipulate the HBC to get better trade arrangements.

The continuing competition and constant movement of people through the region had devastating consequences. As early as 1816 there had been reports that the region's beaver population was in trouble, and heavy pressure on scarce food resources led to repeated reports of food shortages through the 1820s, 1830s, and 1840s; thirteen Abitibi Native people died of starvation in 1826, and HBC officials at Mattagami were told of many other deaths throughout their district. In 1833 an epidemic of measles or scarlet fever (or possibly both) ravaged the district from Lake Huron to Mattagami. Tuberculosis was reported to be widespread in the Temiskaming District in 1843. Not surprisingly, people began to panic. Rumours of cannibalism repeatedly surfaced at Mattagami, and some First Nations trappers withdrew from the trade. In the winter of 1831–32 a religious leader convinced his people to destroy the HBC post at Hannah Bay (about a hundred kilometres east of Moose Factory), and nine people at the post were killed.[56] At Flying Post in 1851 an attempt was made to assassinate the HBC trader Donald Grant and take over the post. Grant survived only by a lucky accident, and he retreated to Moose Factory with the women and children of the post as soon as the rivers were open.[57]

In spite of the conflict, comparatively permanent settlements were growing around the fur trade posts. People in these hamlets could count several generations of fur trade employment, and there were little cemeteries nearby giving silent witness to their lives and work. These post settlements were not isolated islands in a northern sea. Kinship networks linked them to families living according to more ancient traditions in the surrounding bush, and economic networks linked them to Canada, Scotland, and England. The fur trade continued to attract newcomers from these places, newcomers in search of economic opportunity, personal freedom, or adventure. Some came only for the duration of their contracts; others stayed on.

The most important of these settlements (and a focal point for the entire region from 1821 to the 1860s) was Moose Factory on James Bay at the mouth of the Moose River. The first post on the site had been built in 1673 on Hayes Island, and for a time Moose served as the residence of HBC Governor Charles Bayley. Between 1686 and 1696 it changed hands several times as the British and French fought over it. When the British finally regained the post, they demolished the original buildings. A new establishment rose in 1730 a little farther upriver and was named Moose Factory for the first time. It was, wrote one observer some years later, "a fort built for defence, with thick walls and loop-holes, and a communication all round outside upon the roof. This was the whole of the original building, shut in like an old castle with gates, and enclosing a kind of octagonal area within."[58] It became an important and busy centre, where cargo ships from England anchored and traders from the vast network of inland lakes and rivers arrived to do business. Meanwhile, a comparatively permanent Native campsite developed nearby, where the post's provisioners and labourers lived. Gradually the HBC expanded the site, so that by the mid-nineteenth century a little village had developed, described by the visiting Anglican Bishop, David Anderson, as being "far prettier than I had expected":

The Fort, with its double verandah and a sort of belvidere above, the church with its little spire (though it boasts not of architectural beauty), and the modest parsonage on one side of the Fort; and stretching, in the other direction, some neat cottages with little gardens in front ... lying more irregularly along the bank of the river. This gives more of a village appearance, making it prettier than York [Factory], or most of the forts in the country, which are generally all of one type, a quadrangle enclosed with pickets.[59]

Moose was a cosmopolitan place in the nineteenth century. Along with the senior HBC officers in residence and others visiting the post, there were ships' crews in from overseas; English, Scots, French, and English Canadian workers; an Anglican mission and school; visiting Native traders from the interior; and a sizable permanent mixed-ancestry population of employees and their families. By the turn of the century, Moose had a permanent population of about three hundred and a summer population of six hundred.[60] Goings-on there were followed with lively interest throughout the district, even after the HBC began to supply its interior posts from Montreal via the Canadian Pacific Railway (CPR). As the Roman Catholic missionary Jean-Marie Nédélec described it, "C'était un charmant village anglais ... une capitale en miniature."[61]

The interior posts also became settlements, although on a much smaller scale than Moose Factory. Perhaps the most important was Abitibi. By the mid-nineteenth century, the post was located on a long point jutting out into Lake Abitibi at the mouth of the Duparquet River. It consisted of two houses, two storehouses, plus a cold cellar for potatoes, a stable, and a "cow byre," as well as the tents of visiting Native traders or provisioners. Next in importance was Mattagami Post on Lake Kenogamissi. By the mid-nineteenth century, Mattagami Post consisted of "a large and well built house for the master, houses for the servants, stores, cattle sheds"[62] and facilities for storing the crops of potatoes and other root vegetables that were grown on a few cleared acres adjacent to it. An Anglican church and missionary's house rounded out the establishment. After the completion of the CPR, which ran only two to three days' travel from the post, the HBC imported a larger variety of livestock, and in 1890 counted a bull, a calf, a cow, two heifers, two oxen, and five pigs.[63] While there were only four or five HBC employees stationed at the post at any one time, a number of Native families built homes nearby. When the census was recorded in 1901, Mattagami had a population of forty-six, including Hannah, the Ojibwa wife of HBC chief trader James Miller and their nine children. English, Scots, French, Cree, and Ojibwa families must have helped lend the little village a rather interesting atmosphere.

The third most important settlement in the region by the turn of the century was something of a latecomer. In 1865 the HBC opened a post to compete with "free traders" on the narrows of Lake Matachewan, just under a hundred kilometres east of Mattagami Post. Its heyday was during the 1890s, when trader James Mowat (with his wife and children) oversaw the establishment of three log houses, a storehouse, a workshop, a stable to house a cow and bull, and a little log chapel. Although the HBC contingent consisted only of the chief trader and three assistants, about forty Native families lived in the vicinity, and in 1905 the population was ninety-seven, not counting the HBC personnel.[64] Farther west on Groundhog Lake near the Groundhog River (a tributary of the Mattagami) was Flying Post, established in 1800 by the NWC. By 1901 it was home to 114 people.

These settlements were bases not only for fur traders and their families but now also for a new class of European visitor. Christian missionaries began their work in the 1830s and 1840s from two entry points: Protestants through Moose Factory in the north, and Roman Catholics though Temiskaming in the south. Both initiatives brought important and often unanticipated changes. Although a Jesuit father, Antoine Silvy, had accompanied de Troyes's expedition through the area in 1686 and had held religious services at Lake Abitibi, it was not until the 1830s that there was sustained church interest in the region. The Roman Catholic bishop of Montreal decided to extend the influence and services of his diocese up the Ottawa River to the growing community at Fort Temiskaming. Priests had already been serving the lumber camps along the Ottawa Valley;

Temiskaming was merely a logical extension of the work, and there was a growing population of baptized Roman Catholics there.

Sulpician Louis-Charles de Bellefeuille and parish priest Jean-Baptiste Dupuy were sent in the summer of 1836 to Temiskaming, where they conducted mass, erected a cross, and visited nearby Native camps.[65] They returned to Montreal with favourable reports of the need for northern missions, so the following year the bishop of Montreal organized a more ambitious expedition, this time with the assistance of the Hudson's Bay Company. Abbé Bellefeuille spent two weeks at Fort Temiskaming and then headed north with guide George Wabimango to Abitibi, arriving on 14 July with a letter of introduction from the HBC officer at Temiskaming. Although the chief trader's wife, Mrs. Fraser, welcomed the priest and provided him with accommodation in the officers' quarters, other local people were less enthusiastic. Few were willing to permit the baptism of their children, and when Bellefeuille finally succeeded in organizing a baptismal service, a sudden storm came up and scattered the congregation. Nevertheless, the priest persisted, and by the time of his departure eight days later he claimed to have baptized some forty children and had been invited to visit the people at Grand Lac the following year.[66] Bellefeuille duly returned in the summer of 1838, but he died in Montreal shortly after his second trip. The new mission field was turned over to Father C.E. Poiré, who constructed the first chapel at Temiskaming in 1839, then announced his plans to extend the mission all the way to James Bay.

At this point, Protestant officials with the HBC sat up and took notice. Several members of the company's London Committee were committed Protestant Evangelicals with a strong antipathy to Roman Catholicism. Others, like the governor of the Northern Department, George Simpson, had more practical concerns. What would be the effect of "foreigners" from Canada living on the doorstep of the HBC posts? Would they provide a foothold for trade competition? Would they subvert the trade by encouraging Native people to settle at mission sites instead of trapping in the bush? To forestall such possibilities, Simpson proposed that a Wesleyan Methodist minister from England come to Moose Factory under the auspices of the HBC so that the company could keep a careful eye on his activities and be in a position to control him if necessary. Thus, in 1840, the English Wesleyan Methodist Missionary Society sent four missionaries into HBC territory. One of them, George Barnley, came to Moose Factory with instructions to give any attention he could to the Abitibi region as well. Barnley remained at Moose for seven years. Apparently, he never did visit the post at Abitibi, but in the summer of 1844 he spent three months at Mattagami conducting services for HBC employees, teaching their children, and trying to make contact with the area's First Nations.[67]

The Roman Catholics responded immediately to this challenge. In 1841 Father Poiré asked for HBC permission to visit Moose Factory, but he was turned down. He complained to the bishop of Quebec, who attempted to negotiate an agreement with the HBC in 1842 – but to no avail. So the church took another approach. In 1843 Bishop Bourget of Montreal gave responsibility for northern mission work to the Oblates of Mary Immaculate (OMI), a French missionary order that had recently arrived in Canada. Bourget applied to the HBC to allow the Oblates to work in Abitibi-Temiskaming. George Simpson finally agreed to a compromise and gave permission for the construction of buildings at Mattawa, Temiskaming, and Abitibi so that the missionaries could visit each year for a few weeks' work.[68] Father Nicolas Laverlochère took responsibility for these missions in 1844 and began a career of extensive travel through the region, establishing a key base at Abitibi, where a chapel was constructed in 1846. The following year the bishop of Quebec tried a new tactic and simply informed the HBC that he was sending Laverlochère to Moose Factory. Once there, the missionary and his assistant, Father Garin, announced that they intended to build a permanent mission near the post. The HBC had no difficulty in preventing the construction of a chapel, but thereafter the OMI missionaries visited annually.[69] The post at Mattagami was not forgotten in this expansion, although it remained on the outskirts of the work. In 1849 Father Clément visited it briefly but was unable to return there until 1853, after which no priest visited until 1868, when Father Jean-Marie Pian held a summer mission at the post.[70]

While the Roman Catholics were establishing their work in the interior, the Methodist mission at Moose Factory was going through considerable upheaval. George Barnley had a series of disagreements with the HBC officer in charge there, and he sailed home to England in disgust in 1847. Meanwhile, Church of England missionaries at Red River had been instrumental in creating the Anglican Diocese of Rupert's Land, and in 1851 they sent the Reverend John Horden to Moose Factory, where he remained until his death in 1893. At first, the region was administered from the diocesan centre in what would become Winnipeg, but in 1872 the Diocese of Moosonee was created and John Horden was consecrated as its first bishop. It was thus the Anglican Church, not the Methodists, that came to have the most enduring impact on the Protestant religious history of the region.

In the autumn of 1854, Horden made the first of many trips into the Kenogamissi District, spending a week at Mattagami Post, where he baptized some of the HBC employees' children, married one couple, and baptized several Native women and children. He received the enthusiastic support of the HBC officer in charge (Richards) and his wife, who helped him with a translation of the catechism that Horden intended to publish on the printing press he had recently imported to Moose Factory.[71] In 1856 Horden obtained the services of T.H. Fleming to extend the Anglican presence more permanently to Mattagami, Flying Post, and New Brunswick House. Unfortunately for Horden's plans, Fleming became seriously ill and had to return to England after just four years. Not until the 1870s, when Horden obtained the services of the Native catechist John Sanders, could a permanent Anglican mission be established at Mattagami.

Thus, by the middle of the nineteenth century, a new society had become rooted in the Abitibi-Kenogamissi region. The important HBC posts at Mattagami and Abitibi were at the centre of two villages inhabited permanently by HBC employees and their families and visited periodically by missionaries. Many of the HBC employees were Scots from the Orkney Islands or were descended from those Scotsmen, for by now there were families that had been part of the trade for generations. These men had married women from the area and therefore had extended networks of relatives throughout the country beyond the posts. The population of mixed ancestry (which today we would call Métis) also continued to grow. Some were of Scots and Aboriginal ancestry, but there was also a considerable population of Aboriginal and French Canadian ancestry, dating from the older fur trade contacts. Some of these families identified primarily with their First Nations heritage, while others were practising Christians who were bilingual or multilingual. The posts, village settlements, and transportation networks on river and trail had laid the groundwork for patterns that would persist into the present, in spite of dramatic changes that reoriented the geographic distribution of places that came to be considered "important" in the twentieth century.

Scattered throughout the bush, First Nations families continued their annual round of fishing, hunting, and gathering. Some came regularly to the posts while others came less often, preferring to rely on the resources of the country. A handful congregated seasonally at the two posts to fish or hunt for provisions to supply the post families. And since only a relatively limited range of trade goods was available at the posts during this period (for it was awkward and expensive to ship goods upriver from the depot at Moose Factory), in many ways, people continued to live in the same way as their ancestors had lived for several thousand years. They had reached an accommodation with the EuroCanadian newcomers for which the long-term consequences were not yet apparent.

Finally, there was a degree of movement in the region that will surprise modern readers. People from Moose Factory travelled regularly upriver to Mattagami, Abitibi, and other places, just to visit and see what was happening. People at Mattagami travelled regularly south over the height of land to Whitefish Lake or Sault Ste Marie for the same purpose. News could travel through the entire northland with impressive speed. And ethnic distinctions such as "Cree" and "Ojibwa" were becoming considerably blurred. While in the eighteenth century it might have been possible to consider the people who lived north of the height of land to be culturally distinct from those who lived south of it, by the middle of the nineteenth century it was less easy to categorize the nations. It was a fluid and mobile community, celebrating multiple ethnicities and different religions, and incorporating with grace and generosity the newcomers who were willing to abide by community expectations. It was scarcely a golden age, as it is sometimes imagined through the haze of nostalgia, but by the mid-nineteenth century, something of a social and economic equilibrium seems to have been achieved.

CHAPTER THREE

"The Best-Laid Plans ..."

And build ye a race, toil-bred sons of the Northland,
　As your stately pines, straight, as your granite hills, strong.
Thew-knit, supple-sinewed, soul and body puissant,
　Britain's vanguard in right, and her bulwark 'gainst wrong.
　　　　　　　　　　　　　　　　J.B. MacDougall[1]

By the 1860s, a new breed of Canadians was beginning to eye the lands beyond the lower Ottawa Valley. The best farmlands had been settled and cleared in the St Lawrence Valley and along the north shores of Lakes Ontario and Erie. Lumber companies were cutting more and more deeply into the great pine forests of the Ottawa Valley and the shores of Georgian Bay. Railway promoters were touting the promise of economic development through networks of rail lines to link producers and markets. Other promoters were considering the vast plains and parkland of the continental interior and calling for expansion of the agricultural "frontier" as the guarantee of a better future for the colonies. Not all of these promoters looked west, however. A handful saw promise closer to home, in the lands north of Lake Nipissing. Empire Ontario was poised to strike.

Pressure seems to have come first from the lumbering sector, for in 1862 a group of timber companies lobbied the colonial government of the Province of Canada for a survey of the lands from the Montreal River to Lake Superior. Four years later, the survey team of Duncan Sinclair and A.P. Salter travelled from the upper Ottawa to Michipicoten, reporting on the variety of resources along the route. In 1868 the recently created provincial government of Ontario began to promote agricultural settlement with the Free Grant and Homestead Act. Based loosely on the American homestead program, Ontario's version offered certain crown lands on generous terms to farmer-settlers, on condition that they build a suitable shelter and clear a minimum area of land within three years. The first lands available under the scheme were in the Muskoka District between the Ottawa River and Georgian Bay. By 1896, lands in the Algoma District around Sault Ste Marie had also been surveyed and opened to homesteaders.

In 1869 the HBC agreed to relinquish its monopoly charter rights in Rupert's Land, which included the territory north of the height of land from Mattagami and Abitibi to Moose Factory. The Province of Ontario and the Dominion of Canada were both interested in controlling these lands because of their resource and development potential, so a dispute arose over new boundary locations. A provisional agreement to extend Ontario north to James Bay along the meridian at 79°30′ from Lake Temiskaming was reached in 1872, but the province and the dominion government were not able to agree on the western limit for another sixteen years. In 1889 legislation confirmed the Ontario boundary north to James Bay, northwest along the Albany River, and west to a point just west of Kenora. In 1890 William Ogilvie of the Geological Survey of Canada (GSC) surveyed the line between Lake Temiskaming and James Bay in response to agitation from Quebec for an extension of its boundaries in the north.

While quibbles over boundaries went on, various interested parties moved ahead to investigate the development potential of the northern interior. The GSC commissioned Robert Bell to travel the Kenogami River in 1871, and then the Mattagami and Moose in 1875. His colleague A.S. Cochrane did a similar river survey of the Abitibi in 1877. They reported on an intriguing variety of timber and mineral resources. Two years later, the Ontario government sent E.B. Borron, a magistrate in the Nipissing District, on the first of what became a series of "inspection tours" through the lands that Ontario hoped to control in the northeast. On that first tour, Borron travelled up the Ottawa River to Lake Abitibi and down the Abitibi River to Moose Factory, and then back up the Moose and along the Missinaibi route to Michipicoten on Lake Superior. On his second tour, in 1880, he visited lands in the vicinity of Moose Factory along the James Bay coast, with brief inland forays. The following year, he travelled the Missinaibi River to Flying Post, followed a fur trade route to Mattagami Post, then headed downriver to Moose Factory and by sea to Albany. From Albany, he went inland to Marten's Falls, Osnaburgh House, Lac Seul, and Wabigoon Lake in what is now northwestern Ontario. The Ontario government was delighted with his reports of the region's extensive natural resources, agricultural potential, and transportation routes. The government was also pleased by his recommendation that it take immediate steps to obtain direct jurisdiction over the area, including that it pressure the dominion government to negotiate a treaty with the Aboriginal peoples of the region, and that it commission fur trade officers as justices of the peace to represent the extension of provincial authority.[2]

Borron saw these measures as merely preliminaries. For him, the grand vision was one of a vast agricultural development that would benefit the province as well as the farmers. "I frankly admit," he wrote in one report, "that the development of agricultural resources of this territory must be the work of time; that it will require capital, intelligence, experience and energy." Fired with the optimism (and chauvinism) of his generation, he believed that the people of Ontario were better fitted for the task than anyone else. Of the lands along the Mattagami and Moose Rivers north of the height of land he enthused, "Once opened up by means of roads and railways and the soil reclaimed, there cannot be a doubt that the agricultural resources will alone be sufficient to employ and maintain a large population in comfort, if not in affluence."[3]

Meanwhile, Quebec had also been eyeing the potential for northern settlement, but here it was Roman Catholic clergy who took the real initiative. The Oblate mission at Fort Temiskaming had become almost a regular village with the arrival in 1866 of a contingent of Grey Nuns from Ottawa to provide medical and educational services. In 1881 a retired fur trader named Angus McBride brought thirty Métis families to settle at the head of the lake where they supported themselves largely by farming. The following year, Charles Alfred Paradis, an energetic young priest originally from Michigan, arrived and began a publicity campaign to promote Roman Catholic French settlement of the Temiskaming region. Father Edmond Gendreau of the University of Ottawa also visited the area, liked what he saw, and in 1883-84 organized the Société de colonisation du lac Témiscamingue under the auspices of the OMI in Ottawa.[4] The colonisation society chartered a railway company with the intention of improving access for settlers, and it briefly operated a steamboat on the lake.[5] The first colonists arrived in 1886, settling around what would become Ville-Marie. The timing was perfect. Honoré Mercier and his Parti National took power in Quebec early in 1887 and began a series of programs to promote agricultural settlement to keep French-speaking Canadians in Quebec. Paradis's initiatives now had state support.

While fathers Paradis and Gendreau were making plans for railway access to Temiskaming, a more enduring railway project was under construction a little to the west. In 1885, the Canadian Pacific Railway completed the section of its transcontinental line from Sudbury to Port Arthur/Fort William (now Thunder Bay). The route took the line northwest from Sudbury through a new station called Biscotasing, then on to a new divisional point at Chapleau, and finally across the old fur trade route between Missinaibi and Michipicoten. Suddenly, a key region was easily accessible to independent fur traders. The HBC responded by opening a new post at Biscotasing, as well as raising the prices it offered for furs at Moose Factory and lowering the prices it charged for goods and provisions.[6] In 1888 it bought out the stocks of small competitors at Abitibi and Matachewan. But it was soon clear that the company was fighting a losing battle. Its profits at Moose Factory were reduced, and the Kenogamissi District was decimated. At Chapleau, a company employee lamented that the railway had "ruined what was once our richest Fur country," not only because of the appearance of competing traders but because it was "now overrun" by non-Native trappers anxious for some quick profits.7 Within just two years, the HBC post at Biscotasing had a sizable loss of over $2,000 on its books,8 and Native trappers were complaining that the beaver population was seriously depleted. A series of epidemics, including influenza and measles, swept through the region; they began in the southern parts of the district among people who had the most contact with the CPR and with the human tide the railway had released. By 1890 the epidemics had extended as far as Abitibi, and in 1891 they reached Mattagami Post. Deaths were recorded at each outbreak, but the total extent of the tragic loss will never be known.

The HBC responded with corporate changes and diversification. The size of the staff at each post was reduced, new retail outlets were opened at Sudbury and other places, and the company began to sell hay from its properties at Temiskaming to the lumber companies that were moving up the valley from Ottawa. After 1890 the post at Mattagami stopped shipping through Moose Factory and turned its face to the CPR station at Biscotasing. If the changes brought by the railway could not be stopped, the HBC at least hoped to realize what advantages it could. But the changes meant that fewer families were needed to provide crews for the smaller canoe brigades or to supply them with food and clothing.

Clearly, the fabric of the old fur trade society had begun to unravel. Some employees decided to retire to other regions of Canada or to the growing settlements on the shores of Lake Temiskaming. A handful with strong family connections remained at their posts – for instance, the Moores at Moose and Abitibi and the Mowats at Matachewan – overseeing a much-depleted enterprise. Many Native families simply carried on their lives in the bush camps, taking advantage of eager new traders when they could, or doing occasional work for the railway. Others worked as guides for the handful of southern travellers who had begun to appear in search of summer adventure. One enterprising HBC retiree, C.C. Farr, turned the changing situation to his considerable advantage. He established a farm on the western shore of Lake Temiskaming in 1887 and began a lengthy campaign to attract English-speaking settlers to counterbalance the strong French-speaking colony that Father Paradis had promoted across the lake.9 Between Farr's lobbying efforts with the Ontario government and personal booster campaigns in England, he eventually succeeded in introducing a new element to the regional population, settling them on lands surveyed by the province in 1887 at the head of the lake.

These campaigns also drew the attention of entrepreneurs with grander schemes. In 1895, the railway promoters William Mackenzie and Donald Mann obtained financial backing from a group of Toronto businessmen and applied for a charter to build a railway from Parry Sound (at the northern limit of "Old Ontario") to James Bay. The following year, that charter was amended to permit the investors to lay track from Toronto to Parry Sound, linking Toronto to any future development in a new hinterland and providing access to an ocean port for marketing purposes. Mackenzie and Mann then began a campaign to obtain the dominion government's support for their initiative.[10]

In 1896 the Ontario government joined the bandwagon of northern development in earnest with a series of initiatives to facilitate and promote northern settlement. Over two summers, surveyor Alexander Niven ran a baseline for 480 kilometres, straight from the CPR line northwest of Sudbury to the Moose River. The line was a preparation for more extensive surveys to follow. Ten parties were sent out in 1900 to gather information on the agricultural potential of these lands, and their reports proclaimed enthusiastically that a huge Clay Belt suitable for farming stretched across Ontario from the Quebec border into the Lake Superior region. Lands in the Algoma District were surveyed first, and some were offered to settlers under the terms of the Homestead Act. To jump-start settlement, the Ontario government introduced a program that offered free land to veterans of the Boer War of 1899–1902 and the Fenian Raids of the 1860s; the remainder of the Clay Belt lands were to be sold at what the government claimed were bargain prices.

Meanwhile, the Ontario government turned its attention to the question of access. By 1898, Mackenzie and Mann had still not begun construction of their James Bay railway, so the province provided a $4,000-per-mile cash subsidy to get them started on the first stage of the line, between Parry Sound and Sudbury. The following year (with still no evidence of construction), the government sweetened the deal with an additional subsidy of $2,000 per mile in cash and 5,000 acres (just over 2,000 hectares) of land per mile for track on the stretch between Sudbury and Lake Abitibi.[11]Still nothing happened. So in 1902 the Liberal government of Premier George Ross announced that it would build such a line itself, as a public works project. Dubbed the Temiskaming and Northern Ontario Railway (TNO), it was officially begun in May 1902. North Bay was chosen as its northern gateway instead of Parry Sound or Sudbury. The decision to build the line at public expense was initially very controversial. The Conservatives alleged that the plan was merely an election campaign of smoke and mirrors, and the Conservative mayor of North Bay even declined to participate in the sod-turning ceremony.[12]

The TNO was not to be the only line built through the region with public involvement. The British-managed Grand Trunk Railway had been toying with plans to construct a railway across the continent to compete with the CPR, but it had become concerned about the considerable expense that construction through the Canadian Shield would entail. So in 1903 the dominion government of Wilfrid Laurier announced a deal with the company. The Canadian government would build a National Transcontinental Railway (NTR) from a terminus in Moncton, New Brunswick, through Quebec City, then across northern Quebec and Northern Ontario to Winnipeg. Once the line was built, the government would lease it to the newly incorporated Grand Trunk Pacific Railway (GTPR), which would operate it. For its part, the GTPR agreed to build the rest of the line from Winnipeg to the BC coast at Port Simpson.

The deal precipitated what one historian called (with considerable understatement) a "bitter and prolonged debate" in the House of Commons.[13] Nevertheless, in 1905 the Canadian government sent survey parties into Northern Ontario and Northern Quebec, and Wilfrid Laurier himself turned the ceremonial sod at Fort William in September. It was decided to run the NTR's line north of Lake Abitibi, across the Abitibi and Mattagami Rivers, then west toward Lake Nipigon. Construction contracts for the northeastern Ontario section were let in 1906. E.F. and G.E. Fauquier won the contract to build the 160 kilometres of track west from Abitibi Crossing, and M.P. and J.T. Davis of Ottawa won the contract for much of the rest of the construction through the Clay Belt. Once the route was announced, Toronto politicians decided to extend the TNO line north to join the NTR at a junction that would soon be named Cochrane. But progress on both lines was slow. Not until 1911 did the Fauquiers complete their stretch of the NTR from Abitibi to Hearst, and another four years passed before trains were running regularly from Quebec City to northwestern Ontario.[14]

Meanwhile, Mackenzie and Mann had not entirely abandoned their interest in Northern Ontario. In 1899 they had adopted the name Canadian Northern Railway for a project they hoped would ultimately link a series of separate railway projects into a single company operating from Toronto and Quebec City to Vancouver. Because of the terms of the CPR charter, Mackenzie and Mann had to build their railway north of the CPR tracks, so from Sudbury their line was to go through what would become a new divisional point at Capreol, then northwest along a route that would take it much closer than the CPR to the old HBC posts at Mattagami and Groundhog Lake. Although the Canadian Northern line was completed by 1905 between Port Arthur and Edmonton, another ten years passed before service was inaugurated through northeastern Ontario.[15] By then, the Canadian Northern was awash in scandal and debt, as was the National Transcontinental. Following a royal commission inquiry in 1916, the Canadian government began the process of taking over both lines, and in 1923 the two were amalgamated under the name Canadian National Railways (CNR).

By 1905, then, there were four major railway lines either built or being planned to cross the region: the CPR, Canadian Northern, and the NTR, all with tracks running from east to west; and the TNO going from south to north. As had happened in western Canada, the coming of the railways precipitated a series of shifts in settlement patterns from the old river routes and HBC trading centres. A combination of railway politics and engineering necessities determined new corridors through different parts of the country than those that had suited canoe flotillas. The skeleton for a new community was being pieced together.

Meanwhile, First Nations people throughout the region watched the early manifestations of these developments with growing alarm. Non-Native trappers who eliminated the beaver and moved on were one kind of threat, but plans for farming and extensive lumbering were another matter altogether. People were well aware that treaties had been signed in 1850 with the bands south of the height of land (the Robinson Treaties) and in 1873 with the people to the west at Kenora–Rainy River (Treaty 3). As early as 1888, the people at Brunswick Lake, Flying Post, and Mattagami had complained to E.B. Borron that the CPR had been laid through their lands without their consent.[16] Eleven years later, having heard nothing in response to their concerns, the people of Missinaibi Lake sent a delegation to meet with the annual party of the Robinson-Huron Treaty. The northern delegates complained that surveyors, railways, and prospectors were trespassing on their lands.[17] The acting Indian agent at Sault Ste Marie, William L. Nichols, visited Missinaibi, Biscotasing, and Chapleau in 1902 and relayed the people's continuing concerns. To the list of problems, they now added fishermen and the bush fires set by the increasing numbers of trains, work crews, and prospectors. The following year, the Indian superintendent at Parry Sound reported to Ottawa that four hundred people at Lake Abitibi and others around Mattagami Post were anxious for a treaty to deal with similar concerns.[18] Still hearing no official response in the summer of 1905, Louis McDougall and Mr and Mrs John Chechabesh of Abitibi went in person to Ottawa to ask for a treaty, a reserve, and regulations to prohibit alcohol in the region.[19]

The issue had at last become urgent for government officials in Toronto and Ottawa. In 1903, as the TNO track was being laid through the Temiskaming District, rich veins of easily dug silver ore were discovered. Hordes of eager speculators and prospectors rushed into the region, now dubbed Cobalt, convinced that the Klondike was about to repeat itself – and right beside a railway track a few hours north of Toronto! There would be no toiling over treacherous mountain passes for these riches. And as in the fabled Klondike, the precious metal was easily removed with a minimum of equipment; anyone might make a fortune. The minority government of George Ross was ecstatic that its costly (and controversial) railway project had been justified so quickly. During the same summer as the Cobalt discovery, survey parties were laying out the main township lines from west of Nighthawk Lake to just southwest and west of Lake Abitibi, and plans had been made to extend the TNO north of its original terminus in the Temiskaming region to "open" these Clay Belt lands for farmer-settlers. In 1904, as had been done farther south, the first homestead grants in these new townships were assigned to Boer War and Fenian veterans, most of whom had probably never seen their property. Canadians were simply moving in and helping themselves without consideration for the people already living in the region.

Officials in Ottawa with responsibility for Indian affairs fretted and debated. Should the Aboriginal peoples of the area be brought into the existing Robinson–Huron Treaty through what was called an adhesion, or should an entirely new treaty be negotiated? Should the treaty include people in both Ontario and Quebec? What role should the *provincial* governments play in any negotiations and subsequent arrangements? There was an additional problem because Ontario and the dominion government were embroiled in a long-standing dispute over who was responsible for the annual payments under the Robinson Treaties, which had been signed before Confederation, when responsibility for "Indians and lands reserved for Indians" had been given to the dominion government under the British North America Act. Furthermore, concerns had been raised about some aspects of Treaty 3 in northwestern Ontario, including whether the Métis had a legitimate claim for inclusion. The Ontario government was reluctant to get involved in a new treaty until some of these basic questions had been settled by the courts.[20] Eventually, an agreement was hammered out between Ontario and Ottawa on what a northeastern treaty should include and how reserves should be selected. Curiously, the idea of a treaty with the First Nations on the Quebec side of the border was dropped with apparently little discussion. Deputy Superintendent General of Indian Affairs Frank Pedley stated that Indian title had never been officially recognized in Quebec, as it had in Ontario and the Northwest, so a treaty was not necessary in Quebec.[21] This proposal received no opposition whatever from the Government of Quebec!

Thus it was in the summer of 1905 that an official delegation set off from Ottawa to arrange Treaty 9 with the First Nations of Ontario north of the height of land. Conferences were held at Osnaburgh, Fort Hope, Marten's Falls, Albany, Moose, and New Post before the treaty party had to retreat south in the face of approaching winter. The following summer, the officials visited Matachewan, Mattagami, and New Brunswick House to secure the adhesion of these communities. All did not go smoothly. The

Family at Mattagami Post during the signing of Treaty 9 in 1906. The photographer's caption read "At the Feast" and, tellingly, did not identify any of the First Nations people by name. (Department of Indian Affairs and Northern Development, Library and Archives Canada [LAC], PA59589)

Abitibi people found it a "very unpleasant surprise" when they were told that only those who hunted on the Ontario side of the border were eligible to participate. As Samuel Stewart, a member of the treaty party, later recorded, "It was a matter beyond the comprehension of the Indians why this distinction should be made between a community the members of which were equally the subjects of His Majesty the King, and who were also in many instances, blood relations."[22] Faced with this protest, the dominion government tried unsuccessfully to convince the Quebec government to create a reserve for the Abitibi people in order to prevent the "serious consequences" that would obviously result from splitting the band for legal purposes. The issue was settled in 1908 when the dominion government told the Abitibi people in Quebec that they could be brought into Treaty 9 if they agreed to abandon any claims to a reserve on the Quebec side of the border. The Abitibi people in Ontario agreed to share their reserve lands, so the Quebec Abitibi people unanimously accepted the offer at a meeting on 22 June 1908.[23] As far as the provincial and dominion governments were concerned, the issues of Indian title and rights had now been settled forever. As we shall see, the First Nations would soon make clear that they saw it otherwise.

With what it believed was clear title to the land, the Government of Ontario ploughed ahead with an ambitious plan to promote agricultural

Michel Batise and his wife, of Matachewan, at the signing of Treaty 9 in 1906.
The Canadian government recognized him as chief at that time. (Treaty 9 Commission, LAC, PA059613)

settlement in Northern Ontario, a plan that was larger in scale but not dis-
similar to its promotion of settlement in the Parry Sound–Muskoka region
in the 1850s and 1860s. Surveys of more and more townships were commissioned, following the TNO line as it inched northward. In 1907 the minister of agriculture, Nelson Monteith, and the minister of lands, forests,
and Mines, Frank Cochrane, visited the area north of Lake Temiskaming
to select a site for a provincial "demonstration" farm to serve the needs of
future farmers in the northern districts of the Clay Belt. (A similar farm
was already under construction at New Liskeard for the Little Clay Belt.)
The farms were clearly an imitation of a dominion government initiative
to encourage prairie agriculture. A site was chosen where the TNO crossed
the Driftwood River; it was named Monteith to honour the minister.

The following year (1908), the TNO railway commissioners created a
Land Department under the direction of Frederick Dane. The new department coordinated lot surveys, prepared maps that laid out future concession roads and 160-acre (65-hectare) farms, and launched publicity campaigns. These included booths at agricultural fairs in "Old Ontario" and a
blizzard of promotional pamphlets.[24] The department organized and
hosted special northern train excursions of politicians, members of the
press, representatives of boards of trade, and sometimes even potential settlers. Accounts of these trips were reported in many Ontario newspapers,

usually thinly disguised as news reports. For example, following a visit along the TNO line, Toronto MPP J.W. Johnson told a newspaper, "Astonishment and admiration were expressed in every form as the travellers proceeded ... It was evident that the 'clay belt' containing 16 million acres of arable land, for the most part alluvial soil, thickly covered with the woods of commerce and indented with lakes and rivers and bays, with their attendant waterfalls, all wholesome, beautiful, picturesque, and ready to be made the handmaidens of every form of industry, and intensified the pride which every citizen of Ontario should feel for his heritage."[25]

The government made another use of the railways in its campaign. In 1912 the Department of Lands, Forests, and Mines created a Demonstration Car in a specially fitted train that travelled through Ontario for three years with displays of potential crops and with pamphlets entitled "Opportunities in New Ontario," "Progressive Ontario," and so on. It offered "colonization tickets" for travel on the TNO so that would-be settlers could spend up to forty days looking over the land possibilities for themselves.[26] To coordinate these activities, in 1912 the Conservative government of James Whitney created the Northern Development Branch. One of its first announcements was a promise to spend five million dollars on road development to ensure access to northern farmland back from the railway lines. A few years later, the Ontario government commissioned the construction of a log "settler's home" at the Canadian National Exhibition in Toronto to house exhibits of crops from across Northern Ontario, and it brought in representatives from demonstration farms like that at Monteith to promote the cause. The display was repeated for several years.[27]

The promotion of immigration was a slightly more delicate part of the program. Under the British North America Act, the dominion government was responsible for immigration policies and recruiting, but the Ontario government did not trust the dominion government to act in the best interests of Ontario, and it took matters into its own hands. "No direct canvassing for immigrants is allowed by the laws of this country," admitted the minister of lands, forests, and mines in 1914, "but by means of literature and through the agency of friends and otherwise everything is being done to encourage settlement of these people."[28] While officials preferred settlers from Old Ontario who were accustomed to the hard life of frontier farming, the Ontario government also actively sought German and Scandinavian settlers, reflecting the racial ideas of the day about hardy northern Europeans. As the minister, William Howard Hearst alleged, "Many of the people who have gone into the Western Provinces [from southern Europe] are not adapted for a country like Northern Ontario ... Even our English, our Irish and our Scotch settlers ... are much better fitted for settlement in Northern Ontario by spending two or three years in Older Ontario and adapting themselves."[29]

The lands that were being promoted in these schemes were depicted as places of plenty, opportunity, and potentially great wealth. "It is a land of wonderful richness," enthused Hearst.[30] A TNO pamphlet printed in 1911 promised "Fortunes for Farmers" and urged the city dweller to get off "the tread mill of city life" and head to the "new North," where "the opportunities that he so much desires, which if he grasps them, will make him his own master and will give him the independence and the competency that otherwise are beyond his fondest hopes and dreams."[31] Northern Ontario was contrasted favourably to alternative destinations for would-be settlers. "The land in the Clay Belt is more fertile than most of Old Ontario," claimed the president of the Sudbury Board of Trade.[32] Northern Ontario was particularly contrasted to the Prairie West. In a 1909 interview with the Toronto *Globe*, TNO chair J.L. Englehart referred to the North as "the front garden of the province" and claimed, "There is no need ... to sit down like they do in the west in the winter to await the coming of the sun again. There is no opportunity for rusting in the front garden of Ontario to those who desire to be busy. There is the summer season to till and garner and market. There is the winter for work in clearing the pulpwood and wood for the mills."[33] When the dominion government publicity trumpeted the ease of establishing a prairie farm because there were no trees to clear, Ontario promoters responded that "the growth of vegetation and timber is proof that the soil is exceedingly fertile.[34] In any case, alleged one pamphlet (in a grossly exaggerated claim), spruce tree roots seldom grew deeper than the top few inches of soil, "so that stumps can be soon removed after the land is once well burned."[35] Furthermore, the Ontario government liked to depict the forest cover as an actual advantage to settlers, because they could sell the wood for pulp as they cleared the land, making some cash income to subsidize the establishment of their farms.

Both the TNO railway commission and the Ontario government tried to downplay the idea that these were northern lands; clearly, they were afraid that images of ice and snow would deter prospective farmers. The preferred name became "New Ontario," with its connotations of progress and fresh beginnings. Typical newspaper articles pointed out "that in relation to the City of Winnipeg, Cochrane, and a large portion of the great clay belt lie to the south-east"[36] (mistaking latitude for soil quality and climate). Some took the claims even further. In an address to the Canadian Club in Toronto, W.H. Hearst enthused, "Much of what we call Northern Ontario lies south of the International boundary. Mr. Whitson [of the Northern Development Branch] can tell you of the beautiful weather they are having in the country around Cochrane now (November). When coming down he found snow and cold only when he came to North Bay. He knew nothing of it in the North where they were enjoying summer weather in 'the great banana belt.' "[37]

Northern Ontario

Big Game Abound in Northern Ontario

THE Great Clay Belt of Northern Ontario extends Westerly from Quebec to the Manitoba boundary, lying one degree south of Winnipeg.

Its bush relieves the monotony of the scene, protects from storm and wind, furnishes timber for the settler's dwelling and fuel for his winter need, as well as a source of income; large rivers and lakes and many lakelets water the land and offer fine inducements to stock raising and dairy farming.

Thousands of miles of colonization roads and steam railways are spreading like a spider's web over that vast new land. A settler can ride from the big cities of Ontario or the West in a Pullman if he wishes almost to his own door. This is something new in pioneer life.

Southern Ontario people should think of this great opportunity lying right at their own door, with its farming sections peopled mostly by their kindred or their own race.

And intending settlers from the British Isles should consider that North Bay (the eastern entrance to it) is only 350 miles from Montreal, whereas Winnipeg is 1,420 miles, Regina 1,771, and Calgary 2,251.

This rich agricultural land may be had by returned soldiers and sailors in 160-acre blocks free; to others 18 years and over 50c. per acre.

Our literature descriptive of this great country may be had free on application.

G. H. FERGUSON,
Minister of Lands, Forests
and Mines

Write **H. A. MACDONELL,**
Director of Colonization,
Parliament Buildings,
Toronto, Canada

This full-page advertisement is typical of the Ontario government's campaign for the colonization of New Ontario. Note the deliberate challenge to Prairie settlement and the positive spin put on the timber. The original photo is indistinct but appears to be of two young moose browsing in a clearing surrounded by scrub and some very small trees – a landscape totally unlike the lots that most settlers would be required to clear. (*Canadian Annual Review*, 1918, 834)

Certainly there were voices urging caution. The first dean of forestry at the University of Toronto, B.E. Fernow, took an extensive tour through the country along the National Transcontinental and reported in 1913 that, in his opinion, wildly exaggerated claims based on little actual knowledge were setting the public up for disappointment. "Too sanguine expectations are being entertained," he wrote, "and should be guarded against." He noted that "no real soil examination in the field" had been undertaken, and even on brief inspection he could see that the soil depth varied considerably, leaving only pockets potentially fit for farming. "This fact is apparently not fully realized in the attempts at settlement," he explained. "Indeed, there seems to be a widespread misconception that the whole country is *immediately* fit for farming." He also pointed out that claims that tree growth indicated good soil were misleading; they reflected soil drainage rather than the "chemical composition" of the soil. Equally problematic, he noted, was the fact that "the climatic conditions of the region" were "still imperfectly known." A reliable thirteen-year record at Abitibi indicated a frost-free period only from mid-June to mid-September in the best years – too short a time for any but the most hardy root crops and grains, and suitable primarily for hay.[38] But the Ontario government dismissed even this moderate caution and plunged in with its programs.

Settlement was organized under the provincial Free Grant and Homestead Act, a somewhat misleading name, since unlike the dominion government's homestead policy on the prairies, the Ontario government actually offered very few lands free. Only lots reserved for veterans of the Boer War and Fenian Raids were true homesteads. Otherwise, settlers were expected to pay a nominal 50 cents per acre for 160-acre (65-hectare) plots. Like prairie homesteaders, however, they also had to live on the land for a minimum period (in this case, three years), during which they had to build a house and cultivate at least 10 percent of the land. Even the minimum dimensions of the house were specified – 16 by 20 feet (4.9 by 6.1 metres) – in order to prevent token shacks being passed off as homes. Initially, settlers had to pay half the purchase price in cash up front and the remainder within two years, but in 1912, following complaints that too many settlers could not manage even this modest scheme, the Whitney government changed the terms to one-quarter in cash and the remainder within three years. Homestead inspectors were appointed after 1903 to ensure that settlers were complying with the legal conditions. All of these requirements were intended to prevent unscrupulous individuals from bypassing the forestry regulations and claiming to be settlers when their aim was to strip the land of its timber or pulpwood while avoiding the licences and fees required in that business. Through these homestead provisions, the Ontario government claimed (by 1908) to have on offer almost 280,000 acres (113,400 hectares) in 231 townships across the

A settler's house in "New" Ontario, c. 1936. This image was apparently intended for use in the Ontario government's promotional material, though one wonders why. The considerable effort required to clear the land was downplayed with promises of the cash income to be derived from the pulpwood sold. (Department of the Interior, LAC, PA43197)

North.[39] Along the TNO, the railway commission was authorized to lay out townsites, which the province hoped would become major agricultural service centres.

The first of these townsites to attract attention north of the Lake Temiskaming region was at McDougall's Chutes, home of the Native family of Bazil and Philomene McDougall, and something of a meeting place for the region's First Nations. An Ontario survey party worked through the area in 1904, in advance of the railway (and the treaty), and a number of lots were designated for the veterans' homestead program.[40] Close behind the surveyor was John McChesney of the Toronto-based Veterans' Locating Association, who had been hired to select lots on behalf of interested veterans. Then an organization called the Canada Lands Improvement Company signed an agreement with the provincial government to locate settlers on farmland in nearby Taylor and Carr Townships. In the summer of 1905, Walter Monahan of Huntsville, Ontario, came to McDougall's Chutes on the company's behalf to establish a base. McChesney built a small frame retail store at the Chutes to supply groceries and hardware to incoming settlers. A first-aid station (optimistically called a hospital) was erected, apparently even before the TNO survey parties had determined exactly where the rail line would go. Nearby, in 1907, the TNO established its main construction headquarters for the section of the line running north to meet the Transcontinental. Crews and equipment poured in, boarding houses and "hotels" sprang up, and McDougall's Chutes became a lively gathering place for the newcomers. The tracks reached the site in 1908. A sense of optimism about the future was palpable. "Every hotel and boarding house was full to overflowing," recalled a Treaty 9 commissioner.[41] Officials of the Canada Lands Improvement Company claimed that some three hundred people had already been settled on lands nearby, and the Ontario government opened its first two crown lands agencies there and at Cochrane.

There were hints about hard times to come, though. In the fall of 1908, the newly appointed crown lands agent reported that only nine men were occupying the lots that had been assigned to them: Walter Monahan, J.B. St Paul, and George Jefferies (in Carr Township) and W. Bailey, Alex Hardy, Theodore Bryson, Albert Taylor, James Cope, and H. Greatreaz (in Taylor Township).[42] Soon afterwards the TNO sent an agent to inspect the farm settlement, and he reported that only twelve families had taken up residence in Taylor and Carr Townships, contrary to the claims of the land company. "There is no doubt whatever, that the Canada Lands Improvement Co., have not put the matter fairly and honestly before us," wrote W.D. Cunneyworth, adding that the company was forcing the settlers to purchase all supplies at its store in McDougall's Chutes that it required a formal contract, in which "some of the conditions are pretty hard."[43]

Not all settlers came in groups or by corporate arrangement. Many were exactly those whom the Ontario government had targeted: frontier farmers from Parry Sound–Muskoka, German families encouraged through the work of a Lutheran pastor, and immigrants from England. By the fall of 1911, about twenty-six families were reported to have settled in the townships around Matheson, including Thomas Mitchell and W.J. Douglas at Matheson, John Critchley and William Clark a little farther north at Monteith, E.J. Kelso at the station stop that was becoming known as Kelso, and W.J. Strothers to the east.[44] Often, the men came alone or with teenage sons to begin the process of clearing the land and building a shelter. Those from Ontario had the advantage of being able to bring in many of the necessary supplies and sometimes even a few cattle.[45] Wives and daughters would join them later, like Mrs William Bailey, who came from England to join her husband at Watabeag in 1905, even before the railway could provide her with passenger service.[46] By 1912, Ontario's road commissioner J.F. Whitson was claiming that "fair progress" had been made by the settlers around Matheson, which was being heavily promoted as some of the best land in the district. Whitson boasted, "There are some

Typical settler's shelter near Monteith, pre-1914. This family could not afford a horse for transportation. (United Church Archives [UCA], 93.049, P/3563N)

large clearings and there is every appearance that, in the not distant future, Matheson will be the centre of a prosperous farming community."[47] To provide a showcase for the district, construction was finally begun on the Monteith Demonstration Farm in 1912, and by 1915 small plots of wheat and oats were being planted under the direction of manager John Whitton, just to prove that it could be done.[48]

While a few hardy souls were trying to establish themselves along the rail lines as farmers in New Ontario, others were looking for faster ways to make a fortune. In the summer of 1905, while Treaty 9 was being discussed, a handful of prospectors had begun to make their way north from the Cobalt silver discoveries, led by instinct, rumours, and tantalizing references in GSC reports. Interest focused initially on Nighthawk Lake, some thirty-five kilometres west of the proposed TNO route. A few claims were staked there in the summer of 1905, and in 1906 a New Brunswick-born veteran of the Klondike named Reuben D'Aigle began scouring the bush west of Nighthawk Lake, convinced that there was something even better here than the Cobalt silver – gold. In 1907 the Finnish prospectors Victor Mattson and Henry (Harry) Pennala[49] made the first confirmed finds of gold on an island in Nighthawk Lake where they sank a small shaft; but

they abandoned the project after early showings did not persist and a fire
destroyed their developments in 1908.

Rumours of the finds spread quickly through the north country. Even
Father Paradis resurfaced to get in on the action. No longer a member of
the OMI, he had been travelling through the area scouting for development opportunities when in the summer of 1907 he noticed some quartz
outcrops on the Frederick House River, whereupon he staked some claims
and brought in ten men to work them.[50] But the area seemed to be more
productive of rumours than gold, and the public's imagination was captured instead by allegedly spectacular gold discoveries at Larder Lake
(1907) and Gowganda (1909). Cobalt latecomers "rushed" to the new
fields in a flurry of excitement. Hotels and suppliers mushroomed
overnight at Cobalt, Haileybury, New Liskeard, and at points along the
routes into the goldfields. Then, in the summer of 1909, three separate
finds of genuine significance in the area west of Nighthawk Lake brought
the area dramatically onto the international stage. These discoveries were
to shape the destiny of the region for the rest of the century. All were made
by relative amateurs with limited capital, so it was other investors who realized the value and developed the finds into three of North America's
largest gold mines.

Jack Wilson had come to the North as a railway labourer. He prospected
in several other districts before investigating the mineral possibilities in
newly named Tisdale and Whitney Townships west of Nighthawk Lake in
1907. He liked what he saw but realized that he needed funding for more
extensive prospecting, so he returned to the area in 1909 with Harry
Preston, George Burns, and the brothers Frank and Cliff Campbell – all
equipped through two Chicago investors, one of whom Wilson had met
when the businessman came to Northern Ontario to fish. On 9 June the
prospectors came upon a rocky outcrop of quartz containing clearly visible
specks of gold, which they nicknamed the Dome. The Chicago investors
could not afford what was needed to develop the claims, so one of them,
W.S. Edwards, went to Toronto to secure further financing. Torontonians
were skeptical. Fraud and scandal had accompanied too many previous
gold "finds" in Ontario, and the investors stayed away in droves. Finally, in
1910, Edwards made an agreement with two of the men who had organized International Nickel of New Jersey – Joseph de la Mar and Ambrose
Monell. Dome Mines Company Limited was incorporated in March 1910
with an authorized capital of $2,500,000, and work began to develop the
property in December of that year.

Rumours of the Dome strike reached Haileybury in the summer of
1909, where a young barber from the Ottawa Valley named Benny
Hollinger heard the stories and decided to try his luck. He and his friend
Alex Gillies persuaded some local contacts to underwrite their costs, and

they headed by canoe and on foot into Tisdale Township, which they reached early in October. West of the Dome property they found the remains of what was probably Reuben D'Aigle's early exploration, and nearby they discovered a vein of quartz with visible showings of gold. Back in Haileybury to record their claims, they ran into a McGill University mining student named Alphonse Paré, who visited their claims, liked what he saw, and advised his uncle Noah Timmins to invest in the property. Noah and his brother Henry were Mattawa storekeepers who had already made a small fortune through a partnership with the brothers John and Duncan McMartin and the Mattawa lawyer David Dunlap. The partners had already invested in what had become one of Cobalt's most successful mines, and now they were looking for new opportunities. Benny Hollinger sold his claims to them, and Alex Gillies sold his to another Cobalt mine owner, M.J. O'Brien. This might have presented difficulties, because O'Brien and the Timmins brothers had been involved in a nasty dispute over the ownership of some Cobalt mining property. But O'Brien was apparently disappointed with the results of an assay conducted on samples from his claims, and he dropped his option on them. The Timmins-McMartin-Dunlap partnership took them over,[51] obtained additional financing, and began to develop the property as the Hollinger Mine. For $330,000 they had purchased a property that would become one of the continent's richest mines and lay the foundations for a Canadian financial dynasty.

A third significant find also was precipitated by news of the Dome discovery. Alexander Oliphant, a railway labourer (who was calling himself Sandy McIntyre after leaving his native Scotland under somewhat obscure circumstances), and a German acquaintance named Hans Buttner whom McIntyre had met in Haileybury, decided to head into the vicinity of the Dome claims in the hope of getting lucky. They did. Their claims between Dome and Hollinger on the shores of what became known as Pearl Lake turned out to have important gold deposits as well. Developing these deposits proceeded more slowly, however, because the financing of the property ran into a series of difficulties. Buttner sold his claims for $10,000 within weeks, but McIntyre held out for more. He offered them to Noah Timmins, but the two men could not agree on a price. In 1910 McIntyre tried to interest another Cobalt mine owner, who refused on the grounds that McIntyre had misrepresented the property. Finally, McIntyre was able to sell his claims by dividing them among the manager of the Union Bank in Haileybury, yet another Cobalt mine owner, and a North Bay speculator.[52] What happened next is a little unclear, but a company was formed to operate the mine under the presidency of Albert Freeman, an American entrepreneur, but he soon found himself at the centre of a court case in the United States over "a series of colourful prospectuses soliciting support for a string of phoney mining companies" which he had set up in Canada.[53] The property was then taken over by a group of Toronto investors that included Sir Henry Pellatt (of Casa Loma fame), and a wealthy speculator named J.P. Bickell was named president.[54] At last, development could proceed at the McIntyre Mine.

Of course, the news of the Dome find attracted dozens of other prospectors and speculators through the summer of 1909, and by spring break-up in 1910, hundreds of people and dozens of "mines" – which were little more than log shacks built over holes in the ground – suddenly materialized in what the attentive southern press was calling the Porcupine Camp. Men milled around the mining recorder's office in Haileybury awaiting the chance to snap up the latest options, especially if they were in the vicinity of a known find like the Dome. Prospectors capitalized on the gullible by calling everything the "Dome-something." A skeptical reporter commented in *Saturday Night* magazine:

The "North Dome" is the latest appendix to "The Dome."
Formerly it was the Feldon; more recently it was the Kirkgaard; now a firm of
Curbsters designate it as the "North Dome," notwithstanding its distance from
"The Dome" is calculated to disenchant those who rush for the shares ...
The Dome Extension – which has more than a fighting chance.
The Preston East Dome – which is extremely doubtful.
The West Dome – which has a "rocky road" to travel.
The Dome Lake – which is in the "Stoneham class."
The North Dome – which has been totally condemned.
Next!!![55]

A small settlement sprang up on the shore of Porcupine Lake. The provincial government got involved by providing prison labour to build road access; a post office was opened and a telephone line strung in. An electrical generating station was built at Sandy Falls on the Mattagami River. Two Roman Catholic priests, an Anglican minister, and two Methodist theology students arrived to attend to people's spiritual needs. Even a little newssheet called the *Quill* was printed for local circulation. The developing properties needed plenty of labour, so carpenters, teamsters, general labourers, and skilled miners flowed in. Many of the latter were Americans with experience in Cobalt, and they knowingly formed Local 145 of the Western Federation of Miners to protect their interests. Businesses followed, and in March 1910 the Porcupine Board of Trade was organized to promote *their* interests. First they lobbied for a better access road, then upped the stakes and demanded a branch line of the TNO. In the winter of 1911 the Ontario government announced plans to comply – and none too soon, according to the board of trade. Several townsites were

First Nations family assisting new arrivals on the Porcupine Trail, c. 1910. People took advantage of the gold rush to supplement their income through guiding and the sale of food, canoes, and other goods. (Archives of Ontario [AO], 3976, C320-1-0-1-2)

laid out. "Tisdale will be a real town with the conveniences which will safeguard health and make business possible," one developer advertised, adding for good measure, "Tisdale is not a promotion enterprise for the sale of forest land at city lot prices."[56] The editor of the Cobalt *Daily Nugget* noted, "Anything with Roof on Will fetch From $200 to $500."[57] The excitement of the rush was palpable.

As well as speculators and fraud artists, more and more serious investors were taking note. International corporations such as Consolidated Goldfields of South Africa moved in to purchase proven properties; options on unlikely claims were quietly let go. Serious mining investors soon realized that unlike the Cobalt silver, the Porcupine gold would not make a "poor man's camp." The gold appeared as small particles embedded in hard quartz veins, chemically bonded with other elements, so removing it would be technically difficult and very expensive. A great deal of money was required to build the mills to crush and refine the ore, while research was necessary to find ways to deal with the unique problems of Porcupine geology. It was not long before the opportunities for small-time investors had been sifted out, but the gold seemed to exist in sufficient quantities to merit the significant capital outlay required. For the believers, the future of the Porcupine Camp looked promising indeed.

Then, on a hot summer day in 1911, disaster struck. Spring had been dry and several small bush fires foreshadowed what was to come. On the 11 July a high wind sprang up, gathering a series of little fires into a single raging inferno that ripped through the tinder-dry trees and then bore down on the Porcupine Lake settlements. Terrified men, women, and children made a dash to the lake, scrambling into canoes and boats where they could, or simply wading in where they could not. Choking from the smoke and ash, they watched in horror as the flames engulfed the camps they called Pottsville and South Porcupine and then licked at the edges of Golden City. A railway car loaded with dynamite exploded, sending debris and a shock wave across the lake, upsetting some of the boats. Little Mervyn Strain drowned, an ironic death by water in the midst of fire. At the West Dome Mine, manager Robert Weiss made a desperate attempt to escape the flames by leading his wife, child, two other couples, and some twenty workers down into the shaft they had been sinking. Tragically, the voracious fire sucked the oxygen from their shelter, and all perished. When the monstrous fire had finally satiated its appetite, people dazedly emerged from their shelters to take stock. Seventy were confirmed dead, and there were fears that an unknown number of others scattered through the bush might also have succumbed. The fire had raged from the Mattagami River to Iroquois Falls and north to the new railway town of Cochrane, consuming some 200,000 hectares of forest.

Everyone in the region rallied to help the victims. The Porcupine Relief Committee was formed, doctors from Cobalt, Haileybury, and New Liskeard boarded a special train to head north to help, and donations from that area were used to buy provisions and wood for coffins. The T. Eaton Company in Toronto sent a railcar loaded with supplies, and the dominion government sent in a militia unit with tents and blankets.[58] The TNO put on extra trains to evacuate some 1,200 people and to carry the seriously wounded to hospital in the Sudbury area. Within a few weeks, donations from the Toronto City Council, the Toronto Board of Trade, the City of London (Ontario), the Masonic Order, the Canadian Bank of Commerce, and other groups, as well as private individuals such as Noah and Henry Timmins and the McMartin brothers, had amounted to over $50,000.[59] Reconstruction was quickly underway. Certainly, some people decided to leave the area, never to return, but others came back to build anew, defying the powers of nature with more substantial buildings that visibly declared, "We intend to stay." As will be seen, the 1911 fire quickly became the symbolic centrepiece of an emerging sense of community identity.

That same year Frank Harris Anson, the vice-president of the Atlantic

Sugar Refineries in Montreal, was looking for new investment opportunities, and he hired two students to visit the Porcupine mining camp and report. The students returned with a mixed message: the best mining options were already sold, but there was considerable potential for pulp production in the spruce and jack pine of the Abitibi district just east of Porcupine. Intrigued by his students' report, Anson apparently visited the region himself in the summer of 1912. He liked what he saw and returned to Montreal to organize financing for a pulp project.

Anson approached Shirley Ogilvie of the flour-milling enterprise in Montreal, perhaps because he had once worked for Ogilvie's. Ogilvie apparently made an attempt to raise funds through connections in England, but he failed; there were doubts that sufficient pulpwood could be obtained in the region to justify the cost of a pulp mill. So the two men themselves scraped enough together to finance four months of preliminary operations through a company they called Anson and Ogilvie. In August 1912 they purchased a twenty-one-year pulp concession from the Ontario government along the Abitibi River and the shores of Lake Abitibi. In return for the exclusive rights to cut pulpwood (but not any prime timber) on this land, they agreed to build a pulp mill on the Abitibi River with a minimum output of 100 tons per day and to employ a minimum of 250 men for an average of 10 months in the year. The new company also agreed to spend $50,000 to clear land near the mill, on which to build housing for the mill workers, and to maintain a force of forest-fire rangers, with the Ontario government paying half the bill. To power the pulp mill, the company was given a lease for hydro rights at Iroquois Falls and Couchiching Falls on the Abitibi River.[60]

With the agreement in place, there was a mad scramble for investors. This time a group of Americans took the bait, but they wanted full paper production, not just a pulp mill. So, in October 1912, Anson and Ogilvie transferred their personal interests to a new company, which they named Abitibi Pulp and Paper Mills, Limited. The first work parties set out from Montreal, commissioned to clear a site for the mill and power plant and to cut a road from the site to the nearest point on the TNO in preparation for a rail spur connection.[61] In December 1912 the company was reorganized for a third time, possibly because it clearly required greater financial resources for the rising costs of its construction and operation. This time, under a new name, Abitibi Pulp and Paper Company, Limited, $5 million in stock was put on offer in $100 shares. Frank H. Anson was appointed president, Shirley Ogilvie was made vice-president, and J.A. McAndrew of Toronto became the company's secretary; other executive officers came from Toronto and Montreal. Among the first stock subscribers were the Montreal lawyers who were handling the new company's business: V.E. Mitchell, E.M. McDougall, J.J. Creelman, and Pierre F. Casgrain.[62]

More than three hundred men were hired through contractors to build the mill. Even before it was finished, dozens of others had been hired directly by the company to begin cutting pulpwood at two bush camps established for the purpose. Early in 1914 the company was again reorganized, this time to permit it to develop the hydroelectric sites necessary to power the mill; its new (fourth) name was Abitibi Power and Paper Company. The mill officially began production in the spring of 1914. Another Canadian corporate giant had been launched.

The Ontario government was delighted with these developments because its earlier efforts to interest investors in the forestry potential of the area north of North Bay had not been a success. In 1901 it had created the Temagami Forest Reserve, which was expanded in 1903 north to the Mattagami River, as part of a program to manage forest resources through fire control and regulated cutting.[63] Although the government had publicized the reserve as the last great stand of pine timber in Ontario and a storehouse of riches for future generations, there had been little commercial interest in the trees, either inside or beyond the reserve. The government had then tried to promote interest in the pulp potential of the forests north of the height of land, emphasizing timber but hinting also at pulpwood. In 1908 Aubrey White, deputy minister of lands and forests, had told the Canadian Forestry Association, "Here in the not distant future will, in my opinion, be found our greatest timber asset." He had painted a vibrant picture of "seven or eight large rivers all flowing north towards the railway line" through which would be floated "enormous quantities of saw logs and pulpwood to feed the mills that will certainly be erected at points where these rivers cross the railway."[64] But all of White's enthusiasm had not succeeded in attracting any serious prospects for commercial forestry either along these rivers or along the TNO line. When the government had offered the pulp limits around Lake Abitibi for sale in 1911, there were no takers.[65] The Chicago *Tribune* had sent a delegation to investigate the area as a resource for its paper but had decided that development costs would be too high.[66] Anson and Ogilvie were the first to be willing to take the risk and the first to be able to convince a sufficient number of investors to join them. Even as construction began, however, the doubting continued. Kaspar Kechner, who worked on the first crew at Iroquois Falls, recalled that one New York consulting engineer advised against the project because it would be impossible to get men willing to work so far north. Kechner also said the workers on the site claimed that "it was a venture whose future, in some quarters, was regarded as so dubious that ... the fellows on the job 'would call a man an old timer if he stayed three days.'"[67]

Nevertheless, Abitibi Power and Paper was an instant political darling, courted devotedly by the Ontario government and promoted as a sign of the success of its policies. In a 1914 pamphlet, the Whitney government claimed that Abitibi was "developing on an enormous scale and will have an investment, when completed, of about three and a half million dollars. Their mills will produce 150 tons of pulp and 200 tons of paper every 24 hours and they will give employment to from 1,500 to 1,800 men." Behind the scenes, though, Abitibi's secretary J.A. McAndrew was forecasting a rather less grandiose investment of less than half the amount and employment for just 250 to 300 men.[68] Indeed, the company was already finding itself in difficulty. Southern optimism about northern resources was giving way to reality; Abitibi had been expecting to cut ten cords of pulpwood per acre but was able to obtain only about four. So in 1916 Anson went to the current minister of lands, and forests, and mines, Howard Ferguson, and cut a deal. If the Ontario government would provide additional cutting rights with sufficient pulpwood, Abitibi would enlarge its plant to double its output capacity. Believing that he had a guarantee, Anson began the expansion. Two years later, with no new rights in sight, the company complained that its pulpwood supply could last only another twenty-five years.[69] Finally, in 1919, the Ontario government made its affection for Abitibi tangible when Ferguson gave the company a gift by selling it pulp-cutting rights to just under 4,000 square kilometres without tendering for bids. Ferguson defended the decision by saying, "My ambition has been to see the largest paper industry in the world established in this Province, and my attitude toward the pulp and paper industry has been directed toward assisting in bringing this about."[70] Locally, too, there was some initial enthusiasm for the Abitibi venture. When the company announced its plans for a dam across the Abitibi River, the Cobalt *Daily Nugget* dismissed concerns about the resultant flooding, noting that there were few settlers in the area anyway. There was no consideration of the impact on the Aboriginal people whose homes and lands would be directly affected.[71]

In spite of the enthusiasm about the Abitibi project, many southern Ontario politicians preferred to see the real future of the North in agricultural development. Empire Ontario would meet and surpass the successes of the dominion in the Prairie West by using the same combination of ingredients: Indian treaties to clear title and prevent conflict; railways to open the lands for commercial agriculture and to export its products; a police force to maintain order; and the promotion of immigration to bring settlers. There seemed to be an unstated cultural assumption that great civilizations began with an agricultural base and that industry would "naturally" follow. The hardy farmer-entrepreneur was endowed with an almost mythical stature in promotional literature and speeches; his character was the moral justification for northern development. Ontarians were not rapaciously removing the precious resources of the earth; rather (in the words of school inspector J.B. Mac-Dougall), they were enjoined:

Bow ye not, sons of battle, to man-made traditions
   Of greatness by plunder, that sap by their sway,
But, yield ye alone to these God-fashioned visions
   That crown you by night, and that gird you by day.[72]

In this grand scheme, mining was highly suspect. Widely perceived in southern Ontario as a game for shysters and confidence men, no one was very surprised by the wild speculation and inflated claims associated with the early days of the Porcupine Camp. It was beset by "the evils of exaggeration, ove[r]-capitalization and mismanagement," according to one mining publication, and *Saturday Night* ran a sarcastic campaign about events at Porcupine in which it made such observations as "The New York Evening Post fell into a singular economic error when it assumed that 'the most profitable business in the whole world in 1911 was that of selling claims, or options, at Porcupine.' To be profitable a thing must represent its money's worth – otherwise it cannot be a 'business' transaction."[73] Porcupine would be yet another flash-in-the-pan and therefore merited little government encouragement and support. The most charitable credit given to mining among Toronto businessmen was that it would ultimately be a support to agriculture, as explained in a 1912 Board of Trade publication: "To mining the North we owe a great deal ... It has also given the Temiskaming and Northern Ontario Railway, the government road, a strong revenue foundation upon which agricultural settlement may be more easily assisted. In addition, it has been an excellent advertisement for Northern Ontario."[74]

Forestry was perceived with slightly more enthusiasm in the halls of power in Toronto. New ideas about conservation and scientific management were beginning to permeate political consciousness through the efforts of such men as the University of Toronto's Dean of Forestry, Bernard E. Fernow, and the Ontario College of Agriculture's Edmund John Zavitz (who became deputy minister of forestry in 1925 and chief forester of the province in 1934).[75] Forestry was just beginning to be considered a kind of farming, with sustainable harvests. But it was given a secondary place to agriculture. Ontario had appointed a "clerk of forestry" in 1883, stationed within the Department of Agriculture, and although forestry matters were moved to the Department of Crown Lands for a brief time, in 1905 they were moved back to the Department of Agriculture, where, according to historians Robert and Nancy Wightman, they were "gradually submerged into the rising Colonization Branch."[76] It was clear where development priorities lay. In most circles, even the announcement of Abitibi Power and Paper's grand plans was greeted more for its potential to help northern settlers than for its intrinsic importance. As the minister of lands, forests, and mines reported in 1912, the main significance of Abitibi's plans was that they would "cause a large expenditure for wages," which in turn would "create markets for natural products, and ... enable the settlers to dispose of their spruce timber removed in clearing their land, at prices which will afford them some profit."[77]

It has been customary in the Canadian historical imagination to see the arrival of agriculture or extensive resource development as a sudden break in the history of a region. The Aboriginal population and the fur trade society suddenly disappear from the stage, displaced irrevocably and sometimes even inevitably by "progress." According to the development promoters of the day, the treaties had taken care of any residual obligation that the Government of Canada might have, and now it was up to the First Nations to accommodate themselves to the new realities. The stories that are told, whether in local oral traditions or in more formal, scholarly texts, accord no place to Aboriginal people in the new economies of "development." But as historian Rolf Knight first demonstrated for British Columbia, Aboriginal men and women had plans of their own for dealing with the new economy.[78]

The opportunities that the gold rush offered were the first to be taken up. The early prospector Reuben D'Aigle worked in partnership with a Métis, William ("Billy") Moore, later of Temagami, while the Métis prospector Sam Otisse made one of the few successful finds in the Elk Lake area.[79] Anahareo, the Mohawk wife of Archie Belaney (better known as Grey Owl), tried her hand at prospecting between 1929 and 1933.[80] Noah Timmins credited a group of unnamed Porcupine Lake "Indians" with bringing reports of possible coal resources to Cobalt and thereby generating the first prospecting efforts, and "Indian" Tom Fox was credited with tipping off the Dome prospectors about possible deposits at Frederick House Lake.[81] The fact that Aboriginal people were instrumental in providing useful information about minerals suggests that they were themselves interested in obtaining possible benefits from the exploitation of these resources. Indeed, some appear to have staked their own claims, as did Tournene of the Larder Lake area, who located a claim on his hunting grounds which subsequently became part of an operating mine.[82] Others took advantage of the opportunity for work. The first officially recorded Porcupine claims were registered to E.O. Taylor, but local tradition has it that the actual staking was done by a crew of Aboriginal men,[83] and Reuben D'Aigle hired five Métis men to operate his modest mine works in 1908.[84] Countless unnamed Native people served as canoemen, guides, and bush assistants to the inexperienced argonauts who came to the area.

At the same time, others signed on with railway construction crews, road-cutting crews, and any of the other seasonal or occasional jobs that served as an income supplement in lean fur-trade years. Women provided meals for travellers in the bush and continued to sell the moccasins and snow-shoes they had been making for the Hudson's Bay Company and which now proved popular among the newcomers. Just as the Aboriginal families of the region had learned to incorporate the fur trade into their lives in the eighteenth and nineteenth centuries, now, in the early twentieth, they hoped to take advantage of the promise of the new development economy to augment and enrich their traditions.

The hopes and intentions of the Ontario government for this new economy were somewhat different from the Aboriginal expectations, however. On the eve of the First World War, successive Ontario govern-ments had put in place a system and transportation infrastructure to colo-nize the lands of Northern Ontario as a great agricultural hinterland that would provide internal markets for southern districts, thereby strengthen-ing the province's economy and political power within the dominion. The old world of the fur trade would have to give way to "progressive" men, buoyed by a sense of moral purpose and even divine right, who would clear the forests and cultivate the earth. Things had already not quite turned out as planned; gold fever had sidetracked too many gullible or greedy arg-onauts, and the farmers seemed more interested in cutting pulpwood for quick cash than making long-term investments in the land. Nor could what appeared to be the most significant industrial development in the region (at Iroquois Falls) be said to have resulted from government plans or pro-motion. Nevertheless, the promoters remained hopeful.

All was "progress" and "development" as the wonders of modern tech-nology, scientific planning, and financial wizardry swept through the northern forests and blasted into the ancient rocks. The Ontario minister of lands, forests, and mines, W.H. Hearst, enthused in 1914, "The people of the north, from Lake Abitibi to the Lake of the Woods, are united in a determination to build up the great Empire of the north and do their part in the development of the greatest Province in the greatest Dominion in the greatest Empire the world has ever seen ... New Ontario ... will provide a strong, vigorous and manly race to carry on the glorious work and tradi-tions of the great nation to which we belong. New Ontario offers splendid inducements for the building up of young Canada."[85]

CHAPTER FOUR

Building the Towns

If all had gone according to plan, the most important new settlement in the region would have been at McDougall's Chutes, which was intended to be an agricultural service centre. Although settlers were slow to come, the future of the site seemed confirmed when reports began to trickle out of the bush that fabulous gold deposits lay just to the west. The population increased more quickly. Shopkeepers set up small frame buildings to supply construction materials and necessities of life. Building on the area's fur trade heritage, Revillon Frères (which at that time was the Hudson's Bay Company's primary competition in the North), established a retail outlet. Two churches, a school, and a bank went up, and local boosters promoted the Black River as a transportation route into the potential farmlands and the "unlimited supply of pulpwood"[1] that lay to the northeast. In 1912 McDougall's Chutes was optimistically incorporated as a town (not a village) and was officially renamed Matheson to honour A.J. Matheson, the provincial treasurer in the government of J.P. Whitney, whose financial dealing had put the Temiskaming and Northern Ontario Railway (TNO) on a firm footing. The first mayoralty race was a tight contest in which Dan Johnson, manager of the Revillon Frères store, won by six votes. The first town council included representatives of the business, farming, and transportation sectors, reflecting the diversity of the nascent economy.[2] Two years later, there were enough farm women in the area to found a Women's Institute. It looked as if Matheson was well on its way to becoming the most important regional service centre between the head of Lake Temiskaming and Cochrane, where the TNO met the National Transcontinental Railway.

Matheson was not, however, located at the most suitable railway stop for access to the Porcupine goldfields. Prospectors, construction crews, and mine developers found it more convenient to travel a few kilometres north of town on the TNO to Mile 222, then head west into the bush to the

First parsonage, Union Church at Matheson, a building purchased from a nearby
Aboriginal family. The men in the doorway are Presbyterian student minister E.L.
Longmore (later of Hollinger Mine) and Methodist Milton Beach, holding his
puppy Teddie. (UCA, 90.162, P/1032)

Frederick House River along trails and water routes well worn by Aboriginal traders and travellers. Where the newcomers disembarked from the
Toronto train, they needed supplies and a place to stay. In 1910, Mile 222
grew from a single railcar parked on a siding to a bustling place with
hotels called Miller House and The Prospect, and with retailers such as
Davies and Dunn Dry Goods. The name Mile 222 hardly seemed suitable
for such a promising place, and it was renamed Kelso in honour of a local
retailer. The biggest business in town was freighting, and the biggest
freighters were the New Liskeard–based Jamieson Meat Company, which
put up a livery stable at Kelso to house as many as 1,200 teams. Big business was already displacing the individual Aboriginal guide. For $1.50,
argonauts could purchase wagon transport for the two-hour trip to the
Frederick House River, where they transferred to boats or freighter
canoes for the next leg of a two-day journey (for an additional cost, of
course). Other businesses and services were quickly established at Kelso,
including Anderson's Sawmill, two hotels, a bank, a drugstore, three
general stores, and a barbershop. Dr James Reid occupied a log cabin that
doubled as a hospital, and the townspeople built a small school to serve
the families of the storekeepers and hotel proprietors. Even the provincial
police arrived to keep an eye on the freighting crews and to intervene in

disputes over land and property.[3] As the reputation of the Porcupine Camp grew, local boosters began to refer to Kelso as "Goldlands" to reinforce the connection and to attract potential residents.

Matheson and Kelso lobbied hard against each other to become the junction point of the railway spur line that the TNO agreed to build into the Porcupine Camp late in 1910. But TNO surveyors argued that the best place for the junction was at another place entirely. So they selected a point at Mile 225, just north of Kelso, and announced that it was to be called Iroquois Falls. The name didn't stick for long, because it was appropriated for Abitibi Pulp and Paper's proposed settlement to the east. Instead, the TNO decided to call the site Porquis Junction, the meeting place of Porcupine and Iroquois. The Ontario government, on the advice of the TNO, decided to lay out a "government townsite" there, in part because of its proximity to the "unlimited water power" on the Abitibi River at the falls, and in part because the land along the railway at Mile 222 was being claimed by the owner of a nearby timber limit.[4] Porquis became the next major boom town in the winter of 1911 as the track construction from there into Porcupine proceeded rapidly from January to May, covering the fifty kilometres to the new Hollinger Mine. Easy access to rail transportation and the potential for pulpwood development attracted attention; within a few years, the population of Porquis Junction was over a hundred. Among the new arrivals was John Rowlandson, a general merchant and pulpwood dealer, who eventually had a significant impact on the area as an outspoken municipal and provincial politician.

North and south of Matheson, two other townsites were being developed with slightly less fanfare. The first was Ramore, twenty-four kilometres south, which began as a railway siding and station, where business congregated in anticipation of serving an agricultural region. Thomas O'Coughlin built the first store and post office there in 1910; the name Ramore was apparently chosen in memory of prospector Louis Ramore, who had been killed by a disgruntled colleague.[5] A number of French-speaking Canadian settlers were attracted to the nearby farmland, though they were not provided with a chapel and resident priest until 1917.

The second town was Nushka, which developed rather independently of provincial promotion. Lying about ten kilometres north of Matheson, it began when a group of families from Quebec arrived as farmer-colonists under the auspices of the Roman Catholic Church. A parish church, school, and post office formed the nucleus of the settlement as Abbé Bourassa and then Abbé W. Gagné helped to organize a town that, unlike the business orientation of Kelso and Ramore, emphasized social services.[6] Bourassa made a point of visiting other French Canadian farm families in neighbouring townships, making Nushka something of a spiritual centre as well. Nushka was (at least initially) a community apart, ignored by the

Ontario government and the TNO commission, and more of an extension
of northern Quebec than of Ontario.

Finally, there was Mattagami Landing, an agricultural settlement that
was soon to be completely overshadowed by unanticipated events. It had
attracted a few hardy souls by 1908 to some promising land along the
Mattagami River – downstream from the old HBC post and accessible at the
time only along the fur trade trail between Nighthawk Lake and the river.
The setters' apparent lack of access to railway or road was no deterrent, for
in 1908 they petitioned the Ontario government for a school, optimistic
that they were laying the foundations of a new agricultural district.[7]
Undoubtedly, their faith was being placed in government promises of
extensive colonization road projects, which were supposed to provide a
transportation network to connect the outlying townships with the main
railway line.

None of these agricultural service centres was particularly planned or
systematically developed. Entrepreneurs erected buildings along the
railway line, and gradually private homes were constructed beyond the
businesses as the dictates of geography permitted. Simple log shacks were
soon replaced by very basic wooden frame buildings in which utility predominated over aesthetics. In a few cases, store owners splurged with false
fronts designed to make the establishments appear more impressive.
People's energy went into making money, not making beautiful surroundings. And since few people in these towns made any large amount of
money, there was little to distinguish one home or business from the next
in the early years. Matheson was the largest settlement of the group, with
a population that may have reached six hundred by the beginning of the
First World War.[8] But they all held high hopes for the future, accepting the
Ontario government's propaganda about the promise of Clay Belt
farming. The newcomers believed that they were founding a new society in
the North that would some day be the envy of the South, if not of the
world.

Scarcely had these hopes been whispered when disaster struck. As
described in the previous chapter, a forest fire in 1911 swept the bush from
Porcupine to Cochrane, destroying most of the buildings at Kelso. Worse
was to come. Five years later, another fire roared along the TNO. Ramore,
Matheson, Nushka, and Kelso were essentially obliterated, and Porquis
Junction was severely damaged. At Matheson, almost a hundred people
escaped on a freight train while others huddled under wet blankets on a
burned-over spot near the river. Without proper fire-fighting equipment,
the hastily organized fire brigades could do little to save the buildings.[9] At
Nushka, families frantically loaded their children onto a passing train,
then returned to try to save their homes. As a wall of flames descended on
the settlement, Abbé Gagné heroically led thirty-five terrified men and

women into a rock cut for shelter. Tragically, they and twenty-nine others nearby were killed. At Kelso, Dr James Reid died trying to save the school. Altogether, more than two hundred people died in the surrounding countryside. The magnitude of the human tragedy seemed to take the heart out of the newcomers, and many of the little towns along the railway never recovered.

Kelso was not rebuilt, and although the TNO station, a general store, and a school remained open into the 1960s, today only a couple of buildings and a cemetery mark its existence. Nushka was renamed Val Gagné to honour the priest who had lost his life in the valiant attempt to save others. The parish was rebuilt, but the town never grew as had been anticipated. Ramore, too, tried to re-establish itself, but only when a Pine Tree Line radar site was built there during the Cold War was there any real injection into its economy. A few people trickled back into Matheson after the fire, but the town was struggling, losing people and businesses, and in 1919–20 losing an actual section of the townsite when the water level was raised in the Black River, flooding some of its land.[10] In 1922, Frank Ginn, the town clerk and crown lands agent, reported that there were 306 people in Matheson, most of whom were "of the labouring classes who are dependent, not upon a steady payroll (there are no factories here) but upon odd jobs in the neighbourhood."[11] The town council soldiered on, struggling with perpetual debt, unable and unwilling to spend scarce money on "improvements" such as sewers and electricity. As Ginn explained somewhat apologetically to the provincial government, "With these figures before you, you will see that in order to keep Matheson on the map and prevent an exodus of its inhabitants, the strictest economy is compulsory for governing bodies." The town's leaders feared that any increase in taxes would push the struggling residents either out into the bush or to nearby settlements that were unincorporated and hence levied no taxes or fees.[12] It was not until the 1960s that Matheson's population again approached its pre-fire numbers, but the lack of economic opportunity in the region continued to hamper the town. In 1968 the municipality was finally dissolved although a small population soldiered on.

At the beginning of the twentieth century, as has been discussed, officials and politicians in the Ontario government were promoting agriculture as the only sure and permanent basis for economic development in New Ontario, and they were dismissing as fraudulent or base speculation any claims about mining development. Ironically, it was, of course, that very mining development that led to the creation of the largest and wealthiest cluster of towns in the region. Some of these mining towns were at least partially planned, while others developed haphazardly, providing variations on the social experiment that provided very different platforms for community development.

Not everyone was planning to make money in Porcupine mining. In this photo, taken c. 1912, a townsite that was never developed is being advertised by promoters. (AO, 3980, C320-1-0-10-8)

Although the goldfields around Porcupine Lake were initially called the Porcupine *Camp*, promoters quickly set about making proposals and plans for more permanent (and profitable) towns. If a piece of property wasn't promising as a mining claim, it would be promoted as a townsite development, and more than one opportunist put up signs and took out advertisements offering "city" lots for sale. "Tisdale will be a real town," enthused one speculator in December 1910. "Tisdale has no boom features, but is to be a business town looking for a permanent future."[13] Tisdale, of course, had no future at all. It was never built.

The first real town to be developed in the camp grew out of an investment by three Haileybury entrepreneurs: Howard C. Dunbar, Hugh H. Sutherland, and Henry J. ("Harry") Potts. In January 1910 they began construction of the Porcupine Camp's first hotel, at the northwest end of Porcupine Lake. It was a thirty-bedroom wonder that advertised a reception hall and a dining room with real china and silver for discerning clientele. They named it the Shuniah Hotel, *shuniah* being rumoured locally to be the "Indian" word for gold.[14] Around the hotel they laid out a street grid and offered lots for sale in what became known as Pottsville, after Harry Potts and his wife, who came to manage the hotel. The first to join them were branches of businesses already established in northeastern Ontario,

Main "Street," Pottsville, 1910. The Revillon Frères store was then the most substantial in town. (Geological Survey of Canada, LAC, PA45236)

including Jamieson Meats (of New Liskeard and Kelso) and Gibson and Sterling's general store (of McDougall's Chutes). Revillon Frères constructed one of the most imposing buildings in town (a two-storey tarpapered frame affair) and took it upon themselves to dig a well for public use even before the stumps had been removed from the main "street." In the summer of 1910 someone imported a "herd" of cattle for fresh beef. Already Potts was growing vegetables behind his hotel, and a Mr Lloyd was raising hens to provide fresh eggs to the camp. They were followed that autumn by the Imperial Bank of Canada and the Bank of Toronto; in December a telephone line connected Pottsville to Kelso (but not, apparently, to anywhere else in the world).[15]

At about the same time that Pottsville was being laid out, rumours began to circulate that the Ontario government was going to develop a townsite of its own to the east of Pottsville on Porcupine Lake, allegedly on a veteran's claim registered to a Mr. Crombie of Toronto. Other competing townsites were also advertised. A veteran named Galloway had his property on the west side of the lake surveyed as a townsite, and the Porcupine Development Company of A.E. Way and J. Arthur Griffith registered a town plan for the south end of the lake.[16] Through a sequence of events apparently lost to the historical record, the "government site" passed quickly into private hands and became known as Golden City (although its official name was registered as Porcupine). Hotels such as the Strathcona (opened February 1910) and the Golden Leaf were just simple wooden

Golden City, 1911. The photographer had produced a panorama to impress the
audience with the scale of the endeavour. Photo has been cropped. (Canada
Patent and Copyright Office, LAC, PA30923)

frame buildings, but they looked very substantial next to Henry Yates's
hotel, which was a tent. The grandly named Porcupine Stock Exchange
and the provincial Mining Recorder were located at Golden City, too, but
by the spring of 1911 even the boosters at the Cobalt *Daily Nugget* had to
admit that "Porcupine today is certainly in a crude state in spite of the
great improvements that have been made during the past year." But locals
were not to blame – apparently, it was the fault of the Ontario government
for not moving quickly enough with railway access. As the *Nugget*
explained, "There are many things that are awaiting the arrival of the first
railroad trains and the resulting reduction in freight rates."[17]

When the Ontario government announced plans for construction of a
railway spur to link the camp to the TNO main line (not a minute too soon
for the local boosters), there was another flurry of activity, because instead
of passing through Pottsville on the north side of the lake, the line was surveyed through the bush along the south shore. A.C. Brown, who had staked
claims at the southwest end of the lake, now found it more profitable to take
over the old plans of the Porcupine Development Company; in partnership
with businessman Cliff Moore, he renamed the streets and began to advertise "South Porcupine," which the partners promoted as "The Pay Roll
Town."[18] "Real Estate Activity Reaches Fever Heat," trumpeted the *Daily
Nugget* in mid-December 1910.[19] A few months later, more excitement
ruffled the waters of Porcupine Lake as a conflict developed between mining
and other interests. In May 1911, South Porcupine entrepreneurs formally
organized the Corporation of the Township of Tisdale and announced the
appointment of a reeve and four councillors. The Cobalt *Daily Nugget* was
outraged: "If the business men and mine owners go to sleep at the switch
and allow an irresponsible crowd with selfish aims to get control, they will

deserve what comes to them."[20] Lawyer J.E. Cook, who was leading the organizational effort, backtracked and then regrouped his men; a new slate of candidates, representing a slightly wider constituency, was presented. The proposed reeve, Harold Kingsmill, was manager of the Rea Mines, and the councillors consisted of a real estate developer, the manager of a mining supply company, an assayer, and a retailer. For a few days it looked as if this slate was going to be challenged by some rival business owners, but in the end the reeve and council took office by acclamation.[21]

Across the lake at Pottsville and Golden City, the entrepreneurs decided that instead of organizing as municipalities, they would form a board of trade to represent business interests, which they assumed were synonymous with the public good. The first board of trade's executive included representatives from both settlements: Henry Potts (hotel owner-manager), George Bannerman (prospector and co-founder of an early success, the Scottish-Ontario Mine), Colonel A.M. Hay (soon to be named president of the McIntyre Mine), and Sylvester Kennedy (store owner).[22] As a coalition of senior mine and retail interests, they shared concerns about improving road (then rail) access to the camp and keeping order among the growing crowd of construction crews – whom they seemed to perceive as a necessary evil and somewhat ominous threat, because they were "foreigners" with no family ties to keep them responsible and under control. Already, class and ethnic tensions were beginning to materialize.

The real-estate boom and town development were in full swing by the summer of 1911 when the terrible fire, described in chapter 3, swept across the Porcupine Camp, killing about seventy-five people. Pottsville was almost completely wiped out, and South Porcupine suffered heavy losses; only Golden City was relatively unscathed. Unlike the situation at Matheson, Nushka, and Kelso in 1916, the people of the Porcupine Camp had sufficient economic motivation to regroup. After a few days of stunned silence, broken only by the hiss of smouldering brush, the camp was suddenly alive again with the clang of hammers and the rasping of saws. New and more substantial buildings replaced the log cabins and canvas tents, while waves of entrepreneurs snapped up lots that were no more than ugly, black, scarred plots, but at least were easy to clear. With rail access complete, the process was amazingly fast. Golden City and Pottsville made a symbolic statement of optimism by formally incorporating the Township of Whitney in September 1911, with Gordon H. Gauthier (one of the first lawyers in Pottsville) as reeve. One of the four councillors was Thomas Strain, a stonemason by trade, who dabbled in prospecting and whose young son Mervyn had died in the fire.[23] The composition of the Whitney council set it apart from the Tisdale council in the early years. Less dominated by big mining interests, it was run by a coalition of professionals and small-scale business owners.

Schumacher, a photo probably taken during the annual Dog Derby. Note the substantial false front on Mr Dunn's general store. (UCA, 93.049, P/4351)

Meanwhile, a few kilometres to the west, other mining developments were shaping two new towns. The first was Schumacher, named for mine developer Frederick W. Schumacher, an Ohio patent medicine manufacturer who, in partnership with geologist Shirley Cragg, had purchased some veterans' lots between the Hollinger and McIntyre claims in 1910 (and, later, others adjacent to the Dome Mine).[24] When gold showings on the properties looked promising, Schumacher approached the TNO for a railway station and in 1912 registered over a hundred lots for a new townsite on his property, not far from the McIntyre Mine. Since the lot sales were slow, Schumacher encouraged development by constructing a number of houses for married mine employees and donating funds for the construction of a school and a hospital.[25] Without formal incorporation, the village remained in a rather raw state for some time. As resident Mrs J.S. Kitchen recalled, "In 1915, Schumacher was sparsely settled, with unpaved roads and one long uneven boardwalk. The hill from the present town park to the McIntyre Road was a mixture of stumps, rock, and sand, with a creek running from it."[26] Schumacher's mine was officially incorporated in the summer of 1914; it produced gold briefly but ceased production in 1918. The mine property was purchased by Hollinger a few years later. However, the townsite was convenient both for McIntyre employees (who had only a short walk north to the mine) and for Hollinger men (who had to travel just a little west), so the end of the Schumacher mine proved to be the beginning of the town. Frederick Schumacher maintained a personal connection with it over the years, although he never lived there. Schumacher was never a true company town, but the financial thread that tied it to Frederick Schumacher, however fine a silk thread it was, sustained a peculiar sort of proprietorship by the absentee "master."

The second townsite development west of Porcupine Lake proved ultimately to be the largest in the region. Through 1910, as Noah Timmins oversaw development of the Hollinger Mine, he realized the need to provide his workers with a place to live that was closer than the townsites around Porcupine Lake (which were a considerable commute even after the rail spur was completed). So in the summer of 1911, after the fire, he commissioned a survey to lay out a townsite on his property just to the northwest of the mine. To manage the business, he incorporated the Timmins Townsite Company. The focal point was to be a slight rise at the southeast corner of the site, reserved for salaried managers and professionals. West of "The Hill," a regular grid of half a dozen streets was laid out with numbered avenues running east-west. Running north-south were streets optimistically named Spruce, Pine, Cedar, Balsam, and Birch, even though they traversed mostly blackened and burned-over stumps. At a public auction on 1 September 1911, some of the lots were offered for sale to commercial and individual owners, ensuring that there would be an element of private development. However, the Timmins Townsite Company reserved ownership of some of the land, and Noah Timmins personally advanced loans to several purchasers as start-up capital for their businesses. The town of Timmins was thus established as a sort of "open" company town, with a mix of individual and corporate development. Noah Timmins's role in its development reflected a version of corporate paternalism that was already old-fashioned elsewhere in North America but which Timmins seemed to relish in his new-found role of industrialist.

The new town rose rapidly. The Hollinger Mine's management led the way by commissioning the construction of three large bunkhouses for single workers, the Goldfields Hotel (which also served partially as a more commodious bunkhouse for technical and managerial staff), and a row of four- and five-room houses for married employees. These houses were offered on a rent-to-own purchase plan, but those who eventually owned the houses were required to sell only to other Hollinger employees.[27] Through the corporate body that controlled the Hollinger Mine (the Canadian Mining and Finance Company, Limited), Noah Timmins commissioned the construction of a hospital and the development of electrical and water supplies capable of serving a population of 10,000, all to be completed within less than a year.[28] Residents petitioned the province for incorporation, and the Town of Timmins was officially created on 1 January 1912. In the spring, the town council announced the construction of cement sidewalks throughout the townsite, claiming to be the first town north of New Liskeard to do so – and pointing out that even New Liskeard

Timmins in 1913, one year after the lots had been laid out. Hollinger Mine can be seen on the horizon. Although the electricity poles are already in place, some business is still being conducted from tents. (Arthur Tompkinson, LAC, PA30044)

had sidewalks on only a few streets.[29] That first summer, growth at the Hollinger Mine proceeded so rapidly that there was an acute housing shortage. So in the summer of 1913, the company built twelve more houses for employees along Tamarack Street (at a time when only three privately built homes were up) and three more bunkhouses at the mine site.

The company was involved in other early development as well. Mine manager P.A. Robbins commissioned the construction of a small frame church on the hill next to the houses of the senior staff. It was turned over to an eager Anglican congregation and became St. Matthew's. Noah Timmins, whose father had been instrumental in establishing the Roman Catholic Church in Mattawa in the upper Ottawa Valley, provided the Reverend Charles-Eugène Thériault with a substantial sum to build a Roman Catholic church in a commanding spot overlooking the townsite.[30] The church was dedicated to St Antoine-de-Padoue, patron saint of Noah *Anthony* Timmins. Symbolically, it was destroyed by fire in 1936 while Father Thériault was in Montreal attending Noah Timmins's funeral. In 1915 Hollinger donated two townsite lots to the local Presbyterian congregation so that they could build their own church, and it donated a further eight lots at the heart of the townsite, plus the plans for a public school, pushing through the project over the objections of town ratepayers.[31] Making money was clearly more important to the townspeople; there was no need to throw it away on frills like teachers' salaries and school upkeep.

In the coming years, Hollinger continued to build employee housing and other facilities including a hockey rink, a ball field, a golf course, an employees' library, and a community recreation hall. In 1919 it added twenty-five small frame houses on Birch and Spruce Streets at a construction cost of $2,200 each.[32] Two years later it announced a much larger construction project: one hundred and fifty rental houses, to be placed on "The Flats," a sandy plain just west of the original townsite. The one-and-a-half storey houses were square boxes consisting of four rooms: a living room (complete with sink and water tap) and three bedrooms, plus a small kitchen and toilet at the back. Rows of these boxes were packed together tightly in nine-metre lots, with only their tarpaper siding in alternate red and green to distinguish them. Even the usually enthusiastic *Porcupine Advance* admitted that they were "not of pretentious appearance," but it claimed that they were "built for comfort, convenience and warmth" – which seems rather unlikely, given that they had no insulation and were heated only by a stove in the living room.[33]

In 1922 the Hollinger Mine added another hundred of these houses, along streets with names such as Vimy, Cambrai, Messines, and Borden – which, like the housing project itself, could be interpreted either as a celebration of Canadian achievement or as a harshly realistic commemoration of mud, crowding, and human despair. One Communist Party organizer who visited Timmins chose the latter view. "The sum total produces an effect that would almost deceive a jack rabbit into thinking it was an enlarged rabbit establishment," wrote Becky Buhay in the *Worker*.[34] Hollinger attempted to improve the houses in the summer of 1936 by adding peaked roofs that allowed two extra rooms and initiating an annual gardening contest to encourage tenants to plant flowers and vegetables on their tiny lots. But there was really very little that could be done to make the Hollinger Houses (as they were dubbed) even slightly more attractive. Nevertheless, the rent was cheap, and Hollinger always had more applications on file than houses available.

Not everyone elected to apply for a company house or to buy a lot in the company townsite. Beginning in 1912, a Toronto firm called Standard Canadian Investors Limited offered lots in Mountjoy Township on the east bank of the Mattagami River in a development called Mattagami Heights; by 1920, some eighty to one hundred people were living there, many apparently in "cottages" owned by C.M. Auer.[35] On the other side of the Timmins townsite, J.P. Bartleman, a New Zealand immigrant who was both a machine salesman and a real estate speculator, obtained some choice property on the Hill adjacent to the Hollinger senior staff "cottages"; the lots were released for sale in the summer of 1922 and became the site of homes owned by retailers and lawyers.[36] Just south of the town of Timmins, the Moneta Porcupine Mining Company (whose president was Sir Henry Pellatt of Toronto) briefly attempted to extract gold from its

Some of the (in)famous Hollinger Houses. These ones, on
Hollinger Lane, Timmins, are seen in 1946, after the addition of the peaked roofs. Hollinger and town boosters were
very proud of these buildings, but clearly they provided only
the most basic shelter. (Bud Glunz/NFB, LAC, PA113472)

claims and then, during the First World War, discovered a more lucrative
business in selling lots for town-building purposes.[37] A ramshackle collection of houses, dubbed Moneta, began to sprout up on and near the properties, many of them occupied by a growing population of Italian workers,
who often combined mine work with entrepreneurial ventures. Among
these businesses, complained Hollinger Mine officials, was the liberation
of construction materials for Moneta housing from the adjacent Hollinger
Mine property. In 1923 the town of Timmins officially annexed Moneta
after a lengthy campaign by Moneta residents to get water, sewer, and
street lighting installed. They had first approached Tisdale Township but
had been put off by the unpleasant reception their submissions had been
given by the Tisdale businessmen-councillors, who made no secret that
they considered the people of Moneta to be undesirables and troublemakers.[38] That same year, Timmins also annexed the townsite in Mountjoy
Township after an acrimonious debate about the expense involved. Then
the Timmins Townsite Company subdivided some of its remaining land

adjacent to Moneta, which it opened for sale in the spring of 1924. Just under half the lots sold were intended for warehouse development along the TNO tracks; Pine Street was extended southward to a site which the company reserved for a "children's park."[39] So private and company development continued in tandem.

While Noah Timmins and his Hollinger Mine were pursuing their unique version of a company town, Dome Mines decided to take another approach. As it rebuilt its plant (which had been completely destroyed in the 1911 fire), it decided to provide accommodation only for senior staff (both married and single) right at the mine site. Initially, there were just five houses, three small bunkhouses, and three "foremen's houses," but by 1914 the property had expanded to twenty-seven houses as well as recreational facilities, a school, and a small hospital.[40] The Dome miners and other workmen were expected to fend for themselves. Many found rooms or homes in South Porcupine, while others (notably Italians) began to squat on company property near the mine.

When Dome acquired some adjacent property from the Dome Extension Mines Company in 1915, the managers decided to build a "village" for their workers on the new site, for there was insufficient housing in South Porcupine for the expanded workforce that the mine now required. A three-storey dormitory to house ninety-two men and ten "double-houses" went up first, in 1916; others followed.[41] The houses were rented to employees at relatively low rates, and the company established a commissary, which tried to match the prices at the larger, privately owned stores in Timmins. Some recreational facilities were provided on the site, and Dome contributed most of the funds required to build a skating rink at South Porcupine. By providing these services, Dome hoped to retain its employees during an era of labour shortages. Unfortunately, the houses at Dome and Dome Extension had been cheaply and hastily put up, so they deteriorated rapidly and caused maintenance problems for the company. In the mid-1930s the mine's assistant general manager reported that the four double-houses at Dome were being called "the black shacks" and their "very damp and undrainable location" had contributed to the problem. The four single-family houses "in what is known as Cyanide Alley," he reported, required such extensive repair that "their continued use is not greatly to our credit." At Dome Extension, the "cottages" were in better repair but were far too small to house the large families (some with boarders) who were renting them.[42] Nevertheless, their convenience and cheapness, and perhaps an unwillingness to invest in real estate in a place that no one thought would last a lifetime, meant that the Dome houses remained in high demand.

Over time, other mines in the area initiated small housing developments on their mine sites, which became known locally as the "properties." The

Postcard image of the completed Abitibi Power & Paper Company plant. Note, at left, the enormous pile of logs awaiting processing. (UCA, 93.049, P/4328)

number of these properties increased, especially during the rapid growth of the 1930s. They included Buffalo-Ankerite (1932–53; houses sold in the mid-1960s); Delnite (incorporated 1934 with production commencing 1937); and Noranda Mines properties at Pamour (incorporated 1934–35), Hallnor (incorporated 1936), and Aunor (1939–40). Most of the housing was very basic, consisting of frame "double-houses" with tarpaper siding for the workers, and small wooden frame single houses for the salaried staff, who generally lived in a distinctly separate street or section. Some properties (like Delnite) had a small community hall and convenience store. At the Aunor property, housing was provided for salaried staff only, and the houses were larger and noticeably more attractive than many in the area, with their fireplaces, white clapboard siding, and coloured shutters. It was one of the last housing projects built, and one oral tradition has it that the first mine manager's wife put her foot down and demanded that something better than what she considered the appalling "Noranda housing" be built on the site.[43]

While companies were building a variety of corporate and private housing in the Timmins region, another much more elaborate experiment in company towns was being designed and built to the east. The story of Iroquois Falls is an interesting and important chapter in the physical and social development of the region. Frank Anson had no doubt that his paper factory was a permanent investment, and he appears to have decided early in the planning that it warranted proper facilities to attract, house, and retain a stable and loyal workforce. An elaborate town would

Aerial photo of Iroquois Falls, c. 1936, with the Abitibi plant in the foreground. The photograph has been carefully shot to exclude Ansonville. (Department of the Interior, LAC, PA43948)

also be effective advertising in attracting potential investors who were still concerned at the risky venture of operating a paper mill this far north. Anson hired a Chicago architectural firm to design the housing and landscaping of his town, and in the spring of 1913 work crews arrived to begin clearing the site. Abitibi chose the name Iroquois Falls for the new town. Curving residential streets intersected with a grid focused on the centre of town, with its park and commercial development, which was clearly separated from the industrial plant. Attractive single and double homes, designed to look rather like New England farmhouses, were complemented by an imposing school, a hospital, and a company hotel (really a guest and boarding house). The company store, Iroquois Falls Mercantile, was designed as part of a central civic complex that included a meeting hall. Lots were reserved in the townsite for churches, which were to be built by private initiative, but otherwise every facility was to be company-owned. Clearly, this was to be a "closed" company town.

Anson's Folly, as it was known locally for a time, was in fact very avant-garde – at the forefront of an American movement to abandon the heavy-handed paternalism of company towns like George Pullman's experiment near Chicago, which had culminated in a disastrous strike in 1894. An investigation ordered by President Cleveland had concluded that the blame for the strike lay in Pullman's attempt to be "both landlord and employer," but American industrialists had not entirely rejected the concept of the company town. Instead, by the turn of the century, they had begun to think of it in terms of modern scientific management principles. As historian Margaret Crawford put it, designers of the "new" company town "tried to translate new concepts of industrial relations and social welfare into new physical form."[44] Between 1909 and 1913, several towns in the United States were conceived and constructed to reflect these ideas. One of them, a U.S. Steel Corporation town near Birmingham, Alabama, bears a decided resemblance to the plans for Iroquois Falls.[45] So while Noah Timmins's plans for his town reflected a previous generation's impulses to corporate paternalism, Frank Anson (the American business-man) was ready to experiment with the very latest industrial scientific man-agement principles.

Visually, Timmins and Iroquois Falls could not have been more differ-ent. The forest fire of 1916 had stripped the Iroquois Falls townsite of trees. But its curving streets, planted vegetation, and large green spaces eventually created an appealing, natural atmosphere, whereas the relent-less, treeless grid of Timmins streets made no concessions to topography or nature. The houses in Iroquois Falls were significantly larger than those in Timmins, and the design varied slightly from neighbour to neighbour, creating an atmosphere of homey comfort and warmth. Utilities and other services were tucked behind the houses along access lanes. The public buildings of Iroquois Falls were designed to impress but also to coordinate visually with the architecture of the homes, while the Timmins equivalents were utilitarian at best and coordinated with the houses only because everything looked like a square wooden box. In both cases, though, an employee's position in the workplace was reflected in his home. In Iro-quois Falls (at least initially), senior managers lived on separate streets from the papermakers, and supervisors were offered single-family houses while their men lived in double houses.

Although Iroquois Falls was a wholly owned, closed company town, it did have at least the trappings of independence. It was incorporated as a town in 1915 and annual elections were held for the mayor and town council. A board of trade was chartered in 1926 to promote retailers' interests and the usual range of sporting, fraternal, and social societies was organized. The Roman Catholic parish built its own school (Ste Anne's) in 1921, and the Royal Bank set up business in the commercial block in 1919. However, because Abitibi owned the townsite and most of its buildings, the town's government could levy few taxes in the usual sense, and it had to fund its activities from licence fees and fines, which seriously limited its scope for action. In the early years, the company frequently advanced loans to cover expenses for such things as running the public school, so cynics may be forgiven for seeing the town council as merely an administrative department of Abitibi Pulp and Paper. Indeed, the first mayor, S.G. McCoubray, who served from 1915 to 1920, was initially the Abitibi office manager and later was "private secretary" to general manager Robert A. McInnis.[46] However, the second mayor (1921–24) was John Vanier, president of the Pulp and Sulphite Union at the plant and an active promoter of the "workmen's" interests.[47] He ran as a candidate for the Independent Labour Party in the dominion riding of Cochrane in the early 1920s. So it would be wrong to conclude that Iroquois Falls municipal government was solely an arm of Abitibi management.

Although Abitibi announced its intention to provide accommodation for every married employee and quite a few single men, many of its employees were put off by the idea of living in a company town, and a number of business people who were shut out of the townsite believed that there was still money to be made from the Abitibi payroll. Still others wanted to protect themselves from a notoriously unstable sector of the economy by working for Abitibi but operating small businesses or farms as a backup, which they would be unable to do as residents of the company town. The result was the development of a ramshackle collection of cabins and shacks in Calvert Township, across the railway tracks from Iroquois Falls. Known initially as "The Wye" because the rail tracks split at this point, the settlement was eventually christened Ansonville in a perhaps slightly ironic salute to the founder of Iroquois Falls. Calvert Township was incorporated late in 1918, after which it had its own reeve and municipal council. But at Ansonville there was no town planning and little regulation. People built whatever and wherever they pleased. The first residents were primarily French-speaking Canadians, such as the grocer Auguste Trottier; they were soon joined by a group of Jewish entrepreneurs, including Barney Nosov and Alex Abramson. In 1918–19, a number of non-Jewish Russian emigrés arrived, forming a local subculture with a group of Ukrainian workers.[48]

The main business of the village in the early years seemed to be a collective project to irritate the Abitibi Power and Paper Company at every opportunity. At one of its first meetings, Calvert Township Council sent notice to Abitibi demanding that it cease its habit of winter snowploughing along the main road through the township, which "made it difficult for teams to pass," and it informed Abitibi that "it was expected the necessary turning out places would be arranged at intervals."[49] The residents of Iroquois Falls retaliated by condemning Ansonville as a dark den of foreigners engaged in regular street brawls, illegal alcohol consumption, and other unsavoury activities. "The 'Wye' ... is achieving an unenviable reputation as a shooting and stabbing town," claimed the Iroquois Falls newspaper in 1920.[50]

The people who chose to live in Ansonville accepted a clearly lower standard of living in order to escape the company town. There was no electrical service, no water and no sewer, nor even graded roads for some time. Insurance companies would not accept clients there because the fire hazard was deemed too high; conflagrations periodically swept through the shanties, destroying dozens at a time before a fire brigade was organized. Nevertheless, Ansonville residents celebrated a sense of superiority based on their perception of themselves as independent. In the mid-1940s, Ansonville even attempted to take over the town of Iroquois Falls through an application to the Ontario Municipal Board. Calvert Township's reeve, Elmo Lefebvre, explained, "Iroquois Falls is not guided by the wishes of the people living in it. A company town should not be dominated by the company that owns it; it should be controlled by the people living in it."[51] Ansonville to the rescue! Yet even Ansonville was too restrictive for some of its individualists. When the township began to levy taxes in 1921, a group emigrated to freedom (saying Ansonville was becoming "too crowded") and set up a new settlement beyond the clutches of the township council, which they called Victoria (later known as Montrock).[52]

Besides the farm service centres, the company towns, and the anti-company towns, a fourth type of mixed-function town flourished in the region, at least for a brief time in the boom years before the Second World War. Perhaps the most important of these was known initially as Driftwood City – it was situated in a pretty spot among the rolling hills where the TNO tracks crossed the Driftwood River (a small tributary of the Black). Here, John McCosh put up a boarding house for railway construction crews, and Robert Kelso built a general store, while Fred Little organized the construction of several sawmills to take advantage of the pocket of larger trees found here that were suitable for railway ties or construction lumber for the anticipated tide of incoming settlers.[53] As noted earlier, the TNO renamed the settlement Monteith in honour of the provincial agricultural minister, Nelson Monteith. At first, Monteith was little more than a flag stop, but it seemed destined for greater things when the Ontario government established a demonstration and experimental farm there. The original modest plans for the farm were redrawn on a grander scale in 1918, when the provincial government announced that it was expanding the facility to train returning First World War veterans in preparation for settling them on their new farms under the Soldier Settlement Act. An optimistic little town began to emerge next to the demonstration farm, with Critchley's General Store serving as post office, meeting hall, and the source of a range of necessaries.[54]

The activity attracted the attention of a young Finnish-born resident of Sault Ste Marie named A.E. (Ernie) Wicks, who was looking for opportunities as a pulpwood contractor. In 1920 he arrived in Monteith and set up the Hawk Lake Lumber Company with a sawmill at Monteith (and later he set up another just west of Cochrane on the National Transcontinental Railway); he obtained a licence to cut timber and pulpwood in Bond Township. Wicks offered lumber, pulpwood, lath, and ties, as well as timber cut to order.[55] Although the company went into receivership in 1931, as did so many others in that troubled industry during the Depression, Wicks was able to reorganize his finances and get back into business, eventually expanding with mills at Timmins, Island Falls, Wasach (on the TNO), Brander, and Edlund (on the CNR).[56] He later moved to Cochrane, where he served as mayor and president of the board of trade; his Monteith mill remained an important local employer.

Meanwhile, the demonstration farm had run into difficulties, so the Ontario government turned it into the Northern Academy, a facility that offered high school courses to children of farmer-settlers scattered throughout the region. The academy also promoted courses in practical agriculture and domestic science in the hope of improving the success rate of Clay Belt farms. As those farms failed, though, enrolment at the academy steadily declined until the expense could no longer be justified. During the Second World War the buildings were refitted as a prisoner-of-war and internment camp (Camp Q), and after the war, it became a correctional facility. Thus, with a slightly broader economic base than places like Val Gagné and Ramore, Monteith was able to struggle along, although it never evolved into a community of any size.

A second mixed-base community developed at Connaught, located on the TNO spur line into the Porcupine area, about halfway between Porquis Junction and Timmins. Sometime before the Porcupine rush, the TNO had established lumber camps in the area to cut logs for ties,[57] and once the tracks had been laid through, a small settlement sprang up where the line crossed the Nighthawk River as it flowed into Frederick House Lake. While the village provided shops and services to the handful of farmer-settlers in the vicinity and to the work crews at a small mine nearby, Connaught was more important as a lumber town during its heyday in the 1920s. Two companies, the St Maurice Lumber Company and the T.S. Woolings Company, obtained licences to cut timber from lots near Nighthawk Lake and float it downstream to their mills at Connaught. These two mills employed over a hundred men, plus bush crews, at their peak production.[58] The lumber was sold mainly to the TNO. In 1923 a fire at the St Maurice site caused significant damage, and although Mr and Mrs Frank Little and their family escaped safely, it appears that the company never recovered. Only the Woolings mill was still operating there in the mid-1930s.[59]

These economic developments and the new settlement distribution they produced obviously posed a considerable challenge to the First Nations

population. On the one hand, the new economy dictated urban development at sites not normally settled by First Nations families. On the other
hand, the railways, roads, and townsites often straddled what had been
their trapping territory. So they were both bypassed and interfered with at
the same time. In response, people who had formally congregated at
Mattagami Post began to drift south to Gogama on the Canadian Northern Railway line, where they could get better prices for their furs. Others
moved west to Chapleau, where they were joined by Cree families from
farther north who were attracted to railway work or wanted to be near their
children attending school there. A sizable new population of Aboriginal
families thus developed at these places, and old sites like Mattagami Post
declined in significance.

Some First Nations settlements, including Matachewan (on the lake that
feeds the Montreal River) and Barber's Bay (just east of Connaught on
Frederick House Lake), remained less affected by the new economy, at
least initially. During the Porcupine gold rush, people at Barber's Bay
helped to guide and provision the argonauts, and after the railway was
built through they returned to trapping and living off the land, supplementing their income with small-scale vegetable growing. Trapping along
the Nighthawk River remained relatively good for people such as Paddy
Gilmore, who carefully husbanded the fur-bearing animals to sustain production from his trapping territory until well after the Second World
War.[60] Unfortunately, fluctuating fur prices and the devastation of
traplines in other areas meant that it had become a very hard life for those
who attempted to maintain their old ways. Living conditions at Barber's
Bay were described as very poor in 1918, compounded by the death of at
least five people in the Spanish influenza epidemic of that winter – some
of the first people in the region to succumb to the epidemic.[61] By the mid-
1930s about fifteen families were still living at Barber's Bay, but in 1938 a
dam was built to raise the water level of Frederick House Lake to turn it
into a storage basin for the massive Ontario Hydro project at Abitibi
Canyon downstream. The village had to be abandoned. Unfortunately, the
families there were not on an official reserve, nor did they have legal title
deeds to their properties, so they were forced to relocate at their own
expense.[62] Another important Aboriginal settlement on St Peter's Bay at
the south end of Nighthawk Lake (in Carman Township) remained less
affected by the changes going on around it. Its people went to visit the new
resource towns and then returned to their own homes in these small segregated settlements.[63]

Thus, within this relatively limited district of northern Ontario, a dozen
settlements were established from the eighteenth to twentieth centuries.
Some flourished; many faded. As a group, they represent an interesting set
of variations on the theme of "town." From the detailed planning and tight

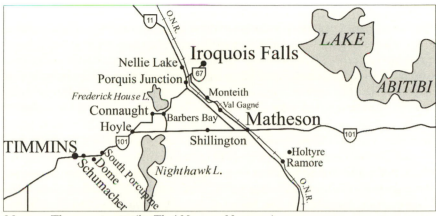

Map 3   The new towns (by Thai-Nguyen Nyguyen)

control of Abitibi Pulp and Paper's company town at Iroquois Falls to the exuberant free-for-all of Pottsville and Ansonville, people could find themselves in very different circumstances from those living only a few kilometres away. For some, as at Timmins and Iroquois Falls, the town was distinctly urban (though not necessarily large). Housing an industrial workforce in class-defined neighbourhoods, these towns offered a full range of services, from health care to churches to schools and sports, and they were instantly supplied with the modern conveniences of electricity, water and sewer facilities, paved roads, street lighting, and movie theatres. For others, such as Matheson and Kelso, the town was essentially a rural village commons, providing services and a social focal point for folk on the surrounding lands. Places such as Monteith and Connaught were somewhere in between, providing services for a small hinterland but also providing employment in primary-sector production of lumber and building materials. Other towns, such as Moneta and Ansonville, were essentially bedroom suburbs for the industrial centres of Timmins and Iroquois Falls. However, unlike late-twentieth-century suburbia, these settlements were haphazardly developed, offered few organized services, and presented a physical face of eccentric individuality rather than the relentless conformity of developer-built tract housing. Finally, there were settlements such as those at Barber's Bay and St Peter's Bay, which were ethnically segregated, materially poor, and so marginalized that their real names were known only to their Aboriginal inhabitants.

While Iroquois Falls was the most elaborately planned town in the region, it would be incorrect to claim that the other resource-sector towns were completely unplanned. Commercial interests dictated their form from the beginning. In nearly every case, an individual or a group of investors obtained title to a block of land for relatively little outlay, then registered a street plan with the provincial government before advertising lots for sale. As might be expected with entrepreneurs looking only for a quick profit, most of these town "plans" were unimaginative affairs, with streets arranged in a basic grid lined up with the railway tracks or with the lakeshore (in the case of Pottsville), or just dropped on the nearest convenient spot between a lake and a swamp (Timmins). The most popular street names on the original plans were King, Queen, and utilitarian numbers. No provisions were made for public parks, other than in Iroquois Falls (and eventually in Timmins), and towns with a lake frontage or riverbank might just as well have been located on the open prairie for all the attention paid to enhancing the natural setting. These were to be utilitarian towns, focused on the business of making money. The only town plan that showed any degree of imagination (with the exception of Iroquois Falls, of course) was Porquis Junction, which was originally laid out as a broadly curving street that fronted on the TNO railway yards, with other streets radiating outward from a central hub, like spokes in a wheel.[64]

Unlike many towns in other parts of Canada, most of these places did not include a clearly delineated commercial street or section. Certainly, in the smallest of them – Kelso and Ramore for instance – businesses located primarily on the street nearest to the railway. In Iroquois Falls, of course, the commercial sector was carefully planned as a discrete unit, and in the original part of the Timmins townsite the lots along two main streets were sold for commercial establishments; but over time, as properties were developed around the original site, businesses migrated through what were otherwise residential areas. In the other towns, commercial and residential activities developed alongside one another from the beginning. For example, the 1913 map of South Porcupine shows a church, a bottling works, a bank, the firehall, a foundry, a pool room, a theatre, and a "club," all scattered among the private houses in one two-block area. Commercial activities were located on almost every single block in the townsite.[65]

The rate of population change varied considerably among the resource-sector towns in the region. Timmins experienced steady growth, interrupted by brief periods of dramatic growth, from 1912 to the Second World War. The biggest boom was just after the First World War, lasting into the early 1920s. The rate of growth picked up again in the 1930s because gold production (unlike almost every other sector of the Canadian economy) suddenly became much more profitable – a result of the American government raising the price to $35 per ounce. These good times were reflected in the growth rates of South Porcupine and Tisdale Township more generally. After the Second World War a slow decline set in. The pulp and paper sector, on the other hand, seemed to struggle at

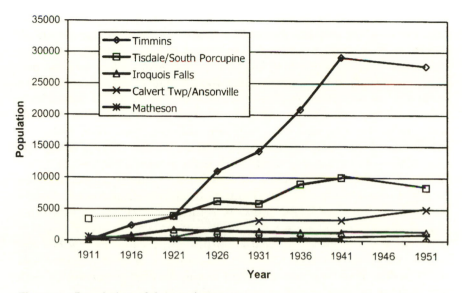

Figure 1   Population of the area's towns

Sources: Census of Canada and municipal returns, Archives of Ontario, RG19-142. Census data and municipal returns rarely tally exactly. Where both are available, priority was given to the municipal returns.

exactly the times when gold was booming. The population of Iroquois Falls peaked in 1921, then slowly declined until the Second World War, when it gradually began to regain ground in the boom of the 1950s.

Population growth and decline in the resource towns had rather less impact on the development of town infrastructure than one might expect. Although Iroquois Falls, as a company town, did not have a municipal tax base in the usual sense, it scarcely lacked amenities, because the basic infrastructure was all provided by Abitibi. Only the church congregations (and particularly the Protestants) found some difficulty as the numbers declined. In the Timmins-Porcupine area, municipal tax accounts suffered because so much property was owned by mining companies, and the issue of mining taxation was a perennially vexing one. Originally, under Ontario law, mining companies had paid only provincial taxes, and only on their profits. Then, just as the Porcupine fields were being developed, the law was changed so that mining companies would pay a percentage of this profit tax to the municipalities in which they were located. But some municipalities, notably Timmins, Tisdale, and Whitney, complained that the law put them in a bind. They alleged that because so much land within the municipal (or township) boundaries was owned by the mines (untaxed), the municipality could never hope to develop it and obtain

revenues from it. Furthermore, the councils argued, since the mines paid
tax only on profits, no money would flow during the development phase
of a mine, when it was most needed by a growing municipality. During the
inflationary period of the First World War, the revenue problem was particularly acute, because municipalities found their costs rising, while the
mine taxes were fixed at low, prewar rates. Other taxpayers in the community (notably retailers) complained that they were being asked to shoulder
the costs of the town unfairly.[66] Thus, the amount of money available for
infrastructure construction and maintenance in the mining towns was
allegedly less than that in a southern town whose economic base was manufacturing products other than gold, for there the municipality could draw
on a tax base enriched by contributions from industrial property assess-
ments. In addition, town and township councils were well aware of the fact
that their residents, like those of Matheson noted earlier, had the option
of simply moving out to the nearby bush if the tax burden was laid too
heavily on their shoulders. So the development of infrastructure and
public works in the mining towns had less to do with population growth
(or decline) than with political manoeuvring and negotiation.

Certainly, patterns of development in these towns were very different
from patterns of development in southern Ontario. In fact, they were
more like other urban places across Canada's resource frontier rather than
like those in the agricultural zones of the Prairie West or in the ocean-
facing towns of the East and West coasts. First, there was not the same
spatial mobility that followed social change in southern cities. Here, new
immigrants did not arrive, crowd into inner-city tenements or rooming
houses, then gradually move outward to more "respectable" neighbourhoods as they climbed the social ladder, while a new wave of arrivals filled
their original homes. As will be discussed in chapter 8, the class dynamics
of these towns was unlike that of the rest of urban Canada. Here, people
came, settled into a particular neighbourhood depending on the nature of
their jobs, and either remained there or moved on to another job in
another town.

A second difference was the significant degree of "squatting" as people
simply chose a plot of land and built a home on it, not bothering with the
niceties of legal title deeds. For some, it was undoubtedly a necessity; lot
prices in the boom years were high, and many newcomers were clearly very
poor in a material sense. For others, it may have been an economic decision, for few people expected the mines to last, and pulpwood cutting was
a young man's game. It made no sense to invest a significant amount of
money in a house or in land if you planned to use it for only a short time
and believed the resale value was negligible. Interestingly, there seems to
have been little general public concern about squatters unless they posed
some sort of threat through disorderly behaviour or through disease

arising from unsanitary conditions. Since there was no real competition for land and space among the twentieth-century newcomers, the question of squatting never became a major issue. Squatters meant, of course, that even the planned towns did not develop in an entirely regular way. Satellite pockets of shanties on the edge of the defined urban space were like the frayed edges of a tapestry, unravelling randomly into the surrounding bush.

A third important difference in development patterns was that these towns did not diversify economically over time. If anything, the economic base shrank as early hopes for agricultural development faded, and one by one, the gold mines closed. In his study of the development of urban centres on the Ohio frontier in the nineteenth century, Richard Wade proposed that these communities began as commercial centres but developed economies of "increasing specialization" as they grew, with the result that "lines sharpened, class divisions deepened, and the sense of neighbourliness and intimacy weakened ... The easy familiarity of small-town life more and more gave way to the impersonality of city living."[67] In this region of northeastern Ontario, the communities were based on specialized economies almost from the beginning (with the exception of the brief construction period), and they certainly did not immediately develop a cheerful, small-town sense of "neighbourliness" – probably because so few people knew one another or shared common past experiences (or even languages). It took time for a sense of community to grow. The process by which that happened will be explored through the remainder of this book.

Finally, unlike towns on resource frontiers in the United States, which historian Paula Petrik claims were "never intended to be permanent,"[68] developers in northeastern Ontario assumed that the towns would at least have a very long life, even if they were not expected to be permanent. The farm townsfolk, of course, believed in permanency from the beginning, accepting the false premise of southern politicians that agriculture was commercially viable in the Clay Belt. In the forestry sector, officials wrote about the spruce forests of Northern Ontario as so extensive that they were virtually limitless. By the end of the First World War, Abitibi Power and Paper had adopted a more cautious approach and had begun to seed and replant, in keeping with new principles of scientific forest management.[69] As far as Abitibi was concerned, Iroquois Falls was a permanent town. Surprisingly, even in the mining sector the idea of permanence took hold. Of course, initially the Porcupine goldfields were seen by most as an opportunity to get rich and then move on. But the incredible extent of the ore bodies, unlike anything Canadians had seen before, encouraged people to think of the mines as long-term propositions. When the Fesserton Lumber Company tried to convince the Timmins Town Council to approve the construction of a railway spur to its proposed plant, councillor E.L. Long-more (then mill superintendent at Hollinger) objected, saying, "They'll have their [timber] limits cut down long before the mines are gone."[70] A dozen years later, the editor of the *Porcupine Advance* claimed vindication for this view as a number of new mines came into production and Hollinger, McIntyre, and Dome were still going strong: "In the old days of Timmins, the saying was common that five or ten years would see the end. But the 'end' gets farther and farther into the future as new ore comes into sight and new mines come into production ... People don't ask for con-crete sidewalks and paved roads, knowing that they themselves will have to bear the cost, if they don't regard their town as their home."[71]

There was, of course, an element of self-delusion in the belief that mining was forever. First, people concluded that the massive capital invest-ment involved at Dome, Hollinger, and McIntyre meant that the owners were in the game for the long term. In reality, the investment was required because of the complexity involved in extracting the gold from the rock, and the value of the gold made the heavy investment economically realis-tic. Obviously, the gold was not hidden underground in limitless quanti-ties. But the retailers in particular hoped people would think of places such as Timmins and South Porcupine as permanent, and the local news-papers promoted both themselves and the towns as solid, orderly, and in the game for the long haul – partly in response to campaigns arguing the contrary in southern papers such as the Toronto *Globe.*

Boosterism was, perhaps, the main thing these towns shared with "fron-tier" development in western Canada. It began in Cobalt, with the editor of the *Daily Nugget* taking a leading role. In a 1910 article proposing the creation of "A Million Population Club," he wrote, "The Daily Nugget is irrevocably committed to this policy of booming the farming districts. We ... will work early and late, day and night, in season and out of season to promote and increase the interests of Northern Ontario, whether it be mining, farming, lumbering or manufacturing, but above all the farming will be the lasting industry."[72] To that end, the *Nugget* provided extensive and enthusiastic coverage of early developments in the Porcupine Camp. A competing paper in Haileybury upped the ante by establishing a news-paper in the camp itself, sending a teenaged employee named George Lake to publish it.

Lake, an energetic and restless young man from Orillia, Ontario, had left school at the age of thirteen to apprentice as a typesetter with a paper in Georgetown, before going north in the Cobalt rush to take advantage of the opportunities in newspaper work, prospecting, and hockey. After his arrival in the Porcupine Camp, he had a disagreement with his employers, took a cash settlement and was soon publishing his own newspaper, which he dubbed the *Porcupine Advance.* In 1916 he hired George Allan Macdonald as editor. Macdonald was older than Lake, with experience of editing local papers in southern and eastern Ontario, but both men clearly shared an interest in the business of promoting business. For them, the camp was a development that merited the attention of government and serious investors; it was no flash-in-the-pan fraud being perpetrated on a gullible public. The *Advance* ignored the speculators and covered the respectable businessmen, their families, and their substantial buildings – all with a dash of irreverence and excitement that reflected both the growth of the towns and the youth of the newspaper.[73]

Not to be outdone, Abitibi funded a paper of its own for Iroquois Falls, to promote awareness of company activities in only slightly less breathless columns than the *Advance*. Abitibi's paper was named the *Broke Hustler*, a play on the name of the most junior worker in a paper mill – the boy who gathered up the torn bits of paper (the "brokes") from the floor of the paper room. There were other venues for area boosters. Local boards of trade issued promotional material and banded together periodically in such groups as the Association of Northern Ontario Municipalities – or its predecessor, the 1920 Northern Ontario Development Committee – to lobby the provincial government and the Toronto Board of Trade for more attention to local growth issues.

But while Northern Ontario's boosterism was a feature in common with that of western urban promoters, there were details unique to the North. Here, boosterism was a peculiar mix of attempts to imitate "the South" and attempts to distinguish the North from it. The *Advance* angrily denied reports in *Saturday Night* and the *Globe* about northern lawlessness and immorality. "We Are Not a Bunch of Law Breakers," sniffed the *Advance* indignantly in one headline. "What utter bosh and rot all this talk about the illegal sale of liquor and non-enforcement of the law."[74] The editor underscored the point by running articles that described middle-class ladies' teas, or noted the construction of a businessman's "fine new residence," or detailed the lives of local residents such as the wife of Dr M.A. Heil of Timmins, who was alleged to be the Countess Kolencki-Langer of Vienna.[75] But at the same time that they were trying to outdo Southern Canada in matters of taste and refinement, area boosters also tried to distance themselves from the South. The Timmins *Daily Press* proposed that far from being criminals and deviants, the people of Northern Ontario might even be morally superior to those of the South. "There is no attempt to hold the Porcupine aloft as an example of virtue and righteousness," wrote the editor, "but the crime records do show a community of better behaviour than most of the old established centers in Ontario."[76] In 1920 the *Porcupine Advance* complained that the new Union of Northern Ontario Boards of Trade and Municipalities was "of little advantage to the real North Land" because it was dominated by representatives from

Undated illustration of Iroquois Falls, identified in the source as a
"model company town." (G. Blouin, LAC, PA111478)

Sudbury and North Bay, which were "absolutely ... 'Old Ontario' town[s]
in style, methods and ideals."[77] Historian Karen Dubinsky dubbed this
"moral boosterism," in which "discourses" of "national economic and
social development, gender relations, sexual morality and crime" combined in a response to southern accusations of northern immorality.[78]
Clearly, it required a difficult balancing act to accept southern values but
not southern judgments of the North.

The large corporations were also involved in boosterism, though of a
slightly different type. Abitibi Power and Paper, in particular, campaigned
to publicize its plant at Iroquois Falls with articles in the *Pulp and Paper
Magazine of Canada* and other journals and with pamphlets such as "An
Illustrated Story of the Development of the Newsprint Paper Mill of the
Abitibi Power & Paper Co." (1924), which modestly described Iroquois
Falls as "the most beautiful and modern town in all Canada."[79] These
efforts were obviously intended to encourage investors, to promote good
relations with governments, and possibly to attract the kind of workforce
that the company preferred. Even the basic idea of a planned company
town or company housing was a kind of boosterism, through which companies could promote themselves as generous, progressive – and in full
agreement with southern leaders who wanted to keep the potential for
frontier disorderliness under a tight lid. Corporate boosterism was in no

small sense a way of currying government favour for company-friendly policies or support in times of crisis. The Timmins interests showed how effectively they could call in those favours during the labour unrest of the late 1930s, when they asked for Ontario premier "Mitch" Hepburn's help in keeping the CIO union organizers out. The infamous confrontation at General Motors' Oshawa plant was a result of Hepburn using Oshawa for his "showdown" against American industrial unionism.[80]

One feature of these northern towns that boosters were eager to exploit was the symbolism of the town's physical appearance. Rather than seeing the basic grid layout as a sign of unimaginative planning or material greed, they celebrated it as a sign of order, progress, and modernity, imposing a sense of structure on the wild chaos of the northern "wilderness."

As columnist Frederick Griffin enthused in the *Toronto Star Weekly*, "Up there you may watch civilization marching, smashing forward, pushing the frontier north with giant gains."[81] The physical appearance of buildings was also used in this attempt to characterize the northern towns. Since most were purely utilitarian wooden boxes, any adornment, however basic, was pointed out as worthy of attention. When Hollinger opened the Goldfields Hotel in 1912, the *Porcupine Advance* commented on "the large balconies overlooking Gillies Lake" (actually, some distance away) as "a very attractive feature of the hotel which bods [sic] fair to become a popular summer home for many people."[82] The "cement finish" on the first houses that Hollinger built was noted as a sign of modernity, and the "verandas" that were added later to the company houses on Tamarack Street were a touch of poetic whimsy permissible in a town that had come of age.[83] The *Advance* lavished particular praise on the physical appearance of Iroquois Falls after a Labour Day visit there in 1917. "Iroquois Falls is the handsomest and neatest town in the North land today," wrote the reporter, noting particularly the fact that the houses were painted as soon as they were built, while the streets were "macadamized" and the bunkhouses were "up-to-date." He added, "While there is practically every modern convenience in the town, Iroquois Falls is happy in being absolutely free from lawyers practising there."[84] The appearance of flower gardens and lawns was also presented as a sign of the permanence of the communities, particularly in Timmins, where boosters were especially sensitive to the idea that somehow their town was only a temporary "camp" until the gold ran out. "Timmins is quickly becoming a town of homes – not houses," wrote the editor of the *Advance* in 1935. The proof was in the flower gardens and "other beautifying efforts" that were cropping up around town.[85]

Real progress was deemed to have begun, though, once brick began to replace wood as the siding of choice on commercial buildings. J.W. Reed is remembered in Timmins primarily because he commissioned the first brick-sided building in town,[86] and Leo Mascioli was careful to make his claim to a position in the local elite by putting brick on his Empire Hotel when it went up in 1924. Brick became such a symbol of status in the region that a tarpaper product used to sheath houses was preferably called by its trademark name, Insul-brick.

A curious attitude to trees also made its imprint on the region. In 1882 the American Forestry Congress had initiated a campaign for Arbor Day, which was to be celebrated to educate the public on the value of forest management.[87] Soon afterward, the Ontario government adopted the idea, and the Department of Education helped to promote it through annual school participation. At the same time, ideas about beautifying cities through the use of parks and trees were becoming popular in Canada. Frank Anson's plan for Iroquois Falls reflected this ideal, and although the townsite was initially denuded of greenery partly through the construction process and partly through the devastation of the 1916 forest fire, trees were planted and eventually became a significant part of the urban landscape. In all other towns in the region, however, visitors even today are often struck by the scarcity of trees on both private and public property. Local horticultural societies promoted gardening, and Hollinger held a regular contest for the tenants of the Hollinger Houses, but tree planting had little general appeal. Of course, in the early years, fear of forest fires encouraged authorities to keep wide clearings around the towns in the hope of stopping the onrush of flames. But removing trees was also seen as a sign of progress, as the wild "uncivilized" life of the bush gave way to the order and regularity of an industrial city. "Arbor day was fittingly observed in the South Porcupine school," noted the *Advance* in May 1912. "No trees were planted, as is the general custom, but instead many were removed and the grounds surrounding the school were otherwise greatly improved." The Cobalt newspaper explained further, "Arbor Day does not posses the same significance in this section as it does in the older part of the province. There is no need to plant trees, the biggest difficulty being to get rid of them."[88]

The environmental impact of the new economic development was of little concern to the builders, but it was considerable. Trees were at best a source of profit, at worst a nuisance or even danger. Industrial capitalism had an insatiable appetite for electrical power, and hydroelectricity meant flooding lands to maintain reservoirs, cutting swaths through the bush for transmission lines, and building generating stations and dams on the most important transportation routes of the old economy. The sprawling mine and paper mill plants laid waste great blocks of land, while noxious fumes poured into the air and fine dust from the ever-growing piles of mine waste blew everywhere. Patchwork clearings for potential farms destabilized the thin layers of topsoil, encouraging erosion in the sandy areas and gumbo in the clay. The detritus of town life began to spread beyond the formal boundaries. And increased human activity initiated the frequent forest fires that disrupted the natural cycle of fire and regeneration. For the First Nations, who felt the effects of these changes directly, they were of considerable concern. But for the newcomers, these changes were merely the result of progress and modernization – developments to be celebrated, not challenged.

Within a decade, the lands of the Mattagami, Abitibi, and Matachewan people had been transformed. Industrial capitalism was replacing commercial exchange. Symbols of progress were being drawn in relentless lines across the land. While many of the lines remained only dreamlines in the minds of outsiders, other lines had been made tangible in the railway tracks, colonization roads, power-transmission lines, and townsite grids that were being cut through the bush, bypassing or bisecting the old waterway travel routes. Money was to be made by maximizing the efficiency of the infrastructure. So a new physical map was built, reflected in the new mental map of the newcomers. Moose Factory was displaced as the social and economic hub. Lands were flooded as the insatiable industrial demand for power took precedence over the lives of hunters and trappers. New social spaces, designed to meet new needs, were sawn out of the bush in places where previous inhabitants had generally passed through rather than settled.

Yet for all the changes, some things remained. The posts at Mattagami, Matachewan, and Abitibi, although now barely perceptible spots on the newcomers' mental maps, continued to exist for a time, and when they were closed, they were replaced by new fur trade depots at more convenient sites. The lines of travel, communication, and social contact continued to run largely north-south, although now it was along the steel of the Temiskaming and Northern Ontario Railway rather than along the Mattagami and Abitibi Rivers. The new economic system, like the old, linked the region to the economic system of a broader world, so the rise and fall of price and demand, reacting to far-off events, continued to have a local impact. And as in the fur trade era, the region's resources drew outsiders, who drifted in and out in search of material gain, adventure, personal independence, or perhaps a new beginning.

The new towns that people built in the region were a product of commercialism, economic necessity, imported ideas, and ideas dictated by internal realities. Whether the towns were carefully planned (Iroquois Falls), partially planned (Timmins), or just grew (Monteith), the original intentions were always modified as the dictates of space, economy, or the ongoing interaction of townspeople shaped life within their boundaries. The process by which they built houses and turned them into homes, neighbourhoods, and communities is the subject to which we now turn.

PART TWO

CHAPTER FIVE

Ethnicity and Immigration

There are some tricky phases in the business of Northern Ontario, chiefly found, perhaps, in the facts that a part of the population is floating and temporary and that a part comes from foreign lands, where ideas of honest business are somewhat elastic.

Toronto Board of Trade, 1912[1]

The Ontario government had done its best to encourage the immigration of Germans, Scandinavians, and southern Ontarians. Instead came Italians, Ukrainians, Chinese, and natives of the Balkans, to say nothing of French-speaking Canadians, all of whom posed challenges to the values and assumptions of the English-speaking settlers and the Toronto politicians behind them. Ethnicity and immigration were the central parameters in the shaping of the Porcupine–Iroquois Falls society in the twentieth century. Both as barriers to the formation of a sense of community, and eventually as a mythologized centre of community identity, they deserve close scrutiny.

In fact, it would be a mistake to begin such a discussion with the twentieth century, for the entire history of the land between the Abitibi and Mattagami Rivers has been a continuing story of meeting and adjusting to newcomers who were drawn to the region for its resources. For the First Nations, the rivers and streams criss-crossing the territory provided access and facilitated mobility, both within the region and to distant lands. While the height of land did provide a boundary of sorts, it was not an impenetrable barrier, and it was undoubtedly crossed for many generations before fur-trading opportunities encouraged greater interaction. Thus, it is difficult to characterize the Aboriginal population of the region as constituting a single "ethnic group." In fact, there is little evidence to suggest that they even saw themselves as a single entity in the centuries before Europeans arrived and began to apply strange new labels to the populations here.

Today it is commonplace to see maps with neatly delineated "tribal" or "national" territories that place the "Cree," "Ojibwa," and "Algonkin" in the region. Unfortunately, these labels obscure more than they reveal. It

would be more realistic to think of the area's precontact Aboriginal population as a collection of semi-autonomous bands, who shared fundamental
ideas about religion and social organization, whose lives were based on the
same economy, and who developed links through marriage, political
alliances, and perhaps a clan system. They shared a basic language but
developed regional variations over time. They referred to themselves first
as members of a particular region or group, and secondarily as "the
people" (Anishinabe). Those who hunted and fished at Lake Abitibi were
the Abitibi people; those who lived along what we now call the Abitibi
River were the Monsoni people, their name for the river.[2] Nighthawk Lake
was known as Piscoutagamy, and hence the families there were the Piscoutagamy people.

The confusion about names began when the French started to investigate
these people in the seventeenth century. Before they made direct contact,
the French relied on information gathered from more southerly nations.
Names used by outsiders were applied with a very broad brush. For example,
the Jesuits used a single name for all the people who lived on the lands
draining into James Bay, which they spelled with at least a dozen variations,
ranging from *Kristinons* to *Cri*. Over time, as the French became better
acquainted with these people, they began to record more specific names.
When Father Charles Albanel and Paul Denis, Sieur de St Simon, travelled
from Tadoussac to Hudson Bay in 1671–72, they noted there were "many
different nations" along the Moose River; they even learned two different
names for that river (Kichesipiou, or Big River, and Mousousipiou, or Moose
River).[3] Through the eighteenth century and into the early nineteenth
century, English-speaking fur traders also recognized these local divisions,
though they tended to refer to people in association with a trading post
rather than with a geographic feature. For example, in 1824, the HBC trader
Thomas Fraser described the "Abitibie Indians," the "Matawei[a?]gamangue
Indians," and the "Moose Factory Indians."[4] It was not until governments
began to take an interest in the region in the late nineteenth century that
the more collective designations of "Cree" and "Ojibwa" crept back into official usage.[5] Early anthropological studies picked up on these general names
and applied them primarily on the basis of language distinctions, deciding
that the "Cree" lived in the lowland areas of the James Bay drainage system,
the "Ojibwa" lived on the south side of the height of land or at the heads of
the river systems, and the "Algonquin" lived in the Temiskaming-Abitibi
region.[6] More recently, anthropologists and historians have noted that these
groupings create artificial distinctions that are misleading and in some ways
meaningless to the people themselves.[7] People now often refer to themselves in association with a particular reserve, such as the Mattagami First
Nation, which in one sense is a return to the older idea of an association
between people and specific places.

Before the arrival of Europeans, trade networks for valuable materials such as Lake Superior copper, Cobalt silver, or good flint for tools encouraged interaction among regional groups. For example, in 1906 the Treaty 9 commissioner Samuel Stewart reported that near the falls on the Montreal River there was a village where "for hundreds of years" people from the Montreal River, Lake Temiskaming, and Lake Temagami had met and "to this day numbers of flint arrowheads, sheets of white mica, and lumps of pure plumbago [black lead or graphite] are discovered, denoting the existence at one time of an extensive workshop."[8] After the introduction of the fur trade, even more travel and interaction seems to have taken place. People from Temiskaming and the Missinaibi River might visit Kenogamissi Post to try to get a better trade deal or to avoid paying for advances they had received at a post closer to home.[9] At Mattagami Post, the HBC encouraged the visits of distant trappers by offering special low prices and extra gratuities if the company believed it could draw trade away from independent competitors. Such was the case with the "Horse People," a band of seven brothers from an area near the north shore of Lake Huron, who went north to Mattagami periodically.[10] In the 1840s steamboats began to cross Lake Huron, bringing independent traders with bulkier goods than could be transported by canoe along the northern rivers, so people from the Mattagami area were attracted south. In times of shortage and hardship, people had another motivation to travel, as Joseph Fortescue noted at Moose Factory in 1889–90 when the beaver population was in serious decline in the interior. "The Indian hunters of Abitibi and Kinogummissee," he wrote, "… having no employment in the Summer, come down near the Coast, and hunt up the Beaver of the Moose and Rupert's House Indians, thus depriving them of their anticipated food and hunts in Winter."[11]

These travels led, of course, to greater integration among the bands. The Anglican missionary John Horden noted marriages between Moose women and Abitibi men and between Moose women and Kenogamissi men,[12] but there were undoubtedly many more intertribal unions. Partnerships also were formed between Native women and Canadian and European fur traders. Such names as Batise/Baptiste, McDougall, Moore, Navue, Polson, Black, Sinclair, and Beads began to appear on the HBC account books through the nineteenth century. Not all the children of these mixed marriages participated in the fur trade. John Sanders, born at Mattagami Post in 1845 to an HBC canoe builder named Valentine Sanders and a Native mother named E. Leblanc, was ordained as an Anglican clergyman in 1879 and worked as missionary and minister in the region until his death in 1902.[13]

By the beginning of the twentieth century, then, the inhabitants of the region had experienced generations of cultural interaction. Ethnic and linguistic boundaries had blurred. New ideas, technologies, and materials had been incorporated. Porcupine quills had been replaced by beads and then by embroidery silks, and patterns had shifted from geometric to floral, but the principles of exquisite work and honour for those able to do it remained. Canvas walls and wooden floorboards might be incorporated into housing designs as people spent more time camped near fur trade posts, but those who travelled to their hunting grounds in winter used the old tent-construction techniques.[14] Roman Catholic and Anglican missionaries had provided printed catechisms or prayer books, which people carried in beautifully decorated boxes and covers, but they continued to fear the wentigo (or weetigo) and practised ancient rituals at the behest of visionaries or shamans.[15] While the fur trade clearly caused disruption (notably, wars with the Iroquois, heavy demands on scarce resources, diseases, and territorial adjustments), the number of newcomers and the nature of the economic change were not so dramatic as to prove unmanageable. People incorporated trapping for trade relatively easily into the annual round, and the newcomer traders had to adapt their expectations and behaviour if they wanted trade to proceed. Mutual interest bound the society of the fur trade together.

The newcomers of the early twentieth century, however, had very different interests. They knew nothing of the region's inhabitants and clearly considered them irrelevant. Furthermore, the immigrants arrived so quickly and in such large numbers that this era of interaction had an utterly different character. The First Nations and their European trading partners adapted as well as they could, but the society and economy that emerged was one that increasingly marginalized the older system and ultimately replaced it almost entirely.

In 1904 and 1905 the first farmer-settlers arrived in the region, coincidentally at the same time as Cobalt prospectors began to make their way north. Most of the first farmers were English-speaking Canadians, like Robert and Philip Dawson from Brock, Ontario. The Dawson brothers had served in the Fenian campaign of 1866 and were granted homesteads for that service in Hoyle Township (north of Porcupine Lake) in February 1905.[16] The earliest prospectors also tended to be Canadians – men such as Reuben D'Aigle from the coal-mining community of Chipman, New Brunswick, and Jack Wilson, who had been living near Massey, just west of Sudbury. But other groups were represented as well. The Finnish prospectors Victor Mattson and Henry Pennala were at Nighthawk Lake in 1907. Father Charles A. Paradis, expelled from the OMI in 1888, had made his way into the area by then. Scouting for French Canadian settlement and mission possibilities, he was sidetracked by prospecting and the business of providing accommodation for other prospectors.[17] Not surprisingly, all of this first group had either roots or connections in nearby

Table 1   Native population of main centres

	1850	1883	1902	1907–8	1909–10	1914–15	1924–5	1928–29
Abitibi	–	380	405	146[1]	141 - QC 115 - ON	281	125 - QC 68 - ON	? - QC 86 - ON
Mattagami	191	105	210	94	89	87	88	88
Matheson / Matachewan	–	87	75	96	93	82	75	n/a

Sources: Mattagami Journal (for 1850 column), LAC, RG19/D16, vol. 2, p 79; Borron's population estimates, 73 (for 1883); Indian Affairs Branch, Treaty 9 File, Inspector Macrea to Superintendent General for Indian Affairs, based on figures received from Roman Catholic priests (for 1902), LAC, RG10 (microfilm reel C11,314); Department of Indian Affairs Annual Report for 1910, *Sessional Papers*, no. 27, p. 68 (for 1907–8); Annual Report for 1911, *Sessional Papers*, no. 27 (for 1909–10); Annual Report for 1916, *Sessional Papers*, no. 27 (for 1914–15); and Annual Report for 1928-29 (for 1928–29).

[1]Probably for Ontario side only, but not specified

parts of Canada, where rumours about the Porcupine region's possibilities were first heard.

When rumour was replaced by actual news at Cobalt in 1909 of the big find at the Dome, the Porcupine rush brought hopefuls of many other nationalities into the area immediately, because the Cobalt mines already had a cosmopolitan mix. Crews of Italian labourers, hired mostly from Montreal where they had landed, were working on the TNO or erecting buildings at the mines. Finns from the mines of Michigan had arrived alongside others from the western United States after a labour strike at Cobalt in 1907 had discouraged many of the first miners of Canadian (and particularly Nova Scotian) origins from coming north.[18] There were also many Ukrainians working on railway construction crews, some possibly the sons of recently settled prairie farmers who were earning cash to help their families get established. Cobalt was also home to a group of Syrian shopkeepers and several Jewish businessmen from various parts of Eastern Europe. Representatives from all these groups were drawn to the promise of riches in the Porcupine district.

There were some French-speaking Canadians among the Cobalt group, but a more significant expansion in that part of the population began from a different direction. In 1910, after the route of the National Transcontinental Railway had been decided, the first settlers began arriving in the Abitibi region of northwestern Quebec under the auspices of clergy in southern Quebec, who were promoting the colonization of the region. In 1912, Abbé Ivanhoe Caron began escorting parties of settlers into Abitibi country, and by the end of the First World War there were some 1,500 families in nine new communities scattered through the Abitibi bush.[19]

The colonizing priests also looked across the provincial border, where they received some assistance from a handful of French Canadians already resident on the Ontario shores of Lake Temiskaming. In 1913 a Hailey-bury group raised a thousand dollars to advertise the agricultural potential of Northern Ontario to Quebecers,[20] and it was about this time that Abbé Bourassa began to settle families at Ramore (south of Matheson) and Nushka (north of Matheson) on the TNO line.[21] By 1916 the parish at Nushka could boast a school, a chapel, and a postmaster, but sixty-four of its early residents were killed in the Matheson fire that year and the town was re-named Val Gagné, as described earlier. As employment opportuni-ties became more widely available in the expanding mines, paper mills, and pulpwood bush camps, sons and fathers of these French-speaking fam-ilies on both sides of the provincial border were drawn into new sectors of the regional economy.

It was only in the rural agricultural areas that the settlers were likely to be of the type encouraged by the Ontario government. In the spring of 1913, crown lands agent Frank Ginn at Matheson reported that all the "useable" lands in Carr, Walker, Taylor, and Calvert Townships had been sold and that others toward the Porcupine district were filling up. Most of the settlers in these townships were English-speaking Canadians, and more often than not they hailed from the marginal farm regions of Parry Sound–Muskoka or Grey–Bruce in Old Ontario.[22] Given that the Ontario government was aiming its heaviest promotion at experienced English-speaking farmers and that settlers in central Ontario had found their lands less productive than they had hoped, it is not surprising that many decided to try their luck in the Great Clay Belt.

By the First World War, therefore, people from Ontario, Quebec, the Maritimes, the US, the British Isles, and Northern, Central, and Southern Europe had been attracted to the region. While occupations were fluid, some segregation did appear early on. Ukrainians and Italians were likely to be found as general construction workers or surface labourers at the mines. French-speaking Canadians farmed or worked in technical jobs at the mines or at the Iroquois Falls pulp and paper mill. Finns could be found everywhere: on farms, underground at the mines, in the bush camps, and running boarding houses and hotels. Fledgling retail outlets might be run by Syrian merchants or Jews from Central and Eastern Europe. Aboriginal men provided transportation and guiding services, while their families supplied potatoes and other foodstuff to prospectors and travellers.

There was another kind of social segregation evident in the ethnic mix as well. Many of the immigrants from Italy, Ukraine, and the Balkans – and all of those from China – were single men whom historians of immigration have described as "sojourners." They came for the work, with no intention of making a permanent home in the region. They might be saving in preparation for marriage to girls from their home regions, or they might be sending money home to support wives and families already established there. They congregated in boarding houses and hotels, relying on the services of laundries and restaurants to replace the domestic support structures of a family home. The situation was very different among the English- and French-speaking Canadians and the Finns. While some came as single men (or women), most brought their families with them right from the beginning, or at least had families whom they could visit regularly in neighbouring regions. Thus, ethnicity was overlaid with two very different sets of social systems.

The First World War precipitated some significant changes to the ethnic mix. By 1915 the workplace had become an increasingly hostile place for Ukrainian, "Austrian," and other workers from what were now enemy countries. The situation was partly economic, because problems in the mining sector had forced a contraction of the workforce, and employed foreigners were resented by British subjects. Moreover, wartime passions legitimized attacks on non-British workers, and by the end of the war, many had simply had enough and moved away. Some may have returned to Europe to assist their compatriots in the war effort, while others probably moved on in search of work, hoping for more welcoming surroundings.

Toward the end of the war, as soldiers began to return to the area, the mines and the Abitibi mill quietly began preferential-hiring campaigns, regarding foreign workers as labour agitators and troublemakers. Then, in 1919, the dominion government revised the Immigration Act and issued a series of orders-in-council to prevent further immigration from wartime enemy countries; in 1923 it placed major restrictions on Chinese immigration that essentially closed it down until 1946.

The decline in population from Asia and Central and Eastern Europe coincided with a labour shortage at the mines, and Dome's manager H.P. DePencier decided to recruit Cornish tin miners from England, who were only too happy to leave an industry that was experiencing a serious depression. In November 1920, 108 men arrived (30 of whom went to work at the McIntyre Mine) and in October 1922 another 120 came to work at Hollinger.[23] Managers considered these men to be workers "of the highest type" and "very desirable additions to our staff."[24] Indeed, DePencier seems to have toyed briefly with the idea of replacing Dome's entire workforce with Cornish miners, but he dropped the idea when he ran into difficulties with the Ontario Ministry of Labour on the subject.[25] The Cornish miners were received with considerable fanfare by the British and the English-speaking Canadians who clearly saw them as reinforcements to an increasingly beleaguered minority.

The 1920s were boom years at Abitibi Power and Paper, and the mines of the Timmins area experienced overall expansion, despite periodic set-backs. Indeed, it began to appear that the gold mines were far richer than anyone had believed, and it seemed almost as if they would last forever. Families came to join workers who had once seen the job as only tempo-rary. Even in the troubled agricultural settlement, there seemed to be a new degree of stability by the end of the decade, as the Cochrane District agricultural office was opened (1927) and vigorous promotion of that sector was renewed. The ethnic mix of the region also seemed to stabilize. Newcomers were often encouraged to immigrate by relatives already in the area, and marriages were celebrated within the ethnic enclaves.

Through the 1920s, national groups began to sort themselves by towns within the region and even to some extent by neighbourhoods within the larger towns. Although there had been a sizable Italian population at Matheson before the war (employed in railway construction), by the 1920s, it had all but disappeared. In Timmins, on the other hand, the Italian population was growing steadily, centred largely on the district called Moneta, south of the business section. French-speaking Canadians constituted one-third of the population of Timmins but only 8 percent of the population of South Porcupine and Tisdale Township. The Iroquois Falls townsite had become overwhelmingly anglophone by 1931, with 66 percent of the residents citing British or English-speaking Canadian ances-try. But across the tracks in Ansonville, French Canadians dominated at 60 percent of the population. There were no Finns at all in Matheson and only a few in Iroquois Falls/Ansonville, but by 1931 they constituted 8 percent of the population of Tisdale Township. Slightly fewer lived in Timmins; although they had been the third-largest component of its pop-ulation in 1921, they had dropped to fourth place by 1931 (behind the Italians). A group of Croatians became an important part of the commu-nity of Schumacher during the 1920s.

The 1930s were difficult years at Iroquois Falls and in the agricultural sector, but as noted above, gold mining did relatively well after the price of gold was raised by the U.S. Government. The population of Timmins doubled and the surrounding districts grew by nearly the same propor-tions, while the population of Iroquois Falls and the rural districts declined slightly. In the Timmins area, the French-speaking population grew slightly faster than the English-speaking Canadian portion, so that by 1941 each represented about one-third of the population. French Cana-dian farmers were a little more likely to stay on their land during those difficult years. The Finnish population of Timmins declined somewhat, but there was a corresponding increase in the Finnish population of nearby Tisdale Township. There was also an element of outmigration. In the 1920s a number of communist idealists from Timmins and South Por-cupine emigrated to the USSR,[26] and in the early 1930s parties like that

Table 2 Ethnic Origin of the population, 1911–1951, as percentages

		British Isles	French	Italian	Finnish	Ukrainian
Timmins	1911	-	-	-	-	-
	1921	37.5	31.6	4.8	6.2	3.8
	1931	40.3	35.0	6.2	4.0	2.5
	1941	39.6	36.4	5.4	3.0	2.1
	1951	36.3	41.4	5.6	2.2	2.8
Tisdale Twp.	1911	44.0	22.5	6.3	2.0	up to 15.5
	1921	48.6	15.7	11.2	4.3	0.9
	1931	49.5	8.6	7.9	8.1	0.4
	1941	52.5	3.0	6.2	8.4	2.3
	1951	?	?	?	?	?
Iroquois Falls	1911	-	-	-	-	-
	1921	54.3	29.0	4.6	0.3	0.1
	1931	66.1	23.5	1.9	0.3	0
	1941	66.7	23.9	1.7	0.08	0.2
	1951	?	?	?	?	?
Calvert Twp.	1911	41.9	16.1	0	0	0
	1921	33.5	60.2	0	2.7	0
	1931	22.8	56.1	0.9	0.5	4.9
	1941	23.1	58.5	1.5	0.4	4.3
	1951	?	?			
Matheson	1911	29.4	14.9	10.6	0	0
	1921	74.8	20.0	0.7	0	0
	1931	89.6	5.2	0.5	0	0
	1941	72.3	14.5	2.1	0	0
	1951	?	?	?	?	?

Source: Census of Canada

escorted by Ivar Seppala of Port Arthur visited the Soviet Union to investigate conditions there, although it is not clear exactly how many participants actually decided to emigrate there for political reasons.[27] Overall, however, the ethnic mix of the region did not change significantly during the Great Depression.

The declaration of war in 1939 brought national identities and allegiances into sharp focus once again. As had happened during the First World War, unnaturalized immigrants from enemy countries were made to feel so unwelcome that some left if they could. There was a slight decline in the number of Italians in Timmins, for example, that does not appear to correspond with an increase in their numbers elsewhere in the region. However, these changes were slight, and by the end of the Second World

War the ethnic distribution in the region remained much as it had before the war, with only minor variations. English- and French-speaking Canadians each continued to constitute about one-third of the population; in Timmins the French-speaking population was slightly larger, at 41 percent. The Finnish and Italian populations declined slightly, perhaps because of emigration during the war, but the Ukrainian population grew slowly. Some Dutch immigrants arrived during and after the war, though their numbers were relatively small. First Nations people still were not attracted to the newcomer towns in any significant numbers, and after the Second World War they were almost invisible in town, preferring to live on the reserves or at Moosonee or Chapleau, where residential schools had been built. Population growth slowed as the gold mines began to produce less, as the pulp and paper industry stabilized with no significant new markets, and as rural depopulation continued. Growth mainly represented a local population reproducing itself as second and even third generations married and established households. For children who had grown up in the region, there was nothing unusual about the variety of languages, religions, food, and music enjoyed by their neighbours. The new generation came to think of ethnicity in different terms. The process by which that happened is a complex and fascinating one and is a major theme of this study.

Because ethnic borders were so tightly drawn in the first decades of the twentieth century, it is worth examining the diverse experiences of the groups that established the new resource-based economy. Why and how they came and the values they brought with them were important patterns in the intricate dance they performed as they reacted to the challenges of their new lives.

ENGLISH-SPEAKING CANADIANS

It may seem odd to consider English-speaking Canadians as an ethnic group, for by conventional definitions of the term they were (and are) not a single cultural unit. However, those who settled in the region came from a surprisingly similar background and brought with them a consistent set of aspirations, values, and expectations. Furthermore, they were perceived by many immigrants as a cohesive group. Thus it is worth examining them more closely through the lens of ethnicity.

Until the Second World War, English-speaking Canadians were the largest single group in all three sectors of the regional economy. Proportionately, their numbers were the largest in the rural townships and in villages such Matheson and Connaught that emerged as service centres (the only exception being Nushka/Val Gagné). Although detailed statistics are not available, impressionistic comments by observers of the time suggest that English-speaking Canadians tended to be employed in skilled and technical positions in the mines and paper mills, shunning underground or heavy manual labour.[28] They clearly dominated the small group of senior management, though they did not hold a monopoly here, as a number of Americans were among these ranks. As might be expected, they also filled most of the small cadre of professional service providers: doctors, dentists, teachers, and clergy. They were fairly evenly divided between Protestants and Roman Catholics, with Roman Catholics holding a slight majority everywhere but Matheson until 1941. The largest single Protestant group was Presbyterian (before church union) and United Church (after it).

In the earliest days of the Porcupine Camp, a significant number of miners arrived from Cobalt, most of whom were apparently originally from Nova Scotia (and Cape Breton in particular).[29] The Porcupine Camp strike in 1912 precipitated a general exodus of these men, who clearly were aware of alternative employment opportunities elsewhere in Canada.[30] Thereafter, English Canadian migrants to the region came almost entirely from Ontario and Quebec. The Ottawa Valley had been home to the largest group that could be traced. Farmers and bushworkers from Renfrew County, Pembroke, Carleton Place, Shawville, and the Gatineau followed the lead of the Mattawa brothers Noah and Henry Timmins in seeking the economic opportunities that were no longer available in the Ottawa Valley. George F. Helmer's story is typical. Born in Shawville, Quebec, across the river from Renfrew, he came to the area in 1917 and bought a farm just north of South Porcupine. There his dairy cattle provided a local supply of milk for a time. Then he sold part of his farm for a townsite subdivision, and this enabled him to invest in business endeavours in the area. He played an active role in municipal politics, serving several terms on Tisdale Township council.[31] Then there was Leonard S. Newton, a farm boy from the Gatineau Valley in Quebec (just north of Ottawa), whose life illustrates the occupational mobility of many in this group. He had worked in lumbering and then as a miner in Cobalt before deciding to come to the Porcupine in 1909 with his two brothers. For a time he worked at the mines and became active in the miners' union and the Independent Labour Party. Then he ran a hotel at Golden City and was on the Timmins Board of Trade. In 1929 he returned to mining at Rouyn, Quebec, while his family remained in Timmins. He was an active member of the Church of the Nativity (Roman Catholic), served as a separate school trustee, and was elected to five terms on Timmins town council.[32] Indeed, so many Porcupine–Iroquois Falls residents hailed from the Ottawa Valley that the *Advance* described a 1934 political meeting as "a regular family re-union, as it were," in an editorial headlined "Good Old Killaloe."[33]

Of course, not all the English-speaking Canadians hailed from the Ottawa Valley. A smaller but significant number came from the Huron-Grey-Bruce region of central Ontario, and others were from the Eastern Townships of Quebec. All these regions had run out of good farmland and had not developed significant employment opportunities for their surplus populations. Northeastern Ontario offered economic opportunities a short train trip from home.

English-speaking Canadians were well represented in the commercial and retail sector. Sylvester Kennedy and his wife Mary (Kelly) of Quebec operated the first hotel and general store at Golden City, and both became active in promoting education at South Porcupine.[34] Dayton Ostrosser, who was of Loyalist ancestry and hailed from Norfolk County, Ontario, ran a clothing store in Timmins and also the Schumacher post office for many years, serving on the Timmins Board of Trade.[35] The brothers Charles and John Dalton were from the Goderich area of Ontario. They operated a livery service that was converted to taxis and buses in the 1930s, and Charles was also active in municipal politics.[36] One of the best known of these businessmen was Roy Thomson of Toronto, a high school dropout who came to Northern Ontario as a radio salesman in the early 1920s. When he discovered that people were not interested in his wares because no radio signals could be received in the area, he bought his own transmitter and in 1930 opened station CFCH in North Bay. He then branched out with stations in Kirkland Lake, Timmins, and, later, Rouyn, Quebec. In 1934 Thomson bought his first newspaper, the infant Timmins *Press*, which occupied space in the same building as his radio station. He used the paper to make turbulent waves of local events (in contrast to the more reserved columns of the *Porcupine Advance*). Thomson parlayed this modest beginning into an international media and business empire that led to his elevation to the peerage in 1963.[37]

English-speaking Canadians who came to farm clearly hoped to put down permanent roots in the region, and even some who came to work at the Abitibi mill anticipated a long-term residency. But in the early years, those who came to work at the mines were largely transients. There was a widespread belief that mines generally lasted no more than ten years,[38] so it made little sense to uproot one's family or purchase substantial housing. Thus, many of the miners were single men in their twenties who were hoping to make some quick money to get themselves established elsewhere; or they were young married men, who had left their wives and families behind on marginal farms, hoping to earn sufficient cash to buy seed or equipment and keep the enterprise going. Over time, this pattern changed somewhat. Certainly, transients continued to dominate the mining workforce, but more and more miners brought or established families, putting their faith in a seemingly endless supply of gold.

The fact that a significant number of English-speaking Canadians who came were from Quebec or were Roman Catholic must have tempered their attitude toward French-speaking Canadians specifically and toward culturally diverse communities in general. Nevertheless, they came to northeastern Ontario assuming that they were simply re-establishing the dominant patterns of Canadian society in this new outpost and therefore assumed that they were entitled to leadership positions here. The Loyal Orange Lodge organized and paraded, particularly at Matheson and Porquis Junction, and Ontario law made English the primary language of instruction in the schools. While many French speakers learned English, few English speakers found it necessary to learn French. The first Timmins town hall had a bilingual sign, but its grander replacement in 1937 somehow managed to drop the French. The English-speaking Canadians simply assumed entitlement as the dominant culture.

FRENCH-SPEAKING CANADIANS

The movement of French-speaking Canadians into the region was part of the larger migration out of Quebec that had begun in the late nineteenth century as young people went in search of industrial employment. Many emigrated to the factories of New England, but not all left the country. Railway and lumber companies had actively recruited them to come to work-sites in Northern Ontario, and the mines of the Sudbury region had been a major draw in the 1880s and 1890s.[39] The Roman Catholic Church had responded to the exodus from Quebec with a series of colonization projects to encourage young people to stay on farms, which the church and other Quebec leaders saw as a core component of Québécois national identity. While the focus of the colonization movement was northwestern Quebec, there was an almost natural spillover across the border from Abitibi-Témiscamingue, and priests began to organize group settlements on the Ontario side as well.[40] During the First World War, the newly established pulp and paper companies responded to local labour shortages by recruiting experienced bushworkers from Quebec.[41] Thus, French-speaking newcomers were represented in all sectors of the regional economy from the early days of the boom. For a time, they were the largest single cultural group at Ansonville and Timmins, and always they represented a sizable minority everywhere else except in the town of Matheson. In 1929 the workforce of Abitibi's Iroquois Falls mill was 52 percent French Canadian, although most did not live in the company townsite.[42] The industrial workforce of the region was quite different from that which historian José Igartua found at the Alcan plant at Arvida, Quebec, where initial recruitment was done outside rural francophonie. It "took a number of years to coax them off the farms in any large numbers to work indoors," recalled one engineer there.[43]

As with the English-speaking Canadians in Porcupine–Iroquois Falls, many hailed from the Ottawa Valley and Gatineau, with other significant numbers from the Eastern Townships, the Beauce, and the Charlevoix regions. One group came to Iroquois Falls from a paper mill in Watertown, New York.[44] Later, families who were not part of formal colonization schemes also began to spill across the border from northwestern Quebec. Although such people had grown up on farms, many had experience cutting logs in winter bush camps or working in pulp mills. Those who went to work for the mines appear to have worked first in construction and carpentry-related positions, putting their woods skills to use, and later moved into other underground jobs. The motivation for migration was clearly economic, for their home regions had generated a surplus labour pool which the limited or marginal farmlands could not absorb. For the most part, the migrants moved into occupations that they had pursued at home, although once established in the region, they might move into other positions. They tended to raise large families and, perhaps as a result, were less likely to move households frequently, though there was a high degree of mobility from mine to mine within the Porcupine area.

Almérie Bouchard's story is a typical example. Born near Sherbrooke in the Eastern Townships, he worked first near home in a paper mill. In 1913 a friend enticed him to Timmins with the promise of better pay. Bouchard joined Hollinger as a machinist and began to raise a family that eventually numbered ten children. In 1920 he left Hollinger to go into business with a fellow French Canadian producing lathes. He remained in business until ill health forced him to retire. Many of his children and grandchildren stayed in the area, and although one daughter married a man from near her father's original home, she and her family eventually returned to become permanent residents of Timmins.[45]

While most wage-earning French Canadians were employed as labourers or as skilled craftsmen such as carpenters or blacksmiths, they could also be found among the small middle class, particularly in Timmins. In 1913 the senior Roman Catholic priest in the area, Father Charles Thériault, recruited a group of teachers, businessmen, and office workers from the Eastern Townships,[46] but there were others who had come on their own, such as Osias Sauvé, a Timmins lawyer originally from Ottawa, who founded *Le Nord Ontarien*, a newspaper that served the French-speaking community.[47] The French-speaking population had other representatives in the most senior places. Perhaps the most important were the Timmins brothers themselves – Louis Henry and Noah. Actually of mixed anglophone and francophone background, they moved easily in both worlds and were claimed by each. Their father was of mixed Scots, Irish, and French ancestry and was known as both Noah and Noë; their mother, Henriette Mineur, was French-speaking. Their sister Louise married Arthur Ferland, Louis

Henry married a Lachine girl named Paré, and Noah married her sister Leila.[48] Their nephew Alphonse Paré, an engineer from Montreal, was also well known in the community, through his role in the construction of the Hollinger Mine.[49] With francophone connections to the "owners" and francophone influence among the local leadership, it is not surprising that the French-speaking population of the region saw itself as the establishment and not as the victim of anglophone oppression and prejudice. The francophones' sheer numbers and their distribution through all social levels and occupations made them a force to be recognized.

The Roman Catholic Church was of central importance to the French Canadians, in part because it had been important "back home," but also because it was one of the most stable, well-staffed, and well-funded institutions in the region. The parish provided an immediately available focal point for newcomers, and priests tended to serve in the community for much longer periods than Protestant clergy or Jewish rabbis. The most imposing building in each town (except, of course, in Matheson) was the Roman Catholic church. Church-sponsored organizations such as the Knights of Columbus provided social interaction and benefits to the wider community, and priests led the way in the establishment of separate schools, including those in Timmins, Iroquois Falls, Ansonville, and Clute Township (Frederickhouse), where French-language instruction was provided (Ontario's infamous Regulation 17 notwithstanding). The Cercle canadien, a social organization that promoted French culture, was not officially a church group, but the priests were always active in encouraging it. The church also had the benefit of nonordained staff. The Sisters of Providence ran a small hospital for the Hollinger Mine, beginning in 1911, and founded and managed what became St Mary's General Hospital at Timmins after 1925. Undoubtedly, it was partly because of Noah Timmins's patronage that the Roman Catholic Church and the French-speaking population flourished in the Timmins area. Timmins's father had been a strong promoter of the church in Mattawa,[50] and his son carried on the family tradition. Noah largely funded the construction of the first church of St Antoine and brought the Sisters of Providence to run his hospital. He and Father Thériault became personal friends.

The prominent Canadian sociologist S.D. Clark once proposed that French Canadians were relegated to unskilled and marginalized positions in the "new industrial communities" of northern Ontario and Quebec in spite of their early potential to move into positions as "industrial entrepreneurs." Clark blamed the Roman Catholic Church, concluding that church programs to encourage farm settlement even in the face of severe difficulties kept French Canadians out of leadership roles in mining and papermaking and helped maintain "a large pool of part-time workers" for those industries.[51] While this argument may partially hold true at Iroquois

Falls, it is utterly incorrect with regard to the mining sector in the Porcupine region. The Timmins family, with its roots in Franco-Ontario, were
the most successful "industrial entrepreneurs" of the region, and their
patronage opened the door for a large and influential francophone population.

FINNS

By the time the northeastern townships had been surveyed for farmers and
the mines had begun to operate, there were already sizable groups of
Finnish settlers in Northern Ontario, clustered at the Lakehead and
Sudbury. There were also growing numbers of Finns in northern Michigan
working in mining and papermaking. Hence, the first Finns to settle the
region came mostly from these nearby places, where they had worked as
labourers in mines and forestry, often in addition to having a home base
on a nearby farm. In fact, they were reproducing patterns of life that they
had followed in Finland, and they were doing so in a countryside of strik-
ingly similar appearance. These first settlers sent word back to Finland
about their new homes, and more and more of their friends and relatives
were attracted to the region. It was a small part of a much larger outmigration from Finland that lasted from the 1870s to the 1930s, drawing
people from rural areas that had suffered famine and unemployment.
Most of the Finnish settlers in Porcupine–Iroquois Falls came from the
region known generally as Ostrobothnia, and specifically from Vaasu
province (on the west coast of Finland), which had a large pulp and paper
industry and which, by the early twentieth century, was facing a "potentially
explosive" situation with a growing gap between wealthy landowners and
poor peasant-tenants.[52] Thus, many of the immigrants to Northern
Ontario not only had bush and mill experience but had developed a sense
of what scholars call industrial worker alienation, and they were aware of
political philosophies such as socialism and communism that promised
workers a better life.

    The CPR and other companies recruited Finns at the turn of the century,
and Canadian government agents had recruited Finnish farmer-settlers for
the Lakehead region, but by 1919 Canadian officials were much more
ambivalent about the desirability of Finnish immigrants, given their role in
labour disputes in Canada and the outcome of the 1918 Finnish Civil War,
in which the Reds had shown considerable strength even though the
Whites were victorious. The Canadian government seemed to fear that the
losers would come to Canada and spread their communist ideas here.
Thus, it appears that Finns who came to Porcupine–Iroquois Falls came
not through official immigration promotion schemes but through personal contacts: word of mouth and chain migration. Not surprisingly, the

Lempi Mansfield and her family, photographed in Cobalt in 1914, before their arrival in the Porcupine region. Like so many others, this family came to Porcupine from Cobalt. (F. Askar/Ontario Studio, LAC, PA126796)

names of neighbouring villages – Ilmajoki, Kurikka, Jalasjärvi, and Jauja-joki – crop up repeatedly in the Finnish biographies. One girl recalled an event in the 1920s when seven women from one village arrived in Timmins for prearranged marriages: "The whole Finnish population of Timmins turned out to meet the train, to watch this mass meeting of grooms and brides who had never laid eyes on each other before ... They all married, though there was some gossip about trading back and forth, but actually, nobody knew who had come for whom in the first place."[53] Unlike other European immigrants to northeastern Ontario, many Finns came with their families right from the early boom years. And the Finns were organizers. They formed sewing circles and Finnish-language schools; they held endless socials, dances, and community picnics; and they established gymnastics clubs for young people. They organized the first consumers' cooperative in the region, and they were active promoters of organized labour, even publishing a bulletin in Italian to raise awareness of the labour movement among their co-workers.[54] They also published what was probably the first newspaper in the area: the *Piiskuri*.[55]

Finns settled throughout the region and worked at the mines, pulp mills, bush camps, and farms, though they were more likely to be employed in mining than at the Iroquois Falls mill. The largest group congregated in Timmins, but they were more visible in South Porcupine, where they constituted a higher proportion of the population (up to 8.4 percent by 1941). One very common pattern was for a family to purchase a homestead, clear some land (selling the logs for pulpwood), and then send the adult men to work in the mines or to cut pulpwood for the winter while the women managed the farm. Another common pattern was for a woman (or married couple) to run a boarding house or "hotel" in town for the transient single male workers. Some women also worked as cooks in the pulpwood camps or as household domestic help, to supplement family income. Each family unit thus became something of a mixed economy unto itself. The strategy was highly successful. It also may be a clue that most Finns came to the area intending to make it a permanent home. As one veteran of the Porcupine rush later recalled, "When this was a town of 'tar-papered packing cases,' the houses of the Finnish colony were distinguished by their neatness, cleanliness and general tidiness."[56]

Sophie Haapala's life mirrored this pattern. Born in Vaasa Province, Finland, in 1881, she came to Canada at the age of thirty-three. Together with her husband Salomen Poikkimaki, she established a farm in the mostly Finnish settlement at Beaver Lake, near Sudbury, and raised eight children. To help make ends meet, she went to Pottsville in the 1930s to work as a housekeeper to Mr Sulo Harris. Three of her sons remained with their father at Beaver Lake to work the farm, but at least one other went into mining, and another possibly took up bush work. When she died in 1938 following an illness, her bilingual funeral (in Finnish and English) was held in the South Porcupine United Church by the Reverend A.I. Heinonen, and her untimely death was mourned by a network of friends across northeastern Ontario.[57]

Not all Finns remained as suppliers of the pool of labour that fuelled the regional economy. At least one became an "industrial entrepreneur" (to use S.D. Clark's phrase). A. Ernie Wicks was born in Finland in 1896 and came to North America with his parents, first to Michigan and then to Sault Ste Marie, Ontario. He began as a bush worker, turned contractor at the age of twenty, and four years later established his own sawmill at Monteith, calling it the Hawk Lake Lumber Company. After some initial difficulties, he founded A.E. Wicks, Ltd, and expanded operations into Timmins and Cochrane. As a member of the local socio-economic elite, he served two years as mayor of Cochrane and became a director of the Ontario Forest Industrial Association.[58]

The Finns who came before 1918 were politically moderate (often social democrats); they were literate, Lutheran, and motivated by the same economic factors that brought the English- and French-speaking Canadians to the area. After the Finnish Civil War, a number of radicalized and even communist Finns began to arrive, driven out by the turmoil at home. They pointedly rejected the Lutheran Church and were openly scornful of what they saw as the ignorance and complacency of Canadian workers. They carried bitter memories of their treatment at the hands of the Whites during and after the civil war, when some 90,000 had been held prisoner and up to 9,500 had perished of "starvation and neglect" – not counting those who had died in "bloody reprisals" following the White victory.[59] They formed alliances with the Workers' Party of Canada (later the Communist Party of Canada) and with local communist Ukrainians. They sponsored May Day parades and became leaders in the union movement at the mines, including the campaign against the One Big Union movement. At the Iroquois Falls plant they were not very successful at influencing the papermakers' locals, so they turned to the bush camps and began a campaign to organize the bushworkers.[60] From 1921 to 1924 they ran Investigative Committees to screen new immigrants from Finland in an attempt to keep the Whites from getting work in the bush.[61] For a time they even succeeded in taking control of the co-operative stores in Timmins and South Porcupine. Needless to say, the Finnish community in the region was deeply divided, and a bitterness was generated that echoes even today.

The influx of communist Finns was diluted over time through a combination of outmigration and the successful suppression of communism by an alliance of state, industry, and church. In 1921 a group called the Suomalainen Maanviljelyskomuuna Kylväjä (Finnish Farmers Commune Sower) was founded at Kirkland Lake to promote the emigration of Finns to the USSR in response to a call from the Soviet government.[62] The first groups began to leave in 1922. In 1930 the Soviet government called for knowledgeable bushworkers to come to the Finnish border region to facilitate Karelia's five-year-plan obligations.[63] The Finns of Timmins and South Porcupine responded with particular enthusiasm and accounted for a significant number of what may have been as many as 10,000 emigrants from northeastern Ontario.[64] Idealists such as the families of Alexander Jokela and Yrjo Lauri were among them.[65] The remaining Finnish population, together with mine managers, noncommunist union leaders, and Roman Catholic and Lutheran clergy, campaigned to suppress the vestiges of communism in a process that will be explored in a later chapter.

Throughout the 1920s and 1930s, the Finnish enclave remained very isolated within the region. Like Finns elsewhere in Canada, they preferred to marry other Finns; historian Varpu Lindström-Best describes a popular song of the 1920s that mocked Finnish women who dated non-Finns.[66] If spouses could not be found locally, they could be found at no great distance. A Canadian official complained in the 1930s that there was a shortage of domestic workers in Montreal and Toronto because so many Finnish girls were leaving to marry in Northern Ontario.[67] The result was a community that was big enough to permit relative self-sufficiency and was alienated by cultural and political distance from its Canadian-born neighbours. As Aili Schneider recalled, "The Finnish population in Timmins lived entirely within its own tightly knit circle ... Mastering the English language was still difficult. Ties with the old country were fresh and strong ... We knew very little about what was going on in our town, or the new country where we now had homes, and cared less ... We had our own Finnish newspaper ... We were like a Finnish island adrift among strangers."[68]

ITALIANS

The patterns of Italian immigration to the region were very different. Neither the Canadian nor Italian government wanted to promote Italian emigration, but from the turn of the century, thousands of migrant workers came anyway for the lumber, mining, and particularly railway-construction opportunities in Canada. They were the classic sojourners: single men who came only for the paycheque, which they sent back to Italy, and who had no intentions of staying permanently. Some apparently did not even stay year-round: in the early years at least, some came only for the summer construction season and returned to Italy for the winter.[69] Italian workers were often recruited by employment agents; Montreal was the entry point for many who came to Porcupine-Iroquois Falls. For some time, sociologists considered these men to be landless peasants, either bypassed or displaced by modern industrial capitalism, travelling the world in search of economic opportunity. But historian Bruno Ramirez has more recently argued that this snapshot misses much of the bigger picture. Overseas work allowed many young men to save money and gain status at home; their sojourning labour "became the main mechanism responsible for integrating Italy within the North Atlantic economy" by providing "precious financial resources for the capital-hungry northern Italian industries."[70] Hence, these young men may be seen as part of an international industrial labour pool that had become an integral part of the Italian economy and culture by the First World War. It is difficult to determine the specific regions from which the majority of these migrants to northeastern Ontario came, but they seem to have included the mountainous south-central regions of Abruzzi, Molise, and Campania, as well as the southern region of Calabria – all areas that contributed substantially to the migrant labour pool in other parts of Canada as well.[71]

The first Italians came to the region as work crews on the TNO. They were then drawn to the better-paid construction opportunities of the early mining rush and eventually took jobs underground. Only a handful found employment at the pulp and paper mills, though they were consistently one of the two largest groups of European immigrant workers living at the Iroquois Falls townsite.[72] None farmed. They congregated in residential enclaves of boarding houses and shacks, notably Moneta south of the original Timmins townsite, and "Little Italy" on the Dome Mine's property.[73] Without literacy skills and with only a limited knowledge of English, the men kept to themselves. They tended to congregate with others from their home villages and regions, and in the early years men from Calabria were likely to be found in South Porcupine, men from Abruzzi in Timmins, and men from more northern villages in Schumacher.[74]

After the First World War the pattern began to change. Some men married, brought their brides to the region, and started families. Some put down roots by establishing businesses. The residential patterns began to shift as well, as business owners drifted a few blocks north from Moneta to live above their shops on Third Avenue in Timmins.[75] In the interwar years, some Italians later recalled, men from the same village often collaborated to buy or build a house and even to facilitate the emigration of families: "Men would pool their money in order for one or more of the investors to pay for passage of his wife to Canada. In many cases such as this the woman would be called upon to care not only for her husband's needs but also for a number of *boardanti*, who would pay each month for room and board."[76] As more families were reunited or established, Father Thériault contacted an Italian-speaking priest from a religious order that was founding Italian parishes across North America, and the Sacred Heart parish was created in Moneta in 1936. The parish church was built only a few blocks from St Antoine, symbolizing the distinctness of the Italian sector.

Scholars have noted that an important feature of Italian migration around the world was the padrone system, in which one individual would sponsor groups of men and arrange employment for them. Some of these padrones were notorious, as was the Montreal immigration agent Antonio Cordasco, whose activities precipitated a royal commission investigation in 1904. Others were genuinely admired by both the migrant labourers and the North American employers they served. Timmins had its very own padrone, Leo Mascioli, who came to wield tremendous influence in the wider community while amassing a personal fortune. He had left his home in Cuccollo, Italy, as a child, charmed his way onto ocean-going vessels, and done odd jobs across the United States. He arrived at the Sydney steel mills in Nova Scotia at the age of nineteen, by which time he was already organizing his countrymen into work crews and contracting out their labour. In his late twenties he returned to Italy to marry Raffaela De Dominicis. He brought her to Canada, and two years later they were in Cobalt for the silver rush, supplying some hundrd and fifty workers for the mines and other construction projects. In 1909 he took forty of his work crew to Porcupine for the season. They returned the following year, when he and his brother Antonio and their crew signed on with Hollinger.

Mascioli made himself indispensable, recruiting miners through a network of connections in Montreal and Abruzzi. During the 1912 strike, he protected Hollinger's interests by providing strikebreakers; in the process, he managed to get himself arrested and fined for assault and for carrying a concealed weapon, following an affray at the Timmins train station. That same year, Mrs Mascioli returned to Italy for health reasons. She died there in 1914, leaving him with two daughters and a son to raise. After the strike, Mascioli expanded his contracting activities as the town of Timmins expanded, winning major contracts for sidewalks, water and sewer, and building construction and maintenance. Eventually, he was the owner of the finest hotel in the area (the Empire at Timmins) as well as a chain of movie theatres, an automobile dealership and garage, and a construction company. He joined a variety of local organizations, including the Kiwanis, the Legion, and the Knights of Columbus, becoming a prominent figure in the local elite. He even played a role in getting Roy Thomson into the newspaper business. Mascioli's son Daniel graduated from Osgoode Hall and was celebrated as the region's first native-born lawyer. Leo died in 1952, and his grave is marked by the most elaborate monument in the Timmins cemetery.[77] It is possibly because Mascioli recruited workers from his home region of Abruzzi that many Italians in the region hail from there, though Abruzzi also supplied a large proportion of Italian immigrants to other parts of Canada during the years of heaviest migration to northeastern Ontario.[78]

The emphasis on single male sojourners should not obscure the fact that some Italians did come to the area with their families from an early date. In the summer of 1912, Domenic Purificate brought his wife and children to Timmins. Within a year, his daughter Cecilia had married the Hollinger miner Hector Marinacci, who had arrived in Timmins a few months before his bride's family. In 1919 Marinacci left Hollinger and went into business, first as the proprietor of a pool hall and later of a bottling works. Then in 1934 he built the Maple Leaf Hotel, which gained fame in later years as one of the venues that brought Stompin' Tom Connors and Shania Twain to the public. Cecilia and Hector Marinacci raised four children, and although not all of them remained in Timmins, the family was sufficiently enmeshed in local society by the 1930s that the couple's twenty-fifth wedding anniversary was featured on the front page of the *Porcupine Advance*.[79]

Most Italians in northeastern Ontario led much less visible lives than the Masciolis and the Marinaccis. During the phase of the single male sojourners into the 1920s, social life focused on the boarding house. As more families were established in the 1930s, the focus shifted to the Roman Catholic parish. Since many men worked with fellow Italians in crews at the mines, there was little need to learn English among the first generation, and many were not literate. Thus, like the Finns, the Italians remained a closed community for some time. However, they did become known in wider circles for their love of music. In South Porcupine, an Italian orchestra of mandolins, accordions, and guitars played every Sunday, to the delight of those leaving church,[80] and semi-professional orchestras were popular performers at community dances. The Italians tended to be politically conservative and did not participate in large numbers in the labour unions, in spite of attempts by more radical workers to draw them in. For this reason, mine managers considered them desirable workers (at least, until the Second World War) even if the Canadian immigration department did not.

UKRAINIANS

Like the Italians, Ukrainians came into the region in railway work gangs and general construction crews. They tended to move into employment at the mines, rather than at the Abitibi mill, and hardly any took up farming. At first they were sojourners, but over time a core group established families and became a permanent feature of the community. Unlike the Ukrainians who settled on prairie farms, the men who came to the Porcupine Camp appear to have originally been part of a pool of workers who had already established sojourner patterns elsewhere in Ontario.[81] As with the Italians, industrial labour does not seem to have been their life goal. Instead, they hoped to use the cash to return to Europe and purchase land.[82] They had come largely from Galicia, a region of small and increasingly unprofitable farms, which was the principal region of emigration to other parts of Canada as well. Not all the members of this first group of arrivals were men. Mary Kramaruk and Eva Kremyr were remembered for their attempt during the 1912 Porcupine strike to stop the arrival of strike-breakers by sitting on the TNO tracks.[83] These workers were joined by the sons (and a few daughters) of Ukrainians who were homesteading in the prairie provinces and needed cash income to subsidize the early settle-ment costs.[84]

Although these sojourners were largely illiterate, they had been influ-enced by the socialist ideals that were spreading through Galicia by the turn of the century.[85] They were not passive and compliant workers. In 1907 they complained to the Austrian consul general in Canada about the TNO's employment practices, alleging that they had been charged exorbi-tant fees for transport and accommodation and had been held as virtual prisoners at work camps.[86] They brought their ideals into the mines, were active participants in the 1912 strike, and continued to play a role in the union movement throughout the history of the region.

During the First World War, of course, the Ukrainians were required to register as enemy aliens, and they faced hostility and harassment from fellow workers. A number appear to have left the region as a result. Then, in the 1920s, as their numbers were being reinforced by a new wave of arrivals, world events brought new divisions. Pro-Soviet communists chal-lenged those who hoped for an independent Ukraine, and the Ukrainians of northeastern Ontario became bitterly divided into Reds and Whites in much the same way as the Finns. In the late 1920s, Ukrainian "labor temples" were built at Ansonville, South Porcupine, and Timmins; in 1932 the Ukrainian nationalists at Timmins responded by building their own Prosvita hall, named for the *Prosvita* ("enlightenment") societies of prewar Galicia.

Religion, of course, was rejected by the communist Ukrainians. Interest-ingly, though, it did not play a particularly strong role in the lives of the nationalists in northeastern Ontario either. The point is an intriguing one, because the Lutheran Church among the Finns and the Roman Catholic and Orthodox churches among Ukrainians elsewhere in Canada played active roles in the movement to counter communism. However, the Timmins area was served only irregularly by Ukrainian clergy; in 1936, the archbishop of the Greek Orthodox Church in Canada visited the north for the first time.[87] In 1940 Timmins Ukrainians founded the Roman Catholic parish of St George's, but they did not have their own priest until 1948 or their own church building until 1950.[88] In the mid-1930s a Ukrainian priest travelled among the mining communities to encourage people against communism and to persuade the mines to hire noncommunist workers, but at least one mine manager did not credit him with much success. "The Ukrainians are the worst communists and pull the wool over their priests of this type," he claimed.[89]

After the Second World War, the texture of the Ukrainian population in the region began to change. The second generation was less politically radical than the first, and it had begun to marry outside the Ukrainian community. Furthermore, significant numbers began to leave the region, particularly for better job opportunities in southern Ontario. One source reported that they left at least in part because of the persistent and ongoing "red baiting" in northern Ontario.[90] Membership in the Ukrainian Labor Farmer Temple Association dropped, and eventually the old hall was sold because those remaining found it difficult to pay the taxes on it.[91] In the 1970s and 1980s there was briefly a revival of interest in Ukrainian identity in the region, but the days of visible public radicalism were over. Indeed, concluded Mary Stefura, by the early 1980s, "in most northern Ontario communities, the Ukrainian group as an identifiable social entity had virtually disappeared."[92]

FIRST NATIONS

As the demographic balance shifted dramatically in the early years of the twentieth century, Aboriginal families were increasingly marginalized – socially, politically, and, ultimately, economically. Although the newcomers of the resource boom were initially aware of and interested in the Native residents of the region, once the services of Native guides or porters were no longer required, a gap developed between the communities, both literally in the distribution of settlements and figuratively in the mental map each group had of the region.

Certainly, continued participation in the fur trade economy helped to set the First Nations apart from the mining, pulpwood, and farming activities of the newcomers. The new resource exploitation clearly had the potential for devastating the fur trade, but initially this did not happen, and the fur trade actually experienced something of a boom. As the Cobalt *Daily Nugget* noted in 1913, "The opening of the north as the greatest mining centre of the continent and a country with a farming future ... has awakened the biggest furriers in Canada and the United States."[93] The Hudson's Bay Company, Revillon Frères, and dozens of smaller buyers competed for the furs before and during the First World War, paying cash and (along the CPR line) introducing new and cheaper merchandise. Continued participation in the fur trade was a reasonable and viable economic choice in those years.

However, cash payments and new retail opportunities were not the only changes. At Iroquois Falls and Matheson and in the Porcupine, resource development activities drove out the trappers, in some places literally taking over their lands and routes. For example, a trail cut by Henry Dokis north from the Abitibi River to access his traplines was taken over by the National Transcontinental Railway as a useful path for hauling timber to

construct its bridge across the Abitibi River.[94] Meanwhile, pressures generated within the new fur trade also encouraged a geographic shift. Independent traders, lacking the HBC or Revillon infrastructure, simply came
in by train and set up seasonal buyers at the main station stops, and the
HBC realized that it would be much cheaper to supply the inland posts by
rail from Montreal instead of by the old canoe brigades out of Moose
Factory. The changes were reflected first in the south. The HBC closed Fort
Temiskaming in 1902 while opening new posts at Biscotasing on the CPR
main line in 1888 and at Gogama on the Canadian Northern (which
became a major depot for the HBC by 1922). One by one, the important
posts of old were closed: Flying Post (1914), New Brunswick House
(1917), Matachewan (c. 1920), Mattagami (1924), and Abitibi (1930).
People around Lake Abitibi now took their trade to La Sarre on the
Transcontinental Railway (later the CNR), which became a central depot,
shipping furs from that region to Montreal instead of to Moose Factory.[95]
By 1902–3, La Sarre was registering the largest dollar value in sales of any
HBC post in the Huron District.[96] The Mattagami people appear to have
taken their trade primarily to Gogama, giving that depot the third-largest
sales in the HBC's Huron District. Reflecting these shifts, the Anglican
Church moved its Mattagami mission under John Sanders to Biscotasing
and planned to open a new mission at Abitibi, but it lacked the money and
personnel to do so. The Chapleau area, west of Gogama, also drew people
because of the Anglican-run boarding school built there in 1907. As the
Canadian government stepped up its pressure on First Nations families to
put their children in school, some people chose to move to be near their
young ones. At Moose Factory, when the TNO finally reached James Bay in
1931, a new townsite was laid out across the river channel from the old
post. Christened Moosonee, it too began to attract a First Nations population from the surrounding country.

These new settlements tended to be more "mixed" than those of the
nineteenth century. Indeed, the anthropologist William H. Jenkins, who
visited La Sarre in 1937, considered that the people there constituted a
unique group, living as they did surrounded by Cree, Ojibwa, and Algonquin neighbours. Another anthropologist in the 1930s described them as
"an off-shoot" of the Ojibwa.[97] Both Cree and Ojibwa met at Chapleau,
Timmins, and elsewhere, and eventually "Oji-Cree" became the more
useful term for the Aboriginal population of the region. There was also a
growing population that had Aboriginal and French Canadian ancestry
(referred to by various names depending on the recorder and the time).
As early as the 1890s a woman named Koo-koo-mis proposed that "most of
the 'Indians'" in northeastern Ontario were "only half breeds."[98] Andrew
Clement, who taught in the Missinaibi area in the 1920s, later said of his
students that "those whose parents took treaty money could be identified

as Indian though the great majority were part Caucasian. Except on reserves, it was difficult to find a purebred Indian."[99]

The continuing importance of the fur trade should not obscure the fact that many First Nations people also began to take advantage of the new economic opportunities. In the early years, prospecting either for oneself or on contract for someone else proved popular.[100] Few Native people show up on the payrolls of the major mines or pulp and paper companies; they preferred to take on seasonal work close to home in the bush camps or on the railway maintenance crews.[101] Casual and contract work could fit easily with hunting, fishing, and trapping and make up for lean times in the bush. Edwin Bradwin, in his study of early-twentieth-century bush-camp life, noted that Native men rarely worked an entire season in camp, preferring to earn just enough for ready-made clothing or a few other luxury purchases.[102] The growing popularity of tourism in the Temagami region to the south drew a number of men into guiding and outfitting, work that could pay very well indeed. In 1920 the Northern Ontario Outfitters and Guides Association set the rate for a head guide at six dollars a day.[103] At that time, skilled mine hoistmen might earn five dollars and fifty cents a day, a top-paid mechanic at the Abitibi mill seven dollars, and the best log cutters in the bush camps just three or four dollars. Some people chose to settle their families off-reserve with them in order to take advantage of employment opportunities. In the fall of 1920, for example, five families who were eligible to live on the Mattagami Reserve were living by the lake at Gogama; the men were working as guides, drivers, and log cutters in the bush, as well as doing fishing and trapping.[104] Women began to find a market for moccasins, baskets, and similar products. In the 1930s the HBC post at La Sarre coordinated the production and sale of "hundreds of pairs of moccasins ... large quantities of baskets, fishing creels, small canoes," and other handiwork, which were sent to markets in Montreal and other parts of eastern Canada.[105] When the Department of Indian Affairs calculated the value of the Chapleau Agency's economy during the 1920s, wage income and money from the sale of farm products accounted for nearly one-third of family income (not counting government annuities).[106] By the 1930s, even during the Great Depression, income from wages had increased so much that it often equalled income from hunting and trapping. Nevertheless, in the printed report that accompanied these statistics, the superintendent general reported that people were "of necessity, more or less nomadic and consequently live in tents most of the year." And the monetary value of the income of the Chapleau Agency's people was consistently one of the three lowest in Ontario.[107]

During these early years of the new resource-based settlement, the First Nations were a visible presence in the region, and they were a source of

Table 3   Chapleau Agency economy, 1930s

Year	Hunting/trapping income	Wages earned	Received from timber	Farm products value	Other earnings
1931	$7000	$5000	–	$1000	0
1932	not available	–	–	–	–
1933	5000	4500	$446	850	0
1934	5000	5000	102	700	0
1935	5000	6000	0	800	0
1936	5000	5000	102	875	0
1937	not reported	–	–	–	–
1938	5000	5000	378	900	0
1939	5000	4000	1990.53	1050	0

Source: Data from annual reports, Department of Indian Affairs

fascination to the newcomers. When a party carrying mail from Moose Factory passed through Cobalt en route to Montreal, it was front-page news, and when the Mattagami First Nation held its annual powwow at Mattagami Landing just west of Timmins in 1915, town residents turned out in large numbers to watch the spectacle.[108] Such people as Mary and Tom Fox of the Matachewan area and Maggie (Buffalo) Leclair of Nighthawk Lake were considered well known in the wider community, while the southerner Edwin Bradwin called the Natives of the area "exotic" and "primal."[109]

But the townspeople's awareness of their First Nations neighbours seems to have diminished through the 1930s and 1940s. Comments about Aboriginal people in the columns of the newspapers declined as the newcomers became increasingly preoccupied with themselves. When notice was made of Native people, it was either negative (as in a report on a measles epidemic or a comment about dire poverty) or a romanticized description of a lost history and culture, usually precipitated by the discovery of an arrowhead or the reminiscences of an "old-timer." These stereotypes served only to further the distance between peoples. The First Nations were left on their own in their ongoing struggle for recognition and control of their own affairs.

The 1920s and 1930s were years of increasing hardship both on- and off-reserve. The Mattagami Reserve was all but abandoned – until a new townsite was built in the 1950s[110] – because a better living could be had at Gogama. Elsewhere, the fact that the game was so depleted was a major cause for complaint. The Ontario government responded by creating the Chapleau Game Preserve in May 1925 and establishing closed seasons for beaver and otter throughout the entire territory north of the French and Mattawa Rivers. But the new regulations only added to First Nations' difficulties. Charges were laid against a woman from the New Brunswick Reserve for killing a deer in the preserve, and twenty-five muskrat were seized from Chief Joseph Whetung. Native people across the region were outraged. Thomas Kuskichee of Biscotasing protested to the Department of Indian Affairs: "I want to enquire a few things about the Indian rites in Trapping. I had a couple of Beaver traps out The Game Warden F. Legace of Chapleau Game Park picked them up and took my traps away. Now I am in a desperate way. There is a number of Indians here no place to trap and Starvation is facing us. My Wife is sick & one child I cant go far to hunt and there is no game to hunt as Foreigners & white men has the country pretty well cleaned up here."[111] Ottawa's response was unequivocal: "Indians are held to be subject to the Game laws of the Province."[112]

Although fur prices were high throughout the 1920s, Native trappers right across Northern Ontario were unable to meet the demand. There were even reports of malnutrition and death from starvation farther north.[113] Then came the collapse of the fur market during the Depression and into the Second World War. "During the war years no one trapped," recalled bush pilot George Thériault (with slight exaggeration). "After the war there was a lot of outside work, so trapping wasn't a serious business again until the 1950s." By then, both the game and the fur market had recovered somewhat.[114]

Officials responsible for Indian affairs experimented with a variety of proposed solutions. In the early 1940s two tracts of land were obtained from the Ontario government south of James Bay and designated as beaver and fur preserves – one of about 18,000 square kilometres and the other about 23,000. Beaver restocking programs were introduced here with the help of First Nations employees.[115] In 1945 and 1946 a program to register "Indian" traplines was initiated, the intent being to award each family exclusive trapping rights to about 93 square kilometres (the equivalent of one township). The program worked best in the James Bay region, where there was little alternative demand for the land. But it encountered difficulties in the districts of Cochrane, Chapleau, and Nipissing, where negotiating trapping rights proved highly controversial.[116] At about the same time, a very different experiment was initiated when a group of James Bay people were taken to Guelph, Ontario, to work in a tannery.[117] Meanwhile, the anomalous position of the Abitibi people on the Quebec side of the border was addressed with the creation of the Abitibi Agency (in 1940), which encompassed some 155,000 square kilometres between La Tuque and the Ontario border, with a population of 1,500 on twelve reserves. This development occurred three years after a typhoid epidemic in the region had killed "many" people before medical help could be dispatched.[118]

By the 1950s, although the fur market rebounded, it was too late for many First Nations families. They had been forced to turn to alternate means of support. Some struggled to hang on to life on the reserves, while others had begun the process of moving to town in the hope of finding a regular paycheque. Their non-Native neighbours had long since ceased to see them as "exotic"; now they were just another group in the community trying to make a living. But the First Nations never gave up their hope of being recognized as more than "just another ethnic group." The generation that came of age in the 1970s and 1980s would participate in an artistic and cultural renaissance as well as a new round of political activism in defence of their Aboriginal rights.

OTHERS

Although their numbers were much smaller than the groups discussed so far, there were several other ethnic communities in the region that played significant roles in its development. Among them were the Chinese and people from the Balkans (notably Croatia). The Jews, while not an ethnic group,[119] also formed a cohesive and identifiable segment of the population that should be considered.

There were Chinese men in the Porcupine boom camp from its earliest days, providing restaurant and laundry services to the prospectors and to single men in the work crews. By 1916, even before the town was completed, Lee Sing was operating a laundry at Iroquois Falls. The cafés and "lunch clubs" run by the Chinese seem to have been welcome gathering spots for Canadian workers, who did not have the same social opportunities as immigrants who lived with compatriots in boarding houses.[120] Notable among these places was the Canadian Club Café, on Pine South in Timmins, run by Lett Fong for many years. John Chew, who found it difficult to obtain fresh ingredients for his restaurant, purchased land in Mountjoy Township just west of Timmins. By 1918 he had forty acres cleared, and he was raising poultry and more than a hundred and fifty pigs – it was one of the largest such operations of the day.[121] Few other Chinese appear to have taken up homesteads, and hardly any were employed by the mines or at Abitibi in manual labour. The Canadian government all but closed the doors to Chinese immigration between 1923 and 1946, so those who came to the region had nearly all been residents elsewhere in Canada before arriving in northeastern Ontario. Apparently, some came with sufficient means to invest in more than just small-scale businesses. For example, by 1917, W. Wing owned or was a partner in four restaurants in Timmins and South Porcupine.[122] Others came with only their labour to invest. As far as can be determined, however, regardless of economic standing, no women accompanied them. Indeed, most were supporting families who had remained behind in China, and they clearly intended to return home when they could; only as time passed and brought the upheavals of Chiang Kai-shek's government and war with Japan did they become naturalized British citizens.

The rest of the population in the region was very ambivalent about the Chinese, who were mocked in the columns of the local English-language newspaper. In the court of public opinion, they were constantly accused of illegal gambling, drug use, and white slavery, in spite of the fact that genuine court appearances were few and far between. Faced with such hostility, it is hardly surprising that they kept to themselves and generated their own networks for socializing and support. A Chinese grocery on Pine Street South in Timmins provided meals and rooms to unemployed Chinese newcomers until they were able to get established, and a community club was maintained in the basement of a Second Avenue business. In 1937, during the war between China and Japan, the men mobilized and within a few days raised more than a thousand dollars between them to send to Shanghai to help war victims.[123] It was not until the 1950s that families began to join their male relatives in the area, following the upheavals of the communist revolution and the relaxation of Canadian immigration laws.

Another group that came initially as sojourners but eventually stayed were migrant workers from the Balkans. Because the Canadian census and area employers did not always distinguish who was who among this group, it is difficult to be precise about their origins and experiences. Yugoslavs from various regions were employed on TNO railway construction projects in northeastern Ontario, and they later moved into mining and pulpwood cutting, though apparently not into the Abitibi mill itself in any numbers. Like the Italians, they were part of a long-term pattern of migration that saw entire villages in Serbia and Croatia depopulated of their men because the tiny family farms could no longer support the population.[124] The men sent money home, and although most were illiterate, they managed to maintain close contact. Meanwhile, they nursed the fabled Balkan ethnic hostilities in the boarding houses and bush camps. As one mystified Canadian reported, "In unaccountable ways the latest information pertaining to events in Europe seems to reach these men in distant work groups. During the months of threatened hostilities in the Balkans, in 1910–11, the new arrival … was besieged by these eager-eyed men for news from the front. For like all other Jugo-Slavs, they nurse resentments … Even in the hinterland they would attempt to settle rooted differences."[125]

In the mid-1920s a group of Croatians came to Schumacher, possibly recruited by McIntyre Mines. Because they constituted a sizable and focused group, they soon organized social and support networks. The Croatian Club established an orchestra in 1927 which became a big hit at community events; the club also provided support services, such as room and board for one of their number who was ill for two years and unable to work.[126] They arranged visits by such dignitaries as Dr J.K. Krnjevic, a deputy in the Croatian parliament and former Croatian delegate to the League of Nations.[127] Krnjevic made several visits to the Porcupine and was a wildly popular speaker, even among the non-Croatians. The Croatians also built a community hall in Schumacher with a dance floor, a performance stage, dining facilities, and quarters for unemployed Croatians in need of temporary accommodation.[128] Gradually, as with the other groups, more and more women came from home to marry and settle in the area. The sojourners had become settlers.

The Jewish people of the region were utterly different. They did not come from any single part of Europe, they did not live together in a neighbourhood, and they came (from the beginning) accompanied by their families with the intention of staying as long as the natural resources held out. What they did share with one another was a high level of education, a focus on the synagogue, and an occupational segregation: almost all were small business owners and hardly any went to work at the mines or mills.[129] Because of their relative permanence, they had an influence on the region out of proportion to their small numbers. "Sam" Bucovetsky, a Polish-born merchant, parlayed a tiny Cobalt clothing store into a retail chain with branches in Schumacher, South Porcupine, Kapuskasing, Rouyn, and Noranda, as well as the original store in Timmins, which today remains a centrepiece of downtown. Others, like Charles Pierce, invested some of their business proceeds in mining and lumbering ventures and thus helped turn the wheels of the economy in less visible ways. As good business managers, they realized the importance of community networks, so they were not an inward-looking closed circle like some other groups. The men joined everything, from the Kiwanis Club and the Masons to the town councils, while the women organized endless Purim Balls and Hadassah Bazaars, which were attended primarily by those outside the Jewish congregations.[130] Between their long-term residence patterns and their active promotion of good community relations, the Jewish population experienced little overt hostility and clearly became a key part of the stable core of the region during the period covered by this study. It was not until the 1950s that families began to leave, and the synagogue was eventually closed in the 1970s.[131]

Of course, many other groups were represented in the regional population, including Poles, Germans and Austrians, Czechs and Slovaks, Romanians, and Russians. Some, like John Gregulski of Shumacher, were lifelong miners with international experience. Born in 1885 in Saturnia, Poland, he began his career at the age of sixteen in the local coal mines. In his early twenties, he moved on to mines in Germany, then came to Cobalt in 1911, where he worked at the Beaver Mine for ten years. Finally the lure of gold brought him to the Porcupine, where he worked until his death at age fifty-two.[132] Others, like George Speroff of Ansonville, ran businesses that catered in large part to their compatriots. Speroff owned a restaurant with a small rooming house above it, in which three fellow Russians lived during the later years of the First World War.[133] Many of these ethnic groups were too small to provide the formal support systems and cultural organizations enjoyed by the Canadians, Finns, Italians, and Ukrainians, so they made do with what was available and maintained informal social networks. When the Syrian businessman A.G. Shaheen died at Timmins in 1937, having been a resident there since 1914, his funeral was held at St Matthew's Anglican Church, but the rector was assisted by the Reverend Father Zarbatany of the Greek Orthodox Church in Montreal. Tributes at the service were given by the Ayoub, Habib, and Assad families.[134]

For a relatively small population, the Porcupine–Iroquois Falls region had attracted a surprising range of humanity. Indeed, the only group that never really appeared were African Americans, of whom there were just five in 1921 (all in the Timmins-Porcupine region) and none at all by the Second World War. Each sector of the region's economy developed its own mix of nations. Farmer-settlers were almost entirely English-speaking or French-speaking Canadians, with a scattering of Finns. Canadians were well represented at the mines and in pulp and paper production. But the mines were more likely to have Italian and Ukrainian workers, while the Abitibi mill had a larger percentage of French-speaking workers. Chinese, Italians, Ukrainians, and Croatians came initially as migrant workers, while Finns, French Canadians, and Jews came to stay. Just how all of these diverse groups interacted forms the focus of the remainder of this study.

CHAPTER SIX

Work

Plenty of good food, sound sleep in comfortable quarters, good companionship ... Good pay, the kind of life he likes ... a vigorous, healthy life.
Abitibi Power and Paper recruiting advertisement, 1947[1]

Since it was work or the hope of work that brought the mass of outsiders to the region in the early twentieth century, it is hardly surprising that work came to define the basic structure of the new community. What you did at work (or what your husband did) shaped your life in many ways, from the practical nature of daily rhythms to the abstraction of your personal identity. And the aggregate of these personal identities came to form a large part of the community identity. Each of the towns in the region was organized around its own distinct economy, so there were important differences in the nature of the work in each place. But each town did not exist in isolation from the others, because personal contacts, recreational interaction, and economic cross-fertilization created a web of relationships that helped contribute to shared values as well as an awareness of difference. Work was the starting point for much of it.

The mining sector employed the largest number of people, almost all of whom were male. Many outsiders have a perception of mine work as unskilled manual labour, but by the twentieth century, hard-rock mines had become complex industrial organizations that demanded a range of skills and knowledge.[2] Certainly, unskilled labour was required, but many positions were highly specialized. The mines were organized as a hierarchy, both in obvious and subtle ways. In the Porcupine gold mines, the general manager was at the top of the pyramid. In the large mines he was a salaried employee, but he could also be a part owner or member of the board of directors, especially in some of the original small mines. Depending on the size of the operation, he could be assisted by several senior supervisors of various departments, the two largest of which were the underground workings and the mill. Then there were smaller departments that included the accounting or payroll office and the technical division that employed a small number of university-educated geologists

Hollinger Mine, c. 1912. This was the view from the company's Goldfields Hotel. (Henry Peters, LAC, PA29927)

(to identify where the gold-bearing ore could be found) and engineers (to determine how to get at it).

Underground workers considered themselves the aristocracy of the labour force, taking great pride in their skills and productivity. The process of extracting the ore was divided among a range of specialists. First, shafts were blasted down into the ground, and tunnels called drifts were extended outward from the shafts to permit access to the streaks of rock that contained the gold. In order to extract the gold-bearing rock, it had to be blasted out in excavations called stopes. Before the Second World War, heavy piston drills run by compressed air were lowered into place. Then crews drilled into the seams of gold-bearing rock, and others packed the holes with explosives. Diamond drilling was heavy, noisy, and tricky work, since the huge drills were not easily manoeuvred and needed constant maintenance. The crews who set the explosive charges had the most dangerous job of all. If it went well, their efforts produced a pile of rubble that was loaded onto carts and trams to be hauled to the surface. The process of removing the broken ore is known as "mucking," and those who did it were "muckers." Other workers, who specialized in construction and carpentry, were required to build extensive timber bracing to support the walls and ceilings of the network of underground tunnels and the areas where ore had been removed. Later, "cut and fill" mining was adopted in many of the region's mines: waste rock and sometimes sand were used to fill areas no longer required for access. Work went on twenty-four hours a day in three shifts: morning, afternoon, and "graveyard." Each underground crew was supervised and coordinated by a "shift-boss," usually a miner who had been promoted after years of experience.

McIntyre Mine's no. 11 shaft and newly completed concentrator, 1931. Note the large quantity of timber required for underground work. (Ontario, Department of Mines, LAC, PA14412)

Above ground, the headframe housed the mechanical workings of the elevators that provided access underground. Men and materials were hauled up and down in the "cage," while ore was raised separately. Special handling and maintenance skills were required to run the elevator system, so the hoistman held a position of particular responsibility and was among the highest paid workers. Other important surface positions included electricians, pipefitters, and teamsters (to drive the horses that were required for hauling jobs until the 1940s). Above ground, the mines also required a small army of relatively unskilled workers, who cleaned, carried, and fetched as needed. Often young men would begin their mining careers in such jobs.

Work within the mine operations department was tightly organized in a quasi-military chain of command. At Hollinger in 1935, for example, there were about 1,900 employees in that department. It was headed by one development superintendent and two superintendents of ore production. Reporting to them were six mine captains and their assistants. Beneath the mine captains were eight foremen, plus one designated as foreman of underground mechanical operations. Each foreman in turn supervised crews of diamond drillers, muckers, machinists, and their helpers.[3]

The other major department of a gold mine is the mill, where the gold is extracted from the ore and ultimately poured into gold bars. First, the broken rock from underground has to be further pulverized. In the early years, this was done using "stamp mills" in which the ore was simply pounded beneath a heavy weight dropped from a height. Over time, more complex ball crushers (giant rotating drums with steel balls inside to crush the rock) were adopted. Once the ore was sufficiently crushed, the gold had to be extracted. When the Porcupine mines first went into operation, the standard technique to remove the gold from the crushed ore was called "amalgamation." The powdered ore was passed over special plates to which most of the gold would adhere, although some gold would fall and have to be collected below on screens.[4] However, the Porcupine ores did not adhere readily to the amalgamation plates, and because the ore contained a relatively small proportion of gold, tremendous amounts of rock had to be processed in order to get paying quantities of gold.[5] The larger mines hired chemists to experiment with cheaper and more effective processes, and during the First World War era a technique using cyanide was developed to chemically separate the gold. Maurice Williams and E.L. Longmore (who later became mine manager) at Hollinger played a key role in discovering a way to make this process work for local conditions.[6] Thereafter, the mines required knowledgeable machinists for repair and maintenance at the mill, and technicians to prepare and monitor the chemical process. At the end of the milling, the nearly pure gold was poured into gold bricks. The bricks were then shipped to customers, including (eventually) the Canadian Mint. At the mint, some further refining might be done, depending on the purity required.

Far from being merely a resource extraction process requiring only physical labour and producing only raw materials, gold mining in the Porcupine region should be considered an industrial process, in which a relatively finished product was manufactured by a highly structured and specialized workforce. Production required a significant capital investment; unlike the early silver mining at Cobalt, millions of dollars were needed to build the extraction and processing plants. And the unique conditions of the geology necessitated considerable research and experimentation to determine the most effective methods of extracting and refining the ore. Local innovation was crucial. Finally, each worker was a specialist filling a singular niche in the process of production. Although much of the work was hard physical labour, it required particular skill and knowledge.

Like other twentieth-century industrial employees in Canada, most underground and surface workers were paid by the hour or day (rather than for piecework), although in the first years of the Porcupine Camp, some workers were hired under contract. The contract workers usually included teamsters and carpenters or timbermen. Office workers, such as managers, accountants, clerks, geologists, and engineers, were salaried. Wages varied considerably, based on the worker's experience, the price of gold, and the general state of the economy. Mine managers maintained among themselves

Interior, McIntyre Mill, 1936 – technological innovation and sophistication. Archival collections and the books of the day are filled with such images, indicating great pride in the technology. (Ontario, Department of Mines, LAC, PA17526)

an unofficial communication about wages, so there was a fair degree of consistency among the Big Three: Hollinger, Dome, and McIntyre. They also kept themselves informed about mining camps across North America.[7] Within each mine there was a considerable wage range, reflecting the hierarchy of labour. At the McIntyre Mine in the early 1920s, for example, a general helper was paid $3.50 to $4.00 per day, a mucker might get $4.25 to $4.75, and an experienced hoistman $5.00 to $5.50 per day.[8] Based on the work week of the time, monthly pay amounted to between $90 and $140. At that time, McIntyre paid its female stenographer $80 per month. At the other end of the scale, Dome paid its general manager a $5,000 bonus in 1923, in addition to his regular salary, which may have been over $1,000 per month.[9] Through the growth years of the 1930s, wages steadily improved, and by the beginning of the Second World War, Porcupine miners were earning significantly more than many Canadian workers. The pay scale at the Buffalo Ankerite Mine in the late 1930s is shown in table 4. At the time, the average industrial worker in Canada was earning a little over $90 per month,[10] so the area's mining men were comparatively well paid.

Table 4   Mine earnings, 1939

Position	Monthly salary
Mine manager	$1250
Geologist	320
Mine captain	260
Paymaster	230
Chief engineer	225
Shift boss	195
Underground average	120

Source: Compiled from Buffalo Ankerite personnel list, 23 October 1939, in Buffalo Ankerite Papers, LAC, MG28 III 81, vol. 12; and Report of Mineral Production, August 1936, in Buffalo Ankerite Papers, LAC, MG28 III 81, vol. 15

If the wages were good, the same could not be said for the working conditions. Mining was a dangerous affair at the best of times, and the Porcupine mines seem to have been more dangerous than most, particularly in the early years. The first fatality occurred in January 1911, when an experienced miner, Albert Brunet, was killed and Fred Carroll was seriously injured in an explosion at the Norrington works in Deloro Township.[11] By the end of the year, four others were dead, the causes of death being typical of the tragedies that would punctuate the history of the mines. On 27 March a young Polish drill helper named Joseph Knash and a French Canadian drill runner, Fred Dupuis, were killed at Hollinger when an explosion went off prematurely in an untamped drill hole. On 27 October a married 35–year-old drill helper, Otto Nemine, was killed in a rockfall at Dome. A few weeks later, also at Dome, a 56–year-old Canadian labourer, Marvin Sommers, died when he broke his neck in a fall. If a man was not actually killed, he could be very seriously injured. John Karpela had to have both arms amputated when he was "overcome by gas" and fell on a candle at Hollinger in October 1911. J. Glasskowski and Robert Richardson sustained serious head injuries at Dome and McIntyre that year; one was hit by a falling drill and the other fell from a ladder when he was surprised by a burst of gas.[12] In 1912 at least seven men were killed and twelve seriously injured in similar circumstances. As the provincial mining inspector (and later general manager of Dome) J.H. Stovel recalled, the pressure and excitement of building fortunes seemed to overcome safety cautions. "All was 'haste and hurry' in their underground work," he noted, "and, as is nearly always the case in such conditions, some of the work was not too well done. A group of men, slightly younger than I was, were running the show and were apt to look down on inspectors as a nuisance."[13]

Some of these deaths triggered community outrage, and local juries were inclined to lay the blame on corporate indifference or carelessness.

Early in July 1912, the labourer Gilbert Martin was killed at the McIntyre Mine when he fell on an exposed high-tension wire in the electrical transformer house. Public pressure led to a coroner's inquest, in which the jury concluded that "death was due to carelessness on the part of the mining company." But as the newspaper report predicted, the issue seems to have gone no further, "there being no blood relation, so far as we can learn, to sue for possible damages or cause other legal procedure."[14] In September 1915, young Adolph Maurice, who had been married just five weeks, was killed when a loaded ore car at Dome broke away and landed on him. Again, a coroner's inquest was demanded, and again the jury blamed the company, recommending that it change its procedures and provide more rigorous inspections.[15] In 1924 the Ontario minister of mines visited the Porcupine mines and was greeted at Timmins by a delegation from Local 145 of the Western Federation of Miners, who petitioned him for a royal commission to investigate "the cause of large numbers of accidents." The minister dismissively responded "that this could not be entertained."[16]

The larger mines took small steps toward improving workplace safety, such as an initiative at Dome in the mid-1920s to train a group in St John Ambulance first-aid techniques. But it was not until a horrific fire took thirty-nine lives at Hollinger in 1928 that serious attention was finally turned to workplace conditions. It seems that most people believed that underground fires could happen only in coal mines, so when a pile of debris 150 metres underground at Hollinger began to blaze, there was no special equipment, no rescue expertise, and no disaster plan in place to help the miners trapped below. A mine-rescue team with a special breathing apparatus used in coal mine fires was brought in by rail from Pittsburgh, but it arrived too late. Although the fire was eventually extinguished, only a dozen of the trapped men survived, and that was thanks to the quick actions of G. Zoleb, who used a compressed air pipe to supply breathable air and to fend off the flames.[17] Both a coroner's jury and a government commission were established to investigate. The local coroner's jury reported a month later, concluding that the fire had been caused by "gross negligence on the part of Hollinger management," who had permitted the storage of flammable materials underground.[18] The provincial investigative commission, led by T.E. Godson, took rather longer to decide that everyone was to blame: the manager for not knowing what was being done with the garbage, foremen and captains who did not speak enough English to understand the regulations, and miners who should have known the practice was dangerous and reported it.[19] The most important recommendation of the Godson Report was that mine rescue stations be established at Timmins, Kirkland Lake, and Sudbury with standard equipment and trained staff. Undoubtedly, the greater sensitivity to potential problems also helped contribute to a slow decline in the fatality rate through the 1930s. But the scientific management approach to mine safety did not prevent a second large-scale tragedy, in which sixteen men at Paymaster were killed in February 1945.[20] Mine work could be deadly work.

Injury also remained a constant fact of life at the mines. Bones were broken in falls or when men were run over by tramcars. Limbs were lost in premature explosions underground or with exposed conveyor belts in the mills. Severe burns were common in the days of steam-driven machinery. And the heavy physical work took its toll in early deaths from heart attacks. Even supervisory personnel could be at risk. McIntyre Mine's superintendent George Harris had to be sent to Toronto for treatment after the cage in which he was riding snagged on something in the shaft, dislodging a load of steel into his leg.[21] Certainly, some mines had much better safety records than others. In 1941, for example, McIntyre Mine had the lowest accident rate in the district, with one in forty men injured in some way; Aunor Mine had the highest, with an incredible one in six having been injured. At the time, the average provincial mine accident rate indicated that one in every sixteen miners in Ontario had received an injury; twelve of the Porcupine area mines were above the provincial average and only two (McIntyre and Hollinger) were below it.[22]

The other major hazard of gold mining was less visible, more insidious, and much more controversial. The Porcupine gold is found in quartz, and when quartz is drilled and crushed, its fine particles collect in miners' lungs and cause a potentially fatal disease called silicosis. When the Porcupine mines were being developed, the exact nature of the problem was not understood locally, but miners in the western United States were well acquainted with it, where it was called "miner's consumption" or "miner's asthma."[23] By the 1920s, Porcupine miners were also suffering from the complaint and demanding help. In 1925 the Ontario Department of Health checked about two hundred of the area's miners and found thirty cases of silicosis complicated by tuberculosis, forty-five straightforward cases of silicosis, and an additional forty-seven cases with "suspicious signs."[24] The findings indicated that the disease tended to kill its victims an average of two years after diagnosis, and at the average age of forty-three.[25] Armed with such information, in 1926 the Ontario government placed silicosis under the Workmen's Compensation Act so that sufferers could receive sanatorium treatment. Two years later, the Ontario Mining Act was amended to make annual x-rays compulsory and to require all new employees to take a physical examination. Then, in 1934, the Ontario Mining Association established a committee to research silicosis and provided funds to the Banting Institute at the University of Toronto to encourage work that Dr Frederick Banting had been doing on the problem for some years.[26] Just two years

later, the McIntyre Mine metallurgist James J. Denny, working with Dr
W.D. Robson of the Banting Institute, discovered that powdered aluminum reacted with quartz particles and prevented the body from
absorbing them. After clinical trials at the Timmins hospital, in 1943
McIntyre began adding aluminum powder to the air in its shower and
change-room facilities. Shortly afterwards, it claimed to have almost eliminated silicosis,[27] though aluminum continued to be used until the
1970s. Better methods of dust control and underground ventilation were
also introduced. (Today, of course, one gasps at the thought of whether
breathing quartz or aluminum was the more hazardous.)

For many miners, however, the second-worst problem to actually contracting silicosis was getting treatment and financial assistance. The disease
causes fibrous nodules to form in the lungs, so it is easily confused with
such diseases as tuberculosis, and indeed silicosis can often be complicated
by a secondary onset of tuberculosis or pneumonia. Because the mine
managers agreed to deal with silicosis (as a workplace hazard) but not the
other diseases, there were frequently differences of opinion over diagnosis. In 1936 the Timmins Town Council was asked for assistance by a man
who had worked at Hollinger for seven years, was diagnosed by his doctor
as having silicosis, but was turned down for compensation by a company
doctor who concluded that the man actually had TB. Timmins mayor J.P.
Bartleman was irate. "'This is another case in which they call it silicosis
until it comes up for compensation; then they call it tuberculosis,' said the
mayor. 'What are we going to do about it?'"[28] Others found the compensation insufficient. For instance, George Couture of Timmins was paid
$500 on his release from Hollinger but spent nearly half of it to pay his bill
at the Haileybury Sanatorium and was forced to sell his home and apply
for relief in order to feed his family.[29] Still others were offered a place at
the sanatorium but would not go because it meant leaving family and
friends behind. John Rowlandson, the member of the Ontario legislature
for the district, lobbied to have some abandoned educational buildings at
Monteith turned into a sanatorium closer to home, but the plan came to
nothing.[30] Miners continued to contract silicosis, and problems in treating
it persisted. "There is intense bitterness and resentment amongst the
miners in regard to silicosis," reported the area's MPP W.J. Grummett, in
1948. "You never hear so many complaints about other forms of compensation, but you certainly do about silicosis."[31]

Even if a man was fortunate enough to escape injury or illness,
working conditions underground were unpleasant at best. A Toronto
visitor to the Paymaster Mine in the 1930s recorded, "What an experience that was! We had to sign that they would not be responsible to what
might happen to us. There was running water on all sides of the small
skip that took us down. The rock drills made a deafening noise. You

wouldn't know your best friend [in the dark and dirt]. Took me a long time to get over it."[32]

The constant threat of danger at work clearly shaped people's lives. Many men dealt with it by developing a habit of masculine braggadocio, celebrating their courageous ability to face and conquer death at every shift. Office workers and surface handymen were looked down upon; the "real" work was done by the muckers and others underground. Inspectors allegedly knew nothing of that real work, and their visits served only to interfere with a man's ability to make the best living as quickly as possible. A man might be at the bottom of a semi-military chain of command, but it was he alone who faced the dangers, so he deserved respect as an individual equal to any and better than some. The work might be demanding, dangerous, and dirty, but men took great pride in their ability to do it well. This was not the alienated industrial labour force of neo-Marxist theory.[33]

Women dealt with the threats very differently, as historian Nancy Forestell has explored. At home, miners' wives and mothers worried silently and listened anxiously for an unscheduled siren or a dreaded diagnosis. They rallied to do what they could for a new widow or helped with the funeral of a man who had died alone and far from home.[34] And some took an active role in local union activities in an attempt to protect their men from injury in the first place. Perhaps many others, both men and women, preferred to put the dangers out of their minds, as Bill Williamson found in his study of work in a Victorian English coal mine. "All that could be done was to trust to luck," his contacts told him. "The busy-ness of daily routines has a soporific effect: to be occupied is a way of avoiding contemplating the unthinkable."[35] Nevertheless, awareness of very real dangers always lurked and had an effect on how both men and women saw themselves.

Another important feature of mine work was the tendency to ethnic segregation in particular jobs or departments. As a 1917 royal commission on natural resources reported, "For common labour and shovellers, Italians and Russians are mostly employed; underground drilling is mostly done by Finlanders, Swedes, and Austrian Poles. Canadians, Irish and Scotch are employed as mechanics, woodworkers in the mills, and for other surface operations, while the engineer's staffs are practically all Canadian."[36] These patterns remained remarkably consistent throughout the period studied in this book.

The men who worked in the Porcupine mines were certainly a diverse group – ethnically, linguistically, and in terms of religion and job skills. However, they all tended to be relatively young (in the period before 1950) and mobile, with experience in mines across North America and sometimes in Europe and Africa as well. For example, Hollinger employee Len Bound was born in London, England, and emigrated to

work underground at mines in Iowa and Utah. He enlisted in the British
army in 1917 and was posted to Canada as an instructor. After his dis-
charge in British Columbia, he went to Cobalt and then to the Porcupine
in 1922, where he remained at Hollinger until his retirement in 1952,
rising through the ranks to become a mine captain.[37] The Nova Scotian
George Doane mined in South Africa, South America, and Yukon before
arriving at the Porcupine in the mid-1920s to work underground at
Hollinger and then as shift boss at Dome.[38] There was also some occupational mobility in and out of mining among men who had portable skills.
John C. Draves had operated heavy machinery in a sawmill, on road construction (driving a bulldozer), and on prairie harvest gangs before
joining the Ross Mine at Holtyre (near Matheson) in 1938.[39] Scottish-
born Robert Sims was a machinist who began his working life in a factory
in Sherbrooke, Quebec, then worked for the Quebec Central Railway, and
later prospected at Cobalt and the Porcupine. When he failed to make
any significant finds, he hired on with Hollinger and then with two other
mines in the area. After a few years he returned to factory work, moving
to Connecticut. Seven years later, he took a job in an American pulp and
paper plant. When he died at the age of sixty-six in 1938, he had family
scattered across California, Connecticut, Quebec's Eastern Townships,
and southeastern Ontario.[40]

Mining work might be only one stage in a lifetime of work options.
George Vartinuik, who was born in Romania, came to Canada in 1912 and
found work in Montreal at the Canada Car and Foundry Company. In
1917 he headed west to try his hand at farming, but after three years he
decided to try mining and hired on at Hollinger. Six years later, he decided
to go into business for himself and opened a grocery store. After three
years as a grocer, he went into the hotel business where he finally settled
down. He served for a time as secretary of the Cochrane District Hotel-
man's Association. In 1938 he branched out into the business of manufacturing soft drinks in Timmins.[41]

Technical and professional workers had similarly mobile careers. M.B.
Scott, who retired as Hollinger's chief chemist in 1952, had been born and
educated in Scotland but had his first job in Italy at Tenuta Etruscan
Mines. He emigrated to Canada in 1910 and worked in a number of positions before joining Hollinger in 1915 to work on developing a new refinery process. In 1942 he was promoted to run the mine's laboratory and
assay office. Then there was E.L. Longmore, who served as Hollinger's
general manager 1946–53. He was born near Kingston, Ontario, and
graduated from Queen's University in mining and metallurgy in 1912,
having paid his way through school as a prairie schoolteacher, as a lay minister at Matheson, and as a surveyor in British Columbia. After graduation,
he worked briefly at an Ontario mine and then returned to Queen's for

research work before joining Hollinger as a helper in the assay office. During the Second World War he left Hollinger to serve as general manager of the Wartime Metals Corporation, a crown corporation formed to coordinate mine production for the Department of Munitions and Supply. After the war he returned to Hollinger to be general manager.[42]

Longmore was unusual among the senior managers because he had risen through the ranks locally and had no international experience. More typical was the second Hollinger general manager, Percy A. Robbins (1911–18). Born in Chicago and educated as a mechanical engineer at Cornell University, he had his first job in Philadelphia. In 1896 he moved to South Africa, where he worked for a number of mining companies in the Transvaal and then in Durban for the General Electric Company, before returning to mining with De Beers (while acting as an examiner of engineering students at the University of Cape of Good Hope). In 1907 he returned to the United States to work as a consulting engineer in New York. Then he moved to Cobalt as general manager of the McKinley-Darragh Mine before the Timmins brothers brought him to Hollinger as general manager. He left in 1918, intending to take up a private consulting practice in Toronto, but instead he enlisted with the U.S. Army Corps of Engineers when his native land entered the First World War. After the war, he returned to mining in the United States. At the time of his death in 1938, he was president of a placer mining and exploration company operating in Alaska.[43]

At the top of the mining hierarchy were the "owners," many of whom either lived in the region or were such regular visitors that their presence was well known and carefully watched. Strictly speaking, few of these men were owners; rather, they were presidents of the boards of directors, because the larger mines all offered stocks for sale on public exchanges. But locally, these men were looked upon as the money and power behind the work. Louis Henry Timmins and his brother Noah lived in Haileybury until the late 1920s, when both moved to much grander houses in Westmount, Quebec; but Noah's brother-in-law J.B. Paré and Paré's son Alphonse were residents of Timmins for a time. Louis Henry Timmins does not appear to have been well remembered in the Porcupine, but Noah regularly attended company banquets, local hockey games, and mass at St Antoine Roman Catholic Church. On the occasion of the twenty-fifth anniversary of Father Thériault's ordination, Noah Timmins came to town and gave an afterdinner speech (in French) in which he reminisced about their shared experiences of early "camp" days.[44] Colonel Alexander Marshall Hay, president of McIntyre Mines from 1915 to his death in 1917, was also a resident of Haileybury (having, like the Timmins brothers, first made his name in the Cobalt rush) and was a regular visitor to town. Frederick Schumacher lived in grand style in Columbus, Ohio, and seldom visited the Porcupine Camp, but he was as well known as any permanent resident through his largesse to the community, which included the donation of an organ to Trinity United Church.[45] Only the presidents of Dome and Buffalo-Ankerite (among the larger mines) do not appear to have had much of a local profile.

After mining, the next largest employer in the region was Abitibi's pulp and paper mill at Iroquois Falls. Partial production began in the summer of 1914, and by the boom years of the mid-1920s, more than a thousand men were employed each day, producing 508,000 kilograms of newsprint, 178,000 kilograms of ground pulp, and 46,000 kilograms of sulphite pulp (a pulp with longer fibres that adds strength to newsprint).[46] The plant operated twenty-four hours a day and sent much of its paper to the expanding American newsprint market; the largest customer for many years was the Chicago *Tribune*.[47] Logs from bush-cutting operations were stockpiled, then fed into huge revolving drums that removed the bark. The peeled logs were pulverized in the groundwood mill to separate the fibres. Some of this material went to the sulphite mill, where it was "cooked" in a pressurized acid solution that produced a longer fibre for stronger paper. The mechanically produced pulp and the chemically produced pulp were then blended together, water was added, and the mass was spread on moving screens, dried, and pressed to produce a continuous wide strip of newsprint that was rolled into enormous cylinders. Nothing was wasted; the bits of paper that came off in the process (called "brokes") were gathered up and recycled into the wet pulp mix. The process remains much the same today, though some wood is now received as wood chips and the plant produces specialty paper in addition to newsprint.[48]

The process of producing pulp and paper required a significant capital investment, a skilled labour force, and ongoing research into the required chemistry and engineering. Thus, like a gold mine, the pulp and paper mill was a highly structured industrial workplace that produced a relatively finished product. It was organized into departments around the different stages of the process, and by the 1920s the Abitibi plant also had a research division to develop better paper and processing techniques adapted to local conditions, and a nursery to grow seedlings for reforestation projects. The job opportunities ranged from straightforward manual labour to research positions that required university degrees. The plant could offer a man a lifetime of promotions. He might begin as a youth at the bottom rung as a "broke hustler," gathering the bits of paper that came loose from the processing screens. Then he might learn the skills of a machinist or papermaker, and eventually he might supervise a crew or even a department, although rarely did anyone move from such a career to the position of general manager. As in mining, occupational mobility had its limits.

Most of the workers who came to the Abitibi plant in its early years appear to have had experience in paper manufacturing, often in New England. John Stillman Foley, for example, had been born in Nova Scotia but worked for thirty years at a paper plant in Rumford, Maine, before bringing his family to Iroquois Falls in 1923.[49] Office manager S.G. McCoubrey grew up in a paper-mill town near Belfast in Northern Ireland, and Frank K. Ebbitt had worked for the Ottawa Valley timberman J.R. Booth before joining Abitibi in 1913.[50] Technical and professional employees could be just as mobile as their peers in mining, with an international circle of connections. Engineer A.T. Hunter, for example, was born in England, educated in Switzerland, began his career in England, and then spent three years in the Balkans until a financial crisis there encouraged him to emigrate to North America. He worked at paper mills in Quebec and Newfoundland, then joined a firm in New York State, before coming to Abitibi in 1929.[51] H.G. Schancke Jr, an engineer who became manager of Abitibi's Forestry Division in 1919, had been educated at Pennsylvania State College and worked in paper mills in Quebec and the central United States before coming to Iroquois Falls.[52]

Typical of the career paths of senior management was that of R.A. ("Bob") McInnis. Born in Gravenhurst, Ontario, about 1884, he went to work at the age of sixteen in the sales division of an international forest products company. In 1914 he joined Abitibi as a managerial assistant in the Montreal head office, and in 1917 he was assigned to the new Iroquois Falls plant as general manager, in which capacity he served for a decade before moving on to another pulp and paper firm. While at Iroquois Falls, he played an active role promoting Northern Ontario, including doing a stint as president of the Northern Ontario Board of Trade and then serving as vice-president of the provincial association. Forestry ran in his family. An uncle, Colin C. McInnis, had been a depot manager for timber baron J.R. Booth in the district north of Sudbury.[53]

The pulp and paper industry was also like gold mining in that company "owners" were a visible presence in the community for most of the period before the Second World War. Although Frank Harris Anson never lived in Iroquois Falls, he visited frequently, and his mother (Mrs A.H. Anson) had a house in town for three years before her death in 1925. As the company newspaper reported sentimentally, "The mill and the town were a constant reminder of the great work done by her son." Anson's son Frank H. Jr ("Fritz") was a fixture at the mill, for he was groomed to take over his father's role. Frank Jr arrived in January 1913, worked at a number of odd jobs, then joined the engineering department briefly before being put in charge of assembling machinery in the grinding mill. Eventually (in 1925) he was promoted to assistant manager. He married and raised a family at Iroquois Falls.[54]

While both the mines and the paper mills required skilled labour, the mines could draw on men from a wider range of experiences. A man could learn to handle explosives while working on a railway construction crew, for example, or learn how to maintain machines in a southern factory. Some skills were unique to papermaking, however, so the area mills had a narrower base on which they could draw. One of the reasons why French-speaking Canadians so dominated the papermaking trades[55] was that many came from Quebec regions where mills were already established. They were able to make a place for themselves in the early years of production in northeastern Ontario and to maintain a sort of "chain hiring" process from among friends and relatives still in Quebec.

Work in the paper mills was far less hazardous than work in the mines, but injuries and fatalities did occur. The worst accidents occurred on the dam across the Abitibi River at Iroquois Falls, rather than in the plant. Two men died on the dam while it was under construction in the spring of 1914, and four men died trying to repair it in February 1920. Both times, the victims drowned when water breached supposedly secure gates and dragged them downstream in a roar of whitewater.[56] Accidents in the mill itself were less likely to be deadly but nonetheless remained a fact of life.

Wages at the Abitibi plant fluctuated considerably over the period in question. During the boom of the 1920s, they compared favourably with mining wages, perhaps because they had to compete within a similar labour pool. During those good years, general labourers could earn from $3.20 to $4.30 per day while skilled mechanics might earn $5.76 to $7.28.[57] After the company went into receivership, the workforce was cut in half and wages dropped almost as dramatically. For a number of years during the 1930s, since work was available only part time, people who remained on the payroll found themselves in serious difficulty. Reports of scurvy and malnutrition among their families began to surface. When times were good, they were very, very good, but when times were bad, they were horrific.

Abitibi was not the only producer of pulp and paper in the region, but it was the only one to survive the Depression. The Mattagami Pulp and Paper Company ran a mill at Smooth Rock Falls on the Mattagami River from 1916 to 1927, when it sold the plant to Abitibi;[58] it ran its bush-cutting operations (which employed up to seven hundred men per season) out of a base at Timmins.[59] T.S. Woolings built a pulp mill on the Frederick House River near Connaught in 1921.[60] The Monteith Pulp and Timber Company built a small facility at Monteith during the First World War; it was leased for a time by the Fesserton Lumber Company (primarily for its sawmill) and was then taken over by the entrepreneur A.E. Wicks. The site included a dam on the Driftwood River, a boarding house, a store, and employee "cottages."[61]

These pulp and paper companies obtained some of their wood from individual suppliers such as farmer-settlers who were clearing their land, but most came through the process of contracting out. The Ontario government issued licences that gave companies the exclusive right to cut particular species of trees on a defined area of crown land. Each season, contractors bid for the right to cut the wood in specific zones of these "pulpwood limits." Temporary bush camps were built to house and feed the workers over the winter months, when most of the cutting was done. For example, over the winter of 1933–34, Abitibi contracted with four men to run five camps that would supply its Smooth Rock Falls mill: J.B. Gibson (two camps), A. Girard, R. Turpin, and L. Silver.[62] These camps employed a great many horses, which consumed considerable amounts of hay, so sometime in the 1920s Abitibi established its own farm on the Abitibi River below the Iroquois Falls townsite. There, it raised hay to feed the bush teams and also (by the mid-1930s) raised dairy cattle to supply milk to the town.[63]

Work in the pulpwood bush camps differed in several significant ways from work in the mines and mills. First, it was seasonal, so unions were less effective. Second, men were paid for what they produced rather than receiving a fixed wage. Although the work was supervised, each cutter was, in a sense, an individual entrepreneur. The men generally supplied their own tools, such as the prized "swede" saw. Finally, the bush camps offered employment for women as cooks and laundresses. Many people have the mistaken impression that the bush camp was an exclusive male world, but in a surprising number of cases there were working single women or women and children accompanying their husbands, particularly in the camps run by Finns.

There was considerable variation in the size and quality of these camps. Some of the smaller ones run by less scrupulous "jobbers" (contractors) still resembled their nineteenth-century counterparts, with hastily erected log cabins for shelter and poor (or non-existent) sanitation facilities. But after the First World War, many of the camps in northeastern Ontario were much more modern and even comfortable. This was especially the case in those that were run by men who contracted regularly for Abitibi, as well as in the handful of camps that Abitibi ran directly. One Abitibi camp near Iroquois Falls in the mid-1920s consisted of a two-storey "sleep camp" of solid frame construction with tarpaper exterior, a cookery, a stable and blacksmith shop, a storehouse, an office, and the "jobber's shack," where the contractor lived apart from the men. The camp had electricity and employed seventy-five men, plus a camp staff that probably included a clerk (who ordered supplies and kept accounts), a cook (and the cook's assistants), a man to take care of the horses and barn, possibly a blacksmith, and a crew foreman. Half of the workers here were French-speaking Canadians, 20 percent were "Slavs," 15 percent were Finns, 10 percent were English-speaking Canadians, and a handful were from the British Isles.[64]

Workmen, 1930. An instructor at Frontier College took this
photo of two of his students. Identified only as Yugoslavian
employees of Abitibi, the two men are nameless "types,"
presented for the edification of "real" Canadians. (LAC,
c64844)

Bushworkers were among the most poorly paid of the region's workforce and they worked long hard hours for what they got. Six days a week,
at the first morning light, they trudged out through the snow for up to
three kilometres to their assigned "work strips," and where they worked
until dark, felling the spruce and jack pine. After the trees were cut, the
logs were trimmed into sixteen-foot lengths (just under five metres), then
piled for collection. A strong, experienced cutter might manage a
hundred of these logs per day, earning him $3 or $4; newcomers could get

much less. The value of the logs depended on their size, and there was always a dispute with the scalers who measured them to determine what the logger would get. A handful of men worked under contract for $30 to $45 per month.[65] The men who managed the dangerous work of driving the logs down the rivers in spring were earning about $2.60 per day by the late 1930s.[66]

If male bushworkers were paid less in comparison to men working at the mines or in the mills, women who worked at the bush camps, particularly as cooks, found themselves earning very good money in comparison to what was available elsewhere. In the early 1920s a cook could earn $45 to $60 per month.[67] Certainly, the hours were long and the work demanding, but those who did it seem to have found it very satisfying. Elsa Silanpää arrived in Northern Ontario as a teenager in 1926 and began as a cook's assistant in a Finnish-run camp. She became a full-fledged cook and worked her way from season to season into increasingly large camps with greater responsibilities. She married a bushworker whom she met along the way, and she raised her children to school age in the camps. She liked the work because it was "clean" and well paid; furthermore, it was easy to save her wages because there was little to spend them on in camp.[68]

At each bush camp, the cut and trimmed logs were picked up by a small army of men with teams of horses (the teamsters), who hauled the logs through the snow to a central collection point. One Abitibi camp required twenty teams to transport the 60,000 cords cut by its men.[69] The Mattagami Pulp and Paper Company cut logs upstream from its Mattagami River plant, so it was able to use the river to float the logs to processing in the spring, following the time-honoured tradition. However, much of Abitibi's pulpwood limits were *downstream* from the Iroquois Falls mill (which had been situated for its proximity to electrical power generation capacity), so the river could not be used. Instead, the company built a railway line in 1922 to connect its pulpwood limits to Iroquois Falls so that the logs could be carried directly to the mill on train cars. Of course, not all of Abitibi's wood came from downstream. For some years, the company maintained an office at Matheson under Frank K. Ebbitt to manage the big annual log drive down the Driftwood River. At the end of each season, Shillington (then called Driftwood City) became a temporary city, where the cutters and drivers celebrated their year's work.[70]

Because bush work was seasonal and the earnings low, it was not possible for anyone to support a family entirely from it. Thus, bush work became just one component of family survival strategies, particularly among Finnish and French-speaking Canadian farmer-settlers. While the men went off to camp in the winter, the women stayed behind to manage the farms. The cash income was crucial for buying seed or buying hay for animal feed, as well as for such necessities as food and clothing. Not all bushworkers were from farm families, however. Some came from families who lived in town. A small army of men moved constantly within the region from summer mine work to winter bush work to road-construction jobs when they were available. These, of course, tended to be young men just getting started in the work world, or they were men with limited technical skills. Because of their job transiency, it is difficult to track their specific numbers or personal stories. In 1921 one report noted that of 1,275 men in bush work around Timmins that year, 105 had families living in Timmins, but the writer had no idea where the remainder lived when they were not working in the bush.[71]

Working life on the farm was clearly a struggle. The marginal soil, the extremely short growing season, and a climate that produced little rain in the spring when it was needed and plenty in the fall when it was not, meant that even if markets had been available, sustainable commercial agriculture was not feasible, regardless of the wild claims of government promoters. Thus, most farms were at best subsistence affairs. People struggled to clear the land and build setters' "shacks" with little or no road access. They then planted mostly potatoes for their own use, and hay – the one cash crop as long as large numbers of horses were still employed in the mines and bush camps. Few farmers could afford to hire help, so everyone in the family was put to work. Not surprisingly, lands were abandoned almost as quickly as they were taken up. Between 1913 and 1931, over 1.5 million acres of Clay Belt lands were "located" as homesteads, but by 1931 only 6.5 percent of those lands had actually been cleared, and an even smaller percentage was in crop.[72] In the Matheson area in 1922, there were only three farms with enough land cleared to be even potentially self-supporting.[73] The life of these farms was artificially extended in the 1930s when many families collected relief in order to feed themselves. As the relief commissioner recorded early in 1936, "The settlers in this District are having a great difficulty eking out a mere existence ... Only those who have lived in the North can really appreciate the magnitude of these problems."[74] Indeed, the following spring, little Lillian Leduc of Stock Township died of malnutrition because her mother was so badly nourished herself that she was unable to nurse baby Lillian. The coroner's jury at Ansonville recommended that "a thorough investigation be made of this family's living conditions, as well as that of the other relief recipients in this district."[75]

Few settlers recorded their experiences, but glimpses of the life may be seen in a report written by a homesteader near Cochrane, which was passed along to Alfred Fitzpatrick of Frontier College in the late 1920s. It is worth quoting at length:

Now I have manuvred in all parts of the world but how I am fixed now would make a dog squeal. Let me acquaint you with my deplorable position ... I began operations on Lot 9, Concession 13, with $45.00. I paid cash for lumber and vegetables and fought the H. lake [Hawk Lake Lumber Co.] like a million dollar man but they got a [pulpwood] contract out of me for 85¢ stumpage because I did not know better ... I built my first camp and had left in the bank $15.00. I lived on rice, beans, pancakes and spuds and a concoction called tea. I got credit from H.L. slept on bags but later bought blankets. Put out a little Socialistic speeches, captured two men, put them to work with a promise ... I guess I can go on the roads now as a tramp ... I do not want to lose the horses but they must eat as well as me and I don't want to hire them out for their board either.[76]

Hungry, cold, ill-fed, and in debt, those disillusioned settlers who could afford to move eventually left. There was a major exodus from the Matheson area after the fire of 1916, and another more gradual emigration during the 1930s as people abandoned hope at last.

A handful of farmers persisted. The French-speaking settlers around Val Gagné managed better than most, perhaps because they had experience in marginal farming and also because the close community with its focus on the church helped sustain them emotionally. They may have organized through the parish such arrangements as the Cercle agricole, which would purchase equipment that could then be shared by all members.[77] Several farms west of Timmins in Mountjoy Township and east near Porcupine Lake were able to take advantage of the local urban market, in spite of setbacks such as the 1934 epidemic of "hog cholera," which necessitated the slaughter of the entire hog population.[78] Some were small operations, such as that of the Barr brothers who raised strawberries in Mountjoy in the 1920s. The largest two were the closest the region came to "agribusiness." Lawyer Gordon Gauthier, a resident of the Porcupine region from 1910, invested in land near Porcupine and had some 200 acres producing potatoes and oats, the latter harvested with the region's first threshing machine in 1917.[79] The Dalton brothers, John and Charles, who came from a farm near Goderich, Ontario, arrived in 1911 with horses to provide transportation around the camp. John purchased land in Mountjoy Township to raise hay for the horses, and the family eventually became suppliers of horses and hay to the mines. Then, as times changed, they opened a motor taxi business and turned the farm into a popular harness-racing track.[80]

Most others who stayed on their farms were far less successful, and one wonders if some stayed simply because they could not afford to leave. In a study of French-speaking Canadian migrants who came to the Hearst area between 1916 and 1930 (and were still there in 1985), Roger Bernard discovered that almost 79 percent had come in the first place with no money whatsoever, and another 12 percent had less than $250 worth of personal possessions and cash.[81] These were very poor people indeed, and their marginal farms could scarcely improve their material condition or even provide them with sufficient capital to get established elsewhere. Others may have stayed on because, although the life was hard, it did offer certain compensations. As one settler recalled of farm life in the Abitibi region in the 1940s, earnings were "plus que modeste," but "it was pleasant all the same to live in the beauty of nature, to lead a healthy life, to enjoy the tastiest and freshest of foods. Country life inspires serenity, in work free from unnecessary noise."[82] This settler took considerable pride in his knowledge (born of necessity) of so many job skills, entitling his book of memoirs *L'homme aux 56 métiers.*

This flexibility and resourcefulness is illustrated by the career of Noah Taillefer. Noah's parents had worked in bush camps in Quebec and the United States before moving to North Bay where he was born in 1889. At the age of sixteen he got a job as a labourer with the TNO. After about seven years, he married Dora Demers from Hull, Quebec, and took a job cutting logs in the burned-over area between Val Gagné (Nushka) and the Porcupine Camp. During the course of their married life, Dora raised their twelve children on the farm at Val Gagné while Noah took work where he could find it. He helped on the farm, worked as a miner at Preston East Dome, spent time with a firm that raised horses to supply the mines, and put in a stint as a prison guard.[83] Occupational flexibility was a key survival strategy. The availability of wild resources also helped. Hamer Disher, who arrived at Matheson in 1919, recalled, "If it hadn't been for moose and pike and pickerel, we'd have seen some pretty rough times." He remembered the need to snare rabbits to eat when nothing else was available, and sharing moose meat with neighbours.[84]

Through the 1930s, the district's agricultural representative D.J. Pomerleau made heroic efforts to find crops suitable for the conditions and to encourage local markets. The town of Timmins sponsored a farmers' market for a number of years. But everyone was facing an uphill battle as the availability of alternative employment drew people off the farms. Most of those who remained clearly lived in poverty – though, incredibly, they were still able to laugh at their plight. One Cochrane district joke was that the Department of Agriculture had challenged northerners to breed a potato that grew its own overcoat – ordinary jackets were quite inadequate![85] But agriculture could never be anything but a marginal part of the area's economy – a source of work but not of income.

If the mines and mills never came to depend on a local food supply as government promoters had hoped, they did require another local resource: lumber. While most of the region is forested with trees suitable only for pulp production, some stands of large pine were found in the more southerly townships, particularly along the Mattagami River, and the mines had a voracious appetite for timbers. In the early years, of course, lumber was needed for construction of above-ground facilities. Then, as mining proceeded, timbers were needed to support the ceilings of underground tunnels, to serve as ties in the network of underground cart tracks, and for repairs to buildings under constant wear from heavy industrial use. The TNO also was in need of a seemingly endless supply of ties. Local entrepreneurs rushed to meet the demand, and eventually three main companies emerged: the Feldman Timber Company, the Fesserton Lumber Company, and Rudolph-McChesney's. By 1938 they collectively employed about three hundred men in their mills at Timmins and Schumacher. These were sizable, family-run operations. The Feldmans (father Michael and sons Abraham, Alexander, Samuel, and Louis) had emigrated from Russia to Englehart in 1907 and came to the Porcupine in 1910 to provide transportation services that brought construction materials into the camp. They eventually built a large mill on the Mattagami River to produce lumber themselves. They and their families became active members of the Jewish congregation in Timmins, and the Feldman Lumber retail outlet remains a fixture on the highway between Schumacher and Timmins.[86] Other companies that operated from time to time in the area included the Hawk Lake Lumber Company at Monteith (one of the Finnish immigrant A.E. Wicks's enterprises), the Mountjoy Timber Company (a subsidiary of Hollinger that supplied most of the timber used in the mine's construction), and, at Connaught, the St Maurice Lumber Company and T.S. Woolings Company, both of which operated for a relatively short time.

The lumber companies, like the paper companies, obtained timber limits and let out contracts for the bush camps where the logs were cut. However, conditions in these camps were notoriously bad in comparison with the pulp-cutting camps. In 1934 the area's member of parliament, J.A. Bradette, observed in the House of Commons, "Talk of sweatshops and of people being underpaid!" He had visited some camps in the region and noted that while some were well run, "in certain camps a human being should not be allowed to live much less sleep. There seemed to be no attempt at cleanliness, in fact, filthiness seemed to reign supreme."[87] It seems that the smaller companies, as marginally profitable undertakings, attempted to cut corners wherever possible. Certainly, wages in the lumber business were low, even lower than for pulpwood cutters and paper mill workers. In the late 1930s, sawmill workers in the Timmins area were earning about $2.20 per day, compared with a mine mucker's $4.64 or an Abitibi mechanic's $4.32.[88]

Another way of earning income in the natural resource sector of the economy was by trapping. Paradoxically, the settlement and mining boom initially improved the situation for trappers. In 1913 the Cobalt *Daily Nugget* noted that the fur trade in the Cochrane district was one of the best in many years, for some twenty-five buyers had been attracted by the publicity given to northern development and were paying high prices in competition with the Hudson's Bay Company.[89] In fact, trappers had been enjoying a measure of strong competition among fur buyers since 1904. That year, the French fashion furrier Revillon Frères had opened its first posts on James Bay to buy directly from trappers for its clothing business. By the First World War, it was operating at Fort George, East Main, Rupert House, Moose, and Albany, with a network of smaller inland posts, including a store in the Porcupine Camp for a brief period during the rush and a post at Abitibi built within hailing distance of the HBC.[90] As mentioned in the previous chapter, although the HBC had closed its more southerly posts, it continued to operate posts at Abitibi, Matachewan, Mattagami, and Flying Post, in addition to the new post at Biscotasing on the CPR line; and since construction of the railway, much of the business had been conducted on a cash basis.

The First World War was a major disruption to the fur trade, but it rebounded in the 1920s as demand and prices rose. Unfortunately for First Nations trappers, the boom was a double-edged sword. Non-Natives began to trap in the region, attracted by the relatively easy access. These non-Natives paid no attention to the trapline territories that had long been recognized by Native families. As was happening throughout northern Canada, they saw the work as a temporary get-rich scheme rather than as a long-term sustainable harvest. There were even reports of some non-Native trappers threatening the Natives off their lands. Dr J.J. Wall of the Department of Indian Affairs reported that along the National Transcontinental railway line east of Cochrane, "Some of these white trappers have even gone to the length of poisoning the Indians' dogs, and each year it becomes harder for the Indians to obtain a living."[91] Aboriginal trappers throughout the district, like those across the rest of the Canadian North, saw a significant decline in their trapping income through the 1920s. Meanwhile, fur prices were rising, as were the incomes of non-Native trappers.

These non-Native trappers were more than just a challenge to trapping income. They represented a threat to the survival of a people, because they often used strychnine instead of traps, and the poison killed everything that sampled it, including species important as food. Native trappers were not prepared to sit idly by as their economy was destroyed. They called repeatedly on the government to address the problem. Chief John Fletcher at Moose Factory wrote to the Department of Indian Affairs in 1927: "There are six white men who came in on my hunting ground and left nothing but devastation through the use of strychnine and other drugs, in ruining practically all the fur-bearing animals in my territory." Another group at New Post wanted to know if these men had permits to trap, and what the government intended to do to protect Native livelihoods.[92] Tragically, the answer was nothing, other than occasional fines for illegal possession of furs out of season.

Problems continued for Native trappers when the Depression hit the trade hard, affecting everyone. The HBC district office at North Bay was moved to Winnipeg in 1930 to consolidate operations. The following year, when the TNO line was extended to Moose Factory, the HBC incurred a major loss, for it was forced to sell its stock (imported at sea-shipping costs) for the new, lower, railway-import prices. The historic post at Mattagami was phased out because the First Nations traders there preferred to go to Gogama on the railway's main line where groceries were cheap and plentiful.[93] In 1936 a struggling Revillon Frères was taken over by the HBC and its Northern Ontario posts closed. As both demand and prices fell, non-Native trappers lost interest. Only a handful made periodic forays into the bush; many of them seem to have been struggling French Canadian farmers who trapped as part of their diversification-for-survival strategy.[94] By the Second World War, trapping was no longer feasible as the sole source of income. Not until the 1950s did it enjoy something of a small revival.[95] The old fur trade community was gone forever.

One other option for earning income in the natural resource sector of the economy was blueberry picking. The sandy soil and acidic conditions in parts of the district make an ideal nursery for wild blueberries, which had always been an important part of the First Nations' food supply. Newcomers quickly discovered them as well. Countless families in both town and country were soon supplementing their diets with local blueberries, and before long the commercial possibilities were being exploited. In the 1920s Toronto fruit dealers began to advertise for berries in the local newspaper, and within a few years it had become a regular business that occupied up to five thousand people each August. Boxcars full of berries were hauled south at the end of the season.[96] One particular site east of Matheson became famous and was nicknamed Blueberry Lake. A shantytown of huts built from birch poles and tarpaper mushroomed there, complete with a store, a barber shop, and police patrols. Some pickers went for the fun, but for others it was serious business. Entire families were put to work, for collectively they could earn up to a thousand dollars a season, enough to see a family through the winter on the farm. The size of the harvest varied considerably from year to year, of course, as did prices, but blueberry picking continued to be profitable until well into the 1950s. In 1943 the agricultural representative for Cochrane South estimated that blueberries had brought over $124,000 into the district, making it the most important cash "crop."[97] But it wasn't always easy money. In 1938 the medical officer of health closed the Blueberry Lake camp because of a dysentery epidemic; there were two thousand people living at the site without any sanitary facilities. Six people were sick enough to be hospitalized.[98]

Another important employment opportunity was provided by the various railways that ran near or through the region. Crews were needed both in the construction phase and in ongoing maintenance. As was described in chapter 3, the Canadian Pacific, Canadian Northern, National Transcontinental, and, above all, the Temiskaming and Northern Ontario railways became important features of the economic landscape between 1881 and 1931. Initially, construction workers were recruited in Montreal, Toronto, and other large cities. Firms such as Davis and Nagle of Montreal hired immigrants as they landed or recruited men through agents stationed in the United States and elsewhere.[99] Gangs of workers were then brought north and housed in camps not unlike those of the pulp-log cutters, though the sleeping accommodation was more comfortable, since the men were housed in boxcars fitted with bunk beds (hence referred to as "bunk-cars"). Meals were served in another railcar, which was fitted out as a cookery, and in the larger camps there might also be a commissary car where clothing, tobacco, and other supplies were sold to the crews. At one TNO camp in 1927, an observer described the food as "good and plentiful in the camp, but the cold lunches served on the track were often a source of dissatisfaction." He also reported that "sanitary conditions were poor, the latrines not screened nor water chlorinated."[100]

The men usually signed on for a fixed wage (two dollars a day on the National Transcontinental in 1912), and the cost of "room" and board and other incidentals was deducted by the employer. Sometimes, the company would pay a man's transportation costs if he remained on the work crew for a minimum of six months, but very few men ever did. Thus, while the wages looked enticing, many men actually earned very little in railway construction work. Edwin Bradwin, who wrote about labour conditions in the northern camps in the years before 1915, calculated that a worker at Abitibi Crossing on the National Transcontinental might get $15.80 (after expenses) for two and a half months' work, but then he faced the cost of getting out of the bush, and after paying a train fare to Matheson, he might have as little as 65 cents left in his pocket.[101] Some men, especially the Italians, tried to avoid some of the costs by cooking for themselves.[102] It is hardly surprising that the railway contractors complained constantly that men were leaving to work in the mines or the pulp and paper industry.

Canadian- and British-born workers were rarely interested in the heavy labour required in railway construction and maintenance, so the crews were dominated by immigrant workers, usually Ukrainian, Italian, Slavic, and Finnish men. At Island Falls in 1927, for example, contractor H.F. McLean's crew was 90 percent "foreign born," including of 65 percent Slavic workers and 20 percent Italians, with only 5 percent French-speaking Canadians and 2 percent English-speaking Canadians.[103] Ten years later, in a CNR crew in the Capreol district to the south, 40 percent were Ukrainians, 10 percent other Eastern Europeans, 20 percent Italians, 10 percent French-speaking Canadians, and 10 percent English-speaking Canadians.[104]

It seems that, over time, fewer men were recruited in central places such as Montreal, and more and more were hired through local networks. As sociologist Rex Lucas has observed, railway workers tended to be hired through "the informal and vital continuing relationships between particular people within a particular community; the local hierarchy reflects the ethnic groups, the status locally given to particular jobs, and to a large extent, the history of the community and its peoples ... Employment is a local and often merely an incidental matter."[105] Not surprisingly, then, recruitment within ethnic groups and a tendency for specific jobs to be associated with particular nationalities were also features of the railway workforce.

The Temiskaming and Northern Ontario Railway had a particular impact on the region's workforce. Historian Robert Surtees noted that through the 1920s the railway had some 2,100 employees in northeastern Ontario and "everyone who did not make a living from the T&NO was either related to or knew someone else who did."[106] Men with families would establish a home in such towns as Timmins and South Porcupine, but they moved about from job to job as needed until they gained sufficient seniority. Hours were long, conditions of year-round outdoor work difficult, and many jobs were physically very demanding. Men took pride in their ability to do this work in the same way that miners and loggers developed a sense of camaraderie and masculine pride through their work.

The service sector of the local economy was not large but because those who worked in it tended to be less transient than those in other sectors, it had an influence on the region out of proportion to its size. This sector was composed of two parts: the professionals and the business people. Doctors, dentists, lawyers, and some teachers were either hired by the major companies (such as the Hollinger and Abitibi doctors and the teachers at the Dome School) or they came to set up their own offices and provide services to the general public. Most business people operated independently as well, though Hollinger, McIntyre, and Abitibi all ran company stores, which were managed for them by experienced retailers. The area also produced an active co-op movement, which will be examined elsewhere. Clergy were paid by their congregations and their mission boards, but Hollinger and Abitibi assisted occasionally with land and sometimes with money. Thus, the service sector was either directly tied to the major employers or was closely dependent on them.

With the exception of Sam Bucovetsky's department store chain, most retail outlets were small businesses that employed family members and

Table 5 Typical daily wages: comparisons by work sector

	Mining (mucker)	Abitibi Mill (mechanic)	Bush camps (cutter)	Railways (labourer)	Farming[1] (labourer)	Canadian manufacturing
1911–15	$2.75	–	$1 – $2	$2.00	?	$1.34
1916–20	$3.50	$4.05	$2 – $3	?	$2.50	$2.44
1921–25	$4.24	$5.76	$1 – $2	?	$2.50	$3.49
1926–30	$4.60	?	$1 – $2	$2.40	$1.40	$3.10
1931–35	$4.24	?	$1 – $2	?	?	$3.19
1936–40	$4.64	$4.32	$1.64	?	$1.00	$2.79

Sources: Compiled from McIntyre employee cards for McIntyre Mine; Department of Labour [Canada], Strikes and Lockouts, no. 45, 1917, LAC, RG27, vol. 306 (microfilm reel T2693); no. 106, 1921, LAC, RG27, vol. 326 (microfilm reel T2709); *Porcupine Advance*, 29 April 1937, p. 7; Buffalo Ankerite correspondence, 1933-60, LAC, MG28 III 81, vol. 15; Annual Report of the [Ontario] Bureau of Mines for 1911, Ontario *Sessional Papers*, no. 4, 1912, p. 14; Leacy, *Historical Statistics of Canada*, tables E41–8, E86–103; Radforth, *Bushworkers and Bosses*, apps. 5 and 6; Department of Labour [Canada], *Wages and Hours of Labour in Canada* (supplement to the *Labour Gazette*)

[1] Wages only, not including board

perhaps one or two others, so it is difficult to evaluate the wages or overall economic significance of this sector. Clearly, it provided one of the few opportunities available for women to work outside the home, and women were well represented among both owners and employees. Three of the most important services for a population containing a large group of single men were the boarding houses, restaurants, and drinking establishments, ranging from the "blind pig" (illegal) to the "beer parlour" (clearly refined!). Young single men apparently preferred to leave their domestic support to others. So they enjoyed the camaraderie of the boarding house (where meals and other services were provided), rather than moving into individual apartments or private houses (where they would have to fend for themselves). Some of the boarding houses were quite large and, in fact, indistinguishable from small hotels; they were almost always managed by women and frequently owned by them as well. Finnish women were reputed to run the best houses, while Chinese restaurants and laundries were well patronized.

Teachers tended to be the most transient of the service-sector workers, but some remained in the area for many years and had a considerable impact. Bertha Shaw arrived to teach at the South Porcupine school in January 1916 and taught in Tisdale Township until her retirement in 1945. She was beloved as a teacher, honoured for her tireless work during the influenza epidemic of 1918, and admired for the two books of memoirs she published in the 1950s.[107] She is buried by the shores of Porcupine Lake. Another local teacher was given a permanent tribute on her retirement when Moneta School was renamed Flora MacDonald Public School after the woman who was a teacher and then principal there from 1916 until her retirement in 1954. She was remembered by her multinational collection of students for her unfailing interest in their languages and cultures and the fact that she encouraged them to celebrate these gifts from their forebears rather than hiding them in embarrassment.[108] Although such teachers were much loved, they were not well paid. In 1915 the Timmins Public School Board offered its male teacher-principal $100 per month and its female teachers $85, at a time when an experienced machineman at the McIntyre Mine was earning about $120 per month and the accountant there was paid $150 per month (*and* free board).[109] Teachers in the rural school districts did even worse – when they were paid at all by cash-strapped trustees.

Beyond these recognized and officially sanctioned work opportunities, the region had a thriving underground economy that provided very different kinds of services. Given the large population of young men living away from their families and earning good money if they were employed in the industrial sector, it is hardly surprising that drinking, gambling, and sex were favourite pastimes and that there was money to be made in providing them. It would certainly be wrong to portray the region as a wild and lawless "frontier" in the tradition of the Hollywood western, but there was a significant and semi-tolerated unlicensed business sector.

The blind pig (an unlicensed drinking establishment) might be anything from a regular gathering in someone's front room to a shanty on the edge of town, maintained solely for the purpose. And during the Prohibition years, several Ansonville drugstores were operating primarily as bars. There was a high degree of ethnic segregation among these operations, which functioned mostly as social clubs where men could gather after their shifts, speak in their own language, and relax in the comfort of known company as a sort of substitute family. Historian Varpu Lindström-Best has noted that bootleggers were a "well-established part of urban and frontier life" among the Finns, whose *koiratorppas* were generally run by women, who were "at once despised and spoken of with awe" within the Finnish community.[110] The pattern clearly held true in the Porcupine region. Finns and French Canadians seem to have been the owners of many of the establishments throughout the region. The alcohol sold at the blind pigs was generally smuggled in rather than manufactured locally. Tales of "importer" ingenuity became part of local lore, accompanied by sly winks. "Strange to say," recalled Anglican Bishop R.J. Renison, "long clear bacon, eggs, fruit and lard have been shipped in great quantities to Porcupine."[111] During Prohibition in Ontario, it was relatively easy to obtain liquor in Quebec and bring it by rail into the district.[112]

Early on in the Porcupine gold rush, employers pressured the provincial police to crack down on the blind pigs, and in an attempt at public shaming, the *Porcupine Advance* published the names of those arrested. But then a group of "leading members of the camp" (including some unnamed mine managers) complained when the police had seized *their* Christmas stock of liquor. In the spring of 1912 the *Porcupine Advance* ran an editorial headlined "What's The Use?" in which it explained that it had decided not to publish any more names of those convicted of liquor law contraventions. And when two provincial "liquor spotters" at South Porcupine were convicted for taking a $25 bribe from a "saloon keeper" to head off prosecution, the provincial police themselves began to cry, "What's the use?" They claimed that it was almost impossible to obtain convictions for liquor offences because the accused either pleaded that the liquor was for his (or her) personal use or the provincial police could get no cooperation from the local police to obtain evidence.[113] By the 1930s, only the most serious cases were pursued, as in the 1935 case of a man who opened several blind pigs and "disorderly houses," raising concerns among the authorities that "organized crime might secure a foothold in this town."[114]

Prostitutes arrived very early in the twentieth century, following the railway construction crews and then the prospectors into the region. One enterprising young woman even managed to conduct business for a time among a prison work crew that had been assigned to construction duties on the access road into the Porcupine Camp – a group that was supposedly under close guard.[115] Initially, prostitutes seem to have been largely French-speaking Canadians. Later, Finnish, Italian, and Bulgarian names also came to the attention of the authorities; but French women seem to have continued with the largest part of the business (at least, based on the cases reported in the local newspapers). Many of the women worked for (or were brought into the district by) men, though there were also cases of women who ran brothels. Most seem to have come intentionally for the work, but a few instances came to police attention in which girls had been enticed to the region with promises of good work in restaurants or as domestics. In one sad example, a 26–year-old woman, who was newly arrived from Italy and spoke very little English, was forcibly detained for over a year at a Pine Street café in Timmins while the owners tried to force her into prostitution.[116]

Initially, the townsfolk mostly turned a blind eye. Then, in 1934, increasing complaints from the churches and some employers led the Timmins police to launch a series of raids to "clean up" the "disorderly houses" and arrest the men "found in" them, in order to "make the places unpopular." Clearly, some community leaders felt that society had changed so much that ignoring the situation was no longer appropriate. Over a period of four months, sixteen women and seven "found-ins" were arrested; then, in a single night in three simultaneous raids, police arrested thirteen women and fourteen men. One of the women was Mrs Celia Pigeon, whose notorious establishment at 1 Spruce Street provided bootleg refreshments on the main floor and brothel rooms above. It was clearly doing an excellent business, because she easily produced the $6,000 set as bail.[117] As one Timmins businessman recalled, her "girls" threw a spectacular party for her "on her return from Haileybury Gaol – where she had been languishing for three months for professional reasons."[118] Prostitutes in smaller establishments could also make good money. One had to be brought back to stand trial after she took a taxi to Hull, near Ottawa (at a cost of $125), to get home and avoid the court.[119] The police sweep in Timmins succeeded only in driving the business out to such places as Mountjoy Township where there were too few provincial police officers to do much about it. Thereafter, although prostitutes lived on the fringes of society, they were tolerated as a necessary part of life, as long as they did not make too much of a public display. A local legend has it that in one of the towns, a known prostitute was accepted as a foster mother by the Children's Aid Society, which valued her kindness and generosity over her source of income.[120]

Since it was economic opportunity that brought the newcomer population to the region, it is not surprising that work became the focus of life for most people, even though most jobs were physically demanding and dangerous. If times were good and you were lucky enough to be working for one of the major companies, you were well paid compared with an industrial worker in the South. But times were not always good, and not everyone could work for the big companies. Many people lived in dire poverty, while others survived only by flexibility and mobility. There was constant movement in and out of the region, in and out of the workplace, and from one economic sector to another. Business owners, skilled workers, French-speaking Canadians, and married men with families tended to stay put the longest, so eventually a core group emerged in each town that could count generations of residence instead of seasons. But there was a constant ebb and flow around them.

Employers faced this transience with a wary eye. They were also very concerned about the large population of immigrant workers, many of whom did not speak English or French, at least until the 1930s. Since development of the region coincided with an era of major social and labour unrest in Canada, employers and managers were constantly anxious about the potential for trouble in the workplace. In the early years, they attempted to control their workers with heavy-handed coercion. As time went on, they developed more subtle ways to manipulate behaviour and repress rebellion. The story of social control and worker resistance forms an important part of the story of work in the region.

Policing was a key component of the early approach. Since the 1870s,

the Ontario government had toyed with the idea of a provincial constabu-
lary, and a handful of men had been hired, but it was not until the silver
discoveries at Cobalt and the development of a potentially unruly and
unregulated camp there that action was taken to organize a force more
along the lines of the North-West Mounted Police. In 1905 Constable
George Caldbick was dispatched to Cobalt, the first police officer north of
North Bay.[121] In the fall of 1909, more formal organization began with the
appointment of Major Joseph E. Rogers as superintendent of police. In
1910 Rogers divided the province into four departments, one being the
Northern Division that included Cobalt, Sudbury, and the new camp at
Porcupine. Caldbick was promoted to inspector and put in charge, with his
headquarters at Cobalt, and Constable Gerry Lefebvre was sent to the Porcupine Camp. Shortly afterwards, Lefebvre was replaced by Constables
Charles Piercy, George Murray, and R.J. Smith.[122] Murray and Piercy
became heroes for their role in coordinating evacuations and rescues
during the great fire of July 1911, and Piercy oversaw the construction of
the first lock-up behind the mining recorder's office.[123]

The founding township councils were eager to ensure order within their
borders and quickly established police forces of their own. One of the first
orders of business at the inaugural meeting of Whitney Township Council
was to appoint former provincial constable Charles Piercy as police chief,
and when he resigned a few weeks later, he was replaced immediately with
Chief Gunston. Soon afterwards, Whitney Township took over the provincial jail in the camp on the grounds that prisoners who had been arrested
by the provincial police had been allowed to remain "free of charge."[124]
Tisdale Township also appeared to be dissatisfied with the provincial force
and appointed two township police officers of its own. A combined court,
jail, and police headquarters was built in South Porcupine in 1912, and
the former provincial constable Charles McInnis was appointed chief.[125]
The newly incorporated town of Timmins also decided to create its own
police force. James Ryan was appointed chief, and a jail was constructed as
one of the first municipal council expenditures. Iroquois Falls hired Fred
Sheldon as its first chief in 1914.[126] That town's very first expenses were
$250 for the construction of a lock-up and $67.25 for a constable's
uniform, handcuffs, and other necessities. Only then did town officials
turn to matters such as garbage collection, school plans, and sidewalk construction.[127] Even Matheson decided to build a jail in 1910.

Not everyone was enthusiastic about the various police forces developing in the region. Shortly after the fire of 1911, Father Alex Pelletier wrote
to the premier complaining that Constable Murray had been seen drinking at the home of a man "who was living publicly with two lewd women,"
and another constable had allegedly told a liquor vendor "that he had
nothing to fear in continuing this illicit traffic."[128] Constables Piercy and

McInnis also were apparently unhappy with the provincial force, for they resigned from it to take up positions with Whitney and Tisdale Townships. However, it seems that Piercy found the township police force no more satisfying, for he returned to the provincial force within a few weeks. Thereafter, there appears to have been an almost annual turnover of personnel in the local forces. Concerned that they could not rely on the provincial or local police, major companies took matters into their own hands. The TNO had its own security system. Hollinger contracted out to the Thiel Detective Agency, an American company known for its undercover work against the Western Federation of Miners in Idaho. (Interestingly, the town of Timmins also occasionally paid for the services of Thiel men in addition to the town's own police force.)[129] In 1932 Hollinger created its own police force. Dome's police were supervised initially under contract by M.E. White, who went into business with his own "secret service" company in the early 1920s, with a "special department" for mine, mill, and smelter work.[130] Abitibi, too, had a corporate police force but hired its men directly rather than contracting for the service. These private forces seem to have been brought in initially as industrial spies, to keep an eye on union activity and to report on potential trouble. But they carried revolvers and participated in more open police work, such as crowd control during the miners' strike of 1912 in Timmins, which will be discussed shortly.

Companies did not always need to hire police to try to control workers, however. Historian Donald Avery reports that in 1907 a contractor for the TNO (McRae, Chandler and McNeil Construction) issued firearms to its foremen "to intimidate recalcitrant workers" in the camps, most of which "had jails where 'unruly' workers had been confined after kangaroo court proceedings." That year, some thirty Slavic workers were arrested at gunpoint, held overnight in a freight car, allegedly beaten, and ultimately fined for breaking the conditions of their labour contracts.[131] At one pulp-cutters' camp in 1933, MPP John Rowlandson claimed, the Ontario government had resorted to "gunboats and men-of-war" by keeping "armed forces" in response to a request from a contractor who feared trouble.[132]

The larger companies also employed less heavy-handed techniques to encourage the workforce to be compliant. Company housing, whether in a closed company town like Iroquois Falls or in an open company town like Timmins, was one technique. Company stores, such as the Mercantile at Iroquois Falls or the short-lived Hollinger Stores in Timmins, were another. Recreational facilities were also provided. Both Abitibi and Hollinger built skating rinks, baseball parks, and a golf course. In 1938 McIntyre Mines built a magnificent recreation complex across the highway from the Schumacher townsite that became known across Canada as a centre for championship figure skaters. Dome built a more modest complex in South Porcupine. Every company sponsored a hockey team, partly through direct donations and partly by giving time off for practice or by making jobs available for skilled players who could be counted on to give the team a chance at a championship. Sport would provide a "safe" outlet for aggression, a venue for social activity away from the bars, and a means of generating enthusiasm and solidarity among employees for the company "team" in its broader sense.

The power of the press was also used as a tool for social engineering. Abitibi sponsored the *Broke Hustler* newspaper, which openly stated that its purpose was to foster a sense of unity; implicitly, it was also a booster for company policies and encouraged employee loyalty. In Timmins the *Porcupine Advance* was privately owned but never ran more than a muted criticism of Hollinger. Both Abitibi and Hollinger eventually produced glossy corporate magazines to reach their employees directly. French-speaking audiences found a more specifically Québécois social vision in *La Gazette du Nord*, but it too served to promote an orderly, family-based community. Only with the arrival of the Timmins *Press* (later *Daily Press*) in the mid-1930s was a more independent media service available.

The results of these corporate attempts to structure and control the workforce were mixed. Some workers embraced their circumstances, others opted out in a variety of ways, and still others rebelled. The impact on the workplace and the nature of work was probably unanticipated by either employer or employee.

Perhaps the most visible evidence of worker response to corporate dictates was unionization. Although many company towns in the United States had been built in an attempt to prevent the workforce from unionizing, unions came to the mines and mills of northeastern Ontario right from the beginning. The unions played an important role in shaping the work experience. Companies and other interests in the towns (for instance, the Roman Catholic Church) vainly attempted to limit and control the unions – they were particularly concerned about the communist affiliations of some labour organizers – but ultimately the unions survived. A single union attempted to represent all mine workers at most of the mines in the Porcupine area, while several unions represented the Abitibi workers on the basis of job specialization, as was the case among the railway workers. All were affiliated with the international labour movement, so their histories are part of a broader story of labour mobilization in North America and overseas.

Local 145 of the Western Federation of Miners was organized at the Porcupine Camp in the spring of 1910, even before any real mining was underway. The WFM had been formed in Montana in 1893 and recruited its early members in Iowa and Colorado mines. By 1900 it was embracing an increasingly radical socialism and had broken with the American Federation of Labor. It then commenced major recruiting drives in the copper mines of Michigan (1903), and at Cobalt (1906).[133] The WFM built an imposing two-storey union hall in South Porcupine, and Local 145 soon boasted the largest membership of all the northeastern Ontario mine locals.[134] When several of the mines announced a wage cut in the fall of 1912, the union called a strike, and men at all the mines walked off the job. Hollinger closed its bunkhouses in Timmins; the union responded by opening a boarding house of its own. Hollinger then began to import non-union workers under the protection of its Thiel "detectives." There was a violent confrontation at the Hollinger Mine in late November, and when Hollinger attempted to bring in a train car with replacement workers, a force of some two hundred strikers (and some wives) marched out to meet it. The result was a mob scene on the streets of Timmins, in which two men suffered serious gunshot wounds and the mayor was nearly killed when he tried to prevent one of the Thiel constables from firing into the crowd. The provincial police arrested the four Thiel constables at the scene. Afterwards, the badly shaken mayor petitioned the attorney general of Ontario either to remove the Thiel men from Timmins or to send in the militia to protect the townspeople. Instead, provincial police reinforcements were sent north with orders to disarm the Thiel men and to tell them to remain on private property.[135]

Hollinger's general manager, Percy A. Robbins, was incensed at what he considered a defeat for the mine management, so he called on the company's lawyers in Toronto to lobby the provincial government to take action against the strikers. Robbins succeeded in having charges laid against some seventy men under the recently established Industrial Disputes Investigation Act (sometimes called the Lemieux Act). The subsequent trials were followed with considerable interest, for the local press claimed that they were the first test of that legislation in court; but that is another story. The strike was never officially called off. Many men simply left town to find work elsewhere, while others gradually drifted back to work. Hollinger management, in particular, was taken aback by the events, clearly believing that the wages and living facilities they provided should have prevented such a violent confrontation. In its annual report, Hollinger estimated that the strike had cost it $100,000, and a mystified reporter wrote in the Montreal *Gazette*, "Mining circles ... were [mistakenly] disposed to attach little importance to the strike of miners at Porcupine. For some time there had been unrest among certain of these miners, but this did not apply to Hollinger or the Dome, where employees had received every reasonable consideration ... [It was] as unexpected as it seems to have been unjustified."[136]

The failure of the Western Federation of Miners to obtain any significant concessions during the strike helped pave the way for the 1919 visits of several activists in the One Big Union movement. They succeeded in

Henry Peters, a prominent local photographer, took this
picture of the three primary leaders of the 1912 Porcupine
miners' strike after their arrest on a complaint laid by
Hollinger under the new industrial disputes legislation. The
case became a *cause célèbre* in Canadian labour history.
William Holowaski is in the centre; the other two are Peter
Croft and Peter Cleary. (Henry Peters, LAC, PA029974)

getting Local 145 to withdraw from the International Union of Mine, Mill
and Smelter Workers (as the WFM was called after 1916). But then an internal split developed between politicized radical socialists (notably, Finns)
and more moderate Anglo- and French Canadian workers. A group calling
itself the Porcupine Miners' Union applied to the Mine, Mill international

Union parade through South Porcupine, May Day 1913. Note the contingent of women in the middle. Their banner reads "The Men's Fight is Our Fight." (LAC, PA187042)

in 1920 for re-admission, apparently with the assistance of Mine, Mill organizer John Turney.[137] But for several years, the One Big Union organizers continued to try to recruit workers. Dome's general manager described them witheringly to the company's president, Jules S. Bache: "The union bunch is a bad lot. They are the same class as the Winnipeg men who made trouble a couple of years ago, also in affiliation with the Cape Breton men who have been making trouble for a long time past. They are not after [an] increase in wages so much as to make trouble and upset capital. Many are Finns soaked [in] Sovietism in spite of the Russian debacle."[138] The communist-backed Workers' Unity League also attempted to organize the mineworkers, with some success after 1930. However, for the majority of workers, such as Dome miner James Mulaney, these alternatives were too radical to be palatable. Mulaney explained that he would not join the Workers' Unity League "on account of the Bolshevistic views of its members" and that he was "an advocate of trades unionism, but not of Bolshevism or sabotage."[139] The Workers' Unity League in Timmins was dissolved in 1935.[140] In the interim, though, deep divisions among the workers and ongoing campaigns by the mines to hire non-union men made the union movement largely ineffective through the 1920s and 1930s.

In the spring of 1936, Mine, Mill finally succeeded in reorganizing the miners, with the notable exception of those at Dome, and a charter was granted as Local 241. It represented an agreement between moderates and communists, particularly among the Finnish and Ukrainian workers, and was part of a larger organizing campaign that Mine, Mill had success-fully undertaken in Kirkland Lake and Sudbury. W.R. Armstrong, a mod-erate, was elected president of the Timmins local. The arranged marriage was a difficult one. As some members later told the International Execu-tive with considerable understatement, "The membership in District 8 is divided to some degree on political and religious grounds ... [which] has caused many to refrain from giving their full energies to the big job of building our union."[141] In 1941 the Kirkland Lake local went on strike in one of the sorriest episodes in Canadian labour history.[142] The failure of that strike seriously undermined the credibility of Local 241; its Timmins membership fell to less than 100 in 1943, and its office was closed for several years. Slowly through the mid-1940s it was resuscitated, but then all hell broke loose.

In 1947 Local 241 elected non-communists to nine of its eleven execu-tive positions, and the local leadership made threatening noises to the International Executive that it would consider withdrawing from Mine, Mill if what it considered to be communist influence on the International was not repudiated. A few months later, the Timmins local joined others in Port Colborne and Niagara Falls in refusing to pay dues to the Interna-tional until action was taken. The International Executive retaliated by firing Ralph Carlin (a paid employee of the International) who ran the Timmins office. Local 241 voted to reinstate him and sent a note to head-quarters demanding that the International board "send no more red-tinged organizers to the Porcupine."[143] The International then declared the entire Timmins executive suspended. In response, Local 241 made good on its threat to withdraw from the International.

A rival international union, the United Steelworkers of America, seized the opportunity and proposed that Local 241 join it. Local 241's president Ivan Vachon and the brothers Ralph and James V. Carlin succeeded in leading most of the membership out of Mine, Mill into the waiting arms of the Steelworkers. Those who remained loyal to Mine, Mill were furious. Their International appointed William Kennedy to go in and salvage the remnants; allegations flew on both sides. Vachon and his followers claimed that Mine, Mill had been infiltrated by communists, while Mine, Mill accused Vachon and his henchmen of being "stooges" for Ontario's Con-servative premier George Drew and the mine owners. Kennedy took the new union to court on behalf of Mine, Mill, alleging that it had stolen all the office equipment and kept union dues that rightfully belonged to Mine, Mill.[144] The Canadian Congress of Labour tried to resolve the affair (and probably succeeded in making it worse) by asking both Mine, Mill and the Steelworkers to leave Timmins until things could be sorted out.

The Steelworkers' organizers complied, but Mine, Mill would not, so in 1949 the CCL suspended Mine, Mill's membership – thereby guaranteeing an escalation in the battle to the national level.[145] The Steelworkers (as Local 4305) were ultimately certified in September 1950 at Hollinger,[146] though Local 241 of Mine, Mill continued to maintain an office in Timmins for some time afterwards,[147] and Dome Mines continued to keep the unions out entirely. The Steelworkers union proved its effectiveness in a two-month strike at Hollinger in 1951, which received considerable support from the community including cash donations from Sam Bucovetsky and other merchants, and from the Roman Catholic Club Richelieu and all but one of Timmins's hotels.[148]

Although there were no major strikes in the Porcupine mines between 1913 and 1950, it could scarcely be said that the workers were complacent or silent. Union organization itself became the focus of the power struggle, pitting communist and non-communist against each other. It would be a mistake to conclude, as some have, that the cessation of strikes after 1912 was an indication that mine management had won and Timmins was an "anti-union" town.[149] Rather, workers were pro-union but were deeply divided on the issue of what politics were to sustain union activity. There is no doubt whatever, though, that mine managers were anti-union. Dome succeeded in keeping the unions out until 1969, and Hollinger attempted for many years to claim that it did not recognize any miners' union, even though it met and negotiated with union leaders. Everywhere, potential employees were quizzed about past union membership, and Dome hired detectives to pose as workers and report on attempts to organize.[150] Hollinger's records appear not to have survived, so it cannot be confirmed whether Hollinger also spied on union leaders, but it seems highly likely. There was clearly an informal network among supervisors throughout the northeastern Ontario mines about potential "troublemakers," and one supervisor recalled that they would be reluctant to hire men known to have worked at a mine where the union was strong. There may not have been a formal blacklist (as union leaders claimed), but there was no need for one; the informal network seemed to work well enough for management.

The labour situation in the bush camps was just as complex and troubled. It was clearly difficult to organize seasonal workers who represented different languages and political views, but it was also clear to the workers that low wages and poor working conditions had to be challenged. Here again, tensions between communist and non-communist, between socialist and communist, and Finn and French Canadian spilled over to complicate matters.

Socialist Finns may well have organized informal associations in the very early camps, but little information about them has survived. We do know that in 1919 and 1920 the One Big Union sent Dave Rainville, E. Guertin, and other organizers to bush camps throughout Northern Ontario. They succeeded in signing on a number of French-speaking Canadians, but the Finnish bushworkers were suspicious of the OBU movement, as were their brothers in the Porcupine mines.[151] The OBU quickly petered out in the bush. The Finns were much more successful (at least, in the short term) with a campaign organized by the Workers' Party of Canada, forerunner of the Communist Party of Canada. Between 1924 and 1928, locals of the Lumber Workers' Industrial Union of Canada (LWIUC) were organized across Northern Ontario, including at South Porcupine, Porcupine, Timmins, Connaught, and in an unknown number of seasonal camps.[152] One of its drawing cards was a call for a minimum wage of $50 per month for bushworkers.[153] Originally based at Port Arthur, the LWIUC moved its headquarters to Timmins in 1934 under the presidency of W. Delaney in an attempt to recruit more French-speaking and Quebec-based workers.[154]

The LWIUC led northern bushworkers in a series of almost annual strikes that climaxed in the great convulsion of 1933–34. That winter, perhaps as many as 2,500 men in camps throughout the bush put down their saws, and even some settlers refused to cut and deliver wood. Many striking bushworkers walked to Cochrane where a temporary camp and soup kitchen were established. From this "command central," they dispatched groups to bush camps where the men had not yet walked out, in an attempt to encourage them to do so. A reporter for the Toronto *Star* described one of these expeditions this way:

Strained to the breaking point of exhaustion, footsore and disappointed, nearly 200 strikers straggled out of the Abitibi company camps at Jacksonboro last night, their ranks swelled by only 25 additional men … A lad of 17, Tom Parr, fainted in the snow at the side of the tote road. He was picked up by a sleigh the Abitibi company sent along at the rear … The long walk was something like the return of Napoleon's army from Moscow. It was certainly cold, with a temperature of 15 degrees below zero [−26° Celsius] … "That was the worst walk I ever made in my life … We were lucky that's all. We were 147 jackasses," said William Yoakley … "I'll never take another trip like that."[155]

Other strikers congregated at Ansonville, where they were housed and fed by anti-Abitibi sympathizers.

The following season, tensions escalated. Strikers blocked Abitibi's railway in September and threw rocks at the Ontario Provincial Police as they arrested seven strikers. Then reports began to filter out of the camps that strikers and non-strikers were engaging in pitched battles. At Braconnier's camp north of Iroquois Falls, eighty strikers marched in and allegedly seized the food supplies, badly beat the camp clerk, and drove out the workers. The police made two arrests, but further scuffling erupted when the strikers attempted to board a CNR freight train to make their departure.[156] Ivan Dawkins, the injured clerk, was a veteran of the First World War, and the Cochrane branch of the Canadian Legion "entered very strong protest against the fact that police protection" had not been provided for men who only wanted to work.[157]

After a number of similar incidents, support for the strike began to waver. In late October, 130 men at John Gibson's camp on the Mattagami River near Cochrane erected a log barricade across the bridge that provided the only access to their camp. There they fought a pitched battle against strike promoters, whom they saw as an invading army of "thugs."[158] Settlers began to complain that the strikers were preventing them from doing what they considered to be private bushwork; a group near Cochrane formally petitioned the Ontario government for help.[159] Men began to raise questions about the motivation of the strike leaders, whom they saw as outsiders – professional agitators – and not really qualified bushworkers. At Ansonville, striker Laframboise accused leader Nick Thachuk of not really trying to reach a settlement. "Why should they have the strike settled?" he asked. "If the strike is settled, their occupation will be gone."[160] Another striker told the Toronto *Star*, "If the strike had been a strike of the men, I'd still be out on it." But he said he now believed that "it wasn't a strike at all, it was a Bolshevist uprising."[161] With support in decline, most of the agitation had petered out by the end of December 1934. The men were back at work in the bush on much the same terms and conditions as before. Support for the LWIUC was further eroded when the more conservative workers rallied to the new Canadian Bushman's Union, which became an affiliate of the Canadian Labour Congress. It was explicitly anti-communist as well as "blatantly nativist" in its appeal to Anglo-Saxon workers.[162] In response to the troubles, Bishop Rhéaume of the Roman Catholic Diocese of Haileybury began a campaign in January 1935 to organize a Union of Catholic Farmers on the Quebec side of the border. The name may have implied an agricultural association, but the purpose was to draw in bushworkers who were mostly farmers or farmers' sons and "to guard against inroads by communists and other subversive influences."[163] Although the radicalized Finns were disgusted at the failure of Canadian workers to see what was in their own best interests, they realized that strong-arm tactics and appeals to class solidarity would not work; thereafter, both tone and strategy were moderated.

The situation was rather different at the Abitibi mill itself. Here, the workplace was organized differently, with separate unions for each major skill category. Curiously, although acrimonious strife within the labour movement was largely shut out, there were far more strikes at the plant

than there were in the mining sector. In 1947 the area's MPP, W.J. Grummett, attributed the relative peace at Abitibi to the fact that "the man in
charge of the paper industry rose from the ranks ... They have been union
men themselves." By contrast, in mining, he said, "the man in charge was
born with the silver spoon in his mouth, he did not know what it was to use
pick and shovel, he never knew the problem of the miners and he has no
thought or consideration for them."[164]

The International Brotherhood of Pulp, Sulphite and Paper Mill
Workers appears to have been the first union at the mill, possibly arriving
with a group of French-speaking Canadian workers hired by Abitibi in New
England. This union had been formed in 1906 as a breakaway group from
an older organization of paper makers; it was an affiliate of the American
Federation of Labor and later of the Trades and Labor Congress of
Canada. The Pulp and Sulphite, as it was known, organized as Local 90
and represented the largest group of workers. By 1922, there was also a
branch of the International Order of Machinists (Local 1371). The International Brotherhood of Papermakers (the parent union of the Pulp and
Sulphite) organized as Local 109, and a Firemen and Oilers union was also
represented. In 1919–20 the OBU sent in organizers but made few dedicated converts at Abitibi. "About all the local O.B.U. succeeds in doing at
Iroquois Falls," reported an observer, "is to prevent the men forgetting
about petty grievances."[165] When the communists of the LWIUC proposed
that the Abitibi Pulp and Sulphite workers join them in a new, industry-
wide organization in the mid-1930s, the Iroquois Falls executive
responded by filing the invitation "in the waste basket."[166] With a membership dominated by politically moderate English- and French-speaking
Canadians, the handful of radicalized Ukrainians and Finns were apparently unable to solicit sufficient support to cause any sort of dissension in
the ranks.

Although the radicals complained constantly of the complacency of the
established unions, a series of strikes at Abitibi made it clear that the
workers were far from compliant. Some of the strikes were part of indus-
trywide stoppages called by the unions' international executives, while
others were purely local affairs not sanctioned by headquarters. The first
appears to have been for five days in April–May 1917 when the Pulp and
Sulphite joined the Papermakers in calling for higher wages and a "closed
shop" (only union members could be employed). The union leader
Maurice LaBelle explained, "These are the best conditions in the American paper industry but the location and high cost of living compelled us to
get higher wages than elsewhere."[167] Abitibi conceded to both demands.
The following summer, Local 109 walked out for four days to protest a
ruling by the U.S. War Labor Board against the wage demands of their
fellow workers in the United States. Then, in 1921, a more serious dispute

closed most unionized paper mills in Canada and the United States when owners collectively proposed a 20 percent wage cut. The Papermakers and Pulp and Sulphite walked out in Iroquois Falls, forcing the mill to cease production. After twenty-four and a half days and intensive negotiations by the International Executive and conciliators in New York, the men agreed to return to work with essentially the same wages as before.[168] During the bushworkers' strikes of 1933–34, there were no work stoppages at the Abitibi plant, but members of the Pulp and Sulphite donated one hour's pay each week to help the strikers.[169] In February 1937 the men in the paper-finishing department walked off the job in an action not sanctioned by the International Executive. They had been having problems with their supervisor, and when he hired a new man for a senior position without considering men already in line for a promotion, some forty-five or forty-six of the department declared they were quitting. A.P. Burk, president of the International, came to Iroquois Falls to negotiate a solution.[170]

Unlike the violent strike of 1912 in Timmins or the nasty bushworkers' strikes of the late 1920s and early 1930s, the strikes at the Abitibi plant appear to have been relatively civil and orderly affairs. The area's MP, J.A. Bradette, noted in 1929 that the unions at Iroquois Falls were "working quite well as the newsprint manufacturers in that section of the country are satisfied to work in cooperation with the labour element."[171] Indeed, when the big international strike of 1921 began, the Northern Ontario press was somewhat taken by surprise. How could this have happened? asked the Cobalt *Daily Nugget*. Negotiations in the past had always been so "conciliatory"![173]

Unionization came early to the Temiskaming and Northern Ontario Railway. As in the pulp and paper sector, locals were affiliates of international organizations, in this case the Cleveland-based Brotherhood of Railroad Trainmen and the Brotherhood of Locomotive Engineers. Only once, in 1939, does there appear to have been an attempt to organize an all-Canadian union among TNO workers.[173] These unions do not appear to have been particularly radical, and there were no organized strikes or major disputes in the region during the entire period to the end of the Second World War. Historian Albert Tucker has suggested that this labour peace was a result of the men's awareness that the TNO was government-owned, so "any expression of radical views, of overt sympathy with an opposition party, or an aggressive stand on trade-union membership" would be problematic. He also suggested that the TNO was a small railway in comparison with the CPR and CNR, so its workers carried relatively little weight in the large international unions.[174] While these theories are interesting, it seems more likely that labour peace was a result of a different labour tactic: dissatisfied men simply walked away. As a Frontier College instructor reported from a TNO construction camp near Island Falls in 1927, some 250 to 300 men quit the work gang during a single summer: "Men would come round, [and] get acquainted ... when they would be away again ... Towards the end of July desertions were so plentiful that it became difficult to get a [literacy] class, 23 men threw down their shovels on one occasion, 12 on another etc ... A hundred men from Montreal & North Bay came in ... and nineteen of them walked out on the second day."[175] These were not passive workers; they were merely choosing a different form of protest than the strike.

Corporate authority could be opposed in many ways other than formal organization. Certain attempts by the police to control morality were openly mocked. In the summer of 1912 the *Porcupine Advance* reported a police raid one Sunday evening in which "a few men were engaging in a pleasant game of black-jack." Seven men were arrested and fined for after-hours gambling. "Every one realizes that in a mining camp and town situated as these are," went on the report, "that there is little in the way of amusement and that the indulgence in small games of chance for six days in the week harms no one, and is much better than mooching about and doing many other things."[176] Juries routinely refused to convict people accused of liquor infractions. In fact, it seems that the miners' union was more successful than the police at regulating the purveyors of unlicensed alcohol. During the 1912 strike, the Toronto *Globe* reported, "The camp has probably never in its history been so sober. Realizing the danger if their men got whiskey, the union sent out a number of their followers to warn all keepers of blind pigs throughout the district that if they sold any liquor to any of the strikers, they would report them at once."[177] People were also willing to use force against what they considered unreasonable use of power. During the Timmins Silver Jubilee celebrations in 1937, a riot erupted when the police attempted to arrest three young Albertans who were entertaining street crowds with "cowboy songs." For nearly two hours, a thousand people rallied downtown, throwing stones at the town hall and shouting; someone cut the wires in the engine of the police car. Tear gas, fire hoses, and nightsticks were freely applied before the crowd finally dispersed at 4 AM.[178] Authority could be flouted in more subtle ways too. For many years, the Timmins jail was located in the town hall cellar, and inmates happily communicated with pedestrians on the sidewalk outside in full view of officials.

Mockery of the police was one form by which social control was rejected; objections to the company town itself were another. As has been discussed, directly across the railway tracks from Iroquois Falls, a ramshackle collection of houses, shops, restaurants, and boarding houses sprang up at what locals called the Wye (later Ansonville). The settlement was established by those who wished to remain independent of company control. A similar settlement, Moneta, developed just south of the Timmins town boundary.

The people who chose to live in Ansonville and Moneta accepted a clearly lower standard of living. Housing was marginal, and there was no electricity, water, sewers, or even graded roads for some time. Insurance companies would not accept clients in Ansonville because the fire hazard was deemed too high – and, indeed, fires periodically swept through the shanties, destroying dozens at a time. Nevertheless, the residents celebrated a sense of superiority based on their belief that they were truly independent. Clearly, it was possible to live in the shadow of mine and mill without feeling in the least compelled to accept all their demands.

Ultimately, the workplace was structured not only by the nature of the work and by managerial attempts to control it but by the workers' responses to those conditions and the attempts (both collective and personal) to modify them to meet workers' needs and aspirations. Whether on the farm, in the bush, underground, or at a paper mill, it was hard physical work, but people were drawn to the promise of the opportunities in New Ontario and the possibility of a better future through economic gain. The structures and tensions of the workplace were necessarily vital to the shape of life off the job as well as at work. These were, after all, fairly small communities in a comparatively isolated setting, so people were bound to be aware of one another's lives in ways that city dwellers often fail to realize. How the relationships between home and work moulded the community will be explored in the following chapters.

CHAPTER SEVEN

Play

If work was the primary determinant of the community structure, play was undoubtedly a close second. Even before church congregations had organized sufficiently to purchase land and build halls for worship, Golden City boasted a formal athletic association to organize and provide facilities for baseball, field, and water sports.[1] By January 1912 the South Porcupine hockey rink was one of the most elaborate affairs in the camp with its canvas roof and a succession of challenges among teams boasting real uniforms. Golden City battled South Porcupine. Bank managers battled mine managers. The "ladies" battled the men. There was even an attempt by the Porcupine Camp as a whole to challenge Cobalt, but the lack of railway access hampered the opportunity for wider competition. Play quickly became a serious business, whether encouraged by corporate sponsorship, organized by energetic community leaders, or adopted informally around the card tables and pool halls that mushroomed throughout the region. For some, leisure time meant participation in a game, a dance, a tea party, or a concert. For others, it meant being a spectator at a race, game, or film. Hunting, fishing, drinking, and gambling also became an important part of life. The ways in which these pastimes developed provide a valuable perspective on the story of community development as a whole.

Hockey was undoubtedly pre-eminent, shaped by and in turn shaping the culture of masculinity of the region. Initially, hockey was a sport for participants, not spectators, and the first games were organized among the business and professional classes. Some early games were taken very seriously indeed, with organized clubs, subscriptions to raise money for uniforms, and regular reports on the games in the local news. Other games were pure fun. One of the first played at the South Porcupine rink in 1912 was a contest between teams named the Has Bins and Never Wazzers: the latter's goalie (Albert) was a dog. The Cobalt *Daily Nugget* duly reported the play-by-play action, though no one was entirely clear about the final score.[2]

Beyond the boundaries of the Porcupine–Iroquois Falls region, hockey was becoming a Canadian passion as well – and an increasingly organized, regulated, and ultimately professionalized passion at that. As early as 1886, Montreal, Ottawa, and Quebec City were competing against each other in the Amateur Hockey Association of Canada, their efforts given official recognition with Governor General Lord Stanley's donation of a victory cup in 1893. Ontario organized its own Ontario Hockey Association (OHA) in 1890. In the first decade of the twentieth century, several more leagues were founded, including the International Hockey League (1904–5), the Eastern Canada Amateur Hockey Association (1906–7), the New Ontario Hockey League (1907), the National Hockey Association (1909), and the Pacific Coast Hockey Association (1911). Because several of the new leagues were semi-professional, Sir Montagu Allan donated a trophy to encourage amateurs. The cup could be won in a challenge match open to any amateur team that had won the championship of its league in the year of competition.[3] Amateur and professional teams competed against each other for players and supporters. When the first "openly professional" hockey league was formed in 1904 in the Michigan mining town of Houghton, the Ontario Hockey Association warned young men, "Keep away from Houghton or Pittsburgh or you go into the darkness of professionalism."[4] But professional and semi-professional hockey soon became widely and enthusiastically accepted by working men and their families.

Northerners and mining interests were active in these developments. M.J. O'Brien, an Ottawa Valley businessman who had made his fortune in a Cobalt silver mine, was instrumental in the organization of the Temiskaming Hockey League in 1907. When the Ottawa Valley Hockey League was formed in 1909, he continued to own three northern teams (including the Cobalt and Haileybury), then was the main organizer behind the National Hockey Association. His Cobalt and Haileybury teams joined this league and continued their now-fabled rivalry. Their games provided more than social activity for some spectators. One northern legend has it that Noah Timmins bet over $40,000 on a game in 1910.[5]

Given the already well-developed interest in hockey in Cobalt and the Ottawa Valley, and the numerous links between those regions and the Porcupine Camp, it is hardly surprising that hockey came early to the new communities; and given Noah Timmins's personal interest in the game, it is also not surprising that he encouraged it through corporate channels. By 1915 the Porcupine mines had entered the arena. Hollinger and Dome began to sponsor teams in regularly organized leagues, under the honorary presidency of the mine managers. In 1914 Hollinger built the area's first indoor rink for these contests (among other uses). Serious – and sometimes nasty – business competition among the mines was given an outlet in these games, which simultaneously encouraged loyalty to the

A collage of portraits to celebrate the championship hockey team from South
Porcupine, 1913. Hockey players had already become local heroes and celebrities. George Lake, owner of the *Porcupine Advance*, is second from the right in the
top row. (Arthur Tompkinson, LAC, C24329)

company and a sense of participation in a broader community of interests.
The games were fast and physical. As one newspaper put it, "The tactics
employed were not altogether 'according to Hoyle' ... and many penalties
were inflicted."[6]

For those outside the mine workforce, there were other hockey options.
One team consisted solely of University of Toronto graduates, and there
were women's teams consisting of the wives of prominent businessmen,
mine engineers, and at least one doctor. During the First World War, the
228th Battalion (the pride of the North) sponsored both a senior and a
junior team in the Ontario Hockey Association. Lest anyone think hockey
too frivolous a pursuit during the serious business of war, the Toronto *Star*
reported on the hard checking and physicality of one game with the observation that "the boys waded into each other as if making a charge on a Hun
trench."[7] Hockey taught strength and character that would serve the
"boys" on the battlefields of Europe.

After the war, hockey supporters began to chafe under the limitations of
local competition. Hollinger employee Angus Campbell was the driving
force behind the 1919 organization of the Northern Ontario Hockey Association (NOHA).[8] Representatives from Iroquois Falls, Timmins, Cobalt,
Haileybury, New Liskeard, North Bay, Sudbury, and Sault Ste Marie met at

Cobalt to draw up an agreement. Each participating municipality donated money for the purchase of a trophy cup, which was engraved with "scenes of northern industry" and was proudly proclaimed to be "made of northern mineral products."[9] Initially, a number of teams with various affiliations participated, but it was quickly acknowledged that the Timmins and Iroquois Falls "municipal" teams were the senior participants from the region. In the NOHA's second season, Iroquois Falls won the Northern Ontario championship and headed south to battle Toronto for the Allan Cup. Iroquois Falls lost, but its team (consisting of goalie Courbould, defencemen Bryde and Wilson, and forwards Quesnel, Fluker, Fahey, Chircoski, and Yancoski) became local celebrities.[10] This new level of interest in hockey led to increased corporate support and the construction of large and comfortable indoor facilities at Iroquois Falls (1920), South Porcupine (1938), and the McIntyre Community Centre at Schumacher (1938), which seated over two thousand people and was advertised as an *improved* version of Maple Leaf Gardens in Toronto.[11] Even the Northern Ontario Junior Hockey League (organized in 1920–21) became so popular that the Elks fraternal order in Iroquois Falls arranged a telegraph link so that reports of away games could be read to audiences assembled at the Knights of Columbus Hall.[12]

The NOHA turned hockey into serious business. Issues such as the size of a particular goalie's pads or whether the Soo, Michigan, should be permitted to play in the league were hotly debated. Abitibi and the five largest mines in the Porcupine area began to provide support through financial aid and by ensuring that there were "places on their staffs for hockey players who were workers"[13] (code for what soon became the accepted practice of hiring workers primarily on the basis of their hockey skills). There was even a scandal in the NOHA one year when a Timmins businessman put up some money for the Timmins coach to pay off two Iroquois Falls players so that they would throw a key game. The *Porcupine Advance* was incensed – not at the impropriety but at the fact that someone thought the Timmins team couldn't win without help. Professional coaches were hired, notably Stan Burgoyne, coach of the Hamilton Tigers, who came to lead the Iroquois Falls team in 1920. He was reported to be receiving a salary of $900 per year,[14] equivalent to that of the most senior levels of management at mine and mill. Another coach was Billy Burch, a retired professional player from the New York Americans, who was hired to coach the Timmins team in 1935. The *Porcupine Advance* enthusiastically placed Burch as "one of the group that put professional hockey over in a big way – with Reg. Noble, Lionel Conacher and others of hockey's hall of fame."[15]

The facilities were almost as important as the coaches, it seemed, and the rinks at Iroquois Falls and Schumacher became particular points of pride for their towns. The local press covered games in detail and helped

make the players into local heroes. A number began to move into professional hockey, including Auriel Joliet and George Lever of Iroquois Falls,
Bill Barilko of Timmins, and, in a later generation, the brothers Frank and
Pete Mahovlich.[16] Pride in the ability of local players ran deep. In 1948 the
Timmins Kiwanis arranged for the Toronto Maple Leafs to come to town
to play against an all-star local team. The event was intended as a
fundraiser, but the game itself was taken very seriously, even though local
pride took a severe blow in its 19 to 5 trouncing at the hands of the
Toronto professionals.[17]

While the earliest hockey in the region had been the sport of the managerial and professional class, the NOHA brought hockey to a new group.
Participation in the new league required a level of skill and commitment
available only to real athletes, and their performances attracted a loyal and
enthusiastic following among working men and their families. Hockey
became a spectator sport through the NOHA, with keen competition and
high expectations. It was professional in all but name. For the players, life
revolved around the rink. As a resident of South Porcupine later recalled,
"We ... made friends with most of the hockey team and their wives ... They
came over for a social time when hockey would permit it."[18] For the fans,
hockey provided an escape from the drudgery of the long winter and gave
them an opportunity to live a moment of physical power, agility, and pride,
if only vicariously. It was a game that mirrored and celebrated the culture
of masculinity that was evolving among the region's population.

The NOHA did not entirely replace the older leagues, however. A new
hierarchy of leagues and players evolved that drew in a wide range of participants. Just below the NOHA on the status ladder were the mine teams,
which competed among themselves almost as seriously. The mine managers supported and encouraged the teams as part of their strategy to
ensure worker loyalty. Players were recruited and hired as employees, while
financial support was provided to the "clubs" that managed the teams. The
only complaints about the system arose in cases of corporate raiding.
When Hollinger "spirited off" two men whom Dome had hired as hockey-
playing miners, the manager at Dome protested officially to the manager
at Hollinger, noting, "This is the sort of thing that I believe should be
stomped on if we are to keep sport on an even footing in this camp. We are
not crying for the players back and we do not want men of that caliber but
we do think that the Hollinger Hockey Club should refund the $25.00
expense money advanced by [Dome's Hockey Club president] Mr.
Wattam."[19] Of all the commitments of mine management to hockey, the
pre-eminent would have to be the McIntyre Mine's president, John Paris
("J.P.") Bickell. Besides promoting local hockey, he was a major financial
contributor to the construction of Maple Leaf Gardens in Toronto and
served as its first president. The Canadian Mining Hall of Fame quotes

Conn Smythe as saying that Bickell was "one of the cornerstones of the whole thing; he was the man who put the thing over."[20]

Below the mine teams in the hockey hierarchy came the "fun leagues," which operated more sporadically from season to season depending on interest and availability. The "Ladies Hockey Club" organized teams from time to time, the high schools (including Northern Academy) supported teams, and youth teams provided recreation as well as training for NOHA hopefuls.

While the organization of hockey in the region was diversifying, the range of participants did not follow suit, at least not until after the Second World War. During the 1920s and 1930s the clubs were managed primarily by the English-speaking professional and managerial class, while the players were almost exclusively English- and French-speaking Canadians. Finns were enthusiastic sportspeople, but usually with smaller clubs organized by and for Finns. Italians and Ukrainians seem to have enjoyed sports that were sociable more than competitive (as will be discussed) and they also did so within their own cultural communities. Historian Nancy Forestell has suggested that the hockey spectators were drawn "from all ethnic backgrounds,"[21] but it is difficult to evaluate the composition of the audiences in the interwar years. In any case, it is clear that hockey became a shared passion for the Canadian-born residents, and whether it was a professional/spectator or amateur/participant activity, the game came to be seen as a focal point for regional pride and identity, even though it was not an activity unique to the North.

The region's summer passion was baseball, which was rapidly becoming a favourite elsewhere in Canada. In the spring of 1911, with the snow barely melted, Golden City residents formed an athletic association, laid out a baseball field, and applied to play in the Cobalt-Haileybury ball league (which turned them down on the grounds that Porcupine had no means of transportation out of the camp). The following spring, Hollinger Mine officials established the Timmins Baseball Club, with matches between the mine managers and Timmins businessmen, for instance. South Porcupine and Dome also fielded teams in 1912. Iroquois Falls soon followed suit, with teams representing the different departments at the Abitibi mill, which played on an athletic field that had been part of the original town plan. Once rail transportation had improved sufficiently, teams from several towns, including Matheson and Cochrane, staged regular tournaments and played for local awards, such as the Marshall-Ecclestone Cup, which had been donated by the hardware retailer. Tournaments staged on Dominion Day and Labour Day often produced hard-fought matches between Timmins and Iroquois Falls, with special trains put on by the TNO transport spectators. During the First World War, teams occasionally arranged matches as fundraisers for the war effort. By the

1930s, the games had become so popular that elaborate athletic facilities were built by the McIntyre Mine (1933) and Hollinger (1938), with grandstands to seat a thousand spectators at each site, plus dressing rooms, showers, and toilets.

As with hockey, the participants were initially drawn from the Canadian-born population, with leadership from the managers and business class, and the teams tended to be predominantly English-speaking. For example, the 1917 Timmins baseball team consisted of Messers Nolan, McAndrews, Pierce, Sheehan, Deacon, Burns, Hagan, Perrault, and Price.[22] For most of the early years, the Timmins Baseball Club was run by the general manager at Hollinger as the club's president, assisted by a slate of officers drawn from senior management. Players on the McIntyre team through the 1920s included Timmins dentist S.H. Gibson, South Porcupine lawyer T.R. Langdon, McIntyre shift boss Harry Cowden, and McIntyre safety supervisor C.C. Wood.[23] Gradually, however, a wider spectrum of participants was drawn to the game, so that today it is remembered as "the favourite sport" of the region in its boom years.[24] Like hockey, baseball facilitated communication among the towns of the area and helped to break down the barriers between economic sectors.

Golf also enjoyed corporate sponsorship, but participation was much more clearly class-based. In 1919 Hollinger announced that it would construct a nine-hole course and club house because "many of the South African mines have golf courses on or near their properties and in every case they have proven most popular."[25] The Timmins Golf Club was organized to manage the course under the direction of senior mine managers and Father Thériault, the senior Roman Catholic priest in the region. Membership in the club was open to non-Hollinger employees, but the club's initial publicity noted that only "ladies and gentlemen of good character" would qualify.[26] For years, the club president was the mine manager and the golfers continued to come from the ranks of the professional and managerial sector.

Curling also flourished under corporate paternalism, but it attracted a wider range of participants. Abitibi, Hollinger, McIntyre, and Dome all paid to construct the rinks while the curlers paid membership fees to maintain the ice. Interest in curling in the region may have been piqued by some former Nova Scotians who had enjoyed the game at home. It attracted largely an English-speaking Canadian crowd in the 1920s and 1930s, drawn from a cross-section of occupations. Indeed, in later years one curler recalled that it was one of the few venues in which mine managers and muckers could play together on an equal footing. One of the most popular events was the annual TNO bonspiel, initiated in 1930, which drew dozens of teams from across eastern Canada and occasionally even the United States.[27] Like hockey, curling developed a seriously competitive branch of quasi-professionals. The Northern Ontario Curling Association served much the same purpose as the NOHA, and in 1946 arrangements were made to permit its champion team to play in the Brier, Canada's national competition.[28]

A wide range of other sporting activities was also established in the first years of the new economy under the sponsorship of various athletic associations, including the Golden City Athletic Association, which was organized by business and professional men in the spring of 1911 with forty charter members. They proposed to "support baseball, football, tennis, canoeing and other land and aquatic sports," to which end they leased and cleared a plot of land for a ballpark, took out an option to purchase additional land for other activities, and planned to build a grandstand and "wharf."[29] By announcing their intention to follow the rules of the Canadian Amateur Athletic Association, they clearly placed themselves in that cadre of middle-class sportsmen who saw themselves as aspiring gentlemen for whom athletics was a mark of social standing and virtue. In 1915 the South Porcupine Athletic Club obtained the services of "Professor" Lovell to teach "regular physical culture lessons" to its membership.[30] This was not sport as mere play. Indeed, when questions were raised about the appropriateness of sports competitions during the First World War – when able-bodied men were expected to be serving their country and levity seemed wrong in view of the desperate news coming from the trenches of Flanders – the verdict was ultimately in favour of maintaining the athletic associations. As the *Porcupine Advance* noted, "All thoughtful people are agreed that for reasons of health, strength and morality there should be a reasonable amount of good sport."[31] Sport would provide a means of social control by giving young men an "appropriate" outlet for their energies, keeping them out of the bars, and brothels. It would also, hoped the middle-class leaders, serve as a class marker or boundary between workers and men "of good family."

This middle-class domination of the local athletic associations did not, of course, mean that working men were shut out from sporting activities. Corporate paternalism and managerial aspirations for social control ensured that there were facilities available for their use. Hollinger, Dome, McIntyre, and Abitibi all cleared "athletic grounds" and built grandstands, changing rooms, and other facilities on them. In 1937–38, the McIntyre Mine built the most elaborate of these company facilities, which it named the McIntyre Community Centre. It featured a 2,000–seat hockey arena, a separate figure-skating rink, and six sheets of curling ice, plus a gymnasium, a 500–seat auditorium, a bowling alley, and a restaurant. McIntyre employees were given coupons each month for use in the community centre. One of its best-loved features was a summer figure-skating school that drew pupils from across Canada and the United States. When Barbara

Ann Scott dazzled the world at the Olympics, northeastern Ontarians claimed parental glory.[32]

If the Canadian-born members of the community liked to organize sporting activities for recreation, the Finnish-born population was even more enthusiastic. Their organizational activities were divided into two distinct branches, since the reds and whites saw the purpose of sport very differently. Here, recreational activities became an expression of politics, particularly during the 1920s.

The Finnish Canadian Organization, which began as a socialist group and later included communist members, used sports as a recruiting device to attract and then educate young people in political matters. Through its subsidiary, the Finnish-Canadian Amateur Sports Federation, it began to establish youth clubs in Northern Ontario in 1903 (the first at Copper Cliff, near Sudbury) and by 1931 claimed some 43,885 members across Canada, including active groups in South Porcupine and Timmins.[33] Gymnastics was by far its most popular activity, but it also sponsored picnics and field days. In 1928 the Young Communist League in Canada organized the Workers' Sports Association, whose branches became synonymous with Finnish communist athletics in northeastern Ontario. Through the Timmins Ilo ("Comets") club, formed in 1917 (the second club in Canada), the South Porcupine Viesti ("Aces") club, formed in 1924 (the seventh in Canada), and the A.T. Hill club at Ansonville, the communists hoped to recruit young people outside Finnish circles, but here they had little success. When the RCMP investigated communist activities in the region in 1934, it reported that the South Porcupine branch of the Workers' Sports Association had sixty-four members, all Finns, and the Timmins branch had seventy-eight members, only fifteen of whom were in the "English section." The Ansonville branch claimed that it was the only "English" branch in the district, but the RCMP agent reported that its twenty members were "mostly young Finns born in Canada."[34]

The non-communist Finns organized their own alternative sports clubs, primarily through the large and successful Consumers' Co-op, which had become the focal point of their community by the early 1930s. In 1934 it helped a group of young women organize the Jousi ("Bow") Athletic Club for archery and gymnastics. In 1936 a wrestling instructor arrived from Toronto, and the Consumers' Co-op briefly rented a hall on Sixth Avenue in Timmins for the expanding activities until it could build its own hall above a newly constructed co-op store. Even that facility quickly proved inadequate, so in 1936 the society purchased the Moose Hall and converted it to Harmony Hall, run by the Suomalainen Edistyssevra (Finnish Progressive Society). The same year, the society purchased a piece of land on the Mattagami River just west of Timmins to create a park with recreational, swimming, sauna, and picnicking facilities. In 1939 those interested in athletics reorganized themselves as the Timmins Revontulet ("Northern Lights"), which was described later as "an independent sports club whose members also belonged to a Finnish hall, a co-operative and a Lutheran church," although the Revontulet "managed to develop its own traditions."[35] The Revontulet became a very important part of the lives of a large part of the Finnish population within the region, and it provided important connections with Finns in other parts of Ontario because its members travelled regularly to festivals and competitions, particularly in the Sudbury area.[36] Young men and women were thus able to spend a great deal of their leisure time socializing with other Finns, thereby reinforcing their personal and community identities within a circle of Finnish language and culture.

The Finns were avid skiers, and here their enthusiasm helped to make contacts with the broader community. For example, in 1927 the South Porcupine Ski Club was organized, and it soon blossomed with the membership of Carl and Anna Kleven and their family of seven boys. By 1936 there were 233 members in the club using the facilities it had constructed about five kilometres from Timmins; by then, many of the members were not Finns.[37] Skiing became a popular sport among families of several nationalities, as something in which one participated rather than as a spectator sport.

One other important contribution the Finns made to the sporting culture of the region needs to be recognized – the place accorded to women. As historian Lynne Marks has pointed out, in southern Ontario by the turn of the century, sports were almost entirely masculine activities: "Women who became involved in most sports were seen as freaks or oddities who were breaching the bounds of appropriate feminine behaviour."[38] The Finns who came to Porcupine–Iroquois Falls brought an entirely different attitude to women and sport. Strong and healthy women's bodies were to be celebrated and hence cultivated. One of the favourite activities for women's "physical culture" was team gymnastics, which attracted large numbers of young women and was part of the broader Northern Ontario activity circuit, as has been noted. These ideals of feminine behaviour may initially have been confined to the Finnish population, but as will be discussed, they eventually permeated the wider population.

Spectator sports rapidly became a passion in the region among working people, in large part because sporting events provided an opportunity for small-scale gambling. Cobalt historians Charlie Angus and Brit Griffin once observed that "mining culture by its very nature is a gambling culture,"[39] and the employees of Abitibi were not immune to the game either. Bets on hockey, baseball, and pool matches added excitement to contests large and small. In 1921 horse races were held at the first Porcupine (Golden City) fair, and they proved such a success that John Dalton decided to develop a regular track on his family farm just west of Timmins. Four thousand people turned up for its grand opening on Dominion Day 1924,[40] and it continued to attract crowds for a number of years.

Dog-team racing was another popular activity. Early in the winter of 1916, a few members of the Porcupine Camp decided to have some fun by putting together dog teams from the motley collection of animals in the district and racing with them between South Porcupine and Timmins. Joe Brisson won, covering the distance of approximately twenty-two kilometres in one hour, thirty-two minutes, and thirty-seven seconds. The event proved so popular that it evolved into an annual affair, with the *Porcupine Advance* claiming it was "One of Canada's Big Three" by 1920. The competition became serious business. Teams were bred and trained under the watchful eye of locals, and in 1919 Hamilton Wills offered a fine silver cup to the winner. Mr W. Martin became a regional celebrity with six consecutive wins from 1918 to 1923. By the mid-1920s the race had expanded into a full-fledged winter carnival, with a parade through Timmins and with hockey and broomball competitions, snowshoe races, a "kettle boiling competition," and $1,500 in prize money put up by local merchants. The whole event wrapped up with a dance called the Moccasin Masquerade Ball. Through it all, however, there is no doubt that the dog race was the main draw – and betting on its outcome the main excitement.[41]

Gambling was not restricted to sports betting, of course. In the towns, dozens of "clubs" sprang up where men went to play poker and other card games, to smoke, and to consume considerable quantities of alcohol. Newspaper magnate Roy Thomson's biographer claimed that men in Timmins "played poker at tables where 'pots' of four thousand dollars were not uncommon – and where one game, at the Mountjoy Social Club, ran uninterrupted, night and day, for three years."[42] One might accuse the author of exaggerating to paint a picture of Timmins as the "wild frontier," but the authorities had a similar image of them and kept a wary eye on these clubs. For example, at the Pioneer Club, run by Archie Miner, 150 men each paid $1.50 for a three-month membership that entitled them to play cards and to purchase drinks (allegedly soft), cigarettes, and meals. Employee Leo Joanisse acted as poker dealer and sales clerk.[43] In the summer of 1935 the police decided to make an example of the Pioneer and levied a series of charges against the owner, including that of living on the proceeds of gambling. Most clubs were smaller and more casual affairs scattered through the neighbourhoods. Some served a French-speaking clientele, while others catered to Italians, Finns, or Ukrainians. They provided a comfortable atmosphere in which men could socialize after a shift's hard physical labour. They helped establish or reinforce networks among cultural groups, and they provided a sort of surrogate family and domestic space for single men living in bunkhouses and boarding houses.

Another important centre for social and recreational sporting activities was the "amusement parlour." Early on in the life of the Porcupine Camp, several of these sprang up, first in tents and then in hastily erected frame buildings. Like the clubs, these "parlours" served as a surrogate family gathering room. They offered facilities for pool, smoking, eating, and sometimes bowling. Iroquois Falls came a little later to the game, but in 1919 it, too, welcomed its first pool hall and bowling alley as an alternative to those already well established in Ansonville.

These games rooms were owned by a culturally diverse group and very quickly gathered ethnically segregated clienteles. The largest in Timmins was owned by Thomas F. King, a Canadian who had come to the camp in its early days. In partnership with a Mr Fitzpatrick he had also established one of the first movie theatres in the area. King's association with the game of pool (considered socially dubious in such places as Toronto, with its much larger middle class) was no hindrance to him in Timmins, and he eventually came to occupy a place of social prominence and respectability. His amusement parlour appears to have been perceived by the local middle class as a valuable service that kept young men away from less desirable pursuits, such as drinking, fighting, and radical politics. King's main competitor was an Italian entrepreneur, Peter M. Bardessona, who took over King and Fitzpatrick's theatre about 1916 and later formed an association with Leo Mascioli to parlay the theatre into big business. There were also many smaller neighbourhood games rooms, which consisted of not much more than a pool table and snack bar. By 1919 there were eighteen such establishments operating under licence in Timmins alone. They were variously run by French-speaking Canadians (A. Champagne, N. Perron, A. Girard, and P. Bigras among them), Finns (V. Ukkala), Italians (M. Menzino, I. Ferri), various eastern Europeans (J. Zalinsky, T. Carpovitch, and O. Yarovenko), and one Chinese proprietor (W. Ling).[44] French- and English-speaking Canadians organized bowling leagues from time to time, such as the 1919 league, with Albert Brazeau as president and A.G. Carson as secretary. Members of the other cultural communities seem to have preferred social games rather than organized competition, perhaps in part because of their smaller numbers.

Formal organization provided a venue for another sort of leisure activity as dozens of clubs, fraternal societies, and youth groups were formed that offered international as well as local options for social gatherings. One of the first was probably the Porcupine Club, an association of mine engineers and managers organized in the early years of the gold rush. They put up a canvas tent and hired a "custodian" to provide temporary accommodation and a social gathering spot.[45] In February 1912 the growing group of managers and professionals organized a Porcupine branch of the Canadian Club to foster "the study of history, literature, art, music and natural resources of Canada, the recognition of Native worth and talent, and the fostering of a patriotic Canadian sentiment." Like their southern counterparts, they held dinners with guest speakers (such as the Anglican archdeacon Robert Renison) and musical entertainment, but unlike other Canadian Clubs they invited those who were not of British citizenship to join as associate members.[46] To these men, class was a more important sorting device than ethnicity.

Soon after these local initiatives came more formal organizations affiliated with international bodies. The development boom in Porcupine–Iroquois Falls coincided with an explosion of interest throughout the industrial parts of North America in lodges, fraternal societies, and clubs. These came to the region surprisingly quickly. Among the most popular were the Order of the Elks (founded in the United States in 1866; formed at Porcupine–Golden City in 1912 and at Iroquois Falls in 1923); the Oddfellows (arrived in the United States from England in 1819 and reorganized as American in 1843; formed at South Porcupine and Timmins by 1916 and at Iroquois Falls in 1927); the Kiwanis (founded in the United States in 1914; formed at Timmins in 1923); and the Lions Club (founded in the United States in 1917; formed at Schumacher and Timmins in 1935). Although these were exclusively men's clubs, many had affiliated women's groups. For example, the Oddfellows' Rebekah Lodge was established in Timmins in 1916 at the same time as the men's lodge. Also important, but more limited in its membership, was the Masonic Order (established at Porcupine in 1912, at Timmins in 1916, and at Iroquois Falls in 1918), along with its women's branch, the Order of the Eastern Star (formed at Timmins in 1925).

Although these fraternities were formed as service organizations, they were noted in the local press more for their social activities. The organizers of the Porcupine branch of the Elks announced as their first order of business the arrangement of billiards, cards, and smoking facilities in rooms on the main floor of the Mining Exchange in Golden City.[47] Others sponsored seemingly endless rounds of dances and euchre parties. In 1921 the North Bay *Daily Nugget* reported that the Timmins Oddfellows "are a very live bunch, and are to be congratulated on the quantity of their social efforts," which included a recent "stag euchre and cribbage party" ; it had begun with a "grand parade" through Timmins, "enlivened by the musical efforts of several of the company." The paper went on to note, "A very original and attractive invitation card was sent out to brother Oddfellows, which contained sundry exhortations, such as, 'Ladies, stay at home with your children' [and] 'Tribesman — had a very serious accident at his home recently. The last batch of home brew fell flat, and now it is so weak that it requires crutches to support it.'"[48]

Organizations with more political aims also seem to have served primarily as social clubs. When the miners' union formed a women's auxiliary in 1918, the *Porcupine Advance* reported that it was "chiefly for social purposes and for helpful co-operation between the ladies of the Camp." The Loyal Orange Lodge arrived in the Porcupine Camp in 1912, where it sponsored a sports day, complete with a "handsome silver cup" for the winners of the baseball tournament.[49] By 1915 there were Orange Lodges at Timmins, Iroquois Falls, Porquis Junction, Goldlands, and Schumacher; within a few years they were also at Matheson, South Porcupine, and Connaught. Almost every year on the "Glorious Twelfth" (of July), one of the larger lodges hosted a gathering that brought Orangemen from across the Porcupine–Iroquois Falls region for a day of parades, speeches, music, field sports, and an evening dance. The Timmins Golden Chapter of the IODE (Imperial Order Daughters of the Empire) was organized in 1919 by the wives of senior mine management and town professionals in the midst of rising concerns about the radicalism of the "foreign" element in town. After all, the IODE's motto was "One flag, one throne, one empire." But it, too, seem to have served primarily as an opportunity for women to get out of the house and enjoy the company of others within a shared social circle. The extent to which groups like these represented their founders' aims is not clear. Two of the senior officers of the Timmins IODE were francophones, and in 1936, when the Timmins Loyal Orange Lodge sponsored the regional celebration of the Twelfth of July, it cooperated with Father Thériault to share the ballpark so that the Roman Catholics could hold a fundraising circus and midway.[50]

The range of fraternal organizations and their contribution to community leisure activities is an interesting feature of regional social development. It contrasts markedly with what historian José Igartua found in Arvida, Quebec, which Alcan built for its workforce in the mid-1920s. There, only church and business appear to have played any role in organizing community activities, and only one fraternal society (the Moose) seems to have been founded.[51] The reasons for this difference are not clear, but it is possible that because of the larger number of Protestants in Porcupine–Iroquois Falls, there was a greater knowledge of fraternal societies and a larger base from which to recruit members.

Certainly, this type of society catered primarily to English-speaking Protestants. But there were numerous other social groups with their own ethnic, linguistic, or religious bases. The Jewish B'nai B'rith Society in Timmins had a high public profile through the 1930s. Perhaps the most influential, however, were groups sponsored or encouraged by the Roman Catholic parishes. The Knights of Columbus were particularly active in Timmins and Iroquois Falls, and each parish had its branch of the Catholic Women's League. During the 1930s, St Antoine's in Timmins had a large

branch of La fédération des femmes canadiennes-françaises, which promoted francophone culture with musical evenings in the Goldfields
Theatre; its smaller Ansonville counterpart held lunches and card parties.
Also in the 1930s, the Timmins Cercle canadien promoted the French language and Roman Catholic religion within a context of Canadian nationalism. At one point, it maintained an "employment committee" to help
French-speaking Canadians find work during the Depression. In 1945 a
French-language, men-only service organization called Le club Richelieu
was established at Timmins, two years after its founding in Ottawa.⁵² Like
the English-language fraternal clubs, it had a stated social service aim (in
this case, to assist underprivileged children), but it also clearly functioned
as a social focal point.

Almost every other cultural group in the region also formed societies
dedicated to a variety of causes and leisure opportunities. There were the
Sons and Daughters of England, the Cornish Social Club (and choir), the
Caledonian Society, the Croatian Club, the Porcupine Young Syrian
Society, the Italian Camille Cavore, and, of course, the myriad groups
organized by the Ukrainian Labor Farmer Temple Association and the
Edistysseura (Finnish Progressive Society) or the Finnish Organization of
Canada.

Organizations for young people provided their own form of recreational
activity. Founded largely by community leaders who were concerned that
teenage boys in particular were at risk of being led astray in the unre-
strained atmosphere of camp life, they were often sponsored or assisted by
the various churches. Timmins's first Boy Scout troop was formed in 1916
under the sponsorship of the Anglican parish, and shortly afterwards its
minister, R.S. Cushing, helped to organize a Girl Guide company as well.
St Matthew's provided both the leadership and meeting space through the
1920s.⁵³ In the early 1930s, Scouting graduated from under the Anglican
wing: a second troop began to meet in the Hollinger Hall as a community-
sponsored association. In 1935 it became even more inclusive and extensive, with Boy Scout troops organized at the Moneta School, the Roman
Catholic parish of St Antoine (French), and the Roman Catholic parish of
the Nativity (English). Within two years, there were more: at the Legion
Hall, at Notre Dame de Lourdes parish hall, and an all-French troop at
Ansonville under the sponsorship of Ste Anne's parish. Iroquois Falls also
had Scout and Guide groups. The movement's activities were very popular.
At Timmins alone, there were some 360 boys in eight Scout troops and six
Cub packs in 1937.⁵⁴

Many other societies, with a range of purposes, came and went over the
years. In 1912 the Porcupine Literary and Debating Society met to discuss
everything from socialism to the liquor laws. One of its meetings concluded "with a concert and entertainment, with a real live ventriloquist

and magician to lend prestige to the occasion."[55] Iroquois Falls for a time
had a Science Club and a Snowshoe Club. The latter fitted up an unused
Abitibi building with a phonograph for dancing and promised hot beans
and brown bread after a winters' tramp through the bush.[56] The Timmins
Volunteer Fire Brigade organized a recreational club in 1919 to purchase
a gramophone, a pool table, and magazines for its members. Even the
salaried staff at Hollinger organized a group for themselves – the Saturday Night Club – at which they had card parties and other social events.[57]
There were active horticultural societies (in Iroquois Falls from 1916 and
at Timmins from circa 1924); and the Iroquois Falls Community Club was
created to coordinate recreational activity through its five divisions:
music, art, literature, dance, and amateur theatricals. Some of the theatricals were original productions, such as the musical review "Abitibi
Follies."[58]

One organization that came to play an important role in the region was
the Great War Veterans' Association (later the Royal Canadian Legion).
The first branch appears to have been established at Iroquois Falls in
October 1917; the Porcupine branch was formed at Timmins in January
1919 after a delay because of the Spanish influenza epidemic. In 1937 veterans in South Porcupine decided to form their own branch because travel
to Timmins for meetings was not convenient, and in 1938 a branch of the
Ukrainian Veterans' Society was created at Timmins. While the main goal
was to protect the interests of men who had served overseas, the Legion
contributed a great deal to the community more broadly. For example, in
the 1930s the Timmins branch sponsored the construction of a community park and purchased life-saving equipment to be kept on the bridge
over the Mattagami River. The Legion and its Ladies' Auxiliary held
dinners, dances, and other activities for its members, eventually becoming
something of a drop-in social centre, as it did in so many small towns across
Canada. On the occasion of Porcupine's fiftieth anniversary, local residents recalled that Legion events were among the top three "unequalled
for fun and happiness."[59]

As if all these organized social opportunities were not enough, church
leaders continued to agonize over the dangers of drinking establishments and amusement parlours, fearing that too many unsupervised
young men were a danger to the community. So the churches began to
provide alternative evening and holiday gatherings that would encourage
a more restrained "family" atmosphere. Euchre parties became a
favourite in Roman Catholic parishes among both English- and French-
speaking parishioners, although the evidence suggests the pastime was
introduced by French Canadians from the Abitibi region across the
border in Quebec.[60] In 1931 the Ansonville United Church initiated a
program of monthly social evenings, with food provided by the Ladies'

Aid and entertainment organized by the church board. These evenings were open to anyone in the community over the age of twelve. First United Church in Timmins purchased land on Nighthawk Lake in 1932 and built Camp Waskesiu, to be used by young people and adults during the summer. The Iroquois Falls (Methodist) United Church sponsored musical activities for young people and adults through the 1920s, as did the United Church in Timmins where the Sunshine Mission Band evolved into a general recreational and social service organization by the mid-1930s.

Throughout the region, various groups organized picnic grounds that were important social venues in summer. Abitibi, Dome, Hollinger, and McIntyre (among others) held annual company picnics. The Buffalo Ankerite Mine built a handsome log "lodge" and swimming facility at McDonald Lake in 1938; it was used by a range of organizations, including the South Porcupine Catholic Men's Club, the Baptist Church, MacKay Presbyterian, the Mine Mill Union's ladies' auxiliary, the Kiwanis service club, and the staff of Timmins Town Hall. The Consumers' Cooperative Society developed a recreational park on the Mattagami River that was used primarily by the Finns, while the Timmins branch of the Ukrainian Labor Farmer Temple Association had its own picnic grounds for a number of years.

Halls were also important centres for leisure activities. Some were paid for by the companies at Iroquois Falls, Dome, Hollinger, and other mines. The Hollinger Hall, for example, was built in 1923, primarily (but not exclusively) for employees and their families, for indoor sports such as basketball and badminton, and for dances, receptions, and private parties. It became in such high demand that in 1951 the company restricted its use to employees. The Masons, Elks, Moose, and Oddfellows built their own halls in the larger towns. The Orange Order had halls in South Porcupine (by 1915) and at Iroquois Falls (by 1929). Cultural communities also built or purchased their own halls. There were Finnish halls in South Porcupine (by 1916) and Timmins (the first in 1915); Ukrainian halls in Timmins (the first in 1922) and Ansonville (1928); a Polish hall in Timmins (by 1933); and a Croatian hall in Schumacher (by 1934). Italians and French-speaking Canadians used their parish church halls for similar purposes. In the smaller communities, such as Connaught and Monteith, church halls were opened to a variety of organizations and recreational use. At Porquis Junction, the Agricultural Society (founded 1918) built a hall that became a valued gathering place, while at Ansonville it was the municipal hall that provided recreational, meeting, and kitchen facilities. The Great War Veterans' Association established the first of the many Legion halls in the district. And in 1912 the Western Federation of Miners built its own hall, which was used for dances and other events besides union business. There was thus an extraordinary number of facilities for public gatherings, but because many served a unique constituency, they often perpetuated divisions within the region and encouraged a sense of community only within a particular subculture.

Two activities to which these halls were put that did cross subcommunity boundaries were music and dancing. Music could be found everywhere, from the farm kitchen to the bush camp to the public theatre. As the labour activist Bob Miner later recalled, "There were more choirs and bands than you could shake a stick at."[61] Residents of South Porcupine had organized a brass band as early as the winter of 1912–13 and had arranged for R.V. Sylvester of Huntsville to lead the group.[62] In the spring of 1915 a group of Italian musicians in Timmins, under the direction of Tommasco Scocco, began to play impromptu (and much-appreciated) concerts on the streets. By the end of the summer they were playing regular concerts, which drew sizable crowds outside the Empire Theatre on Monday and Saturday nights, initiating what became a Timmins tradition of association between Italians and musical entertainment.[63] By 1917 Timmins also had a formally organized and outfitted Citizens' Band, sponsored jointly by Hollinger and the municipality, which gave Sunday evening concerts on the main street. Not to be outdone, Iroquois Falls organized its own band, which gave its first dance in early February 1918; its second public performance that season was a benefit dance at the town hall to raise funds for the Red Cross in the war effort.[64] By the 1930s the list of musical organizations included the Finnish Band, the Croatian Orchestra, the Goldfields Band, the Porcupine Pipe Band, the McIntyre Concert Band, the Cornish Society Choir, the Welsh Miners' Choir (most of whom were Scots-Canadian), the Timmins United Church Mission Band, the Schubert Choral Society, and the Timmins Symphony Orchestra. Amateur night at the Empire Theatre was guaranteed to draw a crowd in the years after the First World War; a typical program included "English songs by the Bowes children, French songs by a young lady singer, and Italian songs by Mrs. Frank Baradiso."[65]

Perhaps the most beloved community musician was Eugene ("Gene") P. Colombo. Born in Detroit, he arrived in the Porcupine Camp as an eighteen year old in 1911 and quickly made a name for himself "because of his clever violin playing abilities." He initially played at the Majestic Theatre in South Porcupine; then after the first Empire Theatre was opened in Timmins, he became a regular fixture, for he and "Scotty" Wilson on the piano accompanied the silent films. When the movie was over, the duo moved down to the basement hall and played for the couples dancing there. Gene Colombo played at many local clubs and events, composing his own music for some occasions. He eventually became manager of Leo

Mascioli's Empire Theatre and was greatly missed when he died in 1940.[66] Perhaps as much as any individual, he helped build bridges between the Italians and other cultural communities in the region.

For most people, music was associated with dances. Right from the earliest days of the gold camp, the pulp mill, and the farm clearing, every community hosted dozens of social evenings that included dancing and, in many cases, elaborate suppers. Early in November 1911 the grandly named Porcupine Mining and Stock Exchange hosted a dance in Golden City that was attended by more than two hundred people, in spite of the fact that women were in scarce supply. Not to be outdone, the Porcupine Barbers' Association imported a "harp orchestra" from Toronto to play for one hundred and twenty couples in the Miners' Union Hall. When Iroquois Falls was still no more than a construction camp of male workers, arrangements were made to escort women from Cochrane to the Abitibi cookery for dances; some women from the developing agricultural centres such as Porquis Junction also attended occasionally. The shortage of women continued to pose a problem even after the First World War, when weekly young people's dances at the Miners' Union Hall in Timmins charged fifty cents to admit "gentlemen" but encouraged "ladies" to attend for free. Special trains were occasionally put on to permit a bigger draw for the dance in the days before automobile travel was feasible. Eventually, dance "pavilions" were erected on Porcupine Lake (the Edgewater) and on the Mattagami River west of Timmins (the Riverside), where summertime dances became the highlight of many young people's lives. As Lempi Mansfield, then a young married woman, later recalled, "We went to the Riverside Pavilion to dance [in the mid-1930s]. It was beautiful there with the lights shining on the water and the lights would throw colours off the decorations hanging on the ceiling. After the dance we would go to our place for a party and break up at 3 a.m. We'd serve lunch. We had no alcohol in those days at our gatherings."[67]

If alcohol was not a part of Lempi Mansfield's social gatherings, she was certainly the exception to the rule. Beer and spirits were both the glue that held social life together – and the acid that corroded it. Alcohol use and abuse was a constant in the history of the region, both when Prohibition was in force and when it was not. "Prohibition does not prohibit – at least in this country it doesn't," observed a reporter for the Toronto *Globe* in 1909. "Here in Elk Lake one will often see more drunks in a day than he would in the city of Toronto."[68] The Ontario police tried vainly to keep alcohol out of the Porcupine Camp; the first seizure of six whisky barrels came in January 1910, before the camp was even well established. But the police had little support from anywhere but Toronto. As noted in an earlier chapter, several Porcupine mine managers had complained in December 1910 that the police had seized their Christmas liquor shipments. And several blind pigs were selling liquor openly to thirsty customers at exorbitant prices, which the hopeful argonauts seemed all too willing to pay. The police were able to lay charges in only one case (in February 1911), when a disgruntled customer who had been ejected from Alfred Bohun's establishment laid a complaint.[69] Failing in the attempt to shut down individual establishments, the police tried to cut off the supply, periodically seizing whisky in boxes labelled "butter" or hidden in crates of apples. For its part, Abitibi resolved to keep alcohol out of the hands of the Iroquois Falls townsite construction crews, but purveyors simply set up shop in the Wye; Ansonville became renowned for its many "drugstores," whose main business was liquor sales. Indeed, in 1921 even the acting police magistrate (and coroner) at Iroquois Falls spent three months in jail for breaching the Ontario Temperance Act.[70]

Few suppliers bothered to comply with provincial liquor laws as the population grew and as well-paid work crews looked for a little socializing and entertainment after their shifts were over. The community leaders themselves could see little point to the provincial authorities' attempts to enforce the law. In May 1912 the *Porcupine Advance* announced that it would no longer print the weekly list of liquor offenders. Instead, it began to report the court proceedings against liquor law infractions as if they were comic entertainment, while also poking fun at Toronto: "Eight residents of South Porcupine dug up $350.00 last Wednesday and contributed the same to the Provincial exchequer without a murmer [sic], notwithstanding the fact that they received nothing in return for their outlay. That's more money than Toronto raised for the Titanic sufferers at a theatrical performance in the big city."[71] On another occasion the paper reported, "Thirty-seven cases of booze were on the sidewalk in front of Magistrate Torrence's office Wednesday morning," bringing "many a wistful look to the faces of passers-by."[72]

The possession and sale of alcohol became a game in which local residents pitted their wits against the provincial police. Blind pigs posted lookouts to watch for police; seized liquor was returned to its owners when they swore before the court that it was for their personal use only; and ingenious devices were created to smuggle alcohol past the authorities.[73] The *Porcupine Advance* particularly enjoyed the efforts of one John Macko, who was observed by sharp-eyed Constable Ed Carmichael to be wearing "unusually large pants." Carmichael investigated and discovered "that a number of cans were suspended inside the wide pants down the legs and so placed that no apparent discomfort was caused to the illicit carrier." The *Advance* (as usual) found the whole affair amusing: "The goods were taken – that is the liquor not the pants – and Macko summoned to appear in Police Court."[74] Some vendors attempted to get round the provincial laws by selling what they claimed was "2½ percent beer" but which the police regularly concluded was of higher alcohol content. "It has been suggested," observed the *Porcupine Advance*, "that the whole bunch who admitted they had that concoction ... should be fined for that offence itself and then granted licenses to sell something decent with a 'tang' to it."[75]

The clientele of the various blind pigs tended to be ethnically segregated because Italian, Finnish, Ukrainian, and Slavic men sought out the company of others who spoke their language or hailed from the same home region. Finnish women seem to have owned quite a few of these establishments, and they in particular did not take kindly to any interference in their businesses. Mary Peterson, for example, was sentenced to four months in the North Bay jail, with no option of a fine, after her third conviction for selling liquor without a licence from her shop in Moneta. Ever defiant, she spat in the face of one of the people who had witnessed against her in the courtroom (for which the judge levied an additional two months).[76] In Timmins, one proprietress of these *koiratorppas* was nicknamed the Queen of Hearts and became the stuff of local legend.[77]

Although infractions of the liquor laws were generally the subject of local humour, alcohol abuse could be very dangerous. Three men became ill and one died in 1923 after drinking homemade liquor at an Ansonville "pharmacy," and the following year a salesman died in Renfrew after a visit to Ansonville in which he consumed what turned out to be wood alcohol.[78] Alcohol consumption was often a prelude to violence, both in public and private spaces. Street brawls outside drinking establishments in the early hours of the morning usually resulted only in a few cuts and bruises and the occasional charge of disorderly conduct, but sometimes the consequences were more deadly. On Christmas Day in 1921, the men at Andrew Bogdnick's boarding house in Schumacher spent the day drinking, and in the evening a brawl erupted between three Austrian and four Russian boarders. John Linsky, a fifth Russian boarder, apparently tried to break up the fight but died from his injuries three hours after the police arrived. Manslaughter charges were laid against three of the brawlers.[79] In another case, at Ansonville in October 1922, a group of Abitibi mill workers spent some time drinking before Karl Kilimnik attacked two of them with an axe, killing Ivan Mulechuk and seriously injuring Joseph Karyck. Kilimnik was sentenced to eight years in a federal penitentiary.[80] Domestic disputes between men and women or between men about a woman also featured prominently in the police court reports, and alcohol was generally a factor. Most cases did not involve weapons, but occasionally sticks, knives, and revolvers were produced and more serious injuries reported.

Excessive alcohol consumption was significant enough to have economic consequences, a fact that was of concern to managers, retailers, and civic officials by the mid-1930s. Someone estimated that $700 worth of beer was sold daily in Timmins at that time – money that could obviously be spent on other purposes. The editor of the *Advance* reported, "At one mine it is said that 150 men failed to show up for work the day after pay-day, beer being blamed for this." Recently, he claimed, eight men had been fired in one week for excessive alcohol use.[81]

Certainly, the widespread availability of alcohol contributed to the problem. In 1936 provincial inspectors closed seven Timmins beverage rooms for liquor law infractions, but that still left twelve licensed beverage rooms, not counting the unofficial neighbourhood "clubs."[82] Historian Nancy Forestell found that there were twenty-eight beer parlours within the municipal boundaries of Timmins in 1939, and she concluded that in the late 1940s Timmins had "twice as many beer outlets per capita as the city of Toronto."[83] But availability is not the only explanation. For young single sojourner immigrants who were far from home and family, the loneliness must have been incredible and the off-work hours long and empty. Shared sociability through drinking and the deadening effects of alcohol must have been appealing. Furthermore, the willingness to drink and the ability to consume vast quantities seem to have been a significant part of the working man's culture in the region from the beginning. It was a display of manhood equivalent to the display of strength and courage underground. Finally, alcohol may have been something of a vehicle of empowerment for men who were relatively powerless at the bottom of a workplace hierarchy, as a little joke used as a filler in the Mine, Mill union newsletter hints:

Joe, the mucker, had his usual Monday hangover.
"Just think," said the shift boss, "If you'd stay sober, you might become a shift boss like me."
"Shift boss, Hell," said Joe, "when I'm drunk I'm a mine manager!"[84]

Drunkenness was, perhaps, one of the "weapons of the weak," to use a phrase coined by political scientist James C. Scott.[85]

The public consumption of alcohol (and its attendant public consequences) appears to have been largely a phenomenon of the resource towns in the Porcupine–Iroquois Falls corridor. Agricultural service centres like Matheson and Monteith were rarely noted in reports of alcohol use and abuse. The reason may be partly economic, for struggling settler-farmers clearly did not have the disposable income to spend on drinks in bars. It is also possible that their alcohol consumption was done privately, at home, and thus came less often to the attention of the authorities. Whether such consumption patterns were the result of economic, cultural, or practical causes simply cannot be determined from the surviving evidence. All that can be said is that the public use of alcohol was primarily a phenomenon of the working man's society in the region.

While the wives of the working men might sometimes be found drinking at the public establishments, their recreation of choice was more likely to be escape through an evening at the movies. Theatres were built at South Porcupine, Ansonville, and Timmins almost immediately with the founding of the towns. In the spring of 1912 the *Porcupine Advance* ran advertisements for the Rex Theatre that promised "3 Reels every night" of "The World's Best Pictures," in addition to live entertainment the week of 22 April by Bartlemes, Lucins, and Valera, who offered juggling, "Comedy Talking and Grotesque Dancing."[86] In 1917, when Leo Mascioli built the Empire Theatre on Third Avenue in Timmins, he laid the foundations for a successful chain of theatres throughout northeastern Ontario. That year, Mr Alinas was running a theatre at "The Wye," and in 1920 Iroquois Falls at last opened its first movie venue. "The pictures will be shown regularly on Friday and Saturday evenings," reported the Abitibi newspaper, "excepting only that for the first few weeks they will not be allowed to interfere with the aSturday [sic] night Hockey fixtures."[87] During the 1920s the Majestic Theatre in South Porcupine became a community focal point with its film serials and romances as well as live stage performances. Lempi Mansfield kept a diary of life in South Porcupine from the 1920s to 1940s, in which she religiously entered the titles of dozens of films she saw each year. Later, she wrote, "One would always get a lift and escape from reality on those days when the ending was satisfactory. Sometimes looking at all the movies we saw [I wonder] how we had time for much else, but we did."[88] For the women, as for the men, it was a hard and often lonely life; movies provided the same sort of escapism and emotional satisfaction as alcohol consumption, but with less destructive consequences.

One other important activity in the region was hunting and fishing, which served to fill both recreational and economic needs for the non-Aboriginal population. The first prospectors made use of local food resources as they worked their way into the bush. Similarly, farm families quickly discovered the necessity of moose meat and fish to feed themselves as they struggled on marginal land. Indeed, a number of them (particularly French-speaking Canadians) added trapping to their mixed economy in an attempt to generate a cash income. Employees at the mines and mills eventually also joined in the seasonal ritual of hunting and fishing, but for pleasure rather than for economic necessity. The satisfaction of providing for one's family permitted a sense of at least some independence from the mine or the grocery retailer. Hunting became an almost exclusively male activity among the non-Aboriginal population and contributed considerably to the culture of masculinity in the region.

At different times, hunting and fishing drew on participants of different classes. In the period before the Second World War, middle-class business and professional men organized "rod and reel" clubs such as the South Porcupine Gun Club (1913), the Dome Mines Gun Club (1916), and the Iroquois Falls Rod and Gun Club (1929). The clubs sponsored trap shooting, stocked local lakes with fish, and even attempted several releases of pheasants for sport-shooting stock. The Iroquois Falls club purchased boats for shared use on several lakes and built "camps" at Perry and Watabeag Lakes for members to use. Clearly, for these men, hunting and fishing of a particular type were hallmarks of the "gentleman," and participation in these clubs was a distinct mark of social status.

The ways in which the residents of the area chose to make use of their leisure time became an important contributor to an emerging social organization and sense of personal and community identity, as will be discussed later. But some observations about the general patterns of recreational activity are appropriate here. How did recreation change over time? Why? Why were particular activities favoured and others rejected? What kind of participatory patterns can be discerned, and what do they tell us about the community?

In the early years of the Porcupine Camp and Iroquois Falls, recreation seems to have been pure play: spontaneous, exuberant, casual, and inclusive (at least, if you spoke English or French). People shared a sense of excitement and optimism about their future, and most were young and just starting out on their adult lives. Reading the columns of the *Porcupine Advance* or the *Broke Hustler*, one is caught up in an infectious zest for life. Dances held in tarpaper shacks with a piano and violin or accordion, with "suppers" made from what could be drawn from a tin, sound in these newspaper columns like gala balls with full orchestra and glittering fancy dress. Participants were often invited to attend in costume, as they did at the "barn dance" in 1911 in Golden City, where the women wore gingham and bonnets and the men wore overalls and smocks. People played at being someone else, testing a variety of identities among a crowd that did not yet know them and would not judge on the basis of past association or family history.

The terrible fires of 1911 and 1916, and the violence of the 1912 strike at the Porcupine mines tempered this early enthusiasm, and the tone of public life hardened a little. At the same time, not only was the growing population more diverse, but differences were becoming more apparent. Recreation became more organized, less fluid, and (in a sense) a more serious business. Teams, clubs, leagues, and organizations were created to direct and control activities. Spectator sports vied with participatory sports for people's time. Class, ethnicity, and gender began to affect recreational patterns in more obvious ways. Corporate sponsorship of elaborate facilities and money for players and equipment introduced a new level of competitiveness and professionalism. It was almost as if the communities were determined to prove to themselves and the world that they were real, permanent, and important – not a flash-in-the-pan gold rush or a minor league bush-cutting operation.

Recreation also became a surrogate battleground for political, religious, and ethnic differences. Communist-sponsored clubs vied with non-communist clubs for young people's patronage. Working men from one nationality drank and played pool together and then fought on the streets with men of another nationality as they spilled out of the bars at closing time. Miners at the bottom of the pecking order waged imaginary battle with their bosses in vigils over beer, while mill workers thumbed their noses at corporate Abitibi as they crossed the tracks to drink in Ansonville. Roman Catholic priests, Lutheran pastors, and United Church ministers organized "family" activities to lure young men and women from the dangers of drinking, gambling, and fighting; in the process, they established yet another kind of competition and social division.

Eventually, however, shared interests in recreational activities began to dominate over the conflicts. Hockey became a symbol of northern masculinity: skill and finesse, combined with brute strength and winter hardiness. If you didn't play yourself, you could always prove your knowledge of the game with a winning bet on the outcome or a memory full of statistics and plays. Hunting represented other characteristics that the community had come to value: individual prowess, an intimacy and visceral connection with "the bush," and a source of personal power in the face of powerlessness elsewhere in life. Gambling (on cards, horses, dogs, and team sports) mirrored the gamble that people had taken with their lives in coming to an unknown world in the hope of a better future. Drinking and movie going provided an escape from the harsh realities of this new life – the ever-present danger on the job, the loneliness of separation from family and home, and the limited opportunities for women. Music could be shared and appreciated across the barriers of language differences.

The favoured pastimes represent a fascinating balance of the individual and the collective, undoubtedly mirroring the community's attempts to balance the personal traits of the individualists and entrepreneurs who were attracted to the region with the obvious need for cooperation to make the project work. Hockey, for instance, is a team sport, but individual effort is applauded and "stars" become heroes. For young Finnish women, gymnastics provided a similar balance, as individual effort was married to synchronized team performance. Baseball, too, is a team sport, but the individual batter and pitcher direct the course of the game.

Recreation was also the site of a delicate balancing act between employer and employee in the company towns. The managers of the mines and paper mills obviously believed that recreational facilities were worth the expense: they would simultaneously attract and create the kind of stable, cooperative workforce the managers wanted. Sporting matches would provide a controlled outlet for aggression while keeping young men away from the dangers of the bar, the brothel, and radical politics. Recreational facilities would attract men with families, who would be more likely to remain on the payroll for a long time, providing stability and a level of expertise. In other words, recreation could be used as a means of social control. Most workers seemed well aware of the purpose of this apparent corporate largesse, but felt no qualms about using it to their own benefit. For the Mine, Mill union's leader, Bob Miner, the situation generated some ambivalence, as he later recalled: "Bickell [president of the McIntyre Mine] took an active interest in the social welfare of his miners and he built the McIntyre Arena, with a restaurant, bowling alley, curling rink, hockey rink and basketball court. To make it even better, he gave every McIntyre miner thirteen dollars a month in coupons for use in the arena. This was good in a sense, but on the other hand it was meant to keep the men quiet."[89]

Certainly, the immense popularity of the McIntyre Arena suggests that, in one sense, it was a successful corporate device for social control. In another way, though, McIntyre employees made the facilities their own, coming to expect such amenities as their due – part of the remuneration owed them for risking their lives underground and working long hard shifts in the mill. The McIntyre centre did not become a symbol like the proverbial "company store," cowering and resentful under the shadow of the nearby headframe. Instead, it became a source of community pride. Iroquois Falls and Schumacher maintained a rivalry for decades over who had the best arena (and hence the moral high ground). Display was clearly a part of sports competition; the team that made the best showing did so not only with its skills but with its uniforms and venue, and if it took corporate sponsorship to put on that show, so be it. When the Iroquois Falls town hall (provided by Abitibi) burned down in 1965, many residents were emotionally devastated. "Perhaps it was an expensive building to maintain and it certainly had its faults," recalled one, "but the many people who took its facilities for granted for so many years felt a deep sense of personal loss after the fire."[90]

Finally, recreational activities undoubtedly became important because of the region's economy and location. Men earning good pay had disposable income. It is not accidental that the struggling farm families were least likely to participate in town-based events. And the relative isolation of a region within which there were half a dozen townsites provided an excellent setting for residents to turn their sights inward for amusement and friendly rivalry. Of course, many spent holidays with family and friends elsewhere; the Italians and Britons, in particular, made regular visits overseas. But during the long winter, with its early dusk, heavy snows, and bitter cold, travel was more restricted and people made an effort to "get out" to socialize. Recluses who withdrew into themselves to the point of incoherence were referred to as being "bushed"; social interaction was the only antidote.

So if work shaped the fundamental structure of society in the region, play was the arena in which the tensions generated by that structure were mirrored, modified, and sometimes even resolved.

CHAPTER EIGHT

Society

Aili Schneider, member of a Finnish family that emigrated to Timmins, recalled, "Mother used to tell us that in Finland out of the way places like this were called 'God's hidden pockets.' But this place could not merit even such a title, and she would not blame God if He forgot the whole mess. 'This Place,' the only way mother ever referred to Timmins ... Mother said, 'That's the way the whole country is built, makeshift and temporary, built for people who drift forever.' "[1] Roy Thomson's biographer was scarcely more positive: "All who came to Timmins from 1911 onwards were either looking for gold or planning to syphon off some of the earnings of those who had already found it. They were not looking for beautiful homes, so they built an ugly town. They were not interested in the Arts ... They were not obsessed with a respect for the law ... They were not all successful, so they formed a tough community, skilled in 'horse trading,' externally aware of the value of a buck, and, above all, warily respectful of those who had not failed."[2] Few but the First Nations expected to make the region a permanent home, and certainly much of what the newcomers built was ugly and makeshift, but there was more to it than that. Drawn by a shared goal of making a good living, people came from many different backgrounds to the mines, mills, and bush lands of Porcupine–Iroquois Falls. Even if they had no intention of staying, they had to make themselves comfortable for the duration. And work did not take up all the hours in the day. In the facilities and activities they arranged for themselves or in those their employers provided, an organized society began to emerge. The dynamics of that new society are the subject of this chapter.

From the days of the fur trade through the resource exploitation boom and beyond, it was economic opportunity that attracted most newcomers to the region, so it is not surprising that social categories and distinctions were derived primarily from work categories. These distinctions were a crucial determinant of people's experiences in the region. People were defined by their sex and ethnicity, certainly, but overlapping these identities was the concept of status and class that emerged from the structures of work and the business of earning a living. Relationships between home and work moulded the communities in both large and small ways.

Understanding class has been a major problem for scholars. Orthodox Marxists are perhaps the only ones who have no difficulty with the concept, subscribing to the materialist position that one's class is determined by one's relationship to the means of production. Either you own it or you work for those who do. In the late nineteenth century, the growing group of managerial, professional, and scientific workers was evidence that this strict definition of class needed modification. These were people who did not own the means of production but who aspired to the status of those who did, and they were clearly in a position to control and exploit the working class. So the concepts of the "petit bourgeoisie" and "middle class" evolved. Then sociologists began to consider the prickly question of how societies defined status in relation to class, and new ideas were debated about the influence of culture, rather than economics, on class systems. Functionalist, structuralist, and then postmodernist variations have left us with a seemingly endless smorgasbord of possible ways to conceptualize "class." As will become clear in the following discussion, seeing class as a product of both economic and cultural construction may be complex and somewhat unwieldy, but ultimately it provides the richest insight.

Aboriginal society before the arrival of the fur trade was neither egalitarian nor class-free, in spite of the wishful thinking of utopianists and the theories of neo-Marxist anthropologists. Certainly, every individual was born with more or less equal opportunity, but life experiences eventually differentiated status within the band and the wider regional society. A man who was a successful hunter would be particularly respected, not merely for his ability to provide for his family but because success at the hunt was tangible evidence of his access to the spiritual helpers and animals who gave themselves to him. Women who were particularly skilled seamstresses or basket makers also were respected, and their knowledge and expertise were sought by others. At the other extreme, people who were disruptive or committed offences against the group were ostracized or actively driven out. Leadership was fluid and every individual was relatively free to follow his or her own mind, but leaders did exist, providing advice or serving as models.

European fur traders brought with them more rigid ideas about social status but their ideas were not entirely foreign to the First Nations. Traders from Canada valued a man with good bush skills in exactly the same way the Native people did, and they too recognized the importance of forging alliances with prominent families through marriage and political negotiation. So it is not surprising that the Canadians slipped easily into the social networks that already existed. Hudson's Bay Company traders, on the other hand, brought ideas about class and status that were somewhat more distant and hence problematic for the First Nations – for instance, the HBC's early attempt to prevent liaisons between its servants and Aboriginal women. The company's quasi-military chain of command institutionalized status distinctions based on accidents of family and birth overseas more than on bush skills. Of course, the HBC system did leave room for promotion based on achievement, defined in corporate terms, but a man's place as chief trader or post labourer dictated what he ate, where he slept, and how he spent his leisure time. Men in position of authority proclaimed the rules to subordinates, who were expected to follow without questioning. In the summer of 1825, trader William Robins at Mattagami Post received a stiffly worded letter from his superior, Alexander Christie, saying, "I now desire you will strictly prohibit the men under your command from any improper connection, or intimacy, with the Indian women. Such irregularities cannot be allowed."[3] Christie himself was in fact married to a descendant of an HBC servant who had made just such an "irregular" connection, so he obviously had no difficulty with the different standards expected of the different classes of men within the company's ranks. We really have no clear evidence about how the First Nations reacted to the status distinctions that were introduced inside the HBC posts in the region, but it must have been one of the characteristics that divided the society in the camps from the society in the posts.

With the arrival of the first farmers and resource developers, the question of status and class became even more complex. In 1960 the Hollinger employee George Holland looked back on his long career and concluded that he liked living in Timmins because "in this community a person can live according to his means and is not rated as a citizen by his position or his possessions." Hoistman Owen Farnan echoed Holland's enthusiasm: "The people are free and easy and there are no social barriers."[4] In a very different vein, Jim Tester, a prominent member of the Mine, Mill union in northeastern Ontario, observed, "I was raised in the 1920s, and my father, who had been very much influenced by the Western Federation of Miners and had heard Big Bill Haywood speak many times, used to talk about him in such admiring terms. But I really didn't know what my father was talking about ... It wasn't until my actual experiences required answers to many of the problems that I discovered there really is a class struggle going on out there."[5] Were Holland and Farnan simply deluded by the comforts of a company house and a company-sponsored weekend baseball league? Were they merely stooges giving the company what it wanted for its corporate propaganda magazine? Or were the dynamics of class and status within the community far more complex than either they or Jim Tester would allow?

In the United States, there is a fairly well-developed debate about class in frontier societies. For many years, following Frederick Jackson Turner, the frontier was associated with individualism and egalitarianism as people allegedly found themselves free of the restraints of older societies. The new frontier society was believed to be a place where anyone could rise through hard work to a position of wealth and influence. American popular culture still reflects these ideas; but for over forty years, American scholars have been challenging them in a variety of ways. In 1959 Richard Wade proposed that although there was considerable mingling of classes in early-nineteenth-century American frontier cities, mingling did not mean egalitarianism. Wade described a stratified society that was led by merchants who occupied a place at the top of the social ladder, followed by lawyers, ministers, doctors, teachers, and journalists, who had as much "prestige" as the merchants but less income. Below them were the clerks, shopkeepers, and labourers. Then came the "transients and rootless," followed by African Americans (whether slaves or free).[6] In the late 1960s, Duane Smith followed this approach in his study of mining camps in the Rocky Mountains from 1859 to 1890. "Society ... in the sense of class consciousness, came early to this urban frontier," he wrote. "Social stratification was also reinforced with the coming of women, who brought with them or quickly copied the prevailing attitudes of the East."[7] More recently, the academic pendulum has begun to swing back again, revisiting the possibility of frontier social openness. Paula Petrik, in a study of Montana mining communities in the late nineteenth century, proposed that this frontier "promoted increased economic opportunity," which in turn encouraged "social equality," especially for women.[8] Most authors seem to agree, however, that the value system that came to dominate these communities was essentially a middle-class ideology, rooted in the business ethic of economic advancement through hard work, and brought to the frontier by the urban merchants who were among the first and most permanent residents in the mining camps and railway towns of the American West.

There is no doubt that merchants played an important role in shaping the class dynamics of northeastern Ontario. Although they were a small proportion of the population, their tendency to longer-term residence gave them an influence out of proportion to their numbers. But the social structure of the region owed far more to the nature of the economy and the structure of the workforce it produced. In both mining and paper-making, production required large numbers of manual labourers (both skilled and unskilled) and a relatively small group of managerial and scientific personnel. And the owners – the "capitalist class" or "haute bourgeoisie" – constituted a very tiny group indeed, some of whom (in the early years, at least) did not even live in Canada. Furthermore, the concept of a class of owners is problematic, since nearly all companies were publicly traded on North American stock exchanges, and many workers themselves owned shares. And, of course, the TNO was a government-owned and hence publicly owned railway. Thus, the class structure in the region developed differently from that of urban Canada during the same period. These were working towns, with very few professionals and managers and even fewer capitalists or owners. The business and service sectors were small. Simply by force of numbers, working people dominated the public discourse. Furthermore, since these were small communities in a semi-isolated setting, people were aware of one another's lives in ways that city dwellers often fail to realize. Household status was gauged by the occupation and work performance of its male head.

If the structures of the regional economy contributed to local ideas about class, so did imported ideas developed in the circumstances of "home" societies. Immigrant workers from the Austro-Hungarian Empire, the British Isles, Finland, and even American mines had learned to see themselves as an industrial working class, locked in a struggle with the capitalist system. If they did not band together to protect themselves, they would be exploited, and the benefits of their physical labour would accrue to those who did nothing but sit and wait for the profits to roll in. Canadian-born workers in Northern Ontario, however, had no such misgivings about capitalism. Industrialization had come late to Canada, and many of the Canadian workers had been born on family farms or were no more than a generation removed from the agrarian life. For them, industrial capitalism was still a sign of "progress" and desirable modernity – a great adventure in which they were participating to build a new nation and a better future.

That is not to say that Canadian-born workers had no sense of class difference. But, for them, class was overlaid with ethnicity and the great chasm between French and English. English-speaking Canadians had a sense of entitlement to a place at the top of the status ladder; French-speaking Canadians were growing resentful of a situation in which "the bosses" invariably seemed to be English-speaking and the workers, French. Whether it was a supervisor in the mill or the directors of a local athletic association, leadership seemed to be in the hands of one "class." Before 1950, however, francophones in the area kept their resentment to themselves. As writer Lola Lemire Tostevin put it in a fictionalized account, "There is a photograph of my mother standing in front of her grandfather's shop, Louis Séguin and Son – Sash and Door, the sign in English because that's where the business was, with the English, and you didn't want to offend them by flaunting your French."9 In Porcupine–Iroquois Falls, the classic Canadian tension was somewhat tempered by the factors that were discussed in chapter 5 – the large proportion of French

Table 6   Occupations of Timmins residents, 1915 and 1920[1]

	1915 %	1920 %
Farmer	1	0.6
Technical, clerical	9	8
Business, professional	28	20
Labour	61	72

Source: Table reproduced from Forestell, "All That Glitters Is Not Gold," 100, table 2.1

[1] as characterized by Nancy Forestell

speakers, the leadership of francophone entrepreneurs such as the Timmins family, and the historic roots of both anglophones and francophones in the Ottawa Valley, where accommodations were being grappled with already. Nevertheless, English was the language of public space, and resentments were building that would lead to the demands for change made (and achieved) by those born after the Second World War.[10]

These divisions of language, religion, politics, and ethnicity were even more pronounced between Canadian-born workers and immigrant workers, so it cannot be said that there was a single, self-conscious "working class" in the traditional Marxist sense. Nor (in spite of the best efforts of dedicated socialists and communists) did a working class "make" itself, in E.P. Thompson's sense, during the formative years of the resource economy. However, clear social boundaries and status designations emerged. Some were imposed by the structures of workplace and townsite geography; others evolved as adaptations to the unique conditions of life in the area.[11]

The hierarchical structure of the workplace was reflected in every aspect of the resource-based community, from where people lived to how they played and where they worshipped. Company housing dictated physical distribution of class within some places, but even when people were free to choose their place of residence, workers at the bottom of the hierarchy tended to congregate in certain neighbourhoods and their bosses in others. In Timmins, where there was sufficient population to support more than one church of some denominations, congregations reflected these divisions. Miners and mill workers were likely to join certain types of clubs or participate in certain sports, where their fellows were other miners and mill workers; the managers and doctors belonged to entirely different organizations. Class may be problematic for scholars to define, but in the mining and forestry-based towns, its impact was very clear to all.

At the top of the pyramid were the corporate directors. Although they were rarely seen in the North, their existence was permanently noted through the company guest house or Directors' Lodge, where they stayed on their occasional inspection tours. Until the Great Depression, the Directors' Lodge at Iroquois Falls was a large imitation-Tudor house with a spacious verandah overlooking the town park. It was clearly meant to impress: "That living-room was graced with a great fireplace, and a wide, curved staircase that reached a balconied mezzanine which opened to various rooms ... At the rear of the building was a dining room, kitchen and stores, and a narrow staircase that twisted through 180 degrees to the quarters of the couple who acted as caretaker, cook and housekeeper."[12]

The larger mines also had guest houses for visiting directors, whose visits were invariably something of an occasion, always noted in the local press. At the opening of the Dome mill in 1912, "twenty-one private rail cars brought guests from as far away as New York and Chicago while several additional cars were laid on by Pullman. A Toronto company was engaged to decorate South Porcupine streets ... There were hourly trains to take guests to see the forty stamp mill turn out real gold bricks. At the banquet ... the potted palms came from the railway conservatory down the line."[13] Frederick Schumacher, original owner of the Schumacher Mine (later part of Hollinger), visited regularly until he was into his eighties, and every year he donated Christmas gifts for distribution to the schoolchildren in the town that bore his name. The gifts were not only appreciated (and commemorated in an outdoor wall mural), but they were clearly a reminder of the paternalistic relationship between owner and worker. Other "owners" were represented by their delegates, who lived in the community and were acknowledged by the workers as a sort of surrogate nobility. Alphonse Paré, nephew of the Timmins brothers, lived in Timmins for many years on the hill at Hemlock Street overlooking the mine on one side and the workers' homes on the other. F.H. Anson's son (F.H. Junior) and Anson's elderly mother lived in Iroquois Falls.

At the next level (below the directors and owners) was the local middle class, which could be divided into two subclasses. The senior group consisted of the mine general managers and the Abitibi plant general manager, who was called the director in the early years. Most mine managers lived on the mine site apart from the homes of all other employees. Abitibi's general manager lived in a designated house on Cambridge Avenue; it was larger than the other houses and on a slight elevation above them. Mine managers tended to be engineers with international experience, for example, Percy A. Robbins (Hollinger, 1911–18) who had been born in Chicago and had worked in the United States and South Africa; Richard J. Ennis (McIntyre, 1913–40s) who had worked in Colorado; and H.P. De Pencier (Dome, 1921–34) who had worked in South Africa. They

were university graduates, as were many of their wives.[14] Dome staff liked
to joke about the McGill connection, while Queen's and the University of
Toronto also were well represented among the Canadian-born managers.
A few, like E.L. Longmore (Hollinger, 1944–51), had lived many years in
the community and were promoted into the position; but most, like Joseph
H. Stovel (Dome 1934–44), were brought from outside directly into senior
management. Obviously, there were fewer Abitibi managers for comparison, but they seem to have fitted the same general pattern. Robert A.
McInnis, for example, (manager 1917–26) had worked for pulp and paper
companies in New York and Montreal before joining the Abitibi head
office and being sent to Iroquois Falls.

General managers (and their wives) played an active role in the community, which seems to have been expected – a sort of *noblesse oblige*.
McInnis was president of the Northern Ontario Boards of Trade
(1922–24) and vice-president of the Ontario Associated Boards of Trade
(1924–26); he was remembered in Iroquois Falls for his public service.
Longmore was director of the Cochrane District Children's Aid Society.
Robert E. Dye, superintendent, general manager, and eventually vice-
president of Dome, was an active supporter of the Victorian Order of
Nurses, while Stovel served on the Tisdale Public School Board and the
National War Labour Board. A cynic might conclude that this public
service was actually, in the words of British scholar Howard Newby, "the
exercise of power" over their workers – a paternalism that was given a
gentle face through an appeal to the idea of community.[15] Nevertheless,
the leadership provided by senior management was useful and probably
necessary.

While playing a role integral to the northern community, the managers
also remained connected to the wider world of international business and
finance, as well as to social networks from their university days. Not all were
products of an urban childhood. Dye was from small-town South Dakota,
De Pencier from the Gatineau region of Quebec, Longmore from a farm
near Ernestown in eastern Ontario, and McInnis from Gravenhurst,
Ontario. Nevertheless, through their education and work experience they
were part of an international, cosmopolitan social system.

The more junior subclass in the region's middle class consisted of the
service-sector professionals (doctors, lawyers, clergy), middle-level managers (department heads in the mines and mills), scientific and technical
personnel who supported production, and the owners of the larger businesses. In the mining and forestry sectors, they were often university-educated and had work experience across the North or internationally; they
socialized with and aspired to be general managers. Stan A. Wookey, for
example, was born in Jamaica, graduated in engineering from the University of Toronto, came to the Porcupine Camp in 1911, was promoted to

assistant superintendent at McIntyre Mine in 1927, and retired to Toronto in 1947.[16] Unlike Wookey, however, most members of this class tended to be highly mobile, pursuing career opportunities wherever they arose. As Gladys Kitchen, a resident of the area, later put it, "These people moved around a great deal ... [They] were well travelled, well educated, so the community had, right from the beginning, a certain amount of culture. It was primitive in the way we lived, but not in the way we had our social gatherings."[17] Those social gatherings were the subject of some fascination for the local press in the early days of the Porcupine Camp. In mid-March 1912, for example, the Cobalt *Daily Nugget* reported on an entertainment that Mrs Charles Auer held for her friends at her "spacious colonial residence" near the Mattagami River on the occasion of the visit of a Toronto friend. Present were the wives of the Hollinger general superintendent (duly given first position on the guest list), the local doctor, the largest dry-goods retailer, several Hollinger middle managers, the assistant general manager of McIntyre, and several others. From the elaborate description of their costumes, the guests had clearly come prepared for a grand occasion.[18] Members of this class took care to establish social boundaries. When members of a South Porcupine club held a card party and dance in 1916, they informed the *Porcupine Advance*, "Admission will be strictly by invitation, and those not having an invitation will not be admitted. The committee have taken this course to characterize a class of citizens from those which as a rule make things very unpleasant in these social affairs ... The members of this society are conducting this dance on firm principles in order to establish and maintain a high standard of sociability amongst the citizens of South Porcupine."[19]

In spite of the small size of the middle class, the social life of its members tended to be divided among the employment sectors. While the occasional golf tournament brought Iroquois Falls professionals in contact with mining professionals, the two circles generally operated independently. Merchants socialized among themselves and might interact with others primarily at church or synagogue. The middle class did come together, however, in public service organizations such as school and library boards. In 1932, for example, the Timmins Public Library Board consisted of two Protestant clergymen, one Roman Catholic priest, a mining engineer, a geologist, a public school principal, the wife of a commercial salesman, and the librarian (whose husband was an independent prospector).[20] The libraries seem to have been of interest almost exclusively to the middle class. As one South Porcupine resident recalled, "How bravely and long Reverend McVittie, pastor of the United Church, had fought, without much help and indeed against a little opposition from town authorities, for the establishment of this important asset to community life."[21] In Timmins, when a vote was held in 1921 to approve plans for a town library,

only forty of a potential three hundred property owners turned out to vote
– and two of them were opposed to the idea.[22]

While there was a degree of residential segregation that helped set the
middle class apart, the differences were not always as significant as might
be expected. In the town plan for Iroquois Falls, the single houses just east
of the town centre (facing the Directors' House) were labelled as homes
for "superintendents, the Mayor, and other dignitaries," while the "double
houses" to the west side were intended for general workers.[23] But over
time, middle managers appear to have become more scattered throughout
the townsite. Nevertheless, they were rarely found in Ansonville, outside
the company town limits. In Timmins, the first "cottages" built by
Hollinger just west of the mine were intended for professional and managerial families, but over time that group spread itself throughout the town.
Still, they were more likely to be found on the streets north of what became
Algonquin Boulevard. South of it lay the working men's neighbourhood of
Moneta, and farther west, Hollinger built the tar-papered rows of miners'
houses. In smaller communities like Schumacher and South Porcupine
there was no obvious residential segregation, primarily because there were
so few residents who could be called middle class. One place where class
segregation was clear, however, was in the numerous housing developments that many of the mines built adjacent to their properties. The
largest of these was at Dome, which even had its own school. Here, managers lived apart from miners and mill men; the distinctions were made
physically and aesthetically with more attractive houses and larger lots for
the managers.

Ethnically, the middle class was predominantly Anglo-Canadian, with a
handful of Americans and French-speaking Canadians among the mine
and mill staff, and a scattering of immigrants from farther afield among
the retailers – such as Charles Pierce, who was born in Russia, and Samuel
Bucovetsky, who was from Poland. The French Canadian members of the
middle class tended to be fully bilingual and considerably anglicized, like
businessman J. Émile Brunette of River Joseph, Quebec, who was
described by one observer as being "half French, half Irish – all Canadian."[24] Another was lawyer Gordon Gauthier, born near Windsor,
Ontario, to a family of Great Lakes fishing-boat captains. Thus, while non-
Anglo members of the middle class did exist, there was the widespread
impression among working people that "those in charge" were invariably
English-speaking Canadians.

By far the largest "class" in the region was that of labouring men and
their families. Some might be classified as unskilled labour, but for the
most part they should be recognized as skilled workers, as has been discussed. In one sense, it is misleading to consider these people a single
"class" because they were deeply divided by language, ethnicity, and reli-

gion. On the other hand, their place in the workforce meant that they shared basic life experiences and a place in the community that permits us to consider them collectively.

Nancy Forestell, in her fine study of the lives of Timmins miners, has pointed out that the hard physical nature of the work shaped a good part of the lives of working people there,[25] and the same could be said of men employed in the bush camps or in the Abitibi mill. Shift work complicated social life and leisure time, while the high proportion of single men and transients dictated a very different social dynamic from that of middle-class workers with their resident families and regular hours.

It would be wrong to conclude that because of these conditions, working people were entirely absent from the public life of the community. In fact, their interests and pastimes dominated it. As was discussed in chapter 7, they were dedicated and enthusiastic sports fans, supporting local hockey and baseball teams from the top level of competition to the amateur weekend pick-up game. Working men also supported the dozens of fraternal organizations that flourished throughout the region.

Euchre parties were a favourite pastime for mixed-sex gatherings, while men-only activities revolved in large measure around drinking – at home, at licensed "beer parlours," or at unlicensed blind pigs. Drinking and smoking provided a bond among strangers; they became such a core of working men's identity in the region that anyone who did not participate was suspect. In 1922 a corporate spy reported at one mine, "Some of the men are inclined to ridicule G— as a shift boss because he does not drink or smoke."[26] When Timmins Town Council tried to have the licence of a local wine store revoked, the motion was opposed by the three working men's councillors, one of whom (a McIntyre labourer and truck driver) explained, "I hate to see a working man deprived of his drink – no matter how cheap it is."[27]

Among labourers, attitudes to class and social status varied considerably because of the influences of ethnicity and history. Union activist Bob Miner recalled that at Dome, miners imported from Cornwall, England, "were class conscious to the extent that they took their caps off whenever they met the boss."[28] Some of the Finnish labour organizers despaired at the willingness of Canadian and especially Italian workers to acquiesce to management's demands. The Finns read and circulated the twice-weekly *Miners' Bulletin* (published in Sudbury), which included an Italian section (the *Bulletinel Minatori*), as well as directing other recruiting and educational efforts toward those whom they considered ignorant of the realities of labour politics.[29]

There were important distinctions of status among the labourers. In the mining sector, underground workers considered themselves the workforce elite because of the physically demanding and dangerous work they

performed. The shift boss held a position of particular power and authority, not only because of his control of day-to-day work activities, but because
he hired (and could fire) men for his crew. For many miners, "the boss"
meant the shift boss; office-based managers were too distant and vaguely
unimportant to matter. When Hollinger built its tarpaper miners' "cottages" in Timmins, the shift bosses were strategically located in every fifth
house along certain streets, undoubtedly because of the control they could
exert, even away from the mine.

Ethnicity, ethnic exclusivity, and attitudes toward other ethnic groups
were also important status differentiators within this group. Finnish miners
tended to be highly literate and politically well educated, so they considered themselves superior to groups such as the Italians, who tended to
have low literacy rates and political docility, at least in terms of complying
with management's dictates. Both English- and French-speaking Canadians considered themselves superior to recent immigrants, especially
during wartime, when they simply assumed that they were entitled to the
first chance at employment opportunities and promotion considerations;
and as was discussed in chapter 5, the Chinese were at the bottom of the
ethnic hierarchy, entirely because of racist attitudes. Aboriginal people
were accorded a peculiar place. Romanticized images of who they once
had been were constructed and integrated into local identity myths, as will
be discussed. But contemporary "Indians" were something else altogether.
Those who had joined the labour force seem to have been considered as
low-status Canadians or as a branch of the French-speaking population,
while those living apart on the fringes of the new society were alternately
ignored or pitied as a regional underclass.

Ethnicity was not the only delimiter of status: place of residence was also
important. Iroquois Falls workers considered themselves superior to
Timmins workers because their community was more attractive and, they
believed, better supplied with recreational facilities and organizations.
And, of course, Ansonville residents considered themselves superior to Iroquois Falls residents because in Ansonville they were independent of
company control.

There may also have been more subtle attributions of status based on
personal and individual criteria. Obviously, these are much more difficult
to distinguish or measure, but in such small towns where everyone knew a
great deal about everyone else, there must have been a place for this kind
of alternative status. The British scholar Bill Williamson observed this phenomenon in a turn-of-the-century English coal-mining town. Because the
miners held similar jobs, lived in similar houses, and knew what everyone
else was paid, Williamson concluded that "claims to be different had to be
based on more abstract qualities such as respectability, bearing, honesty,
integrity, learning." Women were judged on how well they kept their

homes and their children. For Williamson, the significance of this person-alization of social standing was that "any evidence of falling behind was taken as an indictment of the individual concerned and not as a reflection of prevailing social conditions."[30] While I have been unable to find ade-quate evidence of this form of status distinction in Porcupine–Iroquois Falls, it may well have existed, and it may help explain the relative lack of radicalism among the Canadian-born workers that was noted in chapter 6.

While these rough categorizations of class and status are helpful in a general way to understanding the social dynamics of the community, they are also misleading. First, most people did not seem to think of themselves as members of a particular class. There were two exceptions: the small middle class, who self-consciously distanced themselves in subtle and not-so-subtle ways from the workers; and the politicized labour activists, who came to the region with a well-developed class sense that had been nur-tured in labour relations in Europe or the American West. However, the majority of working people looked around them, saw other working people, and agreed with hoistman Owen Farnan that there were "no social barriers." The second problem with these rough class divisions is that a number of individuals in the community did not entirely fit any of the cat-egories, and a certain degree of status mobility over time helped to blur the boundaries.

One of the most interesting examples of an individual who did not fit the class categories easily is Leo Mascioli, whom we met in chapter 5. From a beginning as an immigrant labourer, he quickly built up a business empire that gave him a position of considerable status in the region. His handsome Empire Hotel surpassed Hollinger's Goldfields Hotel as the fashionable place to stay in Timmins, and his chain of well-appointed the-atres in Timmins, Schumacher, South Porcupine, Ansonville, and New Liskeard became focal points for community recreation. He was a major investor in the Timmins *Press* – the first newspaper that offered serious competition to the *Porcupine Advance.*[31]

By 1939 Mascioli had become a very wealthy man. He was a mainstay of the Roman Catholic parish of St Antoine, and he contributed substantially to the construction of Sacred Heart Church to serve the Italian community in Timmins. When the *Press*'s second proprietor, Roy Thomson, lost his newspaper building and radio station in a fire, it was Mascioli who helped him get back on his feet. He sent his children to school in Montreal (where, sadly, one of his daughters died), and his son Daniel attended the University of Toronto and Osgoode Hall, whence he graduated in 1937 as what the *Porcupine Advance* celebrated as the "first Timmins-born barris-ter."[32] Mascioli also sent money regularly to support his family in Italy, and when the Italian government launched its campaign against Ethiopia, he supported the war effort by promoting the collection of cash and gold; by

the spring of 1936, Timmins Italians had contributed over $3,000 –
second in Canada only to the amount collected in Toronto.[33] Mascioli
arranged the founding of a Timmins branch of the Order Sons of Italy in
January 1939, by which time the order was dominated elsewhere in
Canada by fascists and under scrutiny by the RCMP. Mascioli's role in promoting the interests of Italians at home and abroad was recognized officially by Benito Mussolini. Consequently, when Italy declared war against
England and France on 10 June 1940 and Canadian authorities arrested
six hundred Italian Canadians for internment as enemy aliens, Leo and
Antonio Mascioli were among them. The local member of parliament, J.A.
Bradette, the senior Roman Catholic priest, Father Thériault, and Mascioli's fellow businessman, Roy Thomson, all campaigned for Leo's release
from Camp Petawawa.[34] After a brief internment, the Masciolis (and most
of the other Italians) were released, and Leo returned to Timmins to pick
up where he had left off.

Mascioli was clearly eager to be considered a leading member of the
community. Through the 1920s and 1930s, he joined the Knights of
Columbus, the Kiwanis, the Legion, and the Porcupine Pioneers Association; and it is significant that he was a member of the parish of St Antoine,
where other community leaders worshipped, rather than of the smaller
Italian Sacred Heart parish nearby. He made a point of owning large and
expensive automobiles, one of which (he proudly pointed out) "was always
borrowed by the municipality when celebrities came to visit Timmins,"
including the Prince of Wales.[35] The private education that he obtained
for his children and the elaborate stone monument placed over his grave
when he died in 1952 were also statements of his aspirations. But he was
never accepted by the Canadian middle class as one of its own. His arrests
in 1912 and 1940 were clearly an embarrassment, erased from community
memory. And even Roy Thomson's biographer, sympathetic for Mascioli's
assistance to Thomson, called him "utterly alien," with "ludicrous broken
English" – a "mere Italian migrant" who "could never rank equal" with the
Anglo-Saxon elite.[36] In spite of Mascioli's personal fortune, he was still a
"peasant." It would take another generation for the middle class to accept
his children as its own.

Another example of blurred class and status boundaries can be found
among the Finns. A Finnish miner or bushworker could have some surprising connections. When Kyosti Kallio was elected president of Finland
in 1937, Hollinger miner F. Omala gave a public lecture about him at the
Timmins Finnish United Church; Omala had attended school with the
president, and his wife and Kallio's wife continued to operate neighbouring farms.[37] Oskari Tokoi, a Finnish politician who had briefly been prime
minister in the turbulent year of 1917 (the first elected socialist prime
minister in Europe), worked cutting trees in a bush camp near North

Temiskaming with a group of fellow expatriates in 1920–21.[38] Political upheaval and a rural society in transition meant that distinctions in Finland itself were not always clear, and those blurred and permeable boundaries came with the Finns to Porcupine–Iroquois Falls.

Tracing class structure and relations in the agricultural sector is even more difficult. It seems that most farm families came to the area with very little in the way of start-up capital. The price of a 160–acre (65 hectare) homestead was $80, but only a quarter was required in cash; the remainder was to be paid in three annual instalments at 6 percent interest under the terms of Ontario's homestead legislation. So a farm property could be obtained with just $20 cash and a few tools. But getting things going would cost somewhat more. In 1915 the Monteith Demonstration Farm officials calculated that it would cost about $265 to clear 9 acres (3.6 hectares) of bushland. Based on the current price for pulpwood, only about $120 could be raised through the sale of logs cleared from those acres, assuming that about thirty cords of pulpwood were removed.[39] Hence, less than half the cost of clearing the land could be recovered in the short term, and for many families the financial burden was too great, forcing them to abandon partially developed properties. These farms proved attractive to some who had a little more cash on hand. Hamer Disher of South Porcupine recalled buying a farm near Matheson in 1919 for $600; it had three or four cleared hectares, a log barn, and a "nice little frame cottage."[40] Regardless of the route taken to ownership, some initial investment was required even though start-up costs were relatively low, so the very poorest families were unlikely to be able to establish themselves in this region.

While most of the area's farmers began from the same position as small-scale homesteaders, significant variations in the quality of the land and access to road or rail transportation meant that success also varied considerably. Hamer Disher was unable to support himself on his farm, so he took on jobs cutting pulp and building roads to generate cash, while he hunted rabbits or went fishing to feed himself. When Disher married, he moved permanently into South Porcupine, seeing no way he could support a family on the marginal land.[41] Leslie Walker had better luck with his farm near Porquis Junction. When he bought it in 1935, there were fourteen hectares cleared, and within six years he had thirty-six hectares under cultivation, six summer employees, a family home, and a house for one employee; he was in the process of installing electricity. His main crop was potatoes, which brought in from $6,000 to $10,000 in a season.[42] But it seems that Walker was the exception. Most farms were very small. Farms in Taylor Township near Matheson, which was the most successful of the agricultural areas, averaged only about nineteen hectares each in crops by 1941; in more marginal areas, such as German Township a few kilometres to the west, only about seven hectares per farm were under cultivation.[43]

Table 7   Farming in Taylor Township

	No. of farm owners	No. of farm tenants	Average acres in crops/farm	Improved acres/ person	Crop acres/ person	Farms under 50 acres	Farms over 1,000 acres	Total pop.
1911	36[1]	0	0	4.0	1.5	0	0	185
1921	95	1	20	6.4	5.9	4	74	412
1931	–	–	–	–	–	–	–	592
1941	101	5	47	8.0	9.7	1	62	751

Source: Data from Agricultural Census of Canada. Township level statistics were not reported for these categories in 1931.

[1]Includes Clergue and Walker townships

After it had become clear that field crops and livestock were not viable, poultry and egg production were promoted for a time by the district agricultural representatives; but here, too, resources were limited. In 1933 in the Val Gagné area, fifteen farmers owned an average of just fifty-three hens each. The agricultural representative referred optimistically to these farmers as "poultry breeders," but only one of them had any roosters.[44]

Interestingly, the most successful commercial farms in the area were owned by men who had not come with the primary intention of farming. The largest, with over eighty hectares cleared by the early 1920s, belonged to Gordon H. Gauthier, a Timmins lawyer who had served as mining recorder in the Porcupine Camp. He was the first in the district to purchase a "modern threshing machine" for his oats, and he produced potatoes and other crops commercially. He had the largest flock of poultry in the district and was one of only three registered breeders of Ayrshire cattle.[45] The Chinese restaurant owner John Chew purchased a farm in Mountjoy Township west of Timmins, and by 1918 he had sixteen hectares cleared on which he raised pigs and poultry to supply the hotels and restaurants in town. With his 130 pigs, the *Porcupine Advance* counted him "one of the biggest farmers in this district."[46] The Dalton farm west of Timmins was also well known locally – especially after it was turned into a racetrack and recreation spot.

It is almost impossible to develop any conclusions about class and status distinctions in the agricultural sector. Most people were forced to integrate farming with wage earning; very few succeeded as commercial farmers for more than a generation. The few who did were accorded recognition akin to other successful business families, but because there were so few, their impact on the region in social terms was limited.

Because of the continuing problems of transportation in the area, it was difficult for farmers to participate in social activities or in organizations that contributed to community development. Road construction was perpetually promised and perpetually delayed. The first lands opened to farming were along the railway, but these were largely veterans' lands and the majority were not taken up. As a result, incoming settlers were forced to select land farther back in the bush, where there was limited access.[47] As late as 1927, agricultural representative Daniel J. Pomerleau was still complaining that the few existing roads were bad. In most settlements, he reported, roads were either still under construction or utterly "impracticable" because of the conditions of rock and swamp.[48] One homesteader who lived only about two kilometres from Timmins in Mountjoy Township, complained that after five years there still was no road along the first concession, so he had no way of getting a crop to market.[49] A dozen years later, things were not much better in Mountjoy. George Vartinuk was commissioned by the farmers of that township to offer to pay the Town of Timmins to do the roadwork that the provincial government seemed to have forgotten.[50] The farm women of Val Gagné made membership in the Women's Institute an act of heroism, some of them walking several miles through the bush to get to the meetings (as late as 1941) because of the lack of road access. Mrs William Bailey spent forty-five years on her farm in the bush near Watabeag and made only one visit to Timmins and none to any other towns in the area.[51] Clearly, in these circumstances, it was difficult for farm families to have much influence on the wider society of the region. Unless they were working as wage labourers, they remained a people apart, outside the consciousness of the miners and mill workers, and outside their social systems as well.

Next to class, the other crucial structure that shaped social organization was the relationship between men and women, along with the concepts of gender and gender roles that defined life at home and at work. Indeed, class and gender intersected in a number of important ways, some reflecting patterns rooted in the sending societies and others evolving to meet the needs of the new settlements. It has become almost a cliché in North American culture to think of frontier societies as having very few women and being places where daily life revolved around the rituals of male work and male recreation. Yet that was never entirely true in this region. For a brief period, certainly, men outnumbered women quite significantly. However, at no time were women entirely absent, and for considerable periods they formed a substantial proportion of the population and played roles that, although distinct from men's, were equally important in shaping the contours of community. Thus, while the region evolved into a community dominated by a certain version of masculinity and male values, women were complicit in that process.

In the pre-boom Aboriginal society, of course, there were no sex ratio imbalances, and even with the introduction of the fur trade economy, with its male-only European workforce, the ratios were not significantly

Table 8   Aboriginal population of the Mattagami District, 1848–1850

	Adults		Children					
	M	F	M	F	Total	Births	Deaths	Out-migration
1848	81	105	103	85	374	n/a	n/a	n/a
1849	79	97	103	87	366	14	7	15
1850	80	102	95	57	334	9	12	29

Source: Based on Mattagami and Flying Post Journals, 1824–94, LAC, MG19/D16, vol. 2, pp. 37, 39

skewed. By the mid-nineteenth century, the population in the Moose Factory hinterland had adapted to the fur trade economy and absorbed the male newcomers. A relatively stable society had emerged, formed around family and kinship connections. Scots, French-speaking Canadians, and members of First Nations from outside the district had been incorporated into a network of personal relationships that provided both the foundation and the glue that held the fur trade economy together. Within these networks, women played a prominent and public role. Some – such as Tacqua, who traded at Mattagami Post in the 1820s and 1830s – headed bands in their own right and were valued trading partners of the HBC.[52] Others, such as Eleanor Brass, raised families who became important community leaders. Mrs Kellock at Kenogamissi managed the fishery for the post's crucial winter food supply, while other women managed the production and exchange of wild rice from the area west of Flying Post. The widow Misquabawaquey was one of the most important trappers who traded at Flying Post in the 1830s; and there was Caminocama's wife, who came directly to Mattagami for the scissors, cloth, and ribbon that she wanted; she was apparently not willing to wait behind in camp while her husband traded on her behalf. Indeed, the direct participation of women in the trade appears to have been much more extensive in this region than in most other parts of Canada.[53]

Within this fur trade society, nearly all adult men and women married, though a significant number of women outlived their husbands and spent part of their lives as widows. As children, boys tended to outnumber girls slightly, but in adulthood the ratios were reversed, perhaps reflecting women's greater longevity and the smaller chance of accidental death. Birth rates were not high, and families appear to have had only two or three children in the mid-nineteenth century, and three to four by the end of the century. Permanent migration in and out of the district appears to have also been limited, consisting primarily of migration for the purpose of marriage.

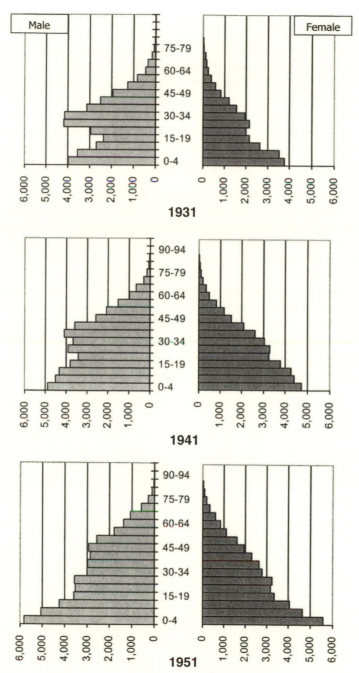

Figure 2   Changing sex distribution, Cochrane District

Source: Census of Canada

The situation began to change in the first decade of the twentieth century – slowly at first, then with a sudden dramatic flourish during the Porcupine gold rush. The advance guard of the new world was almost exclusively male, young, and unattached. First came the railway construction crews, then a scattering of farmers, then the prospectors and mine builders, and finally the Iroquois Falls construction crews – all laying the foundations of the new economy and the society it was to engender. While farming townships and the Iroquois Falls townsite soon had a significant proportion of women, the Porcupine mining fields would require a generation before the ratio of men to women returned to anything like that of the fur trade society.

It has become commonplace to associate resource-extraction activities and "frontier" societies with sex ratio imbalances. Mining camps, in particular, are constantly described as "almost wholly male" – an "uninhibited masculine world" that "confined women more completely to the home and domesticity" than other types of North American societies.[54] Frontier agricultural societies, on the other hand, have been seen by historians as offering new opportunities to women. Some historians have argued that the process of "pioneering" in building new agricultural societies in the Canadian and American West promoted a re-evaluation of cultural attitudes to women and produced reform movements that eventually affected the nation as a whole. In a region that included *both* mining and agricultural sectors, what, then, shaped the relationships between men and women? How did the community come to perceive gender and define gender roles? And how did the different cultural traditions of the inhabitants affect ideas in the new setting?

A survey of the changing demographics of the region is a helpful place to begin. Unfortunately, there are only scattered and often unreliable sources of population data. Only one manuscript census is available, because Canadian census takers did not venture into the unorganized townships north of the Canadian Pacific Railway until 1901, and subsequent manuscript censuses are closed to researchers. Published census data is not much more helpful. The census of 1911 predated the town of Iroquois Falls and only just managed to catch a fleeting glimpse of the Porcupine Camp during the gold rush. Only after 1921 does the published census data become more reliable. Nevertheless, some reconstruction is possible.

The 1901 manuscript census data is difficult to assess because most of the region's population is lumped together simply as residents of unorganized townships. The census takers did visit the HBC posts at Mattagami and Flying Post, which are clearly identifiable in the records, but the information they gathered there is suspect. For example, the section labelled "Matagami Region" is a list of only eight families and two single men resident right at the HBC post; there is no record of the families living beyond the post. In the undifferentiated districts, it is impossible to tell how far north of the CPR or how far away from the posts into the bush camps the data was collected. In general, though, the data confirm two main observations. First, fur trade society was still a healthy balance of men and women, with families of three to four children and a small but significant proportion of elderly people (one as old as Betsie Metewahgeezick, aged ninety-five, at Flying Post). Second, pockets of the new economy were beginning to appear just to the south, probably south of the height of land. Bush camps between Moncrief Township in the District of Sudbury and the Mattagami River consisted almost entirely of men; the only women there were the First Nations women whose families lived in the vicinity, plus a few French-speaking Canadian women and their families who had accompanied their husbands. At every camp that could be identified, even the cooks were men. The majority were young (aged eighteen to forty) with a few older men working as foremen or cooks.

With the inrush of newcomers between 1906 and 1912, the proportion of women to men declined dramatically. Even in the farming townships the men arrived first, having come to investigate the possibilities or to do some initial clearing, with the intention of bringing in wives and/or children later if all went well. When the census was taken in 1911 there was not one woman in German Township, and there were almost two men for every woman in Taylor Township. The most dramatic imbalances were at Matheson, where railway construction crews skewed the ratio to twelve men for every woman, and in the Porcupine Camp where Tisdale Township and some other districts had ten men for every woman.

However, it would be wrong to conclude that women had no role in the area before the First World War. There were, in fact, several hundred women, and they were highly visible in the mushrooming population precisely because of their limited numbers. The arrivals, departures, and activities of women were noted in the local press; they could be found in every sector and in a surprising variety of occupations. An examination of the sources produced during the early settlement years shows that women were an important part of the new economy and society. Only in later years, as a mythology grew up around these times, was the presence of women downplayed. Unlike later residents, the early settlers were anxious to point out the presence of women in order to represent the new community as stable and permanent. Later residents preferred, for different reasons, to de-emphasize that stability; hence, they de-emphasized the presence of women too. Their symbolic pioneer forebears became *men* of action and daring initiative who had left the soft comforts of home behind.

"It is quite remarkable the number of women to be seen in the Porcupine camp," reported the Cobalt *Daily Nugget* in the fall of 1910. Women could be found "not only in the little settlement on the lake, but roughing it in the tents on the claims."[55] Anishinabe women were among those visible to the newcomers. In several camps along the trail into the Porcupine district, they provided a hot meal or a sack of fresh potatoes or a mug of tea to the passersby, while countless unknown others undoubtedly did the same for the prospectors scattered through the bush, many of whom knew little of bush survival skills. One of the women, Maggie Leclair (née Buffalo) of Nighthawk Lake, became a celebrated part of local legend as "Princess Maggie," famed for her trapping prowess and knowledge of bush lore. In 1956 the *Hollinger Miner* ran a feature on her, calling her "one of the most colorful women in all of Canada's history, and certainly the best-known woman in Canada's northland."[56]

Women newcomers were attracted to the region for a variety of reasons. Mrs. Harry Reamsbottom decided it would be an exciting way to spend her honeymoon and accompanied her husband north for a little prospecting in the summer of 1909. Lulu Gibson came to help her brothers run a general outfitters' store at Golden City. Managers of mines that were scarcely more than optimistic holes in the ground built houses and brought in their wives for companionship. Mrs L.P. Silver, Mrs C.S. Steeles, and Mrs R.A. Weiss (doomed to die in the 1911 fire) arrived this way. Mrs Joseph Curry came to manage the Morrow and Beatty staff house at Iroquois Falls while the townsite was being built. Many young women whose names were not recorded came to work in the restaurants and laundries that served the growing population of single men. Others came as entrepreneurs themselves, setting up respectable restaurants, blind pigs, or brothels. Caroline Flowers came to prospect as head of her own team. And of course, there were the farm women, hoping to build new lives for themselves in partnership with their husbands.

The first women newcomers were primarily English- and French-speaking Canadians, with a handful of Americans, most of them wives of mining engineers and managers. In 1911, at the Porcupine Camp, half were married, just over a third were single, and the rest were either widowed or did not inform the census taker of their status. Nearly all were young, just starting their adult lives with high hopes for building a nest egg on the resource frontier. Soon after the initial influx, Finnish women began to arrive, many of whom had been living at Cobalt or Sudbury. They frequently settled with their husbands at South Porcupine or began to clear farm lots in the vicinity. Some came alone for employment as cooks or boarding-house help, sending their wages to families in other parts of Northern Ontario. It was not until after the First World War that Italian, Ukrainian, and other Central European women began to arrive in significant numbers, their sojourner male relatives having decided to settle permanently in areas where the employment opportunities had solidified.

Table 9   Women in the population (percentages)

	1921			1931		
	% Canadian born	% Foreign born	Women % of total	% Canadian born	% Foreign born	Women % of total
Timmins	28	10	38	34	11	45
Tisdale Twp[1]	26	11	37	25	15	40
Iroquois Falls	24	9	33	39	9	48
Ansonville	40	4	44	39	6	45
Matheson	40	8	48	39	10	49
German Twp	26	3	29	36	8	44
Taylor Twp	35	7	42	40	5	45

Source: Calculated from the census of Canada

[1]Includes South Porcupine.

Schumacher, Ansonville, and Moneta became their residences of choice. By the Second World War, the ratio of men to women was approaching the provincial norm in all parts of the region, with the exception of Tisdale Township, which took until 1951 to reach that balance.

It was clearly the hope of economic betterment that drew both men and women to the area, and as has been noted, it was work that came to define people's lives and their place in society most clearly. In some parts of the region, work was sharply "gendered" in that occupations were distinctly divided into men's and women's, and very different values were assigned to each type. In other parts of the region, gender lines were less distinctly drawn. In some places, gendered attitudes toward work arrived with the newcomers and persisted; in others, gender distinctions emerged and evolved locally over time.

Statistical data on employment is problematic as a source of information about women's role in the regional economy. In 1931, for example, the census indicated that Timmins had thirteen male wage earners for every one female wage earner, but other evidence makes it clear that far more women were employed outside the home than the 312 enumerated. Many businesses (legal and otherwise) were run as partnerships between husbands and wives, and women often ran the boarding houses that were home to miners or to men who chose not to live in Abitibi's worker accommodation. Farm women, too, were an integral part of the economy even if the law and the census did not recognize them as such. Work, then, was important to both men and women in the region.

On the farm and in the retail sector, gender distinctions were the least visible. Certainly in the first few years of the twentieth century, aspiring settlers from other parts of Ontario and from Quebec tended to send

Table 10 Sex ratios in selected districts, 1911–1951
(expressed as number of males to 1 female)

	1911	1921	1931	1941	1951
Timmins	–	1.6	1.2	1.1	1.0
Tisdale Twp	10.2	1.7	1.5	?	1.1
Iroquois Falls	–	2.8	1.1	?	1.1
Ansonville	3.8	1.2	1.3	?	1.2
Matheson	12.0	3.2	1.0	?	1.1
German Twp	100% male	2.4	1.3	?	?
Taylor Twp	1.7	1.4	1.2	?	?

Source: Calculated from the Census of Canada. Data were not published for any area other than Timmins in 1941 and not for the rural townships in 1951, by which time they had become so thinly populated that the census compilers probably decided not to include the more detailed data.

Table 11 Employment of men and women, 1931–1951

	Iroquois Falls			Timmins		
	M	F	Ratio M:F	M	F	Ratio M:F
1931	430	79	5.4	4069	312	13.0
1941	383	82	4.7	8342	1123	7.4
1951	449	98	4.6	8109	1756	4.6

Source: Compiled from the Census of Canada. These people are identified in the census as "wage earners."

the men first to select a building site for farm or store, with the women following later. It was a relatively simple arrangement, given that the travel distances were not great. But among immigrants from outside Canada, farmers and tradespeople tended to come as family groups. In the mining and forestry sectors, gender distinctions in the workplace were rigid and clear. No women were permitted underground in a mine (the belief persisting that a woman underground was bad luck), and they were rarities above ground too, with only a handful working as secretaries for senior management. Even the cooks in mining company bunkhouses were usually male. No women worked in the paper mill either, but they could be found as cooks in the bush camps. Women were represented in other parts of the service sector, notably as teachers (but rarely as school principals) and as nurses (but never doctors). They worked as waitresses in the many restaurants that catered to the single male population. Occasionally they can be identified as owners of these establishments, but more often the publicly recognized owner was male.

Only in the illegal blind pigs do women proprietors seem to have predominated.

Gender lines were also clearly drawn in many of the clubs, societies, and other social organizations that sprang up like mushrooms from the first days of the new settlement. Needless to say, women were not part of the senior business and professional organizations such as the Board of Trade and the Canadian Mining Institute. When agricultural societies were organized at Matheson, Porquis Junction, and other places in the 1920s, there were no women officers. Instead, rural women ran branches of the Women's Institute at Monteith, Matheson, Holtyre, Hoyle, Kelso, Shillington, Timmins, Porquis Junction, and Val Gagné.57 The Masons, Elks, and Oddfellows, and other fraternities eventually developed women's sections, but these operated quite independently. Indeed, some of these fraternal organizations made a point of their gender exclusivity, as was noted in the previous chapter. In 1918 the Porcupine miners' union formed its first women's auxiliary. Similarly, the churches usually established separate men's and women's service groups, such as the Catholic Women's League. Only in cultural organizations (for example, horticultural societies and the Cornish Social Club) and political organizations (the Finnish Organization of Canada and the Workers' and Farmers' League) did men and women participate in a more integrated way. In some cases, though, the integration had come at a price. In 1939 the Ukrainian Society in Timmins debated fiercely over whether to admit women as members. Tempers ran so high that the issue led to the police court after a male member was charged with assaulting Annie Bugera, who had advocated integration.58

In Iroquois Falls, Timmins, and South Porcupine, public life revolved so obviously around work from which women were excluded that it would be easy to conclude that they played only marginal roles in these communities. Nancy Forestell called the period 1911–20 in Timmins "Company Town – Bachelors' Town" and traced, during this era, the development of a "pervasive masculine environment" which "the arrival of women and children altered, but did not entirely eradicate."59 A similar pattern would seem to fit Iroquois Falls. As Forestell has demonstrated, for working men's wives in Timmins, not only was there no place in the workforce for them, but there was scarcely any public space at all for them before the 1920s. Dances and picnics provided only "infrequent" opportunity for social gatherings; tiny homes prevented personal entertainment with friends; and there were few other spaces "where women could congregate among themselves or socialize with husbands or boyfriends."60 Forestell proposes that during the boom years of 1920–40, the social dynamics in Timmins began to change as family life became the community focus, but the pervasive value system rooted in the masculine workforce lingered on.

However, two caveats must be raised about drawing connections between women's limited participation in the public workforce and the masculine culture of public life in the region. First, Porcupine–Iroquois Falls may not have been unique in having few women at work outside the home. In her study of working-class life in Halifax in the 1920s, historian Suzanne Morton broke with popular wisdom in pointing out that surprisingly few working-class wives had employment income: only forty-eight in a suburb of over 3,100 households.[61] Yet there have been no claims that Halifax celebrated a frontier culture of rough masculinity rooted in economic realities. Specific concepts of gender undoubtedly existed, derived in part from the workplace experience, but also evolving through other chains of events and experiences, as will be explored.

Second, the economy certainly had an impact on gender relations in the region. But as historian Karen Dubinsky's Ukrainian grandmother asked, "Who do you think did the cooking?" As she put it, "When [Communist Party leader] Tim Buck came to town, when [communist activist] A.E. Smith came to town, who do you think cooked?"[62] Gender segregation may have been an important fact of life, but segregation did not mean marginalization. Social networks established and maintained by women and the "domestic economy" of production to support the household were systems that shaped the community in ways just as significant as the mining, farming, and manufacturing economies.

Company executives saw the value of encouraging marriage and family life in order to stabilize their workforce; hence, the significant investment that Abitibi put into building a company town and the costs that companies like Dome and Hollinger were willing to absorb to provide family facilities. Middle-class Canadian managers believed that women would be a calming and civilizing influence on young male workers, who were supposed to be naturally inclined toward aggression and violence. In the game of boosterism, the area's business leaders used women as a symbol to downplay the region's raw frontier image and to promote the idea that the towns were there to stay.

Although most women were excluded from employment (with the notable exception of farm women, of course), they made public niches for themselves in a variety of places. They supported the Porcupine miners' union both through informal means (providing food for meetings and picnics) and eventually formal means (the women's auxiliary). They may not have literally built the many halls that sprang up everywhere, but they cooked, cleaned, and maintained them as important social spaces. They were a driving force behind the co-op movement in the region, which Finnish women in particular used as an outlet for social and political expression. They provided the bulk of the medical care during the deadly influenza epidemic of 1918, the volunteer labour behind the Children's

Aid Society and other social welfare programs, and they made possible the vibrant parish and congregational life of the region's churches and synagogues. Social networks cultivated by the wives of professionals helped delineate the boundaries of the middle class. Women were active in the socialist movements, particularly Finnish women, who had won the vote at home in 1906 and found it galling – and yet another sign of Canadian backwardness – that Canadian women did not have that right.

Thus, although there were consistently fewer women than men until the 1940s and although men's role in the workforce dictated much of the social dynamics, local conditions ensured that women had both a symbolic and a real influence disproportionate to their numbers. Community boosterism stressed the presence of women as a sign that this was no lawless frontier. Corporate discourse promoted an image of family life centred on the wife and mother. Finnish and other socialist women promoted ideas of women's equality and rights. And perhaps even the fact of scarcity itself promoted a degree of value. It was not until these conditions began to change in the 1940s that images of and attitudes toward women in the Porcupine–Iroquois Falls region began to resemble the Canadian norm more closely. As such, the gendered nature of work in mining, forestry, and railways (plus the failure of the family farm) ensured that women became less apparent in the dominant public discourse.

If society in the region was structured to a considerable degree around class and gender, transience was a third important feature. Transience is widely recognized in both popular and scholarly culture as a characteristic of resource-sector employment. Study after study of American mining and frontier towns has indicated that transience was the central fact of life. "'Just visiting' was an accurate synonym for most people's residency," wrote one historian of Comstock, Nevada, in the 1870s and 1880s.[63] Canadian studies have indicated similar results. Ian Radforth noted that in the late 1920s, Abitibi expected only 10 percent of its bushworkers to return from one season to the next, and Donald Avery reported that among Italian work crews on the CPR, 41 percent lasted less than three months in the job and 60 percent lasted less than six months. In a study of INCO workers in the Sudbury region, Paul de la Riva and Guy Gaudreau concluded that 67 percent worked less than six months, many leaving within days of signing on.[64] Sociologist S.D. Clark, probably the first to comment on transience in the Canadian North, proposed that mobility was actually an intelligent strategy for labourers who were faced with the "ruthlessly exploitative" conditions of work in Northern Ontario and Quebec. "Workers sufficiently mobile that they could be recruited," he wrote, "were mobile enough that they could not be kept for long if conditions of work proved intolerable."[65]

There is no doubt that transience was important in this area of northeastern Ontario, but it varied by economic sector, and those differences are important for understanding the community identity that eventually emerged. Retailers, business people, and some professionals (such as doctors) were more likely to remain for years because their livelihood required considerable capital investment and the gradual creation of a public reputation. However, bushworkers, railway construction crews, homesteaders, and mine employees were very likely to be highly mobile. Workers at the Abitibi mill fell somewhere in between. Difficult times in the pulp and paper market in the 1920s and the downright disaster of the 1930s forced people out of the community; it was not until the market stabilized and Abitibi's affairs were rearranged that more permanent employment was even possible. Eventually, a core of long-term workers evolved at Iroquois Falls, many of whom saw their sons and grandsons set off for the mill.

Statistics are most easily secured for the mining sector. Nancy Forestell reported that in 1917 the Timmins town clerk estimated that only 10 percent of the male population in town was more or less permanent, while half of the rest stayed for only three or four months. That year, she added, Hollinger hired 2,700 men but struck 2,600 off the payroll.[66] My own study of a sample of McIntyre Mine employees in the early 1920s produced similar results. Out of a maximum possible employment of twelve years covered by the records, 85.5 percent of the men worked for less than one year, and only 4.5 percent stayed at McIntyre for more than three years.[67] In 1940, when the area's Cornish miners celebrated the twentieth anniversary of their arrival, only fourteen of the original group of seventy remained.[68] Even during the Depression, when gold mining was the only really secure employment option, a sample of income tax data collected at the Buffalo-Ankerite Mine shows that 30 percent of the workforce was employed for less than a full twelve months in the year, and 5 percent worked less than six months.[69] The story of Robert Mahon provides a concrete example of this kind of mobility. He came to Northern Ontario as a child during the First World War and attended school in Ramore (south of Matheson) where his father owned a hotel. Then he went to work in mining, first moving back and forth among Porcupine-area mines, then to Kirkland Lake, then to Temagami, then to Chibougamau in Quebec, and finally to Cranbrook in British Columbia, where he worked for seven months before being killed in a mining accident in 1937. In his short career, he had changed jobs almost every year.[70] This kind of mobility was a continual problem for the mine managers. When Hollinger's personnel chief H.M. Ferguson went on a hiring expedition to England in the fall of 1950, he cited the high transience rate of Canadian-born men as the rationale for overseas recruiting.[71]

Statistical data from the Abitibi plant were not available, but a similar situation may have existed there. In 1936 the United Church at Iroquois

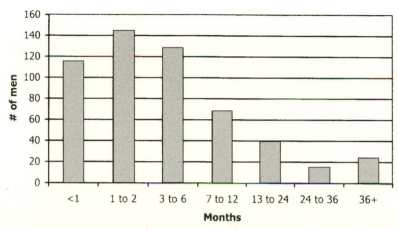

Figure 3   Duration of Employment, McIntyre Mines, 1913–1925

Source: McIntyre Mines, employee cards, Laurentian University Archives, Steelworkers Collection, PO20/1/D/1, 4

Falls was discussing the perennial problem of low membership, and the secretary recorded in the minutes of one of the meetings that "there is a tendency for new arrivals in Iroquois Falls to regard their stay here as of a temporary nature, and to defer transferring their church memberships from other churches." Interestingly, the very fact that the company hoped to attract a stable workforce by providing company housing may have contributed to the problem of transience. "Our population of 1,500 for the time being is largely transient," recorded the church secretary, "all property and homes being owned and controlled by the Abitibi Power & Paper Co. Ltd."[72] The attitude seems to have been that property ownership was a primary goal in life, so employment at Abitibi would be only a way station on the path toward that goal.

In other sectors of the economy, especially bush work and railway work, a small army of floating workers rolled in and out of the region, depending on the season, the wages, and the availability of work. They were part of a labour phenomenon in Canada more generally that has received little attention in scholarly analysis. Largely young single men with no specialized training or trade, they travelled back and forth across the country taking whatever job was available. Some were part of international mobile labour forces, like those from Italy and the Balkans that were described in chapter 5. Others had been born or raised in Canada, but their lives followed the same rhythms. Winter bush work gave way to summer railway maintenance work, which gave way to "harvesters' excursions" to prairie farms in the fall. Edwin Bradwin, who produced a study of work camps in Canada before the First World War, reported that among railway construction crews, transient workers constituted a distinct subgroup known as the "floaters" or "bo's"; Bradwin called them "itinerant navvies." "A restlessness pervades their days," he wrote. "There is the frequent desire to shift work, 'jumping' it is called, even though the move led to little betterment for the individual. It is the fact of change that is desired."[73]

While undoubtedly some of these men enjoyed the life of freedom that mobility allowed, many more were forced into transience by economic circumstance. The career of Ervin Toner illustrates the problem. Toner was born in 1912 at Cobden (in the Ottawa Valley between Pembroke and Renfrew). His father moved the family to Sturgeon Falls (west of North Bay) and took a job at the paper mill there. Ervin joined the workforce in 1929 as a riverman driving logs to the Sturgeon Falls mill. The timing was most unfortunate, for the mill began to cut back production soon after he was hired, and he was laid off. He heard that INCO was hiring at Copper Cliff, so he and some friends headed west to the Sudbury area, and he succeeded in landing a job in the refinery through personal contacts. But after only a few months he was again laid off as financial difficulties began to mount for the nickel-mining sector. Rumours that the gold mines were still hiring took him to Timmins, only to find that no jobs were available. So next he headed to Iroquois Falls, where an aunt offered him a place to stay while he found work. Late in the fall of 1931, he managed to hire on as a casual labourer at Abitibi's Twin Falls station. He worked at different summer and winter jobs for the next ten years before improving economic conditions permitted Abitibi to offer him a permanent position as a pumpman at Twin Falls. With the security of this paycheque, he was finally able to marry (at the age of twenty-eight). He remained at Twin Falls for the next seventeen years, raising three children, and eventually retired to Iroquois Falls. One son, Brian, went to work in the Abitibi mill.[74]

Whether people moved frequently as an economic strategy, as a personal choice, or as an employment necessity, the result for society in the region was significant. The small proportion of the population that was relatively permanent was able to have an impact well out of proportion to its size. Its members dominated the political and social leadership, not because of a sense of bourgeois entitlement or a desire for power (although these may have been important factors in a few individual cases) but because they remained in the region long enough to take on these public roles and to have a stake in the decisions that had to be made. They invested in real estate, businesses, or professional practices that both created and reflected a sense of commitment to place. But their domination of local politics and administration (on bodies such as school boards or recreation councils) was often resisted by the more transient population, which interpreted it as class or ethnic domination.

Transience also had important effects on those who did the moving. In one way, it served to strengthen ongoing ties with family "back home" as the one constant in ever-changing lives. True sojourners, of course, always intended to return home once they had accumulated sufficient cash to marry or to purchase property there. Another group of transient workers does not appear to have intended (or have been able) to return home, but they made periodic visits or otherwise maintained contact. The pages of the Timmins newspapers through the 1920s and 1930s included a surprising number of advertisements for travel agencies or travel services; clearly, those who could afford to travel did. The social notes also made frequent references to women who spent the better part of each summer with their children out of town, staying with family or friends. Tamara Hareven was one of the first historians to comment on this phenomenon, in her study of French Canadian migrant workers in New England. "Strong ties over several generations can still be maintained," she suggested, "under conditions of kin dispersion."[75] These kinds of ties provided a social equivalent to the economic ties that bound the region to international industrial capitalism. Porcupine–Iroquois Falls may have been a peripheral region, a hinterland, in one sense, but in other important ways it was directly and intimately connected to the modern world.

Transience had another, somewhat paradoxical impact, in that it created a pan-northern network. Men migrated from mine to mine across Canada, living in similar surroundings, working under similar conditions, and meeting others who were doing the same thing. Over the course of a working life, a man and his family were likely to encounter others whom they had known at some point along that path – or they met new neighbours who knew former neighbours. It was almost like a large pool of floating "mining people" or floating bushworkers or papermakers. Furthermore, verbal evidence indicates that some "transience" was really just seasonal movement in and out of the paid workforce, particularly among the French-speaking Canadians and Finns who lived on farms. In the 1940s, for example, Jean-Joseph Laurendeau recalled that the French "settlers" in the Abitibi region were being drawn increasingly to mine work, but only for the winter months.[76] Thus, transience did not necessarily produce a social setting of rootless, stakeless, unconnected individuals to the extent that might be expected. Instead, it helped situate the mines and mills of Porcupine–Iroquois Falls in a broader "region" of social and experiential networks. As will be discussed in chapter 10, these networks contributed in no small way to the development of a sense of community and the delineation of its boundaries and perceived characteristics.

Tensions generated through the process of working out class relations, gender roles, and transience meant that the struggle for social order was a fourth important feature of regional social organization. The contest was

both symbolic and real. As Karen Dubinsky has shown, in the early twentieth century, southerners began to see Northern Ontario as "a dangerously
immoral, uncivilized place of vice," contrasted against alleged southern
purity and innocence.[77] Northerners were outraged. So they countered
with campaigns that emphasized how cultured, stable, and modern their
communities were. However, these campaigns should not overshadow the
fact that there were serious social problems in the North – hardly surprising, given the rapid pace of change, the diversity of the population, and
the distance from old networks of social support and control. It would take
decades of adjustment to find a social balance.

Interpersonal violence was common in the early years of the Porcupine
Camp, ranging from shouting matches between neighbours to drunken
street brawls and domestic assaults that occasionally resulted in death.
Suicide was also a sadly regular occurrence. It is impossible to assess
whether violence was any more common in the region than in other parts
of Canada at the time, but there is no doubt that social violence and the
threat of violence were facts of life until well into the 1940s. This was not
the gunfighter violence of American frontier legend; it was a more personal, domestic violence that reflected both individual and community
tensions.

The earliest reports of violence in the Porcupine Camp revolved around
alcohol consumption. Bar fights arising from long-standing disagreements
usually involved only fists, but occasionally knives and revolvers were
pulled. The combatants were just as likely to be Canadian-born as recent
immigrants. Typical was a melee on the streets of South Porcupine at 2:30
AM on a summer night in 1912. E. Tremblay, Thomas Cowan, and several
others were arrested for taking part in a brawl "inspired by love and
whiskey" (as the *Advance* delicately put it). A revolver shot was fired at one
point, though the participants seem to have been too inebriated to aim
dangerously.[78] While similar events punctuated the evenings with some
regularity, surprisingly few repeat offenders seem to have emerged. One
exception was Jimmy Walsh, who in the summer of 1912 was sentenced to
six months for fighting, after two previous warnings and a suspended sentence.[79]

Some of the violence was perpetrated by individuals who clearly were
mentally ill and who drifted around on the fringes of society. One such
case was the murder in December 1921 of farmer Victor Galette, who lived
alone in a shack on his property near Frederick House Lake. Patrick
Dubord, a veteran of the First World War, was indicted as the suspect when
arrested in Montreal on another murder charge. He had twice escaped
from Quebec asylums, and he escaped again from the North Bay jail where
he was being held pending trial.[80] In another case, in January 1924, John
Primak killed Mike Barney and seriously wounded Pete Egnatinn with a

drill steel and a shovel while they were working underground at Dome. Primak was charged with murder, but Dome's manager H.P. De Pencier concluded, "I have little doubt he will be judged insane."[81]

Ethnic conflict contributed to other violent outbursts, ranging from the relatively minor, such as the 1917 fist fight between Italian and Austrian miners at the Dome bunkhouse, to more serious affairs resulting in death, such as that of John Linsky (in a Schumacher fight between "Russians" and "Austrians" on Christmas Day 1921) and of Ivan Melnychuk (in an Ansonville fight between Poles and Russians), as described in the previous chapter.[82] Alcohol and other factors certainly contributed to these disputes, but the combatants used ethnic identity to draw boundaries and to cast their opponents as the threatening "other."

Regular reports of suicide attest to the despair and loneliness of many who had come to the region with high hopes but who found themselves without social support systems when they were desperately needed. The victims included both men and women of all ethnic backgrounds. A 25–year-old male surveyor from Cleveland, Ohio, shot himself in the fall of 1915 while working alone in the bush (probably prospecting). A young waitress attempted suicide in 1918, having been despondent for some time following her parents' return to Toronto and her boyfriend's enlistment for overseas service. A newly married Hollinger draftsman killed himself with two revolver shots in 1923 after his wife left for an extended visit to Montreal. In one two-month period (October and November 1921), the northern coroner investigated seven deaths, three of which were deemed suicide, while a fourth was a suspected suicide.[83]

Finally, quarrels about relationships between men and women accounted for a major proportion of the violence. There were cases in which men attacked or killed in a rage at finding their wives with other men. But it was not always the men who lashed out. In 1927, George Findley was shot and killed by his wife for "showing improper attentions" to their female boarder.[84] There were also a number of incidents in which fathers intervened violently in their daughters' marital affairs, perhaps reflecting a high level of anxiety over the increased sexual freedom demanded by the younger generation. In 1917 E.A. Gentile of Timmins married Tony Salvador's 16–year-old step-daughter Annie McIntyre. Salvador laid charges against Gentile because the girl was underage. Gentile was acquitted, but he ended up in hospital with injuries suffered in a fight with Salvador and two other men. This time, it was Salvador who was arrested – for attempted murder – but the charges were later reduced.[85] In a more deadly case some twenty years later, Louis H. Lee, a farmer near Matheson and the father of ten, shot and killed his 28-year-old neighbour Harold Johnson, whom he believed was paying inappropriate attention to his recently married daughter.[86]

Given the large population of single men and the degree of transience among them, there were surprisingly few incidents of sexual violence. As historian Ian Radforth has noted, women in the bush camps "emphasize that there was no fooling around with the bushworkers," since the women demanded and received respect: Radforth concluded that the lack of conflict was because the women posed no economic threat to the men, did not challenge their masculinity, and provided valuable and appreciated food comforts.[87] Karen Dubinsky explained the lack of sexual danger in the "camaraderie and pioneer spirit of the community," which both included women and "protected them from harm."[88] Certainly, there were problems, as in the case of the bushworker sentenced to six months in jail in 1915 for his "indecent behaviour towards women and girls" at Iroquois Falls; and there were some attempted rapes of teenage girls after nights of drinking and dancing at the somewhat disreputable establishments along the Mattagami River west of Timmins (in the days before the dance pavilion there). There were at least two notorious cases of sexual predators in the 1930s. In one, a widowed miner lured young girls to his shack in Moneta for some time before he was eventually arrested. In another, a well-known real estate agent paid young boys to perform indecent acts in his office.[89] But these were isolated incidents. Angry men lashed out with physical, not sexual, violence. Perhaps women enjoyed a degree of respect because they were service providers or because they were symbols of the mothers and sisters left behind, or simply because they were rare and special commodities.

While the community did not seem prepared to accept serious injury, death, or sexual assault of any kind, it did seem willing to tolerate a certain level of drinking and brawling. There seems to have been an even higher level of tolerance for theft from "the company" (whichever company that might mean). Indeed, in the mining towns it became something of a joke and the subject of local legend. "Highgrading," or the theft of valuable gold ore, was a feature of gold-mining life in the United States as well. The assumption seemed to be that the company had so much gold that a little would not be missed; or that it was a matter of justice – a bonus due to the men who did the "real" work while the owners or managers got rich for taking no risks and never getting their hands dirty. Complaints about the theft of ore began almost as soon as there was ore to be found, and the cases involved men and women, Canadians and recent immigrants, the marginally employed and professionals, and casual thieves and organized rings.

The first attempt to prosecute a highgrading case set the tone for what was to come. In June 1913, Leander L. Keith was arrested for the theft of $1,500 worth of gold amalgam from the McIntyre stamp mill, which he had apparently been collecting in small amounts for some time. The judge found him guilty and offered him the choice of one year in jail or a $500 fine. Much to McIntyre management's dissatisfaction, Keith promptly paid his fine and was released.[90] Hollinger and Dome also attempted to make examples through arrests and prosecutions, but they soon discovered that it was almost impossible to get a jury to convict the accused; even some judges were sympathetic. In a case involving four Dome employees in 1922, two were given suspended sentences and the other two received light jail terms on reduced charges, which caused the mine manager to complain:

The sentences were totally inadequate ... but it is known that Judge [S] is extremely lenient in these high-grading cases, and [D], who was acting as counsel for the prisoners, is the biggest wire-puller in the district ... At first he proposed to have jury trial, but when he learned that there would be no jury trials held for some months owing to the Crown being unwilling to call in the farmers who have [been] recently burnt out as jurymen, and when he learned that Judge [S] would be available he had them elect for speedy trial before the Judge.[91]

Highgrading activities helped to form bonds among different sectors of the community. After Hollinger complained that over $128,000 worth of gold had been stolen in 1927, the authorities attempted to make a public example of one ring. Hollinger miners William Denkow, Adam Klapoushak, Alec Barbas, John Pasichnyk, and Mike Klimovich were alleged to have pocketed ore and delivered it to a local farm owned by Walter P. Wilson, who treated and refined it. The gold was then picked up by Mr and Mrs Abraham Simon, who transported it to Montreal concealed in a special "vest" worn by Mrs Simon under her dress.[92] Other "exporters" sold the gold in various parts of the United States and, in at least one case, directly to the unsuspecting Canadian Mint in Ottawa. There was even a case in which an American laid a complaint against two Timmins men for selling him pellets that turned out not to be gold; the American freely admitted he had been trying to obtain gold illegally. The crown attorney agreed that he had been wronged and took the case to court.[93]

The perception that the North was a dangerous or wild frontier seems to have attracted a steady parade of petty thieves and fraud artists. James Simard, who had already served time in Montreal for theft, cut a swath through Iroquois Falls and Tisdale Township in 1920–21, forging cheques and robbing mail bags while claiming to be named Pearce or McDougall – names of prominent people in the area.[94] In the early months of the Second World War, two young women from Toronto arrived in Timmins recruiting for the Women's Military Training Association, which existed only in their fertile imagination. They managed to extract a two-dollar initiation fee from at least seventy-five women and then skipped town without paying their hotel bill before the authorities caught on.[95] The first armed bank robbery in the area was committed by a New Brunswick man in apparently desperate circumstances, for in the course of the heist, he reportedly told the bank's staff that the Kingston Penitentiary would be "better than the life he was leading now."[96]

Regional society was also shaped by the various attempts at social control and social engineering initiated by company and town leaders. As was described in the chapter on work, the companies wanted a docile, complacent, reliable, and productive workforce. To promote their boosterism campaigns, local politicians and business owners were anxious to depict the region as peaceful and progressive. But while the plans laid systems and structures in place, local residents reacted to them in a variety of ways; their reactions were just as important in making local society as the intentions of others were.

The most visible hand of social control was the police. As has been described, police arrived early in the Porcupine rush, and the area soon supported a surprising number of policing agencies compared with other parts of the Canadian North. The municipal police forces, the Ontario Provincial Police, and private corporate security were all well established by the 1920s. The RCMP (and its predecessors) had detachments at Moose Factory and at Amos, Quebec, that occasionally ran patrols into the Lake Abitibi region. They were very visible in the towns during the First World War when enforcing the Enemy Alien Act and, later, the Military Service Act. There was no period of ad hoc grass-roots regulation and justice as there had been in the mining camps along the Yukon River a few years earlier.[97] The area's police forces seem to have been intended to serve two functions, as identified by Allan Greer in his analysis of nineteenth-century policing in Canada: to keep a troublesome population under control and to participate in "programs of social transformation"[98] – in this case, to enforce middle-class Canadian norms on a population of immigrant workers.

In spite of what would appear to be an oppressive police presence in the region, the police were not particularly effective, at least not until the 1930s. A rapid turnover of personnel was undoubtedly a major part of the explanation, for men rarely stayed long enough to learn much about the community or to earn its respect. Furthermore, there were conflicts between the OPP and the community police, as in 1918 when OPP Constable W.S. Ackeroyd twice complained that the Timmins police and unnamed others were "knocking" and "trying to make trouble" for the provincial force.[99] All of the police forces had difficulty recruiting satisfactory personnel. One OPP constable was discovered drunk on the job by his inspector in 1916. On another occasion, the Roman Catholic priest Alexandre Pelletier complained to Ontario premier J.P. Whitney, "Our police is far from being feared ... Witnesses say that they have seen the officer [—] drinking in the house of a certain André Leroux, who was living publicly with two lewd women ... Another person heard the officer [—] (also of South Porcupine) tell a liquor seller, named Robillurd, that he had nothing to fear in continuing this illicit traffic."[100] Nor did anyone seem to take the police efforts to enforce liquor and gaming laws very seriously. When police arrested seven men for gambling on a Sunday evening and the Porcupine magistrate fined them each five dollars and costs, the *Porcupine Advance* observed, "It would have been cheaper to go to church." It added, "Every one realizes that in a mining camp and town situated as these are, that there is little in the way of amusement and that the indulgence in small games of chance for six days in the week harms no one, and is much better than mooching about and doing many other things."[101] Opposition to the police could be much more physical. When some Timmins police constables attempted to arrest two drunks outside the Moneta Dance Hall on a winter's night in 1924, a crowd of up to fifty men appeared on the scene and battled the constables, who were eventually forced to retreat and give up on the idea of arrests.[102]

People could also make use of the police and court authorities to suit their own ends, as in the case of Rachel Popvitch, who was turned in to police by two fellow countrymen on allegations of illegal liquor selling. The Timmins magistrate discovered that the complainants had "informed the police so as to get Rachel sent to jail because she had caused another Austrian to be sent down." Her lawyer told the court "that he felt there was a regular conspiracy against her among a certain group of Austrians and that she was in fear of her life as a consequence."[103]

Less formally sanctioned systems of social control were also developed. One major concern of the Anglo middle-class leaders was that young men "of good family" would be lured into a life of drinking, gambling, and worse once they were let loose from family ties and set among the large "foreign" population of the North. Through the provision of carefully structured opportunities for social activity, the middle-class moralists attempted to counter the pernicious influences of "camp" life. Smoking and reading rooms, as well as a social club established under the auspices of the Presbyterian and Anglican clergy in 1916, served these purposes.

Even younger people were targeted with these techniques, and youth groups were used to reach out to the children of the foreign-born population. It was an experiment in assimilation sustained by a foundation of moral value judgments made by the Protestant Canadian middle-class. When the Anglicans organized the first Boy Scout troop in Timmins, for example, a concert was held to raise funds to cover the five-dollar cost of the uniforms in order to make membership accessible to that class of boys most "in need" of moral guidance.[104] During the First World War, Porcupine's United Church sponsored a Girls' League for "moral betterment," and Timmins's United Church ran groups such as the Trail Rangers and Tuxis Square for teenaged boys. The latter brought in "at least two new Canadians as members each year" and was pleased to report in 1931 that four of these newcomers were "rapidly assimilating ideas which were before strange to them." Perhaps more important to the boys, however, were the softball tournaments, the hockey games, and the log cabin they built outside Timmins for a ski-trip shelter.[105]

Teachers were obvious agents of social control inside the classroom, but, interestingly, they also attempted to impose their values outside the schools. For example, among the issues discussed at the first annual meeting of the North Temiskaming Teachers' Institute at Monteith in 1918 was the need for "censorship" of "melodramatic and comic movie plays" and the need for laws to enforce curfews and regulate the sale of cigarettes to minors.[106]

It seems that more subtle forms of social control, operated by members of the community themselves, were far more effective than official systems at keeping order. Even for the first generation of residents who were away from home and parental influence, social networks served as a check on uninhibited behaviour. In the bush camps, according to one worker, men did not make advances to the women because "their brothers, cousins etc. might be in camp; you didn't know."[107] Because of the immigration patterns, there were likely to be other young men in town from your village in Italy or Yugoslavia, and you didn't want your reputation ruined at home if you intended to return for a bride some day. Boarding houses also provided a surrogate family and degree of obligation to others, particularly since men tended to congregate in ethnically segregated lodgings. Elisabeth Townsend of South Porcupine recalled Charlie Nikkanen, Franki Maki, Vern Isaacson, and Anton Laino establishing a "co-op" boarding house there because "they couldn't get Finn cooking like they would like it – so they hired a cook and started this."[108] When boarders failed to follow the rules, there were mechanisms for sanction, as in the case of George S— of the Scandia Boarding House in Timmins, whose landlady arranged to garnishee his wages at Buffalo-Ankerite to pay his overdue bill.[109]

More complex is the question of whether the company town itself operated as a form of social control. There has been some debate on the issue in the American context but very little among Canadian scholars. José Igartua discussed Alcan's concept of a company town briefly in *Arvida au Saguenay*, and Eileen Goltz studied Copper Cliff, an INCO company town near Sudbury.[110] Essentially, the discussions have focused on two issues: whether "welfare capitalism" benefited the workers and whether it actually succeeded as a mechanism for social control. In the baldest terms, among the older literature one school proposed that benevolence was actually malevolence, and the heavy hand of capitalism crushed the working class into submission and debt peonage in these towns. "I sold my soul to the company store," goes the refrain. Another school, largely among geographers and urban planners, has preferred to emphasize the positive by examining such philosophies as that of the Garden City movement, which lay behind some company town designs.[111] More recent studies have tended to focus on the interaction of worker and owner in these towns, proposing that the results were ambiguous and that an element of mutual interest eventually emerged.[112] What all of these studies have in common, however, is an emphasis on the role of the company, its intentions and plans, giving only the most general consideration to the workers' aspirations and goals. If we consider what people in Iroquois Falls, Timmins, and other company housing "properties" were actually doing, some very interesting new interpretations are possible.

As has been described, this region had some significant variations on the concept of company town, from the "closed" townsite of Iroquois Falls designed according to the latest principles of scientific management, to the mix of company and private development leavened by old-fashioned direct paternalism in Timmins, to the mine "properties" with limited housing on-site for management and supervisory personnel. Abitibi contracted the management of the Mercantile, a company store, as the only retail outlet in town, while Hollinger ran two stores from 1919 to 1933 (in competition with other Timmins retailers) as an experiment in keeping wages low. Some houses built by Hollinger were sold to employees, but the rent-to-purchase plan gave the company a measure of control, and those who eventually owned the houses had to agree to sell them only to other Hollinger employees.[113] In its rental units, the Hollinger management chose carefully which employees would be "rewarded" with a house; and for some years, as noted above, it strategically located shift bosses on every block, presumably to keep an eye on the men even off the job.[114] The Timmins brothers provided loans for lot purchases and start-up capital to encourage townsite development; the loans undoubtedly had the effect of making and maintaining a particular relationship with the town "fathers." In Timmins, the corporate entity that owned Hollinger was used to build a hospital, develop the electrical supply, and pay for the waterworks system.[115] And, as has been described, most companies also built and sustained infrastructure for recreation.

There is no doubt that one of the companies' main purposes in providing housing, recreational facilities, and commercial outlets was to encourage and maintain an orderly and cooperative workforce. How, though, did these arrangements affect the development of social organization in the region?

First, not everyone who worked for the big companies lived in company housing. The choice to live elsewhere was often a deliberate decision to have some independence, and it reflected the limitations of social control through housing. Living in Ansonville, Moneta, or South Porcupine, or even simply squatting in the bush outside any town limits, were all viable options. In fact, the inhabitants of Ansonville and Moneta seem to have actively engaged in subtle and not-so-subtle attempts to rebel against or goad "the company." These efforts included the theft of construction materials from Hollinger property and attempts to take over Iroquois Falls through legal channels. Second, unions and municipal politics became constructed spaces for similar challenges. As was described in chapter 6, labour energies and conflicts were directed into battles within the unions themselves. And as will be discussed in chapter 9, municipal politics in particular was used by residents as a tool for labour interests, as one anonymous contributor to the *Porcupine Advance* complained in 1939: "The majority of the meetings [of Timmins Town Council] are more like a public entertainment" wherein "resolutions are passed about wage advances at the local mines, which are no business at all of the Town Council."[116] Third, numerous personal acts of defiance, which eventually became part of community culture, permitted an expression of independence at another level. Ask almost anyone about local history, and one of the first stories will invariably be about highgrading or liquor smuggling. Even those who would never dream of committing a crime seem to have regarded these acts as a source of amusement rather than disapproval. Furthermore, recreational activities outside company sponsorship (for instance, hunting, fishing, and blueberry picking) became important pursuits through which people expressed a sense of independence. Participation in these annual rituals certainly helped contribute to a sense of community, as will be discussed, but perhaps their key meaning lay in the image of self-sufficiency, entrepreneurship, and masculinity (in the case of hunting and fishing) which they engendered. People clearly did not see themselves as part of a compliant and submissive company-town workforce.

For those who did live in company housing, perhaps the most important and visible effect was something unconsidered by the proponents of social control. Company housing became in part a divisive force. "Properties" located in proximity to the plant meant that people lived and worked in the same circle, separated from similar circles by physical distance, which became perceptual distance as well. If you lived at Buffalo-Ankerite, you had little opportunity for interaction with Pamour people, and even less with Iroquois Falls people, although your life was very much like theirs. Your "community" was first and foremost the group with whom you, your husband, or your father worked and who lived around you. You had to make an effort to meet other people (perhaps at church, perhaps in a fraternal organization). Even the recreational patterns encouraged you to play in the neighbourhood or to cheer on the company team (and to see the opponents from just down the road as the "other"). Winter kept you close to home anyway. Other divisions were created by the occupational segregation built into the company plans. Of course, class-based neighbourhoods were and are a feature of all North American cities, and perhaps in these small towns the segregation was less rigid than in larger places. Nevertheless, the hierarchical structure of the industrial workplace was reflected in the physical appearance and placement of housing. There were divisions within divisions.

In another sense, however, company housing proved an integrative social force. People who came from around the world, perhaps knowing no one here and perhaps scarcely speaking the same language, found themselves in a setting designed to bring them together. The neighbourhood was ready made. The necessary services were provided. The people in the houses around you had come for the same reasons – good pay, the foundation of a better life, and perhaps an escape from unhappy circumstances back home – so it was not difficult to make contacts and find common ground.

In fact, it could be argued that local accommodations were achieved not so much because of corporate paternalism and effective social control but because worker and management shared certain values and goals. A community ethic emerged in Porcupine–Iroquois Falls that emphasized individualism, entrepreneurship, and materialism. During this period, many miners spent their spare time prospecting in the hope that they would one day become millionaire mine owners like Noah Timmins, and a surprising number were shareholders in the company that employed them. Others came to define themselves through pride in "real" work, which was physically demanding, skilled, and dangerous. Unlike the factory assembly line, there was room in these industries for individual initiative. Obviously, Noah Timmins and Frank Anson saw themselves in similar terms. They were risk takers and self-made men who downplayed the element of luck in their careers. Both the workers and the "owners" also shared a passion for the assumed consumerism that was emerging in North America.[117] Workers assumed status by acquiring and displaying modern technology (notably cars and, later, snowmobiles); Noah Timmins did the same with real estate, culminating in his impressive Westmount home, which locals seemed well aware of. These shared values permitted a common ground that provided space for cooperation in the midst of the many opportunities for conflict.

On the other hand, community consensus was not the entire story. The conflict must not be downplayed. Workers in these towns rejected the

values of the middle class management and defined themselves to a
certain extent in opposition to management. Rather than seeing a working
class that aspired to the status of the middle class, there was in these towns
before 1950 a large self-confident population of workers who *looked down
upon* office workers and professionals, and indeed considered themselves
superior to them. Because the cohort of managerial and professional
people was very small, workers were able to dominate community discourse simply by the force of numbers. Machismo was valued over intellectual attainment; green university-educated "boys" who came to work in
the office were mocked for knowing nothing, and many people seemed to
assume an inverse relationship between the amount of education and real
success in work and life. The life of a working man was celebrated as something vital and important. It was a message that Roy Thomson seemed to
grasp intuitively, and by playing to it in the Timmins *Press*, he built the
foundations of his fortune. If working people were able to define themselves in these terms, they could live in the company's houses, buy from the
company's store, and relax in the company's recreation hall without seeing
themselves as socially diminished – and certainly without believing that
they were submitting to the company's control. It was something the
radical labour leaders never fully understood and a major reason why they
never succeeded in convincing the majority of workers that class warfare
was a reality.

Thus, although Timmins and Iroquois Falls represented different kinds
of company towns (one "open" and one "closed"), a similar dynamic was
at work in both. Conflict and consensus tripped around one another in a
sometimes clumsy dance as both company and worker tried to shape a
living space while exploiting the raw materials of a resource economy,
living in a hierarchical (and male) workplace, and experiencing a degree
of physical isolation in a northern climate. In the end, communities
emerged that reflected the workers' aspirations to a far greater extent than
the social-control model of the company town would allow.

Within the structures of company town, small town, and farm life, it was
class, gender, ethnicity, transience, and a quest for social order that
became the key factors in defining society in the region. Individuals came
and went, attempting to fit into the systems they found, or attempting to
change them through public action or personal behaviour. They brought
ideas about social organization from a range of cultural backgrounds and
attempted to reproduce familiar social patterns in the boarding house,
community club, or neighbourhood. Through force of numbers, imported
cultural attitudes, and economic realities, they replaced the social system
of the fur trade era. The social system that emerged, laid on the foundation of the new economy, became the unplanned and somewhat awkward
frame upon which the structure of community would be built.

CHAPTER NINE

Politics

It may be a cliché to describe politics as a blood sport, but it could not be a more appropriate description in this region. Paradoxically, the two main playing fields were (on the one hand) the local, the immediate, the personal, and the sometimes petty – and on the other hand, the global with its class conflict, grand political theory, and broad-brush idealism. For here, newcomers brought with them the political baggage of European wars, nation building, and labour conflict, to which they then added Canadian debates about language, religion, and economic development. But these games had to be played out in small towns, not on the national or international stage. While this meant that there was less scope for theatrics, the intimate knowledge the actors often had of one another meant that the potential for truly visceral passions was great indeed. Politics became the nails that pulled together some regional relationships but drove deep and lasting wedges between others.

Of course, the skeleton that structured these political activities was imposed from outside. In national elections, Porcupine–Iroquois Falls was initially part of the riding of Nipissing. As the population of northeastern Ontario grew, this large riding was divided and boundaries re-emerged. For the election of 1917, the voters of the area went to the polls in the riding of Temiskaming; by 1925 it was Temiskaming North; by 1933 it was Cochrane. Provincially, the region was initially part of the riding of Temiskaming, then part of Cochrane from 1914 to 1926, and Cochrane South thereafter. In both federal and provincial contests, the vote count was always close, and the riding swung between Liberal and Conservative victories (with an edge to the Liberals), with an occasional win by Labour and later candidates belonging to the Co-operative Commonwealth Federation (CCF). These outcomes are deceiving, however, for labour issues always dominated the campaigns. The political parties may have come from elsewhere, but local interests shaped them to meet local needs.

Municipal politics revolved around the annual ritual of nominations and elections. Timmins, Iroquois Falls, and Matheson each had elected mayors, with town councils consisting of six councillors. The organized townships, such as Tisdale, Whitney, and Calvert, each had elected reeves and four councillors. In the early years there was a pattern of election by acclamation; for example, in Timmins the first real election was not held until 1919.[1] Thereafter, early to mid-December was marked by lively contests that drew in a range of participants, including women. In 1914 the Tisdale Township Council approved a resolution to encourage the provincial government to broaden the Municipal Franchise Act "so as to include married women taxpayers."[2] And when the municipal franchise was extended in 1917 to all women citizens of legal age, the *Porcupine Advance* announced the change with some enthusiasm, although its headline teased, "Any Ladies Admitting They Are Over Twenty-One Can Exercise Franchise."[3] Women did more than vote. Josephine Thomas, a business woman, ran for reeve of Tisdale Township in 1920, though unsuccessfully. She ran again in 1922 and 1923 before winning the prize in 1927 and again in 1933. Ellen Terry became Timmins's first "lady councillor" in 1939, topping the polls by a substantial lead and with a record number of votes.[4] Besides the township and municipal councils, there were school boards, boards of health, and numerous other administrative bodies. And in between the annual elections, dissatisfied residents organized other bodies, such as the Citizens' League and the Ratepayers' Association, which intervened in municipal affairs.

The relationship between municipal administration and the major companies was riddled with tension. There is a widespread belief in the region today that, especially in Iroquois Falls and Timmins, "the company" controlled the town councils and ancillary boards. But a close examination of the historical record reveals a more complex situation. In Iroquois Falls, the mayor and councillors were always Abitibi employees, of course, because only Abitibi employees could live in town. But Timmins Town Council was never dominated by Hollinger management or even by Hollinger employees. Only one elected mayor before 1950 worked directly for the mine (E.L. Longmore, then a mill superintendent, who was mayor from 1926 to 1928). Most municipal politicians in Timmins were business people, doctors, or dentists during the 1920s, with a scattering of labourers serving on the council in the 1930s. Nevertheless, given the economy of the town, many had close ties to Hollinger. The first mayor, W.H. Wilson (1912–16), was a hardware merchant, but he did nearly all Hollinger's teamster work. Dr J.A. McInnis (manager 1919–25) had come to Timmins to practise medicine at Hollinger's hospital. To this day, local mythology has persisted in seeing a close link between company and council. Labour activist Bob Miner complained at length in an interview that "the

Company" ran everything, including the town council and municipal boards. "They used to have school board elections on New Year's Eve," he said, "and with a quorum of six or seven would nominate a board. On the high school board they were all appointed, all company officials, all the time."5

Newspaper reports indicate he was wrong about the dates of the elections, and since only a few complete lists of board members seem to have survived, it is not clear how accurate his other observations might be. But according to the available lists, school board trustees were drawn from roughly the same constituency as the town council. And as will be discussed, labour activists were well represented on town councils, while council and company frequently clashed on such matters as assessment, taxation, and limits to authority. On the other hand, municipal politicians in the company towns were clearly aware of the source of their personal and public bread and butter. When the *Industrial Banner* (a Toronto-based labour paper) printed an article in 1918 accusing Hollinger of running the town, Timmins mayor J.P. McLaughlin hotly denied the suggestion. But he cautiously added that "the Hollinger had been very generous in its assistance to the town and it was a great benefit in every way to Timmins."6

This, then, was the setting. Legal systems that had been developed in other times and places, political ideas and customs that had evolved to suit other needs, and expectations drawn from other circumstances were all established here, and the local people worked both within these systems and outside them to try to meet local needs. Economic and social tensions were sometimes addressed through political channels, while these political channels themselves sometimes created new social tensions.

One of the most visible features of the regional political scene was the strength and influence of communism. The communist movement arrived early, alongside (and sometimes indistinguishable from) more moderate forms of socialism. The timing of the development boom in northeastern Ontario was propitious, because it coincided with important organizational developments elsewhere in Canada, and because sympathy for socialist ideals came with the first Finnish and Ukrainian workers, who had been influenced by them in labour movements in Europe. In 1903 a meeting of labour activists in Vancouver, dissatisfied with the progress of trade unionism in Canada, resolved to form the Socialist Party of Canada out of a loose network of groups across the country. The party's leadership consisted primarily of English and Scots immigrants who called themselves Marxists, though they seem to have been more directly influenced by British democratic socialism. The party's early support came from two very different groups: radicalized Finns and Ukrainians, and more moderate "Christian socialists" of British ancestry. The combination proved difficult to sustain.7 The first to break away were the Ukrainians, who in 1909 established the

Federation of Ukrainian Social Democrats (later renamed Ukraininan Social Democratic Party) in Winnipeg and began publishing the bi-weekly *Robochy Narod* (Working People) to promote class struggle. Then in 1911 the Canadan Suomalainen Sosialistijärjestö (Finnish Socialist Organization of Canada, later the Finnish Canadian Organization) was formally chartered by dissidents in the Socialist Party of Canada. Soon afterwards, the two groups met at a convention in Port Arthur (now part of Thunder Bay) and formed the Social Democratic Party of Canada. They called for labour reforms such as the eight-hour day; political reforms such as initiative, referendum, and recall; and broadly based social change through international affiliation with fellow Marxists.[8] Thus, the radical socialist movement in Canada was in the midst of a major recruiting and organizational drive just when the Porcupine gold rush began.

The Finnish Socialist Organization of Canada founded branches at Pottsville, South Porcupine, and Timmins in 1911 and 1912, urging miners and construction workers to organize to protect their interests; the group also threw its support behind the Western Federation of Miners and the 1912 strike. The Ukrainian Social Democratic Party (USDP) was not far behind. Organizer W. Holowacki founded branches in Timmins and Porcupine in January 1913.[9] At first, these groups seem to have been welcomed as much for their social contribution as for their political ideals. In the summer and fall of 1912, the miners' union collaborated with Finnish and "English" socialist parties to host a series of dances and musical evenings at the Miners' Union Hall in South Porcupine; admission was fifty cents and ladies were invited free of charge. "These entertainments," noted the *Porcupine Advance*, "have been most successful and pleasant affairs."[10] Membership in the Finnish and Ukrainian societies boomed as the number of workers increased. The Finnish Canadian Organization and the Ukrainian Social Democratic Party built substantial halls in Timmins where they held rallies, plays, and concerts. As wages and working conditions deteriorated during the war years, their messages were well received among the increasingly restive workers. The bitter divisions of the 1912 strike, followed closely by the First World War, gave a new, hard edge to the local organizations.

The local authorities were concerned. In October 1917, Tisdale Township police arrested an Austrian visitor identified only as "Silky" for what the *Porcupine Advance* claimed was "talking a great deal about a terrible mixture of socialism, pacifism, revolution and what not. His line of bunkum was that the war was a capitalistic affair and the only way for the people to stop it was to revolute [sic]."[11] A few weeks later, news arrived from Russia that Lenin and the Bolsheviks had seized power. The Russian Revolution was welcomed with considerable enthusiasm in some parts of the region; as historian Martin Robin has noted, "Bolshevism symbolized

Finnish Organization of Canada's hall under construction, Timmins, 1915. (LAC, PA187041)

the overthrow of the hateful Czarist dictatorship from which many of their members had fled."[12] The news precipitated a new round of organizational activity, both locally and across Canada. In 1918 the USDP was reorganized as the Ukrainian Labor Temple Association (later the Labor Farmer Temple Association); it held its first convention at Winnipeg in January 1920, taking its politics more clearly into the realm of Marxism-Leninism and declaring its support for the policies of the new USSR.[13] Also in 1918, the Finnish Canadian Organization was forced to reorganize its socialist political wing under pressure from the Canadian government, which was concerned about its subversive potential in wartime.

In northeastern Ontario, through the late winter of 1918, Felix Consovitch led a campaign to recruit supporters to the communist cause by means of pamphlets, rallies, and speeches. As the crowds grew at these affairs, the local authorities decided to act. Consovitch was arrested at the Finnish Hall in Timmins on charges of sedition in early March; the magistrate refused to grant him bail. On 14 March a crowd of several hundred marched from the hall to the Timmins police station and demanded Consovitch's release. Mayor J.P. McLaughlin failed to convince the crowd to disperse, so Magistrate Atkinson arrived on the scene and offered to release Consovitch on $2,000 bail if the crowd would break up. The terms were accepted, a collection was made among the crowd to raise the bail, and a hearing was held on the spot. Consovitch was escorted back to the Finnish Hall by his jubilant supporters. Now thoroughly alarmed, the town council set about organizing a special police force of allegedly 200 to 300 men and sent an urgent plea to the dominion government for help. It seemed to some that a Bolshevik revolution was about to break out in the Porcupine Camp.[14]

Even the leaders of the miners' union decided that Consovitch and his supporters had gone too far and issued a statement to distance themselves from communist ideas. "This Union can never countenance the destructive and unpatriotic attitude assumed by such people," the statement went, "for we wish to retain our own self-respect and the good opinion of honest law-abiding men and women inside and outside the rank of organized labor."[15] The union leaders revealed that Consovitch had assured them of 500 or 600 new members if the union threw its support behind him. In fact, about 100 members of the union quit in disgust when the leadership made its anti-communism clear. The editor of the *Porcupine Advance* called for calm and urged residents not to start carrying firearms, as some were rumoured to be doing.

In response to Timmins Town Council's appeal for help, a contingent of dominion police arrived and began a sweep of suspected agitators. Over forty were arrested for their role in the mob scene in March, though ultimately only nine cases went to court. Seven men were fined, one was given a suspended sentence, and one failed to appear. The local newspaper referred to the arrested men as "Russians," but their names indicate that most were Ukrainian. Interestingly, though, two were French Canadian ("Saval" Proulx and Mike Leguin).[16] In May, Consovitch was tried at Haileybury, where the jury found him guilty of sedition, but he was given a suspended sentence with a $2,000 personal recognizance that he would not speak at any more public meetings. Of course, Consovitch made very effective use of the trial to promulgate his political ideas. He refused to swear the oath on the Bible, then spoke out in his testimony against monarchs and capitalists and predicted the workers' overthrow of their oppressors, all of which the local press obligingly reported.[17] Consovitch moved to southern Ontario after the trial, but the region's communists were not deterred. Pamphlets continued to circulate and less visible organizers continued to work.

In September 1918 the Canadian government issued orders-in-council to outlaw organizations suspected of promoting Bolshevik revolutionary ideals and to prohibit the publication of "dangerous" literature. The editor of the *Porcupine Advance* was delighted, implying that some credit was due locally for winning over a misguided dominion government. "Those who have worked for the stamping out of these evil organizations here are completely vindicated and upheld," he wrote triumphantly.[18] Within the next few weeks, a Mounted Police sweep of the region led to dozens of arrests under the new law, including that of John Sheniuk and other Ukrainians,

W. Rubanetz and other Austrians, and at least one Finn, Emil Mattson.[19] But neither this crackdown nor the end of the war eliminated communist activities in the region. For the next fifteen years, an open war between the Reds and Whites played itself out in northeastern Ontario.

The first engagement in this war focused on the formation of a local branch of the Workers' Party. In the spring of 1921, when a secret meeting had been held near Guelph, Ontario, to establish the Communist Party, the participants included Finnish and Ukrainian representatives, once again allied with idealistic Canadians of British ancestry such as Tim Buck. Because the party was still deemed to be an illegal organization under Canada's wartime regulations, its founders decided to form an open and legal organization through which it could operate. In the fall of 1921 the CPC sent organizers across the country to promote the idea. John Lawrence MacDonald made Timmins one of his eight national stops, and when the Workers' Party was officially founded in February 1922, Timmins was one of fifteen local branches recognized.[20] MacDonald reported that although the Timmins workers had been rather "apathetic" in reaction to the initiative, he remained optimistic that "it might be possible to organize nine or ten branches within a short time" in the area.[21] The Workers' Party was an attempt to bring together communists of all national backgrounds, but even at its founding convention in Toronto, divisions were evident. Two Finnish delegates applied to have a Finnish section officially recognized, and two Ukrainian delegates made a similar application.[22]

Members of the Workers' Party set about recruiting in the Porcupine area through private persuasion and public shows of strength. They instituted an annual May Day parade, which was particularly well attended in Timmins and provided considerable entertainment value as well as political "consciousness raising." They published pamphlets and handbills – including one entitled "No School on May Day," which exhorted Timmins schoolchildren, "Let's put our heads together and make up our minds not to go to school on May Day!"[23] They hosted films and guest speakers, and sent recruiters among the boarding houses and gathering places to talk to men about their political ideals. In February 1924 an as yet little-known Tim Buck visited the Porcupine area to raise funds and organize an offshoot of the Workers' Party called the Trades Educational League.[24] In 1926 the Workers' Party came very close to running William Moriarty as a candidate for the riding of North Temiskaming in the dominion election.[25] Then, as war clouds gathered in Europe in the 1930s, the Workers' Party sponsored anti-war rallies that attracted crowds of several hundreds. When a fundraising drive was launched for its newspaper, the *Worker*, in 1935–36, supporters in the Timmins area surpassed their goal, raising the third-largest sum in the country – more than either British Columbia or Alberta had raised.[26] Indeed, 1936 seemed to be something of a climactic year for the area's communists. Scottish MP "Willie" Gallacher spoke to an audience of 1,500 in the Timmins Arena in mid-August, and when the nineteenth anniversary of the Russian Revolution was celebrated that November, three hundred people showed up for a "concert-meeting" at the Goldfields Theatre; and anyone not there could listen to the speeches broadcast live over the new radio station, CKGB, that Roy Thomson had established in Timmins.[27]

A backlash against this activity grew slowly, simmering through the 1920s and bursting into the open in the 1930s. From the beginning, mine managers kept a wary eye on the activities; Dome manager H.P. De Pencier had a private detective reporting on what the miners were saying and doing about it, and he even commissioned a detective to report from inside the Workers' Party organizational meetings in Toronto during December 1921 and March 1922.[28] The Roman Catholic Church campaigned against communism (as it did elsewhere in Canada), particularly among the French-speaking population. Anti-communist pamphlets and books such as *Autorité ou revolution* by Gustave Sauvé, OMI, were circulated in the area. "Le communisme," wrote Sauvé, "est la plus grand hérésie des temps modernes: hérésie économique, religieuse, philosophique."[29] The church sponsored "study circles" and educational activities of its own to counter the communists' efforts. The Knights of Columbus invited anti-communist speakers, including the American college professor George H. Derry, who filled the Empire Theatre in March 1939 to "flay communism," according to a newspaper report.[30] The editor of the *Porcupine Advance* launched a campaign of his own. When an editorial appeared in the Ottawa *Journal* criticizing this campaign for its intolerance and suppression of free speech, the *Advance* retorted that the *Journal* simply didn't understand that communists in Northern Ontario had become dangerous and disruptive and had to be stopped.[31]

It was Timmins's new newspaper, the *Press*, that really fanned the flames. But in the process, it reduced the debate over communism to farce, perhaps discrediting the movement more than the *Advance*'s more serious campaign ever could. The Timmins *Press* (soon to be the *Daily Press*) was started by the New Zealand–born salesman and financial entrepreneur James P. Bartleman, who sold it in 1934 to Roy Thomson. Bartleman then ran for a seat on Timmins Town Council, styling himself "the people's candidate" and railing against the entrenched elite at the town hall. "This is a workingman's community and the lifeblood of the town is the miner," he proclaimed to a wildly enthusiastic crowd at the Ukrainian Hall.[32] Bartleman was duly elected to the 1934 council, and he began his colourful political career with full support of the *Press* and was elected in 1936 for what turned out to be four terms as mayor. Thomson and Bartleman parted ways in 1939 for reasons that remain obscure and were very likely personal. Then rumours began to circulate that Bartleman was actually a communist. When someone pointed out that the town band had been practising in the Ukrainian Hall and had played at a rally addressed by communist hero Tim Buck, Bartleman, who apparently believed that Thomson was responsible for the smear campaign, retaliated by proposing that the town take over Thomson's radio station, CKGB. The *Press* reported Bartleman's proposal in tones dripping with sarcasm: "Collected in a cozy group around their samovar early this week, a few members of the Timmins Council hatched the first move in their plan to *sovietise* commerce and industry in Timmins." Bartleman and four members of council retorted (in the *Porcupine Advance*) that they were good anti-communists. A poster campaign followed, in which Timmins residents were enjoined to boycott the "fascist" and "Hitlerite" *Daily Press*. By the time the December campaign for mayor and council was on, a wild battle was in progress that had very little to do with either communism or fascism.[33] The idealism of the early communist movement in the North had been swallowed by the muddy bog of personal vendettas.

Meanwhile, it must be stressed, more thoughtful challenges to the Communist Party and its politics were being raised. One of the most effective was, like the communist movement itself, a product of the labour movement. The Trades and Labor Congress of Canada (TLC), concerned about the radicalism of the Socialist Party of Canada, adopted a resolution in 1906 to endorse any political party at the provincial level that declared principles consistent with the TLC's more moderate democratic socialism. The following year, the Ontario Labour Party was organized, and in 1908 it fielded candidates in four Toronto ridings in the provincial election. Soon afterwards, it seemed to fade into obscurity.[34] Then the pressures of the First World War revived organized labour's interest in political action. The Toronto District Labour Council, through the efforts of its president James Richards and activist Laura Hughes, coordinated the formation of the Toronto Labor Party and then, on 1 July 1917, the Independent Labor Party of Ontario.[35]

Organizers turned their attention immediately to the workers of Northern Ontario. Laura Hughes and James Simpson, vice-president of the TLC and a Toronto *Star* journalist, travelled across the province on a series of lecture tours that included several visits to the Porcupine area. On 11 August 1917 a meeting was held at the Miners' Union Hall to form a local branch of the Independent Labor Party (ILP) amid rumours that Jimmy Simpson would run for the riding of Temiskaming in the next dominion election.[36] The ILP's moderate, British-influenced socialism was an appealing alternative for the region's Canadian and British labourers, who did not feel as alienated from "the system" as many European emigrant workers did. But interest in the new party was also encouraged by the personal popularity in the region of Simpson and Hughes in particular. Simpson (who was always referred to locally as "Jimmy") hailed from Lancashire, England, and was active in the Methodist (and later United) Church. He made a point of developing personal friendships with local labour leaders such as William De Feu and tried to cultivate a diplomatic and conciliatory approach to politics.[37] Hughes was the daughter of a Toronto educator, Dr James L. Hughes, and also a niece of the Conservative politician and dominion cabinet minister, Sir Sam Hughes. She was once described as "the best woman platform orator in Canada."[38] George Lake, owner of the *Porcupine Advance*, had travelled with her father in Europe,[39] and the paper always reported favourably on her visits to the North. Clearly, this was a well-connected socialism with a much broader appeal.

The region's communist sympathizers were unable to mount a political opposition with this kind of influence and appeal, so they increasingly focused on activism within the labour movement. Through the 1920s, persuasion gave way to intimidation and even to the threat of violence, particularly in the bush camps, where increasingly frustrated communist organizers tried to persuade French-speaking Canadians and non-communist Finns that they were being exploited both by subcontractors and by big companies such as Abitibi. Some workers recalled the ongoing debate between Reds and Whites as more of a daily entertainment than a truly serious problem.[40] But others, particularly the White Finns, were terrified, and not knowing where else to turn, they began to appeal to the Finnish Consulate in Montreal for protection. In the summer of 1924, Consul Akseli Rauanheimo took their concerns to the immigration authorities. "Many s[o] c[alled] 'white Finns' avoid to go there," he wrote, "because they are afraid of the Finnish communists, the 'reds' who threaten them. We would be glad to know of camps where loyal 'white' bushmen could work in peace and safety. If the consulate had connections with the big companies it would try to furnish them with dependable workers."[41] A year later, Rauanheimo appealed again to Canadian authorities, citing an incident that had occurred near Connaught, midway between Iroquois Falls and Timmins. Two White Finnish miners had been accosted by a gang of Red Finnish miners, who had corralled the two into a nearby cabin and "had a kind of a court" in which the White miners were "sentenced to be exiled [sic]" and threatened with death if they did not comply. "Lawabiding Finns in said part of the country in a very bad position and in need of protection," wrote Rauanheimo, "as incidents like the above mentioned occur frequently."[42]

The conflict reached a climax in the series of strikes that convulsed the bush camps from Sudbury to Cochrane in the early 1930s. The Lumber Workers' Union of Canada had led smaller walkouts almost annually from

the mid-1920s over wages and working conditions; in the Timmins–
Iroquois Falls area these strikes were invariably led by Finns, among whom
Lauri Niemi played a prominent role. Then, in 1931, Abitibi began to cut
wages and, as described earlier, it went into receivership in 1932, further
reducing both wages and employment opportunities. So in the winter of
1933–34 the area's men joined a series of bush-camp strikes across the
North. The strikes turned ugly very quickly. At Driftwood, the OPP were
called to respond to a complaint that Steve Gyulay had attacked a man who
had refused to stop work. When the police arrived to arrest Gyulay, the
strikers blocked the road with logs so that the police could not leave.[43]
Elsewhere, the intimidation was directed at workers who were reluctant to
strike. Nearly two hundred men marched south from Cochrane in below-
zero weather and knee-deep snow to camps along the Mattagami River to
round up support. Near Iroquois Falls, eighty strikers marched on a camp
and seized the food supplies so that the workers they forced out could not
return; the marchers also pummelled the camp clerk, Ivan Dawkins, when
he tried to resist. When the police arrived and attempted to make arrests,
the strikers would not back down and they fought the police off as fellow
strikers boarded a freight train. Strikers also blocked Abitibi's railway line
and threw stones at the OPP who came to clear it.[44] In the second season
of strikes (1934–35), the RCMP estimated that two thousand workers
between Cochrane and Timmins were off the job.[45] By the time the agitation was over, dozens of men in the area (and many more in Northern
Quebec and other parts of Northern Ontario) had been tried on charges
of assault, inciting a riot, resisting arrest, and disturbing the peace.

Obviously, the strikes had involved far more men than just the communist sympathizers, but the role played by communist labour organizers certainly contributed to the level of passion; paradoxically, it also helped
bring an end to the strikes. As one young man told a Toronto reporter, "I
went out on strike sure. I was a delegate to bring out Silver's camp. If the
strike had been a strike of the men I'd still be out on it. But from what I
saw of the attitude of these organizers of yours I soon realized the men
were not running it. It wasn't a strike at all, it was a Bolshevist uprising."[46]
In a commentary on the strike published in Ottawa's *Le Droit*, Léopold
Richer put the matter in perspective: "It is true that the strikers were
organized by outsiders and they took their authority from the Workers'
Unity League of Canada, one of the affiliates of the Canadian Labor
Defence League. But their demands were just ... In face of our exploitation by the companies, the inaction of government authorities, the
absence of Christian and decisive leaders, the victory of some communist
organizers, we must ask ourselves where our community is going."[47]

The conflict between communists and socialists was played out in a less
violent but perhaps equally emotional battle over control of the co-op

movement in the Timmins area. In 1910 a group of Toronto Finns had initiated the idea of establishing co-operative businesses in Canada, and the
idea had taken root in Timmins–South Porcupine by the early 1920s.
Organizers canvassed door-to-door, selling memberships that would entitle
people to purchase groceries and some dry goods at reasonable prices,
and then receive a share of the profits at the year's end. In 1926 the
Workers' Co-operative of New Ontario was formally organized, and soon
there were co-op stores in Schumacher, South Porcupine, and Connaught,
as well as in Timmins, which had the largest. There, the members hired
Charlie Haapanen from Michigan to manage the business, which soon
included a bakery, a dairy, and a boarding house. According to one
observer, it quickly became "one of the largest and most successful co-operative operations in Canada."[48]

The co-operative leaders represented a rather uneasy coalition, however.
Manager Charlie Haapanen was a social democrat, but secretary Nick
Thachuk was president of the local Ukrainian Labor Farmer Temple Association, with its communist leanings. In 1930 Thachuk attended a meeting
in Port Arthur of the International Co-operative Trading Company, a
Finnish group which the communist organizer A.T. Hill wanted to
promote in Canada. He came to the Porcupine area early in 1931 and led
a campaign to increase the communist influence in the Workers' Co-operative by recruiting a large number of new communist members. At the
regular co-op meeting in February 1931, they succeeded in preventing
Haapanen from being rehired as manager; in his place, a new manager
from Fort William named U. Tynjala was brought in.[49] The social democrats complained bitterly, but they were outnumbered. In letters to the *Porcupine Advance*, they argued that the co-op should be an economic aid, not
a political tool, and that it had become essentially an arm of the Communist Party. The RCMP began to keep an eye on the Workers' Co-operative.[50]

Rather than battle the communists any further, the social democrats
withdrew from the Workers' Co-op and established a separate organization, the Consumers' Co-operative Society, Ltd., with a store in Timmins,
which rehired Haapanen as manager. The Consumers' Co-op soon
expanded to larger quarters in Timmins (on Algonquin Boulevard) and
established branches in Schumacher, South Porcupine, and the Dome
Mines townsite. In spite of a serious fire at the Timmins store in 1939, it
became a successful operation again, with annual sales of half a million
dollars in 1945, making it the largest co-operative in Ontario.[51] It advertised in the local newspapers with banners such as "No Political Affiliations" and "The Consumers' Co-operative Society ... have not meddled in
politics or in other matters outside the scope of their original purpose."[52]
But in spite of its success, bitterness toward the communists remained for
many years. In 1974 Lempi Mansfield recalled in vivid detail the 1931

meeting at which the takeover had occurred – even down to the name of the Toronto organizer who had engineered it, although she had been just a girl at the time.[53]

Meanwhile, other groups were organizing to challenge the communists on several fronts. In the spring of 1931 August Lappala, minister of the Finnish United Church, was sent to Toronto as the Porcupine area's delegate at the founding meeting of the Loyal Finnish Organization. This group hoped to reassure Canadians that not all Finns were preaching revolution, and it intended to counter communist influences among Finnish children born in Canada, who had no direct experience of the history that lay behind the warring factions in Finland. The Loyal Finnish Organization was later renamed the Finnish Organization of Canada; its newspaper *Vapaa Sana* was widely read in northeastern Ontario. Shortly after Lappala returned from the founding meeting in Toronto, a Timmins chapter was organized. Later in that same summer of 1931, the non-communist Ukrainians in Timmins formed a branch of an equivalent organization called the Prosvita ("Enlightenment") Society. And by the spring of 1933, the area's Poles had established a branch of the White Eagle Society with similar intent. Dedicated communists did not take these developments quietly. They sent hecklers to the meetings, and in at least one case the police were called in when fighting broke out between the two sides.[54]

During the 1930s, fascism provided another outlet for anti-communists in the region, though details are very difficult to find because people today prefer to forget about it. As has been discussed, many Timmins Italians were attracted to Mussolini's version of Italian nationalism, and undoubtedly the new ideas were useful tools in the ongoing local battle between conservative Italian miners and their radical Finnish and Ukrainian colleagues. In 1929 the Italian government began to send fascist diplomats to Canada to promote Italian nationalism, fascism, and rapprochement between Italians at home and abroad. As the Italian consul general in 1933 put it, "Fascism is dynamism, and active exaltation of Italian values, the sum of all forces required to reaffirm the greatness of Italy in the world ... Our work aims at educating the mass of our fellow Italians according to Fascist moral principles, at keeping alive in them the flame of love for their country of origin, at maintaining the use of the Italian language, at preventing the loss of the ideal bond between Italians abroad and the homeland."[55] To this end, organizers made use of the Order Sons of Italy, which had been founded in New York in 1905 as a social and mutual benefit society. Under fascist hands, it expanded considerably across North America.[56]

In January 1939 the Order Sons of Italy came to Timmins through the efforts of Antonio Mascioli (Leo's brother) and Mrs Anna Di Critico. At its founding meeting, sixty men and women named the lodge the Stella d'Italia and recognized Giuseppe Giustini as its "venerable."[57] It is not clear to what extent the founding members supported the principles of fascism. Certainly, the organization appealed to immigrant Italians who felt isolated and perhaps even under siege in the region. But fascist politics did play a role, because at the same time, a branch of the Italian Fascist League was organized in Schumacher, and possibly another in Timmins.[58] When Canada declared war against Italy on 10 June 1940, not only were men associated with fascist organizations arrested, but the Timmins lodge appears to have been dissolved, never to be reconstituted.

Although the Stella d'Italia lodge was probably never very large, it seems to have enjoyed a measure of support in the broader community. The anti-communist stance of the fascists appealed to some, including Roman Catholic priests in the region, who like their brothers in Toronto had heard the call of the papal delegate, Archbishop A. Cassulo, to support fascism for precisely that reason.[59] When Leo Mascioli was arrested, the quick support he received from a number of different constituencies suggests that fascist sympathies were not seen as problematic at the time. There is undoubtedly much more to be discovered about right-wing politics in the area as time goes by and heals some of the deep wounds left by the convulsions of the mid-twentieth century.

Of course, the development of fascism in Europe gave local communists another field on which to fight. When civil war broke out in Spain in July 1936, an idealistic band of Canadians formed the Mackenzie-Papineau Battalion under Toronto labour writer Edward Cecil-Smith and headed overseas to fight General Franco and the fascists. Timmins supporters claimed that they had sent the fourth-largest contingent of any Canadian city; many were Finns who served in Ilkka-Antikainen Company, a Finnish unit of the "Mac-Paps" led by Niilo Mäkelä. When the battalion survivors limped home after horrific experiences on the battlefields they received a hero's welcome in Timmins.[60]

Communist politics also dominated much of the union movement in the area, particularly in the mining sector, as was discussed in chapter 6. After prolonged debates had led to a significant weakening of the power of organized labour, Local 241 of the International Union of Mine, Mill and Smelter Workers (chartered 1936) worked hard to walk a middle path locally and, in so doing, repudiated the International leadership in 1948 for its close ties to communist influences. A rival union, the United Steelworkers of America, played the anti-communist card in its bid to recruit disgruntled Mine, Mill members.

As the unions battled for control, hostilities escalated. In the years after the Second World War, a significant number of displaced persons (DPs) began to arrive in northeastern Ontario. Among them was a particularly large group of Ukrainians, who were brought to the Porcupine region to work in the mines on an initial three-year contract. These men were bitter anti-communists because of their experiences under Soviet domination, and they were surprised to find such a strong pocket of support for communism in Canada. In return, they were greeted with suspicion by the socialist and communist Ukrainians of the region. The communists tried to drum up feeling against the DPs, accusing them of taking scarce jobs from local residents – a likely tactic, because many men were finding it difficult to obtain employment in the once-rich gold sector. Then, in November 1949, the Association of United Ukrainian Canadians (successor to the Ukrainian Labor Farmer Temple Association) invited the pro-communist activist Peter Krawchuk to speak in Timmins. The meeting was by invitation only, to avoid problems, but a crowd of some two hundred DPs and other anti-communists rallied outside the Ukrainian Labor Temple on Mountjoy Street. Bricks and stones were hurled through the windows, and the stair railing was torn off for use as a battering ram against the main door. Nine people were hurt, including Tom Kremyr, whose injuries were serious.[61]

More conventional Canadian organizations and issues also appeared from time to time on the public stage. Interestingly, municipal politics turned out to be the forum of choice for the "real" action. Provincial and dominion elections were certainly contested, but it was in the town halls and township council chambers that the important battles were fought. In one sense, it is curious that provincial and dominion politics were relatively orderly, given their politically divisive issues – French-language rights, resource development, immigration policy, conscription, and labour law. But as will be demonstrated, for the region's Canadian-born voters the important issues were those about which other Canadians seemed unconcerned. Here, politics was redefined along local lines.

Conventional party politics came early in the development-boom years. The agricultural district of Taylor Township had a Conservative Association by 1911, and the Liberal Reform Association was organized in South Porcupine in July 1912 with representatives from Timmins, Pottsville, Porcupine, Dome, and South Porcupine. Iroquois Falls had its own Conservative Association in place during the summer of 1915, when most of the townsite was still under construction. Formal political organization of the towns and townships proceeded just as quickly. The first townships to obtain incorporation papers were Tisdale (including the hamlet of South Porcupine) and Whitney (including Golden City) in the fall of 1911. The town of Timmins was not far behind, on 1 January 1912; and that same year, McDougall's Chutes was formally (and optimistically) incorporated as the Town of Matheson. Iroquois Falls was incorporated in May 1915 and Calvert Township (including Ansonville) in 1918. Incorporation was cheered as a sign of progress and permanency, while political associations were taken as a sign of sophistication – proof that New Ontario could play the game just as well as Old Ontario.

Two main voting blocks dominated provincial and national politics. The French-speaking Canadian population brought with it a strong affinity for the Liberal Party in dominion politics, which spilled over into the provincial arena as a succession of Ontario Conservative governments associated themselves with anti-Catholic and anti-French policies such as the infamous Regulation 17.[62] French-speaking voters were further annoyed by these governments' insistence on tight liquor regulation and ultimately Prohibition. In reporting the results of the 1923 Ontario election that returned a Conservative government under Howard Ferguson, *La Gazette du Nord* referred to the new premier as "un orangiste intransigient" whose name the reporter couldn't even bring himself to repeat.[63] The second significant voting interest was labour. The area's politicians recognized the importance of labour issues in the riding, and candidates of all parties attempted to style themselves as "the working man's choice." Since French-speaking Canadians constituted a sizable proportion of labour in the region, it is not surprising that a close relationship developed between the local Liberals and labour interests. That alliance was signalled in 1917 when Arthur W. Roebuck – who had helped establish the Canadian Labor Party and had been chosen as a candidate in the dominion election of 1917 by the newly formed Temiskaming branch of the Independent Labor Party (ILP) – decided to run as a Liberal. J.A. Bradette, who served six terms as Cochrane South's member of the dominion parliament, was officially a Liberal but identified himself in the *Parliamentary Guide* (and locally) as "Liberal and Labour."[64]

In spite of the strength of the Liberals, the Conservative Party was always a factor in both provincial and national elections. The English-speaking farmers around Matheson, Porquis Junction, and Shillington, as well as the business and professional sectors of Timmins, Iroquois Falls, and Schumacher, provided an unwavering support base. Medical doctors such as H.H. Moore of Timmins and C.F. Dorsey of Iroquois Falls served regularly on the executive of the area's Conservative associations, and the Conservative candidates tended to be men such as A.J. Kennedy, a New Liskeard-area farmer; A.F. Kenning, a Timmins insurance agent and mining broker, and R.S. Potter, a Matheson resident. But these segments of the population were too small to carry elections on their own. A Conservative candidate could win only if other factors came into play, as in the 1926 and 1929 provincial elections, when Premier Ferguson offered an olive branch in the matter of Regulation 17;[65] or in the 1925 dominion election, when the vote was split between Liberal and labour candidates (and it helped that the Conservative candidate was Roman Catholic). But it was always a struggle for the Conservatives. In the 1935 dominion election, they did not even bother to field a candidate.

Perhaps the most notable feature of regional politics was the emergence of a labour alternative to the traditional Liberal and Conservative options. Dissatisfaction with the old parties appeared first in 1914, when John Walker contested the provincial riding of Cochrane as an Independent. Then in the provincial election of 1919, John Vanier ran as the first official ILP alternative. Vanier had come to Iroquois Falls from the Ottawa Valley just two years earlier and had quickly made a name for himself in the Pulp and Sulphite union, as well as in a number of Iroquois Falls organizations. Although he was not elected in 1919, he made a very credible showing with more than 20 percent of the overall vote, and he topped the polls at Iroquois Falls, Ansonville, and Schumacher. He turned to municipal politics and was elected mayor of Iroquois Falls in 1921, 1922, and 1923. When he contested the provincial riding of Cochrane again in the 1923 election, he was again defeated, but he had made some progress, polling more votes than the Conservative candidate for a total of just under one-third of the vote.

Meanwhile, in 1920 the Independent Labor Party had made a breakthrough on the national scene in the riding of Temiskaming, where the Cobalt carpenter Angus McDonald was elected to the House of Commons in a by-election following the death of the sitting MP, Frank Cochrane. McDonald's victory was a landslide, with more than two thousand votes separating him from the Liberal candidate, Arthur G. Slaght. Canadian political histories have identified McDonald as a Progressive,[66] but local coverage of the campaign leaves no doubt that he presented himself as a Labour Party candidate. When the results of the by-election were reported in Ottawa, the Conservative member for Frontenac, J.W. Edwards, told the House, "I suppose that they [the Progressives] are willing to claim this man, now that he has been elected, but they were mighty careful to keep away from him when the election was on."[67] McDonald was given a very rough reception in the House of Commons. The member for Algoma, G.B. Nicholson, alleged that "the One Big Union was the organization behind the campaign that elected him to this House," and he added that the union's "professed object" was "to destroy even this institution itself."[68] McDonald hailed from Glengarry County in eastern Ontario; his Scots ancestry, farm background, and Roman Catholic faith undoubtedly contributed to his base of support in the riding. "Long Angus," as he was known locally, was re-elected in the 1921 campaign that introduced Mackenzie King to the prime ministerial office; McDonald was one of only three successful labour candidates in the country in that election. He was in his mid-50s, with no political experience, and found the complex stage of national politics a difficult challenge. He made few speeches in the House of Commons, and when he did rise to his feet he was not very effective. His inexperience showed in his uncertainty about procedure, and he was undoubtedly hindered by the lack of a party support system. Nevertheless, he was later given credit for laying the groundwork for the Co-operative Commonwealth Federation (CCF) in northeastern Ontario.[69]

Through the rest of the 1920s, labour support went primarily to the Liberal candidates. Notable among them was Joseph Arthur Bradette, a fluently bilingual native of the Charlevoix region of Quebec, who claimed what today would be called *pûr laine* Québécois ancestry. A bachelor farmer (and later businessman) in the Cochrane area, he was active in the Knights of Columbus, in several other fraternal organizations, and in Les artisans canadien-français (a cultural-nationalist group). In 1925 he ran unsuccessfully as a Liberal-Independent in the dominion election, but he polled considerably more votes than the recognized Liberal candidate. He ran again the following year as a Liberal-Labor candidate, and this time he defeated the incumbent. Bradette was highly effective in the House of Commons, speaking out on issues that ranged from mining taxes to unemployed youth. He was rewarded for his efforts by being re-elected through the 1920s, 1930s, and 1940s, and was appointed deputy speaker in 1943.

By the mid-1930s, Bradette's kind of moderate labour position was being challenged by a small but vocal segment of his constituents. The communists finally became sufficiently organized to field candidates in the 1934 provincial and 1935 federal campaigns (W. Lehtinen and Tom Ewen, respectively). And the recently formed CCF came to town. In 1934 Alex M. Stewart represented the new party in the provincial election with a surprisingly strong third-place finish, and Harry Beach ran for the CCF the following year in the dominion election. It did not take long for CCF support to build. In 1943 party member William J. Grummett was elected to the Ontario legislature for Cochrane South for the first of four terms of office.[70] He seemed an unlikely candidate for the CCF. He had grown up in the Owen Sound region of central Ontario and had come north to practise law. A veteran of the First World War, he remained an officer in the army reserve until he was in his fifties. He was an Anglican and an active member of the Masonic Order. In a generation when CCFers were more likely to be Presbyterians, pacifists, and farmers or intellectuals, he must have been a rarity. However, he had important local connections to both the francophone and labour constituencies. His wife was Marie Gaouette, a francophone who had grown up in Timmins, and they and their five children lived in Ansonville. Grummett clearly appealed to the moderate democratic socialists who were emerging as the passions of the old left-wing politics faded. That new politics found a home in the CCF.

It must be emphasized, however, that for many residents, provincial and national politics were almost irrelevant. Voter turnout was regularly reported to be in the range of just 20 to 30 percent. And as the Reverend G. MacVittie of South Porcupine United Church later recalled, "While they were not completely negligible of questions relative to the Province or the Dominion, the central core of sensitivity arose from local matters."[71] Perhaps it was because men (and a few women) who felt alienated from the system believed that they could have more impact at the municipal level. Perhaps it was because people who came to northeastern Ontario from abroad had little opportunity to learn how the political system at Queen's Park or Ottawa really worked, whereas they had ample opportunity to learn from and shape the system locally. Or perhaps it was, to paraphrase a well-known observation, that the biggest battles occur where the stakes are the smallest. "Porcupine Elections Will Be Exciting," predicted the Cobalt *Daily Nugget* in 1911.[72] It turned out to be something of an understatement.

Each organized township and municipality developed a local political culture that was unique in some ways, though all shared basic rituals and, eventually, similar problems. At Matheson, party politics played a role for many years; elsewhere in the region, traditional party affiliation did not count for much at the municipal level. The Iroquois Falls town government was a curious animal, since Abitibi owned nearly all the property within its boundaries and the town could levy few property taxes in the usual sense. Thus, theoretically, the council had rather limited scope for action, but apparently the elected officials did not place much confidence in theory. Tisdale Township Council became a battleground between socialists and capitalists, while neighbouring Whitney Township carried on with serene efficiency and dwindling resources. The Timmins municipal government was almost a department of the Hollinger Mine until the 1919 revolt of the Timmins Ratepayers' Association turned council meetings and elections into some of the liveliest and most unusual in Canada. When political economist K.J. Rea wrote, "In the north, the role of local government has been even weaker than in the rest of Canada," he clearly could not have been familiar with Porcupine–Iroquois Falls.[73] In spite of local variations, municipal politics in each centre provided both an outlet for socio-economic tensions and a forum in which they were shaped.

Matheson, as a lively railway service centre by 1910, anticipated its future as a major metropolis serving a populous agricultural region, so the full structures of municipal government were put in place early. Incorporated as a town in 1912, it was entitled to a mayor and a council of six. In the first election, voter turnout was high in response to a lively campaign that pitted Daniel Johnson, manager of the Revillon Frères store, against R.A. ("Dick") Douglas; Johnson was elected mayor by just six votes.[74] Frank E. Ginn, the crown lands agent, was appointed first town clerk, a position he held for many years. The first mayors and councillors were all anglophones; the first francophone, Phillipe Gauthier, was elected to council in 1919, but there were many years in the 1920s and

1930s when no French-speaking Canadians participated in any elected positions at Matheson.

After this brave and lively start came the great fire of 1916, which changed Matheson forever. Every house within the town limits was destroyed and many lives were lost. Dozens of families decided to abandon their dreams, never to return. In 1917 the town council was unable to find enough men willing to serve, and one of the six seats remained vacant.[75] The municipality sank deeper and deeper into debt; in 1922 Frank Ginn reported that the debenture debt was now $80,000, far beyond the capacity of the town to cover. The councillors decided that the wisest option was to spend as little as possible, so water, sewer, electrical, and road work were all kept to a minimum, and the local school board barely scraped by. As Ginn pointed out, the struggling residents were highly sensitive to tax or revenue increases and could choose to build homes on nearby lots in the unincorporated townships around Matheson, in order to avoid taxes and water bills that they could ill afford.[76] Nevertheless, by 1922 the town had installed water and sewer service, and there was a small municipal hospital. Electricity came in 1934 from Ontario Hydro.[77] Unfortunately, little record remains of the way in which Matheson's problems were debated or the range of options suggested. The elected officials worked to support the town as best they could until 1968, when the municipality was dissolved and made a part of the larger administrative district of Black River–Matheson.

Whitney Township was another district that organized early amid considerable optimism for future greatness. Located to the north and east of Porcupine Lake, it had been surveyed for homesteads and lots allocated as veterans' grants before the gold rush, but it was as the "gateway" to the goldfields that it was incorporated in September 1911. Pottsville lawyer Gordon H. Gauthier, who was also the mining recorder and magistrate, was proclaimed the first reeve. An Anglican, a Mason, and later an active member of the Conservative Association, he represented the minority middle-class group that seized the opportunity to mould the new settlement in their interests, apparently assuming that it was both their responsibility and their right to do so. Promoting business development was their primary concern, but close behind was an obsession with keeping order among the allegedly unruly and potentially dangerous workforce resident in the township. One of Whitney Township Council's first decisions was to appoint former OPP constable C.M. Piercy as the township police chief and to appoint lawyer J.P. Crawford as town clerk and solicitor. A sober, efficient, and businesslike council saw to it that the streets were cleared, water lines laid, proper forms filled out, and the potential riff-raff closely watched. The liveliest that local politics got in the first decade was during the occasional eruption of competitive animosity between Golden City and

Pottsville (for example, at the "indignation meeting" of June 1911, when Golden City property owners protested against the government's decision to locate the post office in Pottsville).[78] As the *Porcupine Advance* noted on several occasions, the Whitney Township nomination meetings "passed off very quietly." There was a good deal of continuity from year to year as Zack Hart, Irwin P. Wilson, and George D. Hamilton served term after term in office.

But there were some changes. Gordon Gauthier was replaced as reeve in 1914 by a man from a very different background. George Bannerman was a self-made man from near Stratford, Ontario, who had been forced to go to work as a teenager when his father died, leaving a young widow with six children to support. George and his brother William ("Will") went to work on the railway, then headed north in the Cobalt silver rush hoping to strike it rich. But it turned out to be the Porcupine that made their fortunes. In partnership with Tom Geddes, George and Will Bannerman staked what became the Scottish-Ontario Mine north of Porcupine Lake – the first real producer of the area's early mines. Bolstered by their success, the two brothers married. George and his wife Jenny settled at Powell's Point on Porcupine Lake, while Will and his wife Christie eventually decided to homestead near Matheson. Tragically, Christie was killed in the 1916 fire.[79] Although the Scottish-Ontario Mine never developed into a major producer, the proceeds enabled George Bannerman to support his family and to lay the groundwork for other endeavours. Because of his association with the Scottish-Ontario Mine, he was invited to join the first board of trade organized in the camp in 1910. Between 1914 and his retirement, he served six terms as reeve, and he remained a prominent member of the community until his death in 1964. As a man of limited formal education and humble origins, George Bannerman came to represent the second generation of community leaders in Whitney Township. Although he had done well in life, he did not set himself apart from his neighbours and he took his civic responsibilities seriously.

By the 1920s, Whitney Township was clearly being eclipsed by the developments at Dome Mines in neighbouring Tisdale Township and by Hollinger at Timmins. The population dropped from something over 1,800 in 1912 to 275 by 1915 and just 145 in 1922.[80] The character of the township had clearly changed, and the door was left open for a third generation of men such as Pasquale Rotondo to enter municipal politics. The Italian-born Rotondo was a railway worker who had come to Porcupine from Montreal in 1921 with his wife and growing family. He worked as a section foreman for the TNO, and Mrs Rotondo kept a large vegetable garden, chickens, and a cow to help support the family. They joined St Joachim's Roman Catholic Church in South Porcupine and eventually raised eleven children.[81] Rotondo was first elected to Whitney Township

Council in 1927 and served for eleven consecutive terms before being elected reeve in 1938 and 1939. The township government had evolved gradually and peacefully to reflect the changing socio-economic groups that made up its population.

In contrast to the calm of Whitney Township politics, neighbouring Tisdale Township was in more or less permanent uproar, and not always at election time. The township council became a battleground between labour and business, with both sides resorting to tactics other than the ballot in their struggle for supremacy. As resident Uly Levinson recalled, "The elections stirred up much interest, even to fisticuffs and name-calling. It was an all-out fight from start to finish."[82]

Shortly after the township was incorporated in 1911, a group of mine managers and real estate developers constituted themselves a "selection committee" and announced a reeve and township council whom they pro-posed to have acclaimed, allegedly to save the time and expense of an elec-tion, which they deemed "unnecessary." Two local businessmen who had not been consulted raised objections, so the selection committee put them on the council to replace one of the mine owners and an assayer.[83] A busi-ness-mining coalition seemed to have been established and destined to rule. Dissent was brewing, however. The fire of 1911 distracted attention from the proceedings, but when election time rolled round in December, the council's opponents were ready to strike. Six men were nominated for reeve and eleven for the four council seats. After the dust had settled, the township found itself with an almost entirely new council consisting of Sylvester Kennedy (an Ottawa Valley log roller who was attempting to establish himself in business in South Porcupine), Dayton Ostrosser (who was managing a general store in Golden City and operating the Schu-macher post office), Charles A. See (owner of See's Pills and Things), and Irving E. Dunn. Lawyer J.E. Cook, who had been acting as township clerk, was elected reeve. Only Kennedy and Cook had been associated with the original council, and they immediately found themselves under siege. At the first council meeting the newcomers to the council resolved to pursue the "modification" of taxes through an "equalization" of the assessment; they announced that they stood for "equal rights to all and special privi-leges to none."[84] The newcomers lodged a complaint with the Ontario government, alleging that Kennedy could not legally sit on Tisdale Town-ship Council (apparently because he was then a property owner in Whitney Township). Kennedy resigned his seat, weathered the storm, and was resoundingly re-elected.

Then the shaky partnership between business and mining men began to break down over the liquor issue. Under provincial law at the time, prohi-bition of liquor sales could be instituted as a local decision, and the mine owners who had dominated the first municipal government had decided that alcohol would be too disruptive for their labour force; the first council had apparently not approved any liquor licences in the township. Now, business owners in South Porcupine and the nearby Lakeview townsite called for separation from Tisdale Township so that they could be incorporated as towns and go "wet."[85] When their campaign failed, the battle against the old guard was moved to a new front. Late in 1913, allegations were made that Reeve Cook had defrauded the township by misappropriating some funds and had covered it up with an audit done by the local tax collector (and hence illegal). When the tax collector refused to release the township books to the newly elected 1914 council, the province intervened. It commissioned an audit of its own (which strongly criticized the township's management) and laid charges against Cook. In the subsequent election, Kennedy was defeated in his bid for reeve against the challenger E.G. Dickson ("considerable excitement provided in the several voting booths," commented the *Advance*), and all the old councillors went down to defeat with him. They were replaced by men who straddled the boundary between labour and small business, including W.P. Black (a South Porcupine tailor) and J.E. Boyle (a small-scale construction contractor). The charges against Cook were dismissed at trial, were then appealed, and were again dismissed in November 1916.[86] Cook ran for reeve in 1920 but was defeated by Charles Vincent Gallagher, a prospector and surveyor from Warkworth, Ontario (between Peterborough and Trenton), who later served as a Liberal member of the Ontario legislature for Cochrane South. Gallagher presented himself as the "workingman's candidate"; Cook's fate was sealed when his candidacy was endorsed by some supporters of the discredited old guard.

By most accounts, Gallagher was relatively moderate, but his labour sympathies were too much for some conservatives in the passionately divided township. In 1920 the businesswoman Josephine Thomas solicited the support of J.S. Bache, the president of Dome Mines, in her candidacy for reeve, saying, "By electing me to this office you will help get rid of a Local Bolsheviki government who are bouncing on all the investors who come into Camp, and constantly keeping the working man disturbed." She added, "The 'One Big Union' here I believe is weaking [sic] and we want to kill it if it can be done."[87] Bache was enthusiastic, but the mine manager, H.P. De Pencier, urged caution. "I am ... very much afraid that any open support will have the effect of consolidating the labor for their own candidate," he informed Bache, "which is just what happened last year when the election was split up and the radical element won."[88]

That "radical element" didn't wait for the polls to challenge Josephine Thomas. Her candidacy was declared ineligible, and she was forced to withdraw from the campaign. Undaunted, she girded her loins against "the O.B.U.I.W.W. Socialism and so on"[89] and challenged Gallagher again in 1922 and 1923, losing resoundingly both times. Not one to concede defeat gracefully, she headed to Toronto to petition the Ontario government for an audit of the township's books. Her campaign was interrupted briefly when she was arrested on charges of perjury over some disputed mining claim affidavits. Then she was back at it again in December 1926, campaigning against her nemesis, Charles Gallagher, for the reeveship. This time, she apparently managed to defeat him, only to have her qualifications challenged on the grounds that she was still facing legal proceedings over her mine property. The district court judge agreed and overturned the election. Seven years later she finally succeeded in winning an election and actually served out the year in 1933 as reeve of Tisdale Township. But her triumph was short-lived. Gallagher was returned to office for 1934 and served three more terms before moving into provincial politics.[90]

The see-saw battle between labour and "big" business, as personified in the jousting of Josephine Thomas and Charles Gallagher, did not cease once these two were off the scene. Indeed, by all accounts, things heated up. In 1938 the *Porcupine Advance* described a candidates' meeting in South Porcupine this way: "Fists were clenched and attitudes struck, voices raised and faces empurpled, and with the crowd heckling and booing, the speaker made a rush for the other candidate nearly bowling over the chairman who tried vainly to separate them, and the audience saw a melee of waving arms, falling scenery and general bedlam." After the combatants were separated, the chair called for an adjournment, "and the audience was too excited to remember to sing 'God Save the King.'"[91]

Municipal government in Iroquois Falls was much more sedate. Here, a rapprochement eventually emerged between labour and management, and hostilities were directed beyond the town boundaries. The more lively ideological battles were fought against neighbouring Calvert Township, in which the rebellious settlement of Ansonville was located. As an incorporated town, Iroquois Falls was a rather curious creature. As noted above, since Abitibi Pulp and Paper owned nearly all the property within its boundaries, the municipality could levy few property taxes in the usual sense and had limited scope for action with monies raised through licences and fines alone. Abitibi provided all the infrastructure, including water, sewer, road and sidewalk construction and maintenance, and electricity, so the town government did not have to issue debentures to raise funds for these costly undertakings or to manage the tenders and contracts which elsewhere were required to build them. So the town's role was primarily a managerial one. Observers might be forgiven for seeing the council as an administrative department of Abitibi Pulp and Paper. The first mayor, S.G. McCoubrey (acclaimed for five terms in a row), was initially office manager at Abitibi, then private secretary to the general manager. The town's initial correspondence with the Ontario government was written on Abitibi letterhead. Turnout for council "elections" was usually high, but the same men were elected over and over in what amounted to three- or four-year rotations. And the early town councils seem to have consisted entirely of men in supervisory positions at the Abitibi plant. In 1919, for example, the council included W.J. Tierney (millwright superintendent), W.H. Potter (manager of the Railroad Department), George S. Wilson (superintendent of the steam plant), A.W. Hennessy (manager of the Woods Department), and Ed Lavallée (who resigned late in the year to become the town's fire chief).[92] However, it would be wrong to assume that the voters of Iroquois Falls were entirely puppets of the company. They demonstrated a degree of independence when they elected union leader John Vanier as mayor from 1921 to 1923.[93]

It seems that the only issue that generated much debate between 1916 and 1940 was an attempt by the town in 1921 to levy a "poll tax" on occupants of the hotel located just outside the Abitibi property and to charge a sort of "visitors' fee" to residents of Ansonville who came to Iroquois Falls. The town was finding itself in financial difficulties as Abitibi itself was sliding into what would eventually necessitate receivership. The fee question ended up in court when a disgruntled taxpayer challenged the town's right to levy such charges. The judge ruled in the town's favour, noting that Iroquois Falls was "faced with a serious financial problem" (because of Abitibi's problems) and "had adopted a means not expressly prohibited by the Municipal Act."[94]

Meanwhile, the liveliest battle was between Iroquois Falls and The Wye (Ansonville) in Calvert Township. Calvert was formally incorporated on 24 December 1918, but its independent souls did not take kindly to local government. When an attempt was made to levy the first taxes in 1921, a number of residents packed up and moved just outside the township boundaries. The only times there seemed to be much support for Calvert Township Council were the occasions when it challenged Abitibi, the fire insurance companies (who charged very high rates because sections of Ansonville kept burning down), or the "government" (for failing to provide good quality radio broadcast signals in the area). The township government consisted primarily of Jewish and French-speaking Canadian small-business owners such as Arthur Leroux and H.J. Fine. With the exception of Leroux, turnover on the council was rapid.[95] The township was in a perpetual financial crisis, with a significant proportion of its taxes hopelessly in arrears. When the township raised the rates in the middle of the Depression in order to cover its rising relief costs, residents organized the Taxpayers' Protective Association, refused to pay any taxes if the rates went up again, and presented the council with a list of people whom they wanted struck off the relief lists so as to reduce the township's expenses.[96]

In spite of its internal problems, Calvert Township appointed itself guardian of the poor deluded souls of Iroquois Falls and attempted a number of rescue missions to free them from the clutches of Abitibi. The most serious effort came in the mid-1940s, when Reeve Elmo Lefebvre led the charge to the Ontario Municipal Board with a Calvert Township application to formally annex Iroquois Falls. The Ontario Municipal Board ruled against Ansonville's application.[97] It was the economic problems of a later generation that finally forced the two into each other's arms.

Municipal politics in Timmins also reflected and contributed to tensions within the community. The first four town councils were "elected" by acclamation, which would seem to reflect a consensus, but behind the scenes, battles boiled. For example, T.J. McGrath attempted to have the 1913 slate of officers overturned by resorting to the courts, claiming that the voters' list was so gravely in error as to constitute fraud on the part of the 1912 council. The judge ruled against the challenge, noting "neglect" and "dilatoriness" but "no fraud or conspiracy."[98] The scene was set for a lively future.

At first, the conflicts were between Hollinger and the business sector. In 1915 the Timmins Board of Trade lobbied the town council to request beer licences for the town from the provincial licence commissioners, as Ontario's liquor laws then required. The council defeated the motion, with the Hollinger-affiliated councillors (Globe, Moore, and McCoy) leading the charge. Councillors Charles Dalton (owner of a livery business) and E. Laflamme wanted beer licences as a way to regulate the blind pigs and, of course, as a way for legitimate businessmen to get into a potentially lucrative operation. On the other hand, Councillor Globe was paternalistically emphatic about keeping the town "dry." As the *Advance* reported, "He told the Council that during the summer months of the year he had visited a number of mining towns in Colorado, Mexico, Arizona and other western towns and was able to appreciate a good deal better just what the liquor granting could do."[99] This debate was followed by the first real election, when ten candidates presented themselves for the six council seats. In the end, the Hollinger candidates took the top four positions; only two retailers were elected. The four other business-sector candidates were eliminated.

Tensions during the First World War generated the next set of divisions that came to dominate Timmins municipal government for many years. As the cost of living rose and paycheques did not, both the retailers and the mines (and hence the town council) found themselves under fire. The council also seemed deadlocked on the question of building a municipal hospital (the Hollinger hospital served employees only); when the influenza epidemic struck in 1918, the lack of facilities became painfully obvious and the two doctors on the council (McInnis and Moore) were too closely associated with Hollinger to escape censure. Late in 1918, a group of dissidents created the Timmins Ratepayers' Association to challenge the now-entrenched leaders. The association's president, William DeFeu, was a leading organizer of the Porcupine miners' union who worked as a machinist for McIntyre; he had been born in England and so probably had been influenced by the British labour movement. The association's first executive included two French-speaking Canadians, Henri Charlebois and Joseph Thériault, and a prominent labour activist from the forestry sector, Leonard S. Newton. They announced that their purpose was to encourage more public participation in local politics,[100] by which they clearly hoped to engineer a coup and get men on council who would be attentive to labour's needs. DeFeu and Newton were elected to the 1919 town council, with Newton topping the polls. With a foot finally in the door, the Timmins Ratepayers' Association continued to press its influence. Candidates supported by the association were elected through the 1920s. The annual contests drew more and more voters – and more candidates. In 1923 there were twenty-six nominations for the six council seats, and voter turnout tripled.[101] A proposal was even floated to institutionalize the new interest group's place in local politics when W. Ealey suggested that labour and business each nominate three men to ensure labour representation on council.[102]

The ratepayers' association met regularly to criticize the council and press for attention to issues such as poor water service and high taxes. They alleged that unreasonably large amounts of money were going to the public schools at the expense of the separate schools. And they consistently argued that it was appropriate – and, indeed, necessary – for the municipal government to address labour's more general concerns, such as who should pay for silicosis treatment and how to deal with the rising cost of living. They obtained a public voice through a little newspaper initially called the *Citizen*, which was produced by one of their most active members, James P. Bartleman. His paper grew rapidly and was renamed the *Free Press*, probably to disassociate it from the *Porcupine Advance*, which Bartleman considered to be a tool of Hollinger management. After Bartleman sold his paper to Roy Thomson in 1934, it continued to challenge the mine management, the self-appointed elite, and anyone else Thomson thought it might be worth criticizing in order to stir up controversy and sell newspapers.

When challenges at the polls failed to unseat all of the old guard, the Timmins Ratepayers' Association turned to other tactics. In 1933 it tried to have the municipal election overturned on the grounds of procedural irregularities. But in the December elections for the 1934 council the association staged its real coup. Following an energetic campaign by Bartleman, the entire old guard was unseated. All of the elected candidates (besides Bartleman) were working men; all (except Bartleman) were French Canadian. "Startling Declaration of Lack of Confidence," chortled the *Timmins Press*.[103] The new council quickly made it plain where its sympathies lay. For example, overriding objections from some prominent citizens, council permitted a "tag day" to raise money for the bushworkers who were on strike across the region. Two years later the labour lobby succeeded in electing Bartleman to the mayor's seat.

The old guard now felt very threatened and decided to form an association of its own, which it named the Timmins Citizens' League. Rumours circulated that communists were getting undue influence on the council, and two francophone organizations (the St Jean Baptiste Society and Le cercle canadien) began endorsing candidates whom they could trust to be moderates. The Citzens' League candidates who succeeded at the polls included Emile Brunette, an automobile dealer, active member of the Roman Catholic Church, and a francophone. In 1939 Brunette and two others resigned from council to protest the way business was being conducted, and they called upon Mayor Bartleman and Councillors Armstrong, McNeill, and McCabe (a union official) to resign and call a new election. These men, Brunette alleged, had used underhanded tactics to "gain control" of the town government "for their union purposes," turning the council into "a front for certain groups in this town which was [sic] gaining too much control for the good of the municipality."[104]

The battle spilled over into the local media, pitting the *Timmins Press* against the *Porcupine Advance* – until Bartleman lost the support of the *Press* over the radio issue. Roy Thomson had purchased the newspaper in 1933 because he wanted the radio station that came under it. Under Thomson's ownership, the radio station had managed to alienate almost every interest group in town: the francophones (who saw their French-language programming reduced), the retailers (who were attacked in a speech that was broadcast in 1934), residents outside Timmins (who could not pick up the station with its 25–watt transmitter), conservatives (who objected to the broadcast of Communist Party speeches in 1936), and communists (who objected to programs sponsored by local capitalists). In October 1939 the Timmins Town Council waded in with an official statement deploring CKGB for its "over-commercialism," its allegedly excessive profits, and its poor signal. One councillor proposed that the CBC set up a station in town, and the council called for a resident provincial radio inspector to keep an ear on CKGB.[105] Thomson retaliated with an article in the *Timmins Press* alleging that Mayor Bartleman and four councillors were communists who were trying to "sovietise" free-market business activities by proposing to regulate his radio broadcasts.[106]

The municipal election campaign that followed was a bitter one. Bartleman was challenged for the mayor's seat by the Citizens' League candidate

Emile Brunette, who defeated the flamboyant mayor. For council, the Citizens' League candidates included J. Wilfred Spooner (a Roman Catholic businessman, president of the Timmins Underwriters' Association, and later Conservative member of the provincial legislature), and Herbert Warren (a retired retailer, court bailiff, Mason, and Conservative). Opposing them were such candidates as H.R. Anderson (a full-time organizer for the CIO), Wellington Armstrong (also a CIO organizer and a brewing company agent), and Thomas McNeil (president of Mine, Mill Local 241).[107] After Bartleman's defeat, the council meetings were no less lively. Bartleman carried on his campaign from outside the council and in 1941 ran again for a seat, alleging widespread "vice, graft and corruption," including "bootlegging chains" which he said were running amok within the town administration. An anonymous letter in the *Porcupine Advance* put the ongoing battle in equally crude terms:

Our Town was not so bad as towns go ... Now personalities are the order of the day; bitterness reigns at meetings of the council; fanatical religious and political organizations attend the council meetings and dictate their demands; resolutions are passed about wage advances at the local mines, which are no business at all of the Town Council; and the majority of the meetings are more like a public entertainment ... [At election time] we are confronted with a long list of names of people whom we don't know excepting by reading the police court news: some of them bums, bootleggers, high-graders and the like.[108]

Several scholars have noted that the labour front in the Porcupine mining area was relatively quiet, with unions weak or non-existent, and various theories have been put forward regarding the apparent success of mine management in keeping working people quiescent.[109] But it would appear that these theories are misplaced. Rather than fighting labour's battles in the workplace through the unions, working people appropriated the political forum that was available to them and tried to take control of the workplace by municipal edict. Although they succeeded from time to time, their numbers (and perhaps internal divisions on issues such as language and religion) never permitted complete domination of the municipal government. Instead, the Timmins town hall was turned into an arena for the ongoing battle among mine managers, business owners, and labour.

While disparate interest groups struggled for supremacy among the newcomers to the region, an entirely different set of political issues was being played out elsewhere. Apparently, it was invisible to the newcomers, yet it was inextricably linked to their actions. No local member of parliament or municipal politician seems to have raised these questions in public. No citizens' league or ratepayers' association responded. But for the First Nations of the region, these issues struck at the very heart of their survival. As was happening elsewhere in Canada, problems arose over the implementation of their treaty, the allocation of reserve lands, and recognition of resource-access rights. And as has been the case elsewhere, these issues have never been resolved.

Treaty 9, like the other Numbered Treaties, included provisions for land to be set aside for the exclusive use of the Native people who signed the treaty. The Canadian government decided to offer reserves in the vicinity of Matachewan, Mattagami, Lake Abitibi (on the Ontario side), New Brunswick House, Flying Post, Missinaibi, and the railway town of Chapleau, as well as Moose Factory. The idea seems to have been to establish reserves in the vicinity of existing trading posts, and, in the case of Chapleau, the church and school. The treaty commissioners provided a rough description of the area that each band wanted for its reserve, and these choices were ratified by a dominion order-in-council on 12 January 1907 and an Ontario order-in-council on 13 February.[110] The Indian Affairs Branch then established an administrative system of "agencies" through which the reserves could be supervised and the government's assimilation policy pursued. Chapleau Agency, initially under the direction of agent H.A. West, included the communities at Chapleau, Mattagami, Missinaibi, Flying Post, and New Brunswick House. North Temiskaming Agency, under Adam Burwash, was to oversee the people at Lake Abitibi and at the upper end of Lake Temiskaming. Matachewan was added to the Sturgeon Falls Agency (already in existence for people who had signed the 1850 Robinson-Huron Treaty) under agent George P. Cockburn.[111]

Although there were problems in locating almost all of the reserves, the Mattagami site proved to be the most problematic. According to research by historian Jim Morrison, the band wanted its reserve to be set up east of the HBC post in an area rich in deer. The HBC post manager, James Miller, suggested that they choose a site at Kenogamissi Falls where they could take advantage of future income from hydro development of the falls.[112] Ultimately, they settled for a site just north of the HBC post on the west shore of Mattagami Lake. In the spring of 1908, government surveyors were supposed to lay out the boundaries of the reserve, but they deferred doing so because it was discovered that the order-in-council had incorrectly described the location of the HBC post, and since the reserve location was described in relation to the post, the reserve site was obviously also in error.[113] Furthermore, the area which the band wanted turned out to be rich in pine timber – an important stand of lumber-sized trees in an area otherwise mostly good for pulpwood only. The Ontario government balked. Finally, it agreed to permit the reserve on this site "on the condition that the pine timber in the new area measuring over eight inches in diameter be reserved to the Province for a period of ten years from the date of the Provincial Order in Council" of 1907.[114] A new description of the reserve was prepared in the spring of 1909, defining it as "beginning at a point three quarters of a mile North of the Hudson [sic] Bay Company's post, on the North shore of the Mattagami River, thence East a distance of four miles and of a sufficient depth to give an area of twenty square miles [51.8 square kilometres]."[115] But the delay had brought a new problem. Prospectors drawn to the Porcupine region were now eyeing these lands. Surveyor James Dobie reported to Ottawa, "I would like the instructions to be as definite as possible with regard to any mining claims which may possibly be started inside the proposed reserve. That country is full of prospectors now."[116]

Dobie conducted the official survey between 23 June and 4 July 1909 but later admitted, "When I arrived at Mattagami I found it very difficult to tell exactly what was intended by the written description." He further claimed, "I had no idea of the correspondence relating to the difficulty in determining the location."[117] The Ontario government apparently felt no such uncertainty, for in mid-July 1910 the provincial Department of Lands, Forests, and Mines called for tenders on the timber rights to cut red pine, white pine, and jack pine on what was supposedly the Mattagami Reserve. Alarmed, the band wrote to its agent, H.A. West, at Chapleau. He in turn wrote to his supervisors in Ottawa asking for an explanation and reporting that the "Indians seem to be under the impression that it [the timber] belonged to them [and are] almost up in arms about it."[118] The official reply only added to the confusion. Indian Affairs explained that the timber had been reserved to the Ontario government for ten years, but added, "It being understood, however, that the Indians should be allowed to cut such timber as may be allowed for their own use."[119] The band apparently decided it had lost. It abandoned plans to build houses on the reserve, preferring to settle on its hunting grounds off-reserve to the west.[120]

But the Ontario government received no bids for the timber, largely because of the expense involved in cutting it. Since the Mattagami River flows north, logs could not be floated south to the existing major sawmills at Sturgeon Falls and other places. New mills would have to be built at inaccessible points downstream, and no one considered this to be economically feasible. Seeing no action, the Mattagami Band realized that it might not have lost after all. In 1913 a new agent, William McLeod, was hired for the Chapleau Agency, and the Mattagami Band's chief, James Naveau, wrote to him, "wanting to know if the timber on the Indian reserve belong to them or if it was sold would it be of any benefit to the band." The chief pointed out that the band had put considerable effort into extinguishing a recent forest fire on the reserve and thought it "should get some recompense" for its efforts.[121] Still nothing was settled.

Then, in the spring of 1915, the Ontario government succeeded in leasing the timber rights to a Timmins firm in an agreement that permitted it two years to remove the timber. Since the original agreement gave Ontario the timber rights only until 3 February 1917, this lease would run over the end of that period. So the Ontario government applied to Ottawa for an extension.

The application produced a flurry of memos in Ottawa's office buildings. The officer in charge of lands and timber recommended against the extension on the grounds that the band was claiming the timber. Deputy-Superintendent General Duncan Campbell Scott wanted to grant the extension. But the department's legal adviser recommended against it, and ultimately, on that advice, it was turned down. Consequently, the Ontario government did not grant a timber lease.[122] However, that was not the end of the issue. Four years later, early in November 1919, the Boivin Lumber Company in Timmins lobbied Duncan Campbell Scott to grant the Ontario government an extension to the ten-year agreement so that Boivin could purchase the timber rights. Matt Boivin tried to appeal to Scott's emotional and patriotic sensitivities by claiming that the company was representing two "returned soldiers who were three years at the Front the said Henry Boivin having been seriously gassed and shell shocked," and it was they who would benefit from the licence.[123] Within five days, Scott had come up with a plan to circumvent the legal problem. He sent paperwork to the Indian agent, J.T. Godfrey, instructing him to get the Mattagami Band to agree to surrender its timber rights on the reserve. Godfrey warned Scott that this would be no simple matter: "Getting their signatures to any document releasing any rights they may have is going to be a hard proposition as this very thing is a bone of contention at the Matagama Reserve every payment [Treaty Day] as there are some half casts who make it their business to keep the Indians filled up with the idea that they the Indians own the land, timber and everything in connection with it."[124]

Once the Mattagami people learned of the Boivin application, they were furious. Bypassing the Indian agent, they wrote directly to Ottawa and demanded a formal statement in writing that they were the legal owners of both the land and the timber on the reserve. The departmental reply carefully avoided any reference to land ownership, for it was the government's position that reserves were crown lands, merely set aside for Indian use. However, the department did acknowledge that the timber belonged to the band, and it proposed to act on behalf of the Mattagami Band to find a purchaser for the timber if the band voted to release it to the dominion government for a ten-year period. Indian Agent Godfrey organized a meeting of the band and obtained the required vote; an order-in-council dated 19 July 1920 made the timber surrender legal. The band members explained that they were "all in very impoverished circumstances" and hoped that the sale of timber would bring some badly needed income.[125] The dominion government duly advertised with a call for tenders in December 1920.

The apparent compromise failed, and the issue fermented for another thirty years. There were disagreements about the value of the timber. There were complaints that funds from the sales were not reaching the band. During the Depression, the Fesserton Timber Company of Timmins (which then had the cutting rights) repeatedly asked for an extension of its licence because its financial problems (and a fire at its mill in 1932) prevented it from doing any cutting. When the timber was finally being cut, the band complained that the scalers were mismeasuring the logs and it was being cheated of the true value of the timber. Over the years, the band hired a lawyer, obtained the help of Anglican Bishop John Anderson, and threatened civil disobedience – all to no avail.

The real issue seems to have been a basic disagreement between the band and the government over the revenue owed to the band. Chief Neveau and his successors believed that since the band owned the timber, it was entitled to the full proceeds of its sale. Since an early estimate placed the value of the timber at $150,000, the band expected to realize a considerable income. The band members do not seem to have realized how the sale of timber on crown lands actually worked. Governments collected only royalties and licence dues, while the lumber company received the real profits through the sale of the processed lumber. Furthermore, the Mattagami Band seems to have been unaware that the written version of its deal with the government split the royalties in half: 50 percent to Ottawa and 50 percent to the band. So it is hardly surprising that the band was angry when it began receiving payments of $700 or $1,500 a year when it was expecting tens of thousands of dollars. In 1929 Chief James Neveau and Councillors Sam Luke and James Neveau Junior wrote a letter to Indian Affairs that stood as a statement for the entire sorry affair:

We, the Indians of the Mattagami Band, wish to hear from yourself definitely about the sale of timber on our reserve. Many people have spoken to us about the sale but they all tell different stories ... For how much money has the timber been sold? How much of the price will be paid to the Indians and how much will be kept for us by the Goverment [sic]? When will the money be paid to us and who will give it to us?

We have had a very bad Winter hunting as the fur in this country is nearly all killed, and have no money this Summer.[126]

The Matachewan Reserve was also affected by a dispute over timber rights. The reserve site was chosen, approved, and officially surveyed – and

then the Ottawa lumber baron J.R. Booth complained that the reserve had
been located on land to which he already held a twenty-year lease from the
Ontario government. The dominion government initially took the position that Booth was in error because the terms of his lease explicitly
excluded Indian reserves. The Ontario government responded that the
reserve had not been laid out according to the description in the order-in-
council of 1907; rather, it had been surveyed in the wrong place, on J.R.
Booth's timber limits. So the Ontario government refused to recognize the
reserve, as was necessary for the transfer of land from provincial to federal
jurisdiction. The dominion government capitulated; the reserve was
allowed to stand as surveyed and Booth was allowed to remove the timber
from it. "It is, however," wrote the deputy superintendent general,
"urgently desired that a reasonable time limit be placed for the removal of
timber."[127] Caught between feuding jurisdictions, the Matachewan Band
ended up with even less than the people at Mattagami.

The second major ongoing political issue for the area's First Nations was
loss of reserve land, usually because of flooding when dams were constructed to provide hydroelectricity to feed the voracious appetites of the
new mines and mills. In 1915 the chief of the Abitibi Band complained to
Indian Affairs that some eight square kilometres of its reserve had been
flooded because Abitibi Pulp and Paper was maintaining the water levels
too high in the lake; the company denied responsibility and a debate went
on for years thereafter.[128] In 1921 the Ontario government granted permission to Northern Canada Power to construct a dam at Kenogamissi
Falls that would flood some Mattagami reserve lands, including the homes
of Chief James Neveau, his son James Neveau Junior, and Thomas Neveau.
It would also flood the cemetery adjacent to the reserve where some sixty-
four people were buried, including four HBC employees. Northern Canada
Power negotiated an agreement to provide financial compensation, but
when the dam was built, more land than expected was flooded, including
some that contained the contentious prime pine timber. The band
claimed that the lost timber was worth $75,000 to $100,000 and
demanded compensation. A decade-long battle ensued over the question
of the true value of the timber.

The third major political issue for the First Nations was the question of
their right to hunt and fish unimpeded by government regulation. In the
mid-1920s the Ontario government began to demand that Northern
Ontario's Native people pay for trapping licences; the bands objected,
arguing that Treaty 9 had guaranteed them the right to hunt, trap, and
fish, so licences were an infringement on that right. In the spring of 1925
the Indian Affairs Branch ruled unequivocally, "Indians are required to
pay for their licences ... As this is a subject which is held solely within the
jurisdiction of the Provincial authorities this Department cannot interfere

in the matter."[129] Apparently, the department's legal counsel had over-looked the fact that the British North America Act made the dominion government responsible for "Indians." Then the Ontario government introduced restrictions on hunting beaver and otter. Again the First Nations protested; again Ottawa ruled it was a provincial matter. At the same time (May 1925), the Ontario government created the Chapleau Game Preserve, which affected the band at Brunswick House, as well as indirectly affecting the band at Mattagami because the latter also had been using the area for trapping. The game preserve issue went to court when a treaty woman was charged with killing deer inside the preserve. She hired Sudbury lawyer George M. Miller to defend her on the grounds that Treaty 9 exempted her from these game laws. Again, the dominion government declared the issue a purely provincial matter. She lost her case in court.[130] It was not until the 1980s and 1990s that Canadian officials began to consider seriously the question of Aboriginal resource rights and the courts began to reconsider these earlier interpretations.

Finally, there were lengthy political debates in the region about two reserves that never came into being. In 1904 Ontario surveyors had made their way into Bowman Township near the future site of Matheson, where Bazil McDougall demanded that his home and lands along the Black River be recognized as property "reserved" to him. The Ontario government issued what it called a "licence of occupation" to Bazil and Michael McDougall for 18 acres (7.3 hectares). Apparently, the McDougalls considered this to be their own reserve and considered that they were Indians under the jurisdiction of the dominion government. When in 1914 the McDougalls complained that Abitibi's new dam project downriver had flooded some of their property, they got the mayor of Matheson, Daniel Johnson, to write to the Indian Affairs Branch in Ottawa to obtain a settlement. It took some time for department officials to realize that the McDougalls' property was not officially an Indian reserve, but once they had made that determination they washed their hands of the affair.[131] The McDougall family was out of luck. Being registered neither on an official band list nor as property owners in fee simple like other settlers, they were lost in a legal limbo. It was just one example of the plight of the Métis and non-status Indians across the Canadian North.

The second reserve issue developed at Biscotasing, a station stop on the CPR line, which, by the First World War had attracted a growing population of Aboriginal people. Some were from the Flying Post area, others were from the Spanish River area (under the Robinson-Huron Treaty of 1850), and a third group was from Mattagami. All had given up on the reserves allocated to them, partly because of the failure of game at home and (in the case of the Mattagami people particularly) because of the lack of other possibilities of economic support from their reserves. In 1914 the people at Biscotasing obtained the support of the Indian agent at Chapleau in their appeal for the creation of a new reserve. The department in Ottawa refused, but it offered to help the Biscotasing people purchase land. The community was divided; some thought the purchase proposal was a good one, but others felt they could not afford the price, given the low prices they were obtaining for their furs. After six years of repeated petitioning and repeated refusals, the department simply stopped listening.[132] There would be no reserve at Biscotasing. The decision was a particular blow to the Mattagami people, who were forced to make the best of a partially flooded reserve that had few fur-bearing animals and little game, and offered little hope of real income from its timber wealth.

Significantly, very little of the political debates that were convulsing the First Nations of the area permeated the consciousness of the non-Native newcomers. The intervention of a former Matheson mayor on behalf of the McDougalls seems to be the sole exception. Local media reported on Native people only as colourful remnants of a romantic but necessarily disappearing past, and there seems to have been absolutely no awareness that non-Native hunting and trapping was causing an economic disaster for Aboriginal communities. Indeed, the only complaints on that score arose when the Canadian government attempted to register First Nations' traplines in areas to which non-Natives considered they had priority of access. Members of parliament in both Ottawa and Toronto never spoke on Native concerns in the legislature. It is hardly surprising that the chiefs and councillors ignored the electoral system in return. Their only champions were the clergy and bishops of the Anglican Diocese of Moosonee.

Politics was central to the way the emerging community organized and defined itself. Battles over political philosophies dominated much of the public discourse, pitting one group against another while at the same time forging powerful bonds within each faction. Political structures imposed on the region helped to define the battle lines, but in some places, residents appropriated these structures and redefined them, so that municipal politics in Timmins, for example, became a base from which labour activists promoted the interests of working people. Politics could also be a very personal and individual power struggle, as in the case of J.P. Bartleman versus Roy Thomson. And ultimately, politics served some groups very well while leaving others badly damaged. The area's Aboriginal people did everything in their power to promote their own interests, but in the end the power imbalance was simply overwhelming. It would be left to future generations to begin to make up the lost ground.

PART THREE

CHAPTER TEN

Centrifugal Forces

In the mid-1930s the prominent Canadian scholar A.R.M. Lower concluded that the English-speaking population of Northern Ontario believed that there were "three classes of humanity": the "white man," the "bohunks," and the "Indians." The Indians could simply be ignored. The belief, said Lower, is that "French Canadians are white men, as are Scandinavians and Germans, providing they do not come from too far east. Finns are marginal, all Slavs definitely 'bohunks.'" Lower was concerned about the implications of these beliefs. "There is thus an initial disharmony in the average northern community," he wrote, "which is one of its severest handicaps and which will delay, for many years, the building of communities in any real sense."[1] Lower was undoubtedly correct in his belief that culturally rooted attitudes to ethnicity were fundamentally divisive to Northern Ontario. But economic structures and political systems also produced divisions in the region, as did historical events that were unfolding beyond its boundaries. Indeed, it would seem that in the early years of the twentieth century, social divisions were more significant than the forces bringing people together. This chapter is an examination of the centrifugal forces that initially served to create disharmony in the region. However, as will be demonstrated, this very experience of disharmony would eventually draw people together.

Ethnicity (as discussed in chapter 5) became a central defining feature of the region's society from the moment newcomers began to arrive early in the twentieth century. Canadian settlers brought with them a mental map of human society based on the assumption that "white" and northern peoples were the apex of civilized achievement. As one moved outward from the centre, where Great Britain and northern France held sway, lazy southerners like the Mediterranean people and ignorant peasants like the Eastern Europeans were situated where "whiteness" was giving way to "blackness." Thus, Italians and Slavs were "black," with their alleged

swarthy complexions, shifty morality, dangerous sexuality, and violent pro-
clivities. Scholar Noel Ignatiev has demonstrated that in the United States
the Irish were also characterized as "black" at one time.[2] But here in
northeastern Ontario the Irish were firmly and clearly categorized as
"white," a legacy, perhaps, of their place in the British Isles and Ottawa
Valley, the often mythologized "homeland" of "white" settlers in the North.
Africans were "black," of course, but there were so few of them in northeastern Ontario that they were essentially irrelevant to most people. More
important on the cultural map were the "Chinamen" who were placed on
the peripheries even beyond the "blacks." In the minds of some Canadians, they seemed to be scarcely human – incapable of learning proper
English, carriers of disease, and attached not to family and home but to
opium pipes and gambling dens. The place of the "Indian" on the cultural
map of the "whites" was less clear – both admired for what they had been
in the past, and pitied or despised for what they were believed to have
become in the present.

Canadian settlers were also ambivalent about the French-English relationship within their own ranks. Those from the Ottawa Valley, where the
two peoples had long struggled to reach an accommodation, seemed open
to some sort of public rapprochement in the North. Those from other
places were more hostile. Settlers from southern or central Ontario
seemed to see French-speaking Canadians as a vaguely threatening
"other," in large part because of their alleged willingness to follow the dictates of Roman Catholic priests. Anti-Catholicism was still a potent force in
Anglo-Canadian culture in the early twentieth century, and it played out in
northeastern Ontario. French-speaking Canadians from the Eastern Townships were highly sensitized to the politics of English-French relations and
saw the English as a threat to their religion and culture. Many participated
in the colonization movement because they wanted the economic opportunity, but some undoubtedly shared the belief of the colonizing priests
that they could make a more meaningful and satisfying life by getting out
from under the thumbs of the English "bosses" at home. Thus, it would be
a mistake to characterize all Canadians as sharing the same mental map.
Depending on their place of origin, they saw ethnic relations within
Canada very differently.

The various non-Canadian groups represented in the region also had
mental maps of humanity. The Finns considered themselves culturally
superior to the Canadians but seemed to agree that Southern and Eastern
Europeans were even lower on the hierarchy of human achievement. The
physical landscape certainly looked like home to the Finns, but the cultural landscape was utterly foreign. Finnish women found the role of
women in Canadian society galling, especially before women were granted
the vote in Canada. Finns perceived Canadians as politically naïve, sub-

missive, and undereducated. And Finns were utterly perplexed by the Canadian willingness to accept the ugliness and crudity of life in New Ontario, where food was scooped from tins instead of coming fresh from the garden, and where houses were basic utilitarian shelters, with no adornments of flower gardens or window boxes. So rather than adapting to the new society in which they found themselves, they set about trying to change it. First, they established almost self-contained neighbourhoods in which they tried to reproduce the rhythms of Finnish life. Then they became proselytizers – teaching Italians and Ukrainians to read and write, so that they would become more active defenders of workers' rights, and by inviting Canadian young people to participate in the athletic clubs and business co-ops the Finns had been building.

The Italians seem to have been less self-consciously Italian, at least in the early years. They came as labourers intent on helping families back home or establishing their own households, and they identified more closely with immediate family or extended village networks than with a collective national ethnicity. But it would appear that a sense of ethnic identity was emerging by the 1930s, fostered in part by the Italian nationalist movement under Mussolini and in part by the fact that Italians were treated as a distinct group in northeastern Ontario and thus began to respond as one. As scholar Vincent Lombardi has argued in the case of Italian workers in the United States, they "assumed an 'Italian' identity only after their arrival was met with disdain, discrimination and isolation. They responded defensively in turn with a new form of *campanilismo*, an Italian-American provincialism."[3] Fascism definitely cultivated a sense of pan-Italian pride and identity that eventually encouraged the Italians in the region to see themselves as a distinct (and perhaps superior) group, where others had been insisting on seeing them as a distinct (but inferior) group all along.

While Canadians also thought of Ukrainians, Austrians, and "Jugoslavs" as single entities, few members of these groups would have agreed. Rather, they identified with specific home regions and brought with them attitudes toward the other regions near home that were far too subtle to catch the eye of Canadians. The latter had no difficulty in thinking of the Cornish or Highland Scots as distinct and identifiable peoples, but they did not bother to distinguish the Galicians or the Serbs or the Syrians, much less note the differences between Galicians who had come directly from Europe and those whose families had been living for almost a generation in western Canada. Unlike the Italians, though, these Europeans did not find it easy to coalesce into a pan-Ukrainian or pan-Baltic ethnic identity. As will be discussed, differences rooted in history, politics, and religion served to maintain group distinctiveness in spite of the pressures of hostility and discrimination directed towards them in Canada.

Attitudes about ethnicity thus played a central role in dividing one group from another, but there was also a very practical reason for group distinctiveness: language. Many immigrant labourers knew little or no English or French; the chain migration patterns made it unnecessary for them to know much of either language to find their way into the region, and the nature of the workforce permitted them to manage with a very limited vocabulary. The Ontario Bureau of Mines noted in 1911 that within the immigrant labour pool in mining, "many" were "imperfectly acquainted with the English language," so it was not surprising that they did "not mix readily with the English-speaking population."[4] As women and children joined the single male population, it became even easier to use only one's mother tongue for daily living. When a school was opened in 1937 to serve the Italian population of Timmins, just two English class-rooms were provided; the other eight were, of necessity, bilingual in Italian and English.[5] The Roman Catholics of Timmins built two churches on the same property at the centre of town, one to serve the French-speaking pop-ulation (St Antoine) and the other to serve the English (Church of the Nativity). At Iroquois Falls before the First World War, labour organizer Bob Miner recalled, "Many of us couldn't speak to each other because we spoke different languages."[6] Clearly, language barriers formed very real divisions within the community while cultural attitudes, demographics, and the structure of the workplace made it possible for these barriers to be maintained for a surprising length of time.

Ethnic divisions in the region were manifested early on in two nasty inci-dents during the fire of 1911. In a special newspaper issue devoted to the tragedy, the Cobalt *Daily Nugget* reported that at South Porcupine "panic and chaos prevailed." As men rushed to get their families onto boats, the Canadian residents found "it was necessary for the police officer, G.A.D. Murray, with the assistance of Jack Gardner," to push back "the panic-stricken foreigners who stood by and rushed for each boat as it came in." Clearly, the Canadian men deemed the lives of their women and children to be more valuable than the lives of male immigrants, and they were out-raged when the "foreigners" failed to agree. Suspicion of "foreigners" was manifested in another incident during the fire – across the lake at Pottsville. Most of the town was levelled by the flames, but two Italian boarding houses were spared. "Into these Constable Piercy rounded up the Italians," reported the *Nugget*, "and placed them under the charge of Charles Galley, with the warning that a man stirring abroad would be shot."[7]

Canadian hostility to and fear of other nationalities were apparently so widely shared that the *Porcupine Advance* had no qualms about turning its police court column into a sort of running slapstick show on the antics of foreigners. Everything was game for mockery as humour was used to cover up anxieties that lay just below the surface of a population group that held only a slight majority. In 1917 a man charged with unlawful possession of liquor was identified as "a gentleman named Doriyngiorini (honest, that's the name on the official records!)."[8] In 1920 a fight in Schumacher was described as an "affray ... in which another Russian or Serbian or something was badly injured"; he wound up in hospital looking like "the victim of a Bolsheviki prayer meeting."[9] Canadian business owners also played on these fears and hostilities. In 1915 the Sanitary Steam Laundry ran an advertising campaign against the many Chinese laundries in Timmins. "It costs $500 to land a Chinaman in Canada," ran one item, referring to the dominion head tax on Chinese immigrants. "Every shirt, collar, sheet, etc., sent to a Chinese laundry is so much toward that $500. Every $500 means another Chinaman. Why not patronize the Sanitary Steam Laundry?"[10]

While much of the ethnic hostility was expressed in general terms only, on the assumption that "everyone" understood the subtext, the Canadian-born majority sometimes spelled out more clearly what it considered to be the problems with "foreigners." These allegations could reflect actual cultural differences. One big concern of town leaders was the behaviour of children. They saw truancy from school and "running wild" on the streets as the raw ingredients of juvenile crime and ultimately of social disorder. The *Porcupine Advance* campaigned for a children's curfew in 1916, alleging that the "majority" of cases of children roaming the streets were "amongst the foreign element, who evidently have but little control over their off-springs."[11] Immigrant parents were not indifferent to their children; they just had different philosophies of child rearing. Canadian-born residents also alleged that "foreigners" were not civic-minded or willing to put time and effort into undertakings that would benefit others. During the Spanish influenza epidemic of 1918–19, the editor of the *Porcupine Advance* complained, "While the majority of patients are aliens ... none of the foreigners seem willing to assist in any way to combat the disease. At first it was difficult to secure the services of any of them, even for interpreting."[12] Furthermore, the immigrants were criticized for not fully appreciating the civic rights and privileges available to them in Canada. When a Timmins bakery run by Bulgarians was accused of selling underweight loaves of bread, the *Advance* observed, "Someone asks what would happen to a British baker in Bulgaria who made extra money by selling short-weight bread. The answer is that ... he would be spending most of his time, perhaps, thanking the Lord that he was alive at all."[13]

When immigrants did take advantage of civic rights, they could be equally condemned – for instance, for their willingness to take their disagreements to court, which Canadian-born residents tended to consider an unseemly public airing of private laundry. Furthermore, the Canadians seemed particularly surprised at the willingness of immigrant women to assert themselves (often aggressively) in public, either through street confrontations or by resorting to the courts. Clearly, there were different attitudes to women's role in the public sphere and to cultural prescriptions for acceptable feminine behaviour. While class values undoubtedly played a part in these attitudes, the fact that ethnic slurs and stereotypes were often the terms used to define the "problem" indicates that the Canadian-born majority saw cultural differences at least partially at work.

Of course, there were also divisions within ethnic groups, for the definition of "group" clearly varied, depending on whether you were inside or outside it. Especially during the early years of town life, people identified more closely with a specific region rather than the nations they had come from. A young bush camp worker reported to the Italian commissioner of emigration in 1912 that while he didn't mind the work, "he kept repeating that, while there were many other Calabrese about, he was the only one from Mammole and had no one for company but God."[14] Although outsiders may have referred to Italians as a distinct cultural entity, for this young man the idea was remote. Perhaps even more deeply rooted were differences within national groups over politics and religion. These will be discussed more extensively elsewhere in this chapter.

While language may have been the most significant and most obvious barrier between groups, the fact that ethnic enclaves had different sex ratios was also important, because the number of women in a group had an enormous impact on how people lived and socialized. Ukrainian and Yugoslavian male sojourners obviously lived very differently from Finnish or Canadian families, even if those families were also sojourners of a sort. The old fur trade society, with its long-established network of overlapping family and business circles, had no reason or need to take in any of the newcomers (at least, initially). And the newcomers, having come to the region in search of economic opportunity, not life partners, looked homeward (at least until the mid-twentieth century) when it was time to marry. Thus, the economic distinctions were reinforced by demographic differences, helping to keep people apart from one another.

Whether it was real or imagined, ethnic identity forged the most important distinctions in regional society that initially helped to prevent the development of a sense of community. When social values conflicted, ethnicity was blamed. Economic conflict was also expressed in terms of ethnic differences. At the end of the First World War, a labour surplus in the mining sector intensified competition for available work, and complaints began to surface that "too many foreigners are being given employment about the mine while 'white men' go begging."[15] In 1922, when a man was killed underground in a rockfall at the Dome Mine, two fellow miners refused to help remove the body. The two happened to be

Polish, and the Canadian-born miners complained about the incident in ethnic terms. "They said that it is such men as these Poles who are being given preference in the matter of employment over Canadians," reported a company spy, who identified himself as AF.[16] During the Depression, when the pulp and paper sector was particularly hard hit, similar complaints surfaced there. "Foreign agitators" were constantly blamed for the bushworkers' strikes of the early 1930s, prompting Nick Thachuk of the Ukrainian Labor Farmer Temple Association to point out to the *Timmins Press*, "It must be remembered that over 950 men took part in the pulp-wood strike ... of whom 60 per cent were French Canadian workers, and the rest were made up of Anglo-Saxons and other nationalities."[17] Even casual work was so scarce during the Depression that it became a focal point for ethnic hostilities. A settler under the Relief Land Settlement program complained to the Ontario government in 1939 that men in his township had "pleaded for a job" in road work, "but with one or two exceptions were refused for no good reason except they spoke English." Allegedly, "foreign" crew bosses would hire only their fellow countrymen.[18] The same ethnic situation was present in the agricultural sector. A Connaught-area man cleared his homestead then left to earn some cash, only to find the homestead taken from him for non-residency. He complained to the Ontario government saying, "It was given to a Finlander which leaves me under the impression that it was done for political revenge."[19] In every sector during times of scarcity, economic conflicts were expressed in terms of ethnic conflicts.

Religious differences were another source of division in the region, in two ways. First, people tended to conduct important parts of their social lives within a religious congregation. This reinforced networks within the circle but at the same time divided the community into an array of such circles. Second, interdenominational rivalries and conflict between churchgoers and those who rejected organized religion for ideological reasons both generated and sustained important rifts. As will be discussed in chapter 11, the churches could also serve as a unifying factor in regional society, but their role in dividing the towns will be considered here first.

A number of scholarly studies of resource frontier communities have concluded that religion did not play a significant role in people's lives in the unique circumstances of these places. In his analysis of American western mining camps of the late nineteenth century, Duane A. Smith concluded that the "environment was not conducive to the church's activities," and people built instead a materialistic and individualistic society, free from the influences and behavioural constraints of home.[20] In Australia, according to Russel Ward, a "cynical up-country attitude" prevailed among gold seekers, who often shared the "opinion that most clergymen were canting hypocrites."[21] These studies built on the ideas of Frederick

Jackson Turner and his depiction of the American frontier as a place of individualism, where old forms of social control were abandoned. For Turner, religion was evident on the American frontier primarily as a force used by "the East" in an attempt to control and mould the frontier in its own image."[22] Historians Karen Dubinsky and Nancy Forestell have both proposed a similar pattern for northeastern Ontario, pointing out that (at least, in the early years of the twentieth century) some moralists perceived irregular church attendance as a problem.[23] There appears to be some good evidence for this perception. The Cobalt *Nugget* participated in a "Go to Church" campaign in 1914, and in 1917 the *Porcupine Advance* joked about the large crowd spending an evening at the New Empire Theatre by observing, "If the people of Timmins contract this habit of turning out in crowds for meetings every Sunday evening, the first thing they know they will be getting the habit of going to church or something like that."[24]

In fact, church attendance may have been a reflection of underlying divisions in society. Historian Lynne Marks observed that in the small towns of late-nineteenth-century southern Ontario, Protestant middle-class families were more likely to attend church than working-class families were, and women were more likely to attend than men.[25] While I have been unable to obtain congregation lists that would permit similar analysis for Porcupine-Iroquois Falls, it is certainly clear that those who took a leadership role within the Protestant churches were middle class, and Marks may very well be correct in her suggestion that "non-attendance did not necessarily reflect a lack of belief; it might simply point to a rejection of or indifference to the tenets of respectability that were embodied in the churches."[26]

Nevertheless, by the 1920s, religion (or at least church life) had become an important part of the community for a significant number of people. Certainly, the transient sojourner-labourer had little interest in church congregations, but families that intended to stay for the longer term in the retail, mining, paper, or agricultural sectors worked to establish a church life that gave a sense of stability and sociability, as well, undoubtedly, as a source of personal spiritual support in a difficult life. A resident of the Hunta area (north of Iroquois Falls in the vicinity of Cochrane) recalled, "The people were hungry for religion ... The more difficult the lives of the settlers, the rougher the speech, yet the more they craved what was good."[27] Cut adrift from the moorings of familiar places and friends, it is hardly surprising that people sought the spiritual comforts and familiarity of religious observances, and the church provided an obvious base from which to construct a social support network as well as a base for cultural activities. In 1924 Timmins mayor Dr J.A. McInnis noted, "Timmins now a city has reached its maturity in a very precocious manner. The materialistic nature of its industries might have somewhat retarded the cultural and aesthetic aspect of its young life had it not been for the foundation that the church has given to literature, art, music and to those finer things that make life worth while."[28] Furthermore, although many people may have chosen not to join a congregation, the churches, however small, were permanent institutions in the ever-shifting tides of a transient population, and by their permanence they came to have an influence on the life of the region out of proportion to the relative smallness of their membership.

This influence was not always an encouragement to harmony. The emergence of church congregations in the region created additional divisions within the community. As Alex Himelfarb once observed of Canadian single-industry towns more generally, "an accentuated sectarianism" and "deep religious cleavage" prevailed,[29] at least in the 1920s and 1930s. The classic Old Ontario hostilities between Roman Catholics and Protestants took root; different traditions within Roman Catholicism separated others; and theological and social ideas kept the Protestant denominations apart. The Jews, of course, worshipped entirely independently, and the number of Muslims, Hindus, and Buddhists were simply too small to sustain any regular congregational life at all. The division between Roman Catholics and Protestants was perhaps the most visible and important. Brought into the region from the social realities of southern Canada and Europe, it was sustained both through the actions of church officials and through the actions of non-church organizations such as the Loyal Orange Lodge, which had branches throughout the region.

It is hardly surprising that many of the first French-speaking Roman Catholic priests in the area were not inclined toward ecumenicalism, for they saw themselves as missionary colonizers, guiding their Quebec flocks away from the dangers of industrial, urban, English-speaking wolves. These priests saw to it that separate school classes were organized immediately for Roman Catholic children. And Father Charles-Eugène Thériault took an active role in the Timmins strike of 1912, defending the interests of his parishioners against the English-speaking mine owners.[30] A half-century later, he was presented with an award of merit from L'association canadienne-française d'education d'Ontario for "the role that he played throughout his life in the survival of the French-Canadian race in Northern Ontario."[31]

If the Roman Catholic priests saw themselves as defenders of the faith and culture, some Protestant clergy saw themselves as missionaries, and Roman Catholics as potential converts. Many of the early Protestant clergy in the area were student ministers or had been sponsored by home-mission societies to bring the Gospel to frontier settlers who were allegedly in danger of forgetting it. So it is not surprising that these clergymen brought with them a proselytizing zeal that could extend to non-Protestants as well. A United Church minister at South Porcupine claimed some success in this aspect of his missionary work, saying, "Roman and Greek Catholics have become estranged from earlier beliefs. Exhilarating has been their response to genuine religious approaches." He attributed this response to their awakening to the "loathsome incongruities" of their "Mother Church."[32]

Anti-Catholicism was most often expressed privately and therefore seldom appears in the documentary record. It was clearly more pronounced in the rural areas, where the settlement of French-speaking Roman Catholics was interpreted in some circles as a threat to the future of both region and province. As one correspondent put it to Premier Howard Ferguson circa 1916, "I spose they are likely to try to fill up New Ontario so as to get a controll of it … If the French could get a majority in New Ont they could controll Ont … The Catholic French clergy appear to be back of it."[33] Such attitudes were so widespread that some local politicians played on them. In 1937 the editor of the *Porcupine Advance* complained, "Some of this ballyhoo has been particularly vicious, attempting to set race against race and creed against creed."[34] Indeed, Frank Keefer, a Port Arthur Conservative, who served from 1923 to 1926 as Ontario's first (and only) legislative secretary for Northern Ontario, campaigned to promote Protestant settlement in the region "to offset the steady inflow we are having of the French-Canadian, resulting from the Roman Catholic immigration policy."[35] In 1940, when nearly twenty Jehovah's Witnesses were arrested in Timmins for distributing pamphlets deemed to be seditious attacks on the war effort, the police reported that a pamphlet entitled "The End of Naziism" was actually an attack on the Roman Catholic Church.[36]

The Loyal Orange Lodge provided the most important organizational base for the sustenance of this kind of anti–Roman Catholic thinking. Although the LOL functioned in the region primarily as a social club, its roots in Ireland were not entirely forgotten. The Iroquois Falls Lodge was particularly active, holding an annual parade and picnic on "the Glorious Twelfth" to commemorate the Battle of the Boyne. At one such gathering in 1937, nearly five hundred participants heard the United Church minister speak "of loyalty to one's King and country" and "of the necessity for a single flag and one language."[37] When in the fall of 1935 rumours began to circulate that the provincial government was considering the sale of the Monteith Academy buildings to the Roman Catholic Church, the Timmins and Shillington Lodges sent formal letters of protest to Queen's Park.[38]

While suspicions on both sides served to maintain deep divisions between Protestants and Roman Catholics, different traditions within the Roman Catholic Church itself helped to create distinct subgroups in regional society. While the smaller towns like South Porcupine and Iroquois Falls had the population to support only one Roman Catholic church, Timmins (by 1960) had one Eastern Orthodox and eight Roman Catholic parishes. Of the Roman Catholic parishes, four were primarily French-speaking, one was English, one was Italian, and one was Ukrainian. Of the French-speaking parishes, one was served by the Oblates of Mary Immaculate, one by the Redemptorists, and one by the Capuchins; the fourth was the bishop's seat. So language, theology, and tradition served to divide the largest Christian group in the region.

The first priests were French-speaking missionaries sent to meet the First Nations, but the early Roman Catholic mission was never very large, and most of the area's Christians during the fur trade era were Anglicans. The next generation of priests arrived as an extension of their work in the Ottawa Valley. Alexandre Pelletier of the Porcupine Camp (and later at Iroquois Falls), Alexandre Cartier at Timmins, and others such as Roméo Gascon and Jean-Baptiste Bourassa came essentially as visiting missionaries to the settlers, but they also began to serve the construction workers whom they found congregating in the region. With the rapid population growth in the resource boom, Roman Catholicism surpassed Anglicanism as the largest denomination in the region.

It was not only in the agricultural areas that the Roman Catholics became rooted. Noah Timmins saw to it that the Roman Catholic Church was established on a strong foundation in his new town, and his continuing patronage ensured that the church maintained a sort of semi-official status in the western end of the district. He was also fortunate in the arrival of Charles-Eugène Thériault, who established the parish of St Antoine de Padoue in Timmins, which eventually became the bishop's seat. Thériault, born in 1886 at St Eloi, Quebec, was educated at the seminary in Rimouski, and after his ordination was sent to Cobalt in 1910. In 1912 he became the first resident priest at Timmins, and he remained there for over forty years. When he died in 1956 in a Montreal hospital, he was remembered as *l'évêque des mineurs* (the miners' bishop), and memorialized in a play by Sylvie Trudel, a Timmins high school student, as "Le Roi du Nord."[39]

Initially the parish of St Antoine de Padoue served in both English and French, and when Thériault organized the first separate school in Timmins in 1913, classes were offered in both languages. But the timing was problematic. Just then, the province was convulsed in a debate about the use of French in schools, and the Roman Catholic Church in southeastern and southwestern Ontario was bitterly divided between French-speaking and English-speaking (largely Irish) members, lay and clergy alike. The bitterness spilled over into Northern Ontario, and Thériault entered into the fray to protect French-language rights. The situation at St Antoine was undoubtedly tense, and the clergy worked hard to keep everyone satisfied. When Bishop Elie-Ancet Latulipe visited Timmins in

May 1918, the mayor read an appreciation in English, a parish leader read the same address in French, and the bishop replied in both languages.[40] And when a fundraising drive was launched in 1922 to build a new church for the parish, Thériault organized "special canvassers for each nationality in the church, – English, French, Italian, Polish, etc."[41]

These conciliatory gestures were not enough. In the summer of 1926 the bishop, Louis Rhéaume, founded a new parish in Timmins for the English-speaking (and primarily Irish) Roman Catholics. John Robert O'Gorman was appointed its first curate. He was an inspired choice for the position, given his background in both Irish and French Canadian Catholic traditions. O'Gorman had been born at Renfrew, in the Ottawa Valley, in 1881 and obtained a BA at the University of Ottawa under the tutelage of the Oblates of Mary Immaculate. After ordination in 1904, he served at Renfrew and then as a missionary priest in Northern Ontario. He was eventually appointed rector at the cathedral in Haileybury and then founded St Patrick's at Cobalt before being appointed to the new parish at Timmins, which was named Nativity.[42] Within a year, the parish church was ready. It stood behind St Antoine – only steps away – its pseudo-Romanesque architecture a clear contrast to the pseudo-Gothic of its neighbour. O'Gorman oversaw the creation of an extensive parish infrastructure, with the Knights of Columbus and various young people's groups performing much the same functions as those already in existence at St Antoine, but clearly separating the social lives of their participants. Nativity Parish remained for many years the only unilingual English parish in the Porcupine area. When the diocese decided on the next required expansion, ten years later, it was to establish Notre Dame de Lourdes as a French-language parish under Abbé Alphonse Chapleau.

For the growing Italian community in Timmins, churchgoing was problematic. There was a perception outside the region that Italian workers were culturally indifferent to religion. A senior Redemptorist had told the archbishop in Toronto, "We know that the spiritual betterment of these southern Italians is an almost impossible task."[43] And in the United States, one writer observed, "In a coal community of Indiana, where four thousand Italians lived, neither church nor priest was to be found. Everywhere Italians have fallen away from that religion whose earthly capital is still the Italian capital. A Milwaukee Catholic organ, in 1913, estimated (loosely enough!) that a million Italians had already been lost."[44]

Certainly, there seems to have been little interest among the Italians of Timmins for raising the money needed to build a church and attract a priest, but in this they were hardly unusual, for the initiative for all other Roman Catholic parishes in the region had come from outside. And not all Italians had abandoned the church. It may well have been partly a matter of language. Some, like Leo Mascioli's family, spoke English sufficiently well to participate in services at St Antoine or Nativity. Others spoke little or no English or French in the 1920s and 1930s. The problem was noted by outsiders who were concerned on their behalf, and in 1934 a Toronto Italian women's group produced a report that claimed there were 120 Italian families in Timmins but not a single priest to whom they could confess in their own language.[45]

Two years later, Bishop Louis Rhéaume recruited an American priest named Louis Fontana to found an Italian-speaking parish in Timmins. Fontana, who hailed from Woltham, Massachussetts, was a Redemptorist, a missionary order that had been founded in Italy. He stayed initially with O'Gorman, assisting in Nativity Parish while he laid plans for the Italian church. At the end of May 1938, Il Sacro Cuore de Gesù (Sacred Heart of Jesus) on Maple Street South, conveniently located for the Italian district, was officially opened by Bishop Rhéaume.[46]

Ukrainian-speaking Roman Catholics initially worshipped at St Antoine, then moved to the Church of the Nativity after its opening. In 1940 they began to hold special Ukrainian services in the Church of the Nativity once a month, with Abbé N. Charney of Kirkland Lake officiating. They constituted themselves as St George's Parish, and in 1948 their first permanent curate, Redemptorist Father Shawel, arrived and construction of their own parish church began.[47]

Interestingly, the Ukrainian Greek Orthodox Church (established in Canada in 1918) did not become a thread in the religious fabric of the region. Instead, it was a Romanian missionary who first brought the Orthodox Church to the area. In 1933 Father G. Moraru, sent by the mother church in Romania, announced the creation of St Mary's "Roumanian" Orthodox Parish, which was to conduct services in Romanian, Greek, and what was described as "Old Slav."[48] The parishioners built a church at the corner of Maple Street North and Eighth Avenue, which was officially opened amid considerable fanfare in September 1935 by Archbishop Policarp of the Romanian Orthodox Church in Canada. The new parish priest, John Pascari, hoped to attract a larger percentage of the Romanian population of the region, since only about sixty families out of several hundred potential members had joined so far.[49]

Outside Timmins, smaller populations of Roman Catholics necessitated more inclusive parishes. Interestingly, all were led by primarily French-speaking clergy. At Iroquois Falls, Father Alexandre Pelletier arrived in 1914 as a missionary priest, setting up a modest headquarters in a tar-papered shack near the Abitibi mill construction site, from which he served farmers and others at Porquis, Monteith, Kelso, and Matheson. After the fire of 1916, Pelletier arranged for a frame building to be hauled by rail from South Porcupine, and a more permanent (but still very modest) church presence was initiated. A church, school, and residential complex was built just west of the Iroquois Falls townsite, and the parish was consecrated as Ste Anne's. Residents of Ansonville attended Ste Anne's, but the hostilities between them and the residents of Iroquois Falls prompted Ansonville Roman Catholics to petition Bishop Rhéaume in 1923 to create a separate parish for Ansonville.[50] This did not happen until 1949, when the bilingual parish of Saints Martyrs Canadien was formed across the tracks under Abbé Philippe Breen.[51]

Of course, the Roman Catholic Church did not have a monopoly on internal divisions. A proliferation of Protestant denominations throughout the region provided yet another source of social boundaries. The Anglicans had long been a presence through the Diocese of Moosonee's missions to First Nations and HBC personnel, funded in part by the Church Missionary Society of England. Early-twentieth-century development activity brought a flurry of interest from other Protestant denominations, which funded theology students and lay missionaries to bring spiritual support during the summer months and to ensure that the rootless hordes were kept under control, away from the evils of drink and Sabbath prospecting work. In the spring and summer of 1910 at the Porcupine Camp, for example, the Presbyterians had sent Queen's University student A.P. Menzies to hold services in a "reading tent" at Pottsville, and the Methodists had sent the student J.F.G. Morris to initiate its "Porcupine mission" at Golden City.[52] The Presbyterian student E.L. Longmore and the Methodist S. Milton Beach were sent to Matheson, where they cooperated on the construction of its first church buildings in 1909. A log cabin purchased from a local First Nations family and reassembled on the townsite served as the parsonage, and the frame of a small church hovered precariously nearby. The church was officially owned by the Presbyterians, but because of the Methodist support, it was dubbed a Union Church.[53] At Iroquois Falls in the early years, Abitibi provided the use of the town hall for church services; the various denominations chose to meet there separately, despite their very small numbers. At Monteith, Robert Kelso opened his home for religious services, and here, too, the Methodists and Presbyterians preferred to meet on alternate weeks.[54] The Anglicans branched out from their Aboriginal mission work to serve these new settlements, first from their mission base at Moose Factory, and then with theology students from Wycliffe College in Toronto. A number of these students were sponsored by an organization called the Church Camp Mission, which was dedicated to providing services to bush and construction camps throughout Northern Ontario.

As in western Canada, church authorities soon realized that the population was too small to support competing denominations. Mission funds could not sustain the tiny congregations (there were only eighteen members at Matheson, for example, in 1913).[55] Of necessity, "Union" and

The Methodist Church under construction at Matheson. Before the 1916 fire, there were high hopes that a large congregation would eventually fill it as southern Ontarians bought into the provincial government's propaganda. (UCA, 90.162, P/1031)

"United" churches brought Methodists and Presbyterians together at Iroquois Falls, Matheson, Monteith, Porquis, and South Porcupine well before the official formation of the United Church of Canada in 1925. In Timmins, Byrnes Presbyterian Church operated independently until the union created Timmins United Church (later First United Church); a separate Presbyterian congregation was organized in 1940 by those who preferred to remain apart from the Canadian experiment. At Iroquois Falls, it was the Methodists who organized and built the church that became home to the United Church in 1917; at Schumacher, it was also the Methodists who laid the foundations of the congregation that became Trinity United, although it had been turned over to the Presbyterians in 1917 in an arrangement through which the Presbyterians agreed to conduct the services in Schumacher while the Methodists took South Porcupine and the Dome Property.[56]

The United Church in the region was not entirely united, however. In 1903 the Presbyterian Church in Canada's Home Mission Board assigned the Reverend Arvi I. Heinonen to oversee mission outreach to Finns in northeastern Ontario (from Sault Ste Marie to Cochrane). Since non-communist Finns were most likely to be Lutheran, the Presbyterians were clearly hoping to recruit new members, partly for religious reasons and partly as a program of assimilating or "Canadianizing" immigrants. Heinonen travelled throughout his assigned district, holding religious services in Finnish at boarding houses and private homes. He was not always well received because, in keeping with their political views, many Finns in the area were strongly opposed to Christianity. When Heinonen paid his first visit to South Porcupine on 12 December 1913, the owners of the Finnish boarding house where he proposed to hold a service refused him access.[57] In 1926 the Reverend August Lappala was appointed the first permanent minister to the local Scandinavians. He established his headquarters at Timmins and held services in the basement of First United Church until a separate building was refurbished from an old house at the corner of Elm Street North and Sixth Avenue in Timmins.[58] The original congregation also included Swedes and a few Norwegians, but as the Swedish population shrank in the late 1920s and early 1930s, the "daughter" church of Timmins United became primarily Finnish in character and was locally referred to as the Finnish United Church.

The Baptists also came to the region through the auspices of a missionary society. The Reverend Ian F. Cruikshanks (Scottish-born but raised in Toronto) arrived in October 1917 and held services in the Timmins Oddfellows' Hall, then the Old Empire Theatre. Unfortunately for the congregation, Cruikshanks died in the 1918 influenza epidemic, so his plans for the construction of a Baptist church were set back considerably. Nevertheless, a church was finally opened in 1922 on Second Avenue near Maple Street South.

The Anglican Church of Canada built on its early missionary status in the area to establish a highly visible presence, which in some ways was larger and more impressive than membership numbers would indicate. In 1911 the Reverend W.M. Tivett commissioned the construction of one of the most imposing buildings of the day in Golden City. Made of peeled logs with a substantial square tower in front, it was dedicated to St Paul. Shortly after it was built, it was destroyed in the great fire, and the congregation was re-established at South Porcupine instead. Two years later, Anglican churches at Monteith (St Mary's) and Watabeag near Matheson (St Anne's) were erected, followed in 1914 by St Stephen's at Porquis Junction. At Iroquois Falls, construction began on St Mark's Anglican Church in 1917, but it was not consecrated until 1920. Donations solicited through the personal connections of many of the clergy permitted the Anglicans to build substantial churches for relatively small congregations at these places. St Stephen's in Porquis was so named because its chairs were donated by a church of that name in Toronto; St Anne's at Watabeag was named for Anne Clough, mother of its principal endower in England; and St Matthew's at Timmins was dedicated to honour "a generous friend" in England who had helped to pay for much of its original furnishings.[59]

It was undoubtedly the Timmins church that became the most important Anglican congregation in the district. There are different versions of its founding. St Matthew's people's warden, Vincent Woodbury, recalled that Hollinger mine manager P.A. Robbins had commissioned a building for any Protestant denomination the people chose, and the Anglicans won the prize (perhaps because Mrs Robbins was an Anglican, as were assistant general manager A.R. Globe and his wife). However, the Cobalt *Daily Nugget* reported at the time that the building under construction in 1913 had already been designated as Anglican.[60] In any case, the new building commanded an important site on the rise overlooking the new townsite on one side and the Hollinger Mine in the distance on the other, with the homes of senior managers and professionals on the street nearby. St Matthew's became the pro-cathedral church for the Diocese of Moosonee under its fifth bishop, Robert John Renison (1943–54).

Many other religious denominations and organizations established a presence in the region, some through periodic "missions" and pastoral visits, others with a more substantial and permanent presence. A Finnish Evangelical Lutheran congregation was formed at Timmins in 1935; it bought a lot at the corner of Cedar Street North and Eighth Avenue in 1938, but its church building, St Markus, was not begun until 1946.[61] A similar congregation was formed at South Porcupine in 1935, holding services in the Anglican church there until its own building was ready in 1939.[62] Over the years, both these churches had difficulty securing pastors and were often served only by visiting clergy sponsored by mission funds. The Salvation Army held services in Timmins as early as 1915, although its permanent presence dates from 1918 under the "lady officers" Captain Honeychurch and Lieutenant Jones. Eventually, the Salvation Army occupied modest quarters next to the Empire Hotel on Fourth Avenue (now Algonquin Boulevard). In 1936 Major and Mrs William H. Hillier oversaw the construction of a handsome new Citadel on Birch Street, "thanks to the generosity of Leo Mascioli," according to the *Porcupine Advance*. One Timmins resident recalled a rather more cynical version of the story: "There was the Salvation Army sitting beside the Empire Hotel. And to get a [liquor] license, the Mascioli's had to buy the Salvation Army out, and they built the building the Salvation Army is using now, on Birch Street."[63] From 1934–35 to the 1970s, Monteith had a Christian Brethren church called Gospel Hall; the Pentecostals in South Porcupine bought a pool hall for use as a church in 1943; and the Jehovah's Witnesses were active in Timmins and Matheson by 1940. Travelling evangelists, such as G.B. Raymond of Brooklyn, New York, were always popular attractions, drawing crowds with their preaching in local halls and theatres.[64] There was a rabbi, H. Menden, at South Porcupine as early as 1912, and the Jewish population built a synagogue at Timmins that was opened in 1919 to serve the entire Porcupine Camp; a much larger and more elaborate building replaced it in 1928.[65]

Clearly, this considerable variety of religious options produced a series of subgroups in the region which enabled people to worship and socialize independently of other groups and which also sometimes fostered hostility between groups. Divisions within and between religious denominations were not only related to religion. During the 1920s and early 1930s, a significant number of communists spoke out stridently against all religion, particularly within the Finnish and Ukrainian population. They steadfastly refused to marry, considering that sacrament to be a tool of oppression. They organised alternatives, such as sports associations, to eliminate the need for the social functions of the church, and they campaigned against the misguided beliefs of their Christian compatriots. "Professing Christianity among the non-English speaking residents was not easy in our day," one Finn sadly recorded in 1937. "Yet brave Christian men and women and children were found among those old-timers, who dared to come forward."[66] Although the main emphasis of the Communist Party in the region was political and economic, there is no doubt that an element of religious warfare had its impact. Communist activity may not have been particularly challenged by the relatively weak Lutheran Church, but the Roman Catholic Church certainly reacted. The Knights of Columbus (both English and French) sponsored public speakers such as George H. Derry of Michigan, who came to Timmins in the spring of 1939 to lecture on the evils of communism; and Abbé Lionel Brunette led the way in organizing a French-Canadian co-op in Timmins to counter the growing influence of communism there.[67] In 1931, after the Reverend August Lappala was selected as the area's delegate to the Toronto meeting that founded the Loyal Finnish Organization, he set up a Timmins chapter that "ostracized the socialist element among the Finns who would not support a church-affiliated organization even though they were against the communists."[68] Shortly thereafter, the area Ukrainians formed a similar organization, affiliated with the Prosvita movement. The potent brew of politics and religion served to further divide the district.

Economic realities related to the nature of the workplace and the structures of the regional economy also helped divide the population. Although the region encompasses a relatively small geographic space, its economy was divided into distinct sectors that operated independently, had different (and sometimes competing) interests, and had relatively little transfer of skilled personnel from sector to sector. Furthermore, within each economic sector, the workplace was highly stratified with limited upward mobility. Since people came to define themselves socially through their place in the workforce, workplace segregation shaped social divisions more generally. Finally, the high level of transience in certain sectors mitigated against the development of a cohesive community.

It is just sixty kilometres along the old railway line from Iroquois Falls to Timmins, seventy from Timmins to Matheson, and another forty from Matheson back to Iroquois Falls, completing the triangle. The entire trip is not much farther than a drive around the perimeter of Metropolitan Toronto and less than the distance from Moose Jaw to Swift Current, Saskatchewan. Yet within this area, the mining, forestry, and agricultural sectors operated independently, producing towns with their own unique characteristics and sense of themselves. While it is true that some families adopted the strategy of combining farm ownership with wage labour in the mines or bush camps, most people came to the area intending to support themselves in only one economic sector. Even such trades as electrical work or construction, which would seem to be useful in both mining and papermaking, tended to attract workers to a particular industry, where they remained. Among a sample of over a thousand McIntyre Mine employees in the 1920s, more than two-thirds came to McIntyre with previous mining experience (and mostly hard-rock mining at that); only 2.3 percent had worked in pulp and paper, and 3.5 percent in farming. Those who crossed from one sector into another were most likely to be employed in the least-skilled occupations – for example, Ernest Andrews, a 32–year-old native of Bath, England, a labourer who had been laid off by Abitibi and hired at McIntyre as a "crusher helper"; and 21–year-old Paul Demartineux of Longueuil, Quebec, who quit his job in the paper mill at Iroquois Falls to work as a general labourer at McIntyre.[69] While such detailed data is not available from the other economic sectors, anecdotal evidence seems to confirm a similar pattern. Employees at the Abitibi mill tended to come from other pulp and paper mill towns. John Stillman Foley may have been a little older than most new employees at Abitibi, but his experience seems typical otherwise. He came to Iroquois Falls in 1923 as a machine-shop foreman. Born in Nova Scotia, he had worked for thirty years in Rumford, Maine, in the forestry sector before being attracted back to Canada by the opportunities in that same sector in Northern Ontario.[70] Homesteaders, even those who did not stay on the land, were also likely to have grown up on a farm either elsewhere in Canada or overseas – for example, the brothers Charles and John Dalton, who were born on a farm near Goderich, Ontario, and came to the area in 1911 with their horses and wagons seeking land, though they eventually moved into the transportation business.[71]

The creation of company towns helped to reinforce the distinctiveness among the economic sectors, while the corporate sponsorship of leisure activities seemed to discourage people from interacting across sector lines. With the notable exception of the Northern Ontario Hockey Association,

Table 12   Cross-sector movement, McIntyre Mine employees, 1920–1925

Previous Employment	%	Previous Employment	%
Mining total	69.4	Railway	1.9
Hard-rock mines	67.4	Municipal	1.8
Bushwork	5.0	Lumber	1.6
Industry	4.4	Students	1.5
Farming	3.5	Retail/banking	1.4
Construction	2.5	Soldiers	1.3
Pulp and paper	2.3	Self-employed	0.9
Hydro	2.2	Others	0.3

Source: Compiled from McIntyre Mines employee cards, c.1915–25, Laurentian University Archives, Steelworkers Collection, P020/1/D/1,4

most people participated in intramural leagues; only occasionally were golf or baseball tournaments organized to bring teams together. There was no need to travel afield when such a range of sporting opportunity was made available so close to home.

Union organization also worked against cross-sector interaction. When the unions arrived in the region with the establishment of the first mines and mills, there was no significant locally born movement; the large unions were all part of "international" (meaning Canadian/American) networks. The Western Federation of Miners operated entirely independently of the Pulp and Sulphite Workers or the Papermakers and apparently none of the leadership considered the problems of workers to be common across the region. The unions thought of themselves as representing workers whose skills and problems were unique to their workplace. The One Big Union attracted attention very briefly, but even it was apparently seen by miners as an alternative to Mine, Mill and by bushworkers as a protector of their specific interests, rather than as a broadly based alternative to trades unionism. Communist labour activists who visited the region attempted to speak to all audiences but never succeeded in getting enough converts to change the rigidly divided way of thinking about labour. Even within each economic sector, most workers seemed to see their problems as workplace-specific. Consequently, union organizers within Mine, Mill, for example, had very little success in their attempts to bring together workers from Hollinger, McIntyre, Dome, and other mine sites.

Finally, geography must also be acknowledged as a factor contributing to divisions among the economic sectors. Geography permitted the mining, farming, and papermaking sectors to arrange themselves with roughly equidistant town centres, since the gold deposits lay primarily at the west end of the district, the best water power and river systems were at the east end, and the most promising agricultural zone lay to the south. Although the distances were not great, the long and cold winters, with their heavy blanket of snow, discouraged travel for the better part of the year, particularly on the scattered homesteads. People were kept isolated in their towns, too, if not within their individual homes. For townspeople, in some ways, winter became a psychological barrier more than a real one, since train service in the region was frequent and generally reliable; the TNO even put on special trains to facilitate major community events. But for the newcomers, as for the First Nations before them, winter became a time to stay close to home and limit travel to only what was urgent or necessary.

Within each economic sector, the structure of the workforce also conspired to create social barriers. As was described in chapter 6, the mines and mills were organized as strict hierarchies, with the general manager at the top and, at the bottom, the crews of young men who cleared the plant floor or performed odd jobs. Women and families were assigned a place in the social pecking order on the basis of their husbands' places at work. And while a man might work his way up from a general labourer's job to shift boss, further occupational mobility was highly unlikely; so permanent economic (and hence social) divisions were entrenched. John Knox exemplifies one pattern. He came to Timmins in 1924 after a seventeen-year career in managing mines (most lately in Calumet, Michigan) to fill the position of assistant general manager at Hollinger. He retired in 1946 as general manager, having lived for the better part of his career physically and psychologically apart from his employees in the manager's house on mine property.[72] Meanwhile, Walter Avery was pursuing his own career at Hollinger. He arrived in Timmins the same year as Knox, having worked for four years at a tin mine in Cornwall, England. He worked underground at Hollinger for two years in various capacities as a loader, scaler, and chute blaster. In 1926 he transferred to surface work and by 1934 had been promoted to subforeman. After twelve years above ground, he joined the construction department as a mechanic. There he remained until 1955, when deteriorating health prompted him to retire.[73] Similar stories may be found at Abitibi. R.A. McInnis joined Abitibi's head office in 1914 as assistant to the president after fourteen years in the sales divisions of other pulp and paper companies. He was sent to Iroquois Falls as general manager in 1917 and left ten years later for another senior managerial position with Anglo-Canadian Pulp and Paper.[74] Meanwhile, railwayman William H. Potter, who also came to Abitibi in the early years, had become a foreman at its railway yard by 1919. As the plant grew, he was promoted to "general manager" of the rail department, but when he died in 1929 at the age of fifty-three, he was still employed in that capacity.[75]

Finally, the question of transience (as described in chapter 8) needs to be considered as a factor that contributed to a lack of social cohesion.

Highly mobile workers rarely became involved in formally organized activities, preferring to find camaraderie in casual socializing such as drinking, playing games of pool or cards, or being a spectator at sporting events. People who were not planning to stay long did not really care about investing much time or money in their physical surroundings, so the ramshackle bunkhouses and boardinghouses produced a visual landscape that startled those who were accustomed to lawns and paint and flower gardens. For the residents, the quality of the food was more important than the appearance of the building. Finally, transient workers did not bother to join the church congregations and were unlikely to participate in fraternal societies, both of which were at least potentially important parts of the foundation of a community structure. Transience was clearly a major force working against the formation of a sense of community.

If divisions generated by circumstances within the region were important, so too were divisions precipitated by major events that occurred outside the region. Political upheavals in Finland, Russia, Italy, and Ukraine resonated in Northern Ontario. Perhaps most important of all was the First World War, which introduced new levels of tension and anxiety, building on the foundations of hostility and suspicion already in place. While the Second World War also created problems, they were considerably less acute, for reasons that will be explored later. This was no isolated frontier but a place connected immediately and efficiently through human and technological ties to the rest of the world.

Although the majority of Finns who came to Canada did so for economic reasons, Finnish politics continued to influence their lives. In 1809 Finland had been absorbed into Russia when the Russians defeated the Swedes who then controlled it. As a grand duchy, Finland gradually gained considerable control over its internal affairs until the reign of Tsar Alexander III (crowned 1881), who began to assert his authority and limit Finland's autonomy in what became known as an era of "russification." Nicholas II, who succeeded him in 1894, intensified the policy, introducing laws that required Finnish legislation to be reviewed by Russia (1899) and conscripted Finnish men into the Russian imperial army (1901). Finns began to resist, forming the Finnish Labour Party (1899) and assassinating the governor general (1904). A sense of national identity began to coalesce, with a developing interest in the Finnish language and folk traditions. In 1905 the Finns staged a general strike, demanding political reforms, which the Tsar began to concede the following year with the introduction of an elected parliament and universal (male and female) suffrage. The Labour Party, called the Social Democratic Party since 1903, won a majority in all six elections held between 1907 and 1916, although the Russians attempted to maintain some control by repeatedly dissolving the Finnish parliament on a variety of excuses. Finally, in 1917, in the midst of political upheaval in Russia, Finland declared independence, and a bloody and vicious three months of civil war ensued as communists and non-communists battled for control. The Whites declared victory in May 1918; the Treaty of Tartu was signed in 1920 to settle the boundary and other questions, and a new constitution created a republic.[76]

Finnish emigration to Canada in general and to northeastern Ontario in particular thus took place in the midst of this maelstrom. The political polarization between socialists and conservatives was well underway by the time the first Finns came to work in the Porcupine Camp. As the Social Democratic Party turned to Marxism, Finns in northeastern Ontario debated the changes. News of the civil war and subsequent reprisals drove a deep wedge between the Reds and Whites in Northern Ontario, who fought their own battles for control of the unions and the Consumers' Co-operative, as described in the previous chapter. The Red element was reinforced by newcomers who arrived in the early 1920s, fleeing possible reprisals in Finland or simply unwilling to accept the White victory. When they arrived in northeastern Ontario, they found themselves among a relatively moderate Finnish community which had not experienced the horrors of civil war first-hand. The newly arrived Reds began a series of initiatives to awaken their compatriots to political realities and, failing that, to keep them out of positions of potential power and influence. Communist Finns established "investigative committees" to determine the politics of other Finns; they then attempted to keep the White Finns out of the boarding houses and bush camps through intimidation and, sometimes, violence. One such committee was active in South Porcupine by 1921. Few outsiders seem to have been aware of these committees because neither side spoke much English and those who felt threatened (as relative newcomers themselves) probably had little idea of where to turn for intervention from Canadian authorities.[77]

European politics created divisions among other national groups as well. As historian Frances Swyripa put it, "Leaving their homeland at a time when Ukrainian identity was still being formed, turn-of-the-century peasant immigrants were 'Ukrainianized' in Canada as much as in Ukraine."[78] Ukraine's history was much like Finland's – centuries of domination by one power or another. At the end of the nineteenth century, the western regions of Galicia and Bukovina were part of the Austro-Hungarian Empire, and the eastern regions were controlled by imperial Russia. When the Bolsheviks led Russia into revolution, easterners declared the independent Ukrainian People's Republic in 1918. In the west, Ukrainians took advantage of the defeat of Austria-Hungary in the First World War to declare their own Western Ukrainian People's Republic. The two governments united in 1919, but postwar European diplomacy soon divided the

Ukrainian provinces yet again, this time among Poland, the newly formed USSR, Romania, and Czechoslovakia. Ukrainian nationalism was suppressed but not eliminated, and continued to thrive among Ukrainians in Canada.

Nationalism generally meant anti-communism and Christianity, but even here there were divisions among Ukrainian Orthodox adherents (largely from Bukovina) and Greek Catholics and Roman Catholics (largely from the western province of Galicia).[79] There were also social and economic differences among the Ukrainians who had come to northeastern Ontario. Some were children of parents who had settled on farms in the Prairie West between 1890 and 1914. Others came directly from Ukraine, particularly during the post-1918 upheavals. There were also two distinct types: peasant farmers, who emigrated as entire families and who considered mine or railway work as a temporary expedient to support the establishment of a family farm; and industrial workers, who tended to be young single men looking for wage labour or men who had left families in Ukraine and sent back their earnings.[80] The result was a complex set of relationships among Ukrainians in the region. Socialists, communists, nationalists, "polonized" and "russified," farmers and labourers, Greek Catholics, and Ukrainian Orthodox all created distinct units.

The Balkan powder keg also contributed to regional divisions. While most Canadians simply lumped together immigrants from the Balkans as "Jugoslavs," the immigrants themselves maintained distinctions and exclusivities from home. As one resident later recalled, a Serbian shift boss would choose Serbs for his team and reject Croatians.[81] The Croatians maintained their own network through the Croatian Hall in Schumacher, which functioned as a social, political, and self-help centre, but also, of course, maintained a distinct identity.

As mentioned above, perhaps the most important external event that served to divide the region's society was the First World War. Just as the mines were entering production and the Abitibi mill was opening, the catastrophic developments in Europe raised fundamental questions about the new relationships that were still in their early tentative stages. Economically, the war was an important boost for the region, as it was for Northern Ontario generally. Since newsprint was in demand for printing the eagerly anticipated war news, the new Abitibi plant had a larger market than anticipated.[82] At the same time, the production of gold, as a mainstay of the economy, was considered an important support for the war effort. As a speaker to the Canadian Mining Institute put it, "The patriotism of production by the farmers of Canada has been vigourously [sic] and properly preached, but the same arguments apply quite strongly to the mining industry and especially to the production of gold."[83] Socially, however, the war proved to be highly problematic.

Initially, the population seemed to draw together in the excitement of the moment. Young men began to head off to Toronto or Ottawa to enlist with "home" units. Then an organized recruiting drive was initiated in Northern Ontario to fill the 159th Battalion, popularly called the Algonquin Regiment after a militia unit that had been formed in 1903 at Sudbury and Sault Ste Marie. Home Guards were in place at South Porcupine, Schumacher, and Timmins by the summer of 1915. That fall, several dozen Italians were called up for service by the Italian government, and another campaign was initiated to attract men to the 2nd Battalion, Canadian Pioneers, which called for miners familiar with tunnel construction. A large number of First Nations men from Moose Factory and the Chapleau Agency also volunteered. So many men were joining up that the mines, the colonization roads department, and the Abitibi mill began to report labour shortages.[84]

By the spring of 1915, cracks were appearing in this foundation as hostility to non-Canadian or non-British residents began to be expressed openly. The same pattern has been observed elsewhere in Ontario; Barbara Wilson recently attributed it to the sinking of the *Lusitania* in May 1915, which caused the death of many Ontario civilians.[85] A few weeks after the *Lusitania* tragedy, a visiting magistrate in the Timmins police court addressed the participants in a stiffly worded warning that was reproduced at length in the local newspaper under the banner, "Foreigners in Camp Are Strongly Warned." According to the paper, the magistrate said, "I wish to point out ... to those foreigners in this camp that the British Empire is at war with Germany and Austria and the Canadian Government is giving people of those nations very wide privileges as long as they behave themselves and do their work ... This is the first time I have had a chance of talking to so many assembled foreigners and I wish to impress upon you that while I am coming up here I am going to send you to jail, every time you are convicted, for four months."[86] More subtle pressures also were placed on "foreigners." In small communities, gossip and public pressure is a force to be reckoned with. A Timmins police constable named Craft felt obliged to make a public show of presenting his naturalization papers to the town council after allegations circulated that he had some German ancestry.[87] Wild rumours also began to spread to the effect that the Germans had established a naval force in James Bay and could likely count on assistance from a group of "Austrians" who were alleged to be drilling secretly in the bush behind the Dome Mine.[88]

Fearing the threat of large numbers of young men from enemy countries in their midst, representatives of several northeastern Ontario towns drew up a petition in June 1915, calling on the dominion government to institute the immediate "general internment" of enemy aliens. When

nothing was done, the South Porcupine Home Guard sent a formal resolution to Ottawa expressing "its disapproval of the failure of the Government to intern enemy aliens employed in such numbers in the Porcupine
district."[89] The question was debated in economic terms. Allegations were
made that "a large amount in wages" from Porcupine-area mines, amount-
ing to "some $50,000" each month, was going directly "to German bankers
in New York to be forwarded to Austria and Germany."[90] In the summer of
1915, the *Advance* reported, "The alien employment question in the Porcupine district has been a cause for much discontent among workmen who
have been unable to secure employment and many bitter remarks and
comments can be heard."[91] Stories of this discontent reached the outside
world and were reported in the *Canadian Annual Review* for 1915: "From
the Porcupine region many complaints reached the press as to seditious
utterances of alien miners; hostile threats and unpleasant relations with
loyal workers in the mines or the villages. There was alleged drilling by
members of a secret society ... There was an attempt to blow up a powder
magazine at the Nipissing Mine on Feb. 21."[92]

The Finns found themselves under fire because of a slightly more
complex situation. During the civil war in Finland, German forces entered
the country, ostensibly to support the non-communist side, and Germany
assisted in the establishment of the victorious White government. Finns in
northeastern Ontario were anxious to distance themselves from the
German alliance and circulated a letter to that effect from the "Representative in the United States of the People's Republic of Finland."[93] Nevertheless, the Finns were now eyed with suspicion by British subjects in
Northern Ontario. Were the Finns allies of the Germans or not?

Curiously, it was not the Germans or Austrians in the region who bore
the brunt of wartime hostilities. It was the Chinese. There was an outbreak
of vicious anti-Chinese activity directed at the small group of men who ran
restaurants and laundries in the towns. Perhaps because they were visibly
different, did not work among the general population, and were too small
a group to be able to defend themselves very effectively, they seemed to
have become the scapegoats for all the anger and anxiety of the day. In the
summer of 1915 the Timmins Board of Trade began to discuss the question of "white" girls who were employed in Chinese-run restaurants; the
board attempted to get the municipality to pass a by-law to prevent such
employment on the grounds that the girls were in danger of being seized
by their employers for "immoral purposes." When legal opinion pointed
out that the town had no jurisdiction to pass such a bylaw, the campaign
shifted to the sanitary conditions of Chinese-run restaurants. The *Advance*
ran an editorial claiming, "They buy the cheapest stuff they can get –
absolute refuse – which would be consigned to the dump if it were not for
these 'culinary experts' who are allowed by the authorities to cook it up

and feed it to their helpless victims ... We are informed of a car of meat which was refused at Schumacher, owing to its unsanitary condition, and later sent in to Timmins where it found a ready market."[94] The Sanitary Steam Laundry played on these fears with an advertising campaign through the summer of 1915 against the Chinese-run competition. "A case of leprosy is reported to have been traced to a Chinese laundry in Denver, Colorado," ran one item. "Be on the safe side and have the Sanitary Steam Laundry of South Porcupine call regularly on you."[95]

In September 1916 the Canadian government initiated a system to register all "enemy aliens" in the country. Once registered with the military or police, they were required to report monthly to dominion authorities and to apply for permission if they wished to leave a registration district. In the first year of the program, between 700 and 800 people reported monthly at Timmins,[96] rather fewer than the "hordes" of aliens that local gossip implied, but still a considerable number in a community of about 3,000 souls. The registration program seems to have had little effect on the animosity directed at non-citizens. In the summer of 1917 several "foreigners" were arrested and given stiff prison terms for activities deemed to be subversive.[97] The following spring there was a debate about "the large numbers of aliens now in business" in the area and whether business licences could be refused them. They were "bearing no fair share of the responsibilities and burdens of the day while enjoying all the advantages of life in this country," claimed one participant in the campaign, adding, "The multiplicity of their stores has a tendency to increase their habit of grouping together and makes it more difficult to assimilate them into the life of the country." When in the fall of 1917 the Wartime Elections Act explicitly disenfranchised anyone who had been born in an enemy country or who had been naturalized after March 1902, the dominion government was vociferously applauded by the Canadian-born population of the region.

It was not only immigrants from enemy countries who found themselves under fire. In the climate of nasty nativism, even immigrants from allied countries were being attacked. By the summer of 1915, people had begun to notice that military recruits in the area were coming from a very specific segment of the population. In October the *Porcupine Advance* reported that of the hundred men who had enlisted so far in the Pioneers' 2nd Battalion, only two had been born outside Canada or the British Isles.[98] The following spring, Timmins town councillor A.R. Globe (a Boer War veteran) chaired a meeting to inaugurate the 228th Battalion, or Northern Fusiliers, which was advertised as an appeal to the "foreign population who had chosen Canada as their home."[99] The new unit proved to be a hard sell: there were grumbles that the 159th Battalion had been broken up to distribute Northern Ontario men among other units (in keeping with an overall plan of Canadian military leaders). In response, early in 1917 the 228th was reorganized as a railway construction unit and promises were made that "men who joined it would thus be sure of staying with their friends" when the unit went overseas.[100]

As the war dragged on, volunteer enlistment declined everywhere in Canada, and the government eventually introduced compulsory military service through conscription in August 1917. In northeastern Ontario, this policy introduced a new problem. As in other agricultural regions of Canada, the Military Service Act was bitterly resented by farmers who needed their sons' help to run the farms. In May 1918 the military police at Iroquois Falls reported "over seventy" arrests of men who had failed to report as required; forty-seven of these were turned over to the army.[101] However, it was relatively easy to avoid service. As Jack Pecore later recalled, many men simply disappeared into the bush to "prospect," coming out only after the war when they finally felt safe from prosecution.[102] Clearly, these men were very much hated by those who had volunteered for service, and resentments between families cut deeply for some time.

Significantly, the one issue that did not appear to arise during the war was the question of French Canadian recruitment in the area, a question that was hotly debated elsewhere in Canada and even in Northern Ontario. French-speaking Canadians attended the rallies and recruiting drives in large numbers and were represented among the volunteers from the beginning. As will be discussed in chapter 11, in Northern Ontario the First World War appears to have brought English- and French-speaking Canadians together in common cause. The animosity was directed instead toward the shadowy "enemy alien" in their midst.

The end of the war did not bring an end to this hostility. Certainly, many "enemy aliens" simply left, for by the fall of 1918 the number reporting to dominion authorities had dropped by half.[103] But as soldiers began to return and look for work, tensions were renewed, as was happening almost everywhere else in Canada. Men were either turned away because jobs were already filled by immigrant workers or they found themselves working under immigrants who had been promoted to positions of authority while the veterans had been fighting overseas. Veteran A.E. Mortimer of Schumacher expressed the attitude of the day in a letter to the *Porcupine Advance*, published in the early 1920s: "We find 'Aliens' at present 'bosses' and some of them have various other easy jobs. I wonder if some of the 'Shifters' in Camp ever put themselves in the place of the boys who fought to make Canada a 'White Man's Country' … It's bad enough to have fought these people's relations without having to be 'bossed' by them … Some of them are 'well heeled' owing to the war. It's about time they 'beat it.'"[104]

There were widespread allegations that "foreigners" were being given preference in hiring, particularly at the mines,[105] even though it is clear that the managers themselves were extremely anxious about hiring "foreigners" because of a growing fear of the influence of communism, as was discussed in the previous chapter. But as unemployment problems mounted, so did resentment about immigrants. Ontario mining inspector George E. Cole complained in 1924 about the Finns still migrating to the region, "possessing one word of English and that the commercial noun 'job.'" He went on, "My mind turns to the real Canadians out of work and seemingly outcast."[106] The resentment was increasingly overlaid with the growing fear of communism in the postwar world. "Surely a man who has spent months in the Trenches ought to work under a 'White Man' and not a 'Bohunk,'" wrote a correspondent to the *Porcupine Advance*. "A goodly number of these 'Alien' gentlemen have the deepest sympathy with the 'Bolsheviki.'"[107]

Certainly, such kinds of ethnic, political, economic tensions were not unique to northeastern Ontario. Exactly the same kind of sentiments were being widely expressed across Canada at the time, and in no small way they contributed to events such as the Winnipeg General Strike and a cross-country campaign in 1919 for the deportation of all "enemy aliens." Changes to Canadian immigration policy in June 1919 reflected the hostility by strictly regulating the entrance of people from Russia, Finland, and the Ukrainian provinces, as well as completely barring people from Germany and Austria. In small communities like Timmins and South Porcupine the resentment of "foreigners" was not an abstraction; the "enemy alien" was the man working next to you in the stope or the woman hanging out laundry in the yard next door. The effects were direct, personal, and must have been devastating for those at the receiving end of the animosity.

The Second World War also brought divisions into the region, but this time the battle lines were drawn in different places. The Chinese, victims of Japanese aggression in Asia, were now the object of some sympathy, and their fundraising efforts for the people of Shanghai in 1937 were warmly applauded in the *Advance*.[108] The Poles, too, were no longer reviled indiscriminately as "Bohunks"; they were now the courageous victims of Nazi aggression. Various organizations in the region rushed to make public declarations of their loyalty to Canada, anxious perhaps to avoid the kind of nastiness that the First World War had generated.

The Finns found themselves in a particularly awkward situation as the ground at home in Finland shifted. An initial attempt in Finland to remain neutral was crushed by the Soviet invasion that began on 30 November 1939; Soviet strategists feared that Germany might use Finland as a base from which to launch an attack on the USSR. During the winter war that followed, the *Advance* (like other Canadian newspapers) followed events carefully and with considerable sympathy for what it depicted as the unfortunate but brave Finnish people.[109] Various European leaders, including Winston Churchill, also praised the "brave Finns" for their determined fight against communism. White Finns in the region began volunteering for military service at home, much to the disgust of the area's Reds. *Vapaa Sana* reported incidents like one in February 1940 at the South Porcupine train station, when Finnish nationalist volunteers were heckled by a woman shouting, "Russia will win."[110] The nationalists struck back. One winter's night, a gang of nationalists raided the Finnish Organization of Canada's bookstore and then marched to the South Porcupine hall, where a theatrical rehearsal was underway. A fight broke out, the police arrived, and charges were laid.[111] Significantly, the nationalists used the winter war as an opportunity to initiate alliances with Canadians – a process that historian Varpu Lindström has called the "goodwill" campaign of 1940–41, which was intended to "help solidify public opinion on Finland's behalf." Speakers such as August Kuusisto (a member of the Finnish parliament) and journalist E.A. Pulli travelled across Ontario with stops in Timmins, and the child violinist Heimo Haitto played to appreciative audiences on a tour that included Timmins and South Porcupine.[112] Nationalist Finns in South Porcupine publicly warned the Red Cross not to encourage the Finnish Organization of Canada to raise funds for the Finnish Red Cross because of nationalist concerns about "where the monies from their sewing circles, bingo-games, and other collections end up."[113] Certainly, through the early months of the war it appeared that Canada and its Finnish residents were united in a common cause.

Then, in mid-March 1940, Finland and the USSR signed what proved to be a short-lived peace agreement, and the Finns began to look to Germany for military and economic support in the territory that remained beyond Soviet control. By June 1941, the Finns were fighting with German assistance to regain territory they had lost to the Soviets. Considering this cooperation to be essentially an alliance with Germany, the British broke off formal relations with the Finns in early August 1941 and then, on 6 December, declared war on Finland. Canada followed suit the next day. Finns were now officially enemy aliens in Canada, required to register and report to dominion authorities, just like the Germans and Austrians. According to Varpu Lindström, "Among the nationalist Finns, the whole notion of a war between Finland and Canada was laughed off as a joke." They considered the Finnish arrangement with the Germans to be only "a matter of necessity if Finland were to remain independent." Indeed, Lindström argued, "nationalist Finns vehemently asserted that the only enemy Finland had was Russia."[114]

In South Porcupine and Timmins, the subtle complexities of Finnish politics were initially greeted with silent bewilderment. But the actions of nationalist Finns assured that there would be no local outcry against them, no demands for internment of the new enemy alien. A significant number volunteered for overseas service with the Canadian military, and the first two wartime fatalities from the district were Finns: Ahti (Joseph) Aho of Timmins and his cousin Arvo Aho of Gold Centre.[115] The area's Finns also made substantial financial contributions to the Canadian war effort, including a $20,000 pledge to the sixth Victory Loan campaign of May 1944 made by the Finnish Organization of Canada's Timmins branch.[116] Then, in September 1944, Finland and the USSR signed an armistice, one of its terms being a requirement that the Finns remove the Germans from Finnish soil. So between mid-September 1944 and April 1945 Finland was at war with Germany, and the Finns of Northern Ontario could no longer be seen as enemies.

Not all "enemy aliens" were treated like the Finns. Germans were, of course, obvious targets and at least one German family alleged persecution during the war. Helene Kuechmeister complained that her home was vandalized and that the Tisdale Township police had beaten her son Ernest during a campaign of harassment intended to intimidate them into leaving the area.[117] There were official expressions of animosity as well. Early in the war, even before the dominion government had made a move, Timmins Town Council demanded the registration of all enemy aliens.

The Italians also were particular targets. The day before Italy declared war on Britain, Timmins Italians met at the Goldfields Theatre to declare their loyalty to Canada and to reassure their neighbours,[118] but with the declaration of war on 10 June 1940, "a wave of anti-Italian agitation" washed through the district.[119] Local leaders were gravely concerned. J.H. Stovel, manager at Dome Mines, provided information to the police about two unnaturalized Italians on the payroll, in the hope that the RCMP would arrest them so as "to better control the situation with our naturalized Italians."[120] Clearly, Stovel wished to send a message that even a hint of disloyalty to Canada and the war effort would be quickly quashed. When the RCMP did not respond to his request, Stovel fired the two men and nine others who did not have their papers. The McIntyre Mine also instituted a policy of replacing Italian workers with Canadians.[121] As has been noted, several of the area's Italians were interned, including Leo Mascioli and his brother.[122] There is also an oral tradition locally of a nasty "war riot." The graduate student James Louis Di Giacomo was told that in 1939 "rowdies, many of them members of the Algonquin regiment stationed at Timmins," had attacked Italians on the street, hurling rocks and insults, and breaking into a number of homes while the police simply stood by.[123] Unfortunately, I was unable to locate any independent verification of these memories; if such a riot did occur, it is unlikely to have been in 1939 when Italy and Canada were not yet at war. Nevertheless, it is clear that, once again, the pressures of war released the simmering ethnic hostilities of the region.

Interestingly, the hostility exhibited during the Second World War never reached the depths of the vicious and angry campaigns of the first war. Part of the explanation may lie in the fact that many of the most radical immigrants had left the area by 1939 or 1940, discouraged by decades of effort that had failed to convince the workers of Northern Ontario to participate in the class war. Some idealists had returned to Europe to build a new world under communism there, while others had joined European armies to fight for those values more literally. For the immigrants who remained in Porcupine–Iroquois Falls, a degree of assimilation had begun to set in, as will be discussed. After they had lived in the area for twenty or thirty years, raised families there, and participated in work and leisure activities with the wider society, a degree of comfort and familiarity appears to have developed on both sides that helped to smooth the rougher edges of wartime tensions.

Nevertheless, the depth of social division in Porcupine–Iroquois Falls must not be underestimated. Politics, language, religion, and world conflict combined with economic realities in northeastern Ontario to create very real barriers. People may have been attracted to the region with the shared goal of creating a better life for themselves and their families, but they were unwilling to relinquish deeply held beliefs about what made a good life or who were good people. Whether differences were openly and angrily expressed or simply lived out in small daily choices of where to shop or worship, they were a very real part of life in the new settlements. It would seem an unlikely field indeed in which to sow, nourish, or sustain a broader sense of community.

CHAPTER ELEVEN

Centripetal Forces

Not all circumstances conspired against the possibility of consensus in Porcupine–Iroquois Falls. Some socio-economic structures were adopted and maintained that cut across boundaries of class, ethnicity, and gender, while unanticipated local, national, and international events generated reactions that could sometimes draw people together. Early in the resource boom, seeing common cause was difficult and tenuous. But over time, sufficient opportunities and spaces for interaction began to build on one another, gradually developing a base from which the idea of community was at least conceivable. Perhaps it helped that world events drew the more radical segments of the population away, leaving those behind with at least a shallow base of shared values, including the fact that they had been challenged by a common threat. But before a community could be built, space had to be made in which it could be imagined.

In a new place, cut loose from ties of family, church, and social systems, people naturally sought new opportunities for interaction. One of the most popular turned out to be the fraternal society. Scholars have provided a variety of explanations for the popularity of these groups. Some believe they provided an opportunity for a new class of industrial leaders to create networks, proclaim elite status, and maintain exclusivity.[1] In direct contrast, another school of thought sees them as a mechanism for community integration, cutting across class lines.[2] Others see them as products of the new urban life produced by the industrial revolution: newcomers tried to overcome the "anonymity" of city life by joining organizations that echoed "communities roughly the size and character which men until recently had always known, from the prehistoric hunting band to the medieval farming village or artisans' guild."[3] Another scholar preferred to see the societies as primarily a young man's phenomenon, offering a family like setting for "social acceptance at a time of life when other bonds and commitments were in flux."[4] Finally, mass society theorists have argued that these associations are crucial to "mediating relations between individuals and the society's political elites" because they provide power for individuals who otherwise would be relatively powerless. At the same time, this theory proposes, membership in a group serves as a mechanism for socialization and social control.[5] What role did these organizations play in the context of the amorphous and uncertainly structured society of early Porcupine–Iroquois Falls?

Dozens of clubs, societies, and lodges were established in the region over the years, right from the arrival of the first resource developers. Some groups proved ephemeral, serving a temporary purpose of the interests of particular individuals. Others took root and became an important part of life for successive generations. Since membership in all these groups was gender-based but otherwise ostensibly open regardless of religion, ethnicity, or social status, they merit some consideration for the role they may have played in bringing people together.

It is clear that initially some of these groups were far more exclusive than their public pronouncements would admit. The first were founded by men and women from professional, managerial, and business backgrounds and were dominated by unilingual English speakers. The Porcupine Elks, for example, elected the lawyer and businessman Gordon Gauthier as its first "esteemed ruler" (president) and counted among its founding officers two businessmen, T.F. King and Charles Piercy, Dr J.A. McInnis, and a clergyman named Peacock.[6] Active members of the Timmins Kiwanis Club in its first fifteen years included the Buffalo-Ankerite Mine's general manager Phil Kinkel, dentist Dr Lee Honey, lumber company owner Frank Feldman, and businessman Charles Pierce.[7] Potential members had to apply – a convenient gate-keeping device, though none was really needed. Shift-working miners had a practical barrier to attending regular evening meetings, while French-speaking Canadians and recent immigrants came from societies in which these particular fraternal organizations had not taken hold. The more transient men were unlikely to stay in the region long enough to gain sufficient influence to be elected as officers in these groups or perhaps even to become regular members.

Eventually, the fraternity began to pass out of the hands of the self-appointed elite. By the 1930s, men such as Hollinger electrician John Roberts and assistant TNO agent Dariell Coffey could be found among the officers. Meanwhile, the Independent Order of Foresters, the Loyal Order of Moose and other societies with a much more broadly based membership were established. Working men and their wives could also be found in leadership roles. For example, in the 1930s these included:

Independent Order of Foresters – Samuel Morgan, a Hollinger mill worker
Loyal Order of Moose – Thomas H. Richards, a Hollinger first-aid clerk

Sons of England – Ephraim Tomlinson, a Hollinger mill operator
Daughters of England – Mrs C. Rickard, wife of a Hollinger pump repairman
Sons of Scotland – John Roberts, a Hollinger electrician
Women of Mooseheart Legion – Mrs William Pennington, wife of a McIntyre
  labourer
Order of the Eastern Star – Mrs Ruby Heath, wife of a Hollinger mechanic
Porcupine Lodge, IOOF – H. Dariell Coffey, assistant agent for the TNO
Carole canadien français – O. Aubrey, a Hollinger miner
Workers' and Farmers' League (Timmins) – Jalmar Korri, a barber
Croatian Mutual Benefit Society (Schumacher) – Frank Vicevich, a Hollinger
  miner[8]

Furthermore, the work of these societies had gradually become more visible to outsiders, since a public service component was always part of the justification for their existence. The Timmins Kiwanis Club, for instance, specialized in work with underprivileged and troubled children, while the Lions Club provided services to people with eyesight difficulties. Thus, even people from backgrounds in which such societies did not exist now had an opportunity to become aware of them. For the members, by far the most important activities appear to have been social: a seemingly tireless round of card games, dinners, dances, and, obviously, social networking. The women's groups were particularly important in providing a space outside home or church for women to gather against the isolation that many must have feared.

It would seem, then, that just as fraternal societies had provided a sense of belonging to newcomers in an industrializing and urbanizing society in the United States, they now provided that same connectedness for newcomers to the mines and mills. Undoubtedly some of the societies (notably the Masons) were used by certain men to proclaim their status as a local elite, to set up boundaries to define that elite, and to build a network to sustain and manage their hoped-for control over social, economic, and political activities in the region. Most of the societies, however, were made up of people who had no interest in declaring themselves to be holders of the reins of power. Instead, they brought together men (and, separately, women) and gave them a sense of belonging to a group other than the workforce. Over games of euchre and around the dinner table, single men found a domestic space, women found one another, and all found a sense of value in who they were and what they were doing in New Ontario. The men's organizations certainly provided a space for the celebration of masculinity and male privilege, reinforcing the pervasive men's culture in the region which the economy had helped establish in the first place. And the lodge helped create a sense (perhaps partly an illusion) that the place was made up of others who shared one's interests and experiences. The idea that one had a duty to reach out to the less fortunate not only provided common cause for the members but also helped create a sense that there was a wider "community" beyond that warranted one's efforts. It became a mutually reinforcing cycle. Thus, the fraternal organizations provided both a personal sense of belonging in a new society, cut off from family and traditional ties, and a place where individuals could imagine a collectivity where none had existed before.

The organizers themselves clearly recognized the potential value of these clubs in forming a sense of community. Some were even explicit about the stability they might create in a world in flux, even if the purpose of that stability was economic development. In 1916 a group that appears to have been based in the Timmins Presbyterian church began a campaign to establish a social club for young single men that would provide a gathering-place in which to entertain their friends (and keep them out of the bars) and to offer "literary and political" instruction and practical services, such as meals. The *Porcupine Advance* expressed concern that young men "come into the camp for work for a few months and as they have no social ties here the novelty wears off." A social club, it explained, would be valuable in encouraging them to stay on and would promote the stability and permanence that town boosters liked to pretend already existed. When such a club was finally established late in 1919, it was placed under the parental auspices of both the Presbyterian and Anglican ministers and was presented as a sort of home-grown version of the YMCA.[9]

Perhaps the most important impetus to broadly based organization was the First World War. A sense of patriotic duty prompted men, women, and young people to form dozens of groups dedicated to assisting the war effort in a variety of ways. Some, like the Red Cross, were branches of international associations, while others, like the DYB Club, were purely local efforts. The Iroquois Falls Patriotic Association and the Timmins Patriotic Relief Association were primarily fundraising organizations directed by men, while the South Porcupine Patriotic Society was organized by women to knit socks, roll bandages, and sew pyjamas for the men overseas. Perhaps the most important group to emerge from the war was the Great War Veterans' Association (GWVA) and later the Royal Canadian Legion. Established as a self-help group so former servicemen could get hospital care, pensions, and other benefits, it eventually became an important community service group and social meeting place, just as it did in so many small towns across Canada.

Sociology student Peter Vasiliadis once described the Goldfields chapter of the GWVA as "one of the strongest representative organizations for the miners" because it "cut across all class lines," with members that included "miners and mine executives, merchants and politicians."[10] Unfortunately, the surviving evidence only partially supports such an interpretation. The most senior community leaders were not members of the GWVA because very few mine managers, senior business owners, or politicians had served on active duty overseas; most recruits from the area were young men just beginning their working lives, so they were not in managerial positions. Furthermore, army recruiters were looking particularly for experienced miners for tunnel and trench construction, or for loggers and railway construction men (not for clerical or professional workers). In 1915, when the *Porcupine Advance* listed a hundred men who had joined the Pioneer Regiment's 2nd Battalion, only six were identified as professionals and none was a merchant (with the possible exception of one barber and one "storekeeper," a term then generally used for someone who ran a store, not an owner).[11] Nor did the area's veterans represent all the ethnic enclaves, even in proportion to their numbers in the region. Fully 70 percent of the original recruits were Canadian-born, and just over 20 percent were English-born. The rest were mostly Scots or Irish, with one Finn and one "Russian."[12] Eventually, there was a large number of Ukrainian veterans, particularly at Timmins, but most chose to form their own Ukrainian War Veterans Society,[13] and the First Nations veterans also do not appear to have participated in the GWVA/Legion branches in the towns. Thus (and hardly surprisingly), the GWVA reflected the makeup of that portion of the population that supported the war effort and was in a personal position to be able to serve, rather than the broader socio-economic and ethnic profile of the population as a whole.

However, within this group, there was a greater range of men than might have otherwise have considered themselves to have shared interests. When the Iroquois Falls branch of the GWVA was founded in 1917, one-quarter of the members noted were francophones, and the initiator of the movement in Timmins was a sergeant (George Smith) rather than one of the officers.[14] In the mid-1930s, membership and interest appears to have jumped dramatically during and after a "pilgrimage" was organized by the Legion across Canada to bring thousands of Canadians to the unveiling of the great memorial tribute at Vimy Ridge. Mayor J.P. Bartleman of Timmins perhaps reflected the thinking when he said, "A few years ago all the talk one could hear was 'Let's forget the war, etc.' [But] this monster pilgrimage proved that Canada at least will never forget those who served and those who paid the supreme price."[15] As historian Jonathan Vance has proposed, "After four years of war, most people had simply had enough of tragedy, death, and misery." But eventually, he said, people needed to find meaning in the terrible losses, and Canadians "conferred upon those four years a legacy, not of despair, aimlessness, and fatality, but of promise, certainty, and goodness."[16] Thus, in Porcupine–Iroquois Falls, the Legion evolved into a symbol of hope for the future and a celebration of the heroism of those who had served. The shared experiences of that service clearly marked the core of the group. But many others whose lives had been touched by the war also wanted to participate in the process of commemoration, so the Legion and its activities became an important community focal point. When the GWVA announced plans to hold a banquet in South Porcupine on the seventh anniversary of the Battle of Vimy Ridge, a crowd of 350 to 400 turned up to eat roast turkey, listen to rousing speeches, watch skits, and sing "the old-time songs."[17] The anniversary banquet soon became an annual event, and by 1934 the crowd had grown so large at the Timmins version that no local hall could accommodate everyone at one sitting for dinner.[18]

Another very important space in which a diversity of people was brought together was the school. Of course, it is important to remember the fundamental divisions of public and separate (Roman Catholic) schools, as well as the bilingual (and later unilingual French) institutions. Nevertheless, within these broader divisions, children of a range of backgrounds came together every day. Because the towns were small, there was insufficient residential segregation in the catchment area of each school to create differences in the socio-economic profile of the student body. Consequently, students were bound to learn more from one another than the formal curriculum dictated.[19]

Interestingly, the provision of educational facilities was not a priority for many early residents, except for the clergy of the Roman Catholic Church and some middle-class leaders. At Timmins, Hollinger manager P.A. Robbins promoted the construction of an eight-room school in 1916, over what Matthew B. Scott later delicately recalled as "the many objections" of fellow residents "astonished at his audacity in flinging away the ratepayers' money." Indeed, the editor of the *Porcupine Advance* felt compelled to write a column during this debate urging parents to take an interest in their children's schooling.[20] At Porquis Junction, the farmer who had organized the school section found it necessary to visit local families to persuade them to register their children in the school.[21] When the school that served Taylor and Carr Townships was destroyed by the fire of 1916, "repeated attempts" by officials to rebuild failed because of "lack of local interest." By 1934 the majority of children in that area were still receiving "no instruction whatever."[22] In Tisdale Township, a few keen school promoters in South Porcupine battled a recalcitrant township council and the board of trade to raise the money to build a school: the two teachers there were struggling heroically in inadequate rented facilities. Ultimately, most of the funds came from special provincial government grants and relief moneys intended for rebuilding after the 1911 fire.[23] The lack of interest throughout the region in paying for or otherwise supporting schools drew comment from time to time in the *Porcupine Advance*, whose owner (George Lake) and editor (G. Allen Macdonald) were among the handful of school promoters. "Strange as it may appear in this age of the world," ran an editorial in 1917, "there are some settlers who are not over anxious for adequate school accommodation."[24] Rural francophones saw little need for much formal education either. One Abitibi settler recalled that people considered that three to five years' schooling was sufficient to learn basic reading, writing, and "counting"; young people would learn any other skills they might need on the job.[25]

Those who did support expenditure for schools clearly saw them as both symbols and instruments for regional development, as well as tools for social engineering. As the *Porcupine Advance* put it, the settlers with the least interest were "the very ones for whom the schools are the most imperative in the general interests of progress and advancement."[26] Education was "for the good of Timmins," wrote "T.F." to the *Porcupine Advance* in 1927. "Is it not a fact that those countries whose masses of people are the most illiterate, such as, for example, China, Russia, etc., are not only hotbeds of revolutionaries and anarchists, but whose standards of living are indescribably low?"[27] Material gain and social and political stability were the ends; middle-class assumptions shaped the means.

In the rural areas it was largely the work of one man – an outsider – who attempted to overcome the poverty, distance, climate, and indifference. J.B. MacDougall, a former teacher, was appointed the first public school inspector for the districts north of North Bay in 1903–4, and for the next forty years he dedicated himself to the cause of northern education. He founded school sections in unorganized townships, solicited allies in the organized municipalities (then provided them with advice and support), and was the driving force behind the innovative railcar classrooms that began traversing the Canadian Pacific and Canadian Northern railway lines in 1926 to bring education to the children (and some adults) of isolated bush camps.[28] As the population grew, he supervised an expanding cadre of school inspectors who did far more than inspect. MacDougall's contemporary, the scholar A.R.M. Lower, explained: "Inspectors organize school sections, form the school boards in the first place and, if they are tactful men, get the right people on them. They supply the technical knowledge of assessment ... aid and advise in problems of taxation, and generally keep the whole machinery moving. Their influence on teaching is no doubt important but perhaps still more important is their moral support in the face of pioneer school trustees."[29]

Although their motivation was different, the region's Roman Catholic priests were also dedicated to the cause of providing schools that would mould young minds and build an ideal society. The missionary zeal of the colonizing priests was reinforced by their reaction to an issue that was bitterly dividing the Ontario population at the same time as the resource boom was underway. In 1908 a congress of Franco-Ontarians (meeting in

Sunday school class at South Porcupine United Church. Although families
formed only a small minority of Porcupine Camp's population, they were publicized by the boosters as evidence of stability and permanence. The young fellow
on the right clearly found the proceedings worth mocking. (UCA, 90.162,
P/1686)

Ottawa) had called on the province to recognize French-language education rights. Two years later the English-speaking Roman Catholic bishops
of Ontario issued a declaration opposing such a move, and the province
was pitched into a debate that pitted largely Irish Roman Catholics against
those of French Canadian origin. In June 1912 the Ontario government
proclaimed Regulation 17, which required instruction in English as soon
as a child entered school and prohibited instruction in French after the
end of the first form (equivalent of today's grade 3). Provincial school
grants were made conditional on adequate English-language instruction.
For the colonizing priests in Northern Ontario, it was a direct attack on the
heart of their plans. So they went ahead as if Regulation 17 did not exist.
In 1913 Father Eugène Thériault organized the first separate school in
Timmins as essentially a French-language school, which he called L'école
séparée bilingue; it was not until 1915 that an English-speaking teacher
was hired.[30] Schools, he was determined, would preserve the faith and language even in the industrial towns of New Ontario.

Children were not the only targets for social engineering through education. The legion of immigrant workers, many of whom spoke no English

and had no education in their mother tongue either, were feared as potential disrupters whose proclivity to revolution could be tamed through the
guidance of educators. They could also be taught new skills that would
prepare them to "rise above" manual labour and aspire to work as skilled
technicians. Frontier College, known locally as the Reading Camp Association, led the way in sending university students north to work in the bush
and construction camps during the day and to teach classes in English,
arithmetic, and citizenship at night. It also ran adult night schools in
Golden City, South Porcupine, Timmins, Connaught, and on the Dome
Mines property.[31] Frontier College was not alone. In 1916 the "Timmins
Day and Night School for Men" advertised "classes in English, French,
Russian, Polish, Ruthenian, and Italian. Also bookkeeping, shorthand and
typewriting, letter writing and mathematics."[32] Other opportunities were
offered by enterprising individuals like Mr. J.O. Langlois, who ran the "Day
and Night School for English and French" in Timmins for a time; and
beginning in 1920, the Timmins Public School Board ran evening classes
to offer basic arithmetic, more advanced mathematics, and two English-
language classes – one for those who did not speak English but had been
educated in their own language, and one for those who did not speak
English and had never been educated.[33]

By the mid-1930s, the concept of adult education was broadening from
language, civics, and citizenship, in large part because those who were
organizing the courses were looking for more appealing techniques to
draw in students. At Schumacher in October 1935, an event advertised as
Community Night offered a program of entertainment to inaugurate the
year's adult classes. Performances by the Croatian Orchestra, a Ukrainian
girls' dance troupe, a Finnish gymnastic exhibition, and an unspecified
Italian contributor reflected both the intended constituency of the classes
and a growing openness to certain aspects of cultural difference. When
nearly 450 people showed up for the event, the organizers announced
their intention to put on additional classes, including one for "women's
physical culture," which had been demanded by the audience.[34] Classes
such as these provided a space for newcomers to learn English but also to
celebrate their cultural traditions and learn to appreciate those of others.

Beginning in 1936, the Timmins Public School Board arranged for Mr
E.J. Transom, the "supervising principal," and Polish-born Mr S. Kostel, a
graduate of McMaster University, to offer English-language classes to
adults; these proved increasingly popular, with as many as eighty-two students in the spring of 1938. Kostel was introduced as a "new Canadian"
who spoke Russian, Ukrainian, German, "Jugoslavian," "Czechoslovakian,"
and Polish. As a class project in 1938, the students put on an evening of
public entertainment that was in English, but featured the national music,
costumes, and dances of the students' homelands, including Poland,

Ukraine, Lithuania, Hungary, Finland, Yugoslavia, Romania, Italy, and Latvia.[35] The event apparently attracted a large and enthusiastic audience that included many Canadian-born spectators. Gradually and almost imperceptibly, Anglo-Canadian fears of the foreigner were being replaced by a degree of awareness, comfort, and even a little appreciation as opportunities for this sort of non-threatening communication were opened. What had begun as an attempt at assimilation was having the unanticipated effect of introducing Canadians to the immigrants, if only on a superficial level.

Educational outreach to "new Canadians" was not just a feature of formal school settings. The United Church (notably in Timmins, Schumacher, South Porcupine, and Iroquois Falls) was particularly eager to facilitate the assimilation of foreigners, which church members believed was a moral (if not Christian) obligation. Here, the churches in Porcupine–Iroquois Falls were very much in line with the work of the United Church elsewhere in Canada, building on the tradition of the social gospel inherited from its Methodist and Presbyterian antecedents. The Timmins United Church (later called First United) facilitated the organization of a Finnish congregation with a Finnish-speaking pastor, the Reverend A.I. Heinonen, and it continued to support this congregation with fundraisers for the construction of a separate church building and for English-language classes. United Church young people's groups actively encouraged the participation of "New Canadians." The Tuxis Square in Timmins (for boys aged sixteen to eighteen) explicitly aimed to bring in at least two New Canadian members each year.[36] In 1935 the equivalent girls' group (the CGIT, or Canadian Girls in Training) held a Friendship Tea at which cultural displays from Central Europe, China, India, Northern Europe, and the British Isles were accompanied by musical entertainments that included the Finnish singer Miss Ennie Hankola and a display of Ukrainian dancing by Carlene Hodgins and Valerie Morley.[37] At Iroquois Falls, the United Church hosted its first Bazaar of Nations fundraiser in 1930. And when the Ansonville congregation sent two canvassers to solicit funds in Montrock that year, it asked Mr Berdani to go along with them "to help in talking Ukarain."[38] Even though the intent was clearly to draw in New Canadians who could then be exposed to "beneficial" influences, these strategies encouraged old Canadians to be more open to at least the superficial trappings of culture, such as costume, food, and music. And, most importantly, they opened a small door for communication.

Whether the schools and churches succeeded in their plans to inculcate middle-class values and shape a generation of assimilated British citizens can really never be evaluated. Certainly, there is evidence of ongoing frustration among blue-collar workers and their families about the schools' attempts to impose values that they did not share. Schoolteachers and inspectors complained constantly about sporadic attendance and their inability to form an alliance with parents to ensure that the children made an effort to get to school. Union activists, for their part, complained about the curriculum. In the words of Lukin Robinson of Sudbury Mine, Mill, "How many kids ever learn anything about trade unionism in school? Why is it that there is no course of trade unionism in the schools, where the majority of children are children of working people? Who dictates what is taught at school? The working class? Hell no."[39] Even the effectiveness of that curriculum is dubious, considering the problem of obtaining properly qualified teachers (particularly in the first two decades) or teachers willing to stay more than a season. Everything was "make do," with reports in the records about schools with no maps, no books, and even sometimes no heat.

Nevertheless, children did come, including young Nelma Sillanpää and others from the bush camp where her parents were working. As she recalled, "Mr. Brander [the general manager] had the stable-boss drive his sons Ernest and Stanley to school every day. So, all the other children got a ride with them too ... The one-room school was a few miles away, and the lessons there were in French. The teacher, however, was bilingual. We all got along very well, and even managed to learn."[40] Nelma's sense of "getting along very well" was echoed in the memories of many other residents who attended school in the 1920s and 1930s. For the children, ethnic diversity was a fact of life, the only social system they knew. "Growing up in such a cosmopolitan community," recalled Bob Miner of his childhood at the Dome townsite, "you didn't have any prejudices. You grew up with other kids – you'd eat and sleep over at their houses, they'd come over to yours."[41] Neva Lane (née Davis) of Porcupine had similar memories. "The first children we played with was the Brissons and we couldn't speak French and they couldn't speak English but we got along ... So then, the two Makis. We played with them all the time, Finnish children, and then there was Charlie Fera, an Italian boy."[42] Obviously these children were aware of ethnic difference, but it apparently did not matter much. The schools were not the only place where children could meet and mix with others. The appearance of "community" Boy Scout troops at such places as the Hollinger Hall and the Legion, as well as the rather unusual involvement of Roman Catholic and French-speaking groups in Scouting, meant that children could take advantage of non-school opportunities to share new experiences.

While ethnic prejudice may have run deeply among adults, a few significant individuals with different ideas appear to have made a considerable impact on the schoolchildren. Minerva Gram (née Levinson) recalled being harassed as a Jew, but she singled out one teacher, Mrs M.D. Colborne, as unusual. She "left her mark on us, which we liked to think we carried for life," said Mrs Gram. "She was a real humanitarian and all children were the same to her whether they were foreigners or not."[43] Mrs Colborne had begun teaching at South Porcupine in the fall of 1914 after twenty-two years of teaching experience elsewhere in Ontario; she retired in 1930.[44] Timmins's Moneta School had her equivalent in Miss Flora MacDonald, who arrived in 1916 from Cobalt to teach initially at Timmins Public School (later Central School). When the Moneta school was built in 1919, she found the niche that she was to occupy until her retirement in 1954 when the school was renamed in her honour.[45] These remarkable women did not appear prominently in the documentary records of local history, but they clearly had a major impact on the community through its young people.

The schools also produced unanticipated and perhaps unintended changes. In the public schools, English was the language of instruction and of the playground, and increasingly was the language that non-English-speaking children took home with them. Their parents then began to make an effort to learn English, both to prevent the growth of distance between themselves and their children and in the interests of keeping order at home (according to a report given in 1937 by an English-language teacher among the Finns).[46] Mischievous children were forming English-speaking cabals to undermine parental authority and keep secrets among themselves. Student researcher J.L. DiGiacomo, who interviewed Italians in Timmins in the early 1980s, reported another reason why parents learned English: "Many persons interviewed related stories of how their parents stopped speaking Italian when addressing their children in an effort to increase their proficiency in the English language."[47] Knowledge of English had clear benefits in the workplace, so the process was reinforced and perpetuated, gradually building the groundwork for the most basic communication.

It is interesting that English became the preferred second language for most immigrants, rather than French. The Italians, for example, as Roman Catholics could have chosen to send their children to separate schools where French was used, but large numbers went to schools such as Moneta Public for an English-language education. The reasons for these decisions are not clear. Perhaps these parents had absorbed the message that public discourse in Ontario was in English, or that to "get ahead" at work, English would carry a man further than French. It is also possible that clerical leaders like Father Thériault focused their organizational efforts on protecting the French language (as part of the campaign of *la survivance*) rather than proselytizing its cause; it was a defensive strategy rather than a proactive one. Nevertheless, for some families, religious considerations were paramount to language. At Ansonville, where the Roman Catholic school was "entirely French" in the 1930s, the English-speaking Spence family decided to send its children there, rather than to the English-language school where the children would have been exposed to the god-lessness of Protestant instruction. "Making that decision resulted, for the Spence kids, in them all becoming bilingual ... long before 'bilingual' became a household word," recalled their friend Eddie O'Donnell.[48] In another case, the Del Guidice family of Timmins was remembered as "d'origine italienne mais francisés."[49]

The experience of growing up in such an ethnically mixed society produced, by the 1930s, a generation of young adults with some knowledge of one another and of their parents' fears. Some members of this generation began to act as cultural brokers across the divide. One such broker was Dr Peter Wenger, the Canadian-born son of Ukrainian parents who had graduated from Queen's University and come to Timmins to practise medicine. In 1937 the Kiwanis Club there invited him to speak to their regular meeting about the Ukrainian experience at home and in Canada. The *Porcupine Advance* took notice of the event and reported that Dr Wenger had spoken of "the difficulties that the Ukrainian people had to overcome when they first came to Canada, being strangers in a strange land, and how the obstacles had been overcome until at the present time these people were in all professions and businesses."[50] Speaking to an audience that shared a veneration of mythologized "pioneer" forebears, and pointing out the ascent to middle-class status of the second generation, Wenger clearly struck a chord with his middle-class audience. But intermediaries were not limited to the middle class. Countless anonymous "cultural brokers" played a role among the area's workers as well. As Nancy Forestell has observed, "In the 1940s members of Local 241 of the International Union of Mine, Mill and Smelter Workers and its ladies [sic] auxiliary, Local 128, set out to construct their own idea of an idyllic 'family town' ... Overcoming significant inter- and intra-ethnic divisions, and blending together social and political activities, the union and its auxiliary often worked to address issues of joint concern ..."[51]

Some local voices even began to propose that the exchange between old and new Canadians might be mutually beneficial. A 1937 editorial in the *Porcupine Advance*, entitled "Better Canadians" (on the subject of English-language classes), represented a stance that was a major distance from the paper's earlier mockery of foreigners: "In the old lands from which the new Canadians come there are traditions, romance, art, poetry, music, that may be brought to this country. The new land has given much and offers much to the new Canadians. The old lands may give much to the new. These courses of study form the basis on which the greatest mutual benefit is possible."[52]

While all of the efforts to bring people together discussed thus far were deliberate attempts at social engineering, various unplanned events that transpired over time also had the effect of influencing the way people thought about themselves and one another. A series of occurrences generated both inside and outside the region often had unanticipated but nonetheless important consequences for regional society.

The tragic forest fires of July 1911 and July 1916 did not only mark the landscape and those who suffered through the infernos; they also left their mark on subsequent generations, who came to see those fires as defining moments in "their" history. As the flames gathered force, people rallied to protect themselves and the property they had so recently struggled to establish. At Pottsville in 1911, more than 150 people formed a bucket brigade to try to save the commercial centre of the town, and a "relief party" of doctors and other volunteers trekked across the smouldering land to the Dome property to help victims there. At Matheson in 1916, residents organized buckets and wagons to haul water from the Black River in a vain attempt to save their town; others took refuge across the river where they spent a terrifying night. Rita Monahan and Lana Lougheed led the others in hymn singing to keep up their spirits. At Iroquois Falls, Abitibi equipment was put into service by a small army of volunteers. A train plied the track between the plant and the Wye, carrying people to safety. In the Abitibi mill, families huddled together with the horses and a few cattle; one woman gave birth during the night. Nurse Isabella Scott and Mrs Kaspar Lechner attended the injured and frightened, while train engineer Sam McKay and engineer Walter O'Connell risked their lives to save others. Immediately after the 1916 fire, Timmins-Porcupine residents formed the Fire Relief Committee to organize rescue parties and cope with immediate shelter needs, and then to coordinate the reconstruction effort.[53]

The human tragedy of the fires had a considerable emotional impact. There was particular horror in 1911 over what had happened at the West Dome Mine, where twenty-seven bodies were recovered from the mine shaft. Recall that Robert A. Weiss had apparently led his wife, little daughter, and other employees and their wives down the shaft in a desperate attempt to escape the wall of flame that was bearing down on them. But the fire consumed their oxygen, and all perished. The Cobalt *Daily Nugget* reported the horrific details: "It is apparent that at one time an effort was made to escape ... The body of Mrs. Rose Wallingford Burt, wife of Angus Burt, the assayer, was found hanging halfway up the charred ladder where she was trying to escape and was hit by a falling burning timber, the marks of which remain on her body."[54] Some thirty-seven years after the event, memories of the subsequent funerals remained vivid for the Reverend G.B. Maclennan. The body of little Ariel Weiss was laid on the bosom of her mother, Jennie, and a procession of 140 pallbearers began a "solemn march" to the new cemetery, carrying the fire victims through an eerie shroud of smoke and ashes that still hung in the air. "In my long ministry

After the Matheson fire, 1916. Barely settled, this family had lost everything. The lopsided photo captures the disequilibrium of the day. (W.C.H. Dowson, LAC, PA46726)

I have witnessed many touching spectacles," recalled Maclennan, "but none more touching than that. Strong and rugged men wept openly and shed copious tears ... And under the light of a single miner's candle, comrades ... formed a complete circle awaiting the word of prayer and committal of those who so recently had shared with them the fellowship of the mine."[55] As historian Albert Tucker later wrote, the tragedy of 1911 "increased the sense of community in the North," because "people recognized their vulnerability and their dependence on one another."[56]

Although spared by the Haileybury fire of 1922 that killed dozens and left thousands homeless, the people of Porcupine–Iroquois Falls rallied to the cause of these latest victims. Within days, Dome employees had subscribed a thousand dollars and issued a challenge to the other mines to do the same. A benefit dance raised more money at the New Empire Theatre; a few days later, a concert featuring the Timmins Citizens' Band did the same.[57] The emotional impact and necessary collective response had been reinforced in the repetition.

The other major tragic disaster to strike the region was the Spanish influenza epidemic of 1918–19. The disease swept the globe, of course, and although it came slightly later to northeastern Ontario than to the major centres of southern Canada, it arrived nonetheless and with the

Firestorm descending on South Porcupine, July 1911. This photo, one of a series, captures the enormity of the terrifying event. A number of the buildings seen here were destroyed shortly after the picture was taken. (Henry Peters, LAC, PA29808)

same devastating impact. On 9 October 1918, the *Porcupine Advance* published a warning from the provincial board of health that the flu was coming – and within just a few days of the notice, it struck. Almost overnight there were at least two hundred cases, and within ten days there were already thirty-seven dead at Timmins–South Porcupine; at Iroquois Falls, seven unfortunates died in a single day. South Porcupine seems to have been the hardest hit, with the virus raging through the Finnish boarding houses and taking the lives of dozens of young miners. With no hospital or medical staff in South Porcupine, the Timmins doctors did their best, turning the new public school at South Porcupine into a temporary hospital and issuing instructions to the volunteers (many of them young women) who came forward to help. Schools, churches, and other public gathering places were closed throughout the region. By late December 1918, the weekly death toll was in decline and decisions were being made to reopen the churches for Christmas. But the disease had not yet run its course. Occasional deaths continued through the spring and summer of 1919, and it was not until March 1920 that the manager at Dome Mines felt confident in declaring that the epidemic was "practically over."[58]

At first, it did not seem that people were willing to risk their own health to help, preferring to leave the work to medical professionals and town authorities. But as the magnitude of the crisis became apparent, a number of volunteers stepped forward. Miss Dolly Gleason was praised when she and a friend began visiting the Finnish boarding houses in South Porcupine when no one else would, doing "everything that trained nurses could do."[59] At Timmins, one of the first to volunteer was Miss Laura Keon; she was also one of the first to die, the *Porcupine Advance* lamenting her loss in its issue of 6 November. A month later, Timmins Town Council voted to erect a memorial to honour her. Frances Eleanor Faithful (née Foster), the wife of an electrician with Northern Canada Power and an active supporter of Byrnes Presbyterian Church in Timmins, put her religious convictions into practice as another of the nurse-volunteers. Mr L. Steinhart travelled from South Porcupine to Connaught to help when news arrived that a number of the First Nations families there had been stricken; just getting to the village was a challenge because part of the trip had to be made by dog team.[60] At Iroquois Falls, the town organized a special influenza hospital that was run with the help of volunteers, including Miss V. McColl, Miss E. McKenzie, and Miss D. McBurney.[61] As Jack Easton later recalled, this epidemic was an enormous tragedy, but "there was wonderful support forthcoming from voluntary sources."[62]

The influenza deaths were very public and visible in the small towns. "They was just dying like flies," remembered Eva Derosa over fifty years later. "And at the end there was no more coffins. They would just put them in a wagon and cover them up with a blanket and that's the way they were buried."[63] Special trenches were dug in the area's small cemeteries to accommodate the bodies. Many of the dead had never made it to hospital, spending their final hours in the hotels and boarding houses that had been their home. And as most were men without their families, strangers were called on to help them both before and after their death. It was a devastating experience. Across the provincial border in the Abitibi region of Quebec, the epidemic was recalled as *la plus sombre page de notre histoire.*[64]

Other world events which the people of the region faced together included, of course, the two great wars of the twentieth century. While the wars were clearly divisive, as was discussed in chapter 10, the recruiting drives, propaganda, and ultimately the war experiences of returned soldiers contributed to a sense of camaraderie and shared purpose among a large segment of the population. During the First World War in particular, a certain component of the population rallied partly to prove a point to the outside world – that this was a region that mattered, that it was part of important events in the wider world, and had grown into a force to be reckoned with. It was no temporary camp of drifters on the margins of society, and the war in Europe provided an opportunity to demonstrate the coming of age.

The impact of the war was felt early in the region, as rumours circulated in the fall of 1914 that the Germans had succeeded in establishing a naval presence in James Bay and somehow had managed to send an "airship" inland as far south as New Liskeard.[65] More reliable reports of a German presence came in December 1914, when the Ontario government announced an agreement with the dominion government through which German prisoners of war would be brought to northeastern Ontario to work on road construction adjacent to the Transcontinental Railway and to clear land for an experimental farm at Hearst, northwest of Timmins.[66] Young men began to sign up for overseas service, many of the first ending up in the 58th Infantry Battalion, which thus provided a focal point for those left at home.[67] In July 1915 the towns of Iroquois Falls, South Porcupine, Timmins, and Cochrane agreed to collaborate in raising funds to purchase a field kitchen for the unit, with the local boards of trade leading the initiative. A month later, a movement to establish Home Guard units at South Porcupine, Timmins, and Schumacher provided another focal point. Within days, more than a hundred men had signed on in South Porcupine and fifty at Schumacher to protect the region against invasion and sabotage.

More significant recruiting of soldiers began in the fall of 1915, for it was becoming clear that the war was to be no brief skirmish. The first to go were two large contingents of Italians (mostly Hollinger employees) who, as Italian citizens of service age, had been called up by their government.[68] A month later, what the *Advance* called "the first really organized campaign to obtain recruits" was conducted by two officers of the newly organized 2nd Battalion, Canadian Pioneers. The Pioneers were an engineering unit intended partly for road, bridge, and other construction work, but above all for mining and tunnelling under the battlefields of France to lay explosive charges under enemy territory or to provide hidden access routes to the front lines. One of the officers, Lieutenant Alexander Smith, was a former resident of the Porcupine Camp and knew where to come to find men with experience in tunnel construction. But the unit didn't turn down other volunteers, including six from Iroquois Falls and seven from Porquis Junction in the first week. Eventually, about one hundred men enlisted with the 2nd Battalion of the Pioneers.[69] They were given a rousing send-off (which cost the town of Iroquois Falls $79.70), and their subsequent movements were followed with interest.[70]

The next unit to be formed with a significant local membership was the 159th Battalion of the Algonquin Regiment. The Algonquin was a Northern Ontario militia unit that traced its roots back to 1863 at Sault Ste Marie. Before the war, it had maintained depots in Sault Ste Marie, Sudbury, Sturgeon Falls, and Thessalon.[71] Its coat of arms depicted a northern moose, and its motto was "Ne-kah-ne-tah," loosely interpreted as

Ojibwa for "We lead, others follow." With these northern symbols and roots, the unit was a natural to play on a sense of local loyalty. In February 1916, as it began its recruiting drive in Porcupine–Iroquois Falls, it advertised that it was "composed entirely of Northern Ontario men," and it was at pains to point out that its commanding officer, Lieutenant Colonel Dr E.F. Armstrong, was from Cobalt, while its other officers were employees of local mines and mills. Lieutenant W.D. Nicholson (of the Vipond Mine) and Sergeant Ferris toured all the area's schools (public and separate) to give each child a souvenir battalion flag, while Timmins Town Council organized a "patriotic evening" in support of the men, with hockey, broomball, and music.[72] As it had done with the Pioneers' 2nd Battalion, the *Advance* published names of recruits in an enthusiastic honour roll.

The names on these lists were primarily those of British or French Canadian ancestry, a fact that did not go unnoticed locally. So in May 1916, A.R. Globe, Hollinger's assistant general manager (and Timmins town councillor), led a campaign to raise a third northern unit that would appeal to the "foreign population who had chosen Canada as their home." It was designated the 228th Battalion, known locally as the Northern Fusiliers, and boasted a band almost before it had any other members. As men signed on at periodic local rallies, they were sent off to Toronto to drill until the unit reached full strength. In March 1917 the 228th was reorganized as the 6th Battalion, Canadian Railway Troops, under Lieutenant Colonel A. Earchman, to contribute to the massive task of laying railway supply lines in Europe. In order to stimulate declining enlistment, it advertised that government promises had been made to send it overseas as a unit.[73] Once again, patriotic rallies in support of the "boys" of the 228th Battalion periodically galvanized the locals.

Meanwhile, those who could not serve overseas organized countless groups and associations to do "war work." These included the Porquis Junction Patriotic Society (whose main purpose was to support the families of five local married men who had signed up) and the Iroquois Falls Band, founded in 1918 in large part to hold benefit dances for the Red Cross. Women's knitting circles and girls' clubs that rolled bandages all provided new spaces for people to meet and get to know one another. In some ways, of course, these groups simply reinforced ethnic, class, and gender divides. But some made tentative steps toward bridging them. Founding members of the Iroquois Falls Great War Veterans' Association, for example, included Privates Anderson, Boviard, Dinsmore, Falordeau, Lacost, Smith, Wilbrau, and Van Swelded.[74] In other cases, groups were formed as more spontaneous or short-lived reactions to specific opportunities. For example, in November 1915, one of the first returning war heroes was welcomed home with a parade and public reception. The unfortunate Corporal Jamieson of South Porcupine had been seriously injured in one of the first gas attacks of the war and invalided out. Perched on a chair, he was paraded around South Porcupine by a growing crowd, who saw to it that the German Kaiser was "well and truly" burned in effigy along the way. "All were welcome and all went," reported the *Advance*. A week later, when news circulated that Jamieson was having difficulty supporting himself, Tisdale Township Council rallied in a rare moment of agreement and voted him forty dollars a month until his pension was arranged or he found other means of support.[75]

After the war, there was a brief period of shock and mourning, but in the early 1920s returned soldiers and others began to organize events like an annual banquet on the anniversary of the battle of Vimy Ridge, which initially surpassed in popularity the commemoration of Armistice Day on 11 November. For the first time, veterans of the Boer War gained public visibility and support, with newspaper coverage through the 1930s of the annual meeting of the South African War Veterans' Association of Northern Ontario. The region's people participated enthusiastically in the Great Pilgrimage to the unveiling of the Vimy Memorial in France in 1936, and the ceremony was broadcast on local radio for those who could not make the trip. And while local Ukrainians preferred to form their own veterans' association, its activities were reported with solemnity and respect by the *Porcupine Advance*. The Legion in Timmins began to hold an annual Polish Smoker, at which Polish veterans were honoured; the *Advance* observed in its announcement of one of these gatherings, "All of them are friends of all the loyal soldiers of the last great war."[76] Gradually, the Great War was being transformed into the symbol of a terrible trial in which "all" had participated.

Historian Jonathan Vance has argued that Canadians as a whole began to memorialize the war as a sort of object lesson: "the true path through the divisive forces of class conflict, provincial jealousy, and racism, and towards unity, cooperation and harmony between all citizens." Canadians created a mythological set of memories about the war, wrote Vance, that "could turn everyone into better Canadians and make them worthy of the country for which 60,000 men and women had given their lives."[77] While there is little clear evidence that Porcupine–Iroquois Falls people drew direct links between the war experience and the need for community harmony, it is undeniable that for at least fifteen years after the war the strident anti-foreigner rhetoric disappeared from the pages of local newspapers, and features on shared interests and positive activities became increasingly common. "The Finnish people of the district have a well-deserved reputation for successful and pleasing picnics and sports days," enthused the *Advance* in the summer of 1927 in a typical comment. And instead of blaming foreigners for taking jobs from Canadians, now an item in the *Northern Miner* noted, "When the first blush of mining had faded it was found that the more laborious work of the industry had fallen largely into the hands of foreigners, so-called Italians, Finns, Swedes, Slovaks of various nationalities, men who were not afraid to tackle heavy work and to live under rather hard conditions." Canadians, the writer observed, "did not take very kindly to hard mining work."[78] While people may not have directly pointed to the Great War as a moment of reconsideration, it is clear that slowly and almost imperceptibly, public discourse among the majority group was beginning to shift.

As war threatened again in Europe in the late 1930s, the images of heroism and self-sacrifice that had been constructed came head to head with a new reality. At first, events were seen through the warm glow of Great War mythology. As noted, the *Advance* ran regular editorials through 1939 that reported on the unfortunate yet brave Finnish people in their struggle against Russia – and it repeated the theme as Poland fell to the Germans. But when France fell, the shock of reality blew away the fantasies of the Anglo-French population. In the words of one, "Suddenly the war became real and terrible."[79] Proposals were floated to form a local regiment, to form an all-Polish regiment, to form an all-French-speaking unit. Before any of these plans had been attempted, young men began to enlist, and the first organized contingent of sixty-nine left Timmins on 9 May 1940.[80] Others rallied to the Algonquin Regiment, which at the beginning of the war consisted of some 250 militiamen based at Cobalt. By 4 September 1940 they had sufficient numbers to depart for Camp Borden, and eventually fought their way across Belgium and Holland.[81] Women organized in churches and ad hoc groups to raise money and arrange "comforts" to send to the troops. This time, to an even greater extent than during the First World War, there was cooperation and outreach among these groups. In South Porcupine, the Finnish women initially rallied to raise money for the Finnish Red Cross, but when London was bombed in the terrible blitz of 1941, the Finnish women held their teas and concerts to raise money for the English victims.[82] At Iroquois Falls, a variety of women's groups formed a joint committee for war projects.[83] The area's MP, J.A. Bradette, proposed that one of the new corvettes that were coming off the assembly line in 1941 be named HMCS *Timmins* to honour both the family and the town. Under the town's "sponsorship" the *Timmins* became a focal point for community spirit and pride, particularly in the fall of 1942 when it began escort duty off the east coast for merchant navy convoys.[84]

The Second World War brought even more visible changes to the region than the first war had. Victory Loan campaigns were pursued with vigour, officials pitting the towns against one another in an effort to spur donations. "Monster parades" were held, with the participation of everyone, from the Ontario Provincial Police to the Boy Scouts. The old demonstration farm buildings at Monteith, which had served briefly as a prison, were turned into an internment camp where several thousand Germans and other prisoners of war were held. A smaller camp at Timmins was set up toward the end of the war to house prisoners who did bushwork for Abitibi Power and Paper and the Rudolph McChesney Lumber Company. The interned German soldiers provided a new "other" for local animosity. One Iroquois Falls citizen later recalled, "The acrimony that existed in connection with this matter was deep and lasted long, particularly in our little town which was losing many of its sons at that very moment."[85] High schools at Iroquois Falls and Timmins organized cadet corps. In 1942, when the Government of Canada decided that gold mining was not a necessary part of the war effort, it asked mines in Timmins and Kirkland Lake to release 700 workers to INCO for employment in the nickel mines of the Sudbury region. The Porcupine Camp supplied the bulk of the requested workforce, and many of these men took pride in doing what they considered to be war work.[86] From that point, the gold mines began to struggle because they could no longer obtain the necessary supplies for new equipment or basic repairs and maintenance. Everything from ventilation units to steel plates was designated for other purposes deemed central to the war effort. It was soon apparent to everyone dependent on the gold-mining sector that wartime sacrifices were going to mean much more than food rations or donations to the Red Cross. But there was surprisingly little grumbling – in public, at least – as people rallied to make collective sacrifices to win the war.

While events originating outside the region had an impact on how people might cooperate with one another, events generated internally also became opportunities to bridge some of the socio-economic divisions. Some of these events were deliberately staged to encourage socialization; many others began as one-time entertainments but proved so popular that they eventually became expected local rituals. The gradual evolution of shared experience became an important part of community building. The South Porcupine dog-team race was one of the first of these activities (see chapter 7). Although it began as something of a lark to occupy the time of a small circle of friends, it soon attracted attention, evolved into an annual event, and expanded into a full-scale winter carnival, recognized beyond the immediate region. "Porcupine Dog Derby Has Become One of Events of Historic Import to North," proclaimed the Cobalt *Daily Nugget.*[87]

Another event that provided the base for local legend was a one-time adventure that nicely fed a growing sense of local identity. In 1939 Pete Spence of Timmins proposed to paddle a canoe from Timmins to New York City, where the world's fair was being held. Provided with official letters of greeting from the town to present to New York's mayor, Fiorello A. La Guardia, he set off in his "birch" canoe. His progress was followed locally with intense interest. At one point, he disappeared for two weeks when crossing Lake Champlain, and the Porcupine Camp's anxiety level rose perceptibly. Finally, after three months, he paddled down the Hudson River to the city and "portaged his canoe up Broadway" in a moment of triumph for all northerners. Spence's ability to conquer the rigours of the trip while paddling that distance and the fact that he ran out of food and "almost starved" were celebrated as evidence of northern hardiness and character.[88] Everyone shared in the achievement.

A slightly (perhaps only slightly) less rigorous activity was the annual ritual of the Turkey Stag. The first in the region appears to have been held in 1922 at St Anthony's Roman Catholic Church, but the idea spread to Iroquois Falls, South Porcupine, and eventually to Matheson. Apparently it was initially a way to provide Christmas dinner in a family atmosphere for the dozens of single men in the area, but it evolved into a charity fundraiser and a roaring good time. Over its history, different fraternal organizations made the arrangements, including the Knights of Columbus, the Moose, and the Legion. Men of all ages were invited to a supper (sometimes advertised as "all you can eat"), where they played cards, participated in competitions such as moustache growing, step-dancing, or harmonica playing, and bought tickets for a turkey raffle to raise funds for the less fortunate at Christmas. The evening "represented all classes and creeds working together for the common good," wrote the *Advance* of the first Turkey Stag at Matheson in 1936. The claim does not appear to have been much exaggerated. That event was held in the Orange Hall, but the organization committee included two members of the Roman Catholic Knights of Columbus; and at the 1927 stag in Timmins, the list of prizewinners included men with French, Italian, and Finnish names.[89]

Labour Day became another opportunity for annual community gatherings. Initially, Labour Day celebrations took place on 1 May, in keeping with the tradition of the international labour movement, and consisted mostly of parades, with banners and songs organized by the Western Federation of Miners. By the 1920s, however, the activities had been moved to the first weekend in September and had lost most of the overt socialist overtones as more moderate labour leaders appropriated the event. Iroquois Falls led the way, with the various unions at Abitibi organizing a sports day with prizes and refreshments. Timmins followed suit, and for many years the towns took turns hosting the activities, including picnics and games. Special trains brought the participants to the host town. The events in Iroquois Falls appear to have been the most popular, for at Timmins and South Porcupine the ongoing bitter divisions in the labour movement meant that dedicated socialist Finns and Ukrainians persisted in their May Day celebrations, particularly through the 1930s,[90] and occasionally the September activities in Timmins were cancelled for lack of interest.

Other pan-community events were created to mark local anniversaries that were "meaningful" dates for various reasons. Twenty-five years after the Porcupine gold rush of 1909, mine managers and leading business-men decided to hold a week-long Anniversary Fair to celebrate their achievements. When both the Ontario and Quebec ministers of mines agreed to attend, the event took on the stamp of an official celebration. Some 20,000 people eventually participated in the midway, exhibits, and numerous competitions, which included mucking, drilling, first aid, and "bathing beauties."[91] The *Porcupine Advance* discovered the "old timer," defined as a person who had been in the Porcupine Camp before the fire of 1911 – or, at the very least, before the First World War. As will be dis-cussed in the next chapter, the old timer (whose status had nothing to do with age) was gradually constructed as a symbol of community identity. Anniversaries, of course, are arbitrary, and four years later, Timmins decided to host another twenty-fifth anniversary, this time a silver jubilee to commemorate the founding of the town. The Timmins Lions Club wanted to raise funds for a new community centre, so it piggy-backed its fundraiser to the idea of the anniversary, creating the Timmins Silver Jubilee and Porcupine Old Home Week. The Lions Club produced an attractive booklet entitled *The Book of Timmins and the Porcupine*, in which the hardy pioneer builders of the community were celebrated in text and photograph.[92] Participants in a grand banquet listened to speeches from the area's politicians, along with those of religious leaders from the Jewish synagogue and the Romanian Orthodox church, and representatives of the Ukrainian, French, and British population. A week of sporting events, concerts, picnics, and dances drew crowds from the entire district. Two years later, the thirtieth anniversary of the Porcupine gold rush provided yet another opportunity for sports competitions, dancing, a carnival, and this time a "monster bingo."[93] While all these anniversaries were clearly organized by the usual professional-managerial-business coalition, the type of activity was designed to appeal to a broad audience, and the large number of participants and spectators make it clear that the events brought together a much wider spectrum of people than was represented on the steering committees. People played together, listened to the same music, and were made to feel that they were part of a community with a strong sense of history, importance, and unique identity.

Perhaps the most important shared experience across the region was the increasingly regular rhythm of daily life and work. In its repetition, there was a growing awareness of the sameness between one's neighbour's expe-rience and one's own. In a population that consisted overwhelmingly of people in blue-collar jobs, the strength of numbers made it possible to immerse oneself completely in that life and see it as a positive factor – not just something to put up with on the road to acquiring a "superior" middle-class status. Of course, there were exceptions, like the Italian mother who stressed the need for education so that her son would not have to endure the dangers of underground mine work like his father.[94] But in many families, sons followed the paths of their fathers, and daughters their mothers, reproducing the daily rhythms across the generations and giving them a sense of depth, permanency, and value. Given the realities of the region's economic base, the sense of permanence was an illusion, but illusions can shape people's behaviour just as effectively as realities.

A sense of camaraderie in the workplace seems to have begun in a shared understanding of what it meant to be a man. Physical strength, endurance, courage, independence, the ability to drink enormous quantities of alcohol, and a store of stories about sexual prowess defined masculinity in the bush camps and mines, as Ian Radforth and Nancy Forestell have demonstrated for Northern Ontario, and Adele Perry for British Columbia.[95] I have been less successful in determining how the mill workers at Abitibi saw themselves, but the occasional hint seems to suggest that it was much the same as in other sectors of the region's workforce. Farm men, of course, led much more solitary working lives and thus had less opportunity to display or reinforce their sense of manliness among their peers; but farmers who spent seasons in the bush camps certainly participated in the culture of manliness. Indeed, the "pioneer" work of clearing and building a farm could be a tremendous source of pride – not only in the accomplishment of building something from "nothing," but also for the ability to endure the physical hardship implicit in such an undertaking.

Men's sense of manliness was also reflected and reinforced by their recreational activities. First and foremost was the camaraderie of the bottle. Whether in a public bar (licensed or not) or in a boarding house common room, alcohol provided a focal point for leisure time, easing the awkwardness among new acquaintances or dulling anxieties about a new life. It opened a space where the shift boss could be excluded and forgotten (or mocked), giving the mucker or construction worker a sense of personal empowerment. And it was an opportunity to define, display, and reinforce the workingman's sense of masculinity. In stories about sexual conquest and performance, bush skills in hunting or fishing, jokes about the shortcomings of the middle class, or drinking contests, men tested themselves as individuals but at the same time created bonds with others.[96] Gambling, another popular pastime, served much the same purpose. Anything and everything could be used for betting, from the current hockey contest to the next horse race at Dalton's. Perhaps for men who gambled their lives on every dangerous shift or cutting season in the bush, a bet on a sports outcome was a safe outlet that gave them a sense of control. Perhaps it was yet another opportunity to display superior "knowledge" in correctly anticipating the outcome. Or perhaps it was simply an opportunity to make extra money for little effort. Whatever the purpose, gambling pitted individual against individual but brought the participants together in a common cause.

Sporting events, as has been discussed, also became an important focal point for both community and masculine identity. Sporting activity tended to be divided along class lines: golf for the middle class, hockey for the workers; participating in amateur events for the middle class, being spectator at semi-professional events for the workers. Given the small size of the middle class, however, the workers' attitudes and behaviour came to define the norm for sports participation. Formally organized sporting events were particularly important for the role they played in bringing people together from the small towns across the region, and hence across the barriers that tended to separate the economic sectors. As was described in chapter 7, the Northern Ontario Hockey Association was probably the most important in this regard. But the annual Labour Day tournaments that pitted baseball players from Iroquois Falls against those from Timmins or South Porcupine also were significant, as were curling bonspiels and the occasional baseball contests. Play allowed not only an outlet for social tensions but also a space in which personal friendships and a sense of shared experience could develop.

Finally, a sense of siege made unlikely alliances in the region. Elsewhere in Ontario, Anglo-Protestant hostility toward Roman Catholics and French-language speakers had become a deeply engrained part of local culture. But in Porcupine–Iroquois Falls, English- and French-speaking Canadians began to forge something of an alliance to counter the various threats which the "foreigners" were believed to bring. Here in the northeast, unlike in southern Ontario, the non-British population was sufficiently large to be noticed and sufficiently aggressive in defence of its rights and interests to be considered a threat to the authority of both middle-class and blue-collar Canadians. So with a common "enemy," French- and English-speaking Canadians tried to work in a common cause. It was certainly an uneasy alliance, with the French-speaking Canadians making more concessions than the English, but there was a degree of solidarity that was surprising to see at all, and certainly it was very different from relationships between the groups that were developing in Sudbury to the south or Kapuskasing to the north.

Probably because the French-speaking population was so large, it was the business sector that first moved to public rapprochement. After all, a customer was a customer. In the early 1920s, "help wanted" advertisements for store clerks began to solicit those who could speak both French and English. The New Empire Theatre screened French motion pictures from time to time in its early years, and in the 1930s it screened French and English films on alternate nights. The *Porcupine Advance* printed occasional advertisements in French, and then the *Daily Press* went one better and published a special French supplement sponsored by retailers on each St Jean Baptiste Day (June 24). The *Advance* responded with a regular French-language social column during its final years of publication in the 1940s. French also appeared on the airwaves almost from the beginning, with the radio station CKGB broadcasting a French-language newscast from 1934.

Politicians were quick to recognize the value of the French vote, and bilingual candidates placed French advertisements in the newspaper to solicit support, and they made sure that there were French speeches at their meetings. The original municipal building in Timmins had a bilingual sign, and there was much local protest when the new building did not. A special meeting was called to discuss what to do with the stone engraved only with the words "Municipal Building."[97] French-speaking citizens were well represented on municipal councils, particularly in Timmins, Iroquois Falls, and Ansonville/Calvert Township. Indeed, in 1934, the majority of members on Timmins Town Council were French-speaking. When the Timmins Ratepayers' Association was formed in 1919 to challenge the coalition of managers and businessmen who were running the town, Joseph Thériault and Hyacinthe Charlebois were among the five-member executive council, which was led by labour leader (and Englishman) William De Feu.[98] Public administrative bodies also had French-speaking members right from the beginning. The first Timmins Board of Health, for example, consisted of Messers Peters (chair), Belanger, Coyne, Martin, Mascioli, and Sauvé. And when Mayor Reuben Richardson selected the members of his 1935 "striking committee" (which chose other committees), he jokingly remarked that he had chosen a French, an English, and an Irish member to ensure fairness to the local constituencies.[99] It may have been humour used to disarm a critic, but it did reflect a sensitivity to the importance of the French-speaking population.

In small communities, individuals willing to participate in a public capacity were welcomed from both language groups. The first officers of the Timmins Victorian Order of Nurses included Father Thériault and other clergy from the major churches, and two of the five lay members of the executive were French-speaking.[100] Some French speakers seem to have been in particular demand. J. Emile Brunette, it will be recalled, came from River Joseph, Quebec, to work for Hollinger before he started a taxi business with his brother. He parlayed that business into an automobile dealership and began his public service in the parish of St Antoine (and its Knights of Columbus), then he served in the Lions Club, and finally as an elected member of Timmins Town Council in 1937. He was first elected mayor in 1940 and was re-elected repeatedly until 1947. He made no attempt to hide his cultural roots, telling the *Advance* at one point that his "favourite pastime" was to visit his farm in Quebec, and he freely advertised his active role in the cultural-nationalist organization, Le cercle canadien.[101] Another francophone, Hyacinthe Charlebois, somehow managed to be appointed to both the first Timmins separate school board and the first public school board (as well as to the first high school board).[102]

In the workplace, where men had daily contact with others from the range of ethnic groups represented in the region, the French-English alliance was manifested in different ways. Edmund Bradwin observed that in the railway construction camps of 1910–15 there were "two distinct groups of workers," defined by the men as "whites" and "foreigners." The "whites," according to Bradwin, defined themselves as English and French Canadians, British immigrants, and Americans, with a few Scandinavians and the occasional Finn who had distinguished himself through his skill. The "foreigners" were dismissed by the "whites" as "Bohunks," "Hunkies," and "Douks."[103] Historian Laurel Sefton MacDowell believed that a similar division existed among northern miners, and that one of the major barriers to union solidarity among them "was a split between the foreign workers on the one hand and the English and French workers on the other hand." A Timmins labour supporter proposed in 1937 that the local union problem was rooted not so much in political differences as in the fact that "Canadians" were unwilling to accept Ukrainian leadership in the movement.[104] Certainly, part of the English-French alliance was based on the perception that the "foreigners" posed a cultural (as well as economic) threat. But the element of political difference should not be dismissed entirely. The strength of anti-communism among the French-speaking Canadians, reinforced and supported from the pulpit, provided common ground with English-speaking Canadians, who also saw communism as a threat to the individualistic, entrepreneurial spirit that they valued so highly and that had, in many cases, brought them north in the first place. The vigour with which communist-supporters pursued their cause in the region was clearly seen as a threat that warranted unprecedented alliances. The popular mayor Emile Brunette was once described as "half French, half Irish, all Canadian – and a vehement anti-Communist."[105]

The nature of the English-French alliance in the region is perhaps best illustrated through the events of the First World War. Across Canada, and especially in southern Ontario, as the war dragged on, enlistments declined and supporters of the war effort began to point accusing fingers at those still at home. Allegations were raised that French-speaking Canadians had failed in their duty to king and country. Interestingly, none of this acrimony seems to have developed in Porcupine–Iroquois Falls (though it did elsewhere in Northern Ontario). As in other parts of Canada, the first to enlist in the region were mostly recent immigrants from the British Isles – like Albert McGrath at Porquis Junction, who was actually still in the British army reserve while a resident of Canada.[106] But as the Canadian-born began to volunteer, French-speakers were prominently among them – for instance, Adlore Ducharme and Félix Bourdignon of Timmins, who signed up in the first recruiting drive of 1915, and the Desulnier brothers of South Porcupine, who joined the 159th Battalion in 1916. Indeed, in the first week of March 1916, half of the twenty-five men from Timmins and South Porcupine who joined that unit were French-speaking.[107] At a recruiting rally for the 228th Battalion in 1917, organizers estimated that half the audience spoke French, and claims were made that the first volunteer from Timmins had, in fact, been a French Canadian.[108] It appears that the question of francophone contribution to the war effort was not even considered worthy of discussion, for when the *Porcupine Advance* detailed the names, occupations, and nationalities of the first hundred men to enlist with the 2nd Battalion of the Pioneers, it did not bother to break down the category of "Canadian," though the English, Scots, and Irish were listed separately.[109] Early in 1917, the *Advance* ran its first comment on the issue in an editorial entitled "The French-Canadians and the War." Reports had been received, noted the editor, of "much anxiety" in Canada about the French Canadian contribution to the war effort. "From Ontario and the West the French-Canadians have gladly gone by the thousands," went the editorial. "If they have not gone from Quebec Province, it is only because they do not know, because they do not understand, because bold, false leaders have misled them."[110] Clearly, as far as the newspaper was concerned, loyalty and commitment to the cause was simply a non-issue among the French Canadians of Northern Ontario generally, and of Porcupine–Iroquois Falls in particular.

Of course, the rapprochement between French and English Canadians worked best when there was a common threat. At other times, mutual suspicion lurked below the surface, and the francophones tacitly acknowledged the tenuous alliance by being careful to appear conciliatory. Le cercle canadien at Timmins periodically endorsed certain candidates in the municipal elections, apparently without raising hackles. Then, in 1935, the *Daily Press* hinted at an ethnic political conspiracy afoot in these activities, and the representatives U. Aubry and J. Leclerc felt compelled to make a public statement to reassure English voters.[111] When the Roman Catholic parish became involved in the co-op movement in the 1940s, one of its directors reportedly later recalled, "We tried not to be too French."[112] Interestingly, for some of the area's francophones, the biggest cultural threat was not English-speaking Canadians. In 1951, Yves Langevin, the Timmins-based editor of a regional journal called *L'observateur du Nouvel Ontario*, explained that a French-language periodical was necessary because French Canadian families in the region were perpetually in danger of being swamped by a "wave of Americanism."[113]

Specific issues that arose over time provided flashpoints around which people could rally, sometimes initiating collective action and sometimes contributing to a sense of community in response. These flashpoints included the question of management of economic development tools (for example, railway and road construction), Prohibition, taxation policy, French Catholic education rights, and the ongoing problem of the failure of northern agriculture. These issues solidified into symbols that could conjure up considerable emotional response with the incantation of just a few catchwords. Insiders "knew" what was meant, so even the language of these debates provided a device for community formation. A strong sense of grievance was established surprisingly quickly at the core of this sense of identity.

In 1908 indignant residents of Cobalt met to protest decisions being made in Queen's Park and Bay Street regarding the development of the region. "The railway provided a focal point for grievances," wrote historian Albert Tucker, "against the hold of the impersonal financial tentacles of imperial Toronto into the northern country."[114] A secessionist movement was proclaimed and soon spread to Sudbury. Northern Ontario must become a province in its own right in order to protect its own interests. The idea was not new. In 1891 James Stobie had proclaimed its necessity in the pages of the Sudbury *Journal*,[115] and the heat with which the Lakehead (now Thunder Bay) endorsed the idea forced a group of politicians to tour the region in the late 1890s to smooth the waters.[116] In spite of the ridicule heaped on the movement of 1908 by a Sudbury doctor who predicted "We shall likely see in the supplementary estimates a large appropriation for a mammoth lunatic asylum in New Ontario,"[117] the language of grievance set the tone for secessionist movements in 1919–21, 1935, 1939, 1950 (and later in the 1970s). It also proved useful during debates over a variety of issues in which secession was not an option. The main themes were that southerners did not "understand" the North, the South was getting rich at the expense of the North, and northern economic and social woes were the fault of southerners. The imagery attempted to give moral authority to what was essentially a raw power struggle as economic boosters of the new economy in the North attempted to direct it to maximize their personal returns. But the rhetoric seized the imagination of the wider public and became part of a more diffuse sense of public good. A cynic might claim that it was because the small businessmen cloaked their self-interest in the mantle of populism (as when the *Advance* trumpeted, "The People's Railway not for the People")[118] and that others were sucked into the propaganda vortex. But whatever the explanation, the ideas clearly caught on more generally and were guaranteed an important place at election time, whether it was municipal, provincial, or dominion votes that were at stake.

Control over the instruments of economic development was the first flashpoint. Before the gold rush into Porcupine, Cobalt residents were already complaining that the train schedules did not meet their needs, that there were insufficient cars for both freight and passenger traffic, that the freight rates were unreasonably high, and, above all, that the terms accorded the Temiskaming and Northern Ontario Railway made it essentially a monopoly and shut other entrepreneurs out of the potentially lucrative business. As gold finds were reported farther north, locals began to call for more railway construction, and even before politicians in Toronto had been convinced that the Porcupine rush might turn out to be of lasting value, Porcupine hopefuls were demanding a rail link between the camp and the TNO main line. Plans for the pulp and paper plant on the Abitibi River also raised questions about railway access. A group of Sudbury entrepreneurs got in on the action, and collaborative lobbying between the Toronto and Sudbury boards of trade called for a new railway to be built from Sudbury to Porcupine. Apparently, these campaigns were not taken very seriously by TNO management, for in a February 1912 letter marked "Private," the TNO chairman J.L. Englehart wrote sarcastically to the railway's chief engineer, "You will want to get at least three or four of these maps, and you want to go very carefully (pardon me) over whole of correspondence, and if there is room enough on map (do try to find it), you want to outline (even if the lines are imaginary), every blessed railway that good people of Northland, and outside of Northland, want – immediately – constructed."[119] If northerners had any idea of the ridicule, it is perhaps not surprising that the emotional tone of their responses seemed to increase as time went on. Certainly, they had a whipping boy in mining engineer Arthur A. Cole, whom the TNO commissioned periodically to investigate the claims of promoters in Cobalt, Porcupine, and other places. "If there is one Engineer more than another that is conservative," noted Englehart gleefully at one point, "it is A.A. Cole; so much so, that in early days, Cole was the best hated man in any of the Camps."[120] The TNO link to Porcupine was, of course, soon constructed, and it seems to have been constructed with considerable dispatch, being officially opened in June 1911 after six months' work.

Then the ante was upped. In 1919 another Northern Ontario delegation went to Toronto to promote the extension of the TNO to James Bay (to provide a seaport) and to encourage the construction of a network of branch lines connecting to trunk roads in order to expedite development.[121] When rumours circulated that year that the provincial government was contemplating the sale of the TNO, northerners were outraged. As the *Porcupine Advance* put it, "The T.N.&O. despite any faults it may have had is too valuable an asset of the Province to be allowed to be sold." As part of the national railway system, the writer proposed, it would just become a link in the east-west development chain, bypassing and abandoning development in Northern Ontario.[122] Then, when the provincial government announced its commitment to a James Bay extension of the TNO, local boosters expressed their dissatisfaction with the slow pace of construction. Indeed, *L'Abitibi*, a French-language newspaper published in Cochrane, actually dropped its deep-rooted support for the Liberal Party for a time over the issue.[123] In keeping with concerns about railway policy decisions, northerners also kept careful watch over appointments to the TNO railway commission. When Colonel J.I. McLaren of Hamilton and Colonel L.T. Martin of Ottawa and Renfrew were appointed in 1921, the *Porcupine Advance* howled in outrage. There should be northerners on the commission, it proclaimed. "No one can understand the North Land and its needs without residence for some considerable time in the country." Such people "know its needs, they get the spirit of the country and its people."[124]

Control over transportation policies brought the industrial towns and the homesteaders into common cause, although the emphasis for industry was railway access, while the farmers wanted roads. In 1912, the Northern Development Act provided for $5 million to construct colonization roads; within months, about 5,000 men (some of them convict labour) were employed on the project. Under the direction of J.F. Whitson, the new Northern Development Branch intended to lay out the usual concession lines and main roads to connect the most promising farm areas to the TNO line and nearby towns.[125] The branch was inundated with requests for roads and bridges; it is not surprising that many whose requests were not granted began to express the same criticism of distant government as had been expressed in railway politics. Even when roads were completed, there were complaints about their quality. Most roads were little more than cut lines through the bush, and as R.E. Hore described for readers of the *Canadian Mining Journal*, "When first cut the roadway looks promising enough ... After a little use and a few heavy showers, however, it is evident that the ordinary ungraded bush road cannot be relied upon even for occasional service. Once wet, the roads never become dry and firm again, and the effect of a really dry spell is but to make the clay more sticky."[126]

The provincial government took quite a different view. In its 1911 annual report, the Department of Public Works claimed to have "produced an exceptionally high class of Colonization Road." While it admitted these roads were "not by any means up to the finished standard of an ideal country road," it noted that "they can be extended, connected and developed" as the need arose.[127] An anonymous report sent to Toronto's Conservative *Mail & Empire* went even further in its enthusiasm: "I would mention those splendid Whitson roads." "Not even the most careless or indifferent traveller can fail to observe those great wide arteries that penetrate in such direct lines, the dense spruce bush, both east and west from the line of the T.N.&O. Railway."[128] Statements like these outraged northerners; the more exaggerated the government propaganda, the more virulent the response. The *Porcupine Advance* repeatedly published stories like that of a Mountjoy Township farmer who lived less than two and a half kilometres from Timmins but could not market any of his produce because there was no road access.[129] Figures were produced to compare the allegedly massive expenditure on southern roads in contrast to the mere pittance spent in the North. These complaints were soon followed by the refrain that Old Ontario was actually getting the money for southern development out of the riches being sucked from Northern Ontario. As one editorial in the *Porcupine Advance* put it in 1921, "The North land is not objecting so much to the fact that the government alias Mr. Drury, is spending so much money. The kick here is more how and where he gets the money and how and where he spends it." For good measure, it added, "The North is being milked dry to gorge the south."[130]

Complaints about government development policies also became embroiled with complaints about access to patronage – perhaps an inevitable conflation, give the nature of the Canadian political system. Who got the employment, who was awarded the contracts, and who received favourable treatment on the job were all matters for grievance. Here, both business people and labourers had common cause. And in the mid–1930s the question generated a local *cause célèbre*. John Rowlandson, a general storekeeper and small buyer of pulpwood and timber at Porquis Junction, ran for election in 1934 (as a Liberal) in a campaign that largely emphasized "corruption" in the administration of the Northern Development Branch. It was being widely claimed that the branch had become "a political machine"[131] in which money and largesse were distributed freely to Conservative Party friends by "that confounded Finlayson"[132] (William Finlayson, minister of lands and forests). Certainly, there was solid ground for some of the dissatisfaction. Rhetoric aside, historian Peter Oliver probably put it rather too delicately when he described the Northern Development Branch under Conservative Premier Howard Ferguson: "A vision is conjured up of government agents, discreetly doubling as party workers, scurrying about in the north in search of worthwhile projects for government largesse. Despite scattered protests, the development funds were still allotted in a lump sum without scrutiny in departmental estimates ... The opposition itself seemed disinclined to ask hard questions about even the most dubious practices."[133] A businessman in Goderich was more blunt. In passing along some information from "a friend in Northern Ontario" to Liberal leader Mitchell Hepburn, he reported, "There seems to be a sort

of terrorism practised up there."[134] In 1930, the MP for Nipissing produced sworn statements in the House of Commons to the effect that men
who wanted provincial government work "in Northern Ontario were
obliged to swear before a Notary that they had voted Conservative before
they were given pay cheques."[135] There were more sinister allegations,
including a story that one storekeeper had threatened to cut off food supplies if people didn't vote Conservative and that only Conservative-voting
farmers were entitled to have road access built.[136]

Playing into these rumours, John Rowlandson handily defeated the
Conservative incumbent, A.F. Kennedy, in the 1934 election. Indeed, the
province as a whole chose to replace the Conservative government of
Howard Ferguson with a Liberal one under Mitchell Hepburn. Rowlandson's constituents widely expected a clean sweep of the Northern Development Branch, but when nothing materialized they began to grumble
about Rowlandson. Perhaps in a pre-emptive strike, Rowlandson became a
sort of one-man opposition to his own government – "a stormy petrel in
the Liberal ranks," according to the *Mail & Empire*[137] – for he demanded
a full inquiry into the operations of the branch in the riding of South
Cochrane. The government obliged, appointing a commission under
William Belmont Common in mid-May 1935; it became locally known as
the Matheson Inquiry. Common held a series of hearings in Matheson
between 5 and 14 June, listening to 44 witnesses and collecting 2,100
folios of evidence.[138]

The complaints laid before the inquiry seem so petty and pointless that
one might be more than a little perplexed about why it was such an emotional flashpoint in its day. Even Commissioner Common dismissed most
of what he heard: that a foreman on the South Porcupine road crew had
been seen intoxicated, that a private home had been connected to a government-owned hydro generating plant, that a man had been spotted
doing relief work in someone else's name, and that there were personality
conflicts among the staff at the branch's Matheson office. Yet as the
Toronto *Star* reported, one of the hearings was "a stormy session punctuated by angry outbursts from spectators and frequent disorders."[139] It
seems that people had become highly frustrated at the deteriorating
regional economy and felt helpless as they watched their farms failing, the
paper industry struggling, and railway business declining. They blamed
"southern" government for failing to act, for failing to understand, and for
failing to turn over the reins of power so that northerners could do the job
properly.

While the battle for control of regional economic development focused
most tightly and persistently on the issue of roads and railways, the question of deriving public revenue from natural resource extraction came in
a close second. Mining policy was a particularly contested ground. The real

point was a demand from Timmins, Tisdale Township, and other municipalities to derive revenue from the mining property located within their
boundaries. But the issue was expressed in less self-interested terms: the
people of the North had a right to the profits of their labour and "their"
resources; it should not all be siphoned away to government pockets in
Toronto and Ottawa – and, worse, to southern industrialists.

The history of mining taxation in Ontario is a complex one. In 1891, the
Ontario government legislated a royalty of 3 percent on all silver, nickel,
and copper ores produced from crown lands (and 2 percent on iron ores),
although Philip Smith, in his history of Ontario mining, says that the
province "collected nary a dollar from mining royalties" before the system
was abolished in 1900.[140] The system was replaced in 1906 with a sliding
scale of royalties on ores taken within the TNO right-of-way, affecting primarily Cobalt silver mines. Then in 1907 the Conservative government of
James P. Whitney introduced a revenue bill (which was eventually incorporated into the Mining Tax Act) that levied taxes on mining company
profits: a 3 percent tax on profits between $10,000 and $1 million, and 5
percent tax on profits over $1 million. The legislation committed one-
third of the revenue raised to municipalities that had mines within their
boundaries, and (after some hearty lobbying) the government agreed to
make a special case for Cobalt because of its unusually "rocky site"; here,
fully half of the mining tax revenues would go to the municipality.[141] But
municipalities were not authorized to collect any revenue from mining
property located within their town boundaries.

Not only were municipalities excluded from direct taxation of mining
activity, but many outside the mining companies felt that mining in
Ontario was relatively lightly taxed under these provincial policies. Indeed,
in 1930, the deputy minister of mines, Thomas Gibson, produced a report
that claimed Ontario's mines enjoyed some of the lowest taxes in the
world.[142] As a result, the amounts of money in question were quite small.
In 1914, for example, Hollinger paid just under $29,000 in tax (the
second-highest in the province after the Canadian Copper Company at
Sudbury), and Dome paid just over $7,000.[143] Nevertheless, the mining
companies complained constantly about the onerous tax burden, and the
municipalities complained just as constantly that they were getting none of
the supposed riches that were being generated.

The issue heated up in the mid-1930s. Early in the decade, the provincial government revised its tax regime on gold mines in a way that essentially lowered the rates. Unfortunately, the wording of the change was
unclear. There was to be a tax of 1½ percent on profits up to $2.33 million
and "an additional one per centum" on profits above that. The towns of
Timmins and Kirkland Lake read the new regulations to mean that a *total*
of 2½ percent tax was due on the higher profits, while the gold mines

claimed they were required to pay only 1 percent. The municipalities took the issue to court in 1935, and both the district court and the appeal went in favour of the mines' interpretation.[144] Meanwhile, in 1934 the dominion government had introduced a "gold tax" of its own on the bullion produced. The mining companies and the provincial government complained bitterly, but there was little the local communities could really do. Locally, the federal-provincial dispute over the gold bullion tax[145] was probably most significant for its contribution to the rhetoric that was generated by Premier Mitch Hepburn – rhetoric that adapted easily to local concerns. It was in the "public interest," proposed Hepburn, that the people of Ontario should benefit from resource development. Besides, it was the provincial (not dominion) government that had invested in the infrastructure that made gold mining feasible. Northern Ontario residents agreed – but only that it was in their own "public interest," not that of the province more generally. "The mining boom expanded demands for municipal services," historians Matt Bray and Ross Danaker interpreted the argument, "but did nothing to provide much-needed additional municipal income."[146] The *Porcupine Advance* proposed, "All the royalties from the gold mines here should in fairness be paid over by the Government to the Town of Timmins. Anything else is unfair to a mining town and to the people who take a chance to build up such towns."[147] Indeed, the mining tax issue encouraged a shrinking definition of "North" and "northerner." When the mayor of North Bay took a leading role in a booster campaign sponsored by the Union of Northern Ontario Boards of Trade and Municipalities, the *Porcupine Advance* complained that control had slipped to a representative of one of the "old southern towns of New Ontario" – that North Bay was "more of the type of Old Ontario towns" that didn't understand the needs of the real North, where the mining took place.[148]

Hydroelectricity was another lively issue. Power generation stations had been built by some of the big companies (or their subsidiaries) primarily for industrial use, but electricity from these plants was also sold to individuals and to the towns. A campaign for cheaper rates through government ownership was initiated in 1923 by some mining investors, and in 1926 the *Northern Miner* joined the game. Initially, the campaign focused on the costs to the mines, but soon the argument was being expressed more broadly in terms of costs to the municipalities of Timmins and Cochrane (allegedly twelve cents per kilowatt hour in Timmins compared with two cents in Toronto).[149] The *Porcupine Advance* expanded the question further: "To-day, the power situation is the one factor that is holding this country back from unprecedented progress and development."[150] Once again, the North was being hindered by southern policy. Then, in 1932, the Abitibi Power and Paper subsidiary that was developing the massive

Abitibi Canyon hydro project declared bankruptcy. The provincial government responded by beginning the process of integrating electrical-production facilities in northeastern Ontario into the provincially owned Hydro-Electric Power Commission – and northerners found new reason to complain. At first, the change was welcome, particularly since it brought electricity to Matheson for the first time (late in 1935).[151] It also meant considerable construction employment, for the power commission spent over $50 million on hydro development projects across Northern Ontario in 1939–40. In 1944–45 the commission purchased the last of the privately owned plants in the region (including those on the Mattagami River that supplied Timmins and the mines).[152] But in 1950, when the entire system was finally connected to the southern Ontario power grid, the proverbial dam burst. Timmins Town Council petitioned Premier Leslie Frost, complaining that northern electricity was bypassing northern towns en route to the South and that the mines had been unable to purchase sufficient power to keep the men employed. The power commission chairman, R.A. Saunders, countered in a radio broadcast that Northern Ontario's power system would not "lose its identity by reason of this interchange of power."[153] Whether the power was publicly owned or not, the issue was turned into a North versus South competition, with aggrieved northerners once again suffering at the hands of rapacious and anonymous southern interests.

Other issues, social rather than economic, also played a role in uniting the people of Porcupine–Iroquois Falls to rally in a common cause. Chief among these was Prohibition. The "liquor question" convulsed Ontario as a whole for more than a generation, but it took on a unique form in Northern Ontario. First, while there was a clear urban-rural split on the issue, just as in southern Ontario (with the industrial towns of Iroquois Falls and Timmins decisively "wet" and rural areas, including Matheson, firmly "dry"), anti-Prohibitionists in the region chose to see the issue as – once again – evidence of fundamental difference between North and South. "There was nothing approaching an organized agitation for secession until April of 1921," recalled the *Advance*, "when the province voted for the prohibition of the manufacture, importation and sale of alcoholic liquors. The North voted differently to the rest of Ontario." For good measure, it added, "The vote seemed to give a striking illustration of the fact that the North and the South were widely apart in their ideas."[154] The Temperance Act was so reviled that no one seemed to object to the regular and relatively open breaches of it that followed. "The law was so much against the spirit of the North that it had serious effect in lessening respect for the law," commented the *Advance* in 1935. "People in the North appeared to take a delight in circumventing the law."[155] Breaking the law fitted nicely with the image of the independent, individualistic northerner that was being constructed. No northerner was going to submit to unreasonable and arbitrary southern nonsense!

The other unique aspect of the Prohibition debate was that in the South, one form of opposition was framed in terms that "the workingman's source of beer was now shut down by 'class legislation' while no such hardship was suffered by the wealthy."[156] In the North, the class issue does not seem to have arisen. Instead, both working people and their bosses (with the exception of some mine managers) seem to have been united in a common cause. Indeed, it provided fodder for an ongoing run of sly "in" humour. When Dr J.A. McInnis, soon to be mayor of Timmins, spoke at a nomination meeting for a Liberal candidate in the dominion by-election of 1920, he proclaimed that the policies of both dominion and provincial governments "had been to take out of the North one hundred per cent. and give back about two and one-half per cent. 'And you know what poor comfort that two-and-a-half per cent. stuff is,' he concluded."[157]

The education rights of French-speaking Roman Catholic students were another problem area that, surprisingly enough, fed into a sense of community in the region just when it was dividing southern populations. The debate over Regulation 17 played out very differently in Porcupine–Iroquois Falls than in eastern Ontario and even in other parts of northeastern Ontario, where it generated bitter local divisions. There, the authorities actively tried to enforce the law, and English-speaking citizens sometimes intervened directly. At Sturgeon Falls, west of North Bay, the entire student body of one school walked out in silence when the provincial inspector arrived, and at two small towns outside Sudbury a similar walkout was staged to the singing of "O Canada" *en français*. When the Ontario government responded by reducing the school grants, parishes rallied to raise the money themselves.[158] At Sturgeon Falls public school, supporters took the Spanish Pulp and Paper Company to court (and won) for allocating one-third of its taxation to the separate school board.[159] In Porcupine, however, there seems to have been no public objection raised to Father Thériault's École séparée bilingue; indeed, when the student body outgrew its original classrooms, Hollinger contributed $900 (and possibly the land) for the new École St Antoine in 1918 – a not so subtle official sanction.[160] It was not until 1922 that a separate facility was organized for English-speaking Roman Catholic students. (It became Holy Family School in 1926 under Father O'Gorman's leadership). And when it was in operation, a third school, St Charles, was opened and widely acknowledged as a "French Canadian" school.[161] Ste Anne's School at Iroquois Falls was built in 1921 with substantial support from Abitibi (through the municipality);[162] with equitable corporate support provided to both public and separate schools, there was little of the animosity that evolved to the south. Rural schools in predominantly French-speaking districts, such as the Frederick House school, were taught entirely in French and apparently made no secret of the fact when the inspector came to visit.[163] At a flag-stop on the TNO called Devonshire, just north of Nellie Lake, the English-speaking minority initially proposed cooperation in the formation of a separate school board "in the interest of economy"; but the group was eventually persuaded by an outsider, the assistant chief school inspector, J.B. MacDougall, to organize a public school section instead.[164]

Regulation 17 was modified in 1927 and then gradually ignored by the government, so the debate turned to a demand for increased financial support from public tax revenue for separate schools, which in Porcupine–Iroquois Falls meant largely French-language schools.[165] The issue dominated the 1934 provincial election in Northern Ontario. When George Henry's Conservative government was defeated, Henry claimed, "The entire north has deserted us under the influence of the church."[166] Once again, animosity in Porcupine–Iroquois Falls was directed outward at "the government" rather than internally between French and English speakers. In any case, by the mid-1930s the idea of French-language education had come to be taken as natural. Under the headline "Inspectors Pleased With French Classes," the *Advance* reported, "Timmins has one of the very few secondary schools in the province where a section of the curriculum is devoted to French language teaching in the sense that French is the medium through which a subject is taught. French literature and French composition of types equally advanced as English literature and composition in ordinary schools of the province are taught here by Mr. Gauthier."[167] French-language instruction had become a marker of distinctiveness and a point of pride.

There are several possible reasons for these responses. First, the French-speaking population was large and in some parishes formed the majority of the Roman Catholics; the Timmins Separate School Board had a majority of French-speaking trustees; and in some areas the Roman Catholic population as a whole was the majority, as at Iroquois Falls by 1936.[168] Religious solidarity seems to have helped minimize language conflict. Second, there was official corporate support in the early years for the founding of Roman Catholic schools that seem to have been widely assumed to be French-speaking. Third, as has been discussed, there was no overwhelming enthusiasm for expenditure on public schools in any case, so the fierce competition for scarce resources that appeared in other places was unlikely to develop here. Finally, the battle waged by the French-speaking opponents of Regulation 17 used exactly the same imagery as the regional booster campaigns – that the government was at fault and the North was unique. It was a relatively easy matter to see common cause. The enemy was the South – the government – not fellow northerners. So the "French fact" could be enveloped and incorporated into the idea of community.

There were other smaller thorns that provided minor yet persistent irritation. For example, when the itinerary for the 1939 Royal Visit to Canada was announced, northeastern Ontario was bypassed, and "indignation over the snubbing of New Ontario" generated a protest campaign.[169] The Associated Boards of Trade petitioned Prime Minister Mackenzie King with the argument "that the mining areas of the North were admitted by all to have carried Canada through the recent troublous times and so were of essential importance."[170] Another issue was handed to the region periodically by southern politicians who blamed the failure of Clay Belt agriculture on the "class of settler" who had gone north. "This Sort of Thing Tempts to Separation," thundered a one headline in the *Advance* when comments by Manning Doherty, the newly appointed minister of agriculture, implied that northern farmer-settlers were "young and reckless." Don't blame (and insult) the courageous settlers, ran the subtext, blame the short-sighted southern politicians and their foolish policies.[171]

Another festering issue was the question of political representation in Toronto and Ottawa. In the mid-1930s, for example, there was a campaign for a Northern Ontario Senate seat. When R.B. Bennett's government rejected the idea, the angry response was: "This country represents four fifths of the area and an equal proportion of the natural wealth of the province."[172] How dare Bennett fail to recognize its importance?

Finally, even sporting disputes provided an opening for community rallies. In 1935 the Ontario Hockey Association disqualified the Sudbury team in the playoffs because of a disagreement over the eligibility of one player. The Northern Ontario Hockey Association responded with a campaign reminiscent of the battle for political control of economic development. Yet again, northerners were being treated badly by southerners; the only solution was for the NOHA to secede from the provincial body and to run its own game with its own rules.[173] Hockey, that potent symbol of northern identity, was under attack!

While people and events began to build conceptual space for shared experience, we must also recognize the literal construction of physical spaces that permitted the exchange of views. Dozens of halls, built by churches, unions, fraternal societies, and commercial entrepreneurs, became important meeting places for recreation, politics, public service, and pure socialization. The large number of halls might suggest that they served only to perpetuate the religious and cultural divisions by providing each group with a separate meeting place. Certainly, in the early years this was true, but over time the smaller groups found the cost of maintaining a hall too burdensome, and a greater mixing began to emerge. At Iroquois Falls from the beginning, the town hall in the Mercantile was a multipurpose space used by everyone in the town. Hollinger Hall, built in 1923 as a facility for the mine's employees only, was used until the mid-1950s by non-employees as well (until the demand grew so high that management decided to restrict its use again).[174] The Miners' Union Hall in South Porcupine was used for events such as a Barbers' Association dance, a fundraiser for the fire department, and weekly young people's dances in the winter months, besides union-sponsored activities. At Ansonville, "Uke Hall" was a favourite gathering spot where the Ukrainians were joined by others who shared their love of music. And Orange Lodges throughout the area cooperated with Roman Catholic organizations like the Knights of Columbus, as has been noted, when social space was needed. The pleasure that people enjoyed in events that took place in these halls ensured that the halls themselves became important symbols of community, in spite of their modest physical appearance. When Iroquois Falls' Mercantile burned down in 1965, the writers of a community history observed that people felt a "deep sense of personal loss." "This was more than just a town hall," they explained, "it was the heart of our town and served as a type of glue that drew the town residents together."[175]

Finally, it was perhaps a growing sense of permanence that changed fundamentally the way residents perceived themselves and their place in the region. The First Nations, of course, had always considered their place here to be permanent, but most of the early-twentieth-century arrivals either considered themselves temporary residents or soon found that economic circumstances dictated that they had to be. Young men from Europe who came for short-term or seasonal work were not the only sojourners. As has been discussed, Canadians of the day seemed to believe that the "life" of a mine was only a decade long (and that gold mining was suspect in any case) and that forests would last only until a "real" economy of agriculture was established. Farmers who hoped to establish new family roots in the soil found themselves stymied by climate and lack of infrastructure. Pulp and paper workers at Abitibi as well as the smaller factories saw their jobs come and go with the vicissitudes of the North American economy. The Porcupine Camp existed both literally and figuratively.

But by the 1920s it had become clear that the Porcupine mines were unusual. The Big Three were still producing as much as they ever had; and continuing demand for gold in the 1930s meant that the mining sector here never had a Great Depression. Indeed, there were several important new discoveries that considerably expanded the workforce and the economy (including Paymaster, 1930; Buffalo Ankerite, 1932; Hollinger's Ross Mine, 1933; Pamour, incorporated 1934; Hallnor, 1936; and Aunor, 1939). Although Abitibi was in receivership and its dwindling workforce in difficulty, demand for labour at the mines helped to absorb some of the unemployed and to permit a continuing sense of optimism. The regional sex ratio shifted as more of the men married and brought their families to the region; the presence of larger numbers of women and children provided a reinforced sense of "normalcy." New schools and church congregations were organized. A second generation of young men were committed to the region and followed their fathers underground. References to the Porcupine "Camp" began to slip from common usage, and local boosters began to talk of the modern, progressive, and permanent towns that had been built, with brick buildings, concrete sidewalks, and expensive public amenities. Horticultural societies were organized and people competed to beautify their lots. Verandas, second storeys, and even some ornamentation were added to the basic frame box houses in Timmins, and a solid new municipal building went up. Roy Thomson built a fine new home for his media empire in the latest art deco style. People had clearly succeeded in imagining this place as a permanent establishment.

Of course, transience continued to be a fact of life across all economic sectors, as was discussed in chapter 6. And, significantly, this transience continued to mark a boundary between the First Nations and the newcomers. But it was a transience of a peculiar character, one that paradoxically proved fertile ground for community. As was described, men and their families moved back and forth across the country to other mines and mining towns or to other pulp mills, developing pan-regional networks through work and social connections. So even transience was not entirely destructive of the possibility of community. A pan-regional community was evolving in which membership was defined by work skills and social networks, not by the physical place of one's current residence.

Thus it was that the spaces people created for themselves, either in their minds or in their physical surroundings, gradually began to provide room for others. Shared experiences like local disasters and world wars, annual rituals like dogsled races and Labour Day baseball games, perceived threats to shared interests, and the daily contact at work and school may not immediately have bridged the very real divides of language, religion, culture, and class; but they did provide opportunities for those who wished to make contact to do so. As a university student sent north to work among the railway construction crews observed, the summer's experience had "done much to broaden my outlook, and to develop within me a sense of what the spirit of brotherhood can, and ought to, mean. I have been convinced that a smile invites a smile, regardless of creed or nationality, and that good-will can, and will, eventually penetrate the hardest armour."[176]

CHAPTER TWELVE

Creating a Community

The spirit of the north is great – it is not parochial or narrow or intolerant – you find very few animosities, racial, religious or class-wise, and in most of the small mining communities men and women of all the different degrees that exist in a community rub shoulders to the benefit of all.

A.K. Roberts, 1945[1]

Thirty years earlier there had been little evidence for Mr Roberts's enthusiastic characterization of Northern Ontario communities. Indeed, it would be hard to imagine a place less likely to coalesce into a "community" than the region of Porcupine–Iroquois Falls. Distinct economic sectors, a dozen different languages, passionate political differences rooted in dramatic historical experiences, and mutual suspicion sustained through generations of cultural rationalization could only reinforce the attitude of many that they were here only temporarily, until they saved enough to make a better life back home. Those who had hoped to stay, like the farmers, found it impossible to realize their ambitions. Even in the pulp and paper sector, where conditions for permanence seemed most promising, economic changes rooted in distant realities dictated a roller-coaster of employment opportunity. Aboriginal people, marginalized in their own lands, found it increasingly difficult to support themselves. Yet in the region today there is a very strong sense of community. People identify themselves as part of a group that is unique to the North, unique even within the North, and superior in many ways to the urban southern Canadian. By 1951 the image of this community had begun to take shape in the minds of a good proportion of the population. In the words of a francophone observer of the time, "Coming from everywhere, the residents of Timmins form a cosmopolitan city. Each person participates in community life, regardless of which race, of which religion he is. Racial prejudices have given way to the best fraternity. It is unity in diversity."[2] Some fifty years later, a similar perception was expressed by a local resident in a "man on the street" interview conducted by a southern Ontario television journalist. "Up here we all get along," explained the unidentified man, "French – English – the rest of Canada can learn something from us."[3]

Of course, not everyone would agree that a "real" community had emerged. The dozens of Ukrainians who, disillusioned and disappointed, began to drift away to southern Ontario in the 1950s hoping to find a more welcoming situation, would never have accepted the idea that there was a community – except, perhaps, for a community of interests arrayed against them. Finns continued to battle against the stereotype that they were communist troublemakers. In the 1970s the members of the Timmins branch of the Alliance for the Preservation of English in Canada saw themselves under siege from an alleged "French" domination in the region. For their part, a generation of francophones who came of age in the 1960s and 1970s participated in the new Québécois nationalism and rebelled against their parents' quiescence in deferring to "the English." The great divide between Aboriginal people and newcomers persisted, with some residents being totally unaware of the presence of reserves or of ongoing political struggles right on their doorstep. Other groups were similarly invisible in the eyes of those who defined themselves as the community. The organizers of the 1974 Timmins Ethnic Festival intended that the event would "impress upon the English and French citizens of Timmins that there is an ethnic population thriving along side of them."[4] Clearly, a definition of community had emerged that still delineated "insiders" and "outsiders." But that in itself is interesting. How exactly did the widespread belief of community, cooperation, and harmony develop? And what did the participants believe were the characteristics that defined them as a collective?

Before a community can be built, it has to be imagined. The early residents of the Porcupine Camp saw little reason to think in terms of social networks; they were there to make a quick dollar and leave. But as people stayed and the resource base appeared likely to support them for the long term, the sojourners needed more than a paycheque to sustain them and make their lives meaningful. Cut adrift from family and from social systems established elsewhere over generations, people found themselves looking for moorings. They needed connections and activities that felt familiar and safe, but ones that made sense in the new circumstances in which they found themselves. They needed to reach accommodations with others around them. This necessitated the discovery of common ground, perhaps in shared religious practices, similar life goals, or mutual pleasures. In the process, people came to define themselves in terms both of what they believed they were, and what they were not. They began to create boundaries between self and other, although over time the exact location of those boundaries would shift. The *idea* of what might constitute a community played just as important a role in creating the community as the economic and institutional structures that shaped its development or the events that challenged people to respond. In the process, the idea helped define who they were.

The first and most obvious direction in which the newcomers might have looked for a social place was among the Aboriginal population and fur trade society that was already established in the region. Of course, as countless histories of Canada have noted (explicitly or implicitly), Euro-Canadians carried a set of intellectual constructs that laid claim to European cultural superiority and a sense of moral, if not religious, entitlement to the lands and resources. Some newcomers simply ignored the First Nations because of the belief that "superior" civilizations would "naturally" dominate "inferior" ones, and that the Aboriginal population would inevitably disappear. Others, the "progressives" of the day, argued that Aboriginal people should not be ignored, because Europeans had a moral and religious duty to "save" them in both the religious and cultural senses. In either case, the apparent result in region after region was a sudden social disjuncture as Euro-Canadian populations displaced the Aboriginal, leaving First Nations people either completely marginalized from the now dominant economy and community or forced to accommodate themselves so fully into it as to become assimilated. Thus, one might expect that in northeastern Ontario the pattern would be repeated as the mining, agricultural, and pulp and paper economies were established in the early twentieth century. There would be no sense of place for a "white" man among the region's "Indians."

Interestingly enough, this standard story did not play out here in quite the same way as it appears to have done elsewhere. In fact, there was (at least initially) a great deal of interest among Canadian newcomers in the Aboriginal peoples of the area and in the stories of their history, both ancient and more recent. This interest was reflected in early-twentieth-century naming practices. One of the first and best-remembered hotels in Golden City was named the Shuniah, which was said by the proprietors to be the "Indian" word for gold. The Algonquin Regiment chose an allegedly Ojibwa motto (Ne-kah-ne-tah) instead of the traditional Latin. More important, perhaps, was that many geographic features remained associated with Aboriginal peoples. Some places continued to be known by long-standing names from Ojibwa and Cree sources (Abitibi, Mattagami) or their English translations (Nighthawk, Porcupine). Others, such as Iroquois Falls, were not just names but were associated with oral traditions that were circulated among the non-Aboriginal population. Indeed, in 1912 the Toronto Board of Trade mocked the Northern Ontario habit of using Aboriginal names. "While reluctance is natural in abandoning the old Indian names," wrote Fred W. Field, "business interests will not long consent to stumble over such names as Poshokogan, Pikitigushi and Namewaminikan." These impossible names were simply not "modern," he said.[5]

Given the anxiety in the region to be considered "modern," the retention of Aboriginal names is all the more significant.

Many stories were circulated among the newcomers about Aboriginal history, although it is not clear how these were initially transmitted to the non-Aboriginal population or how many of them were purely invented traditions. Nevertheless, the very fact of their existence hints at a fascination among the newcomers for things "Indian." The story of Iroquois Falls was one of the most compelling, for it combined elements of daring, individual initiative, and courage in the face of danger, all of which the newcomers liked to see in themselves. The story was repeated in many variants, but its essential elements did not change. A northern Native woman (sometimes Cree, sometimes Ojibwa, sometimes merely "Indian") tricked a group of Iroquois warriors into driving their canoes over the falls to their death. Sometimes her ruse was presented as an act of revenge for the murder of her band; other times it was supposed to have been to prevent an Iroquois attack. In most versions, the woman herself dies in leading the warriors over the falls, either in an act of noble self-sacrifice or in the blazing glory of revenge. Regardless of the shifting details, stories like this gave the newcomers a sense of ancient connection to the land and a human meaning to otherwise "empty" spaces, in much the same way that the stories had served their Aboriginal tellers. Perhaps, too, this kind of knowledge gave the newcomers a sense of legitimacy. By adopting the "knowledge" of the First Nations, however superficially, the newcomers were in a symbolic sense now a part of the land too. For newcomers from other parts of Canada, this process was scarcely new. All had come from areas where Aboriginal stories were known and shared, so it is not surprising that they looked for regionally specific stories that gave meaning to their new space.

New "Indian" stories were told as well. The most commonly reported of these were ones that linked Native people to the discovery of gold. For example, in 1925 a former Haileybury mining recorder, George T. Smith, told the *Canadian Mining Journal* that interest in Porcupine-area gold had originated in the late 1870s, when two gold nuggets had been discovered in the possession of a Nighthawk Lake "Indian" who had been arrested for the murder of his brother and brought to Mattawa to be judged by HBC Chief Factor Colin Rankin.[6] Mattawa, of course, was also the home of the Timmins family, so a connection was implied (if not literally possible). In another legend, Porcupine prospector Reuben D'Aigle allegedly was attracted to the region after hearing a "Cree trapper" in Cobalt talking about what he had seen sticking out of the ground there.[7] This genre of stories was not, of course, unique to the Porcupine. Across Canada, major mineral discoveries such as those in the Cariboo and the Klondike were explained in tales that originated with Native reports. There may well have been an element of truth in some of these stories,[8] but they seem to represent at the very least an imagined link with the Aboriginal population, perhaps in part to cast the prospectors in a more positive light, suggesting that their finds were based on the more morally acceptable idea of earned knowledge and not merely on dumb luck. At the same time, these "discovery" tales served to distance the newcomers from the First Nations. Invariably, the "Indian" in the story either doesn't realize the value of what he has found or somehow tries (unsuccessfully) to hide the information. The prospector-hero outwits the Indian and gets rich, while the Indian gets drunk, is carted off to jail, or otherwise melts away into insignificance. The prospector-hero has "earned" his reward; and by symbolic extension, so have those who follow the prospector.

Interest in these stories seems to have declined somewhat through the 1920s as people looked to other sources of meaning and definition. But in the mid-1930s they began to enjoy something of a revival. Late in 1933, J.E. Woodall, the Anglican archdeacon at Iroquois Falls, wrote to the *Advance* to inquire about the origins of the name of his town, and in response the editor, G.A. Macdonald, proposed that more systematic efforts be made to collect tales about local history. "It does not seem right that historical data should be allowed to disappear," he wrote, "because so many are engaged in making history rather than in gathering the information from which history is built."[9] It seems that even hard-nosed entrepreneurs dedicated to the business of making money felt the need for some sort of connection to their surroundings and, tellingly, seemed to assume that the "Indian" history of the area was now a part of "their" history.

Through the 1930s and 1940s, interest in and identification with Aboriginal society was not limited to landscape and history. Living "Indians" seem to have been rediscovered by the newcomers. Anglican clergy with missionary experience were sought out as sources of information, and stories about activities in such places as Moosonee began to appear in the local media, with individuals noted by name (no longer the anonymous collective "Indian") and with considerable sympathy evoked for their problems. For example, in the spring of 1936 the *Advance* reported in a page-one story that John Nakoutchee, chief at Attiwapiskat, had arrived in Moosonee with news that his people were starving and that one of them, John Wapano, had died after walking 160 kilometres from his camp to find food. The problem, according to Nakoutchee, was government regulations that prohibited beaver and otter trapping, the mainstays of their economy.[10] While the story played on the element of human tragedy, the unstated subtext was a shared antipathy toward government regulation of all types. The "Indian" was serving a new purpose in the emerging language of regional alienation.

Some individual Aboriginal people became a source of fascination, as much for how they seemed to substantiate the romantic stereotypes as for who they really were. Chief among these publicly visible individuals was Maggie (Buffalo) Leclair, an Anishinabe woman born around 1870 who lived most of her life in the vicinity of Nighthawk Lake and died at Timmins in 1963. She was the personification of much that the newcomers wanted to make of the Aboriginal population. As a handsome woman and a daughter of a prominent family, she was dubbed Princess Maggie and was transformed into the enduring Canadian stereotype of the Indian Princess: noble, beautiful, powerful, and slightly mysterious. As a trapper in her own right, she was admired for her success in building a life from the dangerous and unforgiving land. And she was linked (correctly or not) to a key event in the area's history as "a descendent of the only survivor" of the dramatic Frederick House Massacre (see chapter 2).[11] When Hollinger's magazine for employees ran a story on her in 1956, it picked up on the compelling stereotypes that resonated so strongly: "She is a member of the proud Chippewa tribe, daughter of the greatest hunter of the Chippewas and great-great-great granddaughter of the mightiest of all Chippewa war chiefs." To underscore the dramatic imagery, the article was accompanied by a wonderfully posed photograph, which set Mrs Leclair against a backdrop of luxurious furs, with two nasty looking knives on prominent display.[12] Strength, beauty, and a barely concealed ferocity were unmistakable in the message.

Admiration for, fascination about, and identification with their Aboriginal neighbours did not, however, extend beyond the level of symbolism and stereotype. The newcomers never attempted to interact with First Nations people in a sustained or meaningful way. Aboriginal people were expected to conform to the newcomers' norms and plans. They were not placed among the "foreigners" or "bohunks" on the mental map, but neither were they "white."[13] As makers of a past Golden Age that had paved the way for the modern North, they deserved to be treated with dignity, but they had to realize that "progress" was inevitable and if that meant flooding some land to generate hydroelectric power, so be it. They were neither quite "self" or "other" in the years before 1950, but they were clearly used in the newcomers' early attempts to make some sort of psychological connection with their adopted surroundings, or they were used to criticize government policies toward the North.

If the Aboriginal population was one of the first places where the newcomers looked for a social identity, the physical environment that we encountered in chapter 1 provided a close second. But it was not initially an appreciation of the aesthetic qualities of the landscape that mattered here. Whether the newcomers were farmers, mine developers, bushworkers, railway construction crews, or miners, they were all occupied

A typical scene in the Porcupine–Iroquois Falls region – a small lake among black spruce and other vegetation of the ecosystem that borders the boreal forest. A few kilometres south of this lake, the forest changes to a landscape that once included the large pines that were so highly prized for the timber trade. (Photo by the author)

with the business of tearing down and reshaping their surroundings in conditions that made their efforts difficult, often dangerous, and nearly always unpleasant. If it wasn't the biting cold of winter, it was the wet of spring muskeg and the insufferable blackflies of summer. So it is hardly surprising that the emphasis initially was on nature as a cruel foe to be conquered, subdued, even removed. Progress was measured by the number of trees cleared, the size of the industrial plant erected, and the miles of rail or pavement covering the ground. As the *Porcupine Advance* noted in 1912, "Arbor day was fittingly observed in the South Porcupine school. No trees were planted, as is the general custom, but instead many were removed and the grounds surrounding the school were *otherwise greatly improved*."[14] Coming from societies that defined progress as the subduing of nature to the will of humanity, many of the new arrivals at Porcupine–Iroquois Falls saw in the rapid changes proof that the region was indeed at the forefront of the age while Old Ontario stagnated as a sleepy agricultural backwater. Building a new world was clearly an exciting and satisfying experience in the lives of the newcomers, particularly since many of them were young people just beginning to build their adult lives. The struggle to subdue nature inspired teacher Bertha Shaw to poetry:

Me thinks I see a goddess rise from out an age-old sleep,
Lightly she treads on clay-belt fields and on Laurentian steep,
Her ear attuned to hum of power from mine and forest deep.
Exultant in a hope fulfilled, her smile secret and still,
Aware that brawn and muscle, controlled by brain and skill,
Pitted against her ruthless land have bent that stubborn will.[15]

This shared experience of clearing, digging, sweating, and building became an important source for a set of symbols central to the formation of local identity.

The idea of a fundamental battle against the forces of nature might have remained something of an abstract romance had it not been for the very real and very tragic battles that were forced upon the region in the forest fires of 1911 and 1916. Just when the newcomers were at their most hopeful and busy, great walls of flame descended upon them, apparently from nowhere, sweeping away lives and hard-won property. While some survivors gave up and abandoned the region, those who remained were even more determined to succeed. They had, after all, survived the inferno, whether by luck or by their wits, and now they felt an even greater sense of entitlement. If there had been any doubt about their right to be there based on their "discovery" of the gold or pulpwood, those lingering doubts were now removed. After the fires, they definitely felt they had earned the right to take from the land when so much had been taken from them.

The fires were obviously experiences of enormous drama, but the later reconstruction of their stories was almost as important. The fact that both great fires had probably originated through human carelessness was never discussed. Instead, the stories that circulated for years dwelt on the heroism of individuals during the blaze and the way the community rallied afterwards to help the victims. The fires became symbolic moments in collective local memory in another sense too, for people began to construct a local history measured against the time of the fires. Those who had come before the 1911 fire (Timmins-Porcupine) or the 1916 fire (Iroquois Falls and Matheson) were credited as the founders of the community, and the "real" history of the region was deemed to have arisen from the ashes afterwards.

If images of nature as a foe to be fought and conquered suffused the discovery of the early-twentieth-century newcomers, it was one very specific set of symbols derived from these ideas of nature that dominated. This was the idea of the North. While Toronto promoters tried to downplay the region's northernness in their efforts to attract settlers to New Ontario, local residents very quickly laid claim to the northernness of their setting. It was relatively easy for at least the English-speaking Canadians to co-opt a ready-made set of symbols here, because the idea of Canada as a northern nation was already well developed by the turn of the century.[16] The cold climate was a Darwinian device for weeding out the physically and morally weak, producing a society of hardy individuals superior to those of the places they had left behind. The open spaces were contrasted to the crowded and unhealthy life of the industrial city. The sheer physical effort required to eke out a living under northern conditions was transformed into a positive good. Hard work made for moral superiority and a sense of entitlement. Toronto journalist Frederick Griffin reflected this kind of thinking in a 1931 essay in which he proposed that Northern Ontario was a cure for the black days of the Great Depression: "Go north and find that Canada still advances and that faith, fight and courage still exist in great gobs. I don't mean to Muskoka or some other little near-north, steam-heated till it smirks, but up north to where Ontario begins to edge into a subarctic eternity. Up there men tackle harsh gargantuan jobs with homeric confidence and heroic skill. Up there is a battle front: men against the gods; men against the Abitibi and the Moose. Up there you may watch civilization marching, smashing forward, pushing the frontier north with giant gains."[17]

With time, the emphasis on "smashing forward" gave way to another relationship with the northern environment that proved equally important in constructing the value system upon which a sense of community could be supported. Natural resources in the region were appropriated by ordinary men and women who had developed a sense of entitlement. As was discussed, highgrading received very little censure because it was seen as just the working man taking his share. More importantly, hunting and fishing became a central part of a sense of identity. Adventures in the bush also served to drive a wedge between newcomers and Aboriginal people.

Attitudes to hunting and fishing were eventually dominated by working people's norms. In the early years of the twentieth century, managers and professionals had banded together to establish "rod and reel" clubs that dictated a "gentlemanly" approach. Attempts were made to stock trout for fly fishing or pheasant and ruffed grouse for shooting. Over time, however, these clubs faded away as the popularity of hunting and fishing escalated among working men, who pursued it in very different ways. Now, the game of choice was moose – and the bigger the rack of antlers you put on display, the better. Hunting down a big powerful animal, symbol of masculinity, not only proved your prowess but represented it in a palpable, physical presence. Similarly, the fish of choice was no longer the trout, caught with a silly little rod and a collection of delicate flies; it was a muscular "game" fish, the "muskie" (muskellunge), which required brute force to reel in. And although this kind of hunting and fishing was usually performed in

smaller groups of two or three, the camaraderie of a club soon evolved out
of the shared stories, often told over a beer.

Hunting and fishing obviously drew on and reinforced the definitions of
masculinity evolving in the region: rugged individualism, aggressiveness,
virility, physical courage. But they also gave industrial workers a sense of
freedom and power that was unobtainable in the workplace. Historian
Suzanne Morton's explanation in her study of working-class Halifax partially fits: "Hunting and fishing were the antithesis of work in a warehouse
or shipyard and provided a welcome contrast to modern industrial capitalism, the de-skilling of work, life in a city, and the rise of domesticity.
They played upon the nostalgic appeal of a rural existence."[18] In Porcupine–Iroquois Falls, however, hunting and fishing seem not to have been
so much an alternative to unskilled work or domesticity. Rather, the asser-
tion of masculine individualism and freedom from the constraints of the
workplace seem to have dominated. Hunting also had an aesthetic appeal
that was not often verbalized but should not be underestimated. "The
trade of trapping is very interesting," recalled a French Canadian settler.
"The open air, the smell of the woods, the autumn leaves, the open spaces,
the worthy exercise of walking … How enchanting to live in the beauties
of nature."[19]

Of course, hunting and fishing brought the newcomers into direct conflict with Aboriginal peoples, who considered that the resources were
theirs and that Treaty 9 was a guarantee of their right of access. As has
been described, the First Nations protested persistently to officials, with
little effect. The newcomers, in turn, seem to have simply ignored Aboriginal concerns, if they even heard of them. As game was depleted, government attempts to regulate the hunt were seen as as infringement on a
man's rights, and fed into the anti-government sentiments that underlay
regional alienation. A later generation would see the government's more
generous Aboriginal policies in a similar light, complaining that "Indians"
were unfairly accorded special status by southern governments that simply
didn't understand the North.[20]

Another important dimension of an emerging regional value system was
a very specific concept of development. A faith in "progress" was, of
course, central to the North American social sense of the day, and the
people of Porcupine–Iroquois Falls came to believe that they were living
that dream. The imagery of the headframe and the large industrial plant
that was the Abitibi mill were symbols of progress. But more importantly,
it could all be translated into the starkest material terms – monetary value.
As a pamphlet produced by Byrnes Presbyterian Church in Timmins proclaimed exuberantly in 1924, "Picture a town rising out of the virgin forest
in twelve years; a town of 13,000 people, $500,000 worth of schools,
$160,000 worth of churches, $6,000,000 worth of taxable property, water

One of a series of photos taken in 1936 of Hollinger's tailings disposal system, following the installation of one of its new ponds (known locally as "slimes," for obvious reasons). This particular image shows a 26-metre-high dam holding 9 million tonnes of wastes from the production process. These piles were seen as evidence of progress, not of environmental destruction. (LAC, PA017615)

works, modern fireproof theatre, hotel[,] office buildings ... such a town is Timmins."[21] The local boosters, in both the *Porcupine Advance* and such national publications as the *Canadian Mining Journal*, always measured "progress" in similar terms: value of gold produced, value of the tax base, value of logs in the Abitibi stack, growing population numbers.

On a personal level, value was measured through consumerism. The pages of the local papers were filled with a surprising number of advertisements for automobiles, even before the Ferguson Highway provided a link to the outside world. By the time the highway was semi-passable, Leo Mascioli's Timmins Garage Co. Ltd. was advertising round-the-clock service and a storage garage that could accommodate ninety-five cars.[22] Clothing and jewellery shops were important fixtures in Timmins and South Porcupine, where the larger population could support them. People also had the option of ordering from the ever-popular Eaton's catalogue (as local business owners constantly complained). A good deal of money was also spent on consumables, especially on alcohol, travel, and entertainment, as has been described. Less was spent on durables such as houses

Table 13   Employment in the retail sector, Timmins-Tisdale Township, 1921

Category	No. of Jobs	%	Includes
Food and drugs	18	38	Grocers, butchers, confectioners, drug stores
Clothing	13	28	Men's and ladies' wear, tailors, milliners, shoes
Dry goods	9	19	New and used
Jewellery	4	9	
Transportation	3	6	Automobile sales, horse liveries

Source: Derived from Survey on Vocational Education in Ontario, Lacelle Files, Canada, Department of Labour, LAC, RG27, vol. 257, file 900:02:02, part 9 (microfilm reel T10181)

and land. Of course, there were practical reasons for this pattern – company housing, sojourning, the realities of the resource-extraction economy, and the impossibility of commercial agriculture. But people seem to have transformed their consumer habits into a positive value, making it part of a sense of themselves. Consumerism has been studied primarily as a post-1945 phenomenon in North America, but clearly it had earlier origins and deserves more scholarly discussion.[23]

Because the people of Porcupine–Iroquois Falls saw themselves as succeeding at the twentieth-century game of modernism, materialism, and consumerism, they quickly developed a sense of entitlement. They demanded outside recognition, praise, and support. When such reactions were not forthcoming (or at least not in sufficient quantity), it was an easy step to a sense of grievance. Hostility was expressed primarily toward two recipients: southern "government" and "the Company". Both quickly were reduced to caricature. A sort of shorthand imagery developed that in turn served as an inclusionary device that enveloped all who understood what was "meant." These images became tools in a series of conflicts over what were often quite mundane issues, and the conflicts themselves were eventually assimilated into the set of beliefs about who northerners thought they were.

The first to express a sense of regional grievance directed at government were the early businesspeople, mine developers, and would-be farmers. Complaints were levied about delays in constructing access roads, about legislation governing taxes on mines, about management of the Temiskaming and Northern Ontario Railway, the freight rates and poor passenger service, the distribution of patronage, the process for allocating pulp limits, hunting and fishing regulations, almost every aspect of hydroelectric power generation and distribution, and even about the quality of radio reception. Members of the boards of trade who spearheaded campaigns on these issues during the early years of the twentieth century seem to have grasped (either consciously or intuitively) that merely asking for more from Queen's Park would seem petty and self-serving. But expressing these demands in the language of moral entitlement and indignation gave them the appearance at least of a crusade for the public good. The North was not the South; its resources were different, its needs were different, even its people were different – and southern failure to appreciate these differences meant that the North was being cheated. In the words of the *Advance*, "The interests and objects and ambitions of the North Land are different to those of the rest of Ontario. Even the people of this big North Land are of a distinctive type ... The older parts of Ontario do not understand the great new North, and the people of the North are losing patience with the Provincials of the south." Then, building an image that will be familiar to those who have studied Prairie regional protest, the article stated that northerners feared "that the North is only to be a sort of milk cow for the rest of the Province, milked as long as its riches last and rewarded by little of the fodder of new roads, schools, bridges, railways, etc. that a new country demands."[24]

Unwittingly (and somewhat paradoxically) a group of social campaigners in southern Ontario played directly into this game. As historian Karen Dubinsky has demonstrated, a "social purity movement" emerged in southern Ontario just as "Empire Ontario" was moving north, and this social reform program generated, for its own purposes, images of Northern Ontario as a "dangerously immoral, uncivilized place of vice." White slavery was allegedly rampant in the North, while the male immigrant population was deemed to be a rough and ready bunch of gamblers, drunkards, and sexually promiscuous predators. Young men of good, solid, southern farm families were being lured into this dangerous world beyond parental control.[25] Northern Ontario boosters were not willing to let these claims slip by unchallenged – for obvious reasons – and in their rebuttals they called on the old ideas of the pure, morally superior life of the North, thereby reinforcing the imagery of their political campaigns and perhaps making the idea seem even richer and more meaningful. Some of the rebuttals were defensive, as in the *Advance*'s 1923 response to some Toronto *Star* "slander" of the North, in which the writer threw up his hands. "Perhaps it is useless to reply," he lamented. "The mining camps of New Ontario are famed throughout the world for their orderliness and moral healthfulness. The lumber camps in similar manner compare more favourably with other camps elsewhere ... [Premier] Drury would have the North Land as a cow to be milked; The Star would have it as a bad lad to be kicked."[26] Other respondents went on the attack, playing up the characteristics that the boosters liked to imagine made them unique and superior: "Timmins cherishes the distinction of being rated a 'live' town, and its residents have mostly come from large cities, so have been free from the conservatism which predominates in other places of its size in Old

Ontario, where the penurious agriculturalist and retired farmer are satisfied to live under the same conditions as their fathers and grandfathers did
before them."[27]

Having appropriated cultural images of the North as a place of strength,
courage, manliness, and moral superiority, northern boosters now assimilated these ideas into a sense of who they were, and hurled them back at
southerners. If the imagery had once seemed derivative, it certainly did no
longer, for southerners were now claiming that this specific North was a
place of degeneracy and evil. The idea of North could now take centre
stage in the play of defining self in opposition to "other." It lurked in the
wings of a series of political secession movements, in which Northern
Ontario leaders called for the creation of a separate province that would
free the North once and for all from the constraints of the tired old South.
And what began as the rhetoric of middle-class boosters eventually was
adopted much more widely throughout the population. It gave the con-
glomerate that was Porcupine–Iroquois Falls society something that could
be shared in setting up a mental boundary apparently rooted in geographic space, and in providing a definition of self that was internally satisfying because it conferred a sense of moral superiority. People had left
their homes not to make a quick dollar, motivated by greed, but to make a
better life, motivated by the noble ideals of the age: progress, freedom,
and moral betterment.

Working men and their families developed another set of grievances
that played into their sense of identity in much the same way. "The
Company" was a force arrayed against them, their freedoms, and even
their very lives, in spite of the sacrifices and hardship that workers made in
the company's employ. "The Company" was simultaneously an amorphous
system and a sharply defined personification. When a man said
"Hollinger" or "Abitibi," he did not mean a community of workers; he
meant a distant and uncaring "other." Note the language employed by a
retired miner as reported by local historian Charlie Angus: "McIntyre used
to tell us that it was cheaper to kill a man than to cripple him, especially if
he was a young man and then they'd have to pay him compensation for
twenty-five or thirty years. They didn't want that."[28] A similar sense of
outrage, entitlement, and abstract personification of "the Company" was
expressed in 1934 by a man with bushwork experience: "As you know the
people in this north country have got no protection from the legalized
robbers that think fit to employ them ... The Companies that they work for
rob them right along and get away with it. They have robbed the country
of its' [sic] Natural resources and have robbed the worker and his family
of the wages that was there [sic] due."[29]

This sense of grievance against the company was often merged with anti-
government rhetoric; after all, the government was supposedly responsible

for regulating corporate greed and protecting the working man. Early requests for government intervention were usually rebuffed, as in the case of a delegation of miners who met Ontario Minister of Mines Charles McCrae in February 1924 to ask for a royal commission to inquire into the high accident rate in the Porcupine-area mines. The delegation was abruptly dismissed.[30] The debates over the eight-hour day and workers' compensation went on for years, with the powerful mining lobby making no secret of its opposition. An editorial in the *Canadian Mining Journal* argued, "We have pointed out several times that the miner, of all industrial employees, is probably the best paid, the most comfortably housed, and the most fairly treated. It is, therefore, not seemly that the industry of mining should be experimented on."[31]

Premier James Whitney had responded to this kind of lobbying in 1912–13 by withdrawing the proposed eight-hour day in mining, "frankly admitting that he had been precipitate in presenting his measure."[32] With similar responses to issues of concern to Northern Ontario workers (silicosis, workplace hazards, union recognition, minimum wages, and even Prohibition), it is not surprising that government came to be seen as an ally of "the Company." In this attitude to government, working people found common ground with the business class. Northerners were a breed apart.

The image of what it meant to be a northerner eventually also came to incorporate a series of symbols that were given legitimacy because of their place in "history." For a new settlement anxious to promote itself as modern, progressive, and forward-looking, history was initially something to be forgotten – that load of baggage weighing down the sleepy towns of Old Ontario and holding back the countries of Europe. But eventually, local boosters discovered that history could serve a purpose in providing a selective set of images appropriate to the new setting. Stories attributed to the "Indians" were useful, as has been noted, to connect the newcomers to the land and its traditions and knowledge. Next, the newcomers needed symbols to legitimize their own presence and intentions. As newly transplanted societies seem to do everywhere, the "founding fathers" were made heroes to be venerated and emulated. The "old-timer" and "the prospector," often but not always the same person, became potent symbols.

For the mining sector, "the prospector" became the founder, even though few prospectors actually remained in the region for any length of time and, certainly in a literal sense, contributed little more than the original gold finds. Although hundreds of men (and a few women) participated in the early gold rush, only a handful of names are repeated in the litany: D'Aigle, Bannerman, McIntyre, Hollinger, Wilson, Preston, Mattson, and Pennala (the last in endless variations of spelling). These were lauded either as the first to explore a credible area or as the first big successes. In most accounts, they are referred to familiarly by nicknames – Benny Hollinger, Foghorn MacDonald, Fonsie Rivet, Charlie Auer, Harry Pennala – drawing the storyteller and audience into an invented personal connection with the famous. Details about their lives, obtained from sources unknown, were repeated and embellished to create larger-than-life heroes on grand quests for the holy grail – gold. They were linked whenever possible with significant historical events. Reuben D'Aigle, for example, was unfailingly reported to have been a prospector in the Klondike gold rush. Northern booster and educator J.B. McDougall drew the connection even deeper in Canadian mythology, describing "the prospector" as "the lineal descendant of his dashing prototype, the coureur-de-bois of fur-trading days" with "a brawny arm fitted for the hardships of the trail" and a "firm-set face" that "tells the tale of his stern battle with nature."[33]

The prospector stories all follow the same pattern. A visionary man struggles to convince doubting investors to fund his expedition, then sets off to battle blackflies, muskeg, and unforgiving bush until he comes (almost directly) upon a rock outcrop dripping with gold, thereby proving his superior skills, knowledge, and moral character. He then returns to civilization as a conquering hero, with wealth and fame before him to live happily ever after. In fact, most of the prospectors were young men of limited education and even less knowledge of geology, who by chance happened upon quartz veins with tiny flecks of gold, and often they were unaware of the real significance of their finds. What became the Hollinger Mine, for example, was staked by a teenage barber, Benjamin Hollinger, and his partner, twenty-five-year-old Alexander Gillies, who had been working in the Abitibi country as a railway surveyor. Sandy McIntyre, co-discoverer of the mine that bore his assumed name, apparently realized less than a thousand dollars from his claims.[34] The great majority of prospectors never did succeed in finding minable deposits, even after years of searching, but local tradition conveniently ignored these "failures."

It is interesting that these invented heroes were credited with the founding of the new community when only a handful actually remained in the area for any length of time. Yet after the fact they contributed to the imagined community, representing the values of individualism, foresight, masculine prowess, and knowledge of the land that Porcupine residents wanted to believe they had inherited. In fact, it was perhaps the "failed" prospector who contributed more directly to community building. Consider the story that bush pilot George Theriault tells of his father, who apprenticed as a tailor but whose "real pursuit was prospecting for gold." He worked his way through the bush around Cobalt, then Michipicoten, and finally Timmins, "determined to find a place among his fortunate friends who had become rich and famous. In order to survive until he too hit the jackpot, he opened a tailor shop." Meanwhile, he married and raised a family, whose members made substantial contributions to the social and economic development of the region. Yet Theriault senior never stopped believing that the real measure of his success would be a new mine. "Long after he retired from his trade and lost his eyesight," wrote his son, "he continued to prospect, hoping to find the motherlode."[35] Undoubtedly, it was men like this who helped create and sustain the mythology of the prospector.

The prospector hero was partially a local variant on the eulogization of "the pioneer," another cultural archetype of societies across North America.[36] Although usually associated with the agricultural frontier, the idealized pioneer and the pioneer spirit were adapted easily to the northern setting. "The prospector" was first and foremost among the pioneers, but others who came to supply and support him were also accorded a special place among the revered. Locally, they were originally called old-timers, and at Timmins and South Porcupine the early businessmen in the "camp" became old-timers. At Iroquois Falls, it was the men who built the plant and town – and above all, those who envisioned it – who were eulogized. In the francophone rural settlements, another version of the pioneer mythology was cultivated by the Roman Catholic colonizing priests, who portrayed the settlers as modern-day pioneers repeating the success of their forefathers in the St Lawrence Valley by extending the church into a new promised land.[37] As noted above, other "pioneers" and "old timers" were those who had come before the fires of 1911 and 1916. Since many of them were in their thirties and forties, these terms carried connotations of longevity in place rather than of age. These were not brash new towns; they were established communities with a legitimacy that only time can confer. The term also carried the idea that old-timer values were to be respected and emulated – individualism, personal initiative, materialism, and (perhaps ironically) the willingness to break with tradition.

Identification with the pioneers was simultaneously an inclusionary and exclusionary device. First, the pioneers were depicted as almost entirely male, even though many of them had been accompanied by their wives. They also seem to have been predominantly Canadian (both English- and French-speaking) or were from the British Isles. There were exceptions, such as Timmins's "first" merchant, a Russian-born Jew named Charles Pierce. Interestingly, Pierce seems to have been Canadianized by his family's brief earlier experience as "pioneer" homesteaders near Oxbow, Saskatchewan.[38] The pioneer might have an "Indian" or "halfbreed" entourage, but these people were never depicted as full partners; they

were just employees or assistants. Rarely were they even referred to as
"guides," a term that might have implied they had greater knowledge than
the hero's. Ordinary miners or paperworkers apparently were not considered pioneers; they appear in the stories as a sort of undifferentiated mass
of followers, who arrive in response to the work of the pioneers and toil
anonymously as cogs in the great machine which the pioneers have set in
motion. Finns, Italians, Ukrainians, and other "foreigners" were thereby
excluded, even such prominent individuals as the Mascioli brothers, who
obviously contributed a great deal to the development of the region, both
socially and economically. Also, the pioneers were of middle-class origins
or had been adopted by the middle class as being so entitled because of
their outstanding achievements and acceptable social background. Benny
Hollinger may have been a barber and his brother a railway conductor,
but his roots in the Ottawa Valley, his spectacular discovery, and his acqui-
sition of the material comforts of a middle-class life (including university
education for his two sons) ensured that he could be honoured as a
pioneer.[39]

There was one important difference between the pioneers of the industrial towns and the pioneers of the rural areas. The historical myths of the
towns revolved around the economic engines that drove them. Thus, it was
not "homes" that the fires of 1911 and 1916 destroyed but the newly developed mining properties and Abitibi's plant. Furthermore, the heroes were
individual mining executives and businessmen, not social-service providers
such as teachers, clergy, or doctors, and certainly not the women who ran
the boarding houses or provided domestic support in private homes. In
the rural areas, by contrast, the historical myths venerated the struggles of
pioneer farm *families* and, for the Roman Catholics, the early life of the
parish as a collective. Unfortunately, because of the failure of the agricultural sector and the lack of social continuity, historical myths in rural areas
did not become as deeply rooted or as important contributors to a collective psyche. Instead, as the population consolidated in the towns, it was
their historical inventions that came to dominate.

The cult of the pioneer was never formalized as happened during the
Klondike gold rush with the Yukon Order of Pioneers, founded at Forty
Mile in 1894. Sociologist Thomas Stone has proposed that the Yukon
Order of Pioneers was primarily an attempt to distinguish the latecomers
from the early arrivals, because the former were deemed to be a less desirable class of people; as migrant workers, they were suspected of being criminals, gamblers, and other unsavoury types.[40] The Porcupine–Iroquois
Falls "pioneers" did not have to be formally organized to serve much the
same purpose. Claiming or acknowledging membership was a means of
creating a sense of belonging amongst the most stable portion of the population, of establishing a core set of values which the new community sup-

posedly shared, and of making legitimate one group's claim to economic, political, and social leadership. The two central components were longevity and triumph over adversity. A pioneer had to be a long-term resident, committed to the region (which meant that immigrant sojourners and Canadian migrant workers were excluded) and had to have triumphed over great odds (which conveyed moral legitimacy). So compelling was this set of historical myths that not only locals were aware of them. Journalist Philip Smith, in his history of mining in Ontario, which won the National Business Book Award in 1987, recorded, "It could be said, perhaps, that the indefatigable spirit that animated those northern pioneers, the feeling of belonging that was born of shared adversity – a feeling that still binds together their descendants – was forged in fire, the same fierce element that gave the region its mineral riches so many millions of years ago."[41]

Of course, a series of images constructed by a minority group of middle-class Anglo- and French-speaking Canadians would not necessarily appeal to others in the region. For the French-speaking Canadian mill worker or miner, the idea of North and the northern pioneer had quite a different resonance than it did for his English-speaking Canadian counterpart, as scholar Christian Morissonneau explored in *La terre promise: le myth du nord québécois*.[42] The Italian railway worker, unable to read English and unlikely to be participating in political debates in a system in which he could not vote anyway, probably was not even aware of the entire discussion. The Finnish family in a pulpwood-cutting camp kept aloof from Canadian society and devoted its energy to other political issues. But over time, a series of events forced reaction from all segments of the region's society, and the images that had been generated among one group for particular purposes gradually expanded their appeal. As was discussed in the previous chapter, circumstances did provide for at least some possibility of collective interest and collective response. In the structures of institutions, the work of key individuals, and certain shared goals and values, space was available for people to move beyond the sense of identity they carried with them on arrival. The idea of North provided a set of symbols that all could share in this community space. It took a combination of events and imagined realities for that space to be occupied.

The Great War of 1914–18 posed the first significant set of social challenges to the people of Porcupine–Iroquois Falls, Aboriginal and newcomer alike. The outbreak of fighting in Europe in the summer of 1914 initially seems to have generated little interest in the region; people were preoccupied with establishing their new lives. But by the spring of 1915, war news and enthusiasms were being noticed. The Porcupine mines began a "greater production" campaign to mirror the agricultural campaign elsewhere in Canada, proposing that gold was necessary for the national war effort as much as food.[43] Miners and office staff alike began to sign up for military service; Abitibi faced construction slowdowns as it became more difficult to find workers. As has been discussed, both English and French Canadians heard the call, especially when recruiters made them feel needed for their mining and tunnelling skills or for their knowledge of railway construction and maintenance. And Aboriginal men signed on in significant numbers. In the autumn of 1916, the Ontario minister of lands, forests, and mines reported, "Settlement in Northern Ontario has been almost completely arrested by the war, and the drain of men from farms and industries has rendered an acute labour situation."[44] In the 1917 Victory Bonds campaign, the Temiskaming District tripled its goal, with probably one of every five adults participating.[45] Even at the newly established Iroquois Falls plant, more than a thousand men enlisted for overseas service during the course of the war.[46]

Many of those who served overseas never returned to the North, either through death or the decision to start over somewhere else. But stories of their accomplishments did return, and those left behind basked in the reflected glory of the work of "their boys." In 1946 school inspector J.B. MacDougall wrote:

Heroic deeds of the first Great War are still remembered when the forestry and construction battalions were recruited in the Canadian North. They transformed the entire system of deforestation and timber supply for trench and defence works … The railway battalions were laying steel at the front … And so the spirit and skill acquired in the remote recesses of the northern woods registered for the Empire in far-away France and Flanders against the embattled might of the enemy world. The North was the balance wheel of Canada in those critical days.[47]

One of the most-loved heroes was Private Jack Munroe, an amateur boxer who had first been eulogized as the man who had organized the bucket brigade that supposedly saved Golden City in the 1911 fire. He claimed to have been the first Canadian to step onto French soil, as a member of the Princess Patricia's Canadian Light Infantry, and the *Advance* followed his activities with interest. Munroe was badly wounded at Ypres in 1916 and invalided out, the injury only adding to his legend. While in hospital, he began writing letters to friends in the North (including one to "The Ladies of Matheson"), and these were published in the *Advance* and the Cobalt *Daily Nugget*. Upon his return to Canada, Monroe was paraded through Cobalt and Timmins as part of a campaign to promote the soldier settlement program (agricultural lands for veterans), and he then worked for a time as an army recruiter in Cobalt. After that, he wrote a book of memoirs entitled *Mopping Up! A Dog Story of the Princess 'Pats.' Through the Eyes of Bobbie Burns, Regimental Mascot*, which was published by a New York firm in

1918. Munroe's abilities as a storyteller and speaker, combined with his already established status in the region, ensured that "his" war became Porcupine–Iroquois Falls's version of the war as well.[48] The distant horrors of war were personalized, sanitized (but with just enough blood to make the heroism compellingly real), and incorporated into the regional mythology.

For the young men who served in the trenches of Flanders and returned to tell the tale, the experience certainly brought them into contact with other Canadians and helped contribute to a growing sense of connection with Canada as a nation, as some historians have argued. But it also brought home to them the fact that their experience in Northern Ontario, however brief, had already marked them as something different. First and perhaps most obvious were their skills in tunnelling, forestry, and railway construction. But the North had marked them in less obvious ways too. As Cobalt writer John Patrick Murphy later recalled, the sight of gas creeping across no man's land was described by the British soldiers as "never higher than an English hedge," but the lads from New Ontario said it was "not as high as the bottom branches of a lightning-struck jackpine."[49] The landscape was becoming part of the newcomers' psyche, serving as a convenient symbol with its sharp black spruce and twisted jack pines, and giving a clearly different idea of forest than the soft undulations of the hardwood stands of the South.

The image of the hardy northerner saving civilization turned out to have a broader appeal. Quite possibly, the image that northerners constructed for themselves was fed and reinforced by similar images in circulation through the rest of Canada. Historian Jonathan Vance has argued that one of the most powerful images of Canadian soldiery that came out of the war was that of the "pure and rugged backwoodsman who lived his life far from the stultifying influence of city and university." Vance cites the poetry of Esther Kerry and Goodridge Roberts as examples of this kind of imagery, in which "the soldier is typified as a child of nature, someone who is intimately connected to the untamed wilderness. He is what we believe the essential Canadian should be."[50] Northern Ontarians, in the midst of defining themselves as something distinct, yet anxious to prove they had come of age and were entitled to be seen as contributing Canadians, found in this imagery the ideal combination of myths.

Of course, not everyone saw the war or participation in it on these terms. After the Military Service Act of August 1917 provided for the conscription of men between the ages of twenty and thirty-five, an unknown number of eligible men simply evaporated into the bush. Jack Pecore later recalled that many at Porcupine had been participants in the 1912 strike; unable or unwilling to obtain employment at the mines as a result, they seemed to be prime candidates for military service. "Some of them stayed in there [the bush] all through the war," Pecore claimed. "When they got their army call, they wouldn't go in the army, and they went back in there ... They knew they were safe."[51] At Iroquois Falls in the early spring of 1918, authorities arrested more than seventy men for violations of the Military Service Act, the majority of whom were deemed fit for service and turned over to the army.[52] But the voices of these men were drowned out in the rising chorus of war enthusiasts.

On the home front, one of the most important symbols of the war was the "enemy alien." In August 1914 the War Measures Act gave the government the power to arrest, detain, and deport citizens of enemy countries, but many northeastern Ontarians believed the legislation was totally inadequate. In June 1915 the boards of trade in the main towns organized a petition calling for more stringent measures, and the Cobalt Board of Trade voted to send a delegation to Ottawa "asking that a general internment of aliens be begun immediately."[53] While businessmen and mine managers seem to have led the campaign, it was well received among working men who were finding it difficult to secure work (particularly in the mining sector) and who made the "enemy alien" the scapegoat. "The alien employment question in the Porcupine district has been a cause for much discontent," reported the *Advance* in July 1915. "Many bitter remarks and comments can be heard." At the formation of the South Porcupine Home Guard, a petition for dominion officials was drafted, which read "South Porcupine Home Guard expresses its disapproval of the failure of the Government to intern alien enemies employed in such numbers in the Porcupine District."[54] The government (this time provincial) was further blamed in an incident at the Timmins roundhouse of the TNO. When four Austrian workers accidentally ran an engine into some train cars, they were absolved, but their British foreman was fired. An irate correspondent to the *Porcupine Advance* declared, "Can you beat this? We all know of the various conditions regarding aliens around this camp ... but here is one case where a private corporation is not involved but a Government Railroad, carried on by the representatives of the British people, under British rule and supposed to be British conditions."[55]

Clearly there was an element of economic self-interest that had precipitated this campaign, but it is significant that its leaders began to voice their concerns against government as much as against the aliens themselves. Government (which, of course, was located in the distant South) had failed yet again, they claimed, to understand the "unique" conditions that prevailed in northeastern Ontario. Government did not appreciate that "the foreign population of the Porcupine district far outnumbers the British,"[56] or that vast sums of money earned in the area were allegedly being sent back to Europe to support the German war effort, however indirectly. Government did not fully grasp the fact that enemy aliens would not or could not assimilate and therefore posed a social threat to the North as well. The campaign against the enemy alien became, in part, an exercise in distancing Porcupine–Iroquois Falls from a remote, unappreciative southern government authority. The sense of regional alienation was being reinforced.

Of course, the dominion government did eventually strengthen its measures against citizens of enemy countries – in 1916 with the compulsory registration of "enemy aliens" and in 1918 with restrictions and bans of foreign-language publications and some political organizations. Prisoner-of-war camps were used to intern those considered a particular threat. These measures went a long way to subduing the anti-government outbursts in Porcupine–Iroquois Falls. Local police reported regularly to the public on the number of enemy aliens registered and the number given permits to leave the district; these statistics were published in the newspaper. But the groundwork for an important part of "community" identity had been laid. If you were a British citizen and/or supported the war effort, you were "in." All others were dangerous aliens. Indeed, you did not have to be a citizen of an enemy country to be labelled an "alien" now. A Timmins resident named Mr Hall tried to convince the board of trade in May 1918 that business licences should be refused to all who were not British citizens, though "the aliens of friendly allied nations" might be given special consideration.[57]

The orgy of anti-alien sentiment toward the end of the war spilled easily into the postwar Bolshevik scare that swept across Canada, to which (as we have seen) this region was not immune. Through the 1920s, communism was increasingly perceived locally as something foreign. In the words of a Dome Mines employee, the newly organized Workers' Party "was for the recognition of Russians and such like 'wops' instead of Canadians and it is up to Canadians to steer clear of it and organize among themselves."[58] The enemy alien was transformed into the communist – an evil, vaguely threatening "other" whose presence required constant vigilance and a united front. Finns and Ukrainians were widely considered to be the foreign agitators behind the communist movement, in spite of the fact that its most visible proponents were visiting speakers such as John Lawrence MacDonald, Tim Buck, and William Moriarty. The fact that the most dedicated local communists included Finns and Ukrainians, however, made the equation of foreigner and communist an easy one to maintain for the better part of a decade.

The bitter ethnic divisions of the war and post-war years received a serious check in the tragedy of 1928. On 10 February a fire broke out deep underground at the Hollinger Mine, trapping fifty-one men. Two bodies were removed that day, and periodically over the next three days, processions bearing the bodies of two or three victims at a time emerged from the mine. Eventually, twelve men made it out alive, but thirty-nine others were dead. First came the grief and mourning. Tellingly, the ethnic enclaves rallied and closed in on themselves, organizing separate funerals at the Finnish Hall, the Ukrainian Hall, the Anglican church, and the Roman Catholic church. At St Antoine's, there were separate funeral masses for the Croatian and French Canadian victims. But very quickly thereafter, people emerged to see common cause. A "mass meeting" at the New Empire Theatre in Timmins was addressed by speakers in six languages; participants issued a declaration calling for a government inquiry to determine responsibility. Political differences were set aside when the declaration asked that any board of inquiry include local representatives from the miners' union, the OBU, and the IWW.[59] A month later, a local coroner's jury looking into the tragedy was unequivocal in its conclusions. It blamed Hollinger management completely for "gross negligence" in permitting flammable materials to accumulate underground.[60] Three months later, when the provincial government's own investigative results were announced, there was local outrage. Commissioner T.E. Godson agreed that some blame lay with management but proposed that the miners were at fault for not reporting an obviously dangerous practice. MP J.A. Bradette later recalled, "I heard many fiery utterances which were made against the management and against the government," including allegations that the fire had been deliberately set.[61]

In a place accustomed to death and dismemberment in the workplace, the sheer horror and scale of the tragedy drove a lightning bolt into public consciousness. There was a hardening of the line between worker and manager, and a search began for ways for workers to protect themselves when the government allegedly would not. Municipal politics became a particular focal point for discontent, as was discussed in chapter 9. The communist ranks may not have swelled as the organizers had hoped,[62] but it is clear that local politics was radicalized in another sense. Labour and "progressive" candidates were repeatedly returned at the polls, and a nasty rhetoric about bosses and government crossed ethnic boundaries in a common cause. Government remained the "other," but now the boss or management was more clearly (and widely) identified as a common threat.

This crack in the walls of ethnic exclusivity made possible a growing understanding through the 1930s as events unfolded in Europe that were closely watched in Porcupine-Iroquois Falls. New alliances were formed between the Canadians and certain Ukrainians and Finns as the Canadians began to make more subtle distinctions about which "foreigners" were acceptable. These alliances were facilitated in part by the efforts of the immigrant groups themselves, by the media, and by the shared fear of a common enemy. Of course, these new alliances further alienated the residents who were excluded. However, they also permitted the participants to dominate public dialogue and public space with a sense of collective entitlement.

A group of Ukrainians made the first advances. Across Canada, Ukrainian nationalist activists were organizing *prosvita* ("enlightenment") societies based on a network of the same name that had been started in Galicia at the end of the nineteenth century. In Canada, the Prosvita Society promoted awareness of Ukrainian culture and heritage. I have been unable to determine exactly when the society was formed in Timmins, but in 1932 its members built a new hall on Elm Street North, partly in an attempt to distance themselves from the more radical socialists in the Ukrainian Labor Farmer Temple Association and their hall on Mountjoy. Under their president Walter Rutchynski, the Prosvita Hall provided a focal point for educational campaigns both inside and outside the local Ukrainian population, and brought together conservatives and moderate socialists within that group.[63]

A concern about communism provided a ground where members of Prosvita and the Canadian-born population could meet. In the fall of 1933, participants in a meeting at the Prosvita Hall strongly condemned the Soviet government for its role in the terrible famine that was stalking millions in Ukraine, and they called on Ukrainians in Canada to support the Ukrainian nationalist movement in their homeland.[64] The following year, members of the Timmins Prosvita branch participated in a campaign with the Sudbury branch to disassociate themselves from the Ukrainian Labor Farmer Temple Association, which they considered was full of "disaffected trouble-makers" of the Red variety. Alderman W.J. Cullen of Sudbury went a step further, proposing that the ULFTA should not be permitted to call itself Ukrainian. "Most of its members," he was quoted as saying, "are Finns and it is considered to be a libel on Ukrainians in general." [65] According to the nationalists, no true Ukrainian could be a communist, given the realities of conditions in Soviet-dominated Ukraine.

This link between nationalism and anti-communism became a rallying cry among many Poles in the region as well, particularly through the formation of the Polish White Eagle Society. When a group of communists and labour activists applied for a May Day parade permit in 1933, claiming to represent (among others) the Polish workers, John Opiola, secretary of the White Eagle Society, contacted the *Advance* to make it clear that as far as they knew, there was no local Polish Workers' Association with its communist affiliations. The newspaper responded with the published observation that local Poles were "free from all tendency to 'red' tactics," and their White Eagle Society represented "the loyal Polish people of the town and district."[66] Ethnicity and political tendencies were being separated, and it was now the "communist," rather than the "foreigner" or "enemy alien,"

who was the "other." Clearly, one of the most important elements of this
emerging ethnic rapprochement was the discovery of a shared antipathy to
communism.

Leaders of these nationalist societies were quick to capitalize on this
realization and acted to enlist the alliance of the Canadian-born population. The local media was an important tool in this campaign. When the
Prosvita Society celebrated Ukrainian National Day on 1 November 1933,
it sent a spokesman to the *Advance*, who explained that the activities were
not intended as an expression of disloyalty to Canada. For Canadian
Ukrainians, he said, "their loyalty is to Canada ... but their love for the
Ukraine is of equal depth."[67] Soon afterwards, when a Toronto lawyer
came to speak at their hall, members invited Timmins mayor George
Drew, *Porcupine Advance* editor G.A. Macdonald, and other local dignitaries, giving the event the aura of an officially sanctioned meeting and in
the process generating some favourable publicity. Clearly, anti-communism helped the wider community to accept the Prosvita Society.

Perhaps it also helped that the two heroes of the 1928 Hollinger Mine
fire – George Zolob and Peter Bilenki – were Ukrainian. And it was reas-
suring to the Canadians that the Prosvita Society went out of its way to
affirm publicly that it was possible to be loyal to Canada yet retain an affection for one's homeland. Undoubtedly, the plan to recruit members of the
Anglo-French leadership as allies was also useful. For whatever reasons, the
ice seems to have been broken, and some Canadians began to reciprocate.
In September 1935, W.S. Blake, principal of the Schumacher High School,
arranged with the Schumacher Lions Club to organize a series of winter
activities designed explicitly to bring together "old" and "new" Canadians.
Blake explained that he believed "athletic, recreational, cultural and community progress" could "best be accomplished by a better knowledge of
each other and more frequent intercourse."[68] As was noted in the previous
chapter, a crowd of four hundred showed up at the inaugural meeting, and
the idea proved a great success. When a Ukrainian nationalist army
general came to Timmins in March 1936 on a cross-Canada speaking tour,
the official welcoming committee symbolized the new, tentative cultural
rapprochement: it included the Porcupine District Pipe Band.[69]

Events in Europe had emboldened anti-communist sentiments among
many of the recent immigrants, and they had an impact on the region at
the same time that an awareness of growing political anxieties on other
European fronts was raising new concerns here. For a generation that had
fought and suffered through the "War to End All Wars," it seemed inconceivable that such a disaster might happen all over again. Calls for world
peace simultaneously became calls for local unity, as local leaders looked
for ways to encourage both. Prewar (and then wartime) propaganda connected the region to the world stage, which it rightly deserved to be on,

according to local leaders. But it also clearly had implications for more immediate application.

It was love of music that shaped the first experiment. In 1934 a "Music Festival of Many Nationalities" was organized at Timmins. Held at the Goldfields Theatre under the auspices of the mayor, the general manager of Hollinger, and the manager of the Schumacher Bank of Commerce, it drew a large crowd to performances by both local and imported talent. Among those who competed for prizes were Ukrainian sword dancers, a Cornish choir, a "Venetian Accordion Duo," a bagpipe ensemble, a Finnish chorus, a Spanish dancer, and a Ukrainian mandolin orchestra. Dr J.A. McInnis, who chaired the event, drew considerable applause when he "pointed out how music and art brought all together in harmony and good fellowship" and said that he hoped "the same harmony and co-operation among the nations of the world as was shown by the nations of Timmins would make for world peace and world progress."[70]

A year later, the Silver Jubilee of King George V provided another opportunity for a display of harmony and cooperation. Members of the immigrant groups that had so recently been recipients of the most pointed hostility seem to have decided that it was in their best interests to build on this new spirit of unity in the hope of heading off another round of persecution. When the town of Timmins announced there was to be a celebratory parade for the Silver Jubilee, various national societies organized contributions. The result, held in May 1935, turned out to be an altogether "remarkable parade." Several thousand people turned out to cheer on five kilometres of floats produced by dozens of local groups (even though no prizes were offered, observed the *Advance*). The parade demonstrated, according to the Timmins newspaper, "that people of Italian, Croatian, Jugo-Slav, Czecho-Slovak, Polish, Syrian, Finnish, Roumanian, Ukrainian, and many other origins, carry enshrined in their hearts the love of Britain's flag and Britain's King, the emblems of an Empire's sincere efforts for freedom, democracy, progress."[71] The Italians, whose float represented a national encounter by depicting the landing of John Cabot, went one better in the propaganda campaign by later donating their float to the Children's Aid Society for use as a playhouse.

The idea of cooperation was beginning to catch on. Clearly, all groups involved had their own interests at heart and were not motivated entirely by a vaguely noble goal of world peace. Anti-communists saw the value of an alliance with other anti-communists across ethnic boundaries. Mine and mill managers saw the benefits of a contented and stable workforce, while the most extreme labour agitators were drowned out by the chorus of moderates. Retailers envisioned an expansion of business beyond the ethnically segregated clientele they now tended to draw. Ukrainians from Galicia, who had borne the brunt of Great War nativism but who now saw little hope of returning to a country changed so dramatically under Soviet control, were clearly anxious for a degree of acceptance and social peace. And, of course, the process was very much facilitated by the arrival of the younger generation on the public stage – a generation raised in Canada, if not in the Porcupine–Iroquois Falls region, who had accepted a degree of assimilation and accommodation.

Gestures of cooperation were not limited to crossing the Canadian/non-Canadian divide. In the fall of 1938, for example, the Timmins Hungarian Society held a festival to celebrate the grape harvest and invited a number of Czechoslovakians, who attended in folk costume. Both groups stressed to observers that regardless of current events in Europe, there was a long-standing historical relationship between their nations, and they clearly intended to perpetuate it on Canadian soil.[72]

The *Porcupine Advance* was delighted with this gathering and ran an editorial proposing "that some service club or patriotic society of Older Canadians might sponsor an event to welcome new Canadians." This would provide the latter with an opportunity to show off their "charming costumes," music, "interesting customs," and "unusual but appealing usages." The editor admitted such an event would pose some difficulty, but it would be worthwhile "to show the New Canadians that the Older Canadians are ready to esteem them as they evidently esteem the people of this land."[73] The term "New Canadians" reflected a new way of thinking on the part of the Anglo- and French Canadian middle class. The possibility of citizenship was implied, as was a sense of shared emotional connection to the country. And apparently it was not only G.A. Macdonald of the *Advance* who saw the value of such a project, for nine months later Timmins celebrated its first Great National Festival. For three days, various community groups put on displays of music, costume, and dance at the McIntyre Arena, with prominent local people judging the presentations and awarding prizes. The editor of the *Advance* enthused, "Events like the National Festival emphasize how much they have in common – delight in graceful dancing, love of music, pleasure in beauty in dress and carriage … love of home and family, love of wholesome pleasure, love of freedom, love of independence, love of the right to be men and women in their own right." With an awareness of what was shared, wrote Macdonald, "there will be a united nation that can stand against the world."[74] Although it might be argued that such a festival was a very superficial exchange of cultural values, and a cynic might propose that it was little more than prewar nationalistic propaganda orchestrated by the elite, it was nonetheless a considerable distance from the days when the enemy alien allegedly stalked the streets and drilled in secret behind the Dome Mine. A small accommodation on each side of the divide seemed to be paving the way for more meaningful interaction among a broader-based group than had, to this point, laid claim to being "the community."

There were some surprising elements in this new search for accommodation. The first was a shift in attitudes toward Chinese men, who had once borne the brunt of the most virulent public displays of racism. The second was a sympathy campaign for the plight of European Jews that was totally out of step with Canadian public policy. Finally, there was a rethinking of relations with the Italians, who had once been seen as moderate local allies but had now become a national enemy. In all cases, both local circumstances and international events had combined to force new responses.

By the late 1930s, many Chinese men in the region were long-term residents. Although the Chinese Immigration Act of 1923 had almost completely closed the door to further immigration, the upheavals of war in China in 1911–13 and 1927–37 undoubtedly deterred many Chinese abroad from returning home. They must have felt trapped. In northeastern Ontario, they had lived quietly and kept to themselves, running successful domestic-service businesses such as restaurants and laundries; one had become a wealthy farmer and restaurant supplier. Their names rarely appeared in the police court columns (except for the occasional gambling raid). During the Depression, they seldom applied for relief, relying instead on a network of fellow countrymen when in economic distress. By this time, too, it was popularly believed in the region that many had become naturalized British citizens. In a region where men continued to form the majority of the population, the fact that the Chinese sector was almost exclusively male was not a marker of difference here as it may have been elsewhere in Canada.[75] It was gradually becoming clear to town leaders that the Chinese shared some of their values: a willingness to work hard, to avoid political extremism, to remain committed to the region, and to value success in business. When Hung Ti won the grand prize in a Lions Club raffle during Silver Jubilee Week in Timmins, the *Advance* ran an editorial entitled "A Chinaman's Chance." It read, in part:

In the early days of the Porcupine the Chinamen were among the first to join their paler and redder brethren in taking a chance in this country where everybody took a chance – when it looked as if the country didn't have a Chinaman's chance (old version) and scores of Chinamen have stayed with the land through good and ill unto the present prosperous days when the North has a Chinaman's chance (new version). The Chinaman took a chance on establishing cafes and laundries in this country when others could not seem to make a go of it … If there is anybody that will take a chance, it is a Chinaman, and they are cheerful, industrious, kindly and friendly folk in all their chance-taking.[76]

As patronizing and awkward as this editorial sounds, it was a significant shift from the local mockery of the "Chinks" in earlier years.

After this event, the *Advance* began to run stories on the Japanese invasion of China, including a local perspective. In August the paper reported that the Chinese "citizens" of Timmins had raised more than a thousand dollars to help the people of Shanghai, who were suffering under the Japanese blockade. For the first time, individual Chinese men were identified respectfully by name, including Cheng Fong and laundryman Hop Lee. Their concern that the Japanese attack on China represented the first stage of a campaign of world domination was taken seriously by the *Advance*. And readers were informed that the group had "community club rooms" in the basement of a Second Avenue building – no longer were these rooms represented as dark dens of unthinkable evil and suspicion.[77] Obviously, a more sympathetic and sensitive coverage of Chinese news in the *Advance* did not represent a dramatic shift in public opinion, but certainly the possibility of change was being imagined in one circle at least. Clearly, the Chinese were still on the fringe of the attempts to forge cross-community links. There was no reference to Chinese participation in the 1939 National Festival, for example. Although the new community was beginning to define itself as more inclusive – thus making it increasingly difficult to justify exclusion – some created distances were still far too great to be crossed quickly.

The question of anti-Semitism in the 1930s was another tricky question in Porcupine–Iroquois Falls. As was discussed in chapter 5, a small but influential group of Jewish entrepreneurs across the region seems to have been generally accepted and easily integrated with other members of the professional and business population. Social interaction led the way to more serious political engagement in the 1930s. Early in 1937, the Timmins Lions Club invited businessman Barney Sky (of Russian-Jewish origins) to speak on Jewish history, and Sky used the opportunity to raise alarm bells about Jewish persecution by the Germans and Russians. By the fall of 1938, local concern on this point led to a meeting of prominent citizens, who prepared a petition to Prime Minister Mackenzie King denouncing the persecution of the Jews in Europe and calling on Canada to open its doors to Jewish refugees and others fleeing the Nazis. "We join the Jewish people and the whole civilized world, in mourning the innocent victims of all religious faiths," went the petition. "Let Canada be a haven of refuge to those whose present treatment is a blot on our civilization. May God help them!"[78]

The statement was remarkable in more than one way. Canadian public policy was (and had been since 1931) firm in its refusal to admit refugees of any kind, and Jewish refugees were particularly unwanted, as the incident of the ss *St Louis* was to make clear a few months later. "None is too many," an anonymous government official said to a journalist of the day.[79] But as historian Valerie Knowles has argued, not all Canadians shared this attitude. Among the "select group" who supported a more open immigration policy, she stated, were "leading spokesmen for the Jewish community, prominent members of the Protestant churches, newspaper editors and commentators in English-speaking Canada," and members of the CCF party.[80] It was just such people who participated in the Timmins meeting: Rabbi David Monson; three Protestant clergymen, the Reverends Mustard, Linder, and Baine; newspaper editor G.A. Macdonald; radio broadcaster William Wren; Timmins mayor J.P. Bartleman; several local physicians; two senior managers from Hollinger; and the area's MP, J.A. Bradette, a Liberal with labour leanings. Noticeably absent were any Roman Catholic clergy or French-speaking community leaders (with the exception of Bradette). So it is unclear how far this liberal attitude toward Jews extended. Certainly, not long before, when Victor Nathanson, a Jewish resident of Ansonville, had complained of his treatment on a provincial road construction crew, the foreman allegedly told him, "Your work is excellent Nathanson but you are handicapped because you are a Jew and they are criticising Mr. Rowlandson for appointing you."[81] The anti-Semitism of the political and religious elite in Quebec before the Second World War is well known.[82] Whether similar ideas were being expressed publicly and privately in Porcupine–Iroquois Falls has unfortunately not been recorded or remembered.

Certainly, there appears to have been little support for Nazi ideas in the years before the war. Oddly, it was the strength of local anti-communism that made support for Nazism difficult. When Germany and the USSR signed their non-aggression pact on 24 August 1939, local anti-communists proposed that this was proof positive that the two political philosophies were peas in the same pod. The connection was drawn explicitly by a group of Timmins Slovaks who signed a petition to distance themselves from a movement led by former prime minister and president Edward Beneš, which aimed to rid Czechoslovakia of the Nazis. They considered Beneš to be a communist sympathizer, and observed, "The recent pact between Russia and Germany suggests how little difference there is between Nazism and Communism."[83] It was not a very sophisticated understanding of political philosophy; but, for these Slovaks, despotism was despotism. Of course, opposition to the anti-Nazi Beneš seemed to imply support for National Socialism, so shortly after the first public declaration, Martin Kobzick felt compelled to tell the Daily Press that the majority of Timmins Slovaks were most certainly opposed to Nazism and supported any movement to get the party out of Czechoslovakia.[84] It was a tricky situation, but anti-Nazi sentiment seems to have won out.

The public response to Italians in the region was another complex aspect of the struggle to find accommodation in the 1920s and 1930s. As was discussed in chapter 5, their Roman Catholic faith, their tendency to anti-communism (and hence labour conservatism), their participation in the First World War effort, their increasingly settled family life, and their cultural contributions locally had all made possible at least a superficial acceptance, particularly among English- and French-speaking Canadian fellow workers. They had been perceived as allies in the First World War, though Italians from the area were more likely to have fought in Italian uniform rather than in Canadian or British. In the 1920s they had been favoured by the dominion government as imported labour for Northern Ontario mines.[85] Many had become naturalized British subjects. At the Dome Mines in 1939, for example, fifty-one of the seventy-two Italians on the payroll were naturalized and eight had been born in Canada.[86] By 1940 they had become physically dispersed among the wider population at Moneta and the Dome Mines property. But suddenly, on 10 June 1940, Italy was at war with Canada. The ally was now the enemy. The awkwardness of the situation was symbolically illustrated by the case of an Italian miner at Dome whose French Canadian wife tried to settle a domestic dispute by alleging to the mine manager that her husband had been participating in subversive activities and asking that he be arrested.[87] Their personal struggle was a mirror of the wider social struggle that the Second World War raised in the region.

On the one hand, there was considerable support for the area's Italians on both personal and political levels. The Roman Catholic Church generally and the French-speaking population in particular had already been forging alliances, and they rose readily to the support of Leo Mascioli and his brother when they were interned at Petawawa, as was discussed in chapter 8. When the Ontario legislature held a vote to censure the dominion government for its less than overwhelming war effort, Northern Ontario MPPs either actively opposed the resolution or absented themselves, a choice which historian Graeme Mount attributes to the potential for divisiveness at home, with the French Canadians and Italians on one side and the English-speaking Canadians on the other.[88]

At the same time, ambivalence about fascism stirred the pot. Many Porcupine-area Italians had been drawn to the nationalism of Mussolini's government and joined the Order Sons of Italy, as has been noted. A new sense of pride in things Italian was undoubtedly an appealing response to the thinly veiled prejudice in Canada and to the need to form a sense of community among those from different regions or districts in Italy. There may well have been Sons of Italy who were attracted to fascism as a political philosophy, just as we know there were Canadians who flirted with it in the Parti national chrétien (founded 1934) and in such publications as *Le fasciste canadien.* Unfortunately, very little is known about fascism in the Porcupine district; people seem to prefer to forget. Perhaps those who supported it left the area in answer to Mussolini's call. Those who remained tried to draw a distinction between Mussolini's political move- ment and Italian nationalism, as so many Italians did in eastern Canada.[89] Many families made declarations of their citizenship status or tried to keep a low profile. In the end, in spite of occasional acts of public hostility, the Italians never became what the "enemy alien" of the First World War had been.

The situation for the Finnish-born population was another potential problem, as was described in chapter 10. At the beginning of the war, Canadians saw them as the "brave Finns," fighting heroically against the evils of communism. But when Finland accepted aid from Germany, and Canada and the USSR became allies, the Finns were the enemy. For the many White Finns, Canada's alliance with the USSR in the fight against Hitler must have seemed an awkward arrangement at best. But like the Ital- ians, the Finns were never demonized to the extent that enemy aliens had been in the first war. Perhaps, in part, it was because many were integrat- ing into the wider population – like the first Timmins war casualty, Ahti (Joseph) Aho, who was engaged to be married to an Iroquois Falls nurse, Jean Smith.[90] The Palace Theater in Timmins had begun screening films in Finnish (with English subtitles) early in 1939.[91] Just as importantly, the events of the Winter War had encouraged the Canadian-born to see that not all Finns fitted the stereotype of radical communists or atheist trou- blemakers. So although wartime brought strained relations, it conjured up no widely imagined spectre of Finnish subversives.

The closing months of the Second World War brought one final shock to the people of the region. News of the Nazi concentration camps was, in one sense, merely a confirmation of the validity of the war effort and the allied claims of Nazi treachery. But it was also a horrifying demonstration of the evil of which human beings were capable, and it raised troubling questions for thinking people in Porcupine–Iroquois Falls, as it did for all Canadians. The Women's Association at First United Church in Timmins grappled with these questions at a meeting in May 1945. The Reverend Mr Chidwick was invited as the guest speaker, and the secretary recorded that his presentation addressed two main questions. The first was "what diabol- ical force, social or economic set-up in Germany had changed a people, at one time leaders in culture, music, art, philosophy and even religion, to a nation of sub-humans sunk to the level of concentration camp atrocities." Second, and even closer to home, Mr Chidwick asked what "purposes we are fighting for, and what do we want in the peace to come." Surely it was not, he said, "the subjugation of others; not a return to the old way of life. What the world desires is a new way of life, with war and sin eliminated from the minds of all mankind."[92] That desire for a fresh start was not, of course, unique to the people of Porcupine–Iroquois Falls. But the lessons of group harmony and cooperation clearly had a particular resonance locally. Building on the tentative steps that had been taken in the prewar years, the events of the war seem to have encouraged integration more than division.

Before 1945 there may have been talk of ethnic interaction, but it appears to have gone no further than a symbolic exchange at public events such as parades, concerts, and the national festivals, at least among the adults. But after 1945 the social columns of the area's papers contained irrefutable evidence that things were changing. People born in the years after the First World War were marrying, and their choice of partners was very different from that of their parents. Summer weddings were celebrated in 1948, for example, by Elsie McFadden and Gino Campagnola at First United Church (Timmins), by Annie Barilko and Bernard Dillon at St Joachim's Roman Catholic Church (South Porcupine), by Olga Lucyk and Lauri St Jean at Trinity United Church (Schumacher), and by Lucie Boisvert and Tom O'Loughlin at the Church of the Nativity (Timmins). The records of Trinity United Church in Schumacher show a series of wedding ceremonies for ethnically mixed couples who do not appear to have been regular members of the congregation, but they may have been from different religious backgrounds and found the United Church reasonably neutral ground in which they were welcomed.[93] Within a few years, these "mixed marriages" were being publicly noted and entered into collective memory. Nancy Perger, at one time the curator of the Ukrainian Historical and Cultural Museum in Timmins, recalled that in the 1950s, "young people began to marry outside the Ukrainian community."[94] The abstractions of ethnic and religious harmony were being translated into daily realities for many people. These changes are visible most poignantly, perhaps, in a tour of the Timmins and Tisdale cemeteries. Headstones from the 1920s and 1930s are engraved in a variety of languages and alphabets; those of the 1940s are almost entirely in English or French.

However, the year 1945 was not a kind of magical watershed when a community with common cause emerged from a murky prewar muskeg. Angry conflict was stirred up once again with the postwar arrival of a significant number of DPs – as was described in chapter 9 – and by a potent mix of radical politics and rising unemployment. After the 1949 riot outside the Ukrainian Hall on Mountjoy in Timmins, it looked as if the battles of the 1930s were about to be fought all over again. And while the fundamental rift between nationalist and socialist/communist Ukrainians still existed, the general response to the 1949 riot indicates that some subtle but important changes were taking place. Socialist labour activists interpreted the violence as an attack not just against Red Ukrainians but on labour as a whole, and on the community more broadly. A group calling itself the Timmins Labor Defense Committee was organized in response, and as the first volley in a publicity campaign, it submitted an item to the *Daily Press* entitled "Is D.P. Mob Violence to Rule Our Town?"[95] This committee was evidence that a new coalition had been formed within the left, and the old hard-line Ukrainian and Finnish activists had finally succeeded in making contact with the Canadian-born. The committee's leaders included Art LeBlanc, Stanley Kremyr, and Jim Tester, while its "trustees" were Adelard Houle, Toivo Niemi, Peter Mongeon, and William Kennedy.[96]

This new accommodation among labour interests was also reflected in a revitalized union movement in the mining sector. In 1943 a somewhat moribund Local 241 of the International Union of Mine, Mill and Smelter Workers at Timmins (with only a hundred members) launched an energetic membership drive that succeeded in drawing in between four and five thousand new men. Certification votes were held and won at all the area's mines except Dome. Although the International had initiated the campaign, organizers Bob Miner and William Kennedy[97] would not have been able to attract so many new members without some changes afoot locally. The new Local 241 was a very different creature from its predecessor in the 1920s and 1930s. The original 1920 charter application had been signed overwhelmingly by men with such names as J. Melnyk, Antti Mattson, Mike Mylnychuk, and E. Romouniuk, with only a handful like T.G. McNeil, Norman McKinnon, and William McGinnis; and there had been only one apparently French Canadian name (N. Laport) in the list of fifty-three.[98] But by 1947 the slate of officers included the president Ivan Vachon, vice-president Alcide Brunet, and "warden" C. Fournier, with trustees Walsh, Andrews, Michaud, McInnis, Karcha, Chenier, and Magnusson, clearly reflecting the ethnic mix of the workforce. Secretaries Nick Salome and Stan Jemain rounded out the ethnically diverse leadership.[99] Of course, as was discussed in chapter 6, the new accommodation was tenuous at best, and masked the underlying political differences that eventually led to the acrimonious battle for control and the near-disappearance of Mine, Mill from the Porcupine-area mines. Nevertheless, a coalition of moderates that brought together men (and women in the ladies auxiliary of Local 128) from across the ethnic spectrum was a signal that a sense of shared interests was percolating, even if it was not yet fully brewed.

Bearing in mind that the dedicated communists remained a small but determined and cohesive group apart from the rest of the population, by 1950 it would seem that many among the amorphous collection of miners, mill workers, storekeepers, bushworkers, and railway workers were beginning to see themselves as part of more than just a temporary gathering of transients with little in common. They shared a living space, a working space, and an increasing psychological distance from "home" as time passed; children grew to adulthood in the new surroundings, and world events changed the places their parents had left behind. Key individuals and the local media (whether privately or company owned) were encouraging a sense of community for reasons both practical and idealistic. Gradually, it seemed, the human need for companionship, connection, and a sense of meaning was overcoming the defensive fears of the unknown "other." Perhaps, too, some felt the need to declare that they were creating a new world that was better than the one they had left behind in order to legitimize their absence from that old world. In any case, people had begun to construct a community based on imagined ideals to provide a new human space for the people they were becoming. What did they choose as the primary building materials?

The physical space and a set of values associated with it had become one of the key components. As was discussed earlier in this chapter, the northern setting had been used as a convenient symbol in the boosterism of the first two decades of the century. What had been promoted by the business sector soon provided a useful language for others in the region as well. The rocks, trees, and climate served to set the area apart from Old Ontario, in particular, and allegedly shaped both the bodies and the characters of those who lived in it. The resources that it offered made possible a new kind of life that included a degree of freedom and personal independence, obtainable partly through the material prosperity that came from working the resources and partly through opportunities for such pursuits as hunting and fishing. The North had been constructed as a male space because it allegedly engendered masculine qualities – physical strength, physical and moral courage, ruggedness, and self-reliance. These characteristics echoed the ideas that men who performed hard physical labour liked to believe about themselves. The culture of the male workplace fitted easily with the middle-class ideology of "North," forming a mutually reinforcing dialogue.

The second important building block was the concept of regional society as diverse yet united – something that a later generation would call multiculturalism. What began as a tentative rapprochement between English- and French-speaking Canadians as a device to challenge a common enemy (the subversive, radical foreigner) was gradually evolving into a more inclusive mental map that had been washed with an overlay of moral self-righteousness. Shared experiences, repeated rituals, and necessity had brought people together, and the accommodations on all sides were being perceived as a positive good, not enforced assimilation. French Canadians tried not to be "too French"; Finns stopped speaking about the early battles of camp life; Italians joined the Dante Club instead of the Order Sons of Italy. Not until the 1970s and 1980s did a new generation criticize these accommodations and develop more negative interpretations of what had happened. In 1978, when J-J. Laurendeau published his memoirs of the Abitibi settlers' life, he was almost apologetic for reporting that French Canadian miners used English words as well as some Italian, German, Polish, and others. "It is not a 'crime' to know two or three languages," he wrote. "It is just very useful. It opens borders."[100]

Finally, the emerging community defined itself in relation to a distant and uncaring state. Like so many other "new" societies, people told themselves they were building a way of life that was somehow superior to the old. In this case, superiority was deemed to lie in the values of liberal capitalism. Society in Porcupine–Iroquois Falls was more free, more open, more progressive than in Old Ontario or Europe. And government (always associated with "the South") seemed committed to interfering with all that was best in this new world. Arbitrary regulations and restrictions, policies designed to fill southern pockets, or just lack of well-deserved attention were all obstacles thrown in the path of social and economic development; all had to be vigorously resisted. But it was also a peculiar relationship with government. Like an adolescent who simultaneously rejects his parents as hopelessly out of touch yet is desperate for their approval and recognition, Porcupine–Iroquois Falls promoters tried to "out-modern" the modern. Gold was the economic engine of the nation, and paper permitted the communications networks that sustained it. Both were produced in modern industrial plants with the latest scientific and technological expertise. The people who had accomplished these feats deserved to be treated with respect, not ignored as a fringe settlement on the edges of the wilderness. So the constant struggle in the political arena played into the social and helped shape the images of community.

Thus, in the years before 1950, events generated both inside and outside the region, together with the need to adapt imported ideas to a unique local situation, engendered a public dialogue about what it meant to live in Porcupine–Iroquois Falls. As sojourners became residents, they tried to create new social networks to replace those they had left behind, and they gave these networks meaning by imbuing them with ideas and values that seemed appropriate to the place. They also attempted to legitimize both their flight from "home" and their new claim to residence by creating a set of images about themselves, and by inserting themselves into a created sense of local history that was peopled with heroic Aboriginal men and women who had made themselves a part of the land in times past. These Aboriginal "ancestors" were purportedly followed by brave and hardy "pioneers" such as the archetypical prospector who laid the ground for a new and better life for those who had the vision to follow. The environmental setting was designated as North, and a collection of values was ascribed to both the landscape and the people who came to terms with it.

The sense of a unique identity gradually emerged. Much of this new sense of identity was established in opposition to a series of threatening "others," some imagined and some real, whose presence required a collective defence. But with no single ethnic or religious group in a clear demographic majority, people were forced to live and work together – and to construct a social space in which shared values could be recognized and differences downplayed. Of course, many individuals were never incorporated into this space, and they remained hostile and bitter observers on its margins. But for those on the inside, a sense of community had been formed.

Conclusion

We have observed *how* the processes of community formation and identity development worked themselves out in the Porcupine–Iroquois Falls region. Now we should consider *why*. Why did the economy develop as it did? Why did certain political issues dominate while others were scarcely debated? Why did some employees call for radical solutions to the problems of the workplace while others did not even see the problems? Why did certain individuals and groups come to dominate the public discourse? Why did certain stories get told and repeated while others faded from public memory? Why, ultimately, did a sense of community form here, and why did it take on its particular characteristics?

In the preface, we considered the changing ways in which sociologists and anthropologists have attempted to understand the phenomenon of community, from the characterization of community as something lost to the industrialized world (as posited by Ferdinand Tönnies), to the postmodern critique of community as a creation of industrialization and liberal capitalism. Having toured one specific example of community, it is difficult to find satisfactory explanations in any of these theories. Obviously, since this community could and did form in a "modern" social system, the early theories of Tönnies and his followers do not help. On the other hand, we have seen that the idea of community can be more than a constructed tool through which modernism justifies itself. In Porcupine–Iroquois Falls, thousands of people looked to community as a means of filling the human need for companionship, security, and a sense of connection to something beyond themselves. Furthermore, until recently, social science theory has stressed the tangible – what can be measured – so has missed one of the most important features of community that we have seen at play in this study: the role of the unquantifiables of imagination, memory, and invention. Social science theory has also made the mistake of studying community as a *structure*, whereas we can clearly see that it is equally a historical *process*. Ordinary people play a role in shaping community over time as they respond to events at home and abroad, including the chance encounters of particular individuals and the coincidental intersections of historical trajectories.

How, then, have historians tried to understand community and identity? Have they been any more successful in providing explanations for what we have seen happen in Porcupine–Iroquois Falls? Most historical writing on the subject has focused on the development of the nation as a community, with the concurrent development of a national sense of identity. Thus, it would be appropriate to survey the evolving explanations as they pertained to Canada.

In an attempt to explain the distinctiveness of American society, Frederick Jackson Turner provided one of the first and most compelling explanatory devices – what we now call the frontier thesis. The availability of "empty" land on the margins of established society encouraged a continuous population movement that engendered democratic ideals and a new kind of society characterized by individualism, lack of social convention, and a rejection of established institutions. In turn, this new society in the American West influenced the old society back East, producing an America unlike its European ancestor.[1] The vocabulary, if not all the specifics, appealed to a generation of Canadian academics. The "Canadian Frontiers of Settlement" series of the 1930s set Harold Adams Innis, A.R.M. Lower, and other celebrated scholars to work analysing patterns of development on the "forest frontier" and the "mining frontier," and exploring the implications for political development. As Lower argued, in both Canada and the United States, democracy "has been the spontaneous product of the frontier and the forest."[2] Clearly, however, a thesis intended to explain the uniqueness of American life was problematic for Canadian scholars who wanted to distinguish Canada from the United States. The frontier thesis perhaps contributed vocabulary more than theory to Canadian historiography.[3]

Less well known, but equally provocative, was the "fragment thesis" of Louis Hartz. Hartz proposed that European colonies came to look different from their European parents because only a certain part of the sending society was represented in the colony, which then evolved in a different direction from the parent.[4] By implication, if historical chance had sent a different "fragment," an entirely different dynamic would have been put in place. While the fragment thesis itself appears to have had little direct impact on Canadian scholarship, echoes of it can certainly be heard in the once popular argument that the United Empire Loyalists brought a founding conservatism to Canada, which set us off on a different trajectory from that followed in the United States.[5]

Another grand explanatory device with origins more clearly in Canada was, in part, an attempt to explain the particular patterns of economic development here. There was considerable concern in the 1920s and 1930s that Canada was not industrializing at the same pace as the United States. Our economy seemed to have stalled with the limited extraction of raw materials. In the early 1930s, the professor of political economy H.A. Innis published *The Fur Trade in Canada* and *Problems of Staple Production in Canada*,[6] in which he established his place as a highly original and influential thinker. His interest lay not only in explaining patterns of Canadian economic development but in the complex causal connections he saw among economics, environment, technologies, and human society. Innis influenced a contemporary at the University of Toronto, historian Donald Creighton, who proposed that Canada owed its geographical, economic, and political development to the original east-west dictate of the available water transportation routes, notably the St Lawrence River (hence the Laurentian Thesis).[7] For Innis and Creighton, Canada's political development was distinct from that of the United States, a "natural" consequence of our economic history.

After the stimulus of the Second World War and 1950s consumerism, the industrial development of Canada seemed a less pressing question than the growing regional disparities. The de-industrialization of the Maritimes and the apparent non-industrialization of the Prairies were now the focus for scholarly explanation, particularly since the situation had produced obvious and bitter regional grievances. Canadian historians began to write of "limited identities" instead of focusing on the grand narrative of national development.[8] One of the most influential ideas in this discussion was the metropolitan-hinterland thesis. It was rooted in the theory of economic historian N.S.B. Gras, who studied the relationship between cities and the territory that surrounds them.[9] While Gras was interested in explaining the economic domination of large metropolitan centres, some Canadian historians found the political and social components of metropolitan power to be equally convincing. In 1987 J.M.S. Careless presented a series of lectures for the Donald Creighton Foundation at the University of Toronto that perhaps best demonstrated the explanatory power of the metropolitan thesis in the Canadian context. For Careless, metropolitanism was an important factor in explaining both regional and national identity in Canada. "The policy decisions, the stores of knowledge, and the techniques that were concentrated in such a commanding city were transmitted outward to the hinterland," he said, "working to organize it not in economic terms alone, but in political and social systems, cultural institutions, and built environments as well."[10]

This kind of thinking proved very useful for a new generation of regional historians, but they also rejected the tendency of metropolitanism to emphasize the situation of the metropolis and to consider only the one-way imposition of influence and authority. Doug Owram, who pursued graduate work at the University of Toronto and then moved west to teach at the University of Alberta, studied the ideas of the late-nineteenth century Canadian expansionist movement in *Promise of Eden*.[11] But instead of analysing only the images produced in the campaign to annex the West, Owram turned the mirror to reflect also what the western settlers themselves came to believe about the process and their place in it. Resentful and disillusioned, the western hinterland fought back, and in doing so it reshaped the nation. Clearly, the relationship between metropolis and hinterland was a complex exchange, not simply a one-way imposition of power and influence.

Interest in the hinterland's perspective of these historical processes led to other variations. Kenneth Coates, in a survey history of the Yukon and Northwest Territories, proposed that the northern territories were actually internal colonies, in both the political sense (through constitutional and bureaucratic arrangements) and the economic sense (through an inability to direct development in a way that suited northerners themselves).[12] Others flirted with related ideas, like the applicability of dependency theory, which was originally devised in the context of Third World underdevelopment studies. Historians of Atlantic Canada, for example, have engaged in a vigorous debate in the search for structural explanations of the collapse of nineteenth-century industry and subsequent regional underdevelopment.[13]

Perhaps one of the most subtle and sophisticated analyses of the issues of region, frontier, metropolis, and identity was Paul Voisey's *Vulcan: The Making of a Prairie Community*.[14] In a careful study of a region in southern Alberta through its first decades of agricultural settlement, Voisey argued convincingly that the grand theories of "heritage, metropolis, frontier, and environment" are all too simplistic to explain what happened in Vulcan. Instead, he proposed that we must recognize a "complex interplay" of factors, external and internal, and he scolded historians for being too quick to "employ woolly definitions and assumptions" with only "random illustrations as evidence." The point was not that historians should abandon models entirely but that we should recognize their limitations as "crude tools at best" and should use them more "delicately" to make sense of apparently "random oddities" of the past.[15]

While I agree fully with Voisey on these points, I would add another complaint. All of the models discussed so far in this chapter (and others noted by Voisey) take economics and politics as their core problems and structural devices, even if social identity is part of what is being explained. Society, when it is considered at all, is understood in terms of economic markers (class or occupation, relative wealth, output) or political implications (nation of origin, political orientation, power distribution). Cultural history, which has had a tremendous influence on our understanding of so many other topics, has not been given due consideration in the task of trying to explain regional or national development.[16] Cultural factors need to be given at least equal weight to the economic and political, but they rarely are. One of the few exceptions is Gerald Friesen's challenging *Citizens and Nation: An Essay on History, Communication, and Canada,* in which the author explores the question of how identity is experienced, reproduced, negotiated, and expressed in the "large social group" that is the nation of Canada.[17]

The rather smaller social group that is the region of Porcupine–Iroquois Falls has provided me with exactly the same opportunity to explore the process of identity formation – and in this case, how that identity was expressed in an evolving sense of community. Some things about this place were unique: the specific mix and proportion of cultural influences, the impact of particular individuals, the timing of major events, the physical environment. Other things served to integrate this place into the wider world: economic systems, political structures, personal social networks. A sense of personal and collective identity was both shaped by and had an impact on all these factors. Regional "development" (or "underdevelopment") is not a process dictated purely by economic and political systems, distant metropolises, or geography. These all play a role, but they are also imagined and reconstructed by human beings acting individually and collectively. The mental map is just as important as the physiographic.

Recognizing the role of the cultural in regional development means recognizing a number of features that are often overlooked. In this region, first and foremost, EuroCanadian ideas about race, especially attitudes toward Aboriginal people, were critical. Newcomers were willing to accommodate to Aboriginal social and political expectations when economic gain might result. Hence, the fur trade (after an initial period of tension and adjustment) eventually sustained an integrated, demographically balanced, and relatively successful community. With the ambitions of Empire Ontario, colonizing priests, and industry, however, Aboriginal people were no longer economically necessary. EuroCanadian perceptions of cultural superiority now permitted a one-sided effort to sweep out the First Nations and lay the foundations of a new world, in which the original population was expected either to accommodate or to go elsewhere. Once administrative processes had "cleared away" the issue of Aboriginal title, waves of newcomers arrived with apparently no realization whatsoever that there were living "Indians" on their doorstep. Eventually, when it suited the newcomers, they "rediscovered" the Indian in an attempt to lay a claim to something that distinguished the northerner from the rest of the world. But the Indian they rediscovered was fantasy not reality – another product of the Canadian cultural imagination.[18]

Second, while the demands of mercantilism, industrial capitalism, and political aggrandizement clearly laid the foundations of the twentieth-century developments, cultural factors influenced the shape of the response. The process of migration itself illustrates this point. French-speaking Roman Catholic priests feared the loss of culture among parishioners who were flocking to the factories of New England, so they encouraged migration to a new place where agriculture and the watchful eye of the church would conserve and protect what these men valued most: their religion, their language, and their rural way of life. European labourers came for work so that they could earn enough to support (or establish) families back home; these men, too, had no interest in changing who they were culturally (by moving permanently to a new land) but preferred to use whatever means was at their disposal to sustain their existing way of life. Finnish families who could no longer accept political or economic upheavals at home came to this new place and reproduced what they valued from home in all its dimensions: language, food, recreation, patterns of work, gender roles, even politics. English-speaking Canadians from the Ottawa Valley and marginal lands of central Ontario came as shopkeepers, professionals, or would-be farmers under the impression that they were reproducing the patterns of home, albeit in a renewed and perhaps improved version that would prevent the disillusionment and struggle of their parents' generation. Few newcomers cut themselves off entirely from "home." Sojourners moved back and forth, settlers encouraged others to come (following the classic pattern of chain migration), good incomes and modern technology permitted regular communication, and new tools such as motion pictures and radio permitted ongoing reminders. The result was a complex social arrangement that had as much to do with the dictates of cultural values as it did with the manufacturing of paper or the production of gold.

Of course, with such a variety of people encountering one another in a very short period, it was quickly apparent to all that some expectations were problematic. The third role that culture played in the regional development of Porcupine–Iroquois Falls, then, was in influencing the ways in which people attempted to modify the structures they found in place. Power, particularly in its economic and political manifestations, was challenged. Finns and Ukrainians attempted to convince Canadians that class struggle was the only viable means of challenging the concentration of economic power in the hands of industry; while they never fully succeeded, workers did develop a sense of value based in part on belittling authority through the stories they told and the social and recreational activities they chose. In Timmins and Tisdale Township, imposed structures of municipal government were appropriated and subverted to provide a forum for the protection of the working man's interests. Principles of communal property were softened and adapted to the co-op movement, which itself eventually was given new meaning and reshaped by the postwar generation. Social patterns were also modified as people borrowed or adopted specific cultural elements from one another: Italian music, Finnish skiing and women's athleticism, Chinese food, Canadian hockey. While these changes may not have had much influence on systems beyond the boundaries of the region, there is no doubt that they were real and important in the lives of the people of Porcupine–Iroquois Falls – important even if the attempt at change did not succeed. Participation in the process mattered, too.

What factors, then, seem to have played a role in the formation of the twentieth-century community here? The answer is a complex interplay of the economic, political, and cultural, as well as externally imposed structure, locally constructed systems, and imagined realities.

Whether it was the dictates of the fur market, the structures of the resource-extraction economy, or the design of the workplace, economics was important in shaping the community in both obvious and subtle ways. People were drawn here by the prospect of work, and work took up most of their time. Status distinctions were based primarily on a man's place in the work hierarchy or how he performed his work. Living arrangements were often dictated both spatially and socially by work and the place of work, whether in the company town or private boarding house. Gender roles were shaped by the nature of work and attitudes that maintained strictly gendered divisions of labour. Work provided most of the issues that drove local politics. Fluctuations in distant markets or government policy decisions made in the interests of outside agendas determined in a fundamental way whether there was even any work to be had. People attempted to obviate the strict dictates of the economy with such tools as labour organization, mobility/transience, and participation in mixed household economies of farming, wage labour, and hunting. While these techniques had little impact on the underlying economic structures, they clearly had a significant impact on how people experienced their lives and thus how they came to see themselves. One does not have to be a neo-Marxist or even a cultural materialist to agree that the economy played a fundamental role in shaping the community and people's perceptions of it.

Political systems and ideologies were also important. Local commercial and industrial leaders saw to it that the structures of municipal government were quickly established; clearly, the hope was to take control for the benefit of private profit. Soon, however, other interest groups recognized the utility of the technique, and local politics became a battleground. Issues spilled over onto the provincial and dominion stages where, not surprisingly, they were diluted in the bigger sea of interests; but through the region's contribution to the Independent Labor Party and the CCF, they were not entirely without consequence or influence. Socialism, communism, and fascism, hammered out in foreign contexts, were brought here by those who believed they applied in North America as much as in Europe. And while the political debate was neither sophisticated nor nuanced, it was deeply felt and served as a defining characteristic in many people's lives. Some were drawn together in a shared language; others watched warily across the seemingly permanent divides thus created. Politics was also a tool in the process of regional alienation, as will be noted.

The physical environment, both real and imagined, was another important factor in the shaping of community contours. Obviously, the particular resources that happened to be here and the spatial distribution of the trees, gold-bearing ores, and hydroelectric sources were basic factors. So was the fact that the soils and climate were misunderstood by Toronto promoters, leading to misguided agricultural promotion and so much personal hardship and tragedy. Conflict with Aboriginal people over access to scarce resources contributed in no small way to the exclusion of First Nations people from the new community. The availability of fish, game, and berries drew people out of the towns in part because of economic necessity and in part because of the sense of freedom, power, and self-reliance they offered. The resulting relationship with the land was complex and contradictory. The idea of North, initially borrowed from the rhetoric of southern Canada, was appropriated and expanded by those who came to define themselves as northerners – meaning hardy, rugged, masculine, morally pure, and superior to the degenerate, tired, old southerner. At the same time, the North was not some sort of rhetorical counterpart of the "countryside," offering an idyllic escape from industrial capitalism (perhaps because most residents had had recent exposure to the reality of rural living). Rather, this North was a space in which a new and better industrial capitalism could be "built." Civilization was "smashing forward" here as railways were laid, new towns constructed, and macadamized roads pushed through the bush. The headframe and power plant were symbols of progress, wealth, and importance. Changing the landscape with bush cutting, mine tailings, and massive flooding was not considered problematic. The Northland was vast enough to absorb any human activity.

Finally, the historical accidents that brought particular people to this place must be considered as a key component in the development of community. In the late nineteenth century, at the very time when historical processes were encouraging Ontario and Quebec to look north, there was insufficient "surplus" population locally to feed the voracious appetite for labour which the unanticipated resource discoveries engendered. But there were plenty of workers elsewhere. Experienced American miners were abandoning the shafts of Idaho and Colorado as the mining there was restructured to depend more on new technologies than on labour; or they were leaving the Michigan copper mines after a violent and deadly strike in 1913–14. Problems in the pulp and paper industry of Finland and rising political tensions there were encouraging people to look elsewhere for work. Italy's economy had produced an international labour pool hungry for wages that could be sent home to maintain the economic cycle. Populations in the rural Balkans had expanded to the point where tiny farms could support no more people. The drop in demand for steel following the First World War put many Cape Breton coal miners out of work; they arrived on the labour market right in time for the Porcupine mining boom. Problems in Cornwall's tin mines provided other experienced (and cooperative) workers. European refugees and displaced persons from the Second World War arrived at another propitious time. Events that were the result of historical trajectories, most of which were unrelated to Northern Ontario, coincided here to produce a particular mix of peoples and a unique social dynamic based on an accident of timing. These factors helped make the place different from Sudbury, Thunder Bay, and other communities in Northern Ontario, even though they had a similar mix of resources and physical environment.

With the particulars of economy, politics, land, and individuals in place, people settled down to work and to play. In the process, they were changed both by the original circumstances in which they found themselves and by the changes to these circumstances which they themselves created. Society in Porcupine–Iroquois Falls seems to have been shaped by people's actions in a number of ways. Whether these patterns are unique to the region or common to human experience remains a matter for further research and comparative study.

One of the most important factors in community formation here seems to have been the availability (or the manufacture) of a common enemy or threat. The First World War provided the "enemy alien," a socially acceptable target for animosities that had been building anyway. English- and French-speaking Canadians who had previously emphasized what divided them now discovered an "other" in the immigrants of the Austro-Hungarian Empire, and they were able to imagine new definitions of themselves that had the possibility, at least, of rapprochement. The jingoism and rhetoric of wartime that portrayed the citizen of enemy countries as a danger and a threat to "good" people at home fitted easily with the unstated but apparently widely held sense of threat that Canadians felt about the gangs of immigrant workers who had flooded into the region. Animosity toward one segment of the population was given a public airing and accorded the moral high ground, helping to drive that segment out (sometimes literally, sometimes figuratively). In the process, it helped bring other groups together. There were various similarly manufactured threats – the Chinese, the "boss," the Company, Reds, the government – all of which also served as devices in drawing social boundaries.

Language played a powerful role in this and other parts of the community-formation process. Often, rhetoric produced in one context for a specific purpose took on broader meaning and deeper appeal. For example, community boosters (mostly small businessmen) wanted the mines to pay a larger share of the costs of municipal administration in order to lower the tax burden on small business and property-owning individuals – hardly an issue likely to inflame passion in the heart of a miner renting a room in a boarding house. But the tax campaign stressed the uniqueness of the Northland, the unfairness of southern exploitation, and the potential greatness of the region. Periodic "indignation meetings," at which separation from Old Ontario was proposed, received extensive coverage in both the English- and French-language press. Narrow self-interest quickly ballooned into a much broader sense of regional alienation. Northerners were called upon to unite in common cause. As a full-page advertisement in the *Porcupine Advance* proclaimed, "About the only attention the North now receives from the powers-that-be in the south is when there is a chance to steal something from here. They have filched our resources, squeezed our industries, and squandered our wealth. They would even steal the few little liberties the land now holds. It is up to every man here to know the North, study the North, work for the North, support the North." For good measure, the *Advance* added, "God Save the King. Also the North."[19] And all this was just a promotion to get people to subscribe to the newspaper!

Of course, language that served one context and constituency could not become widely used unless it tapped into something that already flowed beneath the surface. The words were given meaning through people's experiences, but those words also gave experience meaning. Families who had come to farm and build new lives but were struggling desperately just to feed themselves were undoubtedly glad to hear that it was the government's fault, not their personal failings. Abitibi plant workers laid off in the periodic downturns of the paper market could see more easily that provincial policies were to blame rather than the structures of industrial capitalism itself. The widow of a miner killed deep underground would find more meaning in his death if she could call for better regulation of uncaring management than she would if she heard the death blamed on fate or carelessness. The language of common experience became the language of common place. Indeed, one could be a northerner without ever having a clear sense of being Canadian. The language of northern identity provided another conceptual space for community.

Literal space was also necessary. People needed places where they could meet one another, a common ground where difference could be suspended, however briefly and superficially at first. The fact that these were small towns was very important. In large cities, socio-economic and ethnic groups can sort themselves by neighbourhoods, facilitating the maintenance of traditions and values. In Porcupine–Iroquois Falls, such segregation was limited to begin with, and it failed to sustain itself over time. In such small spaces, relatively isolated from the outside world (particularly in winter), people were forced to acknowledge one another at work, at home, in the marketplace, at school. Company paternalism, in the form of housing, recreational facilities, and meeting spaces, also played a role. Sometimes it served to create social divisions – among the towns and townsites, among the mine workforces, between economic sectors – but it also contributed to social exchange within each catchment area. To a lesser extent, the churches also played a role in providing space for people to learn about one another, even though religion served to divide as much as unite. The multitude of meeting halls, and above all the neutral ground of the dance pavilion, provided other important spaces.

Within these public spaces, the performance of social interaction, when repeated, became a ritual that contributed in a significant way to the development of a sense of community. A bit of winter fun with some dogs became an annual display of northern hardiness and achievement. A Christmas meal for lonely bachelors became the annual Turkey Stag, eagerly imitated and anticipated by a range of people. Labour Day parades and baseball tournaments marked a change of season. The rituals of the hockey match were just as important. These activities contributed to the creation of collective identity, but they also (in their repetition) helped to transmit its content, and perhaps also to reshape it as the performances shifted over time.

Performance could take in single occasions when collective action was called upon in the face of unusual or difficult circumstances. The terrifying forest fires of 1911 and 1916 began the process. The nation's call for service during two world wars rallied elements of the community for everything from recruiting and fundraising to knitting. The influenza epidemic of 1919 overwhelmed the limited medical capacities and drew in an army of volunteers. The terrible tragedies of the 1928 Hollinger Mine fire and the 1945 Paymaster cage crash rallied people both to provide immediate assistance and to initiate long-term preventative strategies. All such events provided an opportunity for people to move beyond their differences and come together in a common cause. They also provided new opportunities to identify the reason for the problem and thus provided a new "other" to whom animosity could be directed.

Collective action did not mean only grassroots movements. Leadership and the actions of key individuals played a part in both obvious and subtle ways. In the broadest sense, the choices of industry leaders F.H. Anson and the Timmins brothers influenced community development through both

action and example. Anson's enthusiasm for modern scientific management and the Timmins's more old-style paternalism put very different
structures in place in the two largest towns; different structures generated
different responses. J.P. Bickell, president of McIntyre Mines, provided
leadership of a different sort in his enthusiasm for hockey, which led to the
construction of the McIntyre Arena, with its tremendous impact on the
community. Religious leadership, especially that of Father Eugène Thériault, with his dedication to the interests of French Canada and his ability
to accommodate and encourage other Roman Catholics, was clearly
important as well. The Lake family, owners of the *Porcupine Advance*, and its
longtime editor, G. Allan Macdonald, provided a space for boosterism, for
an expression of identity, and for community debate, while the paper
reflected the changing social face and values of the region in ways that
must have been vital (though impossible to test empirically). The union
leaders William De Feu and Angus McDonald, the politicians J.P. Bartleman, John Rowlandson, J.A. Bradette, and William Grummett, and the
business leaders Leo Mascioli, Sam Bucovetsky, and Roy Thomson all put
their own unique stamp on the life of the community. Leadership was also
provided in less visible ways by the dozens of women who organized the
church clubs and cooked for union meetings, and by such teachers as
Flora McDonald and Bertha Shaw, who influenced countless numbers of
children.

Certainly, space, language, performance, and leadership (both individual and collective) could have had little impact if people had not had at
least some basic values or goals in common. At a superficial level, we can
observe that most people (other than the First Nations) came to the region
to make money and preferably to improve their material status. Not surprisingly, then, people rallied when anything occurred that threatened
their income-earning capacity (layoffs, wage reductions, workplace
hazards, lack of support infrastructure for industry or agriculture). They
were often divided into groups with very different ideas about the cause of
the problems or the solutions, but they sometimes found common ground
in the moderate labour unions and the campaigns to select "working
men's" candidates for the political arena. Other more complex value
systems served to unite specific subgroups, which defined themselves in
part through a common cause and in part through distinction from the
"other." A belief in the value of family and social stability, as well as an
inherently conservative approach to social organization, helped bring
together many English- and French-speaking Canadians, Italians, and
some Finns; the wild single men brawling outside the bars and the radical
labour activists who rejected church and marriage were the common
threat. Roman Catholicism brought together others, including speakers of
English, French, and Italian, as well as some Ukrainians. Above all, a sense

of pride in labour and a sense of entitlement as reward for doing hard and hazardous work proved to be a unifying device.

Over time, one final factor in the formation of community emerged – a factor that only the passage of time could provide. Collective memory (generated in common experience and transmitted mostly through story-telling) organized, explained, and made meaningful the apparently random accidents of time and place that had brought people to this region and shaped their lives here. While some early residents claimed that "history" was one of the things in their old life that was irrelevant in the building of a new world, within only a few decades, residents had fashioned a new kind of "history" for themselves. Peopled with eccentric characters and archetypes alike, these stories gave people a sense of belonging, a sense of rootedness, and a positive justification for their values. The fur trade era became a mythical past of adventure, conflict, and heroism when "Indians" roamed the "wilderness," pitting their wits against nature and the Iroquois invaders. By turns savage and cunning, the Indian had apparently simply melted away into the forests with the "coming of the white man." Then followed the era of the pioneer and the prospector, equally mythical heroes – visionaries who bravely challenged the rugged Northland to make a place for a new and better society of individual freedom, personal wealth, and international admiration. Other stories were told that featured a much darker side – stories of conspiracies in high places far away, conspiracies that aimed to destroy these dreams with secret blacklists on hiring, with underground systems designed to produce wealth and take lives, and with sinister machinations to control the levers of government. Even the death of a hockey star in an airplane crash could not have been the result simply of poor fuel management; secret forces had been at work to bring down a man who had finally "made it" in northern terms. These stories brought into collective memory the endless admiration of and appreciation for individuality and the lack of respect for traditional authority.

Everyone had a story about someone who had come north to escape something at home, and who could blame these fugitives? They were not dubious and potentially disruptive threats to the community; they were eccentrics who could nonetheless be embraced by the community. And if you didn't have a personal connection to tell about, well, there was always someone like Sandy McIntyre. Rather than being viewed as a prospector who had abandoned his wife and left his creditors in the lurch, he was seen as having made a lucky break and a fresh start. Of course, this genre included endless stories about thieving – depicted not as abhorrent but as a source of amusement and admiration. Highgrading was not theft of gold ore; it was thumbing one's nose at authority and a declaration of independence. Stories of events real or imagined gradually built up a store of collective memory that both fed on and contributed to a sense of community identity.

In the end, then, how might we characterize the particular nature of this local identity? Most important is that it was a complex and changeable mental map. A sense of community was not some "thing" – the climax to a historical process. Rather, people experienced multiple identities at the same time. They experienced the impact of changing ideas about how these identities were constituted. They experienced a community that was built on conflict as much as on consensus. And this experience of community was filled with contradictions and ambiguities. Causes in history are not always rational.

Perhaps the most obvious component of the community identity was the domination of blue-collar workers' values. In particular, a very specific definition of masculinity predominated, in which physical toughness, aggression, cunning, and sexuality were admired. There was a sense of pride and of superiority over the middle class whose men did no real "work," whose higher education was mocked as effete, and who were invariably referred to as "the boys" in the office. The capacity to consume large amounts of alcohol and to play as hard as you worked were markers of success. To describe a place as a "shit-kicking town" was a compliment. These were also towns where materialism was valued over aesthetics. Ownership and care of a modern automobile was far more important than maintaining a pretty garden or ornamenting your house. Although Abitibi Power and Paper provided attractive housing at Iroquois Falls, it was a pleasure that many people were willing to forgo in order to maintain their independence.

This sense of independence was sustained and encouraged by the physical setting. People came to identify strongly with the landscape, with its "endless" forests and lakes, its game and fish, and its opportunities for escape from the regulations of the industrial plant and for proving one's manhood. They developed a sense of entitlement to the natural resources, seeing Aboriginal users as competitors and even interlopers. They adopted southern Canadian language and imagery about the North, and made themselves into northerners. Yet at the same time as they were admiring and identifying with the land, they were changing it in fundamental ways. Jobs mattered more than vague ideas about conservation. There were sufficient trees for all the world's paper needs, still leaving enough to sustain the moose population for the annual hunt. The huge growing piles of mine tailings (or slimes) might ooze ghastly coloured liquid, but the vast landscape would take care of it. Perhaps too much space bred a sense of false security.

The idea of community here also vacillated between a strong sense of alienation from the outside world and an equally strong desire to be recognized and approved by outsiders. As northerners, they were misunderstood by rapacious southerners, who wanted to exploit northern labour and resources to fill the vaults of southern banks. Southerners failed to recognize that northerners (if left to their own devices) could outdo them at their own game – the game of progress as defined by modern liberal capitalism. So this alienation was not a rejection of the fundamentals of southern society; it was a sense of outrage at southern unwillingness to let the adolescent strike out on its own and prove to the world that it was an adult who had learned its lessons well.

Community identity was formed and lived on several levels simultaneously. One's personal identity (gender, family, neighbourhood, workplace) coexisted with a local identity, a national identity (not necessarily Canadian), and a transnational identity. In one sense, to call Porcupine–Iroquois Falls a "community" is misleading because people identified with particular towns or townsites in the region, seeing other towns as something foreign. But at the same time, the mental map could (and did) incorporate these other towns, whose representatives you met at the hockey rink, read about in the local newspaper, or shared a meal with at a church picnic. The rivalry among towns, both literal and imagined, ultimately brought them together on one of those levels of collective identity.

The sense of community identity had to be rooted in compromise. Some people had to go much further than others, but everyone had to make some sort of accommodation. The community was perhaps not a "middle ground," being rather too skewed in favour of the English-speaking, Canadian-born, blue-collar demographic majority, but it is interesting to note the changes that people were willing to make. The exchange of apparently superficial things such as music, food, and leisure activities was easiest. Hard-core communist ideas were rejected, but ideas about the need for labour activism, the sense of enduring conflict between worker and "owner," and a sense of frustration with the political system were eventually absorbed. The result was a curious political amalgam of right and left – not quite the Red Tory of classic Canadian politics but a sort of neoliberal socialism with all its inherent contradictions. W.J. Grummett, army officer, Anglican, Mason – and CCF politician – was perhaps its perfect spokesman. Language and religion were eventually fed into this mix of compromise. French, Finnish, Italian, and Ukrainian (among others) continued to be used at home and on the streets, but English became the language of common public exchange. In turn, there was little pressing of the point by English speakers. Unlike other places in Northern Ontario, French-language schools were not condemned (at least, not in public) and French was used at gatherings where organizers wanted to present themselves as "community-minded." The Roman Catholic priests attempted to direct the lives of their parishioners in accordance with the colonizing mission, but the parishioners were not always cooperative, explicitly rejecting such things as Roman Catholic labour unions in favour of broader trade-based or workplace-wide organization. Roman Catholics joined their own traditional religious-based organizations, of course, but they also began to join fraternal societies that are usually associated with Protestant places. Even the Boy Scout movement, a child of British imperialism, was adopted and adapted by French-speaking Roman Catholic parishes. All this accommodation was eventually made very tangible and very personal in the growing number of "mixed" marriages in the region.

Each generation worked with a different sense of community identity. Those of the fur trade era saw themselves as part of a socio-economic system that constituted a "middle ground" (in historian Richard White's words)[20] of significant cultural accommodation for mutual advantage of Native and newcomer. The first generation of new arrivals in the twentieth century saw themselves as builders, constructing something new that not only would put aside the old world of the fur trade forever but would be an improvement even on the world of their youth in its process of transformation from agrarianism to industrial capitalism. The next generation, coming in the 1920s and 1930s, saw themselves as workers in a system already established by others. They found much in the system that was not to their liking, and they expressed their frustration in various ways. Ultimately, they found ways to attempt change, and while not always successful, their activism shaped their sense of who they were. Identity politics here were as much generational as interethnic or economic. Community was in constant negotiation.

We are clearly limited if we attempt to explain social identity as a tangible "thing" or an essence that can be understood as a product of abstract structures like economic systems, political arrangements, or even spatial relationships. These approaches leave little room for human agency, and it is important to understand agency as more than simply action. Above all, agency requires the capacity for imagination. Conceptual maps influence our behaviour in profound and often unrecognized ways. And these concepts are not always rational, consistent, or permanent. We communicate these maps to others through our actions and through the stories we tell. We use these maps to guide us in our response to new situations; the maps are changed as we respond. Memory, in the form of both personal and collective histories, is a selection and sorting device that not only helps us make sense of our experiences and ideas but also helps us give them meaning and purpose. Symbols are the shorthand we produce to encapsulate these meanings. At the same time, identity is not *entirely* "constructed" or "imagined." There are very real structures, processes, and relationships that have an impact, limiting our capacity for action and constraining our imagining, since much of what we do is in reaction to the structures and processes that we find around us.

Community, as one particular form of social identity, is not merely an arrangement rooted in the structures of agrarianism or modern industrial capitalism, nor is it entirely an imagined concept used to legitimize those structures. The human need for cooperation to obtain mutual advantage, for companionship and a sense of security, and perhaps ultimately for meaning beyond ourselves, makes community a potentially useful tool. In this sense, community is a physical and conceptual space where we can set aside some of our differences to make this cooperation possible. But as this study of Porcupine–Iroquois Falls has shown, community does not merely mean harmony and inclusiveness. Rather, the harmony and inclusiveness are selective and are based on conflict with and rejection of others. Conflict and consensus are not dichotomous. Both are part of the same process.

While these broad-brush observations may be helpful in understanding the general idea of community, they tend to obscure the very important fact that there is much about this specific community that is unique. Historical accident or coincidence, the particular and complex interactions of specific individuals, and the unanticipated consequences of choices and actions are equally important factors – and they are not easily accommodated by the practices of modern social science. Nevertheless, as a central part of the human experience, community ought to be considered, in all its complexity, ambiguity, and messiness. To quote Mrs J.K. Kitchen of Schumacher, "My sojourn here has been one of excitement, sadness, and a thankfulness ... I am deeply grateful for the experience of belonging to a community that has survived and thrived through the courage and faith of its pioneers. But things were not easy for the early residents ... In the beginning, circumstances were rather grim."[21]

Notes

PREFACE

1 Available in English translation as Tönnies, *Community and Society*, trans. Loomis.
2 See Tönnies, *Community and Society*, 3.
3 *De la division du travail social; Les règles de la méthode sociologique; Suicide: étude de sociologie; Les formes élémentaires de la vie religieuse: le système totémique en Australie.* The first English translations that I have been able to find are *On The Division of Labour in Society*, trans. Simpson; *The Rules of Sociological Method*, trans. Solovay and Mueller; *Suicide*, trans. Spaulding and Simpson; *The Elementary Forms of Religious Life*, trans. Swain.
4 The three laws cited in MacIver, *Community*, are [1] "Socialisation and individualisation are the two sides of a single process" (214); [2] social relationships are constantly changing in order to fulfill "the principal [sic] of communal economy" (321), which economy exists only within society (322); and [3] social change "involves also a transformation of their common relations to an external world." (359).
5 Mauss, *Die Gabe: Form und Funktion des Austauschs in archaischen Gesellschaften* (1925), apparently first published in English as *The Gift: Forms and Functions of Exchange in Archaic Societies*, trans. Cunnison; Lévi-Strauss, *Structures élémentaires de la parenté*, and *Anthropologie structurale*, apparently first published in English as *The Elementary Structures of Kinship*, trans. Bell and von Sturmer, and *Structural Anthropology*, trans. Jacobson and Schoepf.
6 Parsons, *Structure and Process in Modern Societies*, especially 250–66. Functionalism might be defined as an examination of how a society actually works, based on its purpose. Hence, relationships are more important than the relatively static *systems* that are the focus for structuralists.
7 Thompson, *The Making of the Working Class*, was first published by Victor Gollancz in 1963, revised in 1968, and reprinted repeatedly since.

8 Postscript to 1968 edition of Thompson, *The Making of the Working Class*, 939.

9 De Saussure's *Cours de linguistique générale* was apparently first published in English as *Course in General Linguistics*, trans. Baskin.

10 Barthe's *Le degré zero de l'écriture* and "Eléments de sémiologie," were apparently first published in English as *Elements of Semiology*, trans. Travers and Smith.

11 Geertz, *The Interpretation of Cultures*.

12 Anderson's *Imagined Communities* was first published in 1983 by Verso, which brought out a revised edition in 1991.

13 See, for example, the characterization of the discipline's history in Rousseau, *Self, Symbols, and Society*.

14 Bourdieu, *In Other Words: Essays Towards a Reflexive Sociology*, 9–11, 123 (originally published in French, 1982).

15 Bender, *Community and Social Change in America*, 5.

16 Williams, *The Country and the City*, 104 (first published in 1973).

17 Lyotard, *La condition postmoderne: rapport sur le savoir*.

18 From G.C. Spivak's translation of Derrida's *De la grammatologie*, published in English as *Of Grammatology*.

19 Anderson, *Reality Isn't What It Used to Be*.

20 Foucault's *Folie et déraison: histoire de la folie à l'âge classique* and his *Surveiller et punir: naissance de la prison* appeared in English as *Madness and Civilization: A History of Insanity in the Age of Reason*, translated by Howard, and *Discipline and Punish: The Birth of the Prison*, translated by Sheridan.

21 Butler, *Gender Trouble: Feminism and the Subversion of Identity*. Butler did not originate the idea of performance; it is usually credited to British philosopher John Austin (1911–60) and American John Searle (b. 1932) and is sometimes called the theory of "speech-acts."

22 Saïd, *Orientalism* and *Culture and Imperialism*. Saïd is sometimes seen as a founding father of postcolonialism.

23 Joseph, *Against the Romance of Community*, xix and xxi.

24 References are to Roy Thompson's newspaper empire, the gold mines of Timmins-Porcupine, champion skater Barbara Ann Scott and others who trained at the McIntyre Arena, Maple Leaf star Frank Mahovlich, country music star Shania Twain, the influence of the planned company townsite at Iroquois Falls, and Gordon Thiessen, former governor of the Bank of Canada. Not noted is Nobel Prize winner Myron Scholes and many other influential Canadians and events that are rooted in the region.

CHAPTER ONE

1 Details of the trip are based on a diary kept by Treaty 9 commissioner Samuel Stewart. See Library and Archives Canada (LAC), Samuel Stewart's Journal of James Bay Treaty Trips, 1905–6, and Journal of Visit to Abitibi, 1908, both in RG10, vol. 11,399 (microfilm reel T-6924). Physiographic information is

derived from basic sources on the Canadian Shield and the author's own experiences in the region.

2 Knight, "Prospecting in Ontario: Historical Sketches," *Canadian Mining Journal* 71 (November 1950): 81.

3 Borron, "A Report on That Part of the Basin of Hudson's [sic] Bay Awarded to the Province of Ontario, and Included in the District of Nipissing," in Ontario, *Sessional Papers* 53 (1882): 28–33.

4 Stewart's Journal of James Bay Treaty Trips, 1905–6, LAC, RG10, vol. 11,399, 62 (reel T-6924).

5 Details of this section are taken from Stewart's Journal of Visit to Abitibi, 1908, LAC, RG10, vol. 11,399 (reel T-6924).

6 The following details are derived from Stewart's journals, op. cit.

7 *Saturday Night,* 29 July 1933, 2.

8 Dr Yves Bergeron, Université du Québec en Abitibi-Témiskamingue, to Standing Senate Committee on Agriculture and Forestry, Subcommittee on the Boreal Forest, 28 October 1998. Seen at www.parl.gc.ca/36/1/ parlbus/commbus/senate/com-e/bore-e/09eva-e.htm (accessed 6 July 2000).

CHAPTER TWO

1 Wright, "Prehistory of the Canadian Shield"; Dawson, *Prehistory of Northern Ontario,* 8–11; Marois and Gauthier, *Les Abitibis,* 150–1 and 152–7.

2 Wright, "Prehistory of the Canadian Shield," 94–5; Wright, "Before European Contact," 28; Dawson, *Prehistory of Northern Ontario,* 15–18.

3 Goddard, "Central Algonquian Languages," 586.

4 Francis and Morantz, *Partners in Furs,* 14; Wright, "Prehistory of the Ontario Shield," 91–5; Dawson, *Prehistory of Northern Ontario,* 3.

5 Thwaites, ed., *The Jesuit Relations and Allied Documents,* 46: 289–91.

6 Ibid., 56:183.

7 For example, see the versions detailed in MacDougall, *Two Thousand Miles of Gold,* 216–17, and in the Cobalt *Daily Nugget,* 5 December 1912, 1.

8 Hodgins and Benidickson, *The Temagami Experience,* 17, and Mitchell, *Fort Timiskaming and the Fur Trade,* 8–9.

9 Mitchell, *Fort Timiskaming and the Fur Trade,* 8–9.

10 Francis and Morantz, *Partners in Furs,* 27.

11 Memo, 1 February 1685 Library and Archives Canada (LAC), Archives des Colonies, MG1, series C11A, vol. 7, fos. 212–212v (microfilm reel F-7).

12 Voorhis, *Historic Forts and Trading Posts of the French Regime and of the English Fur Trading Companies,* 26.

13 Francis and Morantz, *Partners in Furs,* 30.

14 Jean Laflamme, "Le Marquis de Vaudreuil et l'Abitibi-Temiscamingue," in Asselin et al., "De l'Abbittibbi–Temiskaming No. 4," 1–25, and Pain, *The Way North,* 35–6.

15 HBC governor's instructions to men, 26 September 1714, quoted in Innis, *The Fur Trade in Canada*, 135.

16 Long, "The Reverend George Barnley, Wesleyan Methodist, and James Bay's Fur Trade Company Families," 45.

17 William Bevan, Moose River Journal, 1734–35, entry for 6 April 1735, Hudson's Bay Company Archives (HBCA), B.135/a/5, fo. 13d (microfilm reel 1M84).

18 Brown, *Strangers in Blood*, 11.

19 William Bevan, Moose Post Journal, 1732–33, entry for 9 October 1732, HBCA, B.135/a/3, fo. 7 (microfilm reel 1M84).

20 William Bevan, Moose River Journal, 1734–35, entry for 23 April 1735, HBCA, B.135/a/5, fo. 14d (microfilm reel 1M84).

21 Ibid.

22 Mitchell, *Fort Timiskaming and the Fur Trade*, 16–17. He also had interests on the Nottaway River.

23 Governor and Council (London) to Governor and Council at Moose, 17 May 1770, Moose Factory Correspondence Inward, 1746–1808, HBCA, B.135/c/1, fo. 82 (microfilm reel 1M375).

24 Governor and Council to John Thomas (Moose Fort), 16 May 1787, Moose Factory Correspondence Inward, 1746–1808, HBCA, B.135/c/1, fo. 187d (microfilm reel 1M376).

25 Mitchell, *Fort Timiskaming and the Fur Trade*, 40–1.

26 Moose Factory Correspondence Inward, 29 May 1794, HBCA, B.135/c/1, fo. 223 (microfilm reel 1M376).

27 Abitibi Post Journal, 1794–5, entry for 26 June 1794, HBCA, B.1/a/1, fo. 2d (microfilm reel 1M1). For information on the construction and supply of the HBC post, see fos. 2–2d and 22d.

28 Cormier, ed., *Jean-Baptiste Perreault, marchant voyageur parti de Montréal le 28ᵉ de mai 1783*, 134.

29 Matawagamingue Post Journal, 1815–18, Angus Cameron to Richard Good, 30 December 1814, HBCA, E41/36, fo. 53d (microfilm reel 4M63).

30 See various reports by Richard Good in Kenogamissi Post Journal, 1812–13, HBCA, B.99/a/14, fos. 5d-9d and 13–15 (microfilm reel 1M66).

31 Matawagamingue Post Journal, 1815–18, HBCA, E41/36, fo. 10 (microfilm reel 4M63). See also a report of the fire in Kenogamissi Post Journal, 1815–16, HBCA, B.99/a/17, fo. 2d (20 July 1815). The HBC blamed the NWC for paying an Indian to do the deed.

32 Matawagamingue Post Journal, 1818–22, entry for 7 October 1819, HBCA, E41/37, fo. 15 (microfilm reel 4M63).

33 Mitchell, *Fort Timiskaming and the Fur Trade*, 233–4 and 237–8; [A. Cameron], Matawagamingue Post Journal, 1818–22, HBCA, E41/37, fo. 24d (microfilm reel 4M63); and HBCA biographies, on file in the reference room.

34 Kenogamissi District Report, 1813–14, HBCA, B.99/e/1, fo. 5 (microfilm reel

IM778); Kenogamissi District Report, 1814–15, HBCA, B.99/e/2, fo. 1d (microfilm reel IM778).

35 Moose Factory Register, Diocese of Moosonee Papers, 1811–1941, Archives of Ontario (AO) MS311, reel 2; St Sulpice Seminary, "Rélation d'une mission ... en 1837." LAC, MG17/A7–2 (microfilm reel C14,008); Kenogamissi Post Journal, 1812–13, HBCA, B.99/a/15, fo. 2d (microfilm reel IM66).

36 *Porcupine Advance*, 27 September 1922, 1; *La Gazette du Nord*, 5 October 1922.

37 See, for example, Kenogamissi reports in Kenogamissi Post Journal, 1815–16, HBCA, B.99/a/17 (microfilm reel IM67).

38 Moose Post Journal, 1732–33, entry for 16 February 1733, HBCA, B.135/a/3, fo. 15 (microfilm reel IM84).

39 Frederick House Journal, 1804–5, HBCA, B.75/a/19 (microfilm reel IM55).

40 Frederick House Journal, 1789–90, entry for 31 August 1789, HBCA, B.75/a/5, fo. 3 (microfilm reel IM54).

41 Frederick House Journal, 1796–97, HBCA, B.75/a/12, fo. 11 (microfilm reel IM54).

42 Kenogamissi District Report, 1816–17, HBCA, B.99/e/4, fo. 2d (microfilm reel IM778).

43 Matawagamingue Post Journal, 1815–18, entry for 1 February 1817, HBCA, E41/36, fo. 35d (microfilm reel 4M63); Kenogamissi Post Journal, 1815–16, HBCA, B.99/a/18, fo. 12d (microfilm reel IM67); Kenogamissi Post Journal, 1816–17, HBCA, B.99/a/19, fos. 12d and 15 (microfilm reel IM67).

44 Frederick House Journal, entry for 31 October 1799, HBCA, B.75/a/14, fo. 6d (microfilm reel IM55).

45 Payne, "Daily Life on Western Hudson Bay 1714–1870," 59, table 3.

46 Goldring, "Lewis and the Hudson's Bay Company in the Nineteenth Century," 32.

47 Moose Factory Correspondence Inward, 1746–1808, HBCA, B.135/c/1, fo. 136 (microfilm reel IM375).

48 Kenogamissi Post Journal, 1794–95, HBCA, B.99/a/1, fo. 10 (microfilm reel IM66); Frederick House Journal, 1793–94, HBCA, B.75/a/9, fo. 34 (microfilm reel IM54); Frederick House Journal, 1799–1800, HBCA, B.75/a/14, np (microfilm reel IM55).

49 Frederick House Journal, 1787–88, HBCA, B.75/a/3, fo. 13d (microfilm reel IM54); Matawagamingue Post Journal, 1815–18, HBCA, E41/37, fos. 18, 19, 19d (microfilm reel 4M63).

50 Governor and Council (London) to John Favell and Council (Moose), 25 May 1769, Moose Factory Correspondence Inward, 1746–1808, HBCA, B.135/c/1, fo. 76 (microfilm reel IM375).

51 Frederick House Journal, 1790–91, entry for 14 March 1791, HBCA, B.75/a/6, fo. 13 (microfilm reel IM54); Kenogamissi Post Journal, 1815–16, entry for 20 August 1815, HBCA, B.99/a/17, fo. 4 (microfilm reel IM67); and

Abitibi Post Journal, 1797–8, entry for 13 August 1797, HBCA, B.1/a/3, fo. 2
(microfilm reel IM1).

52 Brown, *Strangers in Blood*, 96.

53 Alexander Christie, Matawagamingue District Report, 1824–25, HBCA,
B.124/e/1, fo. 1, and Matawagamingue District Report, 1825–26, HBCA,
B.124/e/2, fo. 4 (microfilm reel IM779).

54 Alexander Christie, Abitibi District Report, 1822–23, HBCA, B.1/e/1, fo.1; J.
McRae, Abitibi District Report, 1822–23, HBCA, B.1/e/2, fo. 7; and T. Fraser,
Abitibi Post Journal, 1823–24, HBCA, B.1/a/18, fo. 13 (microfilm reel IM1).

55 Matawagamingue District Report, 1825–26, HBCA, B.124/e/2, fo. 6 (microfilm reel IM779).

56 See Bishop David Anderson's account in *The Net in the Bay; or Journal of a Visit
to Moose and Albany*, 173–4.

57 See his accounts for 3 February 1851, 6–8; 5 February 1851, 10; and 27 May
1851, 18, in Mattagami and Flying Post records, vol. 2, LAC, MG19/D16.

58 Anderson, *The Net in the* Bay, 107–8.

59 Ibid., 105, 108.

60 Anderson, *Fur Trader's Story*, 19.

61 Carrière, *Histoire documentaire de la Congrégation des Missionaires Oblats de Marie-
Immaculée dans l'Est du Canada*, 9:199.

62 John Horden's Journal, Mattagami, 26 September 1854, Church Missionary
Society Archives (CMS), C.1/0, held at LAC (microfilm reel A88).

63 Reports on Matawagamingue, 1885, HBCA, B.124/e/9, fos. 5 and 9 (microfilm reel IM1256).

64 Pain, *The Way North*, 58–9; Samuel Stewart's Journal of Treaty Trips for
1905–6, entry for June 1906, LAC, RG10, vol. 11,399 (microfilm reel T6924);
HBC Reports on Matachewan Post for 1890, HBCA, B.311/e/1 (microfilm reel
IM1256); Indian Affairs Branch, Treaty 9 File, LAC, RG10, file 235,225, parts 1
and 1A (microfilm reel C11,314).

65 Mitchell, *Fort Timiskaming and the Fur Trade*, 174.

66 St Sulpice Seminary, "Relation d'une mission faite en l'été de 1837," LAC,
MG17/A7–2, series II, vol. 26, 14244–14326 (microfilm reel C14,008.

67 See an account of the Mattagami mission in Richard Hardisty's Mattagami
Post Journal, 1843–44, HBCA, B.124/a/18, fos. 16–23; and Mattagami Post
Journal, 1844–45, HBCA, B.124/a/19, fo. 1 (microfilm reel IM78).

68 Cayen, "Les missions catholiques du nord-est ontarien au XIXe siècle,"
26.

69 Carrière, *Histoire documentaire*, 3: 202–11.

70 Ibid., 3: 198–201, and Mattagami and Flying Post records, 1824–94, vol. 2,
LAC, MG19/D16, 40.

71 John Horden, Journals and Letters, 1851–57, Church Missionary Society Collection at LAC, CMS-C.1/0 (microfilm reel A88).

CHAPTER THREE

1 MacDougall, *Two Thousand Miles of Gold*, frontispiece.
2 See Borron's reports, in Ontario, *Sessional Papers* 22 (1880), 44 (1881), and 53 (1882).
3 Borron's report for 1883, in Ontario, *Sessional Papers* 39 (1883): 18.
4 Boucher, "Edmond Gendreau," 394–6.
5 Mitchell, *Fort Timiskaming and the Fur Trade*, 225–6.
6 J. Fortescue, Inspection Report, Moose Factory, 1891, Hudson's Bay Company Archives (HBCA), B.135/e/29, fo. 24 (microfilm reel IM1257).
7 D.C. McTavish to S.K. Parson (at Montreal), Chapleau, 10 November 1890, in Report on Montreal Department, HBCA, B.134/c/3, fo. 16 (microfilm reel IM1257).
8 J. Wrigley to Officer in Charge of Lake Huron District, 25 January 1890, HBCA, B.134/e/1, fo. 40 (microfilm reel IM1257).
9 Tucker, *Steam into Wilderness*, 2.
10 Regehr, *The Canadian Northern Railway*, 71.
11 Ibid.
12 Tucker, *Steam into Wilderness*, 8.
13 Legget, *Railways of Canada*, 122–3.
14 Stevens, *Canadian National Railways*, vol. 2: *Towards the Inevitable 1896–1922*, 157, 159–61, 171.
15 Legget, *Railways of Canada*, 113–18.
16 Borron's report in Ontario, *Sessional Papers* 1 (1888): 15.
17 Morrison, "Treaty Nine Research Report: Treaty Nine (1905–06): The James Bay Treaty," 13–14, 19; Long, *Treaty No. 9: The Indian Petitions 1889–1927*, 2–4.
18 W. Maclean to Department of Indian Affairs, 18 August 1903, in Indian Affairs Branch, Treaty 9 File, 1901–9, Library and Archives Canada (LAC), RG10, vol. 3033, file 235,225, pts. 1 and 1A (microfilm reel C11,314).
19 Burwash to Department of Indian Affairs, 24 June 1905, in ibid.
20 Long, *Treaty No. 9: The Negotiations, 1901–1928*, 1–4.
21 Ibid., 4.
22 Samuel Stewart's Journal of Abitibi Trip, June 1908, LAC, RG10, vol. 11,399 (microfilm reel T924).
23 See the account of these negotiations in ibid.
24 Tucker, *Steam into Wilderness*, 64–5.
25 Quoted in *Canadian Annual Review*, 1909, 340.
26 Address by W.H. Hearst, 16 April 1914, 16, in Sir William Hearst miscellaneous files (Scrapbooks and Minute Books), Archives of Ontario (AO) F6, MU1311, envelopes 16–18.
27 Report of Superintendent R.H. Clemens for 1916, in Ontario, *Sessional Papers*

56 (1917): 7; Annual Report of the Department of Lands, Forests and Mines for 1917, app. 3, in Ontario, *Sessional Papers* 3 (1918): 97–8.

28 Address by W.H. Hearst, 16 April 1914, 15–16, in Sir William Hearst miscellaneous files, AO, F6, MU1311, envelopes 16–18.

29 Ibid., 16.

30 Address to the Canadian Club, Toronto, 18 November 1912, printed in *Canadian Annual Review*, 1912, 68.

31 Quoted in Gourd, "La colonisation des Clay Belts du nord-ouest québécois et du nord-est Ontarien," 249. ("Fortunes for Farmers in New Ontario," 1911).

32 J.F. Black to G.J. Somers, Sudbury, 5 February 1912, in James F. Whitney Papers, file October 1911 to January 1912, AO, F6, MU3132.

33 Toronto *Globe*, 5 November 1909, 9.

34 J.F. Black to G.J. Somers, 5 February 1912, in James F. Whitney Papers, AO, F6, MU3132.

35 "Farm Lands in the Clay Belt of New Ontario," [circa 1912–13], in Sir William Hearst Papers, miscellaneous files, AO, F6, MU1309, envelope 4.

36 George S. Shields's collation of articles descriptive of New Ontario, received 1 November 1912, in Sir William Hearst Papers, miscellaneous files, AO, F6, MU1310, envelope 8.

37 *Canadian Annual Review*, 1912, supplement, 68.

38 "Conditions on the Clay Belt of New Ontario," report by Clifford Sifton and the Commission of Conservation, pamphlet, 1913, 5, 6, and 9, in Sir William Hearst Papers, miscellaneous files, AO, F6, MU1309, envelope 4.

39 Lee-Whiting, "Krugerdorf," 35; Lambert (with Pross), *Renewing Nature's Wealth*, 310; "Northern Ontario: Its Progress and Development under the Whitney Government," pamphlet [circa 1914], in Sir William Hearst Papers, miscellaneous files, AO, F6, MU1311.

40 Report of John H. Shaw, North Bay, 22 and 28 December 1904, Department of Crown Lands, Annual Report for 1906, in Ontario, *Sessional Papers* 3 (1907): 79–80.

41 Journal of Abitibi Trip, June 1908.

42 J. Arch. McDonald, 12 September 1908 in James P. Whitney Papers (March – June 1909), AO, F6, MU3127.

43 W.D. Cunneyworth to J.L. Englehart, North Bay, 20 February 1909 in ibid.

44 "Mr. Doherty's Report," October 1911and J.L. Englehart to John A. Cooper, 12 January 1912, in James P. Whitney Papers, AO, F6, MU3132.

45 Cobalt *Daily Nugget*, 19 June 1913, 1.

46 Lendrum, "Days That are Gone," Timmins *Daily Press*, 22 July 1950, 8.

47 Department of Lands, Forests and Mines [Ontario], Annual Report for 1912, Appendix 36, Ontario *Sessional Papers* 3 (1913), 112.

48 Report of architect F.R. Heakes re Monteith Farm, 1912, Department of Public Works, Annual Report for 1912, in Ontario, *Sessional Papers* 12 (1913); Department of Public Works, Annual Report for 1913, in Ontario, *Sessional*

Papers 13 (1914): 15; Report of Commissioner J.F. Whitson, in Annual Report of the Northern Development Branch for 1915, in Ontario, *Sessional Papers* 63 (1916): 4; "Mrs. Tinney's Report of Monteith," in "Historic Sites and Trails," 1978, 108, held at Iroquois Falls Museum.

49 These names are spelled in a variety of ways in local histories, each variant adamantly defended by its proponent. For example, they are Vintori Matson and Johan Pennanen in Peter Vasiliadis's, *Dangerous Truth: Interethnic Competition in a Northeastern Ontario Goldmining Centre*, 36. I have chosen Victor Mattson and Henry Pennala because they appear this way in a source quoting a person who knew the men; see Frank Lendrum's history columns in the Timmins *Daily Press*, 1949–54 (LAC microfilm reel M5211). Both men had prospected at Cobalt. Mattson was from Port Arthur and Pennala from Ironwood.

50 Cobalt *Daily Nugget*, 4 August 1909.

51 LeBourdais, *Metals and Men: The Story of Canadian Mining*, 156.

52 E.D. Loney, "The Discovery of the McIntyre and Hollinger Mines," *Canadian Mining Journal* 153 (January 1932): 23–4.

53 Smith, *Harvest from the Rock*, 188–93.

54 Fetherling, *The Gold Crusades*, 218.

55 "The Hollinger to Use Sixty Stamps," *Saturday Night*, 3 June 1911, 23.

56 Cobalt *Daily Nugget*, 29 December 1910, 4.

57 Ibid., 16 December 1910, 1.

58 Ibid., special fire edition, 12 July 1911.

59 *Canadian Annual Review*, 1911, 418–19.

60 Sir James Dunn, Royal Commission Inquiring into the Affairs of the Abitibi Power & Paper Company Ltd., 17 March 1941, 7–8. Copy held at AO, RG 8–118. See also Ontario, *Sessional Papers* 13 (1914), app. 33 ("The Abitibi Pulp Limit Agreement"), 77–83.

61 Lendrum, "Days That Are Gone," Timmins *Daily Press*, 26 November 1949, 14; "Memorandum for Mr. Gibson re the Abitibi Pulp Limit," Toronto, 23 October 1913, in Sir William Hearst Papers, AO, F6, MU1309, envelope 1.

62 Abitibi Incorporation Papers, Ontario Corporations Branch, AO, RG95, series 1, vol. 2493; Cobalt *Daily Nugget*, 25 January 1913, 1.

63 Hodgins and Benidickson, *The Temagami Experience*, 77–9.

64 "The Forest Reserves of Ontario," Annual Report for 1908, in Ontario, *Sessional Papers* 3 (1909): 136.

65 *Canadian Annual Review*, 1911, 413.

66 Ibid.; Wiegman, *Trees to News*, 11; Pain, *The Way North*, 229. The *Tribune* located instead at Thorold, Ontario, on the Welland Canal.

67 Lendrum, "Days That Are Gone," Timmins *Daily Press*, 26 November 1949, 14.

68 "Northern Ontario: Its Progress and Development Under the Whitney Government," 6, and J.A. McAndrew to W.H. Hearst, 11 October 1913 ("confi-

dential"), in Sir William Hearst Papers, miscellaneous files, AO, F6, MU1309, envelope 1.

69 Kuhlberg, "We Have 'Sold' Forestry to the Management of the Company," 189–90.

70 Oliver, *G. Howard Ferguson: Ontario Tory*, 69.

71 Cobalt *Daily Nugget*, 5 December 1912, 1.

72 MacDougall, *Two Thousand Miles of Gold*, frontispiece ("To the Builders of the North").

73 *New York Mining Age*, quoted in Cobalt *Daily Nugget*, 29 January 1913, 4; "News of the Mines," *Saturday Night*, 6 January 1912, 23.

74 Field, *The Resources and Trade Prospects of Northern Ontario*, 5.

75 See Lambert (with Pross), *Renewing Nature's Wealth*.

76 Wightman and Wightman, *The Land Between*, 124.

77 Department of Lands, Forests and Mines, Annual Report for 1911, in *Ontario Sessional Papers* 3 (1912): vi.

78 See Knight, *Indians at Work: An Informal Survey of Native Labour in British Columbia, 1848–1930*.

79 Barnes, *Fortunes in the Ground*, 87–8; Hoffman, *Free Gold*, 70; Timmins *Daily Press*, 8 November 1947, 5.

80 *Porcupine Advance*, 14 September 1933, 1.

81 *Canadian Mining Journal* 56 (September 1935): 355–6; Townsley, *Mine Finders*, 95.

82 Lendrum, "Days That Are Gone," Timmins *Daily Press*, 2 August 1952, 16.

83 Ibid., 23 May 1953, 16.

84 Ibid., 8 November 1947, 5; report of an interview with D'Aigle.

85 Address of 16 April 1914 in Sir William Hearst Papers, AO, F6, MU1311.

CHAPTER FOUR

1 Field, *The Resources and Trade Prospects of Northern Ontario*, 99.

2 *Porcupine Advance* 12 April 1912; Lendrum, "Days That Are Gone," columns from Timmins *Daily Press*, 16 December 1959, 7.

3 Cobalt *Daily Nugget*, 31 March 1911, 1; "Historical Sites and Trails," 1978, pamphlet held at Iroquois Falls Museum, 71–3; Southall, " 'A Visitation of Providence': The Matheson Fire, 1916," 37 and 40.

4 Toronto *Globe*, 18 January 1910, 1.

5 Gauthier, "Genese de nos paroisses régionales (nord-ouest québécois et est ontarien)," np.

6 "Historical Sites and Trails," 1978, pamphlet held at Iroquois Falls Museum, np; Tucker, *Steam into Wilderness*, 68; Gauthier, "Genese de nos paroisses régionales," np.

7 MacDougall, *Two Thousand Miles of Gold*, 133–4; Porcupine Prospectors Association, *The Prospector: Commemorating the 30th Anniversary of the Discovery of Gold in Porcupine, 1909–1939*, 15.

8 Field, *The Resources and Trade Prospects of Northern Ontario*, 99. Because Matheson was not incorporated until 1912, it missed the 1911 census, and by 1921 its situation had changed dramatically and it was already in decline. Exact population information for its heyday is not available.

9 Southall, " 'A Visitation of Providence': The Matheson Fire, 1916," 36–7.

10 Frank Ginn (town clerk) to J.A. Ellis, Matheson, 19 February 1920, Matheson Municipal Financial Returns, 1912–40, Archives of Ontario (AO), RG19–142, 988, box 225.

11 Frank Ginn to Ontario Minister of Education, 6 December 1922, Ontario Department of Education Central Registry Files, 1922, AO, RG2/P3, box 100.

12 Ibid.

13 Cobalt *Daily Nugget*, 29 December 1910, 4.

14 Of course, the only "shunia" that really meant gold was not to appear in the community for another seventy years.

15 Details from Cobalt *Daily Nugget*, 6 January to 6 December 1910; Porcupine Golden Anniversary Committee, *Souvenir Booklet Celebrating the Golden Anniversary of the Porcupine Gold Rush, July 1–5, 1959*, 55; MacNab, *Pioneer Ventures: The Story of Will Bannerman in Porcupine*, 1951, interview with resident George Bannerman.

16 Cobalt *Daily Nugget*, 19 January 1910, 1; town plan of Timmins, 1933–61, in Ontario Ministry of Natural Resources files, AO Cartographic Collection, RG1, MNR-ACC 18627.

17 Cobalt *Daily Nugget*, 8 May 1911, 1. See also 30 November 1911.

18 Lendrum, "Days That Are Gone," columns from Timmins *Daily Press*, 15 November 1952, 14; Cobalt *Daily Nugget*, winter 1911, various issues.

19 Ibid., 16 December 1910, 1.

20 Ibid., 14 and 15 March, 1911.

21 Ibid., 5, 12 and 13 May 1911 (all page 1).

22 Ibid., 17 March 1910, 1.

23 Lendrum, "Days That Are Gone," Timmins *Daily Press*, 5 November 1949, 7; W.H. Wilson to Ontario Bureau of Industries, 28 December 1912, Whitney Township Financial Returns, 1912–1960, AO, RG19–142, 707; *Porcupine Advance* obituaries, 12 July and 10 June 1937.

24 Smith, *Frederick W. Schumacher: Portrait of a Renaissance Man*, 13–21.

25 Ibid., 22, 25; *Porcupine Advance*, 18 June 1915.

26 Trinity United Church (Schumacher), Church History File, 1912–1962, United Church Archives (Victoria University, Toronto).

27 Montreal *Gazette*, 16 November 1912, 20.

28 Town of Timmins Municipal Financial Returns, 1912–35, AO, RG19–142, 1080, box 391; *Canadian Mining Journal*, 15 April 1913, 250; Cobalt *Daily Nugget*, 17 February to 8 November 1912.

29 Cobalt *Daily Nugget*, 26 April 1912, 1.

30 Last and Vachon, *Timmins*, 33. They say Timmins provided $10,000.

31 *Porcupine Advance*, 10 December 1915, 1, and 7 January 1916, 8; M.B. Scott,

"A Few Reminiscences of the Early Porcupine," *Hollinger Miner*, 19 May 1952, 3.

32 *Porcupine Advance*, 12 March 1919, 4, and 11 June 1919, 1.

33 Ibid., 23 March, 13 April, 13 July, and 7 September 1921.

34 *Worker*, 6 September 1924. Quoted in Forestell, "All That Glitters Is Not Gold: The Gendered Dimensions of Work, Family, and Community Life in the Northern Ontario Goldmining Town of Timmins, 1909–1950," 79.

35 Cobalt *Daily Nugget*, 20 November 1911, 12; C.M. Macreath to W.J. Fuller, Sault Ste Marie, 27 April 1920, in Correspondence re Mattagami Heights, Timmins Museum 922.10.1; Lendrum, "Days That Are Gone," Timmins *Daily Press*, 16 September 1950, 12; *Porcupine Advance*, 11 June 1915, 8.

36 *Porcupine Advance*, 16 August 1922.

37 *Canadian Mining Journal*, 15 July 1915, 450. It says the company's main income that year was $90,000 from "quite an extensive sale of town lots."

38 *Porcupine Advance*, 15 November 1916, 5; Timmins Municipal Financial Returns for 1923, AO, RG19–142, 1080, box 391.

39 *Porcupine Advance*, 23 April 1924, 1.

40 Dome Inventory, 31 July 1912, in Dome Mines Inventories, 1912–15, AO, F1350, box 96, MU 8782; Dome Mines Summary Property Accounts, 31 March 1913 and 31 March 1914, in Dome Mines Journals, 1911–15, AO, F1350, box 94, MU 8780.

41 *Canadian Mining Journal*, 15 April 1916, 197. The quotation is from Joseph Stovel, Dome manager, quoted in Girdwood et al., *The Big Dome*, 119–20, source not given.

42 Dome Assistant General Manager's Report, 15 April 1935, in Dome Mines General Manager's Files, 1915–34, AO, F1350, box 11, MU 8687.

43 Personal interview with an informant who requested anonymity.

44 Crawford, *Building the Workingman's Paradise*, 45.

45 See the illustration on page 85 in ibid.

46 *Broke Hustler*, 4 October 1919; *Pulp and Paper Magazine of Canada*, 20 March 1919, 285.

47 *L'Abitibi*, July 1929, 4 (obituary).

48 Gauthier, "Genèse de nos paroisses régionales"; Lendrum, "Days That Are Gone," Timmins *Daily Press*, 24 November 1951, 15.

49 Lendrum, "Days That Are Gone," Timmins *Daily Press*, 24 November 1951, 15.

50 *Broke Hustler*, 23 October 1920; *Porcupine Advance*, 27 October 1927, 7.

51 As reported in the Toronto *Evening Telegram*, 14 November 1946. The OMB ruled against the application.

52 Iroquois Falls History File, Iroquois Falls Museum, 8.

53 "Historical Sites and Trails," 1978, Iroquois Falls Museum, 104–5.

54 *Enterprise*, 18 April 1976, in Shillington History File, Iroquois Falls Museum.

55 AO finding aid F242; Correspondence re Finnish Emigration, 1921–25, Immi-

gration Branch, Library and Archives Canada (LAC) RG76, vol. 25, file 651, part 4 (microfilm C4683); Hawk Lake Lumber Company Timber Licences, Ontario Crown Lands Department, Timber Licence Register, Western District (book 8), AO, RG1, microfilm MS894, reel 11.

56 Department of Labour, Strikes and Lockouts no. 67, Northern Ontario Pulpwood Cutters, 1929, LAC, RG27, vol. 343 (microfilm T2755).

57 R.E. Hore, "The Porcupine Trail," in *Canadian Mining Journal*, 15 October 1910, 618.

58 *Porcupine Advance*, 2 May 1923.

59 Ibid., 14 March 1923; Connaught Circuit Register, 1920–c. 1952, United Church of Canada Archives, Acc. no. 96.129L, box 1–1; evidence of J.A. Critchley to Inquiry re Department of Northern Development, South Cochrane (Matheson Inquiry), AO, RG18–111, Box 1.

60 *Porcupine Advance*, 8 April 1948, 1.

61 Ibid., 25 December 1918, np.

62 Ibid., 24 February 1938, 1, and 5 May 1938, 3.

63 Interview of Jack Pecore by John Campsall, 24 March 1975, in Porcupine Historical Society Oral History Collection, Timmins Museum.

64 Plan of Porquis Junction, 22 January 1938, in Porquis History File, Iroquois Falls Museum.

65 C.L. Heath's map of South Porcupine, 10 February 1913, AO, C295–1–149, box 1614.

66 J.W. McBain to Mining Association, 25 June 1938, copy in the Ontario Municipal Affairs administrative correspondence with Tisdale Township, 1946–72, AO, RG19–43, box 226.

67 Wade, *The Urban Frontier*, 203.

68 Petrik, *No Step Backward*, 3.

69 See Lambert (with Pross), *Renewing Nature's Wealth*, 190–4, for Zavitz and his ideas about reforestation.

70 *Porcupine Advance*, 10 October 1923, 1.

71 Ibid., 15 July 1935, 3.

72 Cobalt *Daily Nugget*, 7 October 1910, 1.

73 John Challinor, *CCNA Publisher*, April 1979, on George Lake; interview with Nora Lake, Timmins, 10 September 1996; *Porcupine Advance*, 18 September 1941 (obituary for Mrs. G.A. Macdonald); various early issues of the *Advance*. Lake moved to Langstaff, Ontario, in 1939 although he retained ownership of the paper; his son Merton took over the business in the 1940s, then closed the paper in 1950 to run the printing division exclusively. Macdonald remained editor until the paper closed. In his eighties, he had a popular spot on Timmins TV called "Old Times Talk."

74 *Porcupine Advance*, 2 August 1912.

75 Ibid., 31 March 1939, 1, and first page of 2nd section.

76 Timmins *Daily Press*, 18 August 1939, 8.

77 *Porcupine Advance,* 30 June 1920, 6.

78 Dubinsky, *Improper Advances,* 158 and 161.

79 Schools History File, Iroquois Falls Museum.

80 Morton, *Working People,* 159; Abella, *Nationalism, Communism, and Canadian Labour,* 19.

81 Griffin, "Men against the Moose," *Toronto Star Weekly,* 24 January 1921, general section, 1.

82 *Porcupine Advance,* 7 June 1912.

83 Ibid., 1 November 1912 and 16 August 1916.

84 Ibid., 5 September 1917, 1.

85 Ibid., 15 July 1935, 3.

86 Lendrum, "Days That Are Gone," Timmins *Daily Press,* 31 December 1948, 5.

87 Lambert (with Pross), *Renewing Nature's Wealth,* 179.

88 *Porcupine Advance,* 10 May 1912; Cobalt *Daily Nugget,* 9 May 1912.

CHAPTER FIVE

1 Field, *The Resources and Trade Prospects of Northern Ontario,* 75.

2 Silvy, *Letters from North America, 1673–1708,* 148 and map following 150. Note that the term Monsoni was later applied also to people trading at York Factory. See Bishop, "Territorial Groups before 1821: Cree and Ojibwa," 159.

3 Thwaites, ed., *The Jesuit Relations and Allied Documents,* 56: 203.

4 Thomas Fraser, Abitibi District Report for 1824, Hudson's Bay Company Archives (HBCA), B.1/e/3, fo 2 (microfilm reel IM775).

5 See, for example, Borron's report in Ontario, *Sessional Papers* 22 (1880): 33. Borron refers to the "Swampy Cree" at James Bay and "Chiwpewa" at Lake Abitibi.

6 See, for example, Honigmann, "West Main Cree," 217; Rogers and Taylor, "Northern Ojibwa," 243; and other references in *Smithsonian Handbook,* vols 6 and 15.

7 Wright, "Before European Contact," 35–6, and Rogers, "Changing Settlement Patterns of the Cree-Ojibwa of Northern Ontario," 66. Francis and Morantz, in *Partners in Furs: A History of the Fur Trade in Eastern James Bay 1600–1870,* mistakenly suggest that mid-nineteenth-century missionaries introduced the term Cree, but otherwise they make a useful point about the artificiality of the term (11–12).

8 Samuel Stewart, Journal of James Bay Treaty Trips, 1905–6, LAC, RG10, vol. 11,399 (microfilm reel T6924), no page.

9 See, for example, Philip Good, Kenogamissi Post Journal, 1802–3, entry for August 1802, HBCA, B.99/a/9, fo. 9d (microfilm reel IM66).

10 Hugh Faries, Matawagamingue Post Journal, 1827–28, entry for 27 August 1827, HBCA, B.124/a/5, fo. 1d (microfilm reel IM78).

11 Joseph Fortescue, Moose Post Reports, 1890, HBCA, B.135/e/28a, fo. 23 (microfilm reel IM1257).

12 John Horden's correspondence, 19 September 1862 and 10 February 1865. Church Missionary Society Records, LAC, C1/0 (microfilm reel A89).

13 Smith, "John Sanders," DCB 13: 920–1; John Sanders, "My Autobiography," handwritten copy in his correspondence with the Church Missionary Society, CMS Records, app. B, 1876–77, LAC (microfilm reel A102).

14 See description of housing changes in J.A. Newnham's Diary, Moose, Winter 1892, Newnham Papers, LAC, MG 29/D49, fo. 10.

15 See some interesting accounts of these activities in John Horden's correspondence from Moose, J. Horden to Reverend H. Knight, 3 July 1854, CMS Papers, LAC, C.1/0 (reel 88); 16 June 1860 and Horden to Mr Mee, 7 June 1869 (A203). CMS Papers, LAC, C.1/0, (reel A89).

16 Porcupine Advance, 8 November 1937.

17 Cobalt Daily Nugget, 4 August 1909; Barnes, Gold in the Porcupine! 59–60; Last and Vachon, Timmins, 20.

18 Innis, An Economic History of Canada, 269.

19 Trudelle, L'Abitibi d'autrefois, d'hier, d'aujourd'hui, 44–50; Report on Northern Quebec settlement by CNR Department of Colonization (1944), 2, in Ontario Department of Agriculture Office Files, Archives of Ontario (AO), RG 16-09.

20 Cobalt Daily Nugget, 14 February 1913, 1.

21 Gauthier, "Genese de nos paroisses régionales," np.

22 Cobalt Daily Nugget, 19 June 1913, 1.

23 Correspondence of H.P. DePencier to J.S. Bache (president of Dome) re Dome plans, Dome Mines Collection, General Files, 1920–23, AO, F1350, box 3, MU8689; Porcupine Advance 1 November 1922, 1.

24 Hollinger Mines, Twelfth Annual Report, 1922, 13, Hollinger Mines Collection, miscellaneous reports, AO, MU1382.

25 DePencier to Howard Poillon, New York, 3 November 1920, Dome Mines Collection, General Files, 1920–23, AO, F1350, box 3, MU8689.

26 Raivio, Kanadan suomalaisten historia, 1: 485–91.

27 Winnipeg Division Commissioner of Immigration and Colonization to A.L. Joliffe, Winnipeg, 25 June 1931. Timmins delegates included Alexander Jokela, Martii J. Kyrola, Vaino Urpunen, and Yrjo Lauri. See file on "Finnish Agitators in Northern Ontario," Immigration Branch, LAC, RG76, vol. 219, file 95027 (microfilm reel C7639).

28 Bureau of Mines, re Northern Ontario miners, Ontario Bureau of Mines Annual Report (bound with Department of Lands, Forests and Mines for 1911), in Ontario Sessional Papers 4 (1912): 43.

29 Innis, The Economic History of Canada, 269. Local historian Charlie Angus also notes the presence of Cape Bretoners in Angus and Palu, Mirrors of Stone, 41–2, 44.

30 Toronto Globe, 20 November 1912, 11.

31 *Porcupine Advance*, 9 December 1937.

32 Ibid., 28 September 1933, 1, and 17 October 1917, 8; Timmins *Press*, 25 September 1933, 1.

33 Ibid., 21 June 1934, 4. Killaloe is a village in the Ottawa Valley near Algonquin Park.

34 Porcupine Prospectors' Association, *The Prospector*, 34; *Porcupine Advance*, 12 April 1937 (her obituary), 23 October 1939 (his obituary).

35 *Porcupine Advance*, 13 March 1918; Lendrum, "Days That Are Gone," 1 September 1956 and 1 June 1957.

36 *Porcupine Advance*, 25 February 1920; *Might's City Catalogues* (Timmins), 1934.

37 Goldenberg, *The Thomson Empire*; Braddon, *Roy Thomson of Fleet Street.*

38 *Porcupine Advance*, 15 July 1935, 3. In 1937 the Supreme Court ruled in a contract dispute that the life expectancy of a mine was ten years, a point that the Privy Council upheld the following year; see Manore, *Cross-Currents*, 101.

39 See Dennie, "Sudbury 1883–1946: A Social Historical Study of Property and Class," 27.

40 The editor of *La Vérité* defended these settlements (15 April 1899) because they would gradually extend the boundaries of Quebec; quoted in Grimard and Vallières, *Travailleurs et gens d'affaires canadiens-français en Ontario*, 59.

41 Toronto *Globe*, 12 September 1916, 14.

42 Radforth, *Bushworkers and Bosses*, 32.

43 Igartua, *Arvida au Saguenay*, 62–3.

44 Pauline Larose, "Single Industry Town" (pamphlet), c.1969, 3, in Iroquois Falls History File, Iroquois Falls Museum.

45 Last and Vachon, *Timmins*, 43.

46 Ibid., 21.

47 *Porcupine Advance*, 20 January 1936, obituary.

48 Mattawa Cemetery gravestones; *Porcupine Advance*, 5 June 1930, 1; Montreal *Gazette*, 24 January 1936, 5; Barnes, *Gold in the Porcupine!* 5–6.

49 *Hollinger Miner*, 21 November 1955, 5–6, obituary.

50 F.A. Tortel to Society for the Propagation of the Faith, Ottawa 1864, in Carrière, *Histoire documentaire de la Congrégation des missionnaires Oblats de Marie-Immaculée*, 4: 156 and 164.

51 Clark, "The Position of the French-Speaking Population in the Northern Industrial Community," 62–4.

52 Singleton, *A Short History of Finland*, 92.

53 Aili Grönlund Schneider, *The Finnish Baker's Daughters*, 79, quoted in Lindström-Best, *Defiant Sisters*, 62.

54 Raivio, *Kanadan suomalaisten historia*, 1:406.

55 Lindström-Best, *Defiant Sisters: A Social History of Finnish Immigrant Women in Canada*, 153.

56 Porcupine Golden Anniversary Committee, *Souvenir Booklet Celebrating the Golden Anniversary of the Porcupine Gold Rush, July 1–5, 1959*, 91.

57 *Porcupine Advance*, 22 September 1938.

58 Ibid., 28 April 1938, 1; AO finding aid F242.

59 Singleton, *A Short History of Finland*, 114.

60 See letters from Akseli Ravanheimo of the Finnish Consulate at Montreal on the issue, 1924–25, Immigration Branch Correspondence re Finnish immigration, LAC, RG 76, vol. 25, file 651, part 4 (microfilm reel C4683).

61 Raivio, *Kanadan suomalaisten historia*, 1:464–82.

62 Ibid., 1:485–91.

63 Radforth, *Bushworkers and Bosses*, 125.

64 Raivio, *Kanadan suomalaisten historia*, 1:485–91.

65 A.L. Joliffe, Department of Immigration and Colonization, Winnipeg, 25 June 1931, Immigration Branch Correspondence re Finnish Agitators in Northern Ontario, LAC, RG 76, vol. 25, file 651, part 4 (microfilm reel C7639).

66 Lindström-Best, *Defiant Sisters*, 64.

67 Memo from Director, Immigration Branch, for file. Ottawa, 19 November 1937, Immigration Branch re: Finnish Agitators, LAC, RG76, vol. 25, file 651 (microfilm reel C7639).

68 Schneider, *The Finnish Baker's Daughters*, 39.

69 Di Giacomo, "The Italians of Timmins: Micro and Macro-Ethnicity in a Northern Resource Community," 36.

70 Ramirez, *On the Move: French Canadian and Italian Migrants in the North Atlantic Economy, 1860–1914*, 141.

71 See observations on the Italians in Montreal, 1896–1914, in Avery, *Reluctant Host: Canada's Response to Immigrant Workers, 1896–1994*, 66.

72 The other group was the Germans.

73 On Little Italy, see Girdwood et al., *The Big Dome: Over Seventy Years of Gold Mining in Canada*, 119, quoting J.H. Stovel in *A Mining Trail.*

74 Di Giacomo, "The Italians of Timmins," 47.

75 Interview of Leo Del Villano, 3 September 1975; Porcupine Historical Society, Oral History Collection, Timmins Museum.

76 Di Giacomo, "The Italians of Timmins," 43–4.

77 Story compiled from a number of sources: Timmins *Daily Press*, 27 March 1939, section 3; Braddon, *Roy Thomson of Fleet Street*, 62, 75, 93, 97, 106; Town of Timmins Financial Statement for 1914 in Municipal Financial Returns for Timmins, 1912–35, AO, RG19–142; *Porcupine Advance*, 6 December 1912; Toronto *Globe*, 10 November 1912; *Might's City Catalogue* (Timmins), 1934; Di Giacomo, "The Italians of Timmins," 40.

78 See data on Italian migrations in Foerster, *The Italian Emigration of Our Times*, 38, 529.

79 *Porcupine Advance*, 2 February 1939, 1.

80 Interview of Mrs Minerva Gram by M.E. Stortroen, 4 February 1976, Porcupine Historical Society, Oral History Collection, Timmins Museum.

81 Marunchak, *The Ukrainian Canadians: A History*, 67.
82 Stefura, "Ukrainians in the Sudbury Region," 71; Bradwin, *The Bunkhouse Man: A Study of Work and Pay in the Camps of Canada, 1903–1914*, 106.
83 Perger, "Being Ukrainian in Timmins: A Personal Reminiscence," 114.
84 Ibid., 115; Timmins *Daily Press*, 16 January 1939, 8. For a list of first arrivals, see the Cobalt *Daily Nugget*, 19 July 1911, 1.
85 Swyripa, "Outside the Bloc Settlement: Ukrainian Women in Ontario during the Formative Years of Community Consciousness," 159.
86 Avery, *Reluctant Host*, 39–40.
87 The Rt Revd Ananias Kassab. See *Porcupine Advance*, 6 July 1936.
88 Tremblay, "Timmins: métropole de l'or."
89 Assistant-General Manager, Noranda Mines, to J.H. Stovel, Dome, 28 June 1934, in file "Noranda Strikers," Dome Mines Collection, General Manager's Files, AO, F1350, box 11, MU8697.
90 Perger, "Being Ukrainian in Timmins," 117.
91 Kolasky, *The Shattered Illusion: The History of Ukrainian Pro-Communist Organizations in Canada*, 184.
92 Stefura, "Ukrainians in the Sudbury Region," 71.
93 Cobalt *Daily Nugget*, 14 April 1913, 8.
94 According to Bob Reid, see *Broke Hustler*, 6 April 1926.
95 Voorhis, *Historic Forts and Trading Posts of the French Regime and of the English Fur Trading Companies*, 26.
96 Ray, *The Canadian Fur Trade in the Industrial Era*, 152, table 15: "Huron District Sales, 1922–3." By the early 1930s, La Sarre was also catering to the area's settlers with retail sales and by distributing cheques from Abitibi for pulpwood purchases. See La Sarre Post Journal for 1932–33 and 1935–36, HBCA, B.432/a/1 and B.432/a/4 (microfilm reel IMA36).
97 Jenkins, *Notes on the Hunting Economy of the Abitibi Indians*, 2; John T. McPherson, unpublished manuscript for the National Museum of Canada, 1930, cited in Jenkins, note 2 (original not found).
98 Robert Bell's Notebook on Northern Ontario Indians, gathered from "Mr. Rae," in Robert Bell Papers, 1890, Lawrence Lande Collection, LAC, MG53/B199 (microfilm reel H1466).
99 Clement, *The Bell and the Book*, 56.
100 For example, William Powell of Haileybury hired 27 Moose Factory men to work his claims on the Mattagami River (Cobalt *Daily Nugget*, 19 August 1910, 1).
101 See, for example, the report of Agent H.A. West, 19 April 1910, re the Mattagami Band, in Annual Report of the Department of Indian Affairs, Ontario, *Sessional Papers* 27 (1911): 3.
102 Bradwin, *The Bunkhouse Man*, 104.
103 Hodgins and Benidickson, *The Temagami Experience*, 150, 152.
104 George Shaw to Department of Indian Affairs, 22 September 1920, in

Indian Affairs Branch file on Chapleau Agency, Correspondence re Mattagami Reserve, LAC, RG10, vol. 7835, file 30065–3 (microfilm reel C12,108).

105 J.W. Anderson, in an interview with J.H. Allen Wilmot, 25 June 1958, transcript in HBCA, E93/26, 70 (microfilm reel 4M73); La Sarre, 6 and 15 February 1935, La Sarre Post Journal, HBCA, B.432/a/3, 39 and 41 (microfilm reel IMA36).

106 See annual reports of the Department of Indian Affairs, 1924 to 1929–30. The report for 1924 is in Ontario, *Sessional Papers* 14; the rest were separately published reports.

107 See, for example, the report for 1 November 1931, 19. Other low-income areas were Scugog (near Peterborough) and Golden Lake (west of Ottawa).

108 Cobalt *Daily Nugget*, 3 April 1913, 1 and 6; *Porcupine Advance*, 20 August 1915, 8.

109 Bradwin, *The Bunkhouse Man*, 103; Holley, *Just Passing Through: The People and Places North of Matachewan*, 44, 74; *Hollinger Miner*, 22 May 1956, 10. Tom Fox had guided the prospectors who discovered what became the Dome Mines.

110 Manore, *Cross-Currents*, 56.

111 Thomas Kuskichee to the Department of Indian Affairs, 26 December 1928, in file on Chapleau and the Ontario Game Laws, 1924–29, Department of Indian Affairs, LAC, RG10 (microfilm reel C8103).

112 J.D. McLean, Department of Indian Affairs, to Walter Simons, Christian Island Band Council, 7 November 1924, among other correspondence on the subject in ibid.

113 Anderson, *Angel of Hudson Bay: The True Story of Maude Watt*, 152–4; *Porcupine Advance*, 18 May 1936, 1.

114 Theriault, *Trespassing in God's Country: Sixty Years of Flying in Northern Canada*, 88.

115 Indian Affairs Branch, Department of Mines and Resources, annual reports for 1942 and 1943, pp. 133 and 146, respectively.

116 Indian Affairs Branch, Department of Mines and Resources, annual reports for 1945 and 1946, 166 and 216, respectively.

117 Annual Report for 1945, 165.

118 For more on the typhoid epidemic, see Indian Affairs Annual Report for 1938, 189.

119 There has been some scholarly debate in Canada over whether to consider the Jewish population an ethnic or religious group. I have been convinced by the argument that they should be understood here in religious terms because, unlike the American Jews, they were primarily conservative and Orthodox in their religious beliefs but came from a much greater diversity of national backgrounds: Great Britain, Spain, the Baltic, Poland, Ukraine,

and Russia. See Tulchinsky, *Taking Root*, for the best historical analysis of the Canadian Jewish community.

120 *Porcupine Advance*, 23 December 1936, 1.

121 Porcupine Golden Anniversary Committee, *Souvenir Booklet Celebrating the Golden Anniversary of the Porcupine Gold Rush, July 1–5, 1959*, 41.

122 *Porcupine Advance*, 2 May 1917, 5.

123 Ibid., 14 November 1935 and 23 August 1937.

124 "Quarterly Review of Yugoslav Migrations," (Zagreb), April–June 1930, vol. 4, no. 2, pp 16–17, Immigration Branch Files, LAC, RG 76, vol. 623, part 3 (reel C10,440).

125 Bradwin, *The Bunkhouse Man*, 107–8.

126 *Porcupine Advance*, 23 June 1927.

127 Ibid., 18 August 1938, 1.

128 Ibid., 15 September 1938, 2.

129 The primary exception was some early employment of a group of Jewish men from Europe on the construction of the TNO. An abandoned Jewish cemetery near Krugerdorf was believed to have been the final resting place of some of them. See Lendrum, "Days That Are Gone," Timmins *Daily Press*, 4 April 1953, 16.

130 Historian Gerald Tulchinsky draws a similar conclusion about Jews in other small Canadian towns in the early twentieth century (Tulchinsky, *Taking Root*, 160–1).

131 See, for example, *Porcupine Advance*, 15 August 1917 (re establishment of the Timmins synagogue), 18 June 1919 (re inauguration of Zion Hall); and 18 February 1937 (re Purim Balls as community outreach); untitled booklet in Iroquois Falls Museum History File (re Ansonville Jews); *Scroll*, 23 December 1938, Iroquois Falls Museum Schools History File (re Iroquois Falls Jews).

132 *Porcupine Advance*, 16 June 1938, 1.

133 *Broke Hustler*, 13 March 1918.

134 *Porcupine Advance*, 21 October 1937.

CHAPTER SIX

1 Timmins *Daily Press*, week of 4 November 1947.

2 For an introduction to the scholarly debate on defining labour as skilled or unskilled, see McClelland, "Masculinity and the 'Representational Artisan' in Britain, 1850–80," esp. 80. In *Family Time and Industrial Time*, Tamara Hareven characterizes industrial work as comprising (1) a hierarchical organization/authority; (2) fixed and regulated time; (3) systematic organization of work; (4) a set pace of work; and (5) "machine regulated" rather than "task-oriented" work. I would argue that these definitions apply equally to twentieth-century mining as it was done in this region.

3 Arthur W. Young, "Mining," *Canadian Mining Journal* 56 (September 1935): 373.

4 Newell, *Technology on the Frontier: Mining in Old Ontario*, 25–6.

5 Ralph E. Foster, "Hydro-Electric Power and Ontario Gold Mining," *Canadian Mining Journal* 67 (March 1946): 159.

6 "Hollinger Mine History," 1968, 2–7 in Hollinger Mines Historical Materials, Archives of Ontario (AO), MU8114.

7 Labour Wages File. Includes information on 1920 wage scales in Sudbury, Kirkland Lake, Nevada, and Idaho mines, as well as of hydro workers in northeastern Ontario. In General Files, 1919–24) Dome Mines Collection, AO, F1350, box 1, MU8687.

8 McIntyre Mines Employee Cards, Laurentian University Archives, P020/1/D/1,4.

9 J.S. Bache to H.P. DePencier, New York, 13 June 1923, in Dome Mines Collection, General Files, 1920–23, AO, F1350, box 1, MU8689.

10 Leacy, *Historical Statistics of Canada*, E41–8.

11 Cobalt *Daily Nugget*, 19 and 21 January 1911, 5 and 1, respectively.

12 Report of E.T. Corkill, Chief Inspector of Mines, in Annual Report of the Department of Lands, Forests and Mines for 1910, Ontario, *Sessional Papers* 3 (1911): 66–71, 85.

13 Lendrum, "Days That Are Gone," Timmins *Daily Press*, 4 January 1958, 4.

14 *Porcupine Advance*, 12 July 1912, 1–2. Curiously, the official report in the Bureau of Mines Report for 1912 (Ontario, *Sessional Papers* 4, 1913) says Martin was married and that he died when his skull was fractured by a broken pole winch.

15 *Porcupine Advance*, 1 October 1915, 1.

16 Dome Diary, 12 February 1924, in Dome Mines Collection, General Files (1919–24), AO, F1350, box 1, MU8687.

17 See accounts of the fire in Trotter, "Breakthroughs in Health and Safety in Northern Ontario Mines," 120–1; Smith, *Harvest from the Rock*, 235–7; and *Porcupine Advance*, 16 February 1928, 1.

18 *Porcupine Advance*, 29 March 1928, 1.

19 T.E. Godson, "The Hollinger Mine Fire," *Canadian Mining Journal*, 8 June 1928, 464–8, and 26 October 1928, 878–80.

20 See Raivo, *Kanadan suomalaisten historia*, 2: 272, for a photo montage and identification of the victims.

21 *Porcupine Advance*, 26 July 1912.

22 Ontario Mining Association Report, accidents in 1941 and 1942, in Buffalo Ankerite Collection, Correspondence, 1933–60, Library and Archives Canada (LAC), MG28 III 81, vol. 19.

23 Lingenfelter, *The Hardrock Miners: A History of the Mining Movement in the American West, 1863–1893*, 16.

24 Smith, *Harvest from the Rock*, 241.

25 Knox, *Gold Mining in Ontario*, 77.
26 Report of Ontario Mining Association, 1 November 1935, in Dome Mines Collection, General Manager's Files, 1915–34, AO, F1350, box 11, MU8697.
27 Smith, *Harvest from the Rock*, 243.
28 *Porcupine Advance*, 2 July 1936.
29 Timmins *Press*, 2 October 1933, 1.
30 Dome Assistant General Manager to Ontario Minister of Education, 12 February 1935, in Dome Mines Collection, General Manager's Files, 1915–34, AO, F1350, box 11, MU8697; *Porcupine Advance*, 22 April 1937.
31 Ontario Legislative Assembly, *Debates and Proceedings*, 1948, 2:2027.
32 Townsley, *The Mine Finders*, np.
33 On alienation, see Rinehart, *The Tyranny of Work*, and Wallimann, *Estrangement: Marx's Concept of Human Nature and the Division of Labor*. For a specific study of alienation in a technological world, see Ellul, *The Technological Society*.
34 See more on Forestell's analysis of women's responses to workplace hazards in Timmins in "All That Glitters Is Not Gold: The Gendered Dimensions of Work, Family, and Community Life in the Northern Ontario Goldmining Town of Timmins, 1910–1950."
35 Williamson, *Class, Culture, and Community: A Biographical Study of Social Change in Mining*, 33.
36 Royal Commission on the Nature Resources, Trade and Legislation of Certain Portions of His Majesty's Dominions, 1917, 307, quoted in Innis, *Settlement and the Mining Frontier*, 362, note 11.
37 *Hollinger Miner*, 27 October 1952, 7.
38 *Porcupine Advance*, 10 April 1941, 1.
39 *Hollinger Miner*, 25 October 1954, 10.
40 *Porcupine Advance*, 23 May 1938, 3.
41 Ibid., 2 December 1937 and 21 March 1938.
42 *Hollinger Miner*, 23 March 1953, 2.
43 *Porcupine Advance*, 26 November 1915, 3; 27 March 1818, 1; 2 October 1918, 1; and 25 April 1938, 1. See also *Canadian Mining Journal*, 15 May 1916, 242.
44 *Porcupine Advance*, 26 September 1935, 1.
45 Barnes, *Gold in the Porcupine!* 65–7; see also Smith, *Frederick W. Schumacher.*
46 Toronto *Globe*, 10 June 1921.
47 Guthrie, *The Newspaper Industry: An Economic Analysis*, 241, figures for 1928.
48 My thanks to Jocelyne Guinard of Abitibi Consolidated for this information.
49 *Porcupine Advance*, 14 February 1938 (obituary).
50 *Pulp and Paper Magazine of Canada*, 20 March 1919, 285; *Broke Hustler*, 20 April 1926.
51 *L'Abitibi*, February 1931, 18.
52 *Broke Hustler*, 27 September 1919.
53 Compiled from *Porcupine Advance*, 15 April 1931; *Broke Hustler*, 4 October 1919 and 20 April 1926; Agricultural Representative's Report, 27 August

1949, Ontario Ministry of Agriculture, AO, RG16, G-5-1; and Lendrum, "Days
That Are Gone," Timmins *Daily Press*, 23 July 1955, 4.

54 *Broke Hustler*, 2 June 1925. Details of Frank Jr's life from *Broke Hustler*, 29
December 1925 and 20 April 1926, and from an undated item from late
1925 or early 1926 (clippings at Iroquois Falls Museum).

55 Radforth, *Bushworkers and Bosses*, 32, says that in 1929 Abitibi's workforce at
Iroquois Falls was 52% French Canadian and only 8.2% English Canadian.

56 *Broke Hustler*, 29 December 1925; *L'Abitibi*, 26 February 1920, 4.

57 Department of Labour [Canada], Strikes and Lockouts, no. 45, LAC, RG27,
vol. 306 (microfilm reel T2693); Strikes and Lockouts, no. 106, May–June
1921, LAC, RG27, vol. 326 (microfilm reel T2709); *Porcupine Advance*, 2 May
1923, p 1.

58 Pain, *The Way North*, 230.

59 C.M. Macreath to W.J. Fuller, 27 April 1920, in Correspondence re
Mattagami Heights, 1920, Timmins Museum, 992–10.1.

60 Cobalt *Daily Nugget*, 17 May 1921, 1.

61 *Pulp and Paper Magazine of Canada*, 27 February 1919, 226–7; "Mrs. Tinney's
Report of Monteith," in "Historical Sites and Trails," 1978, 105, Iroquois Falls
Museum.

62 Abitibi Power and Paper to Cochrane OPP, 20 November 1933, in Department of Labour [Canada], Strikes and Lockouts, no. 139, 1933, LAC, RG27,
vol. 357 (microfilm reel T2968).

63 Undated note on "Iroquois Falls: Model Town of the North," in Iroquois Falls
History File, Iroquois Falls Museum; *Porcupine Advance*, 13 August 1936, 8.

64 E.J. Robertson's report, 1926, in Frontier College Collection, LAC, MG28 I
124, vol. 150. For other camp descriptions of the same era, see Sillanpää,
Under the Northern Lights, 24–5, and Radforth, *Bushworkers and Bosses*,
88–92.

65 "The Bush Doctor," reminiscences of Dr Henry Swan in Abitibi History File,
Iroquois Falls Museum; *Toronto Worker*, 17 December 1927, in Department of
Labour [Canada], Strikes and Lockouts, no. 78, LAC, RG27, vol. 339 (micro-
film reel T2751); Sudbury *Star*, 20 October 1928; North Bay *Nugget*, 23
October 1928; Radforth, *Bushworkers and Bosses*, 255 (app. 6, "Logging Wages
in Ontario."

66 *Porcupine Advance*, 25 October 1937, 1.

67 Lindström-Best, *Defiant Sisters: A Social History of Finnish Immigrant Women in
Canada*, 86.

68 Radforth, *Bushworkers and Bosses*, 101.

69 Arthur Lowe, "Headline Fodder," *Maclean's Magazine*, 15 November 1927, 59.

70 Lendrum, "Days That Are Gone," Timmins *Daily Press*, 23 August 1947, 10.

71 Timmins and Tisdale Survey, Survey on Vocational Education in Ontario, in
Lacelle Files, Department of Labour [Canada], LAC, RG27, vol. 257, file
900/02/02, part 9 (microfilm reel T10,181).

72 Frederick Noad, "Ontario's Unsettled Settlers," *Saturday Night*, 4 November 1933, 15.

73 Frank Ginn to Ontario Minister of Education, Matheson, 6 December 1922, in Ontario Department of Education Central Registry Files, 1922, AO, RG2/P3, box 100.

74 W.B. Common, "The Commissioner's Report" (Report of the Matheson Enquiry, 1936), 29, AO, RG18–111, box 1.

75 *Porcupine Advance*, 24 June 1937, 2nd section.

76 Contained in letter from Edward L. Murphy to Alfred Fitzpatrick, Mile 86, Edlund, nd [1927], Frontier College Homesteading Plan, 1921–43, LAC, MG 28 I 124, vol. 199.

77 Laurendeau discusses the operations of a Cercle agricole on the Quebec side of the border in *L'homme aux 56 métiers*, 8.

78 Report of Agricultural Representative D.J. Pomerleau, 1 November 1933 to 31 October 1934, p 3, in Agricultural Representative Reports, Ontario Ministry of Agriculture, 1927–1949, AO, RG16, G-5-1.

79 Porcupine Golden Anniversary Committee, *Souvenir Booklet Celebrating the Golden Anniversary of the Porcupine Gold Rush, July 1–5, 1959*, 39.

80 Compiled from *Porcupine Advance*, 25 February 1920, 1; *Might's City Catalogue* (Timmins), 1934; interview of Jack Andrews, 10 July 1975, in Porcupine Historical Society Collection, Timmins Museum; Porcupine Golden Anniversary Committee, *Souvenir Booklet*, 39.

81 Bernard, *Le travail et l'espoir: migrations, développement économique, et mobilité sociale Québec/Ontario, 1900–1985*, table 6-1, 155.

82 Laurendeau, *L'homme aux 56 métiers*, 466 (my translation).

83 Last et Vachon, *Timmins*, 43–4.

84 Interview with Hamer Disher by M.E. Stortroen, 1 June 1975, Porcupine Historical Society Collection, Timmins Museum.

85 MacDougall, *Two Thousand Miles of Gold*, 13.

86 Compiled from *Porcupine Advance*, 14 August 1930, 1 (obituary for Michael Feldman); Michelle Rocheleau, "An Inventory of Historic Sites in Timmins-Porcupine" (typescript report, for Timmins Roman Catholic Separate School Board, 1979), 77. Copy seen at AO library.

87 Canada, House of Commons, *Debates*, 12 March 1934, 1415–16.

88 *Porcupine Advance*, 30 May 1938, 1.

89 Cobalt *Daily Nugget*, 14 April 1913, 8.

90 See Sexé, *Two Centuries of Fur Trading, 1723–1923: Romance of the Revillon Family*, and Ray, *The Canadian Fur Trade in the Industrial Era*, 92–3. I have been unable to locate details of the Porcupine Camp operation, but the store is clearly featured in early photographs of the camp.

91 HBC London Correspondence, General, A92/corr/257/1, 21, as quoted in Ray, *The Canadian Fur Trade in the Industrial Era*, 203.

92 John Fletcher to Department of Indian Affairs, 1 September 1927, copy in

file of Temiskaming Agency, Abitibi Reserve, Department of Indian Affairs, LAC, RG10, vol. 6613, file 6035–2 (microfilm reel C8017).

93 For descriptions of trade at Gogama in the early 1930s, see the HBC's Gogama Post Journals, HBCA, B.415/a/1 and B.415/a/2 (microfilm reel IMA27).

94 See, for example, complaints of Native people at La Sarre on Lake Abitibi in 1936, La Sarre Post Journal, HBCA, B.432/a/4, 58 (microfilm reel IMA36), and Laurendeau, *L'homme aux 56 métiers*, 53.

95 Theriault, *Trespassing in God's Country*, 88.

96 Report of Agricultural Representative D.J. Pomerleau, 1 November 1930 to 31 October 1931, 14, and 1 November 1931 to 31 October 1932, 16, in Ontario Ministry of Agriculture, 1927–49, AO, RG 16, G-5-1.

97 L.H. Hanlan's report for 1 April 1943 to 31 March 1944, 2, 18, in Ontario Ministry of Agriculture, 1927–49, AO, RG 16, G-5-1.

98 *Porcupine Advance*, 1 August 1935, 8 August 1938, 6, and 25 August 1938.

99 Avery, *Reluctant Host*, 39.

100 William B. Ririe's report, 1927, Frontier College Collection, LAC, MG29 I 124, vol. 150. See also H.L. Sharpe's report, 1927, for a description of a CPR Chapleau Divisional work crew's camp (in the same file).

101 Bradwin, *The Bunkhouse Man*, 65–7.

102 Ibid., 133–4.

103 William Ririe's report, Frontier College Collection, LAC, MG29 I 124, vol. 150.

104 Gordon Armour's abstract of work, 1938, Frontier College Collection, LAC, MG28 I 124, vol. 157.

105 Lucas, *Minetown, Milltown, Railtown*, 114–15.

106 Surtees, *The Northern Connection*, 184.

107 Shaw, *Broken Threads: Memories of a Northern Ontario Schoolteacher*, 11, 48, 55, and 70ff; Lendrum, "Days That Are Gone," Timmins *Daily Press*, 29 October 1955, 4, and "Browsing Around," Timmins *Daily Press*, 29 August 1957, 16.

108 Lendrum, Timmins *Daily Press*, 12 January 1954, 4, and "Days That Are Gone," 26 March 1955, 4; interview with Mr Olaf Pollon, 1997, in Porcupine Historical Society Collection, Timmins Museum.

109 See *Porcupine Advance*, 25 June 1915, 8, for teachers' wages; McIntyre data from McIntyre employees' cards, Laurentian University Archives, P020/1/D/1,4.

110 Lindström-Best, *Defiant Sisters*, 105, 107.

111 Lendrum, "Days That Are Gone," Timmins *Daily Press*, [9 February] 1948, quoting a 1910 news item.

112 Dorothy Pinkney, "The Transplanting," (unpublished memoirs, circa 1920–22), AO, acc. 14904 (microfilm MS712, reel 1).

113 Cobalt *Daily Nugget*, 30 December 1910 and 5 September 1913, 1; *Porcupine Advance*, 17 May 1912; OPP Divisional Inspector's Report, March 1914 and

January 1915, OPP Northern Division Monthly Reports, 1911–21, AO, RG23, B12, box 1.

114 *Porcupine Advance*, 14 March 1935, 4.

115 D. Chalmers to R.P. Fairbairn, Matheson, 1 May 1911, in correspondence of the Colonization Roads Branch, 1911–13, AO, RG52, series 2A, box 5.

116 See sample reports in the Cobalt *Daily Nugget*, 5 February 1910, 1; Rev. Alex Pelletier to James Whitney, 4 August 1911, in James P. Whitney Papers, March to September 1911, AO, F6, MU3131. See also *Porcupine Advance*, 19 January 1916, 1; 22 May 1918, 1; 7 August 1918, 1; 20 February 1924; and 12 and 26 March 1924.

117 *Porcupine Advance*, 30 August 1934, 5; 4 October 1934, 3; and other reports through to 3 and 6 December 1934, pages 1 and 2, respectively.

118 Braddon, *Roy Thomson of Fleet Street*, 65.

119 *Porcupine Advance*, 6 December 1934, 2.

120 Interview with a former resident who wished to remain anonymous.

121 Cobalt *Daily Nugget*, 30 September 1912, 1.

122 AO, finding aid for RG23, 1–2. (Caldbick's name is incorrectly spelled as "Colbeck.") Constable Caldbick's son later became a lawyer in Timmins.

123 OPP Northern Division Monthly Reports, 1911–21, AO, RG 23, B12, box 1; Cobalt *Daily Nugget*, 17 July 1911, 1.

124 Lendrum, "Days That Are Gone," Timmins *Daily Press*, 5 November 1949, 7, from Whitney Township Council Minutes.

125 *Porcupine Advance*, 28 March and 28 June 1912. The name was sometimes spelled "McGinnis."

126 *Broke Hustler*, 6 January 1919 [sic, should be 1920].

127 Iroquois Falls Municipal Financial Returns for 1915, AO, RG19–142, 764, box 186.

128 Rev. Alex Pelletier to James P. Whitney, Toronto, 4 August 1911, James P. Whitney Papers, AO, F6, MU3131.

129 Town of Timmins Financial Statement, 1914, Timmins Municipal Financial Returns, 1912–35, AO, RG19–142, 1080, box 391.

130 M.E. White to H.P. DePencier, Toronto, 20 October 1922, Dome Mines Collection, Miscellaneous Reports, 1912–45, AO, F1350, box 88, MU8774.

131 Avery, *Reluctant Host*, 39.

132 *Porcupine Advance*, 31 March 1935, 2.

133 Wyman, *Hard Rock Epic*, 172–3; Moore, *American Influence in Canadian Mining*, 116–17; Lankton, *Cradle to Grave: Life, Work, and Death at the Lake Superior Copper Mines*, 206, 209; Murphy, *Yankee Takeover at Cobalt!* 96.

134 Cobalt *Daily Nugget*, 4 June 1910, 1; Solski and Smaller, *Mine, Mill*, 60.

135 Ibid., 3, 4, and 5 December 1912; Department of Labour [Canada], Strikes and Lockouts File no. 3618, 1912, LAC, RG27, vol. 300 (microfilm reel T2689).

136 Hollinger Gold Mines Ltd., 2nd Annual Report, 31 March 1913, 2 and 15, AO, MU1382; Montreal *Gazette*, 16 November 1912, 20.

137 "Application for a Charter," 28 July 1920, Western Federation of Miners Collection, University of Colorado at Boulder Archives, box 1, 1920.

138 H.P. DePencier to J.S. Bache, 7 April 1923, Dome Mines Collection, General Files, 1920–23, AO, F1350, box 3, MU8689.

139 "AF" reports, South Porcupine, Dome Mines Collection, General Files, 1920–23, AO, F1350, box 3, MU8689.

140 MacDowell, *"Remember Kirkland Lake": The Goldminers' Strike of 1941–42*, 62.

141 Timmins Mine, Mill Local 241 to International Executive Board, 22 September 1947, Western Federation of Miners Collection, University of Colorado at Boulder Archives, box 133, 1944–47.

142 For an examination of this strike and its repercussions, see MacDowell, *"Remember Kirkland Lake."*

143 Ivan Vachon (president), Art Jones (financial secretary), and J. Carlin (recording secretary), "Notice" dated 11 April 1948, Western Federation of Miners Collection, University of Colorado at Boulder Archives, box 136, 1947–51.

144 John Clark (president IUMMSW) to "All Canadian Locals," dated Chicago, 7 April 1948, in ibid.; Supreme Court of Ontario ruling of 5 December 1949. Mine, Mill won the return of their desk and filing cabinets. See Western Federation of Miners Collection, University of Colorado at Boulder Archives, box 139, 1947–50.

145 Abella, *Nationalism, Communism, and Canadian Labour*, 88–107, has excellent coverage of these events.

146 The vote was 860 in favour of Steelworkers and 269 in favour of Mine, Mill (*Globe and Mail*, 27 September 1950, 5).

147 Abella, in *Nationalism, Communism, and Canadian Labour*, says it had 25 members in 1950 (86).

148 *Globe and Mail*, 4 August 1951, 11.

149 Forestell, "All That Glitters," 52.

150 "AF" reports, South Porcupine, in Dome Mines Collection, General Files, 1920–23, AO, F1350, box 3, MU8689.

151 Dominion Police Security Bulletin no. 49, 11 November 1920, in Kealey and Whitaker, *R.C.M.P. Security Bulletins: The Early Years, 1919–1929*, 190.

152 A. Hautamaki to Department of Labour, Port Arthur, 7 August 1928, Department of Labour [Canada], Strikes and Lockouts, 1928, no. 62, LAC, RG27, vol. 341 (microfilm reel T2753).

153 Sudbury *Star*, 20 October 1928, in Department of Labour [Canada], Strikes and Lockouts, 1928, no. 103A, LAC, RG27, vol. 341 (microfilm reel T2753).

154 Fort William *Times Journal*, 28 August 1934, in Department of Labour [Canada], Strikes and Lockouts, 1934, no. 209, LAC, RG27, vol. 364 (microfilm reel T2975).

155 Toronto *Star*, 2 December 1933, in Department of Labour [Canada], Strikes and Lockouts, 1933, no. 139, LAC, RG27, vol. 357 (microfilm reel T2968).

156 North Bay *Nugget*, 24 September 1934, and an unidentified clipping with a

Canadian Press report from Iroquois Falls, possibly from October 9, in Department of Labour [Canada], Strikes and Lockouts, 1934, no. 209, LAC, RG27, vol. 363 (microfilm reel T2975).

157 *Porcupine Advance*, 11 October 1934, 6.

158 Ibid., 25 October 1934, 4.

159 Ibid., 1 November 1934.

160 Ibid., 14 December 1933.

161 Toronto *Star*, 2 December 1933, in Department of Labour [Canada], Strikes and Lockouts, 1933, no. 139, LAC, RG27, vol. 357 (microfilm reel T2968).

162 Radforth, *Bushworkers and Bosses*, 130. See also an editorial entitled "Orders from Moscow" that appeared in the Toronto *Globe*, 17 September 1934.

163 *Porcupine Advance*, 10 January 1935, 3.

164 Ontario, Legislative Assembly, *Debates*, 1947, 1:166.

165 RCMP Security Bulletin 39, 2 September 1920, in Kealey and Whitaker, *R.C.M.P. Security Bulletins: The Early Years, 1919–1929*, 91.

166 Radforth, *Bushworkers and Bosses*, 135.

167 Department of Labour [Canada], Strikes and Lockouts, no. 45, 1917, LAC, RG27, vol. 306 (microfilm reel T2693).

168 Department of Labour [Canada], Strikes and Lockouts, no. 106, 1921, LAC, RG27, vol. 326 (microfilm reel T2709); Montreal *Gazette*, 22 April 1921, 9. See also Cobalt *Daily Nugget*, 2 May 1921, 8; 11 May 1921, 1; 12 May 1921, 8; and 3 June 1921.

169 J.A. Bradette, in Canada, House of Commons, *Debates*, 26 March 1934, 1839.

170 Canada, Department of Labour [Canada], Strikes and Lockouts, no. 24, 1937, LAC, RG27, vol. 381 (microfilm reel T2990); Toronto *Clarion*, 18 February 1937; *Porcupine Advance*, 18 February 1937, 1.

171 Canada, House of Commons, *Debates*, 8 May 1929, 2373.

172 Cobalt *Daily Nugget*, 11 May 1921, 1.

173 Tucker, *Steam into Wilderness*, 144–5. Charles Beattie led the Brotherhood of Railway Employees with the encouragement of the Canadian Congress of Labour.

174 Tucker, *Steam into Wilderness*, 63.

175 William Ririe's report to Frontier College Collection, LAC, MG29 I 124, vol. 150.

176 *Porcupine Advance*, 26 July 1912.

177 *Globe*, 18 November 1912, 2.

178 *Porcupine Advance*, 2 and 8 July 1937, both page 1.

CHAPTER SEVEN

1 Cobalt *Daily Nugget*, 6 June 1911, 5.

2 Ibid., 30 January 1912, 1.

3 Howell, *Blood, Sweat, and Cheers: Sport and the Making of Modern Canada*, 44–6; James Marsh, "Canadian Amateur Hockey Association" and "Allan Cup" in *Canadian Encyclopedia Online* (accessed October 2001).

4 Quoted in Cosentino, *The Renfrew Millionaires*, 12.

5 Angus and Griffin, *We Lived a Life and Then Some: The Life, Death, and Life of a Mining Town*, 33. For more on M.J. O'Brien and hockey promotion, see Wayne Simpson, "Hockey," in Morrow, *A Concise History of Sport in Canada*, 169–229, and Cosentino, *The Renfrew Millionaires*.

6 *Porcupine Advance*, 17 January 1917.

7 Quoted in the *Porcupine Advance*, 17 January 1917.

8 Campbell later worked for McIntyre (*Porcupine Advance*, 4 April 1935, 7).

9 Description by retiring NOHA president Angus Campbell, in Lendrum, "Days That Are Gone," Timmins *Daily Press*, 20 March 1954, 4.

10 Lendrum, "Days that are Gone," Timmins *Daily Press*, 3 May 1947.

11 *Porcupine Advance*, 12 December 1938.

12 *Broke Hustler*, 6 March 1923.

13 *Porcupine Advance*, 3 May 1922, 1.

14 Toronto *Globe*, 11 November 1920, 15.

15 *Porcupine Advance*, 2 December 1935, 7.

16 Barilko joined the Maple Leafs in 1947, helped win three Stanley Cups, then was killed in a plane crash in 1951, an event that became something of a local legend. In spite of the expert opinion that the plane simply ran out of fuel, many exotic explanations for the "mysterious" crash have been proposed over the years.

17 *Porcupine Advance*, 22 July, 1 and 7 October 1948.

18 Lempi Mansfield, "Aim for a Broom," unpublished memoirs, 1979, Library and Archives Canada (LAC), MG31, H95, file 51, np.

19 J.H. Stovel to John Knox, 20 August 1941, in Dome Mines Collection, Manager's Files, 1939–41, Archives of Ontario (AO), F1350, box 15, MU8701.

20 Viewed on the internet at www.halloffame.mining.ca (accessed 22 January 2004).

21 Forestell, "All That Glitters Is Not Gold," 282.

22 *Porcupine Advance*, 12 September 1917, 6.

23 Lendrum, "Days That Are Gone," Timmins *Daily Press*, 28 September 1957, 4.

24 Girdwood, Jones, and Lonn, *The Big Dome*, 43.

25 *Porcupine Advance*, 12 March 1919, 1.

26 Ibid., 11 June 1919, 1.

27 Ibid., 22 January 1948, 1.

28 Greaves, "Sports and Recreation," 195.

29 Cobalt *Daily Nugget*, 6 June 1911, 5.

30 *Porcupine Advance*, 9 July 1915, 2.

31 Ibid., 19 June 1918, 4.

32 See, for example, Williamson, *The Northland Ontario*, 96. See also *Porcupine*

Advance, 4 and 8 November 1937, 1; 12 December 1938; and 8 July 1948, 1.

33 Raivio, *Kanadan suomalaisten historia*, vol. 1, 448–55.

34 RCMP Security Bulletin 713, 4 July 1934, in Kealey and Whitaker, *R.C.M.P. Security Bulletins: The Depression Years*, part 1, 1933–34, 130.

35 Sillanpää, "Revontulet Athletic Club of Timmins," 76.

36 Ibid., 76–8; Sillanpää, *Under Northern Lights: My Memories of Life in the Finnish Community of Northern Ontario*, 42–4.

37 Stortroen, *An Immigrant's Journal*, 81, 83.

38 Marks, *Revivals and Roller Rinks*, 121.

39 Angus and Griffin, *We Lived a Life and Then Some*, 32.

40 *Porcupine Advance*, 2 July 1924, 1.

41 Ibid., 26 February 1919, 4; 7 January 1920, 2; 10 and 14 March 1923, 1.

42 Braddon, *Roy Thomson of Fleet Street*, 61.

43 *Porcupine Advance*, 1 August 1935, section 2, 1.

44 Town of Timmins Financial Returns for 1916–19, AO, RG19–142, 1080, box 391.

45 Murphy, *Yankee Takeover at Cobalt!* 169.

46 *Porcupine Advance*, 12 February 1912, 1; also 25 March 1912 and 5 April 1912.

47 Cobalt *Daily Nugget*, 20 April 1912, 1, and *Porcupine Advance*, 26 April 1912.

48 North Bay *Daily Nugget*, 9 November 1921, 3.

49 *Porcupine Advance*, 12 June 1918, 1, and 12 July 1912.

50 Ibid., 21 May 1919 and 6 July 1936.

51 Igartua, *Arvida au Saguenay*, 51.

52 Last and Vachon, *Timmins*, 92; Tremblay, "Timmins: métropole de l'or," 22: 25.

53 *Porcupine Advance*, 29 March 1916, 1, and 31 July 1918, 1.

54 Ibid., 29 March 1916, 31 July 1918, 25 February 1935, 28 October 1937, and 9 December 1937.

55 *Porcupine Advance*, 19 April 1912, 9.

56 *Broke Hustler*, 15 November 1919 and 20 November 1920.

57 *Porcupine Advance*, 12 February 1919, 1, and 29 January 1919, 1.

58 *L'Abitibi*, March 1929, 15.

59 Porcupine Golden Anniversary Committee, *Souvenir Booklet Celebrating the Golden Anniversary of the Porcupine Gold Rush, July 1–5, 1959*, 81.

60 *La Gazette du Nord* had regular reports on Knights of Columbus activities in this regard through 1922.

61 Quoted in Solski and Smaller, *Mine Mill: The History of the International Union of Mine, Mill and Smelter Workers in Canada Since 1895*, 72.

62 *Porcupine Advance*, 20 December 1912 ("Local Items").

63 Ibid., 4 June, 13 August, and 17 September 1915. The last item listed the 14 band members and their conductor by name.

64 *Broke Hustler*, 9 February and 4 May 1918.

65 *Porcupine Advance*, 2 April, 1919.

66 Ibid., 15 January 1940, 1, and 24 September 1915, 5; *Daily Press*, 28 April 1951, 16.

67 Mansfield, "Aim for a Broom," Mansfield Papers, LAC, MG-31, H95.

68 "Winter Outlook in the North, " Toronto *Globe*, 5 November 1909, 9.

69 Cobalt *Daily Nugget*, 18 January 1910, 30 December 1910, and 3 and 10 February 1911.

70 Toronto *Globe*, 22 October 1921, 1.

71 *Porcupine Advance*, 17 May 1912.

72 Ibid., 26 July 1912.

73 OPP Divisional Inspectors' Reports, 1914–17, OPP Northern Division Monthly Reports, AO, RG23, B12, box 1, file 1.4.

74 *Porcupine Advance*, 25 June 1915, 2.

75 Ibid., 20 August 1915, 5.

76 Ibid., 3 September 1915, 3.

77 Lindström-Best, *Defiant Sisters*, 105, 107.

78 *Porcupine Advance*, 14 March 1923 and 16 April 1924.

79 North Bay *Daily Nugget*, 30 December 1921, 1, and *Porcupine Advance*, 4 January 1922, 1.

80 *Porcupine Advance*, 25 October 1922, and *La Gazette du Nord*, 12 April 1923.

81 *Porcupine Advance*, 16 August 1934, 4.

82 Ibid., 2 April 1936, 1.

83 Forestell, "All That Glitters Is Not Gold," 301.

84 Issue dated December 1952, in Western Federation of Miners Collection, University of Colorado at Boulder Archives, box 144.

85 Scott, *Weapons of the Weak: Everyday Forms of Peasant Resistance*. Historian Ray Rozenzweig has argued that the alcohol consumption patterns of American industrial workers are evidence of the "alternative culture" of that class (*Eight Hours for What We Will: Workers and Leisure in the Industrial City*). See also the discussion of nineteenth-century drinking in Ontario in Marks, *Revivals and Roller Rinks*.

86 *Porcupine Advance*, 26 April 1912.

87 *Broke Hustler*, 17 January 1920.

88 Mansfield, "Aim for a Broom," Mansfield Papers, LAC, MG-31, H95.

89 Quoted in Solski and Smaller, *Mine Mill*, 71.

90 Abitibi-Price, *Iroquois Falls News*, special 75th anniversary edition, July 1987, np. I am grateful to T.M. Devine of Toronto for making his personal copy available to me.

CHAPTER EIGHT

1 Schneider, *The Finnish Baker's Daughters*, 13, 20.

2 Braddon, *Roy Thomson of Fleet Street*, 61.

3 Flying Post Journal, 1825–26, copy of a letter dated 17 July 1825, Hudson's Bay Company Archives (HBCA), B.70/a/2, fo. 5d (microfilm reel IM53).

4 *Hollinger Miner*, June 1960, 18–19, copy seen at Archives of Ontario (AO), Hollinger Mines Historical Materials, 1911–68, MU8114.

5 "We're Still Here," panel discussion, in Steedman, Suschnigg, and Buse, *Hard Lessons: The Mine Mill Union in the Canadian Labour Movement*, 169.

6 Wade, *The Urban Frontier*, esp. 105–7 and 129.

7 Smith, *Rocky Mountain Mining Camps*, 39–40.

8 Petrik, *No Step Backward: Women and Family on the Rocky Mountain Mining Frontier, Montana, 1865–1900*.

9 Tostevin, *Frog Moon*, 50–1.

10 See, for example, Conrad Lavigne's story as told in Arnopoulos, *Voices from French Ontario*, 37–40 and ff.

11 José Igartua draws a similar conclusion about workers in Alcan's company town (*Arvida au Saguenay*, 9).

12 O'Donnell, *Loose Canon [sic]*, 83.

13 Barnes, *Link with a Lonely Land*, 49.

14 For example, H.P. DePencier's wife Norah (née Thompson) was a graduate of the Hamilton Normal School and had a degree in modern languages from the University of Toronto (Shaw, *Laughter and Tears*, 152). Shaw refers to Mrs. DePencier and Mrs. J.H. Stovel as "First Ladies of the mining community."

15 Howard Newby, *The Deferential Worker* (London, 1977), cited in Williamson, *Class, Culture, and Community*, 21.

16 Lendrum's column, Timmins *Daily Press*, 8 November 1947, 5.

17 Interview with M.E. Stortroen, 7 May 1975, in Porcupine Historical Society Oral History Collection, Timmins Museum.

18 Cobalt *Daily Nugget*, 15 March 1912, 1.

19 *Porcupine Advance*, 8 November 1916, 1.

20 *Might's City Catalogues* (Timmins), 1932.

21 Shaw, *Broken Threads: Memories of a Northern Ontario Schoolteacher*, 110.

22 *Porcupine Advance*, 1 June 1921, 1.

23 *Pulp and Paper Magazine of Canada*, 20 March 1919, 285.

24 Braddon, *Roy Thomson of Fleet Street*, 78.

25 See Forestell, "All That Glitters Is Not Gold" and " 'You Never Give Up Worrying': The Consequences of a Hazardous Mine Environment for Working-Class Families in Timmins, 1915–1950," 199–212.

26 "AF" reports, 6 February 1922 (name removed to protect privacy), Dome Mines Collection, General Files, 1920–23, AO, MU689.

27 *Porcupine Advance*, 6 July 1939, 1.

28 Solski and Smaller, *Mine Mill: The History of the International Union of Mine, Mill and Smelter Workers in Canada since 1895*, 72.

29 Raivio, *Kanadan suomalaisten historia*, 1:406.

30 Williamson, *Class, Culture, and Community*, 68–9.

31 Timmins *Daily Press*, 27 March 1939, entire section devoted to a celebration

of Mascioli's life on the occasion of his 35th anniversary in Northern Ontario. Details on Mascioli's work for the town come from Timmins Municipal Financial Returns, 1912–35, AO, RG19–142, 1080, box 391.

32 *Porcupine Advance*, 23 December 1937.

33 Principe, *The Darkest Side of the Fascist Years*, 212, app. 9.

34 Braddon, *Roy Thomson of Fleet Street*, 106–7.

35 Lendrum, "Days That Are Gone," Timmins *Daily Press*, 2 September 1950, 16, citing undated clipping about Leo Mascioli.

36 Braddon, *Roy Thomson of Fleet Street*, 97.

37 *Porcupine Advance*, 25 February 1937, 1.

38 See correspondence in Immigration Branch, Correspondence re Finnish immigration, 1903–21 and 1921–25, Library and Archives Canada (LAC), RG76, vol. 25, file 651, part 3 (microfilm reel C4683), and RG76, vol. 25, file 651, part 4 (microfilm reel C4683).

39 Report of Monteith Demonstration Farm Director R.H. Clemens for 1915, in Ontario, *Sessional Papers* 62 (1916): 14; price of pulpwood based on $4 per cord as reported in J.L. Englehart to William Clutterbrook, Toronto, 25 January 1912, in James P. Whitney Papers, October 1911–January 1912, AO, F6/MU3132, and Cobalt *Daily Nugget*, 10 March 1913, 1.

40 Interview by M.E. Stortroen, 1 June 1975, in Porcupine Historical Society Oral History Collection, Timmins Museum.

41 Ibid.

42 *Porcupine Advance*, 4 September 1941. Income calculated on quoted price of $1.50 to $2.00 per bag of potatoes. See also Report of the Agricultural Representative for Cochrane South (L.H. Hanlon), 1 April 1940–31 March 1941, in Ontario Ministry of Agriculture, reports from agricultural representatives, Cochrane South, 1938–1941, AO, RG16, series G-5-1, p. 10 (microfilm MS597, reel 7).

43 Agricultural census data, 1941.

44 Report of Agricultural Representative for Cochrane (D.J. Pomerleau), 1 November 1932–31 October 1933, in Ontario Ministry of Agriculture, reports from agricultural representatives, Cochrane, 1927–1938, AO, RG16, series G-5-1, p. 15 (microfilm MS597, reel 7).

45 Compiled from Report of D.J. Pomerleau, ibid., pp. 9 and 5; Porcupine Golden Anniversary Committee, *Souvenir Booklet Celebrating the Golden Anniversary of the Porcupine Gold Rush, July 1–5, 1959*, 39.

46 Porcupine Golden Anniversary Committee, *Souvenir Booklet*, 41; *Porcupine Advance*, 22 May 1918.

47 Agricultural Representative F.C. Hart to J.L. Englehart, 17 August 1911, in James P. Whitney Papers, March–September 1911, AO, F6, MU3131.

48 Report of D.J. Pomerleau, [November] 1927, in Ontario Ministry of Agriculture, reports from agricultural representatives, Cochrane, 1927–38, AO, RG16, G-5-1, pp. 2–3 (microfilm MS597, reel 7).

49 *Porcupine Advance*, 20 August 1924, letter to the editor.

50 Ibid., 10 September 1936, 1.

51 Ibid., 6 February 1941, 1; Frank Lendrum's column, Timmins *Daily Press*, 22 July 1950, 8.

52 Kenogamissi District Report, 1814–15, HBCA, B.99/e/2, fo. 3 (microfilm IM778); Mattagami and Flying Post Journals, 1824–94, vol. 3, Library and Archives Canada (LAC), MG19/D16. See Matawagamingue Indian Debt Book for 1838–39 for an example of her trade. Her band consisted of her son, two daughters, a sister, and her sister's daughter.

53 See, for example, Abel, *Drum Songs*, on the Dene of the northwest.

54 Mann, "The Decade after the Gold Rush: Social Structure in Grass Valley and Nevada City, California, 1850–1860," 487 (on Nevada City); Smith, *Rocky Mountain Mining Camps: The Urban Frontier*, 187 (on the American West generally, 1859–90); Petrik, *No Step Backward: Women and Family on the Rocky Mountain Mining Frontier, Montana, 1865–1900*, xiii (on Montana).

55 Cobalt *Daily Nugget*, 17 September 1910, 1.

56 *Hollinger Miner*, 22 May 1956, 1, 10.

57 See the fine history of these groups by Ambrose, *For Home and Country: The Centennial History of the Women's Institutes in Ontario*.

58 *Porcupine Advance*, 23 February 1939, 6.

59 Forestell, "All That Glitters Is Not Gold," 2, 35.

60 Ibid., 291–2.

61 Morton, *Ideal Surroundings: Domestic Life in a Working-Class Suburb in the 1920s*, 79.

62 Dubinsky, " 'Who Do You Think Did the Cooking?': Baba in the Classroom," 195.

63 Goldman, *Gold Diggers and Silver Miners*, 15; Petrik, *No Step Backward*, 13; Rowe, *The Hard-Rock Men*, 294; Doyle, *The Social Order of a Frontier Community*, 261 (and elsewhere); Curti et al., *The Making of an American Community: A Case Study of Democracy in a Frontier County*.

64 Radforth, *Bushworkers and Bosses*, 34; Avery, *Reluctant Hosts*, 65–6. Avery cites Robert Harney and Vincenza Scarpaci, eds., *Little Italies in North America* (Toronto, 1981). See particularly De la Riva and Gaudreau, "Les ouvriers-mineurs de la region de Sudbury (1912–1930): le cas de l'International Nickel Co.," 126–30. José Igartua also examines transience in *Arvida au Saguenay*, although his emphasis is on worker "perseverance"; see especially 70–2.

65 Clark, "The Position of the French-Speaking Population in the Northern Industrial Community," 64.

66 Forestell, "All That Glitters Is Not Gold," 60.

67 Compiled from McIntyre Mines Ltd., employee cards, c.1915–25, Laurentian University Archives, Steelworkers Collection, P020/1/D/1,4.

68 *Porcupine Advance*, 14 November 1940. Twenty men had died, while the rest had moved.

69 Employers' Income Tax Returns, 1931, in Buffalo Ankerite Correspondence, 1933–60, LAC, MG28 III 81, vol. 15.

70 *Porcupine Advance*, 2 December 1937.

71 *Globe and Mail*, 16 November 1950, 10 ("Hollinger Seeks 300 U.K. Miners; Stability Needed"). Labour leaders, however, believed that management was simply looking for more docile workers.

72 Minutes of meeting on 26 February 1936, in Iroquois Falls United Church Session Minutes, 1935–64, United Church Archives, Victoria University, acc 77.564L, box 2–5; minutes of meeting on 12 September 1916, in Iroquois Falls Pastoral Charge, Miscellaneous Minutes, 1912–17, United Church Archives, Victoria University, acc 77.564L, box 1–1.

73 Bradwin, *The Bunkhouse Man*, 99, 79.

74 *Iroquois Falls News*, special 75th Anniversary edition, July 1987. Copy kindly provided by T.M. Devine, Toronto.

75 Hareven, *Family Time and Industrial Time*, 115.

76 Laurendeau, *L'homme aux 56 métiers*.

77 Dubinsky, *Improper Advances*, 152.

78 *Porcupine Advance*, 19 July 1912, 1.

79 Ibid., 2 August 1912, 1.

80 Cobalt *Daily Nugget*, 27 April and 5 May 1921.

81 *Porcupine Advance*, 23 January 1924; H.P. De Pencier to J.S. Bache, Dome, 26 February 1924, Dome Mines Collection, General Files, 1920–23, AO, MU8689.

82 *Porcupine Advance*, 14 November 1917; North Bay *Daily Nugget*, 30 December 1921, 1; *Porcupine Advance*, 4 January 1922; *Porcupine Advance*, 25 October 1922; and *La Gazette du Nord*, 12 April 1923.

83 *Porcupine Advance*, 15 October, 1915 and 7 August 1918; North Bay *Daily Nugget*, 14 December 1921.

84 *Porcupine Advance*, 29 September 1927.

85 Ibid., 25 July and 1 August 1917.

86 Ibid., 21 July 1938.

87 Radforth, *Bushworkers and Bosses*, 102.

88 Dubinsky, *Improper Advances*, 149.

89 *Porcupine Advance*, 25 September 1915, 1; 4 October 1934, 3; 25 October 1934. See also North Bay *Daily Nugget*, 6 December 1921, 3.

90 Cobalt *Daily Nugget*, 10 and 12 June 1913, 1; AO finding aid for RG23, 79 (OPP investigations).

91 H.P. De Pencier to J.S. Bache, 28 November 1922; Dome Mines Collection, General Files, 1920–23, AO F1350, box 3, MU8689. Names have been changed.

92 *Porcupine Advance*, 30 June 1927, 1.

93 Ibid., 14 February 1935, 1. The two Timmins men were acquitted for lack of evidence.

94 North Bay *Daily Nugget*, 21 November 1921, 1.

95 *Porcupine Advance*, 19 December 1940; and 9 and 30 January 1941.

96 Ibid., 8 December 1938, 1.

97 See, for example, Stone, "Flux and Authority in a Subarctic Society: The Yukon Miners in the Nineteenth Century," 114–32.

98 Greer, "The Birth of the Police in Canada," 43.
99 OPP Divisional Inspectors' Reports for March and August 1918, in OPP Northern Division Monthly Reports, 1911–21, AO, RG23, B12 Box 1 (file 1.4).
100 OPP Divisional Inspectors' Report, September 1916, in ibid.; Rev. A. Pelletier to James Whitney, Toronto, 4 August 1911, in James P. Whitney Papers, March–September 1911, AO, F6/MU3131.
101 *Porcupine Advance*, 26 July 1912.
102 Ibid., 2 January 1924, 1.
103 Ibid., 1 May 1918, 3. The case against Popvitch was dismissed.
104 Ibid., 29 March 1916 and 31 July 1918.
105 South Porcupine Presbyterian Church and Timmins First United Church annual reports for 1930 and 1931, United Church Archives, Victoria University, Toronto.
106 Toronto *Globe*, 24 October 1918, 14.
107 Quoted in Radforth, *Bushworkers and Bosses*, 102 (source not given).
108 Elisabeth Townsend to M.E. Stortroen, 27 April 1975, Porcupine Historical Society Oral History Collection, Timmins Museum.
109 Buffalo Ankerite Correspondence, 1933–60, in Buffalo Ankerite Collection, LAC, MG28 III 81, vol. 14.
110 Igartua, *Arvida au Saguenay*, 33–41, 52; Golz, "The Image and Reality of Life in a Northern Ontario Company-Owned Town," 62–91.
111 For examples of the varieties of this literature, see Garner, *The Model Company Town: Urban Design through Private Enterprise in Nineteenth-Century New England,* and Allen, *The Company Town in the American West.*
112 For examples, see Crawford, *Building the Workingman's Paradise,* and Zahavi, *Workers, Managers, and Welfare Capitalism.*
113 Montreal *Gazette*, 16 November 1912, 20.
114 See Timmins city directories for the mid-1930s.
115 Town of Timmins Municipal Financial Returns, 1912–35, AO, RG19–142; *Canadian Mining Journal*, 15 April 1913, 250.
116 *Porcupine Advance*, 30 October 1939, 5.
117 For a discussion of these developments in a slightly later period, see Parr, *Domestic Goods: The Material, the Moral, and the Economic in the Postwar Years.*

CHAPTER NINE

1 There had been a partial election in 1916, but only a few council seats were contested.
2 "Days That Are Gone," Timmins *Daily Press*, 10 December 1949, 6, citing minutes of the council meeting of 2 February 1914.
3 *Porcupine Advance*, 7 March 1917, 7.
4 Ibid., 27 November 1939, 1; 30 November 1939, 2; and 7 December 1939, 1.

5 Quoted in Solski and Smaller, *Mine, Mill: The History of the International Union of Mine, Mill and Smelter Workers in Canada since 1895*, 71.

6 *Porcupine Advance*, 8 January 1919, 1. The *Banner* was published by "Jimmy" Simpson, vice-president of the Trades and Labor Congress. He served at one point as mayor of Toronto.

7 Robin, *Radical Politics and Canadian Labour, 1880–1930*, 96; Rodney, *Soldiers of the International*, 8; Kolasky, *The Shattered Illusion*, 2–4; Raivio, *Kanadan suomalaisten historia*, 1:399–404.

8 Robin, *Radical Politics and Canadian Labour*, 113.

9 Raivio, *Kanadan suomalaisten historia*, 1:404 and 423; Marunchak, *The Ukrainian Canadians*, 217.

10 *Porcupine Advance*, 11 October 1912.

11 Ibid., 31 October 1917, 1.

12 Robin, *Radical Politics and Canadian Labour*, 145.

13 Marunchak, *The Ukrainian Canadians*, 403–5.

14 *Porcupine Advance*, 20 March 1918, 1.

15 Quoted in *Porcupine Advance*, 27 March 1918, 2.

16 *Porcupine Advance*, 3 April 1918, 1.

17 Ibid., 29 May 1918, 3.

18 Ibid., 2 October 1918, 3.

19 "Chief Agitators in Canada," Public Safety Board, Department of Justice, 1919 Report, in Kealey and Whitaker, *R.C.M.P. Security Bulletins: The Early Years, 1919–1929*; *Porcupine Advance*, 30 October 1918, 3.

20 Rodney, *Soldiers of the International*, 47–8; Robin, *Radical Politics and Canadian Labour*, 194.

21 W.N. Simpson to H.P. DePencier, Toronto, 5 January 1922, in Dome Mines General Files (1920–23), Archives of Ontario F1350, Box 3, MU8689.

22 [R. Allen?] to H.P. DePencier, Timmins, 22 March 1922 in Dome Mines Collection, General Files, 1920–23, AO, F1350, box 3, MU8689.

23 *Porcupine Advance*, 3 May 1934, 8.

24 Dome Manager's Diary, entry for 12 February 1924, Dome Mines Collection, General Files, 1919–24, AO, F1350, box 1, MU8687.

25 Dominion Police Security Bulletin 333, 2 September 1926, in Kealey and Whitaker, *R.C.M.P. Security Bulletins: The Early Years, 1919–1929*, 345, 350.

26 RCMP Security Bulletin 767, 7 August 1935, in Kealey and Whitaker, *R.C.M.P. Security Bulletins: The Depression Years*, part 2, *1935*, 434; RCMP Security Bulletin 793, 12 February 1936, in Kealey and Whitaker, *R.C.M.P. Security Bulletins: The Depression Years*, part 3, *1936*, 77.

27 *Porcupine Advance*, 17 August 1936, 1; RCMP Security Bulletin 833, 18 November 1936, in Kealey and Whitaker, *R.C.M.P. Security Bulletins: The Depression Years*, part 3, *1936*, 505.

28 See Dome Mines Collection, General Files, 1920–23, AO, F1350, box 3, MU8689.

29 Quoted in Fortin and Gaboury, *Bibliographie analytique de l'Ontario français*, 171.

30 *Porcupine Advance*, 9 March 1939, 3.

31 *Ibid.*, series of page 4 editorials over the summer of 1935.

32 Timmins *Press*, 2 December 1933, 1.

33 *Porcupine Advance*, 30 March 1939, 4, and 28 September 1939, 1; Braddon, *Roy Thomson of Fleet Street*, 97–9. Braddon incorrectly gives the date of the radio takeover proposal as late October 1939 (97).

34 Robin, *Radical Politics and Canadian Labour*, 86–7, 90, 115.

35 See Naylor, *The New Democracy: Challenging the Social Order in Industrial Ontario, 1914–1925*, 78–96.

36 *Porcupine Advance*, 15 August 1917, 1.

37 Ibid., 3 January 1935, 3.

38 Naylor, *The New Democracy*, 146.

39 *Porcupine Advance*, 15 September 1920, 4.

40 Radforth, *Bushworkers and Bosses*, 95, quoting Toivo Tienhaara.

41 Akseli Rauanheimo to F.C. Blair, Montreal, 13 August 1924, in Immigration Branch Correspondence re Finnish Immigration, Library and Archives Canada (LAC), RG76, vol. 25, file 651, part 4 (microfilm reel C4683).

42 To A.L. Joliffe, Commissioner of Immigration, Montreal, 15 May 1925, Immigration Branch Correspondence re Finnish Immigration, LAC, RG76, vol. 25, file 651, part 4 (microfilm reel C4683).

43 Toronto *Star*, 24 November 1933, in Department of Labour, Strikes and Lockouts, no. 139 (Cochrane District Pulpcutters), LAC, RG27, vol. 357 (microfilm reel T2968).

44 Compiled from newspaper clippings in Department of Labour [Canada], Strikes and Lockouts, no. 209 (Timmins District Pulpwood Cutters), LAC, RG27, vol. 364 (microfilm reel T2975), and *Porcupine Advance*, 11 October 1934.

45 RCMP Security Bulletin 726, 3 October 1934, in Kealey and Whitaker, *R.C.M.P. Security Bulletins: The Depression Years*, part 1, 341.

46 Toronto *Star*, 2 December 1933.

47 *Le Droit*, 28 November 1933 (my translation).

48 Interview of Lempi Mansfield by M.E. Stortroen, 24 September 1974, in Porcupine Historical Society Oral History Collection, Timmins Museum; Vasiliadis, "Co-operativism and Progressivism," 1, 25; MacPherson, *Each for All: A History of the Co-operative Movement in English Canada, 1900–1945*, 104.

49 Vasiliadis, "Co-operativism and Progressivism," 34–7, 41.

50 See, for example, *Porcupine Advance*, 14 March 1931 and 9 November 1936; RCMP Security Bulletin 679, 3 November 1933, in Kealey and Whitaker, *R.C.M.P. Security Bulletins: The Depression Years*, part 1, 59.

51 Sillanpää, *Under the Northern Lights*, 35–7; *Might's City Catalogues* (Timmins), 1938; MacPherson, *Each for All*, 204.

52 *Porcupine Advance*, 9 May 1935, 6, and 25 October 1934, 3.

53 Interview by M.E. Stortroen, 24 September 1974, in Porcupine Historical Society Oral History Collection, Timmins Museum.

54 *Porcupine Advance*, 3 May 1934, 1.

55 Quoted by Pennacchio, "Exporting Fascism to Canada: Toronto's Little Italy," 52. The source given is Norman A. Robertson Papers, LAC, MG30, E163, vol. 12, file 124, 1–3.

56 Ibid.; Salvatore, *Le fascisme et les italiens à Montréal: une histoire orale, 1922–1945*; Scardellato, *Within our Temple: A History of the Order Sons of Italy of Ontario*.

57 Scardellato, *Within our Temple*, 213–14.

58 Timmins *Daily Press*, 19 January 1939, 1–2, and 31 August 1939, 8.

59 Pennacchio, "Exporting Fascism to Canada," 57.

60 Timmins *Daily Press*, 2 February 1939, 1–2; Raivo, *Kanadan suomalaisten historia*, vol. 2, 491–2. The Mac-Paps served from the autumn of 1937 to September 1938.

61 Kolasky, *The Shattered Illusion*, 104; Perger, "Being Ukrainian in Timmins," 117.

62 Regulation 17 was a measure proclaimed in 1912 that restricted the use of French in Ontario schools by requiring instruction in English to begin immediately on a child's entry to school; no French at all was to be permitted after the first form (equivalent of modern grade 3).

63 *La Gazette du Nord*, 5 July 1923, 1.

64 Bradette was elected in 1926, 1930, 1935, 1940, 1945, and 1949. See *Canadian Parliamentary Guide* for 1946, 151.

65 McKenty, *Mitch Hepburn*, 41.

66 See, for example, Beck, *Pendulum of Power*, 157, 160–1; and Robin, *Radical Politics and Canadian Labour*, 243.

67 Canada, House of Commons, *Debates*, 13 April 1920, 1188.

68 Ibid., 27 May 1920, 2807.

69 Timmins *Daily Press*, 12 June 1948, 5.

70 Grummett was very effective in parliamentary debate and by 1947 was essentially acting as leader of the CCF in the legislature, ensuring that Northern Ontario issues were well represented. His main concerns were mining labour issues, mining taxation, roads, education, and civil rights.

71 Church History File, South Porcupine Presbyterian Church, for 1961, United Church Archives, Victoria University.

72 Cobalt *Daily Nugget*, 22 December 1911, 1.

73 Rea, *The Political Economy of Northern Development*, 142.

74 *Porcupine Advance*, 12 April 1912. Ontario municipal records incorrectly list the first mayor as M.A. Attallah. See Matheson Municipal financial returns, 1912–1940, AO, RG19–142, 988, box 225.

75 Matheson Municipal financial returns, 1912–40, AO, RG19–142, 988, box 225.

76 Frank Ginn to Ontario Minister of Education, 6 December 1922, Ontario
    Department of Education Central Registry Files, AO, RG2/P3, box 100, 1922.
77 Bloomfield, Bloomfield, and McCaskell, *Urban Growth and Local Services: The
    Development of Ontario Municipalities to 1981*, 88, 115, 140.
78 Cobalt *Daily Nugget*, 5 June 1911, 1.
79 MacNab, *Pioneer Ventures*.
80 Whitney Township Municipal Financial Returns, 1912–60, AO, RG19–142,
    707.
81 Interview of Mrs Pasquale Rotondo by John Campsall, 9 September 197[-],
    Porcupine Historical Society Oral History Collection, Timmins Museum.
82 Interview of Uly Levinson by M.E. Stortroen, 4 February 1976, Porcupine His-
    torical Society Oral History Collection, Timmins Museum.
83 Cobalt *Daily Nugget*, 5, 12, and 13 May 1911; letter dated 11 September 1911,
    apparently misfiled in Tisdale Township Municipal Financial Returns,
    1928–47, AO, RG19–142, 660.
84 Cobalt *Daily Nugget*, 3 January 1912, 1.
85 Ibid., 25 September 1913, 1.
86 Ibid., 24 October 1913; Tisdale Township Municipal Financial Returns,
    1911–27, AO, RG19–142, 659, box 1304. See also *Porcupine Advance*, 10
    December 1915, 2; 7 January 1916, 1; 8 November 1916, 1 and 5.
87 Mrs J.A. Thomas to J.S. Bache, South Porcupine, 17 November 1920, Dome
    Mines Collection, General Files, 1920–23, AO, F1350, box 3, MU8689.
88 H.P. DePencier to J.S. Bache, 24 November 1920, Dome Mines Collection,
    General Files, 1920–23, AO, F1350, box 3, MU8689.
89 Thomas to J.S. Bache, 3 December 1921, Dome Mines Collection, General
    Files, 1920–23, AO, F1350, box 3, MU8689.
90 *Porcupine Advance*, 9 January and 13 February 1924; Tisdale Township Munici-
    pal Financial Returns, 1928–47, AO, RG19–142, 660; Frank Lendrum's
    column, Timmins *Daily Press*, 28 November 1956, 34.
91 *Porcupine Advance*, 1 December 1938.
92 Iroquois Falls Municipal Financial Returns, 1915–44, AO, RG19–142, 764, box
    186; *Broke Hustler*, 4 October 1919, 6 June 1920, and 4 June 1922.
93 *L'Abitibi*, July 1929, 4 (obituary).
94 *Broke Hustler*, 23 April 1921; North Bay *Daily Nugget*, 23 November 1921, 1.
95 Lendrum, "Days That Are Gone," Timmins *Daily Press*, 24 November 1951,
    15; List of Calvert Township reeves in Iroquois Falls History File, Iroquois
    Falls Museum.
96 *Porcupine Advance*, 27 July 1936, 8.
97 Clipping from the Toronto *Evening Telegram*, 14 November [1946], in
    Ontario Department of Municipal Affairs, administrative correspondence
    regarding Iroquois Falls, 1931–75, AO, RG19–43, box 83.
98 Cobalt *Daily Nugget*, 3 February 1913, 1.
99 *Porcupine Advance*, 10 September 1915, 1 and 3.

100 Ibid., 1 January 1919, 1.

101 Ibid., 5 December 1923.

102 Ibid., 14 November 1923.

103 Timmins *Press*, 4 December 1933, 1.

104 *Porcupine Advance*, 12 January 1939, 1, and 20 April 1939, 1 and 8.

105 Ibid., 26 October 1939, 1 and 8.

106 Quoted in Braddon, *Roy Thomson of Fleet Street*, 98 (date not given).

107 *Porcupine Advance*, 30 November 1939, 3rd section, 1.

108 Ibid., 30 October 1939, 5.

109 See, for example, Forestell's thesis, "All That Glitters Is Not Gold." Gourd
     makes a similar point in "Mines et syndicats en Abitibi-Temiscamingue,
     1910–1950," 76–8.

110 Superintendent General of Indian Affairs to the Governor General, 16 Feb-
     ruary 1909, in Frank Pedley's Letterbooks, 1908–11, LAC, RG10, vol. 1128
     (microfilm reel C9006); Morrison, "Treaty Nine Research Report," 98, 104,
     114.

111 Department of Indian Affairs Annual Report for 1907–8 (*Sessional Papers* 27,
     1909).

112 Morrison, "Treaty Nine Research Report," 56.

113 Superintendent General of Indian Affairs to the Governor General, Ottawa,
     16 February 1909, in Frank Pedley's Letterbooks, 1908–11, LAC, RG10, vol.
     1128 (microfilm reel C9006).

114 Ibid.

115 J.D. McLean to Surveyor James Dobie, Ottawa, 5 May 1909, in Department
     of Indian Affairs, Treaty 9 Reserve Surveys, 1908–36, LAC, RG10, vol. 7757,
     file 27044–1 (microfilm reel C12,048).

116 James Dobie to J.D. McLean, Thessalon, 5 May 1909, in ibid.

117 Ibid., 6 June 1910.

118 West to J.D. McLean, September 1910, in Department of Indian Affairs,
     Chapleau Agency correspondence regarding the Mattagami Reserve,
     1910–30, LAC, RG10, vol. 7836, file 30065–3, part 1 (microfilm reel
     C12,108).

119 Department to H.A. West, 3 November 1910, in Department of Indian
     Affairs, Chapleau Agency correspondence regarding the Mattagami Reserve,
     1910–30, LAC, RG10, vol. 7836, file 30065–3, part 1 (microfilm reel
     C12,108).

120 Report of Agent H.A. West for 1910–11, Department of Indian Affairs
     Annual Report for year ended 31 March 1911, *Sessional Papers* 27 (1912): 3.

121 William McLeod to Department of Indian Affairs, 31 July 1914, in Depart-
     ment of Indian Affairs, Chapleau Agency correspondence regarding the
     Mattagami Reserve, 1910–30, LAC, RG10, vol. 7836, file 30065–3, part 1
     (microfilm reel C12,108).

122 Departmental correspondence from 16 March to 4 December 1915, in ibid.

123 Matt Boivin to Duncan Campbell Scott, Timmins, 3 November 1919, in ibid.

124 J.T. Godfrey to D.C. Scott, 22 November 1919, in ibid.

125 Various correspondence from 24 March 1920 to 22 August 1929, in ibid. The quotation is from H.J. Bury to the Acting Deputy Superintendent General, 11 August 1921.

126 Chief and Councillors to Department of Indian Affairs, 18 July 1928, in ibid.

127 Correspondence dated 12 November 1913, 1, 6, and 10 October 1919 in Department of Indian Affairs, Treaty 9 Reserve Surveys, 1908–36, LAC, RG10, vol. 7757, file 27044–1 (microfilm reel C12,048).

128 Correspondence dating 3 August 1915 to 25 July 1919 and elsewhere in the file, Department of Indian Affairs, Temiskaming Agency, Abitibi Reserve, regarding lands flooded by Abitibi Power and Paper, 1915–19, LAC, RG10, vol. 6613, file 6035–2 (microfilm reel C8017).

129 J.D. McLean to Frank Edwards, Ottawa, 18 April 1925, Department of Indian Affairs, file on Ontario Game Laws, correspondence regarding the Chapleau Game Preserve, 1924–29, LAC, RG10, vol. 6745, file 420–8A (microfilm reel C8103).

130 Department of Indian Affairs, file on Ontario Game Laws, correspondence regarding the Chapleau Game Preserve, 1924–29, LAC, RG10, vol. 6745, file 420–8A (microfilm reel C8103).

131 Correspondence from 28 July 1914 to 21 April 1915, Department of Indian Affairs, Temiskaming District, file regarding flooding at Matheson, 1914–15, LAC, RG10, vol. 6613, file 6044–5 (microfilm reel C8017).

132 Correspondence from 31 July 1914 to 2 October 1920, Department of Indian Affairs, Chapleau Agency file regarding the Biscotasing Reserve petition, 1914–20, LAC, RG10, vol. 3180, file 452,054 (microfilm reel C11,335).

CHAPTER TEN

1 Lower, *Settlement and the Forest Frontier in Eastern Canada*, 149.

2 Ignatiev, *How the Irish Became White*.

3 Lombardi, "Italian American Workers and the Response to Fascism," 143.

4 Annual Report of the Ontario Department of Lands, Forests and Mines for 1910, Ontario, *Sessional Papers* 3 (1911): 14.

5 Rocheleau et al., "An Inventory of Historical Sites in Timmins-Porcupine," 126. The name of the school was changed to Sacred Heart in 1959 and it evolved into an English-only school.

6 Interview by M.E. Stortroen, 10 February 1976, Porcupine Historical Society Oral History Collection, Timmins Museum.

7 Cobalt *Daily Nugget*, 12 July 1911 (extra edition), 1 and 4.

8 *Porcupine Advance*, 2 May 1917, 5.

9 Ibid., 21 January 1920, 1.
10 Advertisement in the *Porcupine Advance*, 6 August 1915, 8.
11 *Porcupine Advance*, 11 October 1916, 8.
12 Ibid., 30 October 1918, 3.
13 Ibid., 19 June 1918, 1.
14 Quoted in Harney, "The Padrone System and Sojourners in the Canadian North, 1885–1920," 134.
15 "AF" reports, South Porcupine, 30 April 1922, Dome Mines Collection, General Files, 1920–23, Archives of Ontario (AO), F1350, box 3, MU8689.
16 Ibid., 27 May 1922.
17 Timmins *Press*, 20 November 1933, 6.
18 R.W. to Norman Rogers, 31 March 1939, in Ontario Relief Settlement file, Unemployment Relief Commission, 1932–39, Library and Archives Canada (LAC), RG27, vol. 2093 (name changed to protect confidentiality).
19 P.L.B. to Wesley Gordon, Connaught Station, 14 September 1932, in Ontario Inspection Reports File, Unemployment Relief Commission, 1931–33, LAC, RG27, vol. 2071, file 425–4 (name changed to protect confidentiality).
20 Smith, *Rocky Mountain Mining Camps*, 105–6.
21 Ward, *The Australian Legend*, 123.
22 Turner, *The Frontier in American History*, 35. See also Doyle, *The Social Order of a Frontier Community*, 18–19, 26.
23 Forestell, "All That Glitters Is Not Gold," 286–7; Dubinsky, *Improper Advances*, 157–8.
24 *Porcupine Advance*, 2 May 1917, 8.
25 Marks, *Revivals and Roller Rinks*, 12, 14–15.
26 Ibid., 24.
27 Jowett, *No Thought for Tomorrow: The Story of a Northern Nurse*, 54.
28 Byrnes Presbyterian Church, "Bazaar Book … 1924," Church History File, United Church Archives, Victoria University.
29 Himelfarb, "The Social Characteristics of One-Industry Towns in Canada," 33.
30 Last and Vachon, *Timmins*, 34.
31 *Le Droit*, 2 May 1956, 2 (my translation).
32 South Porcupine Presbyterian Church File, 1961, United Church Archives, Victoria University. The minister's name has been omitted to protect confidentiality.
33 C.A. Wartman to Premier Ferguson, Vanessa, Ontario, nd., in Howard Ferguson papers, AO, F8, box 6, MU1022.
34 *Porcupine Advance*, 2 December 1937, editorial.
35 Quoted in Oliver, *G. Howard Ferguson: Ontario Tory*, 213.
36 *Porcupine Advance*, 18 November 1940, 1.
37 Ibid., 15 July 1937.
38 Ibid., 26 September 1935, 6.

39 Last and Vachon, *Timmins*, 32–5; *Le Droit* (Ottawa), 2 May 1956, 2, and 5 May 1956, 10.
40 *Porcupine Advance*, 29 May 1918.
41 Ibid., 1 February 1922, 1.
42 Ibid., 19 December 1929; Rocheleau et al., "An Inventory of Historical Sites in Timmins-Porcupine," 82; Tremblay, "Timmins: métropole de l'or," 31.
43 Quoted in Harney, "Toronto's Little Italy, 1885–1945," 51.
44 Foerster, *The Italian Emigration of Our Times*, 398.
45 Partasso, "La donna italiana durante il periodo fascista in Toronto, 1930–1940," 180.
46 Tremblay, "Timmins: métropole de l'or," 32; Rocheleau et al., in "An Inventory of Historical Sites in Timmins-Porcupine." The latter say the church was opened in 1937 (84); Tremblay says it was opened July 1945 (32); but the *Porcupine Advance*, 26 May 1938, 1, clearly reports the date as 5 June 1938.
47 Tremblay, "Timmins: métropole de l'or," 32 and 34.
48 *Porcupine Advance*, 27 July 1933, 1.
49 Ibid., 5 September 1935, 1.
50 "Ste. Anne's parish celebrates 80 years," *Enterprise* (Iroquois Falls), 28 May 1997.
51 "Histoire de notre paroisse," typescript, no author, c. 1994–95, in Churches History File, Iroquois Falls Museum.
52 Sketch of South Porcupine United Church History in South Porcupine United Church History File, 1952, United Church Archives, Victoria University; Lendrum, "Days That Are Gone," Timmins *Daily Press*, 17 April 1954, 4.
53 United Church Archives, Victoria University, captions on photos 90.162/P1031 and 90.162/P1032.
54 "Historical Sites and Trails," 1978 (typescript), Iroquois Falls Museum, 111.
55 Iroquois Falls Church Membership Register dated 1 June 1913, Iroquois Falls Pastoral Charge, 1912–14, United Church Archives microfilm reel LCM197.
56 *Porcupine Advance*, 23 May 1917, 5.
57 Ibid., 28 June 1937.
58 Ibid., 25 March 1937, 1, and 28 June 1937; Raivio, *Kanadan suomalaisten historia*, vol 1, 260.
59 "Historical Sites and Trails," 1978 (typescript), Iroquois Falls Museum, 92; Lendrum, "Days That Are Gone," Timmins *Daily Press*, 31 March 1956, 4.
60 Lendrum, "Days That Are Gone," Timmins *Daily Press*, 7 May 1949, 5; Cobalt *Daily Nugget*, 17 July 1913, 1.
61 Sillanpää, *Under the Northern Lights*, 103–4. The church was finished in 1947.
62 Raivio, *Kanadan suomalaisten historia*, 1:260–2.
63 *Porcupine Advance*, 2 July 1915, 8; 17 July 1918, 1; 19 July 1934, 1; 30 August 1937. See also interview of Leo DelVillano by M.E. Stortroen, 3 September 1975, Porcupine Historical Society Oral History Collection, Timmins Museum.
64 "Historical Sites and Trails," 1978 (typescript), Iroquois Falls Museum, 111;

Rocheleau et al., "An Inventory of Historical Sites in Timmins-Porcupine," 83; *Porcupine Advance*, 18 November 1940 and 16 January 1941.

65 *Porcupine Advance*, 12 July 1912, 15 August 1917, 16 October 1918, 18 June 1919, 19 January 1928.

66 Ibid., 28 June 1937.

67 Ibid., 9 March 1939, 3; Tremblay, "Timmins: métropole de l'or," 40.

68 Vasiliadis, "Co-operativism and Progressivism," 45.

69 McIntyre Mines Ltd., employee cards, c.1915–25, Laurentian University Archives, Steelworkers Collection P020/1/D/1,4, box 2 (part of C surnames to F surnames).

70 *Porcupine Advance*, 14 February 1938, obituary.

71 Ibid., 14 February 1917, 1, and 25 February 1921, 1; *Might's City Catalogues* (Timmins), 1934.

72 *Porcupine Advance*, 4 June 1924, 1; "Hollinger Mines History," 1968, 5; Hollinger Mines Historical Materials, 1911–68, AO, MU8114.

73 *Hollinger Miner* 24 October 1955, 5; *Might's City Catalogues* (Timmins).

74 *Porcupine Advance*, 15 April 1937; *Broke Hustler*, 11 October 1917, 28 October 1924, and 20 April 1926.

75 *Porcupine Advance*, 28 November 1929; *Broke Hustler*, 4 October 1919 and 6 January 1919 ([sic] should be 1920].

76 See Lindström-Best, *Defiant Sisters*, 14–21, and Singleton, *A Short History of Finland*, 64–116.

77 Raivio, *Kanadan suomalaisten historia*, 1:464–82; Finnish Consul to A.L. Joliffe, Commissioner of Immigration, Montreal, 15 May 1925, in Immigration Branch Correspondence re Finnish Immigration, 1921–25, LAC, RG76, vol. 25, file 651, part 4 (microfilm reel C4683).

78 Swyripa, *Wedded to the Cause*, 8.

79 Marunchak, *The Ukrainian Canadians*, 99.

80 Ibid., 67.

81 Interview by the author, 1995; anonymity requested.

82 Wilson, *Ontario and the First World War*, xxiii.

83 J. Murray Clark of Toronto, quoted in Hopkins, *Canadian Annual Review*, 1915, 545.

84 See, for example, W.E. Kerr to C.H. Fullerton, 31 July 1916, Ontario Colonization Roads Branch, Officials' Files, West Division and Temiskaming, 1916, AO, RG52, series II-A, box 95; Report of Minister G.H. Ferguson Annual Report of the Ontario Department of Lands, Forests and Mines for 1916, in Ontario, *Sessional Papers* 3 (1917): xviii.

85 Wilson, *Ontario and the First World War*, lxxi.

86 *Porcupine Advance*, 11 June 1915, 1.

87 Ibid., 11 June 1915.

88 Wilson, *Ontario and the First World War*, lxx; *Porcupine Advance*, 12 December 1917, 8.

89 *Canadian Mining Journal*, 1 July 1915, 417; *Porcupine Advance*, 23 July 1915, 2.

90 "Condition and Treatment of Aliens in Canada," *Canadian Annual Review*, 1915, 355.

91 *Porcupine Advance*, 23 July 1915, 4.

92 "Condition and Treatment of Aliens in Canada," *Canadian Annual Review*, 1915, 355.

93 *Porcupine Advance*, 26 June 1918, 1.

94 Ibid., 9 August 1916, 4.

95 Ibid., 23 July 1915, 8.

96 Ibid., 17 December 1919, 1. (I have been unable to confirm numbers from other parts of the district).

97 Ibid., 12 December 1917, 8.

98 Ibid., 15 October 1915, 5.

99 Ibid., 17 May 1916, 1.

100 Ibid., 10 January 1917, 1.

101 *Broke Hustler*, 4 May 1918.

102 Jack Pecore to M.E. Stortroen, 24 October 1975, Porcupine Historical Society Oral History Collection, Timmins Museum.

103 *Porcupine Advance*, 17 December 1919, 1.

104 Ibid., 28 January 1920, 6.

105 See, for example, "AF" Reports, South Porcupine, 28 April 1922, Dome Mines Collection, General Files, 1920–23, AO, MU8689.

106 George Cole to Alex Gillies, Assistant Divisional Commissioner, Department of Immigration, South Porcupine, 26 June 1924, Immigration Branch Correspondence re Finnish Immigration, LAC, RG76, vol. 25, file 651, part 4.

107 *Porcupine Advance*, 28 January 1920, 6.

108 Ibid., 23 August 1937.

109 Lindström has detailed a similar attitude expressed in the press across Canada during this episode; see *From Heroes to Enemies: Finns in Canada, 1937–1947*.

110 Cited in ibid., from 8 February 1940, AO, MU3343.09.

111 See account in Lindström, *From Heroes to Enemies*, 65.

112 Ibid., 113–16.

113 Ibid., 112, quoting Minutes of a Meeting of Finland Aid, South Porcupine, 28 January 1940, AO, MU3342.06.

114 Ibid., 173.

115 *Porcupine Advance*, 20 November 1941, 1.

116 Lindström, *From Heroes to Enemies*, 194.

117 Letters from Mrs Helene Kuechmeister and Ernest Kuechmeister to the Department of Municipal Affairs (Ontario), 23 June and 8 July 1952 (referring to incidents in 1945), Department of Municipal Affairs Administrative Correpondence re Tisdale Township, 1946–72, AO, RG19–43, box 226.

118 Di Giacomo, "The Italians of Timmins," 57.

119 J.H. Stovel to Ernest Lapointe, Attorney-General, 28 June 1940, Dome

Mines Collection, Enemy Aliens files, 1940–41, AO, F1350, box 21, section 7.

120 Ibid., 13 June 1940.
121 Di Giacomo, "The Italians of Timmins," 59.
122 Braddon, *Roy Thomson of Fleet Street*, 106.
123 Di Giacomo, "The Italians of Timmins," 56. Local historian Charlie Angus provides a colourful account of this "street battle" in *Mirrors of Stone*, 62–4, which he says is based on Di Giacomo's version, but it contains additional details that I have been unable to confirm.

CHAPTER ELEVEN

1 For example, Acheson, "Changing Social Origins of the Canadian Industrial Elite, 1880–1910," 213–14.
2 Warner, *The Social System of the Modern Family*, as discussed in Maurice R. Stein, *The Eclipse of Community: An Interpretation of American Studies*, 75.
3 Berthoff, *An Unsettled People*, 272–4.
4 Rotundo, *American Manhood*, 63.
5 Laumann, *Bonds of Pluralism: The Form and Substance of Urban Social Networks*, 8 and 135–6. See also Kornhauser, *The Politics of Mass Society*.
6 Cobalt *Daily Nugget*, 20 April 1912, 1.
7 *Porcupine Advance*, 18 November 1937 and 2 February 1939.
8 *Might's City Catalogues* (Timmins), 1934.
9 *Porcupine Advance*, 30 August 1916, 27 November 1918, 3 December 1919, and 10 December 1919.
10 Vasiliadis, "Co-operativism and Progressivism," 15.
11 *Porcupine Advance*, 15 October 1915, 5.
12 Ibid., 15 October 1915, 5.
13 Ibid., 13 and 24 January 1938.
14 *Broke Hustler*, 13 October 1917.
15 Quoted in *Porcupine Advance*, 6 July 1936, 1.
16 Vance, *Death So Noble: Memory, Meaning, and the First World War*, 74, 266.
17 *Porcupine Advance*, 9 and 16 April 1924.
18 Ibid., 12 April 1934 ("Big Crowd Had Big Time at Eighth Annual Vimy Banquet"), 1.
19 This situation changed somewhat in Timmins during the expansion of the school system to accommodate the baby boom, but this discussion is intended to pertain to the period before 1950 only.
20 *Hollinger Miner* 19 May 1952, 3; *Porcupine Advance*, 22 March 1916, 4.
21 "Historical Sites and Trails," 1978, 83–4. At Iroquois Falls Museum.
22 Report of Inspector W.R. McVittie to V.K. Grier, Cochrane, 7 May 1934, Ontario Department of Education, Central Registry Files, 1934, AO, RG2/P3, box 186.

23 *Porcupine Advance*, 28 June 1912, "The School Question in South Porcupine."

24 Ibid., 7 March 1917, 3.

25 Laurendeau, *L'homme aux 56 métiers*, 67.

26 *Porcupine Advance*, 7 March 1917, 3.

27 Ibid., 25 August 1927, np.

28 For an interesting account of life on these cars, see Clement, *The Bell and the Book*.

29 Lower, *Settlement and the Forest Frontier in Eastern Canada*, 109.

30 Tremblay, "Timmins: métropole de l'or," 30; Lendrum, "Days That Are Gone," Timmins *Daily Press*, 20 April 1955, 4.

31 MacDougall, *Building the North*, 153.

32 *Porcupine Advance*, 6 and 27 December 1916 (both on p. 8).

33 Ibid., 29 August 1917, 4, and 24 December 1919, 1.

34 Ibid., 28 and 31 October 1935, and 11 November 1935 (all on p. 1).

35 Ibid., 21 September 1936, 4 October 1937, and 23 May 1938.

36 Annual Report for 1931, Timmins United Church, in First United Church Minutes of Congregational Meetings, 1917–53, United Church Archives, Victoria University, Toronto.

37 *Porcupine Advance*, 27 May 1935, 1.

38 Minutes of a meeting on 10 April 1930, Ansonville Mission Minutes, 1924–55, United Church Archives, Victoria University, Toronto.

39 Comments to a panel discussion, published in "We're Still Here," in Steedman, Suschnigg, and Buse, *Hard Lessons*, 172.

40 Sillanpää, *Under the Northern Lights*, 25.

41 Quoted in Stiff, *Ontario Mining: The Early Years*, 72. Source of quotation not clear.

42 Interview with M.E. Stortroen, 29 January 1975, Porcupine Historical Society Oral History Collection, Timmins Museum.

43 Interview with M.E. Stortroen, 4 February 1976, Porcupine Historical Society Oral History Collection, Timmins Museum.

44 ss1A, Tisdale Township, Ontario Department of Education, Cochrane District Inspection Reports, 1913–35, AO, RG2/F-3-E.

45 Her career is reconstructed from *Porcupine Advance*, 11 October 1916, 3; *The Daily Press*, 12 June 1954 (4); Lendrum, "Days That Are Gone," Timmins *Daily Press*, 26 March 1955, 4.

46 *Porcupine Advance*, 1 March 1937.

47 Di Giacomo, "The Italians of Timmins," 54.

48 O'Donnell, *Loose Canon* [sic], 138 (ellipses in the original).

49 Lavigne, *Tours de force*, 53.

50 *Porcupine Advance*, 15 April 1937, 1.

51 Forestell, "All That Glitters Is Not Gold," 316–17.

52 *Porcupine Advance*, 1 March 1937.

53 Cobalt *Daily Nugget*, 11 and 18 July 1911; Southall, "A Visitation of Providence," 36–8; *Porcupine Advance*, 2 August 1916, 8.

54 *Daily Nugget*, extra edition, 12 July 1911.

55 Letter from G.B. Maclennan to Frank Lendrum, in "Days That Are Gone," Timmins *Daily Press*, 8 May 1948, 5.

56 Tucker, *Steam into Wilderness*, 58.

57 H.P. DePencier to J.S. Bache, 12 October 1922, Dome Mines Collection, General Files, 1920–23, AO, F1350, box 3, MU8689; *Porcupine Advance*, 18 and 25 October 1922 (both page 1).

58 For accounts of events in the Porcupine region, see *Porcupine Advance*, 9, 16, 23, 30 October, 6, 13, 20, 27 November, 4, 11, 18, 25 December 1918, and 30 April 1919. See also H.P. DePencier to J.S. Bache, 9 March 1920, Dome Mines Collection, General Files, 1920–23, AO, MU8689.

59 *Porcupine Advance*, 30 October 1918, 1.

60 Ibid., 25 December 1918; Jack Easton in "Days That Are Gone," *Daily Press*, 10 November 1956, 4; Timmins Financial Statement, 1918, Costs re Emergency Hospital, Timmins Municipal Financial Returns, 1912–35, AO, RG19–142, 1080, box 391.

61 Town of Iroquois Falls Expenses, 15 November 1918, Iroquois Falls Municipal Financial Returns, 1915–44, AO, RG19–142, 764, box 186.

62 Lendrum, "Days That Are Gone," Timmins *Daily Press*, 10 November 1956, 4.

63 Interview with Ruth Reid, 1 March 1974, Porcupine Historical Society Oral History Collection, Timmins Museum.

64 Trudelle, *L'Abitibi d'autrefois, d'hier, d'aujourd'hui*, 133.

65 Wilson, introduction to *Ontario and the First World War*, lxx (no source given).

66 *Canadian Annual Review*, 1915, 462.

67 The 58th was a unit formed at Niagara-on-the-Lake in May 1915 and was sometimes referred to as the "Central Ontario" Battalion. In February 1916, under Lieutenant Colonel H.A. Genet, it was assigned to the 9th Brigade of the Canadian Expeditionary Force.

68 *Porcupine Advance*, 3 September 1915, 5.

69 Ibid., 15 October 1915, 5. See also the list in Hollinger's Annual Report, 1915, 6–7, AO, MU1382 (formerly F1335).

70 In 1915. Iroquois Falls Municipal Financial Returns, 1915–44, AO, RG19–142, 764, box 186.

71 Tucker, *Steam into Wilderness*, 59.

72 *Porcupine Advance*, 16 and 23 February 1916 and 8 March 1916; Lendrum, "Days That Are Gone," Timmins *Daily Press*, 9 April 1949, 5.

73 Details from *Porcupine Advance*, 17 May 1916, 1; 10 January 1917. Also from "Commanding Officers Overseas," app. 1 in vol. 4 of *Canada in the Great War* (Toronto, 1921), 339, 365.

74 *Broke Hustler*, 13 October 1917.

75 *Porcupine Advance*, 12 and 19 November 1915, pp. 1 and 2, respectively.

76 Ibid., 14 November 1940, 1.

77 Vance, *Death So Noble*, 256.

78 *Porcupine Advance*, 25 August 1927; *The Northern Miner*, item quoted in *Porcupine Advance*, 9 February 1933, 2.

79 Braddon, *Roy Thomson of Fleet Street*, 105.

80 Sillanpää, *Under the Northern Lights*, 62.

81 Angus and Griffin, *We Lived a Life and Then Some*, 73. Source cited is George Cassidy, *Warpath: The Story of the Algonquin Regiment 1939–1945* (Cobalt: Highway Book Shop, 1990).

82 Lempi D. Mansfield, "Aim for a Broom," 1979, unpublished manuscript, Library and Archives Canada (LAC), MG31/H95, file 51, np.

83 Minutes of meeting of 11 September 1940, Iroquois Falls United Church, Ladies' Aid Minutes, 1925–33, vol. 2, United Church Archives, Victoria University, Toronto.

84 *Porcupine Advance*, 30 June 1941, 1; display in Timmins Museum, August 1997.

85 O'Donnell, *Loose Canon* [sic], 136. Monteith was designated as Camp 23. See Department of Defence, POW Work Project, Timmins/Monteith, LAC, RG 24/C1, microfilm reel C5386.

86 "Men to Sudbury" file, in Dome Mines Collection, General Files, AO, F350, box 26, MU8712. Nickel was needed for weapons manufacture and for strengthening the steel used in ships and tanks.

87 *Daily Nugget*, 27 April 1921, 3.

88 See reports in Timmins *Daily Press*, summer 1939, and note in the column "15 Years Ago," *Daily Press*, September 1954.

89 *Porcupine Advance*, 4 January 1937, 3; 22 December 1927, np.

90 See, for example, RCMP Security Bulletin 755, 15 May 1935, in Kealey and Whitaker, *R.C.M.P. Security Bulletins: The Depression Years*, part 2, *1935*, 276.

91 *Porcupine Advance*, 10 May 1934, 3; 23 May 1934, 8; 31 May 1934, 1.

92 Lions Club of Timmins, *The Book of Timmins and the Porcupine*.

93 *Porcupine Advance*, 2 July 1937.

94 Di Giacomo, "The Italians of Timmins," 69.

95 See Radforth's *Bushworkers and Bosses*, Forestell's "All That Glitters Is Not Gold," and Perry's *On the Edge of Empire*.

96 These are my own interpretations, based on comments in the oral histories and local publications, as well as personal observations.

97 *Porcupine Advance*, 10 March 1938.

98 Ibid., 1 January 1919, 1.

99 Ibid., 7 January 1935, 1.

100 Ibid., 28 February 1923.

101 Ibid., 2 December 1937.

102 Lendrum, "Days That Are Gone," *Daily Press*, 1 September 1956, 4.

103 Bradwin, *The Bunkhouse Man*, 92, 105–6.

104 MacDowell, *"Remember Kirkland Lake,"* 64.

105 Braddon, *Roy Thomson of Fleet Street*, 98.

106 "Historical Sites and Trails," 92, Iroquois Falls Museum.

107 *Porcupine Advance*, 8 October 1915, 1; 8 March 1916, 1.

108 Ibid., 10 January 1917, 1.

109 Ibid., 15 October 1915, 5.

110 Ibid., 24 January 1917, 4.

111 Ibid., 7 November 1935.

112 Tremblay, "Timmins: métropole de l'or," 40–1 (my translation).

113 Sylvestre, "Les journeaux de l'Ontario français 1858–1983," 3.

114 Tucker, *Steam into Wilderness*, 46.

115 Ashley Thomson, "1900–1910," in Wallace and Thomson, *Sudbury: Rail Town to Regional Capital*, 85, note 108. See also Dennie, "Sudbury 1883–1946: A Social Historical Study of Property and Class," 217–18.

116 Wightman and Wightman, *The Land Between*, 104.

117 Sudbury *Journal*, 9 April 1908, quoted in Ashley Thomson, "1900–1910" in Wallace and Thomson, *Sudbury*, 78.

118 Cobalt *Daily Nugget*, 23–5 June 1909, cited in Tucker, *Steam into Wilderness*, 44.

119 Englehart to S.B. Clement, Toronto, 12 February 1912, in James P. Whitney Papers, October 1911–January 1912, AO, F6/MU3132.

120 Englehart to Premier Whitney, Toronto, 22 June 1912, in James P. Whitney Papers October 1911–January 1912), AO, F6/MU3132.

121 *Canadian Annual Review*, 28 February 1919, 648.

122 *Porcupine Advance*, 24 December 1919 and 31 December 1919, 4.

123 *L'Abitibi*, 15 April 1920, 1.

124 *Porcupine Advance*, 2 February 1921, 7.

125 Schull, *Ontario since 1867*, 174–5; Ontario Department of Lands and Forests, Annual Report for 1912, Ontario, *Sessional Papers* 3 (1912): 88–92.

126 R.E. Hore, "The Porcupine Trail," *Canadian Mining Journal*, 15 October 1910, 620.

127 Ontario Department of Public Works, Annual Report for 1911, Ontario, *Sessional Papers* 12 (1912), 71.

128 "An Ontario Citizen" to *Mail & Empire*, Toronto, 9 October 1919. Typed copy in Sir William Hearst Papers, Miscellaneous Files, AO, F6/MU1309, envelope 6.

129 *Porcupine Advance*, 20 August 1924, letter to the editor signed "Homesteader."

130 *Porcupine Advance*, 20 July 1921, 6.

131 Nelson Hartley to Mitchell Hepburn, 23 April 1934, in Mitchell F. Hepburn Papers, Correspondence Files, May–June 1934, AO, F10-A1/MU4914.

132 W.H. Robertson to Mitchell Hepburn, Goderich Ontario, 3 March 1934, in

Mitchell F. Hepburn Papers, Correspondence Files, March–April 1934, AO, F10-A1/MU4913.

133 Oliver, *G. Howard Ferguson: Ontario Tory*, 340.

134 W.H. Robertson to Mitchell Hepburn, Goderich Ontario, 3 March 1934, in Mitchell F. Hepburn Papers, Correspondence Files, March–April 1934, AO, F10-A1/MU4913.

135 Quoted in Oliver, *G. Howard Ferguson, Ontario Tory*, 368.

136 H. Goode to "Mr. M. Hepurn," Brower, Ontario, 2 April 1934, in Mitchell F. Hepburn Papers, Correspondence Files, March–April 1934, AO, F10-A1/MU4913.

137 *Mail & Empire*, 13 June 1935.

138 Commissioner's Report, Matheson Inquiry, 7 March 1936, in W.B. Common, Matheson Inquiry Papers, AO, RG18–111, box 1.

139 Toronto *Star*, 7 June 1935, as quoted in ibid., 30.

140 Smith, *Harvest from the Rock*, 87.

141 "Northern Ontario: Its Progress and Development under the Whitney Government," pamphlet [circa 1914], 18, in Sir William Hearst Papers, Miscellaneous Files, AO, F6, MU1311, envelopes 16–18.

142 See discussion in Nelles, *The Politics of Development*, 87–102, 429–43.

143 *Canadian Mining Journal*, 15 March 1915, 1.

144 *Porcupine Advance*, 11 November 1935, 1.

145 Other than the role it played in the ongoing tensions of Canadian federalism, at least. For a discussion of this aspect of the question, see Nelles, *The Politics of Development*, 439–43, and Armstrong, *The Politics of Federalism*.

146 Bray and Danaker, *Yesterday, Today and Tomorrow: The Association of Mining Municipalities of Ontario*, 12.

147 *Porcupine Advance*, 3 May 1922, 1.

148 Ibid., 19 November 1919, 4; 30 June 1920, 6.

149 Manore, *Cross-Currents*, 61–5.

150 *Porcupine Advance*, 4 April 1923, 1.

151 Ibid., 16 December 1935, 1.

152 Manore, *Cross-Currents*, 95–103.

153 Ibid., 119–20.

154 *Porcupine Advance*, 16 February 1939, 4, editorial.

155 Ibid., 4 November 1935, 3.

156 Johnston, *E.C. Drury: Agrarian Idealist*, 157.

157 *Porcupine Advance*, 10 December 1919.

158 Lalond, "Le règlement XVII et ses repercussions sur le Nouvel-Ontario," 31.

159 *Canadian Annual Review*, 1915, 498.

160 Tremblay, "Timmins: métropole de l'or," 30; Lendrum, "Days That Are Gone," 30 April 1955, 4; 7 May 1955, 4. Forestell, in "All That Glitters," refers to the land donation (47).

161 Tremblay, "Timmins: métropole de l'or," 35; and Rocheleau et al., "An Inventory of Historical Sites in Timmins-Porcupine," 123.

162 Iroquois Falls Municipal Financial Returns for 1921, AO, RG19–142; "An Illustrated Story of the Development of the Newsprint Paper Mill of the Abitibi Power & Paper Co.," 1924 (pamphlet), in Abitibi History File, Iroquois Falls Museum.

163 See Inspection Reports from 1928 on for SS3, Clute Township, Roman Catholic Separate Schools Inspection Reports, Cochrane District, 1928–33, AO, RG2/F3-F.

164 See MacDougall's report of the incident in a memo to the Deputy Minister of Education, North Bay, 19 April 1924, Ontario Department of Education, Central Registry Files, 1924, AO, RG2/P3, box 130.

165 McKenty, *Mitch Hepburn*, 41.

166 Quoted in Schull, *Ontario since 1867*, 293.

167 *Porcupine Advance*, 7 October 1935, 2.

168 Iroquois Falls Municipal Financial Returns, AO, RG19–142. There were 244 resident students in Ste Anne's and only 184 in the public school.

169 Timmins *Daily Press*, 5 January 1939, 1.

170 *Porcupine Advance*, 5 January 1939, 1.

171 Ibid., 26 November 1919, 4 editorial.

172 Ibid., 25 July 1935, 4 editorial.

173 See coverage of the dispute in the *Porcupine Advance*, from 25 March 1935 to 2 December 1935.

174 *Hollinger Miner*, 26 March 1956, 5.

175 *Iroquois Falls News*, special anniversary edition, July 1975, np. Copy kindly provided by T.M. Devine, Toronto.

176 Arthur Carrington, Instructor's Report for 1927 from CPR Chapleau Division, Frontier College papers, LAC, MG28 I 124, vol. 150.

CHAPTER TWELVE

1 MPP for St Patrick, 11 March 1948, Ontario, Legislative Assembly, *Debates and Proceedings*, 1948, 2:155.

2 Tremblay, "Timmins: métropole de l'or," 22–3 (my translation).

3 ON-TV news broadcast, Timmins, 15 August 1997.

4 DiGiacomo, "The Italians of Timmins," 108.

5 Field, *The Resources and Trade Prospects of Northern Ontario*, 37–8.

6 "Pioneers of Northern Ontario," *Canadian Mining Journal*, 24 April 1925: 426.

7 See, for example, the version in Murphy, *Yankee Takeover at Cobalt!* 168.

8 And, of course, the claims on which the Klondike rush was initiated were indeed worked by First Nations prospectors.

9 *Porcupine Advance*, 7 December 1933, 4, editorial entitled "Preserve History of North."

10 *Porcupine Advance*, 18 May 1936, 1.

11 Text in a display in a 1997 exhibit at the Timmins Museum and National Exhibition Centre.

12 *Hollinger Miner* 22 May 1956, 10 and cover photo.

13 See Lower, *Settlement and the Forest Frontier in Eastern Canada*, 149, on northern Ontario attitudes in the 1930s.

14 *Porcupine Advance*, 10 May 1912.

15 From "The Northland's Challenge," in Shaw's *Broken Threads*, 152.

16 See particularly Berger "The True North Strong and Free."

17 Griffin, "Men against the Moose," *Toronto Star Weekly*, 24 January 1931, general section, 1.

18 Morton, *Ideal Surroundings*, 127.

19 Laurendeau, *L'homme aux 56 métiers*, 466 (ellipses in the original; my translation).

20 See Dunk, "Racism, Regionalism, and Common Sense in Northwestern Ontario," 205–6, 210, 215.

21 "Bazaar Book," 11, in Church History File, Byrnes Presbyterian Church, Timmins, United Church Archives, Victoria University, Toronto.

22 Now known as Highway 11, it was partially open to Matheson in 1927 and to Cochrane the following year. On Mascioli's garage, see, for example, the full-page ad in *Porcupine Advance*, 1 March 1928.

23 See, for example, Parr, *Domestic Goods*. There is a brief examination of working-class consumerism in Halifax in Morton's *Ideal Surroundings*, 45–8.

24 *Porcupine Advance*, 22 October 1919, 1.

25 Dubinsky, *Improper Advances*, 143–62 (chapter 6, "Sex and the Single-Industry Community: The Social and Moral Reputation of Rural and Northern Ontario").

26 *Porcupine Advance*, 6 June 1923.

27 Ibid., 17 May 1916, 4, editorial.

28 Sidebar quotation from Felix Brezinski (source not clear), in Angus and Palu, *Mirrors of Stone*, 42.

29 H. Goode to "Mr. M. Hepurn" [sic], 2 April 1934, Brower PO, in Mitchell F. Hepburn's Papers, Correspondence Files, March–April 1939, AO, FO-A1, MU4913.

30 [Dome Manager's?] Diary, entry for 12 February 1924, Dome Mines Collection, General Files, 1919–24, AO, MU8687.

31 "The Eight Hour Act," *Canadian Mining Journal*, 15 April 1913, 230.

32 *Canadian Annual Review*, 1912, 336.

33 MacDougall, *Two Thousand Miles of Gold*, 90.

34 *Globe and Mail*, 10 January 1940, 4, Alexander Gillies's obituary; Lendrum, "Days That Are Gone," Timmins *Daily Press*, 11 November 1950, 11; Le Bourdais, *Metals and Men*, 154, 156. Sandy McIntyre's real name was Alexander Oliphant.

35 Theriault, *Trespassing in God's Country*, 6–7.

36 See, for example, work by Patricia Limerick, such as "The Adventures of the Frontier in the Twentieth Century," in White and Limerick, *The Frontier in American Culture*; and Bogue, "Social Theory and the Pioneer."

37 See, for example, Morissonneau, *La terre promise: Le myth du Nord québécois*.

38 *Porcupine Advance*, 23 May 1917, 1; 30 January 1918, 1; 3 January 1938, 1.

39 North Bay *Daily Nugget*, 31 October 1921, 5; *Porcupine Advance* 3 December 1918, 1; *The Daily Press*, 15 May 1948, 4.

40 Stone, *Miners' Justice*, 114–15.

41 Smith, *Harvest from the Rock*, 182–3.

42 Morissonneau, *La terre promise*.

43 *Canadian Annual Review*, 1915, 545.

44 Report dated 31 October 1916, in Annual Report of the Ontario Department of Lands, Forests and Mines for 1916, Ontario, *Sessional Papers* 3 (1917): xviii.

45 *Canadian Mining Journal*, 15 December 1917, 482.

46 *Broke Hustler*, 13 December 1919; *Pulp and Paper Magazine of Canada*, 20 March 1919, 286.

47 MacDougall, *Two Thousand Miles of Gold*, 202.

48 See Munroe, *Mopping Up!*; Farmiloe, *The Legend of Jack Munroe*, and miscellaneous items in the *Porcupine Advance* and Cobalt *Daily Nugget*, summer and fall 1916.

49 Murphy, *Yankee Takeover at Cobalt!* 157.

50 Vance, *Death So Noble*, 159–60.

51 Interview by M.E. Stortroen, 24 October 1975, Porcupine Historical Society, Oral History Collection, Timmins Museum.

52 *Broke Hustler*, 4 May 1918.

53 *Canadian Mining Journal*, 1 July 1915, 417.

54 *Porcupine Advance*, 23 July 1915, pages 4 and 2, respectively.

55 Ibid., 18 June 1915, 4, signed "A Timmins Britisher."

56 *Canadian Annual Review*, 1915, 355, quoting from a paper identified as the Porcupine *Herald*.

57 *Porcupine Advance*, 15 May 1918, 2, editorial.

58 As reported by "AF," South Porcupine, 28 April 1922, in Dome Mines Collection, General Files, 1920–23, AO, MU8689 (name not given to protect confidentiality).

59 *Porcupine Advance*, 16 February 1928, 4.

60 Ibid., 29 March 1928, 1.

61 Canada, House of Commons, *Debates*, 8 May 1929, 2373.

62 Vasiliadis, "Co-operativism and Progressivism," 30.

63 See Perger, "Being Ukrainian in Timmins," 117; Swyripa, "Outside the Block Settlement," 159; *Porcupine Advance*, 17 May 1934, 1. The *Advance* identified the first president as William (not Walter) Rutchynski, and his surname was sometimes spelled "Rutchinsky."

64 *Porcupine Advance*, 12 October 1933, 2.

65 Ibid., 17 May 1934, 1.

66 Ibid., 27 April 1933, 8.

67 Ibid., 9 November 1933, 3.

68 Ibid., 23 September 1935, 8.

69 Ibid., 16 March 1936, 1.

70 Ibid., 8 March 1934, 1.

71 Ibid., 9 May 1935, 4 editorial.

72 Ibid., 17 and 20 October 1938.

73 Ibid., 20 October 1938, editorial entitled "The New Canadians."

74 Ibid., 24 July 1939, 4.

75 See Pon, "Like a Chinese Puzzle: The Construction of Chinese Masculinity in *Jack Canuck*," 88–100.

76 *Porcupine Advance*, 15 July 1937.

77 Ibid., 23 August 1937.

78 Ibid., 21 November 1938.

79 See Abella and Troper, *None Is Too Many*, v.

80 Knowles, *Strangers at Our Gates*, 119–20.

81 Affidavit of Victor Nathanson, 15 March 1935, to Matheson Inquiry, in Matheson Inquiry files, AO, RG18–111, box 1.

82 See, for example, Tulchinsky, *Taking Root*, xvii–xviii and throughout.

83 *Porcupine Advance*, 28 August 1939, 1.

84 Timmins *Daily Press*, 31 August 1939, 8.

85 Avery, *Reluctant Host*, 86.

86 J.H. Stovel to Attorney General Ernest Lapointe, 13 June 1940, in Dome Mines Collection, Enemy Aliens files, 1940–1, AO, F1350, box 21.

87 Dome Mines Collection, Manager's Files, 1939–41, AO, MU8701.

88 Graeme S. Mount, "The 1940s," in Wallace and Thomson, *Sudbury: Rail Town to Regional Capital*, 171.

89 Principe, "A Tangled Knot: Prelude to 10 June 1940," says, "When Italy entered the war, Fascists became definitely marginalized even in the Italian community" (36).

90 *Porcupine Advance*, 20 November 1941, 1; see also a comment on this second-generation openness in Schneider, *The Finnish Baker's Daughters*, 39.

91 *Porcupine Advance*, 12 January 1939, 8.

92 Minutes of the meeting of May 1945, Women's Association Minutes, First United Church, Timmins, United Church Archives, uncatalogued.

93 Schumacher (Trinity) United Church Marriage Register, 1935–44, United Church Archives, 96.129L, box 2–2.

94 Perger, "Being Ukrainian in Timmins," 117.

95 Ibid., 115, 117.

96 Ibid., 115. Photocopy of the newspaper item placed by this committee, which lists the names.

97 See 3 August 1944 and 11 April 1945 in Western Federation of Miners Collection, box 133, 1944–7, University of Colorado at Boulder Archives; Solski and Smaller, *Mine, Mill*, 70.

98 Application for a charter, 28 July 1920, Western Federation of Miners Collection, box 1, 1920, University of Colorado at Boulder Archives.

99 List of officers dated June 1947, Western Federation of Miners Collection, box 139, 1947–50, University of Colorado at Boulder Archives.
100 Laurendeau, *L'homme aux 56 métiers*, 60.

CONCLUSION

1 The idea was originally expressed in 1893. See Billington, *Frontier and Section*. Billington's *America's Frontier Heritage* also has a useful discussion.
2 Lower, "Some Neglected Aspects of Canadian History," 65–8.
3 McDougall, "The Frontier School and Canadian History"; Zaslow, "The Frontier Hypothesis in Recent Historiography"; Cross, *The Frontier Thesis and the Canadas*.
4 Hartz, *The Founding of New Societies*.
5 For example, see Wise, "Upper Canada and the Conservative Tradition"; Craig, *Upper Canada: The Formative Years, 1784–1841*.
6 Innis, *The Fur Trade in Canada: An Introduction to Canadian Economic History* and *Problems of Staple Production in Canada*.
7 Creighton, *The Commercial Empire of the St. Lawrence, 1760–1850* (republished as *The Empire of the St. Lawrence*).
8 Careless, "Frontierism, Metropolitanism, and Canadian History"; and "'Limited Identities' in Canada".
9 Gras, *An Introduction to Economic History*.
10 Careless, "Matters of Structure and Perception," in *Frontier and Metropolis*, 9.
11 Owram, *Promise of Eden: The Canadian Expansionist Movement and the Idea of the West, 1856–1900*.
12 Coates, *Canada's Colonies: A History of the Yukon and Northwest Territories*.
13 See, for example, essays in Buckner and Frank, eds., *Atlantic Canada after Confederation*, and Alexander et al., *Atlantic Canada and Confederation*.
14 Published in Toronto, 1988.
15 Voisey, *Vulcan*, 248, 254.
16 For an introduction to the scope of cultural history and cultural studies, see the essays in Mukerji and Schudson, eds., *Rethinking Popular Culture*.
17 Published in Toronto, 2000.
18 See Francis, *The Imaginary Indian: The Image of the Indian in Canadian Culture*.
19 *Porcupine Advance*, 31 August 1921. The theft of "liberties" is a veiled reference to provincial liquor laws.
20 White, *The Middle Ground: Indians, Empires, and Republics in the Great Lakes Region, 1650–1815*.
21 Schumacher-Trinity United Church History File, 1912–62. United Church Archives, Victoria University, Toronto.

Bibliography

ARCHIVAL SOURCES

Archives of Ontario

Anglican Diocese of Moosonee Papers (1811–1941). MS311 (2 reels microfilm).

John C. Bailey Papers (1883–90). F644, MU21

Colonization Roads Branch Papers (1911–17). RG52, series 2-A, box 5; series 1-A, box 408; series II-A, boxes 58, 95, 112

Commission of Inquiry into Soldiers' Settlement Colony at Kapuskasing (1920). RG18–66, box 1

Computerized Land Records Index

Crown Lands Department (Ontario). Inspection of Surveys, Cochrane and Temiskaming District (1905–6), RG1, series CB-1, box 6 (microfilm reel M5924, reel 5)

– Timber Licence Registers. RG1, MS894 (microfilm reels 10, 11, 15)

Department of Agriculture (Ontario). Annual Reports of Agricultural Representatives, Cochrane, Cochrane North, Cochrane South (1927–49). RG16, series G-5-1 (microfilm MS597, reel 7)

– Office Files, 1932–59. RG16, series 16–09, box 69

Department of Education (Ontario). Central Registry Files (1916–39). RG2, P3, boxes 25, 50, 56, 58, 77, 131, 137, 180, 186, 191A, 193, 200, 225

– Public Schools Inspectors Reports, Cochrane District (1913–35). RG2, F-3-E, box 42

– Roman Catholic Separate Schools, Inspection Reports, Cochrane District (1928–33). RG2, F-3-F, box 70

Department of Municipal Affairs (Ontario). Municipal Administration Correspondence (1931–75). RG19–43: Iroquois Falls (box 83); Timmins (box 225); Tisdale Township (box 226); Whitney Township (box 250)

– Municipal Financial Returns. RG19–142: Iroquois Falls (no. 764, box 186);

Matheson (no. 988, box 225); Timmins (nos. 1080 & 1081, box 391); Tisdale Township (nos. 659 & 660, box 1304); Whitney Township (no. 707)

Department of Natural Resources (Ontario). Timber Licence Map Index. Cartographic Collection MNR/ACC 21021

– Town Plans, Timmins (1933–61). Cartographic Collection. RG1, MNR/ACC 18627

Department of Public Works (Ontario). Minister's Office Files. Correspondence (1911–15). RG15–1, box 8

Dome Mines Collection (1915–47). F1350, multiple boxes, MU8687–MU8782)

Howard Ferguson Papers (1913–31). F8, boxes 5–7, MU1021

Sir William Hearst Papers. Miscellaneous Files. FU6, MU1309, 1310, and 1311

Mitchell F. Hepburn Papers. F10

Hollinger Mines Collection (1911–68). F1335

Inquiry re Department of Northern Development, South Cochrane (Matheson Inquiry) papers. RG18–111, box 1

Multicultural Historical Society Collection. Workers' and Farmers' League Records. Timmins (1931–59). MFN593, subseries 062–094, MSR9806

Ontario Provincial Police. Northern Division Monthly Reports (1911–21). RG23, B-12, box 1, file 1.4

Dorothy Pinkney Papers [1920–22]. Unpublished manuscript, "The Transplanting" [listed by Archives as "Memoirs of the North"]. Acc. no. 14904 (microfilm MS712, reel 1)

Porcupine Area Photograph Collection. C320–1

Royal Commission Inquiring into the Affairs of the Abitibi Power & Paper Company Ltd. (1941). RG18–118

St John's Evangelical Lutheran Church Parish Records (1935–70). Microfilm

James P. Whitney Papers (1905–13). F5, MU3115; F6, MU3116–3134

A.E. Wicks, Ltd, Papers (1929–48). F242

Women's Institute Collection. Cochrane North and South Files (1938–64). RG16-87, FFE 8.12 and 8.13

Workers' Farmers' League Records (1931–59). MFN593

Hudson's Bay Company Archives
(on microfilm held at LAC)

Abitibi District Reports (1822–27). B.1/e/1–7

Abitibi Post Journals (1794–1826). B.1/a/1–19

Flying Post District Reports (1823–95). B.70/e/1–9

Flying Post Journals (1823–48). B.70/a/1–21 (microfilm reel IM53)

Frederick House Journals (1785–1805). B.75/a/1–19 (microfilm reels IM54, IM55)

Gogama Post Journals (1931–33). B.415/a/1–2 (microfilm reel IMA27)

S.I. Iserhoff File (nd). E.93/31 (microfilm reel 4M73)

Kenogamissi District Reports (1813–21). B.99/e/1–8

Kenogamissi Post Journals (1794–1821). B.99/a/1–23

La Sarre Post Journals (1932–41). B.432/a/1–7 (microfilm reel IMA36)

Matachewan Post Reports (1885–95). B.311/e/1, 8, 9, 11 (microfilm reel IM1256)

Matawagamingue District Reports (1824–31, 1885–1895). B.124/e/1–7

Matawagamingue Journals, NWC (1815–22). E41/36–37 (microfilm 4M63)

Mattagami Post Journals (1815–48). B.124/a/2–22

Michipicoten District Reports (1833–34). B.129/e/9

Montreal Department Reports (1890–92). B.134/e/2, 3, 6, 7

Moose Factory Correspondence Inward (1746–1864). B.135/c/1–2

Moose Factory Correspondence Outward (1901–02). B.135/b/56 (microfilm reel IM1120)

Moose Post Journals (1730–40). B.135/a/1–7 (microfilm reel IM84)

Moose Post Reports (1888–91). B.134/e/1, 26, 27, 28a, 28b, 29

Moose Reports on District (1814–29, 1885–91). B.135/e/1–25

Peter Spence, "Narrative of Occurances on a Journey and Voyage from Matagamay Lake in Hudson Bay to London." (1816–17). B.124/a/1

Temiscamingue Accounts, North West Company (1798–1802). E.41/28–31 (microfilm reel 4M63)

J.A. Wilmot File (interview with J.W. Anderson, 1958). E.93/26 (microfilm reel 4M73)

Iroquois Falls Museum, Historical Collections

Abitibi Pulp and Paper History File

Churches History File

Clubs History File

Iroquois Falls History File

Porquis History File

Schools History File

Shillington History File

Sports History File

Laurentian University Archives, Sudbury

Jim Tester Collection (1931–82). RG9

Steelworkers Collection. McIntyre Mines Ltd. Employee Cards (c.1915–25). PO20/1/D/1, 4

Library and Archives Canada

CHURCH MISSIONARY SOCIETY COLLECTION

T. Hamilton Fleming. Journals and Correspondence (1857–60) (microfilm reel A87)

John Horden. Journals and Letters (1851–69). c.1/o (microfilm reels A88, A89)
John Sanders, Correspondence (1876–1899). c.1/P1.1 & 2 (microfilm reel A121);
    appendix B (reel A102); appendix D (reel A113)
Original Letters, Incoming (1882–1900). c.1/o, appendix D (microfilm reels
    A110, 111, 112, and 121)
Correspondence, Outgoing (1892–98). c.1/I.1 and c.1/I.2 (microfilm reel A107)

GOVERNMENT RECORDS DIVISION
Corporations Branch. Abitibi Pulp & Paper Co. File. RG95, series 1, vol. 2493
Department of Indian Affairs. Chapleau Agency Files (1930–41). RG10, vol. 7836,
    files 30065–3, parts 2 & 3 (microfilm reels C12,108, C12,109)
– Chapleau Agency Correspondence. Re: Biscotasing Reserve Petition (1914–20),
    RG10, vol. 3180, file 452,054 (microfilm reel C11,335); Mattagami Reserve
    (1910–30). RG10, vol. 7835, file 30065–3 (microfilm reel C12,108)
– Chapleau Agency Land Surveys (1903–08). RG10, vol. 7763, file 27065–1
    (microfilm reel C12,052)
– Chapleau Game Preserve Correspondence (1924–29), RG10, vol. 6745, file 420-
    8A (microfilm reel C8103)
– Deputy Superintendent General's Letterbooks (1903–11). RG10, vols. 1126–28
    (microfilm reels C9005, C9006); (1917–20). RG10, vol. 1131 (microfilm reel
    C9008)
– Duncan Campbell Scott's Journal of James Bay Treaty Trips (1905–6). RG10, vol.
    1028 (microfilm reel T1460)
– Northern Superintendency Correspondence (1895–1917). RG10, vol. 2832, file
    170,073–1 (microfilm reel C9660)
– Samuel Stewart's Journal of a Visit to Abitibi (1908). RG10, vol. 11,399 (micro-
    film reel T6924)
– Samuel Stewart's Journal of James Bay Treaty Trips (1905–6). RG10, vol. 11,399
    (microfilm T6924)
– Temiskaming Agency Files. Re Matheson and Abitibi flooding (1914–19), RG10,
    vol. 6613, files 6035–2 and 5044–5 (microfilm reel C8017)
– Treaty 9 File (1901–09). RG10, vol. 3033, file 235,225, parts 1 & 1A (microfilm
    reel C11,314)
– Treaty 9 Surveys of Various Reserves (1908–36). RG10, vol. 7757, file 27044–1
    (microfilm reel C12,048)
Department of Justice. File re Men Employed by Abitibi Power & Paper Co.
    (1904–14). RG13, series A2, vol. 2141, file 449/1914
Department of Labour. Lacelle Files. Survey on Vocational Education in Ontario
    (1921). RG27, vol. 257, file 900:02:02, part 9 (microfilm reel T10,181)
– Strikes and Lockouts (1912–31). RG27, vols. 300, 306, 308, 326, 330, 335, 336,
    339, 341, 343, 346, 347, 351, 357, 364, 374, 375, 381, 393, 396, 400, 401, 404
    (microfilm reels T2689–T2758)
Department of National Defence. Prisoner-of-War Work Projects (Abitibi). RG24,
    series C1, file 7236-34-3-102 (microfilm reel C5386)

Immigration Branch. Correspondence re Finnish Immigration (1892–1942). RG76, vols. 25 and 219 (microfilm reels C4683, C7369)

– Correspondence re Italian Immigration (1904–49). RG76, vols. 129 and 130 (microfilm reels C4793, C4794)

– Correspondence re Yugoslavian Immigration (1926–32). RG76, vol. 623, file 938267 (microfilm reel C10,440)

– Immigration to Ontario (1893–1947). RG76, vol. 83, file 8529 (microfilm reel C4749)

– Ukrainian Labor Farmer Temple Association (1927–43). RG76, vol. 299, file 274485 (microfilm reel C7848)

Secretary of State. Office of the Chief Press Censor. Re Finnish Newspapers (1917–19). RG6, vol. 624, files 370-F-1 to 370-F-9 (microfilm reel T104); and vol. 625, files 370-F-10 to 370-F-13 (microfilm reel T105)

Unemployment Relief Commission. Ontario Inspection Reports (1931–33). RG27, vol. 2071

– Ontario Relief Settlement (1932–39). RG27, vol. 2093

MANUSCRIPT COLLECTIONS

Archives des Colonies. MG1, series C11A, vol. 7 (microfilm reel F7)

George Barnley Journals and Correspondence (1840–45). MG24, J40 (microfilm reel A20) and MG17, C1 (microfilm reels A268–276)

Robert Bell Papers (1873–1909). MG53 (microfilm reels H1464–6)

Buffalo Ankerite Mines Papers (1933–60). MG28 III 81, vols. 11–20

Dr. William Cowan Papers (1852–71), MG19, 8

Fort Michipicoten Papers (1856–58, 1877). MG19, D22

Frank Lendrum. Timmins *Daily Press* columns (1946–63). MG31, B24 (microfilm reels M5210–12)

Frontier College Papers (1921–43). MG28, I124

May Louise Jackman Papers (1894–1982). MG30, C210

Lawrence Lande Collection (Robert Bell Papers, 1877–1902). MG53 (microfilm reels H1463–6)

Lempi D. Mansfield Papers (1909–81). MG31, H95

Mattagami and Flying Post Journals (1824–94). 3 vols. MG19, D16

"Harry" Falconer McLean Papers (1905–78). MG30, B131

A.H. Moss Collection (1914–39). MG19, D15

Jervois A. Newnham Papers (1888–98). MG29, D49

Saint Sulpice Seminary (Montreal) Papers. "Relation d'une mission ..." (1837). MG17/A7-2, series II, vol. 26, 14244–14326 (microfilm reel C14,008)

Samuel Taylor Diaries (1849–67). MG19, A28 (microfilm reel M1000)

Metro Toronto Reference Library, Baldwin Room

Louis H. Timmins. Business Journals (1880–85). S185, item A

Noah Timmins (Sr). Business Journals (1871–87). S184 (C, K)

Timmins Museum, Historical Collections

Correspondence re Mattagami Heights (1920). 992.10.1
Porcupine Camp Historical Society. Oral History Collection

United Church of Canada, Victoria University, Toronto

Ansonville Mission and United Church Records. Acc. no. 77.564L, boxes 1–5, 1–6,
    2–2
Church History Files (Schumacher, South Porcupine, Timmins)
Connaught Circuit and United Church Records. Acc. nos. 96.129 (boxes 1–2, 1–3)
    and 96.129L (box 1–1)
Iroquois Falls Pastoral Charge, Methodist Church, and United Church Records.
    Microfilm reel LCM197 and Acc. no. 77.564L
Kelso United Church Records
Monteith United Church Records
Schumacher (Trinity) United Church Records (1912–62). 96.129L
Timmins. First United Church Records (1915–53). Manitou Conference, not cat-
    alogued

University of Colorado at Boulder Archives

Western Federation of Miners Records (1920–54). Boxes 1, 133, 138, 139, 144,
    241

PERIODICALS

L'Abitibi (Amos, QC)
The Broke Hustler (Iroquois Falls)
Canadian Annual Review
The Canadian Mining Journal
Daily Nugget (Cobalt), *Nugget* (North Bay)
Le Droit (Ottawa)
Family Herald and Weekly Star (Montreal)
The Gazette (Montreal)
La Gazette du Nord (Amos, QC)
The Globe, The Globe and Mail (Toronto)
Hollinger Miner
Iroquois Falls News
Maclean's Magazine
Might's City Catalogues (Timmins)
Missions de la Congrégation des missionaries Oblats de Marie Immaculée
    (Marseilles)

The Moosonee and Keewatin Mailbag
The Northern Miner
The Porcupine Advance
Pulp and Paper Magazine of Canada
Saturday Night
The Timmins Press, The Daily Press (Timmins)

OTHER SOURCES

Aaltio, Tauri. "A Survey of Emigration from Finland to the United States and Canada." In *The Finns in North America*, ed., Ralph J. Jalkanen, 63–69. Hancock, MI: Michigan State University Press, 1969

Abbott, John. "Ethnicity as a Dynamic Factor in the Education of an Industrial Town: The Case of Sault Ste. Marie." *Ontario History* 79 (December 1987): 327–52

Abel, Kerry. *Drum Songs: Glimpses of Dene History*. Montreal & Kingston: McGill-Queen's University Press, 1993

– "History and the Provincial Norths: An Ontario Example." In *Northern Visions*, ed., Kerry Abel and Ken S. Coates, 127–40. Peterborough, ON: Broadview Press, 2001

Abel, Kerry & Ken S. Coates (eds). *Northern Visions. New Perspectives on the North in Canadian History*. Peterborough, ON: Broadview Press, 2001

Abele, Cynthia. "The Mothers of the Land Must Suffer: Child and Maternal Welfare in Rural and Outpost Ontario, 1918–1940." *Ontario History* 80 (September 1988): 183–205

Abella, Irving M. *Nationalism, Communism, and Canadian Labour: The CIO, the Communist Party, and the Canadian Congress of Labour, 1935–1956*. Toronto: University of Toronto Press, 1973

Abella, Irving M., and Harold Troper. *None Is Too Many: Canada and the Jews of Europe, 1933–1948*. Toronto: Lester & Orpen Dennys, 1983

Abitibi Pulp and Paper. "Iroquois Falls, Ontario." Published by the company (pamphlet for members of the Imperial Press Conference, August 1920). Copy in the possession of T.M. Devine, Toronto

Acheson, T.W. "Changing Social Origins of the Canadian Industrial Elite, 1880–1910." *Business History Review* 47 (Summer 1973): 189–217

Alanen, Arnold. "Finns and the Corporate Mining Environment of the Lake Superior Region." In *The Finnish Diaspora*, vol 2, ed. Michael Karni, 33–62. Toronto: Multicultural History Society of Ontario, 1981

Alexander, David G., Eric N. Sager, Lewis R. Fischer, and Stuart O. Pierson. *Atlantic Canada and Confederation: Essays in Canadian Political Economy*. Toronto, Buffalo, London: University of Toronto Press, 1983

Allen, James B. *The Company Town in the American West*. Norman, OK: University of Oklahoma Press, 1966

Ambrose, Linda. *For Home and Country: The Centennial History of the Women's Institutes in Ontario.* Erin, ON: Boston Mills Press, 1996

Anderson, Benedict. *Imagined Communities: Reflections on the Origins and Spread of Nationalism.* Rev. edn. London & New York: Verso, 1991

Anderson, David, *The Net in the Bay; or Journal of a Visit to Moose and Albany.* London: Thomas Hatchard, 1854

Anderson, J.W. *Fur Trader's Story.* Toronto: Ryerson, 1961

Anderson, Walter. *Reality Isn't What It Used to Be.* San Francisco: Harper and Row, 1990

Anderson, William A. *Angel of Hudson Bay. The True Story of Maude Watt.* Toronto & Vancouver: Clarke, Irwin, 1961

Angus, Charlie, and Brit Griffin. *We Lived a Life and Then Some: The Life, Death, and Life of a Mining Town.* Toronto: Between the Lines, 1996

Angus, Charlie, and Louie Palu. *Mirrors of Stone: Fragments from the Porcupine Frontier.* Toronto: Between the Lines, 2001

Arensberg, Conrad M., and Solon T. Kimball, eds. *Culture and Community.* New York & Chicago: Harcourt, Brace & World, 1965

Armstrong, Chris. *The Politics of Federalism: Ontario's Relations with the Federal Government, 1867–1942.* Toronto: University of Toronto Press, 1981

Arnopoulos, Sheila McLeod. *Voices from French Ontario.* Kingston & Montreal: McGill-Queen's University Press, 1982

Asselin, Maurice et al. "De l'Abbittibbi-Temiskaming No. 4." Occasional Papers, no. 4. Rouyn, QC: Department of Geography, Collège du Nord-Ouest, 1977

Avery, Donald. *Reluctant Host: Canada's Response to Immigrant Workers, 1896–1994.* Toronto: McClelland & Stewart, 1995

Baldwin, Douglas O. "The Fur Trade in the Moose-Missinaibi River Valley, 1770–1917." *Research Report 8.* Ontario Ministry of Culture and Recreation, Historical Planning and Research Branch, Toronto, nd

– "Imitation vs. Innovation: Cobalt as an Urban Frontier Town." *Laurentian University Review* 11 (February 1979): 23–42

Barnes, Michael. *Fortunes in the Ground. Cobalt, Porcupine and Kirkland Lake.* Erin, ON: Boston Mills Press, 1986

– *Gold in the Porcupine!* Cobalt: Highway Book Shop, 1975

– *Gold in Ontario.* Erin, ON: Boston Mills Press, 1995

– *Link with a Lonely Land: The Temiskaming and Northern Ontario Railway.* Erin, ON: The Boston Mills Press, 1985

Barthes, Roland. *Le degree zero de l'écriture.* Paris: Éditions du Seuil, 1953

– "Eléments de sémiologie." In *Communications 4.* Paris: Éditions du Seuil, 1964

– *Elements of Semiology,* trans. Annette Lavers and Colin Smith. London: J. Cape, 1984

Beck, J. Murray. *Pendulum of Power: Canada's Federal Elections.* Scarborough, ON: Prentice-Hall, 1968

Bederman, Gail. *Manliness and Civilization: A Cultural History of Gender and Race in the United States, 1880–1913.* Chicago & London: University of Chicago Press, 1995

Bender, Thomas. *Community and Social Change in America.* New Brunswick, NJ: Rutgers University Press, 1978

Benoît, Émile. *L'Abitibi: pays de l'or.* Montreal: Zodiac, 1938

Berger, Carl. "The True North Strong and Free." In *Nationalism in Canada,* ed. Peter Russell, 3–26. Toronto & New York: McGraw-Hill, 1966

Bernard, Roger. *Le travail et l'espoir: migrations, développement économique et mobilité sociale Québec/Ontario, 1900–1985.* Hearst, ON: Éditions du Nordir, 1991

Berthoff, Rowland. *An Unsettled People: Social Order and Disorder in American History.* New York: Harper and Row, 1971

Betcherman, Lita-Rose. *The Swastika and the Maple Leaf: Fascist Movements in Canada in the Thirties.* Toronto, Montreal, Winnipeg, & Vancouver: Fitzhenry & Whiteside, 1975

Bieder, Robert E. "Kinship as a Factor in Migration." *Journal of Marriage and the Family* 35 (August 1973): 429–39

Billington, Ray Allen. *America's Frontier Heritage.* New York, Chicago, San Francisco: Holt, Rinehart & Winston, 1966

– ed. *Frontier and Section: Selected Essays of Frederick Jackson Turner.* Englewood Cliffs, NJ: 1961

Bishop, Charles A. "Demography, Ecology, and Trade among the Northern Ojibwa and Swampy Cree." *Western Canadian Journal of Anthropology* 3 (1971): 58–71

– "Northern Algonquians, 1550–1760." In *Aboriginal Ontario,* ed. Edward S. Rogers and D.B. Smith, 275–88. Toronto & Oxford: Dundurn Press, 1994

– "Northern Algonquians, 1760–1821." In *Aboriginal Ontario,* ed. Edward S. Rogers and D.B. Smith, 289–306. Toronto & Oxford: Dundurn Press, 1994

– *The Northern Ojibwa and the Fur Trade: An Historical and Ecological Study.* Toronto & Montreal: Holt, Rinehart & Winston of Canada, 1974

– "Territorial Groups before 1821: Cree and Ojibwa." In *Handbook of North American Indians,* vol. 6: *Subarctic,* ed. June Helm, 158–60. Washington: Smithsonian, 1981

Bloomfield, Elizabeth, Gerald Bloomfield, and Peter McCaskill. *Urban Growth and Local Services: The Development of Ontario Municipalities to 1981.* Occasional Papers in Geography No 3. Guelph, ON: Department of Geography, University of Guelph, 1983

Blumin, Stuart M. *The Emergence of the Middle Class: Social Experience and the American City, 1760–1900.* New York & Cambridge: Cambridge University Press, 1989

– *The Urban Threshold: Growth and Change in a Nineteenth-Century American Community.* Chicago & London: University of Chicago Press, 1976

Bodnar, John. *The Transplanted: A History of Immigrants in Urban America.* Bloomington: Indiana University Press, 1985

Bogue, Allan G. "Social Theory and the Pioneer." *Agricultural History* 34 (1960): 21–34

Boon, T.C.B. *The Anglican Church from the Bay to the Rockies*. Toronto: Ryerson Press, 1962

Boothman, Barry E.C. "Night of the Longest Day: The Receivership of Abitibi Power and Paper." *Business History* 15 (1994): 22–32

Borron, E.B. "A Report on That Part of the Basin of Hudson's Bay Awarded to the Province of Ontario, and Included in the District of Nipissing." Ontario. *Sessional Papers*, no. 22, 1880

– "A Report on That Part of the Basin of Hudson's Bay Awarded to the Province of Ontario, and Included in the District of Nipissing." Ontario. *Sessional Papers*, no. 44, 1881

– "A Report on That Part of the Basin of Hudson's Bay Awarded to the Province of Ontario, and Included in the District of Nipissing." Ontario. *Sessional Papers*, no. 53, 1882

– "Report on That Part of Hudson's Bay Belonging to the Province of Ontario." Ontario. *Sessional Papers*, no. 39, 1883

– "Report on That Part of Hudson's Bay Belonging to the Province of Ontario." Ontario. *Sessional Papers*, no. 1, 1884

– "Report ... on Part of the Basin of Hudson's Bay Belonging to the Province of Ontario." Ontario. *Sessional Papers*, no. 1, 1886

– "Return of Cases Brought Forward in Northern Nipissing." Ontario. *Sessional Papers*, no. 64, 1887

– "Report of E.B. Borron, Esq., Stipendiary Magistrate, on That Part of the Basin of Hudson's Bay Belonging to the Province of Ontario." Ontario. *Sessional Papers*, no. 1, 1888

– "Report of E.B. Borron, Stipendiary Magistrate, on the Basin of Moose River and Adjacent Country Belonging to the Province of Ontario," Ontario. *Sessional Papers*, no. 87, 1890

Bouchard, Gérard. *Quelques arpents d'Amérique: population, économie, famille au Saguenay 1838–1971*. Montreal : Boréal, 1996

Bouchard, Robert F. "History in the Porcupine." Young Canada Works Project for the Porcupine Camp Historical Society, 1977. Copy in Timmins Public Library

Boucher, Romauld. "Edmond Gendreau." *Dictionary of Canadian Biography*, 14: 394–6. Toronto: University of Toronto Press, 1998

Bourdieu, Pierre. *Acts of Resistance: Against the New Myths of Our Time*. Cambridge: Polity Press, 1998

– *In Other Words: Essays towards a Reflexive Sociology*, trans. Matthew Anderson. Cambridge: Polity Press, 1990

– "Sport and Social Class." In *Rethinking Popular Culture*, ed. Chandra Mukerji and Michael Schudson, 357–73. Berkeley & Oxford: University of California Press, 1991

Bowles, Roy T., ed. *Little Communities and Big Industries: Studies in the Social Impact of Canadian Resource Extraction*. Toronto: Butterworths, 1982

Braddon, Russell. *Roy Thomson of Fleet Street*. London & Glasgow: Collins (Fontana Books), 1965. Reprinted 1968

Bradwin, E.W. *The Bunkhouse Man: A Study of Work and Pay in the Camps of Canada 1903–1914*. Toronto: University of Toronto Press, 1929. Reprinted 1972

Brandt, Gail Cuthbert. "The Development of French-Canadian Social Institutions in Sudbury, Ontario, 1883–1920." *Laurentian University Review* 11 (February 1979): 5–22

Bray, Matt, and Ross Danaker. *Yesterday, Today, and Tomorrow: The Association of Mining Municipalities of Ontario*. Association of Mining Municipalities of Ontario [1990]

Bray, Matt, and Ernie Epp, eds. *A Vast and Magnificent Land: An Illustrated History of Northern Ontario*. Toronto: Her Majesty the Queen in Right of Ontario, 1984

Bray, Matt, and Ashley Thomson, eds. *At the End of the Shift: Mines and Single-Industry Towns in Northern Ontario*. Toronto: Dundurn Press, 1992

Brodeur, René, and Robert Choquette. *Villages et visages de l'Ontario français*. L'Office de la télécommunication éducative de l'Ontario, 1979

Brookes, Alan A., and Catharine A. Wilson. "Working away from the Farm: The Young Women of North Huron, 1910–30." *Ontario History* 77 (December 1985): 281–300

Brown, Jennifer S.H. *Strangers in Blood: Fur Trade Company Families in Indian Country*. Vancouver & London: University of British Columbia Press, 1980

Brown, L. Carson. "The Golden Porcupine." *Canadian Geographical Journal*, January 1967

Buckner, P.A., and David Frank, eds. *Atlantic Canada after Confederation: The Acadiensis Reader*. Vol 2. Fredericton: Acadiensis Press, 1985

Burnet, Jean, ed. *Looking into My Sister's Eyes: An Exploration in Women's History*. Toronto: Multicultural Historical Society of Ontario, 1986

Butler, Judith. *Gender Trouble: Feminism and the Subversion of Identity*. New York: Routledge, 1990

Campbell, Marjorie Wilkins. *The North West Company*. Vancouver & Toronto: Douglas & McIntyre, 1957. Reprinted 1983

Canada, Department of Citizenship and Immigration, Indian Affairs Branch. *Annual Reports* (1951)

– Department of Indian Affairs. *Annual Reports*, 1905–1935

– Department of Mines and Resources, Indian Affairs Branch. *Annual Reports*, 1937–1949

– House of Commons. *Debates*, 1912–1950

– Standing Senate Committee on Agriculture and Forestry. Minutes of 28 October 1998. www.parl.gc.ca/36/1/parlbus/commbus/senate/com-e/bore-e/09eva-e.htm (accessed 6 July 2000)

Canadian Encyclopedia Online. www.canadianencyclopedia.ca (accessed October 2001)

Canadian Mining Hall of Fame. www.halloffame.mining.ca (accessed 22 January 2004)

Careless, J.M.S. *Frontier and Metropolis: Regions, Cities, and Identities in Canada before 1914*. Toronto, Buffalo, London: University of Toronto Press, 1980

– "Frontierism, Metropolitanism, and Canadian History." *Canadian Historical Review* 35 (March 1954): 1–21

– "'Limited Identities' in Canada." *Canadian Historical Review* 50 (May 1969): 1–10

Caroli, Betty Boyd, et al., eds. *The Italian Immigrant Woman in North America*. Toronto: Multicultural Historical Society of Ontario, 1978

Carrière, Gaston. *Dictionnaire biographique des Oblats de Marie-Immaculée au Canada*. 3 vols. Ottawa: Éditions de l'Université d'Ottawa, 1976–79

– *Histoire documentaire de la Congrégation des missionnaires Oblats de Marie-Immaculée dans l'Est du Canada*. 12 vols (3, 7, and 9 consulted). Ottawa : Éditions de l'Université d'Ottawa, 12 vols. 1961, 1968, 1970

– "Jean-Marie Nédélec o.m.i. 1834–1896." Documents historiques, no. 34. Sudbury : Société historique du Nouvel-Ontario, 1957

Cayen, Daniel. "Les missions catholiques du nord-est ontarien au xixe siècle." In *Aspects du Nouvel-Ontario aux xixe siècle*, 23–40. Documents historiques no. 73. Sudbury: Société historique du Nouvel-Ontario, 1981.

Cerulo, Karen. "Identity Construction: New Issues, New Directions," *Annual Review of Sociology* 23 (1997): 385–409

Chute, Janet E. *The Legacy of Shingwaukonse: A Century of Native Leadership*. Toronto: University of Toronto Press, 1998

Clark, S.D. "The Position of the French-Speaking Population in the Northern Industrial Community." In *Canadian Society: Pluralism, Change, and Conflict*, ed., R.J. Ossenberg. Scarborough: Prentice-Hall, 1971

Clausi, Louis. "'Where the Action Is': The Evolution of Municipal Government in Timmins." *Laurentian University Review* 17 (February 1985): 43–56

Clement, Andrew D. *The Bell and the Book*. Cobalt: Highway Book Shop, 1987

Clement, Wallace. *Hardrock Mining: Industrial Relations and Technological Change at INCO*. Toronto: McClelland & Stewart, 1981

Coates, Kenneth. *Canada's Colonies: A History of the Yukon and Northwest Territories*. The Canadian Issues Series. Toronto: Lorimer, 1985

Coates, Ken and William Morrison. *The Forgotten North: A History of Canada's Provincial Norths*. Toronto: James Lorimer, 1992

Cohen, Anthony P. *The Symbolic Construction of Community*. London & New York: Tavistock Publications, 1985

Cohen, Marjorie Griffin. *Women's Work, Markets, and Economic Development in Nineteenth-Century Ontario*. Toronto, Buffalo, London: University of Toronto Press, 1988

Cormier, Louis-P, ed. *Jean-Baptiste Perrault, marchand voyageur, parti de Montréal le 28ᵉ de mai 1783*. Montreal: Boréal, 1978

Cosentino, Frank. *The Renfrew Millionaires: The Valley Boys of Winter 1910*. Burnstown, ON: General Store Publishing, 1990

Craig, Gerald M. *Upper Canada: The Formative Years, 1784–1841*. Toronto: McClelland & Stewart, 1963

Crawford, Margaret. *Building the Workingman's Paradise: The Design of the American Company Town.* London & New York: Verso, 1995

Creighton, Donald. *The Commercial Empire of the St. Lawrence, 1760–1850.* Toronto: Ryerson, 1937

– *Harold Adams Innis: Portrait of a Scholar.* Toronto: University of Toronto Press, 1957

Cross, Michael, ed. *The Frontier Thesis and the Canadas.* Toronto: Copp Clark, 1970

Cumbler, John T. *Working-Class Community in Industrial America: Work, Leisure, and Struggle in Two Industrial Cities, 1880–1930.* Westport, CT: Greenwood Press, 1979

Cumming, James D. *Now and Then.* Toronto: Northern Miner Press, 1966

Curti, Merle, et al. *The Making of an American Community: A Case Study of Democracy in a Frontier Community.* Stanford, CA: Stanford University Press, 1959

Davies, K.G., and A.M. Johnson, eds. *Northern Quebec and Labrador Journals and Correspondence, 1819–1835.* Vol. 24. London: Hudson's Bay Record Society, 1963

Davis, Donald F. "The 'Metropolitan Thesis' and the Writing of Canadian Urban History." *Urban History Review* 14 (October 1985): 95–113

Dawson, K.C.A. *Prehistory of Northern Ontario.* Thunder Bay: Thunder Bay Historical Museum Society, 1983

Dean, William G. "The Ontario Landscape, circa A.D. 1600," In *Aboriginal Ontario,* ed. Edward S. Rogers and D.B. Smith, 3–20. Toronto & Oxford: Dundurn Press, 1994

Delâge, Denys. *Bitter Feast. Amerindians and Europeans in Northeast North America, 1600–64.* Vancouver: University of British Columbia Press, 1993.

De la Riva, Paul, and Guy Gaudreau. "Les ouvriers-mineurs de la région de Sudbury (1912–1930): le cas de l'International Nickel Co." *Revue du Nouvel Ontario* 17 (1995): 105–43

Delorme, Diane. "Les Indiens du nord-est ontarien au XIXe siècle." In *Aspects du Nouvel-Ontario aux XIXe siècle,* 1–10. Sudbury: Société historique du Nouvel-Ontario, 1981

Dennie, Donald. "The British in Northeastern Ontario: The Ubiquitous Minority," *Laurentian University Review* 15 (November 1982): 65–82

– "Sudbury 1883–1946: A Social Historical Study of Property and Class." PH D thesis (history), Carleton University, 1989

Derrida, Jacques. *Of Grammatology,* trans. G.C. Spivak. Baltimore: Johns Hopkins University Press, 1976

De Saussure, Ferdinand. *Course in General Linguistics,* trans. Wade Baskin. London: P. Owen, 1959

Desrosiers, Richard, and Denis Héroux. *Le travailleur québécois et le syndicalisme.* 2nd edn. Montreal: Presses de l'Université du Québec, 1973

Dick, Trevor J.O. "Canadian Newsprint, 1913–1930: National Policies and the North American Economy." *Journal of Economic History* 42 (September 1992): 659–87

Di Giacomo, James Louis. "The Italians of Timmins: Micro and Macro-Ethnicity in a Northern Resource Community." MA thesis (social anthropology), York University, 1982

- "They Live in Moneta: An Overview of the History and Changes in Social Organization of Italians in Timmins, Ontario." Working paper no. 2, York University Timmins Project (director, Gerald L. Gold), May 1982. Copy at the Timmins Public Library

Dobbs, Arthur. *An Account of the Countries adjoining to Hudson's Bay in the North-West Part of America.* London: Robinson, 1744; Johnson Reprint Corporation, 1967

Douglas, Dan. *Northern Algoma: A People's History.* Toronto & Oxford: Dundurn Press, 1995

Doyle, Don Harrison. *The Social Order of a Frontier Community: Jacksonville, Illinois, 1825–70.* Urbana: University of Illinois Press, 1978

- "Social Theory and New Communities in Nineteenth-Century America," *Western Historical Quarterly*, April 1977, 151–65

Drummond, Ian M. *Progress without Planning: The Economic History of Ontario from Confederation to the Second World War.* Toronto: University of Toronto Press, 1987

Drury, E.C. *Farmer Premier: Memoirs of the Honourable E.C. Drury.* Toronto & Montreal: McClelland & Stewart, 1966.

Dryden, Ken, and Roy MacGregor. *Home Game: Hockey and Life in Canada.* Toronto: McClelland & Stewart, 1989

Dubinsky, Karen. *Improper Advances: Rape and Heterosexual Conflict in Ontario, 1880–1929.* Chicago & London: University of Chicago Press, 1993

- "'Who Do You Think Did the Cooking?' Baba in the Classroom." In *Changing Lives*, ed. Margaret Kechnie and Marge Reitsma-Street, 193–7. Toronto: Dundurn, 1996

Ducin, Livo [pseud]. "Unrest in the Algoma Lumbercamps: The Bushworkers' Strikes of 1933–1934," In *Fifty Years of Labour in Algoma*, 79–99. Sault Ste Marie: Algoma University College, 1978

Dunk, Thomas W. *It's a Working Man's Town: Male Working-Class Culture in Northwestern Ontario.* Montreal & Kingston: McGill-Queen's University Press, 1991

- "Racism, Regionalism, and Common Sense in Northwestern Ontario." In *Social Relations in Resource Hinterlands*, ed. Dunk. Thunder Bay: Centre for Northern Studies, 1991

- ed. *Social Relations in Resource Hinterlands.* Papers from the 27th Annual Meeting of the Western Association of Sociology and Anthropology. Thunder Bay: Centre for Northern Studies, 1991

Durkheim, Émile. *De la division du travail social.* Paris: F. Alcan, 1893

- *The Elementary Forms of Religious Life*, trans. Joseph Ward Swain. London: Unwin, 1954

- *Suicide: étude de sociologie.* Paris: F. Alcan, 1897

- *On the Division of Labour in Society*, trans. George Simpson. New York: Macmillan, 1933

- *Les règles de la méthode sociologique.* Paris: F. Alcan, 1895

- *The Rules of Sociological Method*, trans. Sarah A. Solovay and John H. Mueller. New York: Free Press, 1938

– *Les formes élémentaires de la vie religieuse: le système totémique en Australie.* Paris: F. Alcan, 1912
– *Suicide,* trans. John A. Spaulding and George Simpson. New York: Free Press, 1951
Ellul, Jacques. *The Technological Society.* New York: Knopf, 1964
Erickson, Paul A., and Liam D. Murphy. *A History of Anthropological Theory.* 2nd edn. Peterborough, ON: Broadview Press, 2003
Farmiloe, Dorothy. *The Legend of Jack Munroe: A Portrait of a Canadian Hero.* Windsor, ON: Black Moss Press, 1994
Fentress, James, and Chris Wickham. *Social Memory.* Oxford, UK, and Cambridge, MA: Blackwell, 1992
Fetherling, Douglas. *The Gold Crusades: A Social History of Gold Rushes.* Toronto: Macmillan, 1988
Field, Fred W. *The Resources and Trade Prospects of Northern Ontario.* Toronto: Board of Trade, 1912
Flannery, Regina. *Ellen Smallboy: Glimpses of a Cree Woman's Life.* Montreal & Kingston: McGill-Queen's University Press, 1995
Foerster, Robert F. *The Italian Emigration of Our Times.* Cambridge, MA: Harvard University Press, 1919. Reprint, New York: Russell and Russell, 1968.
Forestell, Nancy. "'All That Glitters Is Not Gold': The Gendered Dimensions of Work, Family and Community Life in the Northern Ontario Goldmining Town of Timmins, 1909–1950." PH D thesis (history), OISE/University of Toronto, 1993
– "Women, Gender, and the Provincial North." In *Northern Visions,* ed. Kerry Abel and Ken S. Coates, 107–16. Peterborough, ON: Broadview Press, 2001
– "'You Never Give Up Worrying': The Consequences of a Hazardous Mine Environment for Working-Class Families in Timmins, 1915–1950." In *Changing Lives,* ed. Margaret Kechnie and Marge Reitsma-Street, 198–212. Toronto: Dundurn Press, 1996
Fortin, Benjamin, and Jean-Pierre Gaboury. *Bibliographie analytique de l'Ontario français.* Ottawa : Éditions de l'Université d'Ottawa, 1975
Foster, Ralph E. "Hydro-Electric Power and Ontario Gold Mining." *Canadian Mining Journal* 67 (1946): 155–68, 253–8, 634–9, 720–5, 788–95, 867–74, 957–9
Foucault, Michel. *Discipline and Punish: The Birth of the Prison,* trans. Alan Sheridan. New York: Pantheon Books, 1977
– *Folie et déraison: histoire de la folie à l'âge classique.* Paris: Plon, 1961
– *Madness and Civilization: A History of Insanity in the Age of Reason,* trans. Richard Howard. New York: Pantheon Books, 1965
– *Surveiller et punir: naissance de la prison.* Paris: Gallimard, 1975
Fowke, Edith. *Canadian Folklore.* Toronto: Oxford University Press, 1988
Francis, Daniel. *The Imaginary Indian: The Image of the Indian in Canadian Culture.* Vancouver: Arsenal Pulp Press, 1992

Francis, Daniel, and Toby Morantz. *Partners in Furs: A History of the Fur Trade in Eastern James Bay, 1600–1870*. Kingston & Montreal: McGill-Queen's University Press, 1983

Friesen, Gerald. *Citizen and Nation: An Essay on History, Communication, and Canada*. Toronto, Buffalo, London: University of Toronto Press, 2000

Gabriaccia, Donna. "International Approaches to Italian Labour Migration." In *The Italian Diaspora*, ed. George E. Pozzetta and Bruno Ramirez, 21–36. Toronto: Multicultural History Society of Ontario, 1992

Gaffield, Chad. *Language, Schooling, and Cultural Conflict: The Origins of the French-Language Controversy in Ontario*. Montreal & Kingston: McGill-Queen's University Press, 1987

– "The New Regional History: Rethinking the History of the Outaouais," *Journal of Canadian Studies* 26 (Spring 1991): 64–81

Garner, John S. *The Model Company Town: Urban Design through Private Enterprise in Nineteenth-Century New England*. Amherst, MA: University of Massachusetts Press, 1984.

– ed. *The Company Town: Architecture and Society in the Early Industrial Age*. New York & Oxford: Oxford University Press, 1992

Gauthier, Annette. "Genese de nos paroisses régionales (Nord-ouest québécois et Est ontarien." Rouyn, QC: La Société St-Jean-Baptiste de l'ouest québécois, January 1972. Unpaginated typescript. Held at the University of Ottawa library

Geertz, Clifford. *The Interpretation of Cultures*. New York: Basic Books, 1973

George, Peter. "Ontario's Mining Industry, 1870–1940." In *Progress Without Planning*, ed. Ian Drummond, 52–76. Toronto: University of Toronto Press, 1987

Gibson, Thomas W. *Mining in Ontario*. Toronto: King's Printer, 1937

Gillis, R. Peter, and Thomas R. Roach. *Lost Initiatives: Canada's Forest Industries, Forest Policy, and Forest Conservation*. New York: Greenwood Press, 1986

Girdwood, Charles P., Lawrence F. Jones, and George Lonn. *The Big Dome: Over Seventy Years of Gold Mining in Canada*. Toronto: Cybergraphics [1983]

Goddard, Ives. "Central Algonquian Languages." In *Smithsonian Handbook of North American Indians*, vol. 15: *Northeast*, ed. Bruce Trigger, 583–7. Washington, DC: Smithsonian, 1978

Goldenberg, Susan. *The Thomson Empire*. Toronto, New York, London: Methuen, 1984

Goldman, Marion S. *Gold Diggers and Silver Miners: Prostitution and Social Life on the Comstock Lode*. Ann Arbor: University of Michigan Press, 1981

Goldring, Philip. "Lewis and the Hudson's Bay Company in the Nineteenth Century." *Scottish Studies* 24 (1980)

Goltz, Eileen. "The Image and the Reality of Life in a Northern Ontario Company-Owned Town." In *At the End of the Shift: Mines and Single-Industry Towns in Northern Ontario*, ed. Matt Bray and Ashley Thomson, 62–91. Toronto: Dundurn Press, 1992

Gourd, Benoît B. "La colonisation des Clay Belts du nord-ouest Québécois et du nord-est Ontarien." *Revue d'histoire de l'Amérique français* 27 (September 1973): 235–56

– "Mines et syndicats en Abitibi-Temiscamingue 1910–1950." Travaux de recherches, 2. Rouyn, QC: Collège du Nord-Ouest, 1981

Grant, John Webster. *Moon of Wintertime: Missionaries and the Indians of Canada in Encounter since 1534.* Toronto: University of Toronto Press, 1984

Gras, N.S.B. *An Introduction to Economic History.* New York, London: Harper, 1922

Greaves, Joe. "Sports and Recreation." In *A Vast and Magnificent Land,* ed. Matt Bray and Ernie Epp, 183–98. Toronto: Her Majesty the Queen in Right of Ontario, 1984

Greer, Allan. "The Birth of the Police in Canada." In *Colonial Leviathan: State Formation in Mid-Nineteenth-Century Canada,* ed. Greer and Ian Radforth, 17–49. Toronto, Buffalo, London: University of Toronto Press, 1992

Greer, Allan, and Ian Radforth, eds. *Colonial Leviathan: State Formation in Mid-Nineteenth-Century Canada.* Toronto, Buffalo, London: University of Toronto Press, 1992

Griffin, Frederick. "Men against the Moose." *Toronto Star Weekly,* 24 January 1931

Grimard, Jacques, and Gaëtan Vallières. *Travailleurs et gens d'affaires canadiens-français en Ontario.* Montreal: Études Vivantes, 1986

Guthrie, John A. *The Newsprint Paper Industry: An Economic Analysis.* Cambridge, MA: Harvard University Press, 1941

Hallsworth, Gwenda. "Towns in Northern Ontario: Some Aspects of Their Municipal History." *Laurentian University Review* 17 (February 1985): 103–12

Hareven, Tamara K. *Family Time and Industrial Time: The Relationship between the Family and Work in a New England Industrial Community.* New York, Melbourne, & Cambridge, MA: Cambridge University Press, 1982

Harney, Robert F. "Italian Immigration and the Frontiers of Western Civilization." In *The Italian Immigrant Experience,* ed. John Potestio and Antonio Pucci, 1–28. Thunder Bay: Canadian Italian Historical Association, 1988

– "Men without Women: Italian Migrants in Canada, 1885–1930." In *The Italian Immigrant Woman in North America,* ed. Betty Boyd Caroli et al., 79–101. Toronto: Multicultural Historical Society of Ontario, 1978

– "The Padrone System and Sojourners in the Canadian North, 1885–1920." *Pane e lavoro: The Italian American Working Class,* ed. George E. Pozzetta, 119–140. Toronto: The Multicultural Historical Society of Ontario, 1980

– "Toronto's Little Italy, 1885–1945." In *Little Italies in North America,* ed. Robert Harney and Vincenza Scarpaci, 41–62. Toronto: The Multicultural Historical Society of Ontario, 1981

Harney, Robert F., and Vincenza Scarpaci, eds. *Little Italies in North America.* Toronto: Multicultural Historical Society of Ontario, 1981

Hartz, Louis. *The Founding of New Societies: Studies in the History of the United States, Latin America, South Africa, Canada, and Australia.* New York: Harcourt, Brace & World, 1964

Harvey, Fernand, ed. *Le mouvement ouvrier au Québec: aspects historiques.* Montreal : Boréal Express, 1980

Hecht, A., ed. *Regional Development in the Peripheries of Canada and Europe.* Manitoba Geographical Studies, no. 8. Winnipeg: Department of Geography, University of Manitoba, 1983

Henry, Alexander (the elder). *Travels and Adventures in Canada and the Indian Territories between the Years 1760–1776.* New York: Riley, 1809

Himelfarb, Alex. "The Social Characteristics of One-Industry Towns in Canada." In *Little Communities and Big Industries,* ed. Roy T. Bowles, 16–43. Toronto: Butterworths, 1982

Hinde, John R. "'Stout Ladies and Amazons': Women in the British Columbia Coal-Mining Community of Ladysmith, 1912–14." *BC Studies* 114 (Summer 1997): 33–57

Hobsbawm, Eric, and Terence Ranger, eds. *The Invention of Tradition.* Cambridge: Cambridge University Press, 1983

Hodge, Gerald D., and Mohammad A. Qadeer. *Towns and Villages in Canada: The Importance of Being Unique.* Toronto: Butterworths, 1983

Hodgins, Bruce, and Jamie Benidickson. *The Temagami Experience.* Toronto: University of Toronto Press, 1989

Hoffman, Arnold. *Free Gold: The Story of Canadian Mining.* Toronto & New York: Rinehart, 1947

Holley, Frank. *Just Passing Through: The People and Places North of Matachewan.* Cobalt: Highway Book Shop, 1988

Holliday, J.S. *The World Rushed In: The California Gold Rush Experience.* New York: Simon and Schuster, 1981

Honigmann, John J. "Social Disintegration in Five Northern Canadian Communities." *Canadian Review of Sociology and Anthropology* 2 (November 1965): 199–214

– "Social Organization of the Attawapiskat Cree Indians," *Anthropos* 48 (1953): 809–16

– "West Main Cree." In *Handbook of North American Indians,* vol. 6: *Subarctic,* ed. June Helm, 217–30. Washington: Smithsonian, 1981

Hopkin, Deien R., and Gregory S. Kealey, eds. *Class, Community, and the Labour Movement: Wales and Canada, 1850–1930.* Wales: LLAFUR/Canadian Committee on Labour History, 1989

Horowitz, Gad. *Canadian Labour in Politics.* Toronto: University of Toronto Press, 1968

Howell, Colin D. *Blood, Sweat, and Cheers: Sport and the Making of Modern Canada.* Toronto, Buffalo, London: University of Toronto Press, 2001

Hughes, Patricia. "The Ontario Northland Railway: Root of a Mini-Empire," *Laurentian University Review* 13 (February 1981): 81–93

Hull, James P. "Research at Abitibi Power and Paper." *Ontario History* 79 (June 1987): 167–79

Humphries, Charles W. *"Honest Enough to Be Bold": The Life and Times of Sir James Pliny Whitney.* Toronto: University of Toronto Press, 1985

Hunter, Albert. *Symbolic Communities: The Persistence and Change of Chicago's Local Communities.* Chicago & London: University of Chicago Press, 1974

Iacovetta, Franca, Roberto Perin, and Angelo Principe. *Enemies Within: Italian and Other Internees in Canada and Abroad.* Toronto, Buffalo, London: University of Toronto Press, 2000

Igartua, José E. *Arvida au Saguenay: naissance d'une ville industrielle.* Montreal & Kingston: McGill-Queen's University Press, 1996

Ignatiev, Noel. *How the Irish Became White.* New York & London: Routledge, 1995

Innis, Harold A. *The Fur Trade in Canada.* Toronto & Buffalo: University of Toronto Press, 1956. Reprinted 1970

– *Problems of Staple Production in Canada.* Toronto: Ryerson Press, 1933

– *Settlement and the Mining Frontier.* Toronto: Macmillan, 1936. (Reprinted by Kraus Reprint, 1974)

Innis, Mary Quayle. *An Economic History of Canada.* Toronto: Ryerson Press, 1935

Iroquois Falls Souvenir Book Committee. *Celebrating 75 Years of Growth. Iroquois Falls, 1915–1990.* [1990]

Jalava, Mauri A. "The Finnish-Canadian Cooperative Movement in Ontario." In *The Finnish Diaspora*, vol. 1, ed. Michael Karni, 93–110. Toronto: Multicultural Historical Society of Ontario, 1918

Jasen, Patricia. *Wild Things: Nature, Culture, and Tourism in Ontario, 1790–1914.* Toronto, Buffalo, London: University of Toronto Press, 1995

Jenkin, A.K. Hamilton, *The Cornish Miner: An Account of His Life Above and Underground from Early Times.* London: George Allen & Unwin, 1927. Reprinted 1948

Jenkins, William H. *Notes on the Hunting Economy of the Abitibi Indians.* Washington, DC: Catholic University of America, 1939

Jestin, Warren J. "Provincial Policy and the Development of the Metallic Mining Industry in Northern Ontario, 1845–1920." PH D thesis (political economy). University of Toronto, 1977

Johnston, Basil. *Ojibway Language Lexicon for Beginners.* Ottawa: Indian and Northern Affairs, 1978

Johnston, Charles M. *E.C. Drury: Agrarian Idealist.* Toronto: University of Toronto Press, 1986

Joseph, Miranda. *Against the Romance of Community.* Minneapolis & London: University of Minnesota Press, 2002

Jowett, Cecelia. *No Thought for Tomorrow: The Story of a Northern Nurse.* Toronto: Ryerson Press, 1954

Karni, Michael, ed. *The Finnish Diaspora.* 2 vols. Toronto: Multicultural History Society of Ontario, 1981

Kaufman, Harold F. "Toward an Interactional Conception of Community." In *Perspectives on the American Community*, ed. Roland L. Warren, 88–103. Chicago: Rand McNally, 1966

Kealey, Gregory S. "The Parameters of Class Conflict: Strikes in Canada, 1891–1930." In *Class, Community, and the Labour Movement: Wales and Canada,*

1850–1930, ed. Deian R. Hopkin and Kealey, 213–248. Wales: LLAFUR/Canadian Committee on Labour History, 1989

Kealey, Gregory S., and Reg Whitaker, eds. *R.C.M.P. Security Bulletins: The Early Years, 1919–1929*. St John's, NF: Canadian Committee on Labour History, 1994

– *R.C.M.P. Security Bulletins: The Depression Years*. 5 vols. St John's, NF: Canadian Committee on Labour History, 1993, 1995, 1996, 1997

– *R.C.M.P. Security Bulletins: The War Series, 1939–1941*. St John's, NF: Canadian Committee on Labour History, 1989

Kechnie, Margaret, and Marge Reitsma-Street, eds. *Changing Lives: Women in Northern Ontario*. Toronto & Oxford: Dundurn Press, 1996

Kero, Reino. "The Background of Finnish Emigration." In *The Finns in North America*, ed. Ralph J. Jalkanen, 55–62. Hancock, MI: Michigan State University Press, 1969

Kidd, Bruce. "The Workers' Sports Movement in Canada, 1924–40: The Radical Immigrants' Alternative." *Polyphony* 7 (Spring/Summer 1985): 80–8

Knight, Rolf. *Indians at Work: An Informal History of Native Labour in British Columbia, 1858–1930*. Vancouver: New Star Books, 1978. Rev. edn, 1996

Knowles, Valerie. *Strangers at Our Gates: Canadian Immigration and Immigration Policy, 1540–1997*. Rev. edn. Toronto & Oxford: Dundurn Press, 1993

Knox, F.A. *Gold Mining in Ontario: Report of the Committee of Enquiry into the Economics of the Gold Mining Industry*. Toronto: Government of Ontario, 1955

Kolasky, John. *The Shattered Illusion: The History of Ukrainian Pro-Communist Organizations in Canada*. Toronto: Peter Martin Associates, 1979

Kornhauser, William. *The Politics of Mass Society*. Glencoe, IL: Free Press, 1959

Krats, Peter V. "'Suomalaiset nikkelialuella': Finns in the Sudbury Area, 1883–1939." *Polyphony* 5 (Spring/Summer 1983): 37–48

– "The Sudbury Area to the Great Depression: Regional Development on the Northern Resource Frontier." PH D thesis (history), University of Western Ontario, 1988

Kuhlberg, Mark. "'We Have "Sold" Forestry to the Management of the Company': Abitibi Power & Paper Company's Forestry Initiatives in Ontario, 1919–1929." *Journal of Canadian Studies/Revue d'études canadiennes* 34 (Autumn 1999): 187–209

Lafleur, Normand, Donat Martineau, and Alice Descôteaux. *La vie quotidienne des premiers colons en Abitibi-Témiscamingue*. Montreal: Lemeac, 1976

Laine, Edward W. "Community in Crisis: The Finnish-Canadian Quest for Cultural Identity, 1900–1979." In *The Finnish Diaspora*, vol. 1, ed. Michael Karni, 1–10. Toronto: Multicultural History Society of Ontario, 1981

– "The Finnish Organization of Canada, 1923–1940, and the Development of a Finnish Canadian Culture." *Polyphony* 3 (Fall 1981): 81–90

– "The Strait-Jacketing of Multiculturalism in Canada." *Archivaria* 10 (Summer 1980): 225–37

Lalonde, André. "Le règlement XVII et ses repercussions sur le Nouvel-Ontario."

Documents historiques nos. 46–7. Sudbury: Société historique du Nouvel-Ontario, 1965

Lam, Lawrence. " 'The Whites Accept Us Chinese Now': The Changing Dynamics of Being Chinese in Timmins." York University, York Timmins Project, Working Paper no. 4, 1983. Copy at Carleton University Library

Lambert, Richard S. (with Paul Pross). *Renewing Nature's Wealth: A Centennial History of the Public Management of Lands, Forest, and Wildlife in Ontario 1763–1967.* Ontario: Department of Lands and Forests, 1967

Lankton, Larry. *Cradle to Grave: Life, Work, and Death at the Lake Superior Copper Mines.* New York & Oxford: Oxford University Press, 1991

Last, Blance, and Cécile Vachon. *Timmins.* Ottawa: Association des enseignants franco-ontariens, 1981

Laumann, Edward O. *Bonds of Pluralism: The Form and Substance of Urban Social Networks.* New York: John Wiley & Sons, 1973.

Laurendeau, Jean. *L'homme aux 56 métiers.* Rouyn, QC: privately printed, 1978

Lavigne, J. Conrad. *Tour de force.* Vanier, ON: Éditions l'interligne, 1993

Leacy, F.H., M.C. Urquhart, and K.A.H. Buckley. *Historical Statistics of Canada.* 2nd edn. Ottawa: Supply and Services Canada, 1983

Le Bourdais, D.M. *Metals and Men: The Story of Canadian Mining.* Toronto: McClelland & Stewart, 1957

Lebovics, Herman. *True France: The Wars Over Cultural Identity, 1900–1945.* Ithaca & London: Cornell University Press, 1992

Lee-Whiting, Brenda. "Krugerdorf." *Beaver,* Spring 1984, 35–9

Legget, Robert F. *Railways of Canada.* Vancouver & Toronto: Douglas & McIntyre, 1973. Reprinted 1987

Le Maistre, Susan Joy. "Social Segmentation in a Company Town: An Internationalist Account." MA thesis (sociology and anthropology), Carleton University, 1981

Lévi-Strauss, Claude. *The Elementary Structures of Kinship,* trans. James Harle Bell and John Richard von Sturmer. Boston: Beacon Press, 1969

– *Structural Anthropology,* trans. Claire Jacobson and Brooke Grundfest Schoepf. New York: Basic Books, 1963

– *Structures élémentaires de la parenté.* Paris: Presses universitaires de France, 1949

Lewis, Gertrud Jaron. "Germans in Northern Ontario." *Laurentian University Review* 15 (November 1982): 21–40

Lindström, Varpu. *From Heroes to Enemies: Finns in Canada, 1937–1947.* Beaverton, ON: Aspasia Books, 2000

Lindström-Best, Varpu. *Defiant Sisters. A Social History of Finnish Immigrant Women in Canada.* Toronto: Multicultural History Society of Ontario, 1988

– "'I Won't Be a Slave!': Finnish Domestics in Canada, 1911–30." In *Looking into My Sister's Eyes: An Exploration in Women's History,* ed Jean Burnet, 33–53. Toronto: Multicultural History Society of Ontario, 1986

Lingenfelter, Richard D. *The Hardrock Miners: A History of the Mining Labor Movement in the American West, 1863–1893.* Berkeley: University of California Press, 1974.

Lions Club of Timmins. *The Book of Timmins and the Porcupine.* Timmins, 1937. Copy in the Provincial Archives of Ontario Library

Lombardi, Vincent M. "Italian American Workers and the Response to Fascism," *Pane e Lavoro. The Italian American Working Class,* ed. George E. Pozzetta. Toronto: The Multicultural History Society of Ontario, 1980: 141–57

Long, John S. "Archdeacon Thomas Vincent of Moosonee and the Handicap of 'Métis' Racial Status." *Canadian Journal of Native Studies* 3 (1983): 95–116

– "Narratives of Early Encounters between Europeans and the Cree of Western James Bay." *Ontario History* 80 (September 1988): 227–45

– "The Reverend George Barnley, Wesleyan Methodist, and James Bay's Fur Trade Company Families." *Ontario History* 72 (March 1985): 43–64

– *Treaty No. 9: The Half-Breed Question, 1902–1910.* Cobalt: Highway Book Shop, 1978

– *Treaty No. 9: The Indian Petitions, 1889–1927.* Cobalt: Highway Book Shop, 1978

– *Treaty No. 9: The Negotiations.* Cobalt: Highway Book Shop, 1978

Lonn, George. *The Mine Finders.* Toronto: Pitt Publishing, 1966.

Lower, A.R.M. *Settlement and the Forest Frontier in Eastern Canada.* Toronto: Macmillan, 1936

– "Some Neglected Aspects of Canadian History." *Canadian Historical Association Report* (1929): 65–72

Lucas, Rex A. *Minetown, Milltown, Railtown: Life in Canadian Communities of Single Industry.* Toronto & Buffalo: University of Toronto Press, 1971

Luxton, Meg. *More Than a Labour of Love: Three Generations of Women's Work in the Home.* Toronto: Women's Press, 1980

Lyotard, Jean-François. *La condition postmoderne: rapport sur le savoir.* Paris: Éditions de Minuit, 1979

McCann, L.D. "The Changing Internal Structure of Canadian Resource Towns." In *Little Communities and Big Industries,* ed. Roy T. Bowles, 61–81. Toronto: Butterworths, 1982

McClelland, Keith. "Masculinity and the 'Representative Artisan' in Britain, 1850–80." In *Manful Assertions: Masculinity in Britain since 1800,* ed. Michael Roper and John Tosh, 74–91. London & New York: Routledge, 1991

McDermott, George L. "Frontiers of Settlement in the Great Clay Belt, Ontario and Quebec." *Annals of the Association of American Geographers* 5 (1961): 261–73

McDonald, Robert A.J. *Making Vancouver: Class, Status, and Social Boundaries, 1863–1913.* Vancouver: University of British Columbia Press, 1996

MacDougall, J.B. *Building the North.* Toronto: McClelland & Stewart, 1919

– *Two Thousand Miles of Gold: From Val d'Or to Yellowknife.* Toronto: McClelland & Stewart, 1946

McDougall, J.L. "The Frontier School and Canadian History." Canadian Historical Association *Report* (1929): 121–5

McDowall, Duncan. *Steel at the Sault: Francis H. Clergue, Sir James Dunn, and the Algoma Steel Corporation 1910–1956*. Toronto, Buffalo, London: University of Toronto Press, 1984

MacDowell, Laurel Sefton. "Relief Camp Workers in Ontario during the Great Depression of the 1930s." *Canadian Historical Review* 76 (June 1995): 205–28

– *"Remember Kirkland Lake": The Gold Miners' Strike of 1941–42*. Toronto: University of Toronto Press, 1983

MacIver, R.M. *Community: A Sociological Study*. London: Macmillan, 1917

McKay, Ian. "Tartanism Triumphant: The Construction of Scottishness in Nova Scotia, 1933–1954." *Acadiensis* 21 (Spring 1992): 5–47

McKenty, Neil. *Mitch Hepburn*. Toronto & Montreal: McClelland & Stewart, 1967

MacNab, Valerie. *Pioneer Ventures: The Story of Will Bannerman in the Porcupine*. Cobalt: Highway Book Shop, 1992

MacPherson, Ian. *Each for All: A History of the Co-operative Movement in English Canada, 1990–1945*. Carleton Library Series #116. Toronto: Macmillan, 1979

Mann, Ralph. "The Decade after the Gold Rush: Social Structure in Grass Valley and Nevada City, California, 1850–1860." *Pacific Historical Review* 41 (November 1972): 484–504

Manore, Jean L. *Cross-Currents: Hydroelectricity and the Engineering of Northern Ontario*. Waterloo, ON: Wilfrid Laurier University Press, 1999

Marks, Lynne. *Revivals and Roller Rinks: Religion, Leisure, and Identity in Late-Nineteenth-Century Small-Town Ontario*. Toronto, Buffalo, London: University of Toronto Press, 1996

Marois, Roger, and Pierre Gauthier. *Les Abitibis*. Mercury Series #140. Ottawa: Canadian Museum of Civilization, 1989.

Marunchak, Michael H. *The Ukrainian Canadians: A History*. 2nd edn. Winnipeg & Ottawa: Ukrainian Academy of Arts and Sciences in Canada, 1982

Mauss, Marcel. "Essai sur le don: forme et raison de l'échange dans les sociétés archaïque." Originally published in *L'Année sociologique*, 1923–24. Reprinted in Mauss, *Sociologie et anthropologie*. Paris: Presses universitaires de France, 1950

– *The Gift: Forms and Functions of Exchange in Archaic Societies*, trans. Ian Cunnison. New York and London: W.W. Norton, 1967

Melville, J.L. "The Canadian Engineers." In *Canada in the Great War*, 6: 37–74. Toronto: Union Publishing, 1921

Mitchell, Elaine Allan. *Fort Timiskaming and the Fur Trade*. Toronto: University of Toronto Press, 1977

– "Frederick House Massacre." *Beaver*, Spring 1973, 30–3

Miyakawa, T. Scott. *Protestants and Pioneers: Individualism and Conformity on the American Frontier*. Chicago & London: University of Chicago Press, 1964

Molohon, Kathryn T. "Contact and Transition in a Northern 'Border' Town." *Laurentian University Review* 13 (February 1981): 22–34

Moore, E.S. *American Influence in Canadian Mining*. Political Economy Series, no. 9. Toronto: University of Toronto Press, 1941

Moore, Phil. H. *Slag and Gold: A Tale of the Porcupine Trail.* Toronto: Thomas Allen, 1924

Morissonneau, Christian. *La terre promise: le myth du Nord québécois.* Montreal : Hurtubise HMH, 1978

Morrison, James. "Treaty Nine Research Report. Treaty 9 (1905–06): The James Bay Treaty." Ottawa: Treaties and Historical Research Centre, 1986

Morrison, Jean. "The Working Class in Northern Ontario." *Labour/Le travailleur* 7 (Spring 1981): 151–5

Morrow, Don, et al. *A Concise History of Sport in Canada.* Toronto: Oxford University Press, 1989

Morton, Desmond, and Terry Copp. *Working People. An Illustrated History of the Canadian Labour Movement.* Rev. edn. Ottawa: Deneau Publishers, 1984

Morton, Suzanne. *Ideal Surroundings: Domestic Life in a Working-Class Suburb in the 1920s.* Toronto, Buffalo, London: University of Toronto Press, 1995

Mouat, Jeremy. *Roaring Days: Rossland's Mines and the History of British Columbia.* Vancouver: University of British Columbia Press, 1995

Mukerji, Chandra, and Michael Schudson, eds. *Rethinking Popular Culture: Contemporary Perspectives in Cultural Studies.* Berkeley & Los Angeles: University of California Press, 1991

Munroe, Jack. *Mopping Up! A Dog Story of the Princess 'Pats': Through the Eyes of Bobbie Burns, Regimental Mascot.* New York: H.K. Fly, 1918

Murphy, John Patrick. *Yankee Takeover at Cobalt!* Cobalt: Highway Book Shop, 1977

Naylor, James. *The New Democracy: Challenging the Social Order in Industrial Ontario, 1914–1925.* Toronto: University of Toronto Press, 1991

Neill, R.F. "The Passing of Canadian Economic History." *Journal of Canadian Studies* 12 (Winter 1977): 73–82

Nelles, H.V. *The Politics of Development: Forests, Mines, and Hydro-Electric Power in Ontario, 1879–1941.* Toronto: Macmillan, 1974

Newell, Diane. *Technology on the Frontier: Mining in Old Ontario.* Vancouver: University of British Columbia Press, 1986

Nicholson, G.W.L. *Canadian Expeditionary Force, 1914–1918.* Ottawa: Queen's Printer, 1962

Nisbet, Robert A. *The Sociological Tradition.* New York: Basic Books, 1966

Nord, Douglas C., and Geoffrey R. Weller. "Establishing Political Institutions for the Periphery: A Comparative Analysis." Research Report no. 7. Thunder Bay: Lakehead Centre for Northern Studies, 1898

O'Donnell, Eddie. *Loose Canon* [sic]: *A Collection of Recollections of Early Days in Iroquois Falls.* Matheson: O'Donnell Enterprises, 1995

Oliver, Peter. *G. Howard Ferguson: Ontario Tory.* Toronto: University of Toronto Press, 1977

Ontario. Bureau of Mines. *Annual Reports*
– Department of Agriculture. *Annual Reports*
– Department of Crown Lands. *Annual Reports*

- Department of Lands and Forests. *Annual Reports*
- Department of Lands, Forests and Mines. *Annual Reports*
- Department of Mines. *Annual Reports*
- Department of Public Works. *Annual Reports*
- Legislative Assembly. *Debates and Proceedings*, 1947–50
- Northern Development Branch. *Annual Reports*
- *Sessional Papers*, Vital Statistics, 1924–51

Owram, Doug. *Promise of Eden: The Canadian Expansionist Movement and the Idea of the West, 1856–1900*. Toronto, Buffalo, London: University of Toronto Press, 1980

Pain, S.A. *Three Miles of Gold: The Story of Kirkland Lake*. Toronto: Ryerson Press, 1960

- *The Way North*. Toronto: Ryerson Press, 1964.

Parenteau, Bill. "The Woods Transformed: The Emergence of the Pulp and Paper Industry in New Brunswick, 1918–1931." *Acadiensis* 22 (Autumn 1992): 5–43

Park, Robert Ezra. "Human Ecology." In *Perspectives on American Community*, ed. Roland L. Warren, 31–43. Chicago: Rand McNally, 1966

Parker, Bruce A. "Colonization Roads and Commercial Policy." *Ontario History* 67 (March 1975): 31–8

Parr, Joy. *Domestic Goods: The Material, the Moral, and the Economic in the Postwar Years*. Toronto, Buffalo, London: University of Toronto Press, 1999

Parr, Joy, and Mark Rosenfeld, eds. *Gender and History in Canada*. Toronto: Copp Clark, 1996

Parsons, Talcott. *Structure and Process in Modern Societies*. London: Collier-Macmillan, 1960

Partasso, Luigi. "La donna italiana durante il periodo fascista in Toronto, 1930–1940." In *The Italian Immigrant Woman in North America*, eds. Betty Boyd Caroli et al. Toronto: Multicultural Historical Society of Ontario, 1978

Paul, Rodman Wilson. "Mining Frontiers as a Measure of Western Historical Writing." *Pacific Historical Review* 33 (1964): 25–34

Payne, Michael. "Daily Life on Western Hudson Bay 1714–1870: A Social History of York Factory and Churchill." PH D thesis (history), Carleton University, 1989.

Pennacchio, Luigi G. "Exporting Fascism to Canada: Toronto's Little Italy." In *Enemies Within: Italian and Other Internees in Canada and Abroad*, eds. Franca Iacovetta, Roberto Perin, and Angelo Principe, 52–75. Toronto, Buffalo, London: University of Toronto Press, 2000

Peressini, Mauro. "Personal and Public Realms: The Views of Italian Immigrants in Montreal." In *The Italian Diaspora*, ed. George E. Pozzetta and Bruno Ramirez, trans. Marie Stewart, 193–208. Toronto: Multicultural Historical Society of Ontario, 1992

Perger, Nancy. "Being Ukrainian in Timmins: A Personal Reminiscence." *Polyphony* 10 (1988): 114–18

Perry, Adele. *On the Edge of Empire: Gender, Race, and the Making of British Columbia, 1849–1871*. Toronto, Buffalo, London: University of Toronto Press, 2001

Petrik, Paula. *No Step Backward: Women and Family on the Rocky Mountain Mining Frontier, Montana, 1865–1900.* Helena, MT: Montana Historical Society Press, 1987

Pilli, Arja. "Finnish-Canadian Radicalism and the Government of Canada from the First World War to the Depression." In *The Finnish Diaspora*, vol. 1, ed. Michael Karni, 19–32. Toronto: Multicultural Historical Society of Ontario, 1981

"Planning the Town of Iroquois Falls." *Contract Record and Engineering Review*, 28 June 1916, 636–7

Pocius, Gerald L. *A Place to Belong: Community Order and Everyday Space in Calvert, Newfoundland.* Athens & London: University of Georgia Press, 1991

Pon, Madge. "Like a Chinese Puzzle: The Construction of Chinese Masculinity in *Jack Canuck.*" In *Gender and History in Canada*, ed. Joy Parr and Mark Rosenfeld, 88–100. Toronto: Copp Clark, 1996

Porcupine Golden Anniversary Committee. *Souvenir Booklet: Celebrating the Golden Anniversary of the Porcupine Gold Rush July 1–5, 1959.* [Timmins] 1959. Copy in Provincial Archives of Ontario Library

Porcupine News Depot. "Porcupine Hand Book." Vol. 1. Toronto: Porcupine News Depot [1912]. Copy in the Provincial Archives of Ontario Library

Porcupine Prospectors' Association. *The Prospector: Commemorating the 30th Anniversary of the Discovery of Gold in Porcupine 1909–1939.* Timmins: The Association [1939?]

Porsild, Charlene. *Gamblers and Dreamers: Women, Men, and Community in the Klondike.* Vancouver: University of British Columbia Press, 1998

Potestio, John, and Antonio Pucci, eds. *The Italian Immigrant Experience.* Thunder Bay: Canadian Italian Historical Association, 1988

Pozzetta, George E., ed. *Pane e lavoro: The Italian American Working Class.* Toronto: Multicultural Historical Society of Ontario, 1980

Pozzetta, George E., and Bruno Ramirez, eds. *The Italian Diaspora.* Toronto: Multicultural Historical Society of Ontario, 1992

Preston, Richard J. "East Main Cree." In *Handbook of North American Indians*, vol. 6: *Subarctic*, ed. June Helm, 196–207. Washington: Smithsonian, 1981

Principe, Angelo. *The Darkest Side of the Fascist Years: The Italian and Canadian Press: 1920–1942.* Toronto, Buffalo, Lancaster: Guernica, 1999

– "A Tangled Knot: Prelude to 10 June 1940." In *Enemies Within: Italian and Other Internees in Canada and Abroad*, ed. Franca Iacovetta, Roberto Perin, and Angelo Principe, 27–51. Toronto, Buffalo, London: University of Toronto Press, 2000

Proulx, Jean-Baptiste. *Au lac Abbitibi: visite pastorale de Mgr. J. Thomas Duhamel dans le haut de l'Ottawa.* 3rd edn. Montreal: Cadieux et Dolorme, 1885

Pugh, Donald E. "Ontario's Great Clay Belt Hoax." *Canadian Geographic Journal* 90 (January 1975): 19–24

Radforth, Ian. *Bush Workers and Bosses: Logging in Northern Ontario 1900–1980.* Toronto: University of Toronto Press, 1987

– "Finnish Lumber Workers in Ontario, 1919–46." *Polyphony* 3 (Fall 1981): 23–34

– "Political Prisoners: The Communist Interns." In *Enemies Within: Italian and Other*

Internees in Canada and Abroad, ed. Franca Iacovetta, Roberto Perin, and Angelo Principe, 194–224. Toronto, Buffalo, London: University of Toronto Press, 2000

Raivio, Yrjö. *Kanadan suomalaisten historia.* Vol 1. Vancouver: New West Press for Finnish Canadian Historical Society, 1975

– *Kanadan suomalaisten historia.* Vol 2. Thunder Bay: Lehto Printers, 1979

Ramirez, Bruno. "Montreal's Italians and the Socio-Economy of Settlement, 1900–1930: Some Historical Hypotheses." *Urban History Review* 10 (June 1981): 39–48

– *On the Move: French-Canadian and Italian Migrants in the North Atlantic Economy, 1860–1914.* Toronto: McClelland & Stewart, 1991

Ramirez, Bruno, and Michele del Balzo. "The Italians of Montreal: From Sojourning to Settlement, 1900–1921." In *Little Italies in North America,* ed. Robert Harney and Vincenza Scarpaci, 63–84. Toronto: Multicultural Historical Society of Ontario, 1981

Rasporich, Anthony W. "Twin City Ethnopolitics: Urban Rivalry, Ethnic Radicalism and Assimilation in the Lakehead, 1900–70." *Urban History Review* 18 (February 1990): 210–30

Ray, Arthur J. *The Canadian Fur Trade in the Industrial Era.* Toronto: University of Toronto Press, 1990

– *Indians in the Fur Trade.* Toronto: University of Toronto Press, 1974

Rea, K.J. *The Political Economy of Northern Development.* Ottawa: Science Council of Canada, 1976

– *The Prosperous Years: The Economic History of Ontario, 1939–1975.* Toronto, Buffalo, London: University of Toronto Press, 1985

Redfield, Robert. *The Little Community: Viewpoints for a Study of a Human Whole.* Chicago & London: University of Chicago Press, 1955

Regher, T.D. *The Canadian Northern Railway: Pioneer Road of the Northern Prairies, 1895–1918.* Toronto: Macmillan, 1976

Reich, Nathan. *The Pulp and Paper Industry in Canada.* McGill University Economic Studies, National Problems of Canada, no. 7. Toronto: Macmillan [1926]

Reid, C.S., ed. *Northern Ontario Fur Trade Archaeology.* Toronto: Ministry of Culture and Recreation, 1980

Reid, Richard M. Introduction to *The Upper Ottawa Valley to 1855,* ed. Reid. Ottawa: Carleton University Press and the Champlain Society, 1989

Repka, William, and Kathleen M. Repka. *Dangerous Patriots: Canada's Unknown Prisoners of War.* Vancouver: New Star Books, 1982

Rinehart, James W. *The Tyranny of Work.* Don Mills, ON: Longman Canada, 1975

Robin, Martin. *Radical Politics and Canadian Labour, 1880–1930.* Industrial Relations Centre, Research Series no. 7. Kingston: Queen's University, 1968.

Rocheleau, Michelle, Carla Comand, Robert Edmonds, and Perry Kelly. "An Inventory of Historical Sites in Timmins-Porcupine." Timmins Roman Catholic Separate School Board, 1979. Copy in Provincial Archives of Ontario Library

Rodney, William. *Soldiers of the International: A History of the Communist Party in Canada, 1919–1929.* Toronto: University of Toronto Press, 1968

Rogers, Edward S. "Band Organization among the Indians of Eastern Subarctic Canada." In *Contributions to Anthropology: Band Societies,* ed. David Damas, 21–55. National Museums Bulletin no. 228. Ottawa: National Museums of Canada, 1969

– "Changing Settlement Patterns of the Cree-Ojibwa of Northern Ontario." *Southwestern Journal of Anthropology* 19 (1963): 64–88

– "Leadership among the Indians of Eastern Subarctic Canada." *Anthropologica,* ns, 7, no. 2 (1965): 263–84

– *The Round Lake Ojibwa.* Art and Archaeology Division Paper no. 5. Toronto: Royal Ontario Museum, 1962

Rogers, Edward S., and Mary Black. "Subsistence Strategy in the Fish and Hare Period, Northern Ontario: The Weagomow Ojibwa, 1880–1920." *Journal of Anthropological Research* 32 (Spring 1976): 1–43

Rogers, Edward S., and Donald B. Smith, eds. *Aboriginal Ontario: Historical Perspectives on the First Nations.* Toronto & Oxford: Dundurn Press, 1994.

Rogers, Edward S., and J. Garth Taylor. "Northern Ojibwa." In *Handbook of North American Indians,* vol. 6: *Subarctic,* ed. June Helm, 231–43. Washington: Smithsonian, 1981

Rogers, Edward S., and James G.E. Smith. "Environment and Culture in Shield and Mackenzie Borderlands." In *Handbook of North American Indians,* vol. 6: *Subarctic,* ed. June Helm, 130–45. Washington: Smithsonian, 1981

Rogge, John, ed. *Developing the Subarctic.* Manitoba Geographical Studies, no. 1. Winnipeg: Department of Geography, University of Manitoba, 1973

Roper, Michael, and John Tosh. *Manful Assertions: Masculinities in Britain since 1800.* London & New York: Routledge, 1991

Rotundo, E. Anthony. *American Manhood: Transformations in Masculinity from the Revolution to the Modern Era.* New York: Basic Books, 1993.

Rousseau, Nathan, ed. *Self, Symbols, and Society: Classical Readings in Social Psychology.* Boulder, New York, Oxford: Rowman & Littlefield, 2002

Rowe, John. *The Hard-Rock Men: Cornish Immigrants and the North American Mining Frontier.* Liverpool: Liverpool University Press, 1974

Rozenzweig, Ray. *Eight Hours for What We Will: Workers and Leisure in the Industrial City.* Cambridge, MA: Cambridge University Press, 1983

Rumilly, Robert. *La compagnie du Nord-Ouest: une épopée montréalaise.* 2 vols. Montreal: Fides, 1980

Russo, David J. *Families and Communities: A New View of American History.* Nashville, TN: American Association for State and Local History, 1974

Ryden, Kent C. *Mapping the Invisible Landscape: Folklore, Writing, and the Sense of Place.* Iowa City: University of Iowa Press, 1993

Saarinen, Oiva. "Municipal Government in Northern Ontario: An Overview." *Laurentian University Review* 17 (February 1985): 5–25

Saïd, Edward. *Culture and Imperialism.* New York: Knopf, 1993

– *Orientalism.* New York: Pantheon, 1978

Salvatore, Filippo. *Le fascisme et les italiens à Montréal: une histoire orale, 1922–1945.* Guernica, 1995

Scardellato, Gabriele P. *Within Our Temple: A History of the Order Sons of Italy of Ontario.* [Toronto?]: Order Sons of Italy of Canada, 1995

Schneider, Aili Grönlund. *The Finnish Baker's Daughters.* Toronto: Multicultural History Society, 1986

Schober, Michaela C. "Austrian Immigration between the World Wars." In *A History of the Austrian Migration to Canada,* ed. F.C. Englemann, M. Prokop, and F.A.J. Szabo, 59–74. Ottawa: Carleton University Press, 1996

– "Austrian Immigration to Canada in the Imperial Period." In *A History of the Austrian Migration to Canada,* ed. F.C. Englemann, M. Prokop, and F.A.J. Szabo, 45–58. Ottawa: Carleton University Press, 1996

Schuessler, Karl, and Mary Schuessler. *School on Wheels: Reaching and Teaching the Isolated Children of the North.* Erin, ON: Boston Mills Press, 1986

Schull, Joseph. *Ontario since 1867.* Toronto: McClelland & Stewart, 1978

Seager, Allen. "Miners' Struggles in Western Canada: Class, Community, and the Labour Movement, 1890–1930." In *Class, Community and the Labour Movement: Wales and Canada, 1850–1930,* ed. Deian R. Hopkin and Gregory S. Kealey, 160–198. Wales: LLAFUR/Canadian Committee on Labour History, 1989

Séguin, Normand. *Agriculture et colonisation au Québec.* Montreal: Boréal Express, 1980

Sexé, Marcel. *Two Centuries of Fur Trading, 1723–1923: Romance of the Revillon Family.* Paris: Draeger Frères, 1923

Shaw, Bertha M.C. *Broken Threads: Memories of a Northern Ontario Schoolteacher.* New York: Exposition Press, 1955

– *Laughter and Tears: Memoirs from Between the Limestone Hills and the Blue Georgian Bay, Ontario.* New York: Exposition Press, 1957

Shields, Rob. *Places on the Margin: Alternative Geographies of Modernity.* London & New York: Routledge, 1991

Sillanpää, Lennard P.C. "The Political Behaviour of Canadians of Finnish Descent in the District of Sudbury." Licentiate thesis (political science), University of Helsinki, 1976

– "Voting Behaviour of Finns in the Sudbury Area, 1930–1970." In *The Finnish Diaspora,* vol. 1, ed. Michael Karni, 101–116. Toronto: Multicultural History Society of Ontario, 1981

Sillanpää, Nelma. "Revontulet Athletic Club of Timmins." *Polyphony* 7 (Spring/ Summer 1985): 76–9

– *Under the Northern Lights: My Memories of Life in the Finnish Community of Northern Ontario.* Mercury Series Paper no. 45. Ottawa: History Division, Canadian Museum of Civilization, 1994

Silvy, Antoine. *Letters from North America, 1673–1708.* Trans. and ed. Ivy Alice Dickson. Toronto: Mika, 1980

Sinclair, Peter. "The North and the North-West: Forestry and Agriculture." In *Progress without Planning: The Economic History of Ontario from Confederation to the Second World War*, ed. Ian Drummond, 77–90. Toronto: University of Toronto Press, 1987

Singleton, Fred. *A Short History of Finland*. Cambridge & New York: Cambridge University Press, 1989

Smith, Donald A. "John Sanders." *Dictionary of Canadian Biography*, 13:920. Toronto: University of Toronto Press, 1994

Smith, Duane A. *Rocky Mountain Mining Camps: The Urban Frontier*. Bloomington & London: Indiana University Press, 1967

Smith, Louise Nightingale. *Frederick W. Schumacher: Portrait of a Renaissance Man*. Timmins: Porcupine Advance [1980]

Smith, Philip. *Harvest from the Rock: A History of Mining in Ontario*. Toronto: Macmillan, 1986

Smith, R.M. "Northern Ontario: 'Limits of Land Settlement for the Good Citizen'." *Canadian Geographic Journal* 23 (October 1941): 182–211

Solski, Mike and John Smaller. *Mine Mill: The History of the International Union of Mine, Mill and Smelter Workers in Canada since 1895*. Ottawa: Steel Rail Publishing, 1984

Southall, Margaret. "'A Visitation of Providence': The Matheson Fire, 1916." *Beaver* August/September 1991, 36–40

Stamp, Robert M. *The Schools of Ontario, 1876–1976*. Toronto: University of Toronto Press, 1982

Steedman, Mercedes, P. Suschnigg, and Dieter K. Buse, eds. *Hard Lessons: The Mine Mill Union in the Canadian Labour Movement*. Toronto: Dundurn Press, 1995

Stefura, Mary. "Ukrainians in the Sudbury Region." *Polyphony* 5 (Spring/ Summer 1983): 71–81

Stegner, Wallace. *Angle of Repose*. New York: Fawcett Crest, 1971

Stein, Maurice R. *The Eclipse of Community: An Interpretation of American Studies*. New York: Harper Torchbooks, 1960. Reprinted 1964

Stelter, Gilbert A. "The People of Sudbury: Ethnicity and Community in an Ontario Mining Region." *Polyphony* 5 (Spring/Summer 1983): 3–16

Stelter, Gilbert A., and Alan F.J. Artibise. "Canadian Resource Towns in Historical Perspective." In *Little Communities and Big Industries*, ed. Roy T. Bowles, 47–60. Toronto: Butterworths, 1982

Stevens, G.R. *Canadian National Railways*. Vol 2: *Towards the Inevitable, 1896–1922*. Toronto & Vancouver: Clarke, Irwin, 1962

Stone, Thomas. "Flux and Authority in a Subarctic Society: The Yukon Miners in the Nineteenth Century." In *Interpreting Canada's North*, ed. Kenneth S. Coates and William R. Morrison, 114–32. Toronto: Copp Clark, 1989

– *Miners' Justice: Migration, Law, and Order on the Alaska-Yukon Frontier, 1873–1902*. New York: Peter Lang, 1988

Stortroen, M.E. *Immigrant in Porcupine*. Cobalt: Highway Book Shop, 1977

– *An Immigrant's Journal.* Cobalt: Highway Book Shop, 1982

Stiff, John. *Ontario Mining: The Early Years.* Toronto: Ontario Department of Mines and Northern Affairs [1971?]

Sturino, Franc. "The Role of Women in Italian Immigration to the New World." In *Looking into My Sister's Eyes,* ed. Jean Burnet, 21–32. Toronto: Multicultural History Society of Ontario, 1986

Sundstén, Taru. "The Theatre of the Finnish-Canadian Labour Movement and its Dramatic Literature, 1900–1939." In *The Finnish Diaspora,* vol. 1, ed. Michael Karni, 77–91. Toronto: Multicultural Historical Society of Ontario, 1981

Surtees, Robert J. *The Northern Connection: Ontario Northland since 1902.* Toronto: Ontario Northland and Captus Press, 1992

Suttles, Gerald D. *The Social Construction of Communities.* Chicago & London: University of Chicago Press, 1972

Swyripa, Frances. "Outside the Bloc Settlement: Ukrainian Women in Ontario during the Formative Years of Community Consciousness." In *Looking into My Sister's Eyes,* ed. Jean Burnet, 155–178. Toronto: Multicultural History Society of Ontario, 1986

– *Wedded to the Cause: Ukrainian-Canadian Women and Ethnic Identity 1891–1991.* Toronto, Buffalo, London: University of Toronto Press, 1993

Sylvestre, Paul-François. "Les journaux de l'Ontario français, 1858–1983." *Documents historiques,* no 81. Sudbury: Société historique du Nouvel-Ontario, 1984

Tanner, Helen Hornbeck, ed. *Atlas of Great Lakes Indian History.* Norman & London: University of Oklahoma Press, 1987

Theriault, George. *Trespassing in God's Country: Sixty Years of Flying in Canada.* Chapleau, ON: Treeline Publishing, 1994

Thompson, E.P. *The Making of the English Working Class.* Penguin Books, 1968

Thwaites, Reuben, ed. *The Jesuit Relations and Allied Documents.* Vols. 46 & 56. New York: Pageant, 1959.

Tilly, Charles. *Stories, Identities, and Political Change.* Boulder, New York, Oxford: Rowman & Littlefield, 2002

Tönnies, Ferdinand. *Community and Society (Gemeinschaft und Gesellschaft* [1887]*).* Trans. C.P. Loomis. New York & London: Harper Torchbooks, 1957

Tosh, John. "Domesticity and Manliness in the Victorian Middle Class: The Family of Edward White Benson." In *Manful Assertions,* ed. Michael Roper and Tosh, 44–73. London & New York: Routlege, 1991

Tostevin, Lola Lemire. *Frog Moon.* Dunvegan, ON: Cormoront Books, 1994

Tough, Frank. *As Their Natural Resources Fail: Native Peoples and the Economic History of Northern Manitoba, 1870–1930.* Vancouver: University of British Columbia Press, 1996

Townsley, B.F. *Mine Finders: The History and Romance of Canadian Mineral Discoveries.* Toronto: Saturday Night Press, 1935

Tremblay, Rodolphe. "Timmins: métropole de l'or." *Documents historiques,* no 22.

Sudbury: Collège du Sacré Cœur pour la Société historique du Nouvel-Ontario, 1951

Trigger, Bruce, and Gordon M. Day. "Southern Algonquian Middlemen: Algonquin, Nipissing and Ottawa, 1550–1780." In *Aboriginal Ontario*, ed. Edward S. Rogers and D.B. Smith, 64–77. Toronto & Oxford: Dundurn Press, 1994

Tronrud, Thorold J. "Frontier Social Structure: The Canadian Lakehead, 1871 and 1881." *Ontario History* 79 (June 1987): 145–65

Trotter, Donald. "Breakthroughs in Health and Safety in Northern Ontario Mines." In *At the End of the Shift*, ed. Matt Bray and Ashley Thomson, 120–9. Toronto: Dundurn Press, 1992

Trudelle, Pierre. *L'Abitibi d'autrefois, d'hier, d'aujourd'hui.* Amos, QC: chez l'auteur, 1937

Tucker, Albert. *Steam into Wilderness.* Toronto: Fitzhenry & Whiteside, 1978

Tulchinsky, Gerald. *Taking Root: The Origins of the Canadian Jewish Community.* Toronto: Lester Publishing, 1992

Turner, Frederick Jackson. *The Frontier in American History.* Intro. Ray Allen Billington. New York: Holt, Rinehart and Winston, 1965

Tyrrell, J.B., ed. *Journals of Samuel Hearne and Philip Turnor.* Toronto: Champlain Society, 1934

Vance, Jonathan F. *Death So Noble: Memory, Meaning, and the First World War.* Vancouver: University of British Columbia Press, 1997

Vanderhill, Burke G. "Agriculture's Struggle for Survival in the Great Clay Belt of Ontario and Quebec." *American Review of Canadian Studies* 18 (1988): 455–64

Van Kirk, Sylvia. "A Vital Presence: Women in the Cariboo Gold Rush, 1862–1875." In *British Columbia Reconsidered*, ed. Gillian Creese and Veronica Strong-Boag, 21–37. Vancouver: Press Gang, 1992

Vasiliadis, Peter. "Co-operativism and Progressivism: Workers' Co-operative of New Ontario Limited." Unpublished essay, York University, nd. Copy at Timmins Museum

– *Dangerous Truth: Interethnic Competition in a Northeastern Ontario Goldmining Centre.* New York: AMS Press, 1989

Virtanen, Keijo. "'Counter-Current': Finns in the Overseas Return Migration Movement." In *The Finnish Diaspora*, vol. 1, ed. Michael Karni, 183–202. Toronto: Multicultural History Society of Ontario, 1981

Visentin, Maurizio A. "The Italians of Sudbury." *Polyphony* 5 (Spring/Summer 1983): 30–6

Voisey, Paul. *Vulcan: The Making of a Prairie Community.* Toronto, Buffalo, London: University of Toronto Press, 1988

Voorhis, Ernest. *Historic Forts and Trading Posts of the French Regime and of the English Fur Trading Companies.* Ottawa: Department of the Interior, 1930

Wade, Richard C. *The Urban Frontier: The Rise of Western Cities, 1790–1830.* Cambridge MA: Cambridge University Press, 1959

Wallace, C.M. "Communities in the Northern Ontario Frontier." In *At the End of the Shift*, ed. Matt Bray and Ashley Thomson, 5–18. Toronto: Dundurn, 1992

Wallace, C.M., and Ashley Thomson, eds. *Sudbury: Rail Town to Regional Capital.* Toronto & Oxford: Dundurn Press, 1993

Walliman, Isidor. *Estrangement: Marx's Concept of Human Nature and the Division of Labor.* Westport, CT: Greenwood Press, 1981

Walton, John. *Storied Land: Community and Memory in Monterey.* Berkeley, Los Angeles, London: University of California Press, 2001

Ward, Russel. *The Australian Legend.* 2nd edn. Melbourne, London, New York: Oxford University Press, 1966

Warren, Hugh Lewis. *Rhymes of a Northland.* Toronto: Frederic D. Goodchild, 1920

Warren, Roland L. "Toward a Reformulation of Community Theory." In *Perspectives on the American Community*, ed. Roland L. Warren, 69–77. Chicago: Rand McNally, 1966

Warren, Roland L., ed. *Perspectives on the American Community: A Book of Readings.* Chicago: Rand McNally, 1966

Watkins, Mel. "The Staple Theory Revisited." *Journal of Canadian Studies* 12 (Winter 1977): 83–95

Weiler, John. "Michipicoten: Hudson's Bay Company Post 1821–1904." Research Report no. 3. Toronto: Historical Sites Branch, December 1973

Weller, G.R. "Hinterland Politics: The Case of Northwestern Ontario." In *Provincial Hinterland: Social Inequality in Northwestern Ontario*, ed. Chris Southcott, 5–28. Halifax: Fernwood Publishing, 1993

– *Northern Studies in Sweden and Canada. An Ontario Perspective.* Research Report no. 11. Thunder Bay: Lakehead Centre for Northern Studies, 1989

Wesley, James. *Stories from the James Bay Coast.* Cobalt: Highway Book Shop, 1993

Wetherell, Donald G., and Irene R.A. Kmet. *Alberta's North: A History, 1890–1950.* Edmonton: University of Alberta Press/Canadian Circumpolar Institute Press, 2000

White, Richard. *The Middle Ground: Indians, Empires, and Republics in the Great Lakes Region, 1650–1815.* Cambridge & New York: Cambridge University Press, 1991

White, Richard and Patricia Limerick, eds. *The Frontier in American Culture.* Berkeley: University of California Press, 1994

Whitnell, Bonny, Dwight Boyd, Monique Charlebois, and Mary Chircoski. "Historical Sites and Trails." Young Canada Works Project [Iroquois Falls], 1978. Copy at Iroquois Falls Museum

Wiegman, Carl. *Trees to News: A Chronicle of the Ontario Paper Company's Origin and Development.* Toronto: McClelland & Stewart, 1953

Wightman, W.R. *Forever on the Fringe: Six Studies in the Development of Manitoulin Island.* Toronto, Buffalo, London: University of Toronto Press, 1982

Wightman, W. Robert, and Nancy M. Wightman. *The Land Between: Northwestern Ontario Resource Development, 1800 to the 1990s.* Toronto: University of Toronto Press, 1997

Williams, Raymond. *The Country and the City.* London: Chatto and Windus, 1972

Williamson, Bill. *Class, Culture, and Community: A Biographical Study of Social Change in Mining.* London & Boston: Routledge & Kegan Paul. 1982

Williamson, O.T.G. *The Northland Ontario.* Toronto: Ryerson Press, 1946

Wilson, Barbara M., ed. Introduction to *Ontario and the First World War, 1914–1918: A Collection of Documents.* Toronto: The Champlain Society, 1977

Wise, S.F. "Upper Canada and the Conservative Tradition." In *Profiles of a Province: Studies in the History of Ontario,* ed. Edith G. Firth, 20–33. Toronto: Ontario Historical Society, 1967

Wisemer, Cathy. *Faces of the Old North.* Toronto, New York, London: McGraw-Hill Ryerson, 1974

Wojciechowski, Margot J. *Federal Mineral Policies, 1945 to 1975: A Survey of Federal Activities That Affected the Canadian Mineral Industry.* Working Paper no. 8. Kingston: Queen's University Centre for Resource Studies, 1979

Wolf, Eric R. *Envisioning Power: Ideologies of Dominance and Crisis.* Berkeley, Los Angeles, London: University of California Press, 1999

Wright, Erik Olin, et al. "The American Class Structure." *American Sociological Review* 47 (December 1982): 709–26

Wright, James V. "Before European Contact." In *Aboriginal Ontario,* ed. Edward S. Rogers and D.B. Smith, 21–38. Toronto & Oxford: Dundurn Press, 1994

– "Prehistory of the Canadian Shield." In *Handbook of North American Indians,* vol. 6: *Subarctic,* ed. June Helm, 86–96. Washington: Smithsonian, 1981

Wyman, Marc. *Hard Rock Epic: Western Miners and the Industrial Revolution, 1860–1910.* Berkeley: University of California Press, 1979

Young, Frank W. *Small Towns in Multilevel Society.* Lantam, New York, Oxford: University Press of America, 1999

Zahavi, Gerald. *Workers, Managers, and Welfare Capitalism.* Urbana: University of Illinois Press, 1988

Zaslow, Morris. "The Dilemmas of the Northern Missionary Diocese: The Case of the Anglican See of Moosonee." *Laurentian University Review* 11 (February 1979): 101–16

– "Edward Barnes Borron, 1820–1915: Northern Pioneer and Public Servant Extraordinary." *Aspects of Nineteenth-Century Ontario,* ed. F.H. Armstrong et al., 297–311. Toronto: University of Toronto Press, 1974

– "The Frontier Hypothesis in Recent Historiography." *Canadian Historical Review* 29 (1948): 153–67

– *The Northward Expansion of Canada, 1914–1967.* Toronto: McClelland & Stewart, 1988

– *Reading the Rocks: The Story of the Geological Survey of Canada 1842–1972.* Toronto & Ottawa: Macmillan for Department of Energy, Mines and Resources, 1975

Zucchi, John E. *Italians in Toronto: Development of a National Identity 1875–1935.* Kingston & Montreal: McGill-Queen's University Press, 1988

– "Neighbourhood and Paesani." *The Italian Immigrant Experience,* ed. John Potestio and Antonio Pucci, 29–40. Thunder Bay: Canadian Italian Historical Association, 1988

Index

Abitibi Indian agency, 131
Abitibi posts: early, 18–19;
  eighteenth century, 22,
  24; missions at, 35–6;
  nineteenth century, 31,
  33–4, 107; twentieth
  century, 99, 107
Abitibi Power and Paper.
  See Abitibi Pulp and Paper
Abitibi Pulp and Paper, 82,
  85, 148–50; founding of,
  60–3; government rela-
  tions, 63–5; promotion
  of, 96, 136; reforestation,
  93; workforce of, 108,
  109, 115
Abitibi region, 107
Aboriginal peoples. *See* First
  Nations
African Americans, 135
agricultural representatives,
  109. *See also* Pomerleau,
  Daniel J.
agriculture: commercial,
  132, 155, 222; early, 8,
  34; legislation regarding,
  39, 43, 52; problems of,
  12, 52, 93, 154–6, 221–2,
  358; promotion of, 41,
  46, 47–53, 55. *See also*
  Monteith Demonstration
  Farm
Albanel, Charles, 18, 104
Albany, Fort, 18, 19, 40,
  46

alcohol: and class, 447n85;
  First Nations and, 45; in
  fur trade, 30; and mas-
  culinity, 343; problems
  with, 163–4, 198–202
Algonkian (culture group),
  15
Algonquin Regiment, 311,
  336
Algonquins, 15, 16, 103,
  128
amusement parlours, 191
Anderson, Benedict,
  xvii–xviii
Anderson, David, 33
Anglican Church, 78, 128,
  300, 302–3. *See also* mis-
  sions, Anglican
Angus, Charlie, 189
Anishinabe, 104
Anson, Frederick (Frank)
  Harris, 60, 82, 84, 98,
  409–10
Anson, Frederick (Franz)
  Harris Jr., 149
Anson and Ogilvie, 61
Ansonville, ON, 89, 91, 117;
  ethnicity in, 110, 115,
  126; founding of, 85–6;
  politics of, 273–4
anti-Semitism, 390–1
Arbor Day, 98, 367
Arvida, QC, 115
Association of Northern
  Ontario Municipalities, 95

Auer, Charles M., 79, 215
Aunor Mine, 82, 143
Austrians, 109, 134, 289
Avery, Donald, 233
Avery, Walter, 307

Balkans, 108, 133–4, 289,
  310. *See also* Croatians;
  Yugoslavs
banks: Bank of Toronto, 73;
  Canadian Bank of Com-
  merce, 60; Imperial Bank
  of Canada, 73; Royal
  Bank, 84
Bannerman, George, 75,
  269
Baptist Church, 302
Barber's Bay, ON, 88, 89
Bardessona, Peter M., 191
Barilko, Bill, 184, 445n16
Barlow-Ojibway, Lake, 14
Barnley, George, 35, 36
Barthes, Roland, xvii
Bartleman, James P., 79,
  144, 256–7, 275–6, 391
baseball, 185–6
battalions: 58th, 336,
  465n67; 159th, 311, 313,
  336–7, 347; 228th,
  313–14, 337, 347
Beads, Charles and John, 26
Beaver Lake, 120
Bernard, Roger, 155
Bickell, J.P. (Jack), 58,
  184–5, 410